D0830219

Langenscheidt

Universal Russian Dictionary

**Russian – English
English – Russian**

Edited by the
Langenscheidt Editorial Staff

Langenscheidt

New York · Berlin · Munich
Warsaw · Vienna · Zurich

Contents – Оглавление

Revised edition by Irina A. Walshe

© 1993 by Langenscheidt KG, Berlin and Munich
Printed in Germany

Preliminary Notes

The user of this dictionary is advised to make himself familiar with the following details of technical arrangement:

Marks of Repetition

1. The sign ~, the so-called tilde, stands either for the whole headword of an etymological word group of for that part of it which precedes the vertical stroke (|):

труд

    '~ный = тру́дный

    ~ово́й = трудово́й

еди́н|ственный

    ~ство = еди́нство

    ~ый = еди́ный

begin

    ~ning = beginning

disast|er

    ~rous = disastrous

A circlet above the tilde ⌀ means: Capital initial letter instead of the small one in the headword or vice versa:

югосла́в   Ита́л|ия

    ⌀ия = Югосла́вия   ⌀ья́нец = италья́нец

2. A hyphen (-) as a mark of repetition has the following functions:

a) It stands for the preceding word, part of which is represented by a tilde:

служи́|а́нка

  ~и́ть, по- = служи́ть, послужи́ть

слы́шать

  ~ся, по- = слы́шаться, послы́шаться

  b) It stands for both aspects (imperfective and perfective) of a preceding Russian verb:

лиш|а́ть, ~и́ть = лиша́ть *impf.*, лиши́ть *pf.*;

  - себя́ жи́зни – лиша́ть *and* лиши́ть себя́ жи́зни;

  ~ся = лиша́ться *impf.*, лиши́ться *pf.*

  c) It stands for a word of the translation or part of it in the same way as does the tilde in the case of headwords:

American америка́|нец, -ка; -ский = америка́нец, америка́нка; америка́нский

Stress

The main stress of each Russian word is indicated by an acute accent (´) above the vowel of the stressed syllable.

An unbracketed word with two accents such as и́на́че can be stressed either и́наче or ина́че.

If the main stress falls on part of a word which follows a tilde, the stress mark given in the translation does not apply:

во́лос

  ~а́тый = волоса́тый, *not* во́лоса́тый

A stress mark above the tilde or the hyphen indicates that the main stress falls on the vowel preceding the added part:

отлич|а́ть

  '~ие = отли́чие

удостове́р|е́ние

  ~я́ть, '~ить = удостоверя́ть *impf.*, удостове́рить *pf.*

A special case are such spellings as «преодоле́(ва́)ть»

which render in a concise form the two aspects of a Russian verb:

преодолева́ть = *impf.*,   преодоле́ть = *pf.*

The Parts of Speech

To save space, the part of speech (*v.* – verb, *adj.* – adjective) is given only in cases of possible doubt. Thus no indication follows the headword ‹sing›, which is clearly a verb, and, accordingly, no indication follows its Russian translation [c]петь.

1. The Verb

As a rule, both aspects of Russian verbs are given. Excepted, of course, are those cases where the Russian verb has only one aspect or where the English translation justifies only one of the two aspects. In such cases the imperfective aspect remains unmarked.

In this dictionary the following methods are used to denote the perfective aspect:

a) In the Russian-English part the perfective aspect stands after the imperfective;

закла́л

~я́ть, ~и́ть = закаля́ть *impf.*, закали́ть *pf.*

пока́з

~ывать, ~а́ть = пока́зывать *impf.*, показа́ть *pf.*

де́лать, с~ = де́лать *impf.*, сде́лать *pf.*

писл|а́ние

~а́ть, на- = писа́ть *impf.*, написа́ть *pf.*

b) In the English-Russian part square brackets are used to show the formation of the perfective aspect:

temper   закаля́ть [-ли́ть]

show   пока́зывать [-за́ть]

do   [с]де́лать
write   [на]писа́ть

As the two last examples show, this method enables the spelling of both aspects to be given in a concise form, which is impossible in the Russian-English part. Here the corresponding perfective aspect forms are listed in their appropriate alphabetic place with a reference to their imperfective forms:

сде́лать → де́лать

написа́ть → писа́ть

c) Where possible, the perfective aspect, in both parts of the dictionary, is marked off by bracketing within the imperfective form:

соб(и)ра́ть = собира́ть *impf.*, собра́ть *pf.*
созда(ва́)ть = создава́ть *impf.*, созда́ть *pf.*
откры(ва́)ть = открыва́ть *impf.*, откры́ть *pf.*

Note: The reflexive particle (-ся) in brackets has nothing to do with the aspects. Spellings such as углубля́ть(ся) [-би́ться] for English ‹deepen› mean: The transitive verb ‹to deepen› is in Russian углубля́ть *impf.*, углуби́ть *pf.* The intransitive usage of the English verb corresponds to the Russian углубля́ться *impf.*, углуби́ться *pf.*

2. The Substantive (Noun)

The gender of the Russian noun is indicated only when it deviates from the following rules:

Nouns ending in any consonant or in -й are masculine:

брус, буго́р, буди́льник, буке́т, май, и́ней, поко́й, поцелу́й.

Nouns ending in -а or -я are feminine:

була́вка, кра́ска, спа́льня, ту́фля.

Nouns ending in -о, -е or -ё are neuter:

окно́, мы́ло, по́ле, мо́ре, ружьё, острие́.

All nouns ending in -ь are followed by the label *m* or *f* as they can be of masculine or feminine gender:

гвоздь *m*, медве́дь *m*, кровь *f*, це́рковь *f*.

Some Russian words denoting people have the same form for male or female persons; accordingly they are marked *m/f*: обжо́ра *m/f* glutton.

Most often, however, such words have in Russian a different form for the feminine. This dictionary gives, as a rule, both forms in the following way:

singer   певе́ц|, -и́ца = певе́ц *m*, певи́ца *f*
writer   писа́тель(ница) *m* = писа́тель *m*, писа́тельница *f*
German   не́м|ец, -ка = не́мец *m*, не́мка *f*.

In the Russian-English part the attributive (that is, the adjectival) use of an English noun is indicated by three dots next to the noun:

зи́мний winter ... (i. e. in such word combinations as ‹winter morning›, ‹winter coat›, etc.).

3. The Adjective

The Russian adjective is always given in its attributive form, in the nominative singular of the masculine. If the Russian adjective has only predicative forms (a very rare occurence), the other nominatives are added:

glad   рад, '-а, '-о, '-ы = рад *m*, ра́да *f*, ра́до *n*;
ра́ды *pl.*

4. The Adverb

Adverbs which follow the regular pattern of English adverb-building (adjective + -ly) or the regular Russian pattern, as ме́дленно ‹slowly› from ме́дленный ‹slow›, are, as a rule, not listed here. However adverbs deviating from the regular word-formation pattern have been included, for example ра́но *adv.* ‹early›, where the adjective ра́нний would suggest ра́нне.

Construction Aids

Each Russian preposition is followed by an indication of the case (or cases) it demands. (See list of Russian abbreviations.)

As the Russian verb very often requires a construction which is different from that of the corresponding English verb, the user will find useful hints how to build the Russian phrase:

помо|га́ть, '-чь (Д).

In Russian you say ‹Я помога́ю ему́› (dative!) for ‹I help him›.

Selection of the Right Word

Apart from suitable abbreviations, which are listed in the next paragraph, the user will find explanatory words. They are intended to facilitate the choice between different translations of the same word. These explanatory words are italicised and are normally placed in round brackets in front of the translation: thin то́нкий; *(hair)* ре́дкий; *(soup)* жи́дкий. This means: The normal word for ‹thin› is ‹то́нкий›, but when speaking of thin hair, you must use ‹ре́дкий›, and when speaking of thin soup, you must use ‹жи́дкий›.

When the explanatory word is not bracketed, it can serve as a possible direct object for the verb which follows:

заноси́ть, занести́ *note* enter, *hand* lift.

adopt *boy* усыновля́ть [-ви́ть]; *habit* усва́ивать [усво́ить].

A colon after the unbracketed word in italics means that it can be the subject of a sentence formed with the verb in question: исте|ка́ть, '-чь *time*: elapse. abate *storm*: утиха́ть ['-хнуть].

List of English Abbreviations

a. and, also и, та́кже

abbr. abbreviation сокра-
ще́ние

adj. adjective и́мя прилага́-
тельное

adv. adverb наре́чие

ae. aeronautic(s) авиа́ция

agr. agriculture се́льское
хозя́йство

anat. anatomy анато́мия

Am. American English аме-
рика́нский вариа́нт анг-
ли́йского языка́

approx. approximately при-
близи́тельно

arch. architecture архитек-
ту́ра, строи́тельное де́ло

attr. attributive(ly) атрибу-
ти́вное употребле́ние

av. aviation авиа́ция

b. s. bad sense отрица́тель-
но

biol. biology биоло́гия

bot. botany бота́ника

Brit. British (English) usage
брита́нское (англи́йское)
словоупотребле́ние

chem. chemistry хи́мия

coll. colloquial разгово́рный

collect. collective noun соби-
ра́тельное существи́-
тельное

comm. commerce торго́вля

comp. comparative degree
сравни́тельная сте́пень

conj. conjunction сою́з

cul. culinary term кулина́р-
ное выраже́ние

dimin. diminutive уменьши́-
тельное сло́во

eccl. ecclesiastical term цер-
ко́вное выраже́ние

econ. economy эконо́мика

e. g. for example наприме́р

el. electrical engineering
электроте́хника

etc. and so on и так да́лее

f. feminine gender же́нский
род

fig. figurative(ly) в перено́с-
ном значе́нии

fin. finance фина́нсовое
де́ло

f/pl. feminine plural мно́-
жественное число́ же́н-
ского ро́да

geogr. geography геогра́фия

geol. geology геоло́гия

gr. grammar грамма́тика

hunt. hunting охо́та

impf. imperfective aspect не-
соверше́нный вид

*(im)pf. imperfective and per-
fective aspect* несовер-

10

шённый и совершённый вид

indecl. indeclinable несклоня́емое сло́во

inf. infinitive инфинити́в

jur. juridical term юриди́ческое выраже́ние

lit. literature литерату́ра

m masculine gender мужско́й род

mar. maritime term морско́й те́рмин

math. mathematics матема́тика

med. medicine медици́на

m/f masculine and feminine gender мужско́й и же́нский род

mil. military term вое́нный те́рмин

min. mineralogy or *mining* минерало́гия, го́рное де́ло

mot. motoring автомоби́льное де́ло

m/pl. masculine plural мно́жественное число́ мужско́го ро́да

mst mostly бо́льшей ча́стью

mus. music му́зыка

n neuter gender сре́дний род

n/pl. neuter plural мно́же-

ственное число́ сре́днего ро́да

o. s. oneself себя́, себе́, -ся

paint. painting жи́вопись

parl. parliamentary парла́ментский

pf. perfective aspect соверше́нный вид

phil. philosophy филосо́фия

photo. photography фотогра́фия

phys. physics фи́зика

pl. plural мно́жественное число́

pol. politics поли́тика

pred. predicative предикати́вное употребле́ние

pref. prefix приста́вка

pres. present tense настоя́щее вре́мя

prep. preposition предло́г

pron. pronoun местоиме́ние

ps. person лицо́

rail. railways железнодоро́жное де́ло

s.b. somebody кто́-либо, кого́-либо

sg. singular еди́нственное число́

s.o. someone кто́-либо, кого́-ливо

s.o.'s someone's чей-либо, чей-то

s.th. something что́-либо,

чего-либо

su. substantive (noun) и́мя существи́тельное

tech. technical science, engineering те́хника

thea. theatre теа́тр

tel. telephone телефо́нная связь

typ. typography книгопеча́тание, маши́нопись

.U.K. the United Kingdom Соединённое Короле́вство

univ. university университе́т

v. verb глаго́л

v/i. intransitive verb непереходный глаго́л

v/t. transitive verb перехо́дный глаго́л

zo. zoology зооло́гия

Russian Abbreviations

И	= имени́тельный паде́ж	*nominative*
Р	= роди́тельный паде́ж	*genitive*
Д	= да́тельный паде́ж	*dative*
В	= вини́тельный паде́ж	*accusative*
Т	= твори́тельный паде́ж	*instrumental*
П	= предло́жный паде́ж	*prepositive*
и т. д.	= и так да́лее	*and so on*
и т. п.	= и тому́ подо́бное	*and the like*

A

a and, but; **~ (не) то** or else, otherwise

абажу́р lamp-shade

абза́ц *typ.* paragraph

абитурие́нт university applicant

абон|еме́нт (*concerts, lectures, etc.*) subscription, season ticket; **~е́нт** (*concert series, telephone*) subscriber

або́рт abortion

абрико́с apricot

абсолю́тный absolute

абсу́рд absurdity; **~ный** absurd

ава́нс *fin.* advance

авантю́ра adventure

ава́рия wreck, accident; break-down; crash

а́вгуст August

авиа|биле́т air ticket; **~ла́йнер** airliner; **~ли́ния** airline; **~но́сец** aircraft carrier; **~пассажи́р** air passenger; **~по́чта** air mail; **~цио́нный** aviation...; **'~ция** aviation

австрали́|ец, ~йка; ~йский Australian

австри́|ец, ~йка; ~йский Austrian

автобиогра́фия autobiography

авто́|бус bus; **~вокза́л** bus station; **~граф** autograph; **~запра́вочный: ~запра́вочная ста́нция** filling station; **~ма́т** slot-machine; sub-machine gun; *coll.* telephone booth; **~мати́ческий** automatic; **~маши́на, ~моби́ль** *m* motor-car; **~моби́льный** motor(-car)...; **~но́мия** autonomy; **~отве́т** auto-answer; **~портре́т** self-portrait; **~стоя́нка** car park; **~тури́зм** motoring holiday(s)

а́втор author; **~ите́т** authority, prestige; **~ите́тный** authoritative; competent; **~ский: ~ское пра́во** copyright

авто|ру́чка fountain pen; **~стра́да** motorway; **~цисте́рна** tank lorry

аге́нт agent; **~ство** agency

агита́ция agitation, propaganda; **предвы́борная ~** election campaign

агра́рный agrarian *adj.*

агре́ссия aggression

агроно́м agronomist
ад hell
адапта́ция adaptation;
~**и́роваться** adapt
адвока́т lawyer
администра́ция administration
адмира́л admiral
а́дрес address; ~**а́т** addressee; ~**но-спра́вочный**; ~**но-спра́вочная кни́га** directory; ~**ова́ть** (im)pf. address
а́дский hellish
аза́рт passion, heat; ~**ный** passionate, heated; (game) gambling, of chance
ази́|ат(ка) ~ **а́тский** Asian
азо́т nitrogen
аи́ст stork
акаде́мия academy
аквала́нг aqualung; ~**ре́ль** f water-colour
аккомпан|еме́нт mus. accompaniment; ~**и́ровать** (Д) accompany
аккордео́н accordion
аккредитова́ть (im)pf. accredit
аккура́тный accurate; neat; punctual
акт act (a. thea.); jur. deed; ~**ёр** actor; ~**и́вный** active; ~**ри́са** actress
аку́ла shark
аку́стика acoustics
акуше́рка midwife
акце́нт accent; ~**и́ровать** (im)pf. accentuate
акционе́р share-holder;

~**ный** joint-stock…
а́кция fin. share; pol. action
алкого́ль m alcohol
аллерг|е́н allergen; '~**ик** one prone to allergy; ~**и́ческий** allergic; ~**ия** allergy
алле́я avenue; garden alley
алма́з diamond
алта́рь m altar
алфави́т alphabet, ABC
а́лчн|ость f greediness; ~**ый** greedy
а́лый scarlet, bright red
альбо́м album
альпини́ст(ка) mountaineer
алюми́ний aluminium
амба́р barn, granary
америка́н|ец ~**ка**; ~**ский** American
амни́стия amnesty
амортиза́тор shock-absorber
ана́лиз analysis; ~**и́ровать**, **про**- analyse
анана́с pine-apple
анга́р hangar
а́нгел angel
англи́йский English; ~**ча́нин**, ~**ча́нка** English|man, -woman
'Англия England
анке́та (official form) questionnaire
анне́ксия annexation
аннули́ровать (im)pf. annul, cancel
анса́мбль m ensemble
анте́нна aerial, antenna
анти́чный antique
антра́кт thea. interval

аню́тин: **~ы гла́зки** *m/pl.* pansl|y, -ies

апа́тия apathy

апельси́н orange

аплоди|ровать (Д) applaud; **~сме́нты** *m/pl.* applause

аппара́т apparatus; instrument; organs

аппети́т appetite; **~ный** appetizing

апре́ль *m* April

апте́ка chemist's shop, drugstore; **~рь** *m* chemist, druggist

ара́б, ~ка Arab; **~ский** Arabic, Arabian

арбитра́ж arbitration

арбу́з watermelon

аргенти́н|ец, ~ка Argentinean; **~ский** Argentine

аргументи|ровать (*im*)*pf.* argue

аре́нд|а lease; rent; **~а́тор** leaseholder, tenant; **~ова́ть** (*im*)*pf.* lease; rent

аре́ст arrest; sequestration; **~ова́ть** *pf.*, **~о́вывать** *impf.* arrest; sequestrate

аристокра́т, ~ка aristocrat; **~ия** aristocracy

арифме́тика arithmetic

аркти́ческий arctic

а́рмия army

армяни́н, ~ка; ~ский Armenian

арома́т aroma

артиллери́|йский artillery...; **~ия** artillery; **~йст**

artilleryman, gunner

арти́ст actor; **~ический** artistic; **~ка** actress

а́рфа harp

архи ... *pref.* arch ...

архите́кт|ор architect; **~у́ра** architecture

астро|на́вт astronaut; **~ном** astronomer; **~но́мия** astronomy

ата́к|а attack; **~ова́ть** (*im*)*pf.* attack

атеи́зм atheism

ателье́ *n indecl. art.* studio; **~ мод** fashion house

атла́с[1] atlas

атла́с[2] satin

атлети́зм (*sports*) body building

атмосфе́ра atmosphere (*a. fig.*)

а́том atom; **~щик** atomic scientist; **~ный** atomic, atom ...; **~ный реа́ктор** atomic pile

аттеста́т certificate; testimonial

аудито́рия lecture-room; audience

аукцио́н auction

афи́ша poster; *thea.* playbill

'африка́н|ец ~ка; ~ский African

ах ah, oh; **'~ать, '~нуть** gasp (*with surprise*)

аэро|бус airbus; **~дро́м** airfield; **~пла́н** aeroplane; **~по́рт** airport; **~ста́т** balloon; **~сни́мок** aerial photograph

Б

ба́б|а (*not polite*) woman; **снежная ~а** snowman; **~ий: ~ье лето** Indian summer; **~очка** butterfly; **~ушка** grandmother

бага́ж luggage, baggage; **~ник** *mot.* boot; **~ный** luggage..., baggage...

багро́вый purple *or* crimson

бадминто́н badminton

ба́з|а base; basis; **~ис** basis, foundation

байда́рка kayak, canoe

байт *tech.* byte

бак tank; (clothes-) boiler

бакале́|йный: ~йный магази́н grocery; **~я** grocery goods

ба́кен buoy

ба́ки *m/pl.* side-whiskers

бал ball, dance

бала́нс *comm.* balance

бале́т ballet

ба́лка *tech.* beam, girder

балл (*in exams*) mark; (*sports*) point

балова́ть, из- spoil, pamper; **~ся** *no pf.* frolic; (T) indulge in

балти́йский Baltic

балы́к balyk (*cured back of sturgeon, etc.*)

бана́льный commonplace

бана́н banana

банда́ж *med.* truss

бандеро́ль *f* (*mail*) small packet; letter packet

банк bank; **~ да́нных** data bank

ба́нка jar, pot; tin; *med.* cupping-glass

банке́т banquet

банк|и́р banker; **~овский, ~овый** bank(ing)...; **~ро́т** bankrupt *su.*; **~ро́тство** bankruptcy

ба́ня (*public*) baths; Russian bath

бар bar; refreshment room; **~мен** barman

бараба́н drum; **~ить** drum; *rain*: patter; **~щик** drummer

бара́к barrack, hut

бара́н ram; **~ина** mutton

ба́ржа barge

баррика́да barricade

барсу́к badger

ба́ртер, ~ный barter

ба́рхат velvet

барье́р barrier; (*sports*) hurdle

бас bass

баскетбо́л basketball

басн|осло́вный fabulous; **~я** fable

бассе́йн *geogr.* basin; **пла́вательный ~** swimming-pool

басто́вать be on strike; **за-** *pf.* go on strike; **~ющий** strike; *adj.* on-strike

башма́к shoe; **у жены́ под ~о́м** henpecked

ба́шня tower; *mil. a.* turret

бая́н accordion

бди́тельность *f* vigilance

бег run(ning); **~á** *m/pl.* horse-race(s); **~áть** run about; → **бежáть**

бегемóт hippopotamus

бег|лéц fugitive, runaway; **~лый** cursory; (*speech*) fluent; **~овáя** и по дорóжка racetrack; **~óм** *adv.* running; *mil.* double-quick; **~ствó** flight, escape; **~ýн(ья)** runner, sprinter

бед|á misfortune; **в тóм-то и ~á** that is just the trouble; **~ный** poor; **~нягá** *m/f* poor (wo)man

бедрó *anat.* hip

бéдств|енный disastrous; **~ие** calamity; disaster; *mar.* distress

бежáть[1], по~ run; *time:* fly; → **бéгать**

бежáть[2] (*im*)*pf.* flee; **~éнец, ~éнка** refugee

без (Р) without; **~ двух (минýт) час** two (minutes) to one

безболéзненный painless

безвéстный obscure, unknown

безвкýсный tasteless

безвóдный arid

безвозврáтный irretrievable, irrevocable; **~мéздный** gratuitous

безвóльный weak-willed

безврéдный harmless, innocuous

безвы́ходный desperate, hopeless

безгрáмотный illiterate; ungrammatical

безграни́чный boundless

бездáрный dull, untalented; (*work of art*) feeble; (*effort, etc.*) bungling

бездéйствие inactivity

безделýшка knick-knack; trinket

бездéльни|к idler, loafer; **~чать** loaf, idle

безденéжье lack of money

бездéтный childless

бездéятельный inactive

бéздна abyss; *coll.* a huge number (of), heaps (of)

бездóмный homeless; (*animal*) stray

бездорóжье lack of (good) roads

бездухóвн|ость soullessness; **~ый** soulless

бездýшный soulless; heartless

безд́мный smokeless

безжáлостный pitiless, ruthless

безжи́зненный lifeless, dull

беззабóтный carefree; light-hearted

беззакóнный lawless

беззастéнчивый shameless, brazen-faced

беззащи́тный defenceless

безлю́дный uninhabited; deserted

безмо́лвие silence
безмяте́жный serene, untroubled
безнадёжный hopeless
безнака́занный unpunished
безнра́вственный immoral
безоби́дный inoffensive, innocent, harmless
безо́блачный cloudless; *fig.* unclouded
безобра́зие ugliness; disgraceful practice; ~ный ugly; disgraceful
безопа́сн|ость *f* safety; security; ~ый safe; secure
безостано́вочный (*train, bus*) non-stop
безотве́т|ственный irresponsible; ~ный meek
безотлага́тельный urgent
безотра́дный cheerless
безоши́бочный faultless; correct; exact
безрабо́тица unemployment; ~ный unemployed, jobless
безра́достный joyless
безразли́чный indifferent; **мне э́то ~о** it is all the same to me
безрассу́дный imprudent; rash
безукори́зненный irreproachable
безу́мие folly
безупре́чный blameless; (*reputation*) unstained
безусло́вный uncondi-

tional; undoubted
безуспе́шный unsuccessful
безуте́шный inconsolable
безуча́стный indifferent, apathetic
безъя́дерный nuclear-free
беле́ть, по- turn white; *impf.* show white
бе́лка squirrel
бело́к (*egg or eye*) white; albumen, protein
белоку́рый fair-haired; ~ру́с(ка), ~ру́сский Byelorussian; ~сне́жный snow-white
бе́л|ый white; ~ая кость *f* blue blood
бельги́|ец, ~йка, ~йский Belgian
бельё linen, underwear; **посте́льное ~** bedlinen
бельэта́ж first floor; dress circle
бензи́н petrol, gasoline; ~обак petrol tank; ~около́нка petrol pump
бе́рег bank; shore
бережли́вый economical, thrifty
бе́режн|ый careful; ~ое отноше́ние (к Д) consideration (for)
берёза birch
бере́менн|ая pregnant; ~ость *f* pregnancy
бере́чь, с- (of) take care (of); spare; *secret* keep
берло́га den, lair
бес demon

бесе́д|а talk, chat; **_овать** talk, converse

беси́ться, вз_ get furious; *animal:* become rabid

бескла́ссовый classless

бескомпроми́ссный uncompromising

бесконе́чный endless; infinite

бескоры́стный disinterested, unselfish

беспа́мят|ность f forgetfulness; **_ство** unconsciousness, swoon

беспарти́йный non-party, independent

беспе́чный unconcerned, happy-go-lucky; (*life*) carefree

беспла́тный free (of charge)

беспло́дный fruitless; barren

беспово́ротный irrevocable

беспоко́ить worry; disturb; **_ся** *v/i.* worry; bother

беспоко́йный uneasy; troublesome; (*child*) restless

беспо́лезный useless

беспо́мощный helpless

беспоря́док disorder

беспоря́дочный: _ перелёт non-stop flight

беспо́шлинный duty-free

беспоща́дный merciless

беспреде́льный boundless, unlimited

беспреко́словно unquestioningly, without demur

беспре|ры́вный, _ста́нный uninterrupted, incessant

бесприме́рный unparalleled

беспристра́стный impartial

беспричи́нный groundless

беспу́тный dissipated, licentious

бессвя́зный incoherent

бесси́лие weakness; impotence

бессме́ртный immortal; (*glory*) undying

бессмы́сленный senseless

бессо́вестный unscrupulous

бессозна́тельный unconscious

бессо́нница insomnia

бесспо́рный indisputable

бессро́чный permanent

бессты́дный shameless

беста́ктный tactless

бестолко́вый muddle-headed; unintelligible

бестсе́ллер bestseller

бесхи́тростный artless

бесхозя́йственность careless and wasteful management

бесце́н|ный priceless; **_ок: купи́ть за _ок** buy for a song

бесчелове́чный inhuman, brutal

бесчи́сленный innumerable

бесчу́вственный insensible; unfeeling

бесшу́мный noiseless

бе́шеный rabid; furious; frantic

библиоте́ка library; **~рь** m librarian

Би́блия Bible

бидо́н (for milk) can; (large) milk churn

бижуте́рия costume jewellery

биле́т ticket; **парти́йный ~:** **~ная ка́сса** booking-office; box-office; ticket office

бино́кль m opera-glasses; binoculars

бинт bandage

би́ржа fin. exchange; **~ труда́** labour exchange; **~ фо́ндовая** ~ stock exchange

бис encore

бискви́т sponge-cake

бит tech bit

би́т|ва battle; **~ко́м: ~ко́м наби́тый** crammed; **~о́к** cutlet

бить¹, по- beat; **~²**, про- clock: strike; **~ся** (с T) fight (with); (над T) struggle (with problem)

бич scourge

бла́го welfare; blessing; **на** ~ (P) for the good (of)

благодар|и́ть, по- thank; **~ность** f gratitude; **~ный** grateful; **~я́** (Д) thanks to

благо|де́тель m benefactor; **~полу́чие** (personal) well-being; **~полу́чно** (arrive) safely; **~прия́тный** propitious; **~разу́мный** reasonable; (metal) precious; **~скло́нность** f favour, good will; **~слови́ть** bless; **~состоя́ние** (public) well-being; **~твори́тельность** charity; **~твори́тельный** charitable, charity ...; **~тво́рный** beneficial, salutary; **~уха́ние** fragrance

блаже́нный blissful; **~ство** bliss

бланк: заполня́ть ~ fill in a form

бледн|е́ть, по- turn pale; **~ый** pale

блеск glitter, shine

блест|е́ть glitter, shine, sparkle; **~я́щий** brilliant

ближ|а́йший nearest; next; **~ний** neighbouring; fellow creature; **~ний Восто́к** Near East

близ (P) near; **~кий** near, close; **мой ~кие** my people; **~ко** adv. near, close by; **~ко от** (P) close to; **~не́ц** twin; **~ору́кий** short-sighted (a. fig.); **~ость** f nearness; intimacy

блин pancake

блинда́ж mil. shelter

блок pol. bloc; tech. unit, assembly; pulley

блока́да blockade

блокно́т note-book
блонди́нка blonde
блоха́ flea
блужда́ть roam, wander; (*in a forest*) ramble
блу́зка blouse
блю́д|о dish; course; **~це** saucer
боб bean
боб|ёр (*fur*) beaver; **~р** *zo.* beaver
Бог, бог God; god; **ей '~у!** by God!; **сла́ва '~у!** thank God!
бога́т|ство riches, wealth; **~ый** rich
богаты́рь *m* (*epic*) hero
бога́ч rich man
боги́ня goddess
Богома́терь mother of god
бого|сло́в theologian; **~служе́ние** church service; **~твори́ть** idolize; **~ху́льство** blasphemy
бо́др|ствовать be *or* keep awake; **~ый** brisk; hale (and hearty); **~я́щий** bracing
боево́й fighting..., battle...
боеголо́вка warhead
боеприпа́сы *m/pl.* ammunition
боеспосо́бность *f* fighting efficiency
бое́ц, *pl.* **бойцы́** fighter
Бо́ж|е: ~е мой! my goodness!; **~ий** God's ...; **~ья коро́вка** lady-bird
бой fight; battle; (*clock*)

striking; **'~кий** smart, ready; **'~ня** slaughter(-house)
бок side; **~ ó~** side by side
бока́л (wine)-glass
бок|ово́й lateral, side...; **~ова́я ка́чка** *mar.* rolling; **'~ом** sideways
бокс boxing; **~ёр** boxer
болва́н blockhead, fool
болга́р|ин, ~ка; ~ский Bulgarian; **2ия** Bulgaria
бо́лее more (+ *comp.*); **~или ме́нее** more or less; **тем ~** all the more
боле́знь *f* illness; disease
боле́льщик (*sports*) fan
боле́ть (3. *ps. sg.* **боле́ет**) be ill; (3. *ps. sg.* **боли́т**) ache, hurt
болеутоля́ющий sedative *adj.*
боло́то bog, swamp
болта́ть[1] (T) dangle; **~ся** *v/i.* hang loosely *or* about
болта́ть[2] chat(ter)
боль *f* pain; **зубна́я ~** toothache; **~ни́ца** hospital; **~ни́чный** hospital...; **~ни́чный лист** sick-leave certificate; **'~но: мне ~но** it hurts me; **~но́й** sick, ill; *as su.* patient
бо́льше more (**чем** than); **~ не** no more; no longer; **~ви́к** Bolshevik; **~ви́стский** Bolshevist
бо́льш|ий bigger, greater; **по ~ей ча́сти** for the most part; **са́мое ~ее** (at

the utmost; _инствó majority; _óй large; big; great

бóмб|а bomb; _**ардирóвщик** bomber; _**ить** coll. bomb; _**оубéжище** air-raid shelter

бор pine forest

борéц fighter; wrestler

бормотáть, про_ mutter

бóров hog

бородá beard; _**вка** wart

бороздá furrow; _**ить, вз-,** fig. **из-** furrow

боронá harrow

борóться fight; wrestle

борт mar. side; board; **нá _, на _ý** aboard; _**проводни́ца** av. stewardess

борьбá fight, struggle; wrestling

босикóм adv. barefoot; _**óй** (foot) bare; (person) barefoot(ed)

босонóжки sandals

ботáник botanist; _**а** botany

ботинок boot

бóчка barrel, cask

боязли́вый timorous; '_**нь** f fear

боя́ться (P) be afraid (of), fear

брази́л|ец, _ья́нка, _ьский Brazilian

брак¹ marriage; wedlock

брак² spoilage; reject(s)

брани́ть scold; abuse; _**ся** quarrel; swear; '_**ный** abusive; _**ь** f abuse; swearing

брасс breast stroke

брат brother; _**áние** fraternization; '_**ский** brotherly, fraternal

брать, взять take; _**взаи́мы** borrow; _ **с негó примéр** follow his example; _ **себя́ в рýки** pull o.s. together; _**ся за** (B) take up; undertake

брáчный matrimonial

бревнó log, beam

бред delirium; coll. nonsense

брéзгать, по_ (T) be squeamish (about)

брезéнт tarpaulin

брéмя n burden

бригáда brigade, team

британский British

бри́тв|а razor; _**енный:** _**енные принадлéжности** shaving accessories

брить, по_ v/t. shave; _**ся** v/i. shave, have a shave

бровь f eyebrow

броди́ть¹ ferment

броди́ть² wander, ramble; _**я́га** m tramp

броне/бóйный armour-piercing; _**нóсец** zo. armadillo; _**танковый:** _**танковые войскá** n/pl. armoured forces; _**транспортёр** armoured personnel carrier

брóнза bronze

брони́ровать, за_ book, reserve (mst. hotelroom)

броня́ armour

броса́ть, **бро́сить** throw; *people* desert; *habit* give up; **-ся** (*на* B) dash, rush (at); **-ся в глаза́** strike (the eye)

брошь *f.* brooch

брус beam; **паралле́льные _ья** *m/pl.* parallel bars

брусни́ка cowberry

бры́згать, **бры́знуть** (T) splash (on *на* B); *pf.* spurt out

брюзгли́вый peevish

брю́ки *f/pl.* trousers

бу́бны *f/pl.* (*cards*) diamonds

буго́р hillock

буди́льник alarm-clock

буди́ть, **раз** *v/t.* wake; *fig.* awaken

бу́дка (sentry-)box; booth

бу́дний: **_ день** *m* weekday

бу́дничный everyday; *fig.* humdrum

бу́дто (бы), (*a.* **как _**) as though, as if

бу́дущее *as su.* future; **_ий** future; **на _ей неде́ле** next week

бу́ер ice-boat

бузина́ *bot.* elder

бук beech

бу́ква *alphabet* letter; **прописна́я _а** capital letter; **стро́чная _а** small letter; **_а́льный** literal; **_енный** (*code, etc.*) *tech.* alphabetic; **_енно-цифрово́й** (*code, etc.*) *tech.* alpha-

numeric

буке́т bouquet

букини́ст second-hand bookseller; **_и́ческий**: **_и́ческий магази́н** second-hand bookshop

букси́р tug(boat)

буксова́ть *wheel:* skid

була́вка pin; **англи́йская _** safety pin

бу́л|ка (*white bread*) loaf; **сдо́бная _ка** bun; **_очка** roll; **_очная** baker's shop

булы́жник cobble-stone

бульо́н broth

бума́г|а paper; **_и** *pl.* (*official*) papers; **це́нные _и** securities

бума́жн|ик wallet; **_ый** paper...

бунт rebellion; riot; **_овщи́к** rebel

бура́в borer, gimlet; **_ить** bore

бу́рный stormy; impetuous; loud

бурово́й: **_ая вы́шка** drilling *or* oil rig

бу́рый: **_ у́голь** *m* brown coal

бу́ря storm

бутербро́д sandwich

бу́тсы *pl.* football boots

буты́лка bottle; **_ вина́** bottle of wine; **_ из-под вина́** wine-bottle

буфе́т sideboard; buffet

буха́нка loaf

бухга́лт|ер book-keeper, accountant; **_е́рия** book-

-keeping; accounts department

бухнуть, раз~ swell

бухта geogr. bay

бушевать rage, roar

буянить, на~ brawl, kick up a row

бы: я сказал бы, если бы я знал I'd say, if I knew

быва|ть be, happen; '-ший former

бык bull

быстр|ота quickness; speed; '-ый quick, fast; speedy

быт (way of) life; ~ие phil. being; existence; ~овой of life; everyday; genre...

быть be; у меня есть (И) I have; ~ в состоянии be able; может ~ perhaps; так и ~! all right! (I don't object)

бюджет budget

бюро n indecl. bureau, office; справочное ~ inquiry office; ~крат bureaucrat; ~кратия bureaucracy

бюстгальтер brassiere

В

в (II or B) in, into; to; at; on; в первый раз for the first time; в этом году this year; два раза в день twice a day; в два раза больше twice as much, twice as many

вагон carriage, coach; ~-ресторан dining-car; спальный ~ sleeping-car; трамвайный ~ tram-car; ~овожатый tramdriver

важн|ость f importance; ~ый important

ваза vase

вакансия (for an office job) vacancy

вал¹ (man-made) bank; mil. rampart

вал² gross output

вал³ tech. shaft

валет (cards) knave, jack

валить¹, по~, с~ (3. ps. sg. валит) throw down, overthrow; fell; -ся fall down

валить² (3. ps. sg. валит): снег ~ snow is falling heavily; толпа ~ the crowd is thronging

валовой comm. gross

вальс waltz

валют|а currency; ~ный; ~ный курс rate of exchange ~ная coll. speculator in foreign currency

валять, с~ cloth felt, full; ~ дурака play the fool

валяться v/i. lie about; wallow, roll

вам (= Д) to you, for you; you; → вы

вами (= Т) by (or through)

you, you; → **вы**

ваниль f vanilla

ва́нн|**а** bath-tub; bath; **ный**; **ая ко́мната** bathroom

ва́рвар ; **ский** barbarian; barbaric

варе́нье jam

вари́ть , **с** boil, cook; *beer* brew; **ся** *v/i.* boil

вас (= P *a.* B) you; → **вы**

василёк cornflower

ва́та wadding; *med.* cotton-wool

ва́фля waffle

ва́хта *mar.* watch, guard

ваш, **-а**, **-е**, *pl.* **-и** your; yours

вбега́ть, **вбежа́ть** (*в* B) come running, run (into)

вби(**ва́**)**ть** drive in, hammer in

вблизи́ *adv.* near by; **от** (P) not far from

введе́ние introduction; preface

вверх up, upwards; up-stairs; **у** above, over-head; upstairs

вви́нчивать, **ввинти́ть** screw in

вводи́ть, **ввести́** introduce; **в заблужде́ние** mislead

ввоз import(ation); **и́ть**, **ввезти́** import

вд(**ав**)**а́ться** (*в* B) jut out (into); **в подро́бности** go into details; **в то́нкости** split hairs

вда́|**вливать**, **и́ть** press in

вдали́ in the distance, far off; **ь** into the distance, far

вдво́|**е** *adv.* double, twice; **е бо́льше** twice as much or as many; **ём** two together; **мы ём** the two of us

вде(**ва́**)**ть** pass or pull through; **ни́тку в иглу́** thread a needle

вде́н(**ыв**)**ать** fit in, set in

вдова́ widow; **соло́менная** grass widow; **éц** wid-ower

вдоль (P) along; *adv.* lengthwise

вдохнове́ние inspiration; **ля́ть**, **и́ть** inspire

вдохну́ть → **вдыха́ть**

вдруг suddenly

вду(**ва́**)**ть** blow into

вду́мчивый thoughtful, pensive

веде́ние[1] leading, con-ducting; management

ве́д|**ение**[2] authority, juris-diction; **омство** depart-ment

ведро́ pail, bucket

ведь: **да э́то Мари́я!** Why, it's Mary!; **э́то пра́вда?** It is true, isn't it?

ве́жлив|**ость** f politeness; **ый** polite

везде́ everywhere

везти́, **по** convey, carry; drive; cart; → **вози́ть**

ему́ везёт he is lucky

век century; lifetime; **сре́дние ~á** *m/pl.* Middle Ages; **~ово́й** ancient, age-old

ве́ко eyelid

ве́ксель *m* bill of exchange

веле́ть (*im*)*pf.* (Д) order, tell

велика́н giant

вели́кий great; **~á, ~ó, ~и** *pred.* (*garment*) too big

Великобрита́ния Great Britain; **2душный** generous, magnanimous; **2ле́пный** magnificent; *coll.* excellent

вели́чественный majestic; grand; **~ество: ва́ше ~ество** your majesty; **~ие** grandeur; **~инá** size; *math.* quantity

велого́нка cycle-race; **~дро́м** velodrome, **~трек** cycling track

велосипе́д bicycle; **~и́ст(ка)** cyclist; **~ный: ~ная доро́жка** cycle-path

ве́на vein

венге́рка, венгр ~ский Hungarian

ве́ник short broom; (*in Russian bath*) bundle of (birch) twigs

вено́к wreath, garland

вентиля́тор *tech.* fan

венча́льный wedding...; **~ние** (*church*) wedding, coronation; **~ть, у-** crown

(*a. fig*); **~ть, по-, об-** *v/t.* marry (*in church*)

ве́ра faith; belief; trust

вера́нда verandah

ве́рба willow (-tree); **~ный: '2ное воскресе́нье** Palm Sunday

верблю́д camel

вербова́ть, за- recruit

верёвка rope; cord

верени́ца file, row, line

ве́рить, по- (Д) believe; trust; **~ в** (В) believe in

вернисáж *art* (*exhibition*) opening day

ве́рность *f* faithfulness; loyalty; correctness

верну́ть *pf.* return, give back; win back; **~ся** *v/i.* return

ве́рный faithful; true, right

вероисповéдание creed, denomination, religion

вероло́мный perfidious, treacherous

вероя́тн|ость *f* probability; **по всей ~ости** in all probability; **~ый** probable

верста́к (*joiner's etc.*) bench

верте́ть twist, twirl; **~ся** *v/i.* turn, revolve, spin

вертолёт helicopter

верфь *f* shipyard

верх top, upper part; *fig.* height; upper hand; **~ний** upper; **~о́вный** supreme; **~о́вное кома́ндование** high command; **~о́вой** *adj.* riding; *su.*

horseman; **~овая езда** riding; **~ом** on horseback; astride; **ездить ~ом** ride; **~ушка** top; apex; *coll.* leaders, ruling clique

верши́на summit (*a. fig.*)

вес weight (*a. fig.*)

весели́ть, **раз-** amuse, cheer; **-ся** *impf.* enjoy o.s., make merry; *pf.* cheer up

весёл|ость *f* gaiety, cheerfulness; **~ый** gay, cheerful

весе́лье merriment; merry-making

весе́нний spring(-time)…

ве́сить *v/i.* weigh

весло́ oar; paddle

весна́ spring(-time); **~ой** in spring; **~ушка** freckle

вести́, **по-** lead, conduct; drive, steer; → **води́ть**; *impf. only in all following meanings:* *war* wage; *books* keep; *conversation* hold; **~себя́** behave

вестибю́ль (*in hotels, etc.*) vestibule

ве́стник herald

весть *f* news; **пропа́сть без ~и** *mil.* be missing

весы́ *m/pl.* scales, balance

весь, **вся**, **всё** *adj.* the whole (of); all; **все** *pl. adj.* all; *pron.* everybody; **всё** *pron.* everything, all; *adv.* → **всё**

весьма́ highly, greatly

ветвь *f* branch

ве́тер wind; **~ерóк** light breeze; **~ровóй**, **~ровóе**

стекло́ *mot.* windscreen

ве́то *n indecl.* veto

ве́треный windy; *fig.* frivolous

ве́тхий decrepit, ramshackle; **2 заве́т** *eccl.* Old Testament

ветчина́ ham

ве́чер evening; **~и́нка** evening party; soirée; **'~ний** evening…; **~ом** in the evening; **сего́дня ~ом** tonight

ве́чн|ость *f* eternity; **~ый** eternal

вече́рка *coll.* evening paper

ве́шалка hall-stand; peg; coat hanger; (*on coat*) tab; **~ть**, **пове́сить** hang (up); **-ся** hang o.s.

веще|вóй **~вóй мешóк** *mil.* kitbag; **'~ственный** material; substantial; **~ствó** substance, matter

вещь *f* thing; piece of work; *pl.* things, belongings

ве́ять *v/i.* blow; *flags:* fly

взад *и* **вперёд** to and fro

взаи́мный mutual, reciprocal

взаимо|вы́годный mutually beneficial; **~де́йствие** interaction; co-operation (*a. mil.*); **~пóмощь** *f* mutual aid; **~понима́ние** mutual understanding

взаймы́: взять ~ (B) borrow; **дать ~** (B) lend

взамён (P) instead of; *adv.* instead

взбега́ть, взбежа́ть run up

взби(ва́)ть *pillow* shake up; *cream* whip; *hair* fluff

взве́шивать, взве́сить *v/t.* weigh (*a. fig.*)

взвод *mil.* platoon

взгляд look, glance; *fig.* view, opinion; **_ывать, взгляну́ть (на** B) look (at)

вздор nonsense

вздорожа́ние rise in prices

вздох deep breath; sigh; **_ну́ть → вздыха́ть**

вздра́гивать, вздро́гнуть *v/i.* start; wince

вздыха́ть, вздохну́ть breathe deeply; sigh; *pf.* take breath; *impf.* _ (**по** or **о** II) sigh, long for

взима́ть *taxes* raise, levy

взлеза́(ть) (на́ гору) climb up (a hill)

взлёт upward flight; *av.* take-off; **_но-поса́дочный: _'-но-поса́дочная полоса́** runway

взлета́ть, _е́ть fly up; *av.* take off

взлом breaking open; **_'-щик** housebreaker, burglar

взмо́рье coast; seaside

взнос payment, instalment; fee, dues

взойти́ → восходи́ть *a.* **всходи́ть**

взор look, gaze

взро́слый grown-up (*a. su.*)

взрыв explosion; *fig.* outburst; **_ать[1], взорва́ть** blow up, blast; **-ся** *v/i.* burst, explode; **_ать[2]**

взрыть plough up

въезжа́ть, въе́хать (на B) drive up, ride up

взыска́|ние punitive measure; *jur.* exaction; **_а́тельный** exacting; **_ивать, _а́ть** exact; *debt* recover

взя́т|ка bribe; (*cards*) trick (*of one round*); **_оничество** bribery

взять → брать

вид look, air; aspect (*a. gr.*); view, sight; kind; *zo., bot.* species; **в _'-е** (P) in the form (of); **в хоро́шем _'-е** in good condition; **под _'-ом** (P) under the pretence (of); **_ де́лать _** pretend; **име́ть в _у́** bear in mind; intend; **_ на жи́тельство** residential permit; **откры́тка с '-ом** picture-postcard

ви́део|за́пись videotape; **_-кассе́та** video cassette; **_-магнитофо́н** video(tape)-recorder

ви́д|еть, у- see; **_имый** visible; apparent; **_но** apparently; **по́езда ещё не _но** the train is not yet in sight; **_ный** visible; conspicuous; notable; *coll.* handsome

ви́за visa; official stamp

визг screech; yelp

визжа́ть, за- screech; yelp

визи́т (official) visit; ~ный: ~ная ка́рточка visiting card

ви́лка fork; *штепсельная* ~ *el.* plug

виля́ть, вильну́ть (T) wag; *fig.* be evasive

вин|а́ guilt; fault; ~и́ть *v.* blame; ~и́тельный: ~и́тельный паде́ж *gr.* accusative

вино́ wine; *coll.* vodka

винова́тый (в П) guilty (of); *кто* ~а́т? who is to blame?; ~а́т(а)! sorry!; ~ник culprit; ~ный (в П) guilty (of)

виногра́д grapes; *bot.* vine; ~ядник vineyard; ~ку́ренный: ~ренный заво́д distillery

винт screw; propeller; ~ово́й: ~ова́я ле́стница spiral staircase; ~о́вка rifle

виолонче́ль *f* cello

висе́ть *v/i.* hang

висо́к *anat.* temple

високо́сный: ~год leapyear

вися́чий *adj.* hanging; ~за́мо́к padlock

витами́н vitamin

витра́ж stained-glass window

витри́на shop window

вить, с- twist; *garland* weave; *nest* build; ~ся

impf. hair: curl; *plant:* twine; *dust:* whirl

вихрь *m* whirlwind

вишн|ёвый cherry ...; ~я cherr|y, -ies; -y-tree

вклад *fin.* deposit; *fig.* contribution; ~ капита́ла investment; ~чик *fin.* depositor; investor; ~ывать, **вложи́ть** put in; enclose; deposit; invest

включ|а́ть, ~и́ть include; switch or turn on; ~а́я (В) including; ~и́тельно inclusive(ly)

вкра́тце briefly

вкруту́ю: яйцо́ ~ hard-boiled egg

вкус taste; *име́ть* ~ (Р) taste (of); ~ный tasty

вла́га moisture

владе́|лец, ~лица owner; ~ние possession; estate; ownership; ~ть (Т) own, possess; *language* know

вла́жный moist, humid

власть *f* power; *(political)* authority

вле́во (от Р) to the left (of)

влез|а́(ть), ~ть (в В) climb in(to), get in(to); ~ на де́рево climb (up) a tree

влече́ние bent, inclination; ~ за собо́й involve

вли|ва́)ть pour in

влия́|ние influence; ~тельный influential; ~ть, по-(на В) influence

вложе́|ние enclosure; *fin.* investment; ~и́ть → вкла́-

дывать

влюб|лённый adj. in love; (*look*) amorous; *as su.* lover; **~ляться, ~иться** (*в* B) fall in love (with)

вместе together; *~ с тем* at the same time, also

вместо (P) instead of; *~ этого* instead adv.

вмеща́ть, вмести́ть contain, hold; seat

вмиг adv. in no time

внаём: *сдать ~* (*flat, etc.*) let

внача́ле adv. at the beginning

вне (P) outside; *~ о́череди* out of turn; *~ себя́* beside oneself

внеза́пный sudden

внести́ → **вноси́ть**

вне́шн|ий outward, external; (*policy, trade*) foreign

внешта́тный not on permanent stoff

вниз down(wards); **~у́** (P) at the bottom (of); adv. below; downstairs

вник|а́ть, '~нуть (*в* B) go deep into, scrutinize

внима́|ние attention; **приня́ть во ~ние** take into account; **~тельность** f attentiveness; courtesy; **~тельный** attentive; considerate, courteous

вничью́: *сыгра́ть ~* (*game*) draw v.

вновь adv. anew; newly

вноси́ть, внести́ carry in;

pay in; introduce, enter

внук grandson; **'~и** grandchildren

вну́тр|енний inner; interior; internal; **~й** (P) inside, within (*a. adv.*)

вну́чка granddaughter

внуш|а́ть, ~и́ть idea suggest; *feelings* inspire; **~и́(те) ему́, что ...** impress on him that ...; **~и́тельный** impressive; **~е́ние** suggestion

вня́тный distinct, audible

во → **в**

вовле|ка́ть, '~чь drag in; *fig.* involve

во́время in time, timely

во́все coll. completely; *~ не(т)* not ... at all

вогна́ть → **вгоня́ть**

вода́ water

води́тель driver, chauffeur

води́ть lead, conduct, guide; drive, steer; → **вести́**; **~ся** be found, exist; (*с*T) consort, mix (with)

во́дка vodka

во́дный water...; *~ спорт* aquatic sports

водо|боя́знь f hydrophobia; **~воро́т** whirlpool; **~измеще́ние** mar. displacement; **~ла́з** (professional) diver; **~па́д** waterfall, cataract; **~прово́д** water-pipe; **~ро́д** m hydrogen; **~снабже́ние** water supply

водяно́й water...

воева́ть be at war, fight

военно...: ~**возду́шные** / ~**возду́шные си́лы** f/pl. air force; ~**морско́й** / ~**морско́й флот** navy; ~**пле́нный** prisoner of war; ~**слу́жащий** serviceman

вое́нн|ый military; war...; as su. soldier; '~**ое положе́ние** martial law; ~**ый трибуна́л** court-martial

вождь m leader

во́жжи f/pl. reins

воз cart; cart-load

возбу|жда́ть, ~**ди́ть** excite, rouse; jur. ~**ди́ть про́тив** (P) bring an action against

возвра|ща́ть, ~**ти́ть** v/t. return, restore; ~**ся** v/i. return, come back

возвы́шенн|ость f geogr. height; fig. loftiness; ~**ый** elevated (a. fig.)

во́зглас exclamation

воздви|га́ть, '~**нуть** erect, build

воздержа́|ние abstention; '~**иваться**, ~**а́ться** (от P) abstain (from)

во́здух air; на ~**е** in the open air

возду́шн|ый air...; ~**ая трево́га** air-raid alarm; '~**ый мост** (or '~**ые перево́зки**) airlift; ~**ый шар** balloon

воззва́ние appeal, proclamation

вози́ть convey, carry; drive, cart; → **везти́**; ~**ся** potter about; (с T) busy o.s. (with)

воз|лага́ть, ~**ложи́ть** (на B) lay (on); hopes set; blame put

во́зле (P) beside, by, near (a. adv.)

возме́здие retribution

возме|ща́ть, ~**сти́ть** (B) compensate for; refund; reimburse for; ~**ще́ние** compensation; refund; reimbursement

возмо́жно it is possible; possibly; ~ **скоре́е** as soon as possible; **ско́лько** ~ as much (many) as possible; **наско́лько** ~ as far as possible

возмо́жн|ость f possibility; opportunity; ~**ый** possible

возмути́тельный disgraceful, outrageous

возму|ща́ть, ~**ти́ть** anger, rouse indignation; -**ся** be indignant; ~**ще́ние** indignation

вознагра|жда́ть, ~**ди́ть** reward; compensate (for за B); ~**жде́ние** reward; compensation; fee

возника́ть, '~**нуть** arise, appear

возобнов|ля́ть, ~**и́ть** renew; resume

возра|жа́ть, ~**зи́ть** (про́тив P) object (to); retort; ~**же́ние** objection; rejoinder

во́ин warrior; soldier; **~ский** military; **~ская пови́нность** f conscription

вой howl; (*wind*) wail

во́йлок thick felt

войн|а́ war; **на ~е́** in (the) war

войска́ n/pl. mil. troops, forces

войти́ → **входи́ть**

вокза́л rail. station (building); mar. arrival and departure building

вокру́г (P) round, around (a. adv.)

вол ox

волк wolf

волн|а́ wave (a. radio); **взры́вная ~а́** blast; **~ова́ть, вз-** excite, agitate; ruffle; **~ся** impf. be excited, worry; pf. get excited or worried

волоки́та red tape

волокно́ fibre

во́лос hair; **~а́тый** hairy; **~яно́й** hair...

волочи́ть drag (along); shuffle; wire draw

волчо́к (*toy*) top

волше́бн|ик magician; **~ый** magic; enchanting

во́льн|ость f liberty; pl ~ости undue familiarities; **~о!** mil. stand easy!; **~ый** free; unrestricted

во́ля will(-power); liberty, freedom

вон adv. out; over there

вонь f stench; **~ю́чий** stinking; **~я́ть** stink

вообра|жа́ть, ~зи́ть (*себе́*) imagine; **~же́ние** imagination; **~зи́мый** imaginable

вообще́ generally; altogether

воодушевл|е́ние inspiration, enthusiasm; **~я́ть, ~и́ть** inspire, fill with enthusiasm

вооруж|а́ть, ~и́ть arm; equip; **~е́ние** armament

вопло|ща́ть, ~ти́ть embody, incarnate; personify; **~ще́ние** incarnation; personification

вопреки́ (Д) in spite of; regardless of

вопро́с question; **~и́тельный** interrogative; question...; **~ник** (*for polls etc.*) questionnaire

вор thief

ворва́ться → **врыва́ться**

воробе́й sparrow

воров|а́ть, с- steal; **~ство́** stealing

во́рон raven; **'~а** crow

воро́нка (*for pouring liquids*) funnel

во́рот collar; tech. windlass; **'~а** n/pl. gate; (*sports*) goal; **~ни́к, ~ничо́к** collar

ворча́ть, про- grumble

восемна́дцат|ый eighteenth; **~ь** eighteen

во́семь eight; **~деся́т** eighty; **~со́т** eight hundred

воск wax

восклиц|а́ние exclamation; **-ца́ть, '-кнуть** exclaim

восково́й wax...; *fig.* waxen

воскрес|а́ть, '-нуть rise from the dead; **'-е́ние** resurrection; **-е́нье** Sunday

воспал|е́ние *med.* inflammation; **-я́ться, -и́ться** become inflamed

воспит|а́ние upbringing; education; **'-ывать, -а́ть** bring up; educate

воспламен|я́ть, -и́ть inflame (*a. fig.*)

воспо́льзоваться → по́льзоваться

воспомина́ние memory, reminiscence; *pl. a.* memoirs

воспре|ща́ть, -ти́ть prohibit, forbid; **-ще́ние** prohibition

восприи́мчивый susceptible; (*mind*) receptive

воспри|нима́ть, -ня́ть perceive; (**непра́вильно**) (mis)interpret

воспроизве|де́ние reproduction; **-води́ть, -вести́** reproduce

восста́|(ва́)ть (**про́тив** P) rise (against); **-ние** insurrection

восстан|а́вливать (*or coll.* **-овля́ть**), *pf.* **-ови́ть** restore; reconstruct; **-овле́ние** restoration; reconstruction

восто́к east; **к -у от** (P) east of

восто́р|г enthusiasm, rapture(s); **-га́ться** (T) be enthusiastic (about) *or* enraptured (with); **-женный** enthusiastic

восто́чный east..., eastern

востре́бовани|е: до -я poste restante

восхо́д (**со́лнца**) (sun) rise; **взойти́** *poet.* → **восходи́ть**

восьме́рка (*cards*) eight; number eight (*bus, etc.*)

восьмо́й eighth

вот *particle* here (is), there (is); **- как!** you don't say!; **- что он сказа́л** that is what he said

во́тум: - (не)дове́рия (Д) vote of (no) confidence (in)

вошь *f* louse

впа|да́ть, -сть (**в** B) fall (into) (*a. fig.*); **'-лый** sunken, hollow

впервы́е for the first time

вперёд *adv.* forward; ahead; in advance

впереди́ (P) in front (of); ahead (of); *a. adv.*

впечатле́ние impression

-и́тельный impressionable

впи́с|ывать, -а́ть enter, insert

вплоть (**до** P) right up (to); down (to) fig.

вполголоса in a low voice

вполне́ fully, quite

впору́ быть ~ (Д) fit

впосле́дствии afterwards, subsequently

впра́ве: быть ~ have a right (+ to inf.)

впра́во (от P) to the right (of)

впредь henceforth; in future; ~ до until

впры́с|кивание injection; **~кивать, ~нуть** inject

впуск admission, admittance

впус|ка́ть, ~ти́ть let in

враг enemy

вражда́|а v/t. enmity, hostility; **~е́бный** hostile

врата́рь m goal-keeper

врач physician, doctor; **вызыва́ть, вы́звать** ~ call a doctor, send for a doctor; **зубно́й** ~ dentist; **вое́нный** ~ medical officer; **~е́бный** medical

враща́|ть v/t. turn, revolve; **~ся** v/i. revolve, wheel; run; **~е́ние** revolution, rotation

вред harm; detriment; **~и́ть, по~** (Д) harm; be injurious to; **'~ный** harmful, injurious, noxious

вре́менный temporary; provisional

вре́м|я n time; **во ~** (P) during; **~я го́да** season; **тем ~енем** meanwhile

времяпрепровожде́ние pastime

вро́де (P) like, such as

врождённый inborn, innate

вро́з|ницу by retail; **~ь** separately, apart

вруча́|ть, ~ить hand over

врыва́ться, ворва́ться (в B) burst in(to)

вряд: **~ли** scarcely, hardly

вса́дник horseman

все → **весь**

всё pron. → **весь;** adv. always, all the time; **~ же** all the same; **~ ещё** still, yet

всевозмо́жный every or all possible

всегда́ always; **раз (и) на~** once (and) for all

вселе́нная universe, world

все|ми́рный world...; world-wide; **~могу́щий** almighty; **~наро́дный** national; **~наро́дный** nation-wide; **~о́бщий** universal, general; **~сою́зный** All-Union; **~сторо́нний** all-round, comprehensive

всё-таки all the same, for all that

всеце́ло entirely

вска́кивать, вскочи́ть jump (up, on, into)

вско́ре soon; shortly after

вскри́к|ивать, ~нуть cry out

вскры́|(ва)ть open; reveal; **~тие** opening; revelation; autopsy

вслед (**за** T) after, following; ~ **послать** send on, forward; **'-ствие** (P) in consequence of, owing to

вслух adv. aloud

всмятку: **яйцо** ~ soft-boiled egg

всплы(ва́)ть (come to the) surface

вспомина́ть, вспо́мнить remember, recall

вспомога́тельный auxiliary

вспоте́ть → **поте́ть**

вспы́льчивый hot-tempered, irascible

вста(ва́)ть rise, get up; stand up

вставл|я́ть, **'-ить** set in; insert; ~**ные зу́бы** m/pl. false teeth

встре́тить → **встреча́ть**

встре́ч|а encounter, meeting; reception, welcome; (*sports*) match; **~а́ть, встре́тить** v/t. meet; *fig.* meet with; ~**аться** v/i. meet; ~**ный** contrary, counter…; **пе́рвый ~ный** the first person you meet

вступ|а́ть, **-и́ть** (**в** B) enter; *fig.* enter into; join; ~ **в брак** marry (*v/i.*); ~**и́тельный** entrance…; introductory

всходи́ть, взойти́ sun: rise; *seeds:* sprout; (**на** B) ascend, mount

всю́ду everywhere

вся → **весь**

вся́кий any; every; anyone; everybody; **на** ~ **слу́чай** just in case

вта́йне in secret

вта́лкивать, втолкну́ть (**в** B) push in(to)

втека́ть, втечь (**в** B) flow in(to)

втира́ть, втере́ть rub in

вторг|а́ться, **'-нуться** (**в** B) invade; intrude into; ~**же́ние** invasion; intrusion

втор|и́чный second, repeated; secondary; **'-ник** Tuesday; **~о́й** (*numeral*) second; ~**остепе́нный** minor; secondary

в(т)уз = **вы́сшее (техни́ческое) уче́бное заведе́ние**) (technical) college

вход entrance; **'-а нет** no entry; ~**и́ть, войти́** (**в** B) go or come in(to); *fig.* enter into; ~**и́ть в соста́в** form part (of); **войди́(те) в моё положе́ние!** put yourself in my place!

вчера́ yesterday; ~**шний** adj. yesterday's

въезд entry, entrance (*for* or by transport); ~**на́я ви́за** entry visa

въезж|а́ть, въе́хать (**в** B) enter; drive in(to); move in(to)

вы you

выбира́ть, выбрать

choose; select
вы́бор choice; selection;
~ы *m/pl.* election(s)
выбра́сывать, вы́бросить
throw out; throw away
вы́везти → вывози́ть
вы́веска sign(board)
вы́вести → выводи́ть
выве́тривать, вы́ветрить
air, ventilate; *smell* let out
вы́вих *med.* dislocation;
~нуть *pf.* dislocate, put
out (of joint)
вы́вод conclusion; inference; **~и́ть, вы́вести** lead
or take out; conclude, infer; hatch; breed; exterminate; **~ок** brood
вы́воз export; taking out;
~и́ть, вы́везти export;
take or convey out; bring
out; **~ дете́й на мо́ре**
take the children off to
the seaside
вы́гляд|еть look, seem to
be; **'~ывать, вы́глянуть**
look out; (**из-за** P)
emerge (from behind)
вы́говор pronunciation; reproof
вы́год|а advantage; profit;
~ный advantageous; profitable
вы́гон pasture; **~я́ть, вы́-
гнать** drive out; *coll.* sack
(*from work*)
выгора́ть, вы́гореть burn
down; fade (*in the sun*)
выгружа́ть, вы́грузить unload

вы́грузка unloading
выда(ва́)ть hand out, distribute; give away; betray;
~ себя́ за (B) pretend to
be, pose as; **~ся** protrude;
stand out; be conspicuous
вы́дача distribution; issue;
extradition
выдвига́ть, вы́двинуть
move or pull out; *fig.* propose, put forward; nomi-
nate; **~ся** move forward;
rise (from the ranks)
выдворя́ть, вы́дворить
evict, throw out
выделя́ть, вы́делить
single out; distinguish;
biol. secrete
выде́рживать, вы́держать
endure, bear; *test* pass
вы́держка endurance; ex-
cerpt; *photo.* exposure
вы́дра otter
вы́дум|ка invention; idea;
coll. made-up story;
'~ывать, ~ать invent; *story
a.* make up
выдыха́ть, вы́дохнуть
breathe out
выезжа́ть, вы́ехать (**из** P)
leave (*by car, train or on
horseback*); move (*from a
flat*)
выжива́ние survival;
~ива́ть, ~ить survive
вы́здоров|еть *pf.* recover,
regain health; **~ле́ние** re-
covery
вы́зов challenge; summons; **~ по телефо́ну**

telephone call

вызыва́ть, вы́звать *person* call out *or* for *or* up; challenge; summon; *feeling* provoke, excite

выи́грывать, вы́играть win; gain

вы́игрыш winnings; *(sweepstake)* prize; gain

вы́йти → **выходи́ть**

вы́кидыш miscarriage; abortion

выключа́т|ель *m el.* switch; **~ь, вы́ключить** switch off; *gas* turn off

выкра́ивать, вы́кроить *dress* cut out; *time* find

вы́лез(а́)ть climb *or* scramble out; *hair:* come out, fall out

вылета́ть, вы́лететь fly out; *av.* take off

вылечи́вать, вы́лечить (от P) cure (of)

вылива́ть, вы́лить pour out; empty

выма́нивать, вы́манить *money, promise* coax (out of y P); *person, animal* lure (out of *из* P)

вымеря́ть, вы́мерить measure

вымира́ть, вы́мереть die out, become extinct; become deserted

вымета́ть, вы́мести sweep (up)

вымога́т|ельство extortion; **~ь (у** P) extort (from)

вымока́ть, вы́мокнуть be drenched

вы́мысел invention, fiction

вы́мя *n* udder

вынима́ть, вы́нуть (из P) take out (of)

выноси́ть, вы́нести carry *or* take out; endure; *sentence* pass; **~ливый** able to endure hardship, hardy

вынужда́ть, вы́нудить force, compel

вы́нуть → **вынима́ть**

выпада́ть, вы́пасть fall *or* drop out

выпи(ва́)ть drink; drink up

выпи́сывать, вы́писать copy out; write out; *newspaper, etc.* subscribe to

выпла́чивать, вы́платить pay (off); pay out

выполня́ть, вы́полнить fulfil, carry out

выправля́ть, вы́править straighten; correct

выпряга́ть, вы́прячь unharness

вы́пуск output; issue; *(literary)* instalment; **~а́ть, вы́пустить** let out; *goods* produce, turn out; issue, publish; **~ из рук** let go; **~но́й: ~но́й экза́мен** school-leaving examination; **~но́й кла́пан** exhaust valve

выраба́тывать, вы́работать work out; manufacture; *coll.* earn

выра́внивать, вы́ровнять

smooth out; *road* level

выра|жа́ть, вы́разить express; **~же́ние** expression; **~зи́тельный** expressive

выраста́ть, вы́расти grow up; increase

выреза́ть, вы́резать cut *or* carve out

вы́ровнять → **выра́внивать**

вырожде́ние degeneration

выруба́ть, вы́рубить cut out; cut down, fell

выруча́ть, вы́ручить come to s.o.'s. aid; help out; (*money*) make, get

вырыва́ть, вы́рвать tear *or* pull out; (**у** P) wring (from)

вы́садка disembarkation

выса́живать(ся), вы́садить(ся) disembark; plant

выска́зывать, вы́сказать *v/t.* state, tell; **-ся** (**о** П) express one's opinion (about); (**за** В, **про́тив** P) declare o.s. (for, against)

выслу́шивать, вы́слушать hear out; *med.* auscultate

высме́ивать, вы́смеять ridicule

высо́вываться, вы́сунуться (**из** P) lean out (of)

высо́кий high; tall

высоко|ка́чественный high-quality...; **~ме́рие** haughtiness; **~ме́рный** haughty; **~па́рный** high-

-flown, bombastic

высота́ height; altitude; (*sound*) pitch

вы́сохнуть → **высыха́ть**

выста́в|ка exhibition; **~ля́ть, вы́ставить** put out *or* forward; exhibit

вы́стрел shot; **~ить** → **стреля́ть**

вы́ступ projection; **~а́ть, ~ить** come out *or* forward; *meeting, etc.* address; *thea.* perform; **~ле́ние** performance; speech

вы́сунуться → **высо́вываться**

вы́сший higher; highest

высыла́ть, вы́слать send (off); *person* send out; deport

высыха́ть, вы́сохнуть *v/i.* dry up; wither

выта́скивать, вы́тащить drag *or* pull out

вытека́ть, вы́течь flow *or* run out; *impf. a.* result, follow (from)

вытесня́ть, вы́теснить force out; oust

вы́течь → **вытека́ть**

вытира́ть, вы́тереть wipe (off, up); wipe dry

выть howl; *wind:* wail

выта́гивать, вы́тянуть draw *or* pull out; stretch (out)

выу́чивать, вы́учить (В) learn; **~ ученика́ языку́** teach a pupil a language; **-ся** (Д) learn

вы́ход going out; way out (*a. fig.*); exit; *agr.* yield; **~и́ть, вы́йти** (*из* P) go *or* come out (of); *book*: be published; **~** за́муж *woman*: marry

выцвета́ть, вы́цвести fade, lose colour

вычёркивать, вы́черкнуть cancel, cross out

вы́честь → вычита́ть

вы́чет (*pay*) deduction; **за ~ом** except; less, minus

вычисля́ть, вы́числить calculate, compute

вычита́ть, вы́честь subtract; deduct

вы́ше *adj., adv.* higher; *prep.* (P) above, beyond; **~ука́занный, ~упомя́нутый** above (-mentioned)

вы́шивка embroidery, needle-work

вышина́ height; **'~ка** (watch)tower; **бурова́я '~ка** rig

выявля́ть, вы́явить reveal; make known; expose

выясня́ть, вы́яснить elucidate; ascertain

вью́га snow-storm

вяз elm

вяза́|ние knitting; crotchet (-work); **~ть, с~,** bind, tie up; knit; crotchet

вя́з|кий viscous; miry, boggy; **~нуть, у~** stick, get stuck

вя́лый slack; flabby; limp; sluggish

вя́нуть, у~ *v/i.* wither

Г

га → гекта́р

га́вань *f* harbour

гада́ть, по~ tell fortunes; *impf.* guess

га́дкий vile; ugly

га́ечный: ~ ключ wrench

газ gas

газе́т|а newspaper; **~ный: ~ная бума́га** newsprint; **~ный кио́ск** news-stand; **'~чик** *coll.* journalist

га́зо|вый gas...; **~вая коло́нка** (*apparatus for heating water*) geyser; **~вая плита́** gas stove; **~вый**

балло́н gas bottle *or* cylinder

газо́н lawn

газопрово́д gas-main

га́йка *tech.* nut

галантере́я haberdashery

галере́я gallery; **'~ка** *thea. coll.* gallery, «the gods»

га́лка jackdaw

га́лстук (neck)tie

га́лька pebbles, shingle

гама́к hammock

гара́ж garage

гаранти́ровать (*im*)*pf.* guarantee; **'~ия** guarantee

гардеро́б wardrobe; cloak-room; **~щица** cloak-room attendant

гарди́на heavy curtain

гармо́н|ика, **~ь** f accordion; **губна́я ~ика** mouth organ; **~и́ст** accordion-player; **~и́ческий**, **~и́чный** harmonious

гарнизо́н garrison

гарни́р cul. garnish

гарниту́р (furniture) set, suite

гаси́ть, по~ extinguish; gas turn off

гастроли́|ровать thea. be on tour; **~ный**: **~ный спекта́кль** m guest performance

гастроно́м (**~и́ческий магази́н**) grocery shop

гва́рдия mil. guards

гвоздь m nail; tack

где where; **~-либо**, **~-нибудь**, **~-то** anywhere, somewhere

ректа́р hectare

генера́л general; **~-майо́р** major-general; **~ьный** general; **~ьная репети́ция** dress rehearsal; **2ная Ассамбле́я** (UNO) General Assembly

ге́ни|й genius; **~а́льный** of genius; (idea) brilliant

геогра́фия geography

герб coat of arms; **госуда́рственный ~** national emblem; **~овый**: **~овая бума́га** stamped paper

герма́нский Germanic; pol. German

геро́й hero

ге́рцог duke; **~и́ня** duchess

ги́бель f death; ruin; loss; wreck

ги́бкий flexible; supple

ги́бнуть, по~ perish

гига́нт giant

гид guide

гидро|самолёт seaplane; **~ста́нция** hydroelectric power-station

ги́льза mil. cartridge-case

гимн anthem; hymn

гимна́зия (secondary school) gymnasium

гимна́ст, **~ка** gymnast; **~ёрка** mil. field shirt; **~ика** gymnastics

гипс plaster of Paris; **~овый**: **~овая повя́зка** plaster bandage

гирля́нда garland

ги́ря (scales or clock) weight

глав|а́ head (fig.); (book) chapter; **~нокома́ндующий** Commander-in-Chief; **~ный** main, chief; **~ным о́бразом** mainly, chiefly

глаго́л verb

гла́|дить, по~ stroke; **~2**, **вы~** iron

гла́дкий smooth; sleek

глаз eye; sg. **~но́й** eye...; **~унь

я** sg. fried eggs

гла́нда tonsil

гла́сность glasnost

гла́сный vowel; adj. public,

open

глин|а clay; **~яный** clay..., earthenware...

глист med. (intestinal) worm

глоба́льный global, world-wide

глот|а́ть swallow; gulp down; **'~ка** gullet; coll. throat; **~о́к** gulp, sip

глу́б|же deeper; more deeply; **~ина́** depth; **~о́кий** deep; profound

глубокоуважа́емый much-esteemed; (in formal letters) dear

глум|и́ться, по~ (над T) sneer (at)

глуп|е́ц fool; **'~ость** f foolishness, stupidity; **~ый** foolish, stupid

глух|о́й deaf; toneless; **~немо́й** deaf-and-dumb; **~та́** deafness

глуш|и́тель m silencer; **~и́ть** stifle; radio jam; **~ь** f backwoods; remote corner

глы́ба clod, clump; block

гляде́ть, по~ (на B) look (at)

гля́нец gloss, lustre

гнать cattle drive; pursue; distil; **~ся за** (T) hunt after, pursue; strive (for, after)

гнев anger; **'~ный** angry

гнездо́ nest

гнёт oppression

гнило́й rotten

гнить, с~ rot; tooth: decay

гно́|иться, за~ fester

гной pus

гну́сный vile, abominable

гнуть, со'~ v/t. bend; **~ся** v/i. bend

гобеле́н tapestry

ро́вор sound of voices, murmur; dialect

говор|и́ть, сказа́ть say; impf. speak; pf. по~ (с T) talk, speak (to)

говя́дина beef

год year (→ a. ле́то); **~тому́ наза́д** a year ago; **~ово́й** annual, yearly

год|и́ться (на B) be fit (for); (Д) fit; **'~ный** fit, suitable

годовщи́на anniversary

гол goal; **заби́ть ~** score a goal

го́лень f shin

голла́нд|ец, ~ка Dutchman, Dutchwoman; **~ский** Dutch

голов|а́ head; **'~ка** (pin, nail) head; **~но́й: ~на́я боль** f head-ache; **~но́й убо́р** head-dress; **~окруже́ние** giddiness

го́лод hunger; famine; **~а́ть** starve; go without food; **'~ный** hungry; **~о́вка** hunger-strike

гололе́дица: на у́лицах ~ the roads are slippery

го́лос voice; pol. vote; **~ова́ть, про~** vote; **~ова́ние** voting; poll голубо́й (light-)blue

голу́бчик! my dear!

го́лубь *m* pigeon, dove

го́лый naked, bare

гольф golf; ~ы knee-length stockings

гоне́ние persecution

го́нка hurry-scurry; ~ вооруже́ний armaments race

го́н|ки *f/pl.* (*sports*) race; па́русные ~ки regatta; ~очный: ~очный автомоби́ль *m* racing car

гонора́р fee; royalties

гонча́р potter

гоня́ть drive (about); → гнать; ~ся за (Т) chase, pursue

гор|а́ mountain; в ~у uphill; под ~у downhill

гора́здо much, far (+ *comp.*)

горб hump; ~а́тый humpbacked; (*nose*) hooked

горбу́ша hunchback salmon

горди́ться (Т) be proud (of); pride o.s. (on); ~ость *f* pride; ~ый proud

го́ре grief, sorrow; ~ва́ть grieve; mourn

горе́|лка burner; ~ть *v/i.* burn

го́рец highlander

го́речь *f* bitter taste; *fig.* bitterness

горизо́нт horizon

гори́стый mountainous

го́рло throat; *anat.* windpipe; ~ышко[1] *dim. of* ~о; ~ышко[2] (bottle-)neck

горнорабо́чий miner

горноста́й ermine

го́рный mountain...; mountainous; mining...; ~я́к miner; mining engineer

го́род town, city; ~ско́й town..., city...; municipal, urban

горожа́не *m/pl.* town-dwellers

горо́|х collect. peas; ~шина pea

го́рсть *f* handful

горта́нь *f* larynx

горчи́|ца mustard; ~чница mustard-pot

горшо́к (*earthenware*) pot; jug

го́рький bitter

горю́чее fuel

горя́чий (*burning*) hot; heated; (*welcome*) warm; ~и́ться, раз- get excited; get angry

гос... *in compounds* = госуда́рственный State...

го́спиталь *m mil.* hospital

господа́ gentlemen

го́спо|ди! good heavens!; ~и́н gentleman; (*with name*) Mr.; ~дство domination, supremacy; ~дствовать (над Т) dominate, rule; ~дь *m* God, the Lord

госпожа́ lady; (*with name*) Mrs., Miss

гостеприи́м|ный hospitable; **~ство** hospitality

гости́ная drawing-room; **~ница** hotel; **~и́ть** (у Р) visitor: stay (with); **~ь** m, **~ья** guest, visitor

госуда́рственный State...; public; national

гото́в|ить, при- v/t. prepare; make ready; coach, train; cook; **~ся** (к Д) v/i. prepare; get ready; **~ый** ready; finished; ready-made

грабёж robbery; **~и́тель** m robber; **~и́тельский** predatory; (prices) exorbitant **~ить, о-** rob; impf. pillage

гра́бли f/pl. rake

гравю́ра print, engraving; etching

град hail; **~ идёт** it is hailing

гра́дус degree; **~ник** coll. thermometer

граждан|и́н, ~ка citizen; **~ский** civil; **~ство** citizenship

грамм gram(me)

грамма́тика grammar

гра́мот|а reading and writing; document; **вери́тельные ~ы** f/pl. credentials; **~ный** literate; grammatical; competent

грана́т pomegranate

грана́та grenade

гранёный cut-glass...; (jewel) faceted

грани́ц|а border, frontier; limit; **за ~ей, за ~у** abroad; **из-за ~ы** from abroad

грани́чить (с Т) border (on)

граф(и́ня) count(ess)

графа́ (book-keeping, etc.) column; **~ик** graph, diagram; schedule

графи́н decanter, carafe

грацио́зный graceful

гребёнка comb

гре́бень m comb; crest

греб|е́ц oarsman; **~ля** rowing; **~но́й** rowing...; **~но́е колесо́** paddle-wheel

грейпфру́т grapefruit

грек Greek

гре́лка hot-water bottle

греме́ть thunder; rumble; clank; **~у́чая змея́** rattle-snake

гренки́ m/pl. toast

грести́ v. row

грести́[2] v. rake

греть warm, give out warmth; fur: keep warm; **~ся** warm o.s.; **~ся на со́лнце** bask in the sun

грех sin

греч|а́нка Greek woman; **~еский** Greek; **~и́ха** buckwheat

греш|и́ть rel. co- sin; **~ник, ~ница** sinner; **~ный** sinful; guilty

гриб mushroom

гри́ва mane

грим (stage) make-up

грипп influenza

гроб coffin; ~**ница** tomb

гроза́ thunderstorm; ~**и́ть** (Д, Т, *inf.*) threaten; **'-ный** threatening; terrible

гром thunder; ~ **греми́т** it is thundering; **как '-ом поражённый** thunder-struck

грома́дный huge, colossal

гро́мкий loud; (*name*) famous; ~**коговори́тель** *m* loud-speaker; ~**овóй** thunder...; thunderous

громозди́ть pile up; **'-кий** bulky, unwieldy

громоотво́д lightning-rod

гро́хот (*noise*) crash; rattle; roar

груби́ть, **на-** (Д) be rude (to); **'-ость** *f* coarseness; rudeness; crudity; **'-ый** coarse; rude; crude; rough

грудно́й breast...; pectoral; ~**но́й ребёнок** baby, suckling; ~ *f* breast; bosom; chest

груз load; cargo; freight; ~**ило** plummet

грузи́н, ~**ка**, ~**ский** Georgian

грузи́ть, **по-** load; *troops* entrain, emplane *etc.*; ~**ови́к** lorry, truck; **'-чик** *mar.* stevedore, docker; loader

гру́ппа group

грусти́ть be sad *or* melan-choly; ~**и́ть по** (D) long for; **'-ный** sad, melancholy

гру́ша pear(-tree)

грыжа *med.* hernia

грызть gnaw; *nuts* crack; *fig.* nag at; ~**ся** *dogs:* fight; *fig.* bicker

гря́дка (*garden*) bed; ~**ущий** approaching, coming

грязелече́бница mud-baths; ~**ная пома́да** muddy; filthy; ~**ь** *f* dirt; mud; filth

гря́нуть *pf.* burst out *or* forth; *song* strike up

губа́ lip; **наду́ть '-ы** pout

губи́ть, **по-** ruin; undo, spoil

гу́бка[1] sponge

гу́б|ка[2] *dim.* lip; ~**но́й** lip; labial; ~**на́я пома́да** lipstick; ~**на́я гармо́ника** mouth-organ

гуде́ть hoot; honk; drone; ~**о́к** hooter; *mot.* horn

гуля́|нье: **наро́дное '-нье** public merry-making; **-ть** (go for a) walk, stroll

гумани́зм humanism; **'-ный** humane

гу́сеница *zo.* caterpillar

густо́й dense, thick; (*voice*) deep

гусь *m* goose

гу́ща sediment, grounds; (*wood*) thicket

Д

да yes; *coll.* and; but; ~
здравствует ... long live
...

да(ва́)ть give; (Д + *inf.*)
let; ~ **доро́гу** (Д) make
way for; **да́й(те)!** give!;
дава́й(те) come on!; +
inf. let us + *inf.*

дави́ть press; (*juice out of
fruit, etc.*) squeeze; (**на** В)
weigh (on); ~**ся, по-** (Т)
choke (with)

да́вн|ий old, bygone; ~о́
long ago; for a long time

да́же *adv.* even

да́лее further; **и так ~**
(*abbr.* и т. д.) and so on
(*etc.*)

далёкий far (away), distant, remote; ~еко́ *adv.*
far

даль f distance; ~**ний** distant; remote; (*way*) long;
~**нови́дный**   far-seeing;
~**нозо́ркий** long-sighted;
~**ше** farther; further; **что
же ~ше** what next?; **чи-
та́й(те) ~ше** go on reading

да́м|а lady; (*cards*) queen;
~**ский** ladies' ...

да́нные data; makings

дань f: **отда(ва́)ть ~** appreciate, recognize, pay
tribute (to Д)

дар gift; donation; ~**и́ть,
по-** give (as a present);
~**ова́ние** gift, talent;

~**ови́тый** gifted, talented;
'~**ом** for nothing; in vain

да́та date

да́т|ский Danish; ~**ча́нин,
~ча́нка** Dane

да́ча dacha, country-cot-
tage; ~**ник, ~ница** summer resident

два m/n two; **ка́ждые ~
дня** every other day; '~-
дцатый   twentieth;
'~**дцать** twenty; '~**жды**
twice

две f two

двена́дцат|ый twelfth; ~**ь**
twelve

двер|но́й door...; '~**ца** (*fur-
niture*) door; ~**ь** f door

две́сти two hundred

дви́гат|ель m motor, en-
gine; ~**ь, дви́нуть** move,
set in motion; advance;
~**ся** *v/i.* move

движе́ние motion; move-
ment; traffic; '~**имый**
moved, prompted

дво́е two; ~**же́нство** bi-
gamy; ~**то́чие** colon

дво́й|ка (*cards*) two;
(*school*) poor mark; (*bus,
tram*) number two; ~**но́й**
double; ~**ня** twins;
~**ственный: у меня́ к
э́тому дво́йственное отно-
ше́ние** I have mixed feelings about it

двор (court)yard; court; **на**

~é outside; **~éц** palace; **²~éц культу́ры** Palace of Culture; **³~éц бракосочета́ния** Wedding Palace; **~ник** yard-keeper; *coll.* windscreen wiper; **~яни́н, ~я́нка** nobleman, noblewoman; **~я́нский** of noble birth; of ancient stock; **~я́нство** nobility

дву́|бо́ртный double-breasted; **~ли́чный** double-faced; **~смы́сленный** ambiguous; **~сторо́нний** bilateral; *(traffic)* two-way; **'~шка** two-copeck coin

деба́ты *pl.* debate

девальва́ция *econ.* devaluation

де́(ва́)ться get to, disappear; **куда́ он де́лся?** what has become of him?

деви́з motto

деви́чий maiden...; maidenly; **'~очка** *(little)* girl; **'~ушка** (unmarried) girl *(a. form of address)*

девяно́сто ninety

девятна́дцатый nineteenth; **'~ь** nineteen

девя́|тый ninth; **'~ть** nine

дёготь *m* tar

дед grandfather; **~ моро́з** Father Frost, Father Christmas; **'~ушка** grandfather, grandad

дежу́р|ить be on duty; **~ный** *adj.* on duty

дезерти́р deserter; **~овать** *(im)pf.* desert

дезинформа́ция misinformation; **~и́ровать** *(im)pf.* misinform

дезодора́нт deodorant

дезорганиза́ция disorganisation

де́йственный effective

де́йстви|е action; activity; effect; **³** *(drama)* act; **~ительно** indeed, really; **~и́тельность** *f* reality; realities; life; **~и́тельный** real, effective; valid; *gr., mil.* active

де́йствовать¹ act, operate; function, work; **~², по~** *(на В)* have an effect (on); act (upon)

дека́брь *m* December

дека́н *univ.* dean

деклара́ция declaration

декора́ция *thea.* scenery

декре́т decree; *coll.* maternity leave

де́лать, с~ do; make; **~ вы́вод** draw a conclusion; **~ вид** feign, pretend; **~ по-сво́ему** have one's own way; **~ся** become; happen

делега́т delegate; **~ция** delegation

деле́ние division; *(thermometer)* point

делика́тный delicate; tactful

дели́ть, раз~ *v/t.* divide (into **на В**, by 3 **на три**); *impf.* share; **~ся** *v/i.* math.

divide; **~ся, по-** (T) share
дел|о affair; deed; cause;
case (a. jur.); **это моё ~о**
that is my business; **как
~á?** how are things?; **в
чём ~о?** what is the matter; **на ~е** in fact, in reality; **в самом ~е** indeed
дел|овой business...; business-like; **'~ьный** efficient; practical, sensible
демократ|ия democracy;
~изация (P) democratization; **~ический** democratic
демонстрация demonstration; (film, etc.) (public) showing
дёнежный money(ed)
день m day; **в наши дни** nowadays; **на другой** ~ the day after; **на днях** the other day; in a day or two; **через** ~ every other day
дёньги f/pl. money
деполитизация depoliticization (Russia: abolition of political party organizations in the Armed and Security Forces and the Judiciary)
дёр|гать, ~нуть (R) pull, tug; **-ся** twitch; fig. worry
деревня village; the country
дёрево tree; (material) wood; (красное ~ mahogany; **~янный** wooden
держава pol. power
держать hold; keep; ~

пари́ bet; ~ **себя́** behave;
~ся (за B) hold (on to)
дёрз|кий impertinent; daring; **~ость** f impertinence; audacity
десант mil. landing (party)
десе́рт dessert
десна́ anat. gum
десяти|бо́рье decathlon;
~ле́тие decade; tenth anniversary; **~чный** decimal
деся́т|ка (cards) ten; coll. ten-rouble-note; (bus, tram) number ten; **~ый** tenth
де́сять ten
дета́ль f detail; tech. part, component; **~ный** detailed
дет|и n/pl. children; **~ский** child(ren)'s ...; childish; **~ство** childhood
дё́ться → девáться
дефицит deficit; shortage; deficiency; **'~ный** in short supply
деше́вле cheaper; more cheaply
дёшево adv. cheap(ly)
дешёвый cheap
децентрализация econ. devolution
де́ятель m: **госудáрствен-
ный** ~ statesman; **об-
щéственный** ~ public figure; **~ность** f activity; **~ный** active
джаз jazz(music); jazz band
джинсы pl. jeans

диван sofa; settee

дивизия *mil.* division

дивный marvellous

дизайн design; **~ер** designer

дик|арь *m,* **~арка** savage; *fig.* shy fellow, shy girl; **'~ий** wild; savage; shy

дикт|ант dictation; **~атура** dictatorship; **~овать, про~** dictate; **'~ор** *radio* announcer

диплом diploma; **~ат** diplomat; (brief)case; **~атия** diplomacy

директор director; (*school*) head|master, -mistress; **~ция** (*group*) management

дирижёр *mus.* conductor

диск disc; (*gramophone*) record; (*sports*) discus

дискриминация discrimination

дисплей *tech.* display

диспут public debate

дистанция distance (*a. sports*)

дитя *n* child, baby

дифтерит diphtheria

дичь *f hunt.* game; *coll.* nonsense

длин|а length; **~ой в три метра** 3 metres long; **'~ный** long

дли|тельный long, lasting; **~ся** last

для (P) for; **~ того чтобы** + *inf.* in order to; **~ чего?** what for?

дневн|ик diary; **~ой** day...; daily

днём by day; in the afternoon → **день**

дно bottom; **вверх ~м** upside down

до (P) until; as far as; before; **~ сих пор** up to here, up to now; **от пяти ~ семи** from 5 to 7

добав|ление addition; **~лять, '~ить** (**к** Д) add (to); **'~очный** additional, supplementary

доби(ва)ться (P) obtain; achieve; *impf. a.* try to obtain; strive (for)

доблесть *f* valour

добро *noun* (*something*) good; **~ пожаловать!** welcome! (*to visitor*)

добро|вольный voluntary; **~детель** *f* virtue; **~душный** goodnatured; **~желательный** benevolent; **~совестный** conscientious; **~та** kindness

добрый kind, good

добы|(ва)ть procure; extract, mine; **~ча** extraction; output; *hunt.* bag

довезти → **довозить**

доверие confidence, faith; **~ять, ~ить** entrust; commit; *impf.* (Д) trust

довод argument, reason; **~ить, довести** (**до** P) lead or take (as far as); *fig.* bring or drive (to)

довоенный pre-war

довози́ть, довезти́ (*до* P) (*by transport*) take *or* carry (as far as, to)

дово́ль|но enough; **_ный** satisfied, content, pleased; **_ствоваться** (T) content o.s. (with)

дога́д|ка guess, conjecture; **_ливый** quick-witted; **_ываться, _а́ться** *impf.* guess; understand; *impf.* surmise

догна́ть → **догоня́ть**

догов|а́риваться, _ори́ться (*о* П) make arrangements (for); *impf.* negotiate; *pf.* come to an agreement; **_о́р** agreement; *pol.* treaty

догоня́ть, догна́ть catch up (with) (*a. fig.*); *impf.* run after

дожд|ево́й rain...; **_ли́вый** rainy

дождь *m* rain; **_ идёт** it is raining; **_ моро́сит** it is drizzling

дожи(ва́)ть (*до* P) live until; live to see

до́йть, по_ milk

дойти́ → **доходи́ть**

доказ|а́тельство proof; evidence; **'_ывать, _а́ть** prove

докла́д lecture; report; **_ывать, доложи́ть** (*о* П) report (on); *visitor* announce

до́ктор doctor (*a. med.*)

докуме́нт document, pa-

per; **_а́льный** documentary

долг duty; debt

долго|сро́чный long-term; **_та́** length; *geogr.* longitude

доле́е → **до́льше**

до́лж|ен: он _ен + *inf.* he must; **он мне _ен пять рубле́й** he owes me 5 roubles; **_но́ быть** probably; **_ность** *f* post, position; **_ный** due; proper

доли́на valley

доложи́ть → **докла́дывать**

доло́й (B) down with ...

долото́ chisel

до́льше (*time*) longer

до́ля part; share; lot, fate

дом house; **_а** at home; **_а́шний** house...; domestic; home-made; **_о́й** *adv.* home

домохозя́йка house-wife

донесе́ние report; dispatch

доно́с information (against); **_и́ть, донести́** (*о* П) report (on); (*на* B) inform (against); **_чик** informer

допус|ка́ть, _ти́ть admit; assume

доро́г|а road; way; journey; **желе́зная _а** railway; **по _е** (*в* B, *на* B) on the way (to), en route

до́рого dear(ly)

дорого́й dear

дорож|а́ть, вз-, по- rise in price; ‿е dearer; ‿и́ть (T) value

доро́ж|ка path; strip of carpet, runner; *бегова́я ‿ка* running-track; ‿ный road...; travelling...

доса́д|а annoyance; ‿ный annoying

доска́ board

досло́вно word for word

досро́чно ahead of schedule

доста́|(ва́)ть get, obtain; *(до Р)* reach, touch; *ему́ не достаёт терпе́ния* he lacks patience; ‿ся *(Д)* fall to the lot; *ему́ доста́нется* he will get rebuked

доста́в|ка delivery; ‿ля́ть, ‿ить deliver; supply with; give, cause; afford

доста́точно sufficient

достиг|а́ть, ‿нуть achieve; reach

доста́ть → *достава́ть*

достиже́ние achievement

дости́чь → *дости́гнуть*

достове́рный trustworthy; authentic; *(source)* reliable

досто́|инство dignity; merit; worth; ‿йный deserving; merited; worthy

достопримеча́тельности *f/pl.* sights

достоя́ние property, possession, fortune

до́ступ access; ‿ный accessible; *(price)* moderate

досу́г leasure, spare time

дота́ция *(state)* subsidy; grant

дотра́гиваться, дотро́нуться *(до Р)* touch

дохо́д income; revenue, return; ‿и́ть, дойти́ *(до Р)* reach, come to; *fig.* end in; ‿ный profitable, lucrative

доце́нт assistant professor

до́чка, дочь *f* daughter

доще́чка *(door)* name-plate

драгоце́нн|ость *f* jewel; *pl.* jewelry; ‿ый precious

дразни́ть tease

дра́ка scuffle, fight

дра́ма drama; ‿ту́рг dramatist

дра́ться, по- fight

древеси́на *(material)* wood

дре́вн|ий ancient; antique; old; ‿ость *f* antiquity

дрем|о́та drowsiness; ‿у́чий *(forest)* dense, thick

дроб|и́ть, раз- crush; split up; ‿ь *f math.* fraction; *hunt.* small shot

дров|а́ *n/pl.* (fire)wood; коло́ть ‿а́ chop wood; ‿яно́й; ‿яно́й сара́й woodshed

дро́гнуть[1], про‿ shiver

дро́гнуть[2] *pf.* waver, falter

дрожа́ть tremble, shake (with *от* Р)

дро́жжи *f/pl.* yeast

дрожь *f* trembling;

tremor; quaver

друг (*pl.* **друзья́**) friend; ~ ~-**а** each other; ~ **с '-ом** with each other; ~ **ой** other; **никто́ ~ой** nobody else; **на ~ой день** (on) the following day

дру́ж|ба friendship; ~**еский**, ~**ественный** friendly; ~**йть** be friends; ~**ный** friendly; unanimous, united

дрянь *f* rubbish, trash

дря́хлый decrepit

дуб oak

дублёнка sheepskin coat; **коро́ткая** ~ sheepskin jacket

дубли́ровать *film* dub; *thea. part* understudy

ду́мать, по~ (*о* II) think (of)

дупло́ (*tree*) hollow; (*tooth*) cavity

дура́|к (*f* = **ду́ра**) fool, idiot; ~**читься** play the fool

дурно́й bad; evil; ugly; **мне ду́рно** I feel bad or faint

дуть, по~ *wind*: blow; '-**ся**, **на~** (**на** B) be sulky (with)

дух spirit; breath; ghost; **быть (не) в '-е** be in high (out of) spirits

духи́ *m/pl.* perfume, scent

духове́нство clergy; '-**ный**

spiritual; ecclesiastical; ~**ой**: ~**ой инструме́нт** wind instrument; ~**ой орке́стр** brass band

духо́вка oven

духота́ closeness; oppressive heat

душ shower-bath

душа́ soul; *fig.* heart; ~**ёвный** mental; heartfelt; ~**и́стый** fragrant; ~**и́ть¹**, за~ strangle; suffocate, stifle; ~**и́ть²**, на~ perfume; '-**ный** stuffy; sultry

ды́б|ом: у него́ во́лосы вста́ли ~ом his hair stood on end; **вста́ть на ~ы** *horse*: rear

дым smoke; ~**и́ть(ся)** smoke; '-**ка** haze; ~**овой** smoke...; ~**ова́я труба́** chimney, (*ship*) funnel

ды́ня melon

дыра́ hole (*a. fig.*)

дыха́|ние breathing; ~**тельный** respiratory; ~**тельное го́рло** *anat.* windpipe

дыша́ть breathe

дья́вол devil; ~**ский** devilish

дю́жина dozen

дюйм inch

дю́на dune

дя́дя *m* uncle

дя́тел woodpecker

Е

Ева́нгелие gospel

евре́й(ка) Jew(ess); **~ский** Jewish; Hebrew

европе́|ец; ~йский European; **~е́йское Экономи́ческое Соо́бщество** European Economic Community

его́ him; his; it(s)

еда́ food; meal

едва́ (ли) hardly; **~ (ли) не** almost, nearly

едини́ц|а unit; *math.* unity; (*school*) bad mark; **~ный** single, single

едино|гла́сный, ~ду́шный unanimous; **~мы́шленник** like-minded person

еди́н|ственный only, sole; **~ство** unity; **~ый** one; united; single, common

е́дкий caustic (*a. fig.*)

её her(s); it(s)

ёж hedgehog

ежеви́ка blackberr|y, -ies

еже|го́дник year-book; **~го́дный** annual, yearly; **~дне́вный** daily; **~ме́сячный** monthly; **~неде́льник** weekly (*magazine*)

ёжиться, съ~ huddle o.s. up; shrivel

езд|а́ drive, ride; driving, riding; travel; **в двух часа́х ~ы́ (от** P) two hours' journey (from)

е́здить, е́хать (*impf.*), *pf.* **пое́хать** drive, ride, go;

travel; **~ верхо́м** ride; **~ на велосипе́де** cycle

ей (to) her; (to) it

ей-бо́гу *coll.* truly, really and truly

е́ле(-е́ле) (*with difficulty*) hardly; only just

ёлк|а fir-tree); Christmas-tree, (*Russia*) New Year's tree; **быть на ~е** be at a Christmas party

ель f *bot.* spruce or (*less exact*) fir

ёмк|ий capacious; **~ость** f capacity; **~ость запомина́ющего устро́йства** storage capacity

ему́ (to) him; (to) it

ено́т rac(c)oon

епи́скоп bishop

ерети́к heretic

ерунда́ *coll.* nonsense; trifling matter

ёрш (*fish*) ruff

е́сли if, in case

есте́ств|енный natural; **~енно** *adv.* naturally, of course; **~о́** nature, substance; **~озна́ние** natural science; nature study

есть¹ there is or are; **у меня́ ~** I have; **так и ~!** so it is indeed!

есть², съ~ eat

ефре́йтор lance-corporal

е́хать → е́здить

ехи́дный malicious; (*remark*) venomous

ещё still; even more; ~ **раз** once more; ~ **один** another, once more; ~ **не(т)** not yet; ~ **бы!** I should

think so!
ею by or through her (it); her, it

Ж

жа́ба toad
жа́бры f/pl. gills
жа́воронок lark
жа́дный greedy
жа́жда (P) thirst, yearning (for); ~**ть** (P) thirst, yearn (for)
жаке́т (lady's) jacket
жале́ть, по~ (B) pity; (о П, **что** ...) be sorry (for, that ...)
жа́лить, у~ sting; snake: bite
жа́лкий pitiful, pitiable; **~о** pitifully; it is a pity
жа́ло sting
жа́лоб|а complaint; **~ный** plaintive; (book) of complaints
жа́лованье salary
жа́л|оваться, по~ (на В) complain (of); **~ость** f pity; **~ь** it is a pity; **как ~ь!** what a pity!; **мне ~ь вас** I pity you
жалюзи́ indecl. Venetian blind
жанр genre; **~овый**: **~овая жи́вопись** genre-painting
жар heat; fever; embers;

~а́ heat; **~еный** fried; grilled; roast...; **~ить(ся)**, из~ fry; roast; **~кий** hot; (argument, etc.) heated; **мне ~ко** I am hot; **~кое** roast
жаронижа́ющее med., su. febrifuge
жа́тва harvest
жать[1] press, squeeze; shoe: pinch
жать[2], с~ reap
ждать (P or B) wait (for); expect, await; **заста́вить ~** keep waiting
же and, but; after all; **и́ли ~** or else; **приходи́(те) ~!** do come!; **так ~** in the same way; **тот ~, тако́й ~** the same
жева́тельный: **~ная рези́нка** chewing gum
жева́ть chew; **~ жва́чку** chew the cud; harp on the same subject
жела́ние wish; **~тельный** desirable; **~ть** (P) wish v.
желе́ indecl. jelly
железа́ gland
желе́з|нодоро́жный railway ...; **~ный** iron...; **~о** iron

жёлоб gutter; *tech.* chute

желт|о́к yolk; **~у́ха** jaundice

жёлтый yellow

желу́док (*organ*) stomach

жёлч|ный *fig.* bitter, irritable; **~ный пузы́рь** gall-bladder; **~ь** *f* gall, bile

жема́н|ный mincing, affected; **~ство** mincing manners, affectedness

же́мчуг pearl(s); **~ина** pearl

жен|а́ wife; **~а́тый** (*man*) married; **~и́ть** (*im*)*pf.* (**на** II) *man:* marry (to); **~и́тьба** marriage; **~и́ться** (*im*)*pf.* marry, get married; **~и́х** fiancé; bridegroom; **~ский** female; feminine; womanlike; **~ственный** womanly; **~щина** woman

жердь *f* perch, pole

жереб|ёнок foal; **~е́ц** stallion

же́ртв|а victim; sacrifice; **~овать, по-** (**на** B) endow; (Т) sacrifice

жест gesture

жёсткий hard; stiff; **~ ваго́н** hard-seated carriage

жесто́к|ий cruel; severe; **~ость** *f* cruelty; severity

жесть *f* tin(-plate); **~яно́й** tin...

жечь, с~ *v/t.* burn; *nettle:* sting

живи́тельный life-giving; (*air*) bracing; **~о́й** living;

(a)live; lively

живо|пи́сный picturesque; **~пись** *f* (*art*) painting; **~сть** *f* liveliness, vivacity; verve

живо́т *anat.* abdomen; *coll.* belly; **~новодство** cattle-breeding; **~ное** animal; **~ный** animal...; *fig.* brutal

животрепе́щущий topical; stirring, exciting

жи́дк|ий liquid, fluid; *fig.* thin, watery; **~ость** *f* liquid

жи́зненный vital; **~ у́ровень** *m* living standard

жизне|ра́достный cheerful; buoyant; **~спосо́бный** capable of living; *med.* viable

жизнь *f* life; *как* **~?** how are you?

жи́ла vein (*a. min.*); sinew

жиле́т waistcoat

жил|е́ц, *coll.* **~и́чка** lodger; **~и́щный**; **~и́щные усло́вия** housing conditions; **~ьцы́** *coll.* tenants (*in a block of flats*)

жи́листый sinewy; *fig.* wiry

жил|и́ще dwelling, abode; **~о́й** dwelling...; habitable, inhabited

жир fat; **ры́бий ~** cod-liver oil; **~ный** fat

жите́йский wordly; everyday...

жи́тель *m*, **~ница** inhabitant, resident; **~ство** residence, domicile

жить live; **жил-был** (once upon a time) there was

жмýриться screw up one's eyes

жонглёр juggler

жрéбий (lottery) lot; fig. fate

жужжáть hum; buzz, drone

жук beetle

жýлик swindler

жýравль m zo. crane

журнáл magazine, journal; diary; register; **~и́ст(ка)** journalist

журчáть brook: purl, murmur

жýткий terrible; uncanny; sinister

жюри́ n indecl. (festival) jury

3

за (T, B) behind; beyond; outside; at; **~ угло́м, '~ угол** round the corner; (T) (run, hunt) after; (send) for; (B) (thank, pay, fight) for; during, within; **'~ день до** (P) a day before ...; **~ по́лночь** past midnight; **ему́ ~ со́рок** he is over forty; **что ~ ...** what (kind of) ...; **~то́** in return

забáв|**а** amusement; fun; **~ля́ть** amuse; **~ля́ться** make merry; amuse o.s.; **~ный** amusing; funny

забастóв|**ка** pol. strike; **всеóбщая ~** a general strike; **~щик** striker

забвéние oblivion

забéг (sports) heat; **~áть, забежáть** (к Д) call (on); drop in

заби(вá)ть drive in; block

or stop up; **~гол** score a goal

забинтó|**вывать, ~вáть** bandage

заб(и)рáть take; capture; arrest; **~ся** (на В) climb (on); (в В) penetrate (into)

заблаговрéменно in good time, well in advance

заблуди́ться pf. lose one's way

заблуждáться err, be mistaken

заболé|**(вá)ть** (3. ps. sg. **~éет**) fall ill; (3. ps. sg. **~и́т**) begin to ache

забóр fence

забóт|**а** (о П) care (for or of), concern (for); **~иться, по-** (о П) take care (of); look (after); **~ливый** solicitous, careful, thoughtful; **~ы** cares

забрако́в|**ывать**, **∼а́ть** reject; **∼анный** rejected; defective

забра́сывать[1], **забро́са́ть** (T) shower (with)

забра́сывать[2], **забро́сить** throw (far away); neglect; give up

забы́|**(ва́)ть** forget; **∼вчи́вый** forgetful; **∼тьё** unconsciousness; drowsiness

зава́р|**ение**, **∼и́ть**: **∼ ча́й** brew tea

заведе́ние institution; **уче́бное ∼е́ние** educational establishment; **'∼о́вать** (T) manage, be (at) the head (of); **'∼у́ющий** manager; head, director

заверт|**ыва́ть**, **заверну́ть** wrap up; *tap* turn off; *sleeve* roll up

заверш|**а́ть**, **∼и́ть** complete, conclude; *fig.* crown; **∼а́ющий** concluding, final; **∼е́ние** completion, conclusion

заверя́ть, **'∼ить** assure; certify

завести́ → **заводи́ть**

заве́т: **Ве́тхий ∼** Old Testament; **Но́вый ∼** New Testament

завеща́|**ние** will, testament; **∼ть** leave (by will); bequeath

завм|**(ва́)ть** *hair* wave, curl

зави́д|**ный** enviable; **'∼о́вать**, **по-** (Д) envy

зави́нчивать, **∼ти́ть** screw down, screw tight

зави́с|**еть** (**от** P) depend (on); **∼имость** f dependence; **в ∼и́мости от** (P) depending on; **∼имый** dependent

зави́стливый envious

за́висть f envy

заво́д factory, mill, works; **кирпи́чный ∼** brickworks; **лесопи́льный ∼** saw-mill; **∼и́ть**, **завести́** *person* lead or take (to **в** B); *home* acquire; *rule* establish; *conversation* start; *acquaintance* strike up; *tech.* wind up or start (*a. fig.*); **∼ско́й** factory...

заво|**ёвывать**, **∼ева́ть** conquer; win; **∼ева́ние** conquest; winning; *fig.* achievement; gains

за́втра tomorrow; **после∼** the day after tomorrow; **∼к** breakfast; **∼кать**, **по-** have breakfast

заву́ч *coll.* (*school*) director of studies

завя́знуть stick, get stuck

завя́з|**ывать**, **∼а́ть** tie (up); start, enter into

зага́дка riddle; puzzle; mistery; **∼очный** puzzling; mysterious; **∼ывать**, **∼а́ть** *riddles* set, ask; think of

зага́р sunburn, tan

загла́вие title, heading

загла́в|**ный**: **'∼ая бу́ква** capital letter; **'∼ая ро́ль** title role

заглуш|а́ть, **~и́ть** *sound* muffle; *pain* soothe; stifle

загля́|дывать, **~ну́ть** peep in; (*к Д*) call (on)

за́говор conspiracy; '**~щик** conspirator

заголо́вок (*book*) title; (*paper*) headline

загора́|ть sunbathe; **~́елый** sunburnt, tanned; **~́еть** become sunburnt; **~ся** catch fire

за́городный country...; suburban

загото́в|лять, '**~ить** lay in, stock; prepare

загра|жда́ть, **~ди́ть** fence in; bar, block

грани́ца *coll.* foreign countries; *жить* **~ей** live abroad; *пое́хать* **~у** go abroad

заграни́чный foreign

загрязн|е́ние: **~е́ние окру-жа́ющей среды́** environment pollution; **~я́ть**, **~и́ть** pollute

ЗАГС registry office

зад hind part, back; posterior

зада(ва́)ть give; *task* set; *question* ask

задави́ть *pf.* crush; *vehicle:* run over

зада́|ние task; *fin.* deposit; **~ча** task; *math.* problem

задви́жка (*door*) bolt

задё|ва́ть (B) touch, brush *or* knock against; **~** *за живо́е* sting to the quick

заде́рж|ивать, **~а́ть** detain, delay; arrest; **~ка** delay

за́дний back; hind; rear; *поме́тить* **~м число́м** antedate

задо́лго (*до* P) long before

задо́р fervour; enthusiasm

задрема́ть fall into a slumber

заду́м|чивый thoughtful; pensive; **~(ыв)ать** plan, conceive; (+ *inf.*) intend; **~(ыв)аться** fall to thinking; (*над* T) ponder (over)

заду́шевный sincere, heart-to-heart

задуши́ть → *души́ть*

задыха́ться, **задохну́ться** gasp; (*от* P) choke (with)

заём loan

заезжа́ть, **зае́хать** (*к* Д) call (on the way) on; (*в* B) drive *or* ride in(to); (*за* T) fetch, collect

зажи(ва́)ть *v/i.* heal; skin over

зажига́|лка (cigarette) lighter; **~тельный** *mil.* incendiary; **~ть**, **заже́чь** set on fire; kindle; *light* switch on; **~ся** catch fire; *fig.* become enthusiastic

зажи́точный well-to-do

заземле́ние *tech.* grounding

зазна́(ва́)ться become

conceited

зайка *m/f* stutterer; **'_ться** stutter

займствовать, по- *fig.* borrow

заинтересовать *pf.* interest; **_ся** (T) take an interest (in)

заискивать (*перед* T) ingratiate o.s. (with)

зайти → **заходить**

заказ *comm.* order; **_ной** (*letter*) registered; **_чик, _чица** customer, client; **_ывать, _ать** order

закалывать, заколоть stab; kill; *pig* slaughter; pin up

закалённый (*steel*) tempered; *fig.* hardened; **_ка** tempering, hardening; training; **_ять, _ить** temper; *fig.* harden

заканчивать, закончить finish; complete; conclude; *university* graduate (from)

закат sunset; *fig.* decline

закидывать[1], **_ать** shower (*with questions, etc.*); *pit* fill up

закидывать[2], **_нуть** throw (*far away*); toss; **_ удочку** cast a line

заклад pawning; **_ка** (*foundation*) laying; **_bookmark; _ывать, заложить** lay; put; pawn; mortgage; *page* mark

заклеи(ва)ть glue *or* stick down; seal

заключ|ать, _ить conclude; contract; close; **_ся** *no pf.* (*в* B) consist (in); **_ение** conclusion; confinement; imprisonment; **_йтель-ный** final, conclusive

заколоть → **закалывать**

закон law; *fig.* legal, legitimate; lawful

законо|дательный legislative; **_дательство** legislation; **_мерный** regular, natural; **_проéкт** *parl.* bill

закончить → **заканчивать**

закоренелый inveterate

закоченеть numb (with cold)

закреп|лять, _ить fasten, secure; consolidate; *photo* fix

закры|(ва)ть shut, close; cover; **_тие** the closing; close

закулисный back-stage ...; hidden, secret

закуп|ать, _ить buy in

закупори(ва)ть stop *or* cork up

закур|ивать, _ить (*mst v/i.*) light a cigarette *etc.*

закуска hors d'œuvres; snack; cold dish; **_очная** snack bar; **_ывать, _ить** have a snack; **– водку** (T) have ... with one's vodka

закут|ывать, _ать muffle, wrap up

зал hall; (big) room; *зрительный _* auditorium; *спортивный _* gymnasium; *читальный _* reading room

зали́в bay, gulf; **~ва́ть**, **~ть** flood, inundate; **-ся** water: pour; (слеза́ми) be drowned (in tears)

заливно́е fish (or meat) in aspic

зало́г deposit; pledge; security; gr. voice; **отдава́ть в ~** pawn

заложи́ть → **закла́дывать**

зало́ж|**ник**, **~ница** hostage

залп volley; **~ом** at one gulp

зама́з|**ывать**, **~ать** soil; paint over; fig. slur over; putty v.; **~ка** putty

зама́лчивать, **замолча́ть** ignore, hush up; keep silent (about)

зама́нчивый tempting, alluring

замедле́ние slowing down; delay; **~ть**, **~ить** slow down; delay

заме́н|**а** substitution, replacement; **~я́ть**, **~и́ть** substitute, replace

замерза́ть, **замёрзнуть** freeze (to death); freeze over

замести́т|**ель** m deputy; **~ель председа́теля** vice-chairman; **-ь** → **замеща́ть**

замета́ть, **замести́** sweep (up); trace cover up

заме́тить → **замеча́ть**

заме́т|**ка** notice; note; **~ный** noticeable; appreciable

замеча́|**ние** remark; reproof; **~тельный** remarkable; **~ть**, **заме́тить** notice; pf. a. sight

замеша́тельство confusion; embarrassment; **~ивать**, **~а́ть** involve, entangle; mix up

замеща́ть, **~сти́ть** substitute, replace; **~ще́ние** substitution

за́мкнутый (person) reserved; (group) exclusive

за́мок castle

замо́к lock; вися́чий **~** padlock

замолка́ть, **~нуть** fall silent

заморá|**живать**, **~озить** v/t. freeze; drink ice

за́морозки m/pl. frosts

за́муж: **вы́йти ~** (за В) woman: marry; **быть ~ем** (за Т) be married (to); **~ество** married life; **~няя** married

за́мш|**а**, adj. = **~евый** suède, chamois leather

замыка́|**ние**: коро́ткое **~ние** short circuit; **~ться**, **замкну́ться** be closed; fig. be or become reserved

за́мысел intention; (artist's) conception

замы́шля́ть, **~слить** plan, intend; conceive

замя́ть pf. hush up; **-ся** coll. falter, get confused; stop short

за́навес pol. thea. curtain;

'**-ка** curtain

занима́тельный diverting, interesting; **-ь, заня́ть**¹ *money, etc.* borrow; **-²** occupy; engange; take; interest; **-ся** (T) be occupied (with), engaged (in); study; (— *спо́ртом*) go in for sports

заноси́ть, занести́ bring, drop, leave (*passing by*); note enter; hand lift; **до-ро́гу занесло́** the road is snowbound; **\'ивый** arrogant; **\'ы** *m/pl.* snow-drifts

за́нят, -а́, -о, -ы *pred.* engaged; busy; **\'-ие** occupation; pursuit, business; **\'-ия** *n/pl.* studies; lessons; **-о́й** (*person*) busy; **-ый** *attr.* за́нят

заостря́ть, **-и́ть** sharpen; give force or emphasis

зао́чно *jur.* by default; **-ый:** **-ое обуче́ние** tuition by correspondence

за́пад west; **-ный** west (-ern); **-ня́** trap; **попа́сть в -ню́** fall into a trap

запа́здывать, запозда́ть be late *or* behind schedule

запако́вывать, **-а́ть** pack (up)

запа́льчивый short-tempered

запа́с stock, supply; *mil.* reserve; **-а́ть, -ти́** stock, store; **-а́ться, -ти́сь** (T)

provide o.s. (with); **-но́й, -ный** spare; reserve...; **-но́й вы́ход** emergency exit

за́пах smell

запа́чкать → па́чкать

запева́ла *m, fig.* instigator

запере́ть → запира́ть

запеча́т(ыв)ать seal up

запеча́т(ле)ть imprint, impress, engrave

запина́ться, запну́ться (*in speech*) halt, hesitate

запира́ть, запере́ть lock; *person* lock in

запи́ска note; *pl. a.* papers; memoirs; **-но́й: -на́я кни́жка** note-book; **-ывать, -а́ть** write down, note; (*на пласти́нку*) record

за́пись *f* entry; record; **- на плёнку** tape-recording

запла́канный tear-stained

запла́та patch

заплати́ть *pf.* pay

запломбирова́ть *tooth* stop, fill

заплы́в (*water sports*) round, heat

запну́ться → запина́ться

запове́дник reserve; reservation; sanctuary

за́поведь *f rel.* commandment

запозда́ть → запа́зды-вать; **-лый** belated

запомина́ть, **-нить** memorize; keep in mind; **-на́ющий: -на́ющее ус-**

тро́йство (ЗУ) tech. memory, storage

запо́нка cuff-link; stud

запо́р bolt, lock; med. constipation

заправ|ля́ть, '-ить cul. season; **– горю́чим** refuel '-**очный**: '-**очная ста́нция** mot. filling station

запра́шивать, запроси́ть (о П) inquire (about); – **сли́шком высо́кую це́ну** ask an exorbitant price

запре́т prohibition; ban; -**ный** forbidden

запреща́ть, запрети́ть forbid; prohibit; **кури́ть ~а́ется!** No smoking! -**е́ние** → **запре́т**

запро́с enquiry; comm. overcharging; **це́ны без ~a** fixed prices; → **запра́шивать**; -**ы** m/pl. needs, requirements

за́просто coll. without ceremony

запу́г|ивать, ~а́ть intimidate

запуск|а́ть, ~ти́ть neglect; rocket launch; (Т) fling (at в В)

запу́т(ыв)ать tangle; fig. muddle up; -**ся** entangle o.s.; get confused

запыха́вшись out of breath

запя́т|ая comma; **то́чка с ~о́й** semicolon

зараб|а́тывать, ~о́тать earn; pf. a. start (working)

за́работок earnings

зара|жа́ть, ~зи́ть infect; contaminate

зара́з|а infection, contagion; **~и́тельный** fig. infectious; **~ный** infectious, contagious

зара́нее beforehand; in good time

за́р|ево fire glow; **~ни́ца** sheet lightning

заро́дыш embryo; bot. germ; zo. foetus; **подави́ть в ~е** nip in the bud

заро|жда́ть, ~ди́ть engender; -**ся** be conceived; fig. arise

зарпла́та (= **за́работная пла́та**) wages, salary

зарубе́жный foreign

заря́: (**у́тренняя**) ~ dawn; (**вече́рняя**) ~ evening glow

заря́д mil., electr. charge; **~ка** charging; (sports) exercises, drill

заря|жа́ть, заряди́ть load, charge

заса́да ambush

заса́живать, засади́ть (Т) plant (with)

заса́ливать, засоли́ть salt; meat corn

засвиде́тельствовать pf. witness; testify

засева́ть, засе́ять sow

заседа́|ние session; meeting; **~тель** m: **наро́дный ~тель** ≙ juryman; **~ть** sit, have a session

заселя́|ть, **~и́ть** populate, settle

засло́н|ка tech. slide valve; **~я́ть**, **~и́ть** screen, shield; fig. overshadow; **– свет** stand in the light

заслу́га merit, desert

заслу́ж|ивать, **~и́ть** deserve; earn (fig.)

заснуть → **засыпа́ть²**

засоли́ть → **заса́ливать¹**

засор|я́ть, **~и́ть** block up, clog

засо́хнуть → **засыха́ть**

за́спанный sleepy

заста́ва: пограни́чная **~** frontier post

заста́(ва́)ть person find; catch; **~влять**, **~вить** force, compel; cram; block up; **– ждать** keep waiting

застё|гивать, **застегну́ть** button up; buckle; **~жка** fastening; buckle

засте́нчивый shy

застиг|а́ть, **~ну́ть** catch; **– врасплох** take unawares

засто́й econ. stagnation, depression

застре|ва́ть, **~я́ть** stick, get stuck

застрели́ть pf. shoot (to death)

заступ|а́ться, **~и́ться** (за B) intercede (for)

засты|(ва́)ть congeal, thicken; coll. get cold; **– от ужаса** be paralyzed with fear

за́суха drought

засу́ч|ивать, **~и́ть** sleeves roll up

засыпа́|ть¹, **'~ать** strew, cover; fill up; fig. shower

засыпа́|ть², **заснуть** fall asleep

засыха́ть, **засо́хнуть** dry up; wither

затаённый secret, repressed

зата́п|ливать, **затопи́ть** (печь) make fire (in the stove); coll. turn on the heating

затво́р (gun)lock, breechblock; (photo) shutter; **'~нический** secluded; **~я́ть**, **~и́ть** lock; shut

зате|ва́ть, **'~ять** venture, start

зате́м thereupon, then

затемн|е́ние darkening; mil. black-out; **~я́ть**, **~и́ть** darken; fig. obscure; mil. black out

зате́я undertaking, venture; piece of fun, escapade

затих|а́ть, **~ну́ть** calm down

зати́шье calm, lull

затме́ние eclipse

зато́ (to make up) for it; in return

затоп|ля́ть, **~и́ть** flood; submerge; ship sink

зато́р blocking; (traffic-)jam

затра́г|ивать, **~о́нуть** affect, touch; infringe upon

затрата expenditure

затрудн|ение difficulty, embarrassment; **~ять, ~ить** hamper; give trouble to, embarrass; **~яться +** *inf.* find it difficult + *inf.*

заты́лок nape

затя́|гивать, ~ну́ть knot tighten; delay; *song* strike up

заура́дный ordinary, mediocre

заусе́ница agnail

зауч|ивать, ~ить learn by heart

захва́т seizure; usurpation; **~нический** aggressive; **~чик** aggressor; **~ывать, ~ить** seize; take; *fig.* thrill, captivate

захо́д: ~ со́лнца sunset; **~и́ть, зайти́ (к** Д**)** call (on); (**в** В) call (at); drop in; *sun:* set; **~ за (**Т**)** fetch, collect

захолу́стье god-forsaken place

захоте́ть → хоте́ть

заче́м what for, why

зачёркивать, зачеркну́ть cross out

зачёт test, examination; **э́то не в ~** that does not count

зачисл|я́ть, '~ить count in, include; enrol; **~ в штат** take on the staff

защи́та defence (*a. jur., sports*); **~тник** defender; *jur.* defending counsel;

(*sports*) full-back; **~ща́ть, ~ти́ть** defend

зая́в|ка (на В**)** claim (for); request; **~ле́ние** statement; application; **~ля́ть, ~и́ть** declare, announce

за́яц hare

зва́ние rank; title

звать, по~ call; invite; *impf.* (Т) name, call; **как вас зову́т?** what is your name?

звезда́ star (*a. fig.*)

звене́ть ring; clink; jingle

звено́ link

звер|и́нец menagerie; **'~ский** brutal; atrocious; **~ь** *m* (wild) beast, animal; *fig.* brute

звон ring(ing); peal; chime; **~и́ть, по~** ring (the bell); (Д **по телефо́ну**) ring up; **'~кий** ringing; loud; *gr.* voiced; **~о́к** bell; (**по телефо́ну**) ring

зво́нница belfry

звук sound; **~ово́й** sound...; **~оза́пись** sound recording; **~онепроница́емый** soundproof

звуч|а́ть, про~ sound; ring; **'~ный** sonorous

зда́ние building

зде́сь; **'~шний** local

здоро́ваться, по~ (с Т**)** greet; **~ за ру́ку** shake hands; **'~ово!** *coll.* well done!, fine!

здоро́в|ый healthy; wholesome; *fig.* sound; **~ье**

health; *за ва́ше ~ье!* your health!

здра́в|ница health resort, holiday resort; **~оохране́ние** Health Service; care of public health; **мини́стерство ~оохране́ния** Ministry of Health

здра́вый sensible, sound

здра́вствуй|(те)! good morning (afternoon, evening); how do you do?; *да ~ет ...* long live ...

зева́ть, ~ну́ть yawn

зелё|ный green; **'~ень** *f* verdure; *vegetables* greens

земе́льный land...; **~ уча́сток** plot of land

земле|владе́лец landowner; **~де́лие** agriculture; **~трясе́ние** earthquake

земля́ earth; land; soil; ground; **~к (~чка)** (fellow) countryman, (-woman); person from the same town *or* district; **~ни́ка** wild strawberry *or* -ies; **~нка** *mil.* dugout; **~но́й** earthen, earth...

земно́й earthly; terrestrial

зени́т zenith; **~ный** zenithal; *mil.* anti-aircraft...

зе́ркало mirror

зерн|о́ grain; kernel; *ко́фе в ~ах* coffee beans; *collect.* corn, bread grains

зим|а́ winter; **~ний** winter...; **~ова́ть, про~** pass the winter

зия́ть gape

зла́ки cereals

злить anger, irritate; **~ся (на** B) be angry (with); be in a bad temper

зло evil, harm; *adv.* maliciously; **'~ба** spite; anger; **~бо́дневный** topical; **~ве́щий** ill-boding, ominous; **~во́ние** stench; **~де́й** villain

зло́й wicked; evil; **~наме́ренный** ill-intentioned; **~па́мятный** rancorous; **~ра́дный** gloating

зло́сть *f* malice; fury

злоупотребл|е́ние abuse, misuse; **~ля́ть, ~и́ть** (Т) abuse, misuse

зме́|й: бума́жный ~ kite; **~я́** snake

знак sign; token; symbol; mark; *tech.* character

знако́м|ить, по~ (с Т) acquaint (with); introduce (to); **~ся (с** Т) make the acquaintance (of); see, visit; **~ство** acquaintance; **~ый** familiar, acquainted; (*person*) acquaintance

знамена́тельный significant, important

знамени́тый famous

зна́мя *n* banner

зна́ние knowledge

зна́т|ный notable; **~о́к** connoisseur, expert

значе́ние meaning; **~ить** mean, signify

зноби́ть: *меня́* ~ I feel feverish

зной heat, sultry weather; **'_ный** hot, sultry

зов call

зола́ ashes

золо́вка sister-in-law

зо́лото gold; **'_й** gold(en)

зо́на zone

зонди́ровать sound (*a. fig.*); *med.* probe

зонт awning; umbrella; **'_ик** umbrella, *складно́й* **'_ик** telescopic umbrella

зоо́лог zoologist; **_па́рк** zoo

зо́ркий sharp-sighted; vigilant

зрачо́к (*eye*) pupil

зре́лище sight, spectacle

зре́л|ость *f* ripeness; maturity; **_ый** ripe; mature

зре́ни|е (eye)sight; vision; **_то́чка _я** point of view

зреть ripen

зри́тель *m* looker-on, spectator; **_ный** optic; **_ный зал** auditorium

зря *adv.* for nothing, to no purpose

зуб tooth; **_но́й** tooth...; dental; **_но́й врач** dentist; **_овраче́бный кабине́т** dental surgery

зубри́ть *coll.* cram, learn by rote

зубча́тый cogged; jagged

зуд itch; **_е́ть** itch

зы́б|кий unstable; **_ь** *f* ripple

зя́блик finch

зя́бнуть feel cold

зять *m* brother-in-law; son-in-law

И

и and; either, too; ~ ... ~ both ... and; ~ *так да́лее* (*и т. д.*) and so on (*etc.*)

и́бо because, for

и́ва willow

игла́ needle (*a. bot.*); *zo.* quill

игло|терапи́я, _ука́лывание acupuncture

и́го yoke

иго́лка (sewing-)needle; *сиде́ть как на ~х* be on pins and needles

игр|а́ play; game; *thea.* acting; **_а́ть, сыгра́ть** play (cards *в ка́рты*); the piano *на роя́ле*); act; gamble; **_о́к** player; gambler; **_у́шка** toy

иде́а|л ideal; **_льный** ideal; '_ **йный** ideological; high-principled; **_оло́гия** ideology; **_я** idea

идентифика́тор *tech.* name

идти́, пойти́ (→ **ходи́ть**) go, come; walk; *events:* go on; *thea.* be on; (*за* T) follow; *дождь (снег) идёт* it is raining (snowing); *эта шляпа вам идёт* this hat suits you

иждиве́нчество dependence, parasitism

из (P) out of (*a. fig.*); from; (*made etc.*) of

изба́ cottage, log-house

избавле́ние deliverance; rescue; *∼ить, ∼ить* (*от* P) save *or* deliver (from); *∼ся* (*от* P) get rid (of)

избега́ть, ∼жа́ть *or* **∼гнуть** (P) avoid, evade; escape; *∼жа́ние: во ∼жа́ние* in order to avoid

изби(ва́)ть beat (up)

избира́тель *m* elector, voter; *∼ный* electoral, election ...; *∼ный бюллете́нь* ballot paper; *∼ный о́круг* (*district*) constituency; *∼ный уча́сток* polling station

изб(и)ра́ть elect; choose

изби́тый *fig.* hackneyed

избы́ток abundance; surplus

изверга́ть, ∼нуть throw out, disgorge; eject; *∼ся volcano:* erupt

извести́ → изводи́ть

изве́стие news; information; *∼ить → ∼а́ть*; *∼ность* fame; (*по*)*ста́вить в ∼ность* inform; *∼ный* (well-)known; notorious; certain; *как ∼но* as is gen-

erally known; *насколько мне ∼но* as far as I know

и́звесть *f* lime

извеща́ть, ∼сти́ть inform, let know

изви(ва́)ться coil, wriggle; *impf. river:* wind, twist; *∼лина* bend; *∼листый* tortuous; winding

извине́ние excuse, apology; *∼я́ть, ∼и́ть* excuse, pardon; *∼ся* (*пе́ред* T) apologize (to)

извлека́ть, '∼чь (*из* P) take out; extract (from); *fig.* derive, elicit; *∼че́ние* extract(ion)

извне́ from without

изводи́ть, извести́ exterminate; *coll.* exhaust, torment

извраща́ть, ∼ти́ть pervert; distort; misconstrue

изги́б bend, curve; *∼а́ть (-ся), изогну́ть(ся)* bend, curve

изгоня́ть, изгна́ть banish; exile

изгото́вля́ть, ∼то́вить make; manufacture

изда(ва́)ть publish; issue; *∼ зако́н* pass a law

и́здавна from time immemorial; for a long time

издалека́, и́здали from afar; from a distance

изда́ние publication; edition; *∼тель* *m* publisher; *∼тельство* publishing house

издева́ться (**над** T) jeer (at); taunt

изде́лие (manufactured) article, *pl.* goods

изде́ржки *f/pl.* costs, expenses

изжо́га heartburn

из-за (P) because of; from behind; from

излага́ть, изложи́ть give an account of, expound

излече́|ние recovery; cure, treatment; **_ивать, _и́ть** cure

изли́ш|ек surplus; excess; **_не** *adv.* unnecessarily; **_ний** superfluous; unwarranted

изложе́ние account; exposition; **_и́ть → излага́ть**

изме́н|а treachery; faithlessness; **_е́ние** change; alteration; **_ник, _ница** traitor; **_чивый** changeable; **_я́ть, _и́ть** change; alter; (Д) betray; be unfaithful to; **-ся** change

измере́|ние measurement; *math.* dimension; **_я́ть, _ить** measure

и́зморозь hoar frost

изму́ченный tired; worn out; exhausted

изна́нка (*cloth, clothing*) wrong side; *fig.* seamy side

изнаси́ловать rape, violate

изне́женный coddled, pampered

изнемо|га́ть, _чь (**от** P) be exhausted (with)

изно́шенный shabby, threadbare

изнуря́|ть, _и́ть exhaust; overwork

изнутри́ from within

изоби́лие abundance

изобра|жа́ть, _зи́ть represent; depict; picture; **_же́ние** representation; picture, image

изобрета́|тель *m* inventor; **_а́тельный** inventive; resourceful; **_а́ть, изобрести́** invent; **_е́ние** invention

изойти́ → исходи́ть

изоля́ция isolation; insulation

изразца́довать → расхо́довать

и́зредка now and then

изуве́чи(ва)ть mutilate

изуми́|тельный amazing; **_ле́ние** amazement; **_ля́ть, _и́ть** amaze; **-ся** be amazed

изумру́д emerald

изуча́|ть, _и́ть learn, study; **_е́ние** study

изъя́н flaw, defect

изы́ска́нный refined; dainty; **_ивать, _а́ть** (try to) find

изю́м raisins

изя́щный elegant; graceful

ико́на icon, sacred image

ико́та hiccup

икра́[1] (*leg*) calf

икра́[2] caviar(e); *зерни́с-*

тая ~ soft caviar(e); *пáюс-ная* ~ pressed caviar(e); *biol.* roe; spawn

ил silt

и́ли or; **и́ли ... и́ли** either ... or

им (to) them; by him

имéние estate

имени́ны *f/pl.* name-day

и́менно just, exactly; namely

имéть have, possess; ~ **мéсто** take place; ~ **в виду́** bear in mind; ~ **успéх** *performance, etc.*: be a success; **имéется** (**имéются**) there is (are) **и́ми** by *or* through them; them; **э́то и́ми ещё не про́дано** they have not sold this yet

иммигрáнт immigrant

иммуните́т immunity

импера́тор emperor; ~**атри́ца** empress; ~**иали́ст** imperialist; '~**ия** empire

и́мпорт import

импрессиони́зм impressionism

имýщество property

и́мя *n* name, *a. tech.*: **от и́мени** (P) on behalf (of); **зал и́мени Чайко́вского** Chaikovsky Hall

и́наче differently; otherwise

инвали́д invalid; ~**ный**: ~**ная коля́ска** wheel-chair

инвента́рь *m* equipment; implements; (*garden*) tools

инд|éец, ~**иáнка**; ~**éйский** (Red) Indian; ~**éйка** turkey; ~**и́ец**, ~**иáнка**, ~**и́йский** Indian

индивидуáльный individual

инициáлы initials *m/pl.*

инициати́ва initiative

индýстрия industry

и́ней hoar-frost

инженéр engineer

иногдá sometimes

ино́й different, other; ~ **раз** sometimes

иностра́н|ец, ~**ка** foreigner; ~**ный** foreign

институ́т institute; institution

инстру́кция instruction; *tech.* manual

инструмéнт instrument; tool

инсу́льт *med.* stroke

инсцени́р|овать (*im*)*pf.* dramatize, stage; ~**о́вка** dramatization, staging; *fig.* faking

интегрáция integration

интеллигéнт intellectual; ~**ный** cultured, educated

интеллигéнция intelligentsia

интервáл interval; space, *a. tech.*

интервéнт interventionist

интерви́дение intervision

интервью́ interview; **дать** ~ give an interview

интерéс interest; ~**ный** interesting; ~**овáть** interest;

~ова́ться (Т) be interested (in)
интерна́т boarding-school
интернациона́льный international
интерфе́йс *tech.* interface
инти́мный intimate
инфекцио́нный *med.* infectious, contagious; **~я** infection
инфля́ция *econ.* inflation
информи́ровать (*im*)*pf.* inform
инциде́нт incident
ирла́нд|ец, ~ка Irishman, -woman; **~ский** Irish
иск *jur.* suit
иска|жа́ть, ~зи́ть distort; misrepresent
иска́ть (В *or* P) look *or* search for; seek
исключ|а́ть, ~и́ть except; exclude; **~ая** (P) except(ing); **~е́ние** exception; exclusion; **~и́тельный** exceptional; exclusive
ископа́емые *pl.*: **поле́зные ~** mineral resources
искорен|я́ть, ~и́ть eradicate
и́скоса askance, aslant
и́скра spark
и́скренний sincere; **~ость** sincerity
искривл|я́ть, ~и́ть bend, crook; distort
и́скриться sparkle
искуп|а́ть, ~и́ть expiate
иску́сный skilful; **~ственный** artificial; **~ство** art;

skill
искуше́ние temptation
испа́н|ец, ~ка Spaniard; **~ский** Spanish
испаре́ние evaporation
испове́довать(ся *v/i.*) *v/t.* confess
и́споведь *f* confession
испо́лин giant; **~ский** gigantic
исполко́м (= **исполни́-тельный комите́т**) executive committee
исполне́ние fulfilment; execution; *thea.* performance; **~я́ть, ~ить** fulfil; execute; *thea.* perform
испо́льзовать (*im*)*pf.* make use of, utilize
испо́ртить → по́ртить
исправл|е́ние correction; **~я́ть, ~ить** correct; improve; repair
испра́вный in good working condition
испу́г fright, scare; **~а́ть → пуга́ть**
испыта́ние trial, test; *fig.* ordeal; **~ывать, ~а́ть** try, test; *emotion* feel
иссле́дова|ние investigation; research; exploration; **~ть** (*im*)*pf.* investigate; explore
истека́ть, ~чь *time*: elapse; **вре́мя ~кло́** time is up
исте́ц plaintiff
истече́ние expiration
и́стин|а truth; **~ный** true,

veritable
исто́к source
истолко́в|ывать, ~а́ть interpret
исто́р|ик historian; **~и́ческий** historical; historic; **~ия** history; story; **~ия боле́зни** case history
исто́чник source; spring; **минера́льный ~** mineral springs
истощ|а́ть, ~и́ть exhaust, wear out
истреб|и́тель m (plane) fighter; **~ля́ть, ~и́ть** destroy; exterminate
истяза́|ние torture; **~ть** torture
исхо́д outcome; end; Exodus; **~и́ть (из** P) issue

(from); proceed (from); **~ный** initial, starting
исцел|я́ть, ~и́ть heal, cure
исчез|а́ть, ~ну́ть disappear; **~нове́ние** disappearance
исче́рпывающий exhaustive
исчисл|я́ть, ~ить calculate
ита́к conj. thus, so
италья́н|ец, ~ка; ~ский Italian
ито́г sum, total; **в ~е** as a result; **~о** altogether, in all
итти́ → идти́
их them; their
ию́ль m July
ию́нь m June

Й

йог yogi; **~а** yoga
йод iodine; **~ный: '~ный**

раство́р tincture of iodine

К

к (Д) to(wards); **к пяти́ часа́м** about five o'clock; **к пе́рвому января́** by the first of January; **к тому́ же** moreover
кабан́ wild boar
кабачо́к vegetable marrow
ка́бель m cable
каби́на booth; cabin; cockpit

кабине́т study; consulting-room; pol. cabinet
каблу́к (shoe) heel
кавале́рия cavalry
кавы́чки f/pl. quotation marks
ка́дка tub, vat
ка́дры m/pl. personnel; staff; mil. cadre
ка́ждый each; every(-one)

карабкаться

каза́к Cossack
каза́рма barracks
каза́ться, по~ (T) seem
каза́цкий, каза́чий Cossack...
каза́чка Cossack woman
казна́ exchequer, treasury; **~чей** treasurer
казн|и́ть *jur.* execute; **~ь** *f* execution; **сме́ртная ~ь** capital punishment
кайма́ border, edging
как[1] *adv.* how; **~ э́то ни тру́дно** however hard it is; **~ ва́ше и́мя?** what is your name? **вот ~!** really!, you don't say so!; **~ когда́** it depends
как[2] *conj.* as, like; **~ ... так ... ~** both ... and ...; **~ того́** after, since; **в то вре́мя ~** while; **~ раз** just, exactly; **~ бу́дто, ~ бы** as if; **'~-нибудь, ~** somehow; **(~-н.** *a.* anyhow)
како́й what, which; **~-нибудь, ~-то** some; **(~-н.** *a.* any)
кале́ка *m/f* cripple
календа́рь *m* calendar
кало́ша galosh
ка́лька tracing-paper
кальсо́ны *m/pl.* drawers
ка́мбала *zo.* flounder
камени́стый stony
ка́мен|ный stone..., stony; **~оло́мня** quarry; **~уго́льный** coal(-mining)...; **~щик** mason, bricklayer; **~ь** *m* stone

ка́мера cell, chamber; (*photo*) camera; **~ хране́ния** *rail.* left luggage (office), *Am.* check-room
ками́н fire-place
кампа́ния campaign
камы́ш reed
кана́ва ditch
кана́д|ец, ~ка, ~ский Canadian
кана́л canal; channel, *a. tech.*
канализа́ция sewers
канаре́йка canary
кана́т rope
кандида́т candidate; кандидат (*holder of the first scientific degree in CIS* ≅ *doctor's degree in Brit.*); **~у́ра** candidature
кани́кулы *f/pl.* vacations
кану́н eve
канцеля́р|ия office; **~ский: ~ские принадле́жности** *f/pl.* stationery
ка́пать drip; drop
капита́л *fin.* capital; **~и́ст** capitalist; **~овложе́ние** *fin.* investment; **'~ьный** main, fundamental; **'~ьный ремо́нт** major repairs
капита́н captain (*a. mil.*); *mar. a.* master, skipper
капка́н (spring-) trap
ка́пля drop
капу́ста cabbage; **цветна́я ~** cauliflower; **брюссе́льская ~** Brussels sprouts
кара́бкаться clamber

кара́кули pl. scribble

кара́куль m (adj. ~евый) astrakhan (...)

каранда́ш pencil

каранти́н quarantine

кара́т (gems) carat

каратэ́ (sports) karate

кара́ть, по- punish

карау́л guard, watch; **крича́ть** ~ shout for help; ~ить guard; lie in wait for; **~ьная бу́дка** sentry-box

ка́рий hazel, brown

карикату́ра caricature; cartoon

ка́рлик, ~ца dwarf

карма́н pocket; ~ный pocket ...

карп (fish) carp

ка́рт|а (playing-)card; map; chart; ~и́на picture; painting; ~о́н cardboard; ~о́нка cardboard box

карто́|фель m potatoes (~шка coll.) potato or -es; ~фель в мунди́ре potatoes in jackets

ка́рточка card; photograph; **визи́тная** ~ visiting card

карусе́ль merry-go-round; *Am* carousel

карье́р[1] quarry

карье́р[2] full gallop; ~a career (fig.); ~и́ст careerist

каса́ться, косну́ться (P) touch; concern

ка́ска helmet

ка́сса cashbox; pay-desk;

сберега́тельная ~ savings-bank

кассацио́нн|ый: ~ая жа́лоба jur. appeal

кассе́т|а cassette; ~ный: ~ный магнитофо́н cassette recorder

касси́р cashier

кастрю́ля saucepan

ката́нье driving, riding etc. (→ **ката́ться**)

ката́ть[1] → **кати́ть**

ката́ть[2] drive, take for a drive; dough roll; ~ся go for a drive; — на ло́дке go boating; — верхо́м ride; — на конька́х skate

ка́тер mar. cutter

кати́ть, по- roll

като́к skating-rink

като́ли|к, ~чка, ~ческий catholic

ка́тор|га fig. drudgery

кату́шка bobbin; spool; coil

кафе́ n indecl. café

ка́федра pulpit; rostrum; fig. univ. chair

кача́|ть, ~ну́ть rock, swing; pump; ~ться rock, swing; reel; ~ели f/pl. swing

ка́чество quality

ка́чка rocking, tossing; **борт|ова́я** ~ mar. rolling; **килева́я** ~ pitching

ка́ша: ма́нная ~ semolina; **овся́ная** ~ porridge; **ри́со|ва́я** ~ boiled rice

ка́ш|ель m cough; ~лять

cough v.

кашта́н chestnut(-tree)

каю́та cabin, state-room

квадра́т math. square

квалифика́ция qualification(s); **_ци́рованный** qualified, skilled

кварта́л (houses) block; (year) quarter

кварте́т mus. quartet

кварти́ра apartments; flat; **_ант, '_нтка** lodger

квартпла́та (= **кварти́рная пла́та**) rent

квас (rye-bread beer) kvass; **_цы́** m/pl. alum

кве́рху up(wards)

квита́нция receipt; **бага́жная _** luggage-ticket, Am. baggage-check

ке́гля ninepin

кедр cedar

кекс cake

кем through or by whom

кива́ть, _ну́ть (T) nod; (на B) motion (to)

кида́ть, ки́нуть coll. throw, fling

кило́(**грамм**) n indecl. kilo; **_ме́тр** kilometer

киль m keel; **_ка** sprat

кинжа́л dagger

кино́ n indecl. cinema; **_журна́л** newsreel; **_карти́на, _фи́льм** film

ки́нуть → **кида́ть**

кио́ск kiosk; **газе́тный _** news stand

ки́па bale; stack; pile

кипе́ть v/i. boil, seethe

кипяти́ть, вс- v/t. boil; **_о́к** boiling water

кирпи́ч brick; **_ный: _ный заво́д** brickworks

кисе́ль m (dessert) fruit-jelly

кисло|ро́д oxygen; **_ота́** acid(ity); **'_ый** acid; sour; acid

кисть f bot. bunch, cluster; (ornament) tassel; **маля́рная _** paintbrush; **_ руки́** hand

кит whale

кита́|ец, (_я́нка) Chinese (woman); **_йский** Chinese

кише́ть (T) teem (with)

кише́|чник intestines; **_ка́** gut, intestine

клавиату́ра mus. keyboard (a. tech.)

кла́виш(**а**) (instrument) key

клад treasure; **_би́ще** cemetery; **_ова́я** store-room; pantry

кла́няться, поклони́ться (Д) bow (to), greet

кла́пан valve

класс class (a. pol.); **class-room**; **'_ный** class(-room) ...; fig. coll. first-rate; **'_овый: '_овая борьба́** class struggle

класть, положи́ть lay or put (down); place

клева́ть, клю́нуть peck; fish: bite

кле́вер clover

клевета́ть, на_ (на B) slander

клеёнка oil-cloth

кле́ить glue, paste

клей glue, paste; '**-кий** sticky; '**-кая ле́нта** adhesive tape

клён maple

кле́т|ка cage; (*pattern*) check; *biol.* cell; **-чатый** chequered

клещи́ *m/pl.* pincers, tongs

клие́нт client; customer

кли́мат climate

клин wedge

кли́ника clinic

клино́к (sword-)blade

клони́ть bend, incline

клоп (bed-)bug

клуб¹ club(-house)

клуб² puff, cloud, wreath

клуб|ни́ка (*garden*) strawberr|y, -ies; **-о́к** ball

клу́мба (flower-)bed

клык *zo.* tusk; fang

клюв beak

клю́ква cranberr|y, -ies

ключ¹ spring

ключ² key; *mus.* clef; **-и́ца** collar-bone

кля́сться, по- swear, vow

кля́тва vow; oath

кни́га book

кни́ж|ка book; *записна́я* **-ка** note-book; *сберега́-* **тельная** **-ка** savings-bank book; *че́ковая* **-ка** cheque-book ...; **-ный** book ...; bookish

кни́зу down(wards)

кно́пка drawing-pin; press-button; *tech.* button

кнут whip

кня|ги́ня (*married*) princess; '**-жество** principality; **-жна́** princess; **-зь** *m* prince

ко → к

кобы́ла mare

кова́рный insidious, perfidious

кова́ть forge

ковёр carpet

когда́ when; **-либо, -нибудь** some time (or other); ever; **-то** (upon a time)

кого́ whom; *ни от* **-** from no one

код, коди́ровать code

кое-... some...; *e. g.* **-ка́к** somehow, anyhow

ко́ж|а leather; skin; **-аный** leather...; **-ура́** (*fruit, vegetables*) rind, skin, peel

коз|а́ goat, she-goat; **-ёл** he-goat; **-ёл отпуще́ния** scapegoat

козырёк (*cap*) peak

ко́зырь *m* trump(-card)

ко́йка bunk-bed; (*hospital*) bed; *mar.* berth

коко́совый coco...

кол stake

колбаса́ sausage

колго́тки tights; *Am.* panty hose

колеба́|ние oscillation, fluctuation; hesitation; **-ть, по-** shake; **-ться** oscillate; fluctuate; hesitate

коле́н|о knee; *стоя́ть на*

_ях kneel; **стать на _и** kneel down

колесо́ wheel

коле́я rut (a. fig.)

коли́чество quantity

коллекти́в group, body; **_ный** collective, joint; **_ное владе́ние** joint ownership

коллекционе́р (amateur) collector

коло́да (cards) pack; **_ец** (draw-)well

ко́локол bell; **_ьня** belfry; **_ьчик** little bell; blue-bell

коло́ния colony

коло́нка (gas) geyser; (street) water fountain

ко́лос bot. ear

коло́сс colossus

колоти́ть beat

коло́ть[1] chop; split

коло́ть[2], **_ьну́ть** stab; prick; impf. (pig) slaughter

колхо́з (= **коллекти́вное хозя́йство**) collective farm; **_ник**, **_ница** collective farmer; **_ный** collective-farm...

колыбе́ль f cradle; **_ный**: **_ная пе́сня** lullaby

колыха́ть, **_ьну́ть** sway or rock (gently); **-ся** v/i. heave, sway; wave

кольну́ть → коло́ть[2]

кольцо́ ring; **обруча́льное _** wedding ring

колю́чка prickle

коля́ска mot. side-car; **де́тская _** perambulator, pram

ком[1] lump; clod

ком[2]: **о _** about or of whom

кома́нд|**а** command, a. tech.; tech. instruction; mil. party; crew; (sports) team; **_ир** commander; **_иро́вка** mission; (official) business trip; **он в _иро́вке** he is away on business or on a mission

кома́р gnat, mosquito

комба́йн harvester

комбина́т factory; **_ бытово́го обслу́живания** multiple-service establishment (repair of household appliances, dry-cleaning, etc.)

коменда́нт commandant; **_нтский**: **_нтский час** curfew; **_ту́ра** commandant's office

коми́с|**сия** commission, committee; **_сио́нный**: **_сио́нный магази́н** commission shop; **_те́т** committee

коммер|**са́нт** businessman; **_ческий** commercial

коммуни|**зм** communism; **_ст**, **_стка** communist; **_стический** communist...

коммута́тор tech. commutator; switchboard; switch

ко́мнат|**а** room; **_ный** indoor...

комо́к lump; *fig.* lump (*in the throat*)

компа́кт-кассе́та compact-cassette

компа́ни|я company; **~о́н** companion; *comm.* partner

компа́ртия (= **коммунисти́ческая па́ртия**) Communist Party

компле́кт complete set; **~ова́ть, у-** complete; staff

комплиме́нт compliment; **сде́лать ~** pay a compliment

компози́тор composer

компо́т stewed fruit; tinned fruit

компромети́ровать: ~ себя́, кого́-либо compromise oneself, somebody

компью́тер computer

кому́ (to) whom

комфо́рт comfort

конве́рсия *mil.* conversion

конве́рт envelope

конди́терская confectioner's shop

коне́ц end; **в ~це́ ~цо́в** after all; in the end; **~е́чно** of course; **~е́чный** final, terminal

конкуре́нт(ка) competitor; rival; **~оспосо́бный: ~оспосо́бные це́ны** competitive prices

конкуре́нция competition

ко́нкурс (*festival, entry into univ.*) competition; **объя-**

~ви́ть ~ (на B) announce a vacancy (for); **~ный: ~ный экза́мен** competitive examination

ко́нн|ица cavalry; **~ый** horse...; **~ый заво́д** stud-farm

конопля́ *bot.* hemp

консерват|и́вный conservative; **'~ор** *pol.* conservative (*noun*); **~о́рия** conservatoire

консе́рвы *m/pl.* tinned food

ко́нский horse...

конститу́ция *pol.* constitution

конструкти́вный constructive

констру́ктор design engineer

ко́нсул consul; **~ьство** consulate

консульт|а́ция consultation; **~и́роваться, про-** (*doctor, lawer etc.*) consult

конта́кт *med., tech.* contact, *a. fig.*

конто́р|а office; **'~ский: '~ский слу́жащий** clerk

контр~ counter...

контраба́нда smuggling; smuggled goods

контра́кт *comm.* contract

контролёр controller; ticket-collector; **'~ь** *m* control; checking; *tech.* check; monitoring

конура́ kennel

ко́нус *math.* cone

конфере́нция conference

конфе́та sweet; *Am.* candy

конфискова́ть (*im*)*pf.* confiscate

конфронта́ция confrontation

конфу́з *coll.* discomfiture, embarrassment; ~иться, с- feel embarrassed; be shy

конце́рт concert; ~ный concert...

конч|а́ть, ~ить *v/t.* end; *university* graduate (from); -ся *v/i.* end (in T); ~и́на decease

конь *m* horse (*a. sports*); (*chess*) knight

конькй (*pair of*) skates; ро́ликовые ~ roller skates

конькобе́жец skater

конья́к brandy, cognac

ко́ню|х groom; ~шня stable

кооперати́в, ~ный co-operative

копа́ть dig; dig up *or* out

копе́йка copeck

копирова́льный: ~ая бума́га carbon-paper

ко́пия copy; duplicate; replica

копна́ rick, stack

ко́поть *f* soot

копчёный smoked, smoke-dried

копы́то hoof

копьё spear; (*sports*) javelin

кора́ (*earth*) crust; bark;

cortex

кораб|лекруше́ние shipwreck; ~естрое́ние shipbuilding; ~ь *m* ship, vessel

коре́йка smoked brisket of pork

корен|а́стый thick-set, square-built; ~но́й radical; native, aboriginal

ко́рень *m* root

корзи́н|а, ~ка basket

кори́ца cinnamon

кори́чневый brown

ко́рка crust; heel

корм forage; fodder

корма́ stern, poop

корми́ть, на-, по- feed

коро́б|ка (small) box

коро́в|а (small) box; ~ник cow-shed

короле́в|а queen; ~ёвский royal; ~ёвство kingdom; ~ь *m* king

коро́н|а crown; ~ка (*tooth*) crown

коро́т|кий short; ~отко́ говоря́ in short

ко́рпус building; *mar.* hull; *mil., pol.* corps

ко́ршун (*bird*) kite

корыстолю́б|ие (*a.* коры́сть *f*) self-interest; ~и́вый self-interested

корь *f* measles

коса́ plait, tress

кос|а́² scythe; ~и́ть¹, с- mow

коси́ть², с- *eyes*: squint; -ся (на B) look askance

(at)

косме́т|ика cosmetics; **_~и́ческий:_ _~и́ческий каби́нет_** beauty parlour

косми́ческий cosmic; **_~кора́бль_** space|ship (~craft); **_~ век_** space age

космона́вт cosmonaut; **_~ика_** cosmonautics

ко́смос outer space

коснуться → **каса́ться**

косо́й slanting

костёр bonfire

ко́сточка (*fruit*) stone

косты́ль m crutch

кость f bone; (*game*) die; **_ры́бья ~_** fishbone; **_слоно́вая ~_** ivory

костю́м suit; costume

косу́ля zo. roe

кот tom-cat

котёл boiler

котле́та cutlet; **_отбивна́я ~_** chop

кото́р|ый which, what; rel. pron. a. who or that; ..., **_дом ~ого ... тот_** whose house; **_~ый час?_** what is the time?; **_в ~ом часу́?_** (at) what time?

ко́фе m indecl. coffee; **_~йник_** coffee-pot; **_~йная ме́лка_** coffee grinder; **_раствори́мый ~_** instant coffee

кочерга́ (fire-) poker

кошелёк purse

ко́шка cat

КПСС (= **Коммунисти́ческая Па́ртия Сове́тского Сою́за**) hist. Communist Party of the Soviet Union

краб crab

кра́жа theft

край[1] land, region; territory

край[2] edge; brim; brink; **_~не_** extremely; **_~ний_** extreme; uttermost; last; **_по ~ней ме́ре_** at least; **_~ность_** f extreme; extremity

кран tap; (подъёмный) crane

крапи́ва nettle

краса́вец handsome man; **_~а́вица_** (a) beauty; **_~и́вый_** beautiful; handsome

кра́с|ить, по- paint; dye; colour; **_~ка_** paint; dye; colour

красне́ть, по- redden; flush; blush

красно|ва́тый reddish; **_~ре́чие_** eloquence; **_~та́_** redness, red spot

кра́сн|ый red; **_~ое де́рево_** mahogany

красота́ (quality) beauty; pl. a. charms

красть, у'- steal; **_~ся_** no pf. sneak

кра́т|кий brief; concise; **_~ость_** f brevity; conciseness

крах crash, bankrupcy, failure

крахма́л starch; **_~ить, на-_** starch

кра́шеный painted; coloured; dyed

кредит *comm.* credit; **покупа́ть в ~** buy on credit; **~ный:** **~ный бала́нс** credit balance

кре́йсер cruiser

крем cream; **~ для о́буви** shoe cream; **~ для лица́** face cream

кре|мато́рий crematorium; **~а́ция** cremation; **~и́ровать** cremate

Кремль *m* Kremlin

кре́мовый cream-coloured

кре́п|кий strong; firm; robust; **~ость** *f* strength; fortress

кре́сло arm-chair

крест cross; **~е́ц** *anat.* sacrum; **~и́ть**[1], о- baptize; **~и́ть**[2] **(-ся)**, перекрести́ть(-ся) cross (o. s.)

кре́ст|ный, **~ый оте́ц (~ая мать)** godfather, (-mother)

крестья́н|ин, **(-ка)** peasant (– woman); **~ство** peasantry

крива́я *math.* curve; **~о́й** crooked; curved; wry

кри́зис *med., econ.* crisis

крик cry, shout; **~нуть →** **крича́ть**

кри́тик critic; **~а** criticism; critique; **~ова́ть** critisize

крити́ческий critical

крича́ть, кри́кнуть cry, shout; (Д) call; **(на В)** shout (at)

кров shelter

крова́вый bloody

крова́ть *f* bed(stead)

кро́вельщик roofer

кро́вный blood...; **(***interest***)** vital

кровожа́дный bloodthirsty; **~обраще́ние** blood circulation; **~проли́тие** bloodshed; **~тече́ние** haemorrhage

кров|ь *f* blood; **~яно́й** blood...

крои́ть, с~ dress cut (out)

кро́лик rabbit

кро́ме (Р) except; besides; **~ того́** apart from that; in addition

кро́на *fin., bot.* crown

кроссво́рд crossword (puzzle)

кроссо́вки *f/pl.* trainers, *Am.* sneakers

крот *zo.* mole

кро́ткий gentle, meek

кро́хотный, кро́шечный *coll.* tiny, wee

круг circle; sphere; **~лый** round; **~ово́й** circular; **~о́м** round, around; *coll.* entirely

кру́жево (*ornamental*) lace

кружи́ть(-ся) turn, whirl; circle, go round

кру́жка mug; tankard

кружо́к (*people*) circle; small disk

круйз *mar.* cruise (*mst. for pleasure*)

крупа́ groats; **гре́чневая ~** buckwheat; **ма́нная ~** semolina; **овся́ная ~** oatmeal; **перло́вая ~** pearl-

-barley

крýпный large(-scale); big; great

крути́ть twist, twirl; turn; **~ся** turn, spin; whirl

крутóй steep; abrupt; sudden; **~е яйцó** hard-boiled egg

крушéние wreck, accident; *fig.* ruin

крыжóвник gooseberries; gooseberry (bush)

крылáтый winged; **~ó** wing; *mot.* mudguard; **~ьцó** porch

крымский Crimean

крыса rat

крыть, по~ cover; roof; (*paint*) coat; **~ся** be covered; *impf.* be hidden

крыша roof; **~ка** lid, cover

крюк hook; *coll.* detour

крючóк hook

кстáти to the point; by the way

кто who; **~ это такóй?** who is that?; **~-либо**, **~-нибудь** somebody, anybody; **~-то** somebody; **~-то другóй** somebody else

куб *math.* cube; **~ик** (*toy*) brick; **~и́ческий** cubic; **~óк** (*sports*) cup

кувши́н jug; pitcher; **~ка** water-lily

кудá (*whither*) where; **~-либо**, **~-нибудь** somewhere, anywhere; **~-то** somewhere; **~ (бы) ни**

wherever; **~ лýчше** much better; **~ мне!** it is out of my reach

кýдри *f/pl.* curls; **~я́вый** curly(-headed)

кузнéц (black)smith; **~éчик** grasshopper; **~и́ца** smithy

кýзов basket; *mot.* body

кýкла doll; **~ольный** doll's ..., puppet ...

кукурýза maize, *Am.* corn; **~ные хлóпья** cornflakes

кукýшка cuckoo

кулáк fist

кулёк (paper) bag

кули́сы *f/pl.* *thea.* wings

культ- *in compounds* → **культýрный**

культýра culture; **~ный** cultured; cultivated; civilized

куми́р idol

кýница *zo.* marten

купáльный bathing...; **~щик**, **~щица** bather

купáть, вы~ *v/t.* bathe; **~ся** *v/i.* bathe; take a bath

купé *n indecl.* *rail.* compartment

купи́ть → **покупáть**

кýпол dome

кури́льщик smoker; **~ть** smoke

кýрица hen

куропáтка partridge

курóрт spa, health resort

курс course; *fin.* rate of exchange; **быть в ~е** be well informed

курсо́р *tech.* cursor

ку́ртка jacket

ку́ры hens, *pl. of* **ку́рица**

курьёз curious *or* funny event; **~ный** curious; funny

курье́р messenger; courier

куря́щий smoker

куса́ть, укуси́ть bite; sting; **~ться** bite (*a.* each other); **~о́к** piece; lump; (*soap*) cake; (*bread*) slice

куст bush; shrub; **~а́рник** bushes; shrubbery

куста́рь *m* handicraftsman

ку́тать, за~ muffle *or* wrap up; **~ся** wrap o.s. up

кутёж carouse, drinking-bout; **~и́ть** be on the spree; revel

кухя́рка cook; **'~ня** kit-chen; *cul.* cooking

ку́ча heap, pile; *coll.* (P) heaps (of)

куша́к waist-belt, sash

ку́шанье food; dish; **~ть, по~, с~** eat

куше́тка couch

Л

лабора́нт(ка) laboratory assistant; **~то́рия** labora-tory

ла́вка[1] bench

ла́вка[2] (*village*) shop; *Am.* store

ла́вровый laurel ...; **~ое де́рево** bay; **~ый лист** bay leaf

ла́герь *m* camp

лад harmony; **на ра́зные ~ы** in different ways; **'~но** in harmony; **'~но!** all right, O.K.!

ладо́нь *f anat.* palm

ладья́ (*chess*) rook

ла́зать → ла́зить

ла́зер *tech.* laser

ла́зить, лезть (*impf.*), *pf.* **по~,** climb, clamber

лазу́рный azure ...

лай bark(ing)

ла́йка[1] laika; Eskimo dog

ла́йка[2] kid(skin); **~овый** kid ...

ла́йнер (*air, sea*) liner

лак varnish, lacquer; **~иро-ва́ть** varnish; *fig.* touch up

ла́комство dainty, choice bit of food; **~ый** dainty

ла́мпа (*radio*) valve; **~очка** *el.* bulb

ла́ндыш lily of the valley

ла́па paw

лапша́ noodles; noodle soup

ларёк stall, stand, kiosk

ла́ска[1] *zo.* weasel

ла́ска[2] caress; **~ть** caress; fondle; **~ться (к** Д) ca-ress; *dog:* fawn upon

ла́сточка swallow

латви́йский Latvian
лати́нский Latin
лату́нь f brass
латы́нь coll. Latin
латы́ш(ка) Lett; ~ский Lettish
лауреа́т laureate; ~ Но́белевской пре́мии Nobel Prize Winner
ла́ять bark v.
лгать, со́~ lie, tell lies
ле́бедь m/f swan
лев lion; ♌ Leo
левко́й gillyflower, stock
левша́ m/f left-hander; ~ый left; left-hand; left-wing; ~ый борт portside
лега́льный legal
леге́нда legend; ~рный legendary
лёгкий light; easy; ~ая атле́тика field and track athletics
легкоатле́т athlete
легково́й: ~ автомоби́ль m (motor-)car
лёгкое lung
легкомы́сленный light-minded; frivolous
лёгкость f lightness; easiness
лёд ice
ледене́ц fruit-drop
ледни́к glacier; ~око́л icebreaker; ~о́вый icy
лежа́ть lie; be situated; ~чий lying, recumbent
лезть, по́~ » ла́зить
ле́звие (metal) blade

ле́йка watering can
лейкопла́стырь adhesive plaster
лейтена́нт lieutenant
лека́рство drug, medicine, remedy
ле́к|тор lecturer; ~ция lecture
леле́ять cherish, foster
лён flax
лени́|вец m zo. sloth; ~вый lazy; ~ться be lazy or idle
ле́нта ribbon; tape
лентя́й(ка) sluggard; lazy-bones
лень f laziness; idleness
лепета́ть babble; prattle
лепи́ть, вы́~ model, sculpture
лес wood, forest; timber; ~но́й: ~на́я промы́шленность timber industry
леса́ m/pl. woods; scaffolding
леска́ fishing-line
лесни́чий forester; ~о́й wood...; forest...; timber...
лесопи́льня saw-mill
ле́стница stairs, staircase; ladder
ле́ст|ный flattering; ~ь f flattery
лёт: на лету́ in the air; on the wing; хвата́ть на лету́ be quick to grasp
лета́ n/pl. years; ско́лько вам лет? how old are you?; ему́ два́дцать лет he is twenty

лета́ть, лете́ть, *pf.* **полете́ть** fly

ле́тний summer...

ле́то summer; **ба́бье ~** Indian summer; **~м** in summer; *про́шлым* **~м** last summer

ле́топись *f* annals

лету́чий *adj.* flying; **~ая мышь** *f* bat

лётчик, ~ица flier, pilot

лече́бница clinic; **~бный** medicinal, curative; **~е́ние** medical treatment; **~и́ть** treat; **~и́ться** undergo a cure

лечь → ложи́ться

лже *in compounds* pseudo-, false ...

лжесвиде́тельство false evidence, perjury

лжи́вый mendacious; deceitful

ли *interrogative particle:* *ве́рно* **ли** *э́то?* Is that true?; *conj.* if, whether: *я не зна́ю,* *ве́рно ли* *э́то* I do not know if it is true

ли́бо *ог;* **~ ... ~** either ... or

ли́вень *m* downpour, cloudburst

ли́дер *pol., sports* leader; **~ство** leadership; *(sports)* lead

лиза́ть, ~ну́ть lick

ликвида́ция liquidation, elimination, abolition

ликёр liqueur

ликова́ть rejoice, triumph

ли́лия lily

лило́вый *(colour)* lilac, violet

лимо́н lemon; **~а́д** lemonade

лине́йка rule(r); **~ия** line; **~ия свя́зи** *tech.* communication line; **~о́ванный** lined, ruled

линя́ть, по~ fade; *zo.* shed hair; moult

ли́па lime(-tree)

ли́пкий sticky

лиса́, лиси́ца fox

лист leaf; sheet; **~ва́** foliage; **~венница** *bot.* larch; **~о́вка** leaflet

лита́вры *pl.* kettle-drum

литера́тор man of letters; **~у́ра** literature

лито́вец, ~овка, ~овский Lithuanian

литр litre

лить pour; **~ся** pour, stream

лифт lift; **~ёр** lift operator

лих|а́ч dare-devil; **~о́й** *coll.* dashing

лихора́д|ка fever; **~очный** feverish

лицеме́р|(ка) hypocrite; **~ие** hypocrisy

лице́нзия *comm.* licence

лицо́ face; person *(a. gr.)*

ли́чина mask

ли́чн|ость *f* personality; person; personal *(a. gr.)* private; **~ый со-ста́в** *mil.* personnel

лиш|а́ть, ~и́ть (P) deprive or rob (of); **~ себя́ жи́зни**

commit suicide; **~ся** (P) lose; forfeit; **~ение** (de)privation; **~ний** superfluous; spare

лишь *adv.* only; *conj.* as soon as

лоб forehead

лови́ть, пойма́ть catch; **~кий** dexterous, smart; **~кость** *f* dexterity; **~ля**: **ры́бная ~** fishing; **~ушка** trap; pitfall

ло́дка boat

ло́жа *thea.* box

ложи́ться, лечь lie down

ло́жка spoon

ло́жный false, faked; erroneous; **~ь** *f* lie

ло́зунг slogan

ло́кон curl

ло́коть *m* elbow

лом crow-bar; *collect.* scrap; **~а́ть, с~** break; **~а́ть го́лову (над Т)** rack one's brains (over); **~ся** break; crack; *coll.* be obstinate

ломба́рд pawnshop

ломо́ть *m* hunk, chunk; **~тик** (thin) slice

лопа́та spade, shovel; **~ка** *anat.* shoulder-blade

ло́паться, ~нуть burst; split

лоску́т rag, shred

лосни́ться have a gloss, shine

лососи́на *cul.* salmon

лосо́сь salmon

лось *m zo.* elk

лотере́я lottery

лото́к (*hawker's*) tray

лохмо́тья *m/pl.* rags

ло́цман *mar.* pilot

ло́шадь *f* horse

луг meadow

лу́жа pool, puddle

лук¹ onion(s)

лук² (*sports*) bow

лука́вый sly, cunning

лу́ковица (single) onion; *bot.* bulb

луна́ moon; **~а́тик** sleep-walker; **~ный** moon(lit)...

лу́па magnifying glass

луч beam; ray; **~ево́й**: **~ева́я боле́знь** radiation sickness

лу́чше better; **~е всего́** best of all; **~ий** better; best

лы́ж|а ski; **~ник, ~ница** skier; **~ня** ski-track

лы́с|ина bald patch; **~ый** bald

льви́ца lioness

льго́т|а privilege; **~ный** privileged; preferential

льди́на ice-floe

льняно́й flaxen; linen...; linseed...

льстец flatterer

льстить, по~ (Д) flatter

любе́зн|ый kind, amiable; **~имец, ~имица** pet, favourite; **~имый** beloved, dear; favourite; **~итель(ница)** *m* amateur; lover; **~ить** love; like; **~ова́ться**

(T) admire; **~о́вник,**
~о́вница lover; **~о́вь** f
love
любо́й any, every
любопы́тный curious, interesting; inquisitive;
~ство curiosity; inquisi-

tiveness
лю́д|и pl. people, men;
~ный crowded; populous
лю́стра chandelier
лю́тый fierce; (frost) severe
лягу́шка frog

М

мавзоле́й mausoleum
магази́н shop; store
магистра́ль f main(line);
highway
магни́т magnet; **~офо́н**
tape recorder
ма́зать, по~, на~ (T)
spread (on B)
мазь f ointment; grease
майоне́з mayonnaise
майо́р mil. major
ма́й(ский) May(...); **~ка**
vest; T-shirt, sport-jersey
мак poppy
макаро́ны m/pl. macaroni
мале́йший least, slightest
ма́ленький little, small
мали́на raspberr|y, **~ies**
ма́ло (P) little, few; **~ того́,
что ...** it is not enough
that; **~ва́жный** unimportant; **~ду́шие** faintheartedness; **~кро́вный** anaemic;
~ле́тний young; **~пома́лу**
little by little
ма́л|ый adj. small, little; as
su. chap; **~ы́ш** little child
or man; **~чик** boy
маля́р (house-)painter

маляри́я malaria
манёвр man(o)euvre
мане́р|а manner; **~ный** affected
манже́та cuff
мани́ть, по~ beckon; impf.
attract, entice
ма́рганец manganese
маргари́н margarine
маргари́тка daisy
маринова́ть pickle
ма́рка stamp; mark (a.
fin.); brand, grade, sort
ма́рля gauze
март March
марты́шка zo. marmoset
марш march; **~ру́т** route;
itinerary
ма́ршал mil. marshal
маскирова́ть, за~ mask,
disguise; mil. camouflage
масл|ёнка butter-dish; oilcan; **~и́на** olive(tree); **~о**
butter; oil; **~яный** oil...
ма́сс|а mass; coll. a lot;
~овый mass...
ма́стер expert, master;
foreman; **~ская** workshop; **~ски́й** (adv. **~ски́**)

masterly; **~ство** skill, craftsmanship

масть f (*animals*) colour; (*cards*) suit

масшта́б scale

мат checkmate

матема́тик mathematician; **~а** mathematics

материа́л material; fabric; **~ьный** material; financial

матери́к mainland, continent

матери́нский motherly; maternal; **~ство** motherhood, maternity

мате́рия matter; material; cloth

ма́тка womb; (*animals*) female; (*bees*) queen

ма́товый (*lustreless*) dull; (*glass*) frosted

матра́с mattress

матро́с sailor, seaman

мать f mother

мах|а́ть, **~ну́ть** (T) wave; wag; flap; **~ руко́й на** (B) give up (*as hopeless*)

ма́чта mast

маши́н|а machine; engine; *coll.* car; **стира́льная ~** washing machine; **швейная ~** sewing-machine; **~а́льно** mechanically, **~ист** *rail.* engine-driver; **~истка** (*girl*) typist; (*пи́шущая*) **~ка** typewriter, **~ный**: **~ная програ́мма** computer program

машинострое́ние mechanical engineering

майк lighthouse; beacon

ма́ятник pendulum

мгла mist; haze; darkness

мгнове́н|ие moment; **~ный** momentary

ме́б|ель f furniture; **~лирова́ть** (*im*)*pf.* furnish

мёд honey

меда́ль f medal

медве́дь m bear

ме́ди|к medical student; doctor; **~ци́на** medicine; **~ци́нский** medical

ме́дл|енный slow; **~и́тельный** sluggish; **~ить** linger, be slow

ме́дный copper...; brazen

медо́вый honey(ed)...; **~ме́сяц** honeymoon

мед|осмо́тр (= **медици́нский осмо́тр**) medical examination; **~пу́нкт** (= **медици́нский пункт**) first aid post; **~сестра́** (= **медици́нская сестра́**) nurse

медь f copper; *collect.* coppers

межа́ boundary (*between fields*)

ме́жду (T) between; among; **~ про́чим** incidentally; **~ тем** meanwhile; **~наро́дный** international **~контине́нтальный** intercontinental; **~плане́тный** interplanetary

мел chalk

меланжевый: **~ая нить** blended yarn

ме́л|кий small(-scale);

petty; shallow; **~очный**
petty; small-minded;
~очь f trifle; fin. small
change; **~ь** f shoal;
(sand)bank

мелька́ть, ~ну́ть flash;
glimpse fleetingly

ме́льница mill

мельхио́р German silver

**мемориа́льный: ~ая до-
ска́** memorial plaque

ме́на change, barter

ме́неджер manager

ме́нее less; **тем не ~** none
the less

менструа́ция menstrua-
tion

ме́ньше smaller; less; **~е
всего́** least of all; **~ий**
lesser; younger; **~инство**
minority

меня́¹ me; **у ~ боли́т зуб** I
have a toothache

меня́ть¹ change; **~²**, **по~
(на** B) exchange (for);
~ся¹ change; **~ся²**, **по~** (T)
exchange, switch

ме́р|а measure (a. fig.); **по
кра́йней ~е** at least

мерз|а́вец scoundrel; **'~кий**
disgusting; nasty; **'~ость** f
vileness; nasty thing

мёрзнуть v/i. freeze

ме́рить measure; pf. **при-
тры** on

мероприя́тие measure, arrangement

мерца́ть twinkle; flicker

меси́ть ~ knead

ме́сса eccl., mus. mass

мести́ sweep

ме́стн|ость f locality,
place; land; **~ый** local

ме́сто place; spot; seat;
post; **~жи́тельство** residence; **~пребыва́ние**
abode; **~рожде́ние** geol.
deposit

месть f revenge

ме́ся|ц month; moon;
~чный monthly

мета́лл|~, ~и́ческий metal;
metal...

мета́ться rush about

мете́ль f snow-storm

метеорологи́ческий mete-
orological; **~ая сво́дка**
weather report

ме́т|ить (в B) aim (at);
aspire (to); **~ка** mark
(-ing); **~кий** well-aimed;
(eye) keen; (remark) apt

метла́ broom

метр metre; **~а́ж** metric
area; length in metres;
**~и́ческий: ~и́ческая си-
сте́ма мер** metric system

метро́ n indecl. underground, subway

мех (pl. **~а́**) fur

меха́ник mechanic; mar.
engineer

мехово́й fur...

меч sword

мече́ть f mosque

мечта́ (day-)dream; **~ть (о
П)** dream (of)

меша́ть¹, с~ mix; stir; **~²**,
по~ (Д) disturb; hinder

мешо́к bag, sack

миг moment; ~а́ть, ~ну́ть blink, (Д) wink (at); '~ом in a twinkling

мизи́нец the little finger or toe

микрофи́льм microfilm; ~фо́н microphone

ми́ксер mixer

милиционе́р militiaman

ми́ло|ви́дный pretty; ~се́рдие charity

ми́лость f favour, kindness; mercy; ~и про́сим welcome!

ми́лый dear; nice; noun darling

ми́ля mile

ми́мо (P) past, by; ~! miss(ed)!; ~хо́дом in passing

ми́на¹ mien, countenance, expression

ми́на² mil. mine

минда́ль m almonds; almond-tree

минера́льный mineral; ~ая вода́ mineral water

минима́льный minimum

ми́нимум minimum; про-жи́точный ~ living wage

министе́рство ministry; '~р (cabinet) minister

минова́ть (В) pass, (P) escape; be over

мино|мёт mil. mortar

мину́т|а minute; сию́ ~у just a minute or this very minute

мир¹ world (a. fig.); universe

мир² peace; ~и́ть, по-re-concile; ~и́ться (с Т) put up (with); '~ный peaceful; peace...

миро|во́й world...; ~воз-зре́ние outlook, philosophy

миролюби́вый peace-loving

ми́ска basin, bowl

ми́ссия mission

ми́тинг pol. meeting

митрополи́т eccl. metropolitan

мише́нь f target (a. fig.)

младе́нец baby, infant; '~ший younger or youngest; junior

млекопита́ющее mammal

мне (to) me; обо ~ about or of me

мне́ние opinion; обще́ст-венное ~ public opinion

мни́мый imaginary

мно́гие many, a great many

мно́го (P) much; many; ~кра́тный repeated; ~лю́дный crowded; ~на-циона́льный multi-national; ~обеща́ющий promising; ~то́чие typ. dots; ~уважа́емый (letter) dear; ~чи́сленный numerous

мно́жество a great number or deal

мной, мно́ю by or through me; me

мобилизова́ть (im)pf. mobilize

моги́ла grave; *бра́тская* ~ communal grave

могу́чий mighty

могу́щ|ественный mighty; ~**ество** might, power

мо́д|а fashion; *войти́ в* ~ come into fashion; ~**ный** fashionable; **fashion...**

моде́ль model; ~**и́рова-ние** *tech.* simulation

мо́жет: ~ *быть* maybe, perhaps

можжеве́льник *bot.* juniper

мо́жно it is possible; one (you) may *or* can; *как* ~ *скоре́е* as soon as possible

мозг brain

мозо́ль *f* corn, callosity

мой, моя́, моё, *pl.* **мои́** my; mine; *по мо́ему* in my opinion; as I think right

мо́к|нуть, вы- become wet; ~**ро́та** *med.* phlegm; ~**рый** wet

мол breakwater; mole

моли́т|ва prayer; ~**ь** pray, entreat; ~**ься, по-** (*о* II) pray (for)

мо́лния lightning; (*за-стёжка-*) zip

молодёжь *f* youth, young people; ~**ёжный** youth; ~**е́ц** fine fellow *or* girl; ~**ня́к** young cattle *or* cubs; ~**ожёны** newly-married couple; ~**о́й** young

мо́лодость *f* youth

молоко́ milk; *сгущённое* ~

condensed milk

мо́лот hammer; ~**о́к** hammer

моло́ть, с- grind, mill; ~ *вздор* *coll.*, *no pf.* talk nonsense

моло́чный milky; milk...; dairy...

молча|ли́вый tacit(-urn); ~**ние** silence; ~**ть** be *or* keep silent

моль *f* (*clothes*)moth

мольба́ entreaty

мольбе́рт easel

моме́нт moment

мона|сты́рь *m* monastery; abbey; ~**х** monk; ~**хиня** nun

моне́та coin

монито́р *tech.* monitor

монопо́лия monopoly

монта́ж *tech.* assembly, mounting, installation

монтёр fitter; electrician

монуме́нт monument; ~**а́льный** monumental

морг morgue

морг|а́ть, ~ну́ть blink; (Д) wink (at)

мо́рда muzzle, snout

мо́ре sea; ~**пла́вание** navigation

морж walrus

морко́вь *f* carrot(s)

моро́женое ice-cream

моро́з frost; ~**и́лка** *coll.* = *моро́зильник* (deep-)-freezer; ~**ить** freeze; ~**ит** it is freezing; ~**ный** frosty

мороси́ть drizzle

морс: клюквенный ~ cranberry water

морско́й sea...; maritime; marine, nautical

морфий morphine

морщи́на wrinkle; '~ить, с- wrinkle; **lips** pucker; – (**a. на-**) **лоб** knit one's brow; **'~иться, с-** make a wry face

моря́к sailor

москви́ч (-ка́) inhabitant of Moscow; **~о́вский** Moscow...

мост bridge; ~и́ть, **вы́мо́стить**, вы́-паве; **~ки́** m/pl. planked footway; **~ова́я** roadway, carriage way

мота́ть, на- wind, reel; **~о́к** skein

моте́ль m motel

моти́в[1] tune; motif

моти́в[2] motive; reason

мотого́нки f/pl. motor-cycleraces

мото́р motor, engine; **~заводи́ть [-вести́]** ~ start the engine

моторо́ллер motor scooter; **~ци́кл** motor-cycle; **~цикли́ст** motor-cyclist

мотылёк (**night insect**) moth

мох moss; **~на́тый** shaggy; hairy

моча́ urine; **~ево́й: ~ево́й пузы́рь** bladder; **~и́ть, на-** wet; **~и́ться** urinate

мочь, с~ be able; **мо́жет быть** perhaps; **не мо́жет**

быть! impossible!; **он мо́жет** he can

моше́нни|к swindler; **~чать, с-** swindle

мо́шка midge

мо́щ|ность f power; capacity; **~ный** powerful; **high-capacity...**; **~ь** f power, might

мрак darkness, gloom

мра́мор marble

мра́чный dark, gloomy; dismal

мстить, ото(о)'- (Д) revenge oneself (upon)

му́др|ость f wisdom; **~ый** wise

муж husband; **'~ественный** manful, courageous; **'~ество** courage; **~ско́й** male; masculine (**a. gr.**); **~чи́на** m man

музе́й museum

му́зы|ка music; **~а́льный** musical; **~а́нт (-ша)** musician

мука́ flour, meal

му́ка torment

мул mule

мультфи́льм (= мульти-пликацио́нный фильм) animated cartoon

мунди́р uniform

мундшту́к cigar- **or** cigarette-holder

мураве́й ant; **~ник** ant-hill

муска́т nutmeg; **~ный: ~ное вино́** muscat

му́скул muscle

му́сор sweepings; refuse,

garbage; **_опровод** refuse chute

мусульман|ин, **-ка** Moslem; **_ский** Moslem

мут|ить, за-, по- make muddy; _fig. impf._ stir up; **-ся** grow turbid or dim; **'_ный** turbid; dim; dull

муфта _tech._ coupling

муха fly

мухо|ловка fly-trap; **_мор** fly-agaric

муч|ение torment, pain; **'_еник** martyr; **_ительный** agonizing; **'_ить**, за- torment; **'_иться** worry, suffer; take pains

мчаться _v/i._ rush _or_ speed along

мы we

мыл|ить, на- soap; **_о** soap; **_ьница** soap-dish; **_ьный** soap...; soapy

мыс _geogr._ cape

мысл|енно mentally; **_имый** thinkable; **_ить**

think; **_ь** _f_ thought; idea; **_собраться с _ями** collect one's thoughts

мыть, вы-, по¹ wash; **-ся** wash (oneself)

мычать low, moo, bellow

мышление thinking

мыш|ца muscle; **_ь** _f_ mouse; **_ьяк** arsenic

мягк|ий soft; mild, gentle; **_ость** _f_ softness _etc._

мяк|иш (_loaf_) soft part; **_оть** _f_ pulp; fleshy part

мяс|ник butcher; **_ной** meat...; **_ные консервы** tinned meat; **_о** meat; **_орубка** mincing machine

мята _bot._ mint

мятеж rebellion; mutiny; **_ник** rebel, mutineer

мять, по¹, с- (c)rumple; trample; '_ся**, по- be (easily) crumpled; hesitate

мяч, '_ик** ball

Н

на¹ (П _or_ В) on(to); (up)on; (П) in; at; (В) to(wards); **_ этой неделе** this week; **_ завтра** till tomorrow; **_ месяц** for a month; **моложе _ год** younger by a year; **опоздать _ час** be an hour late

на² _int._ (_take it!_) here you

are; **вот тебе '_!** (_unpleasant surprise_) well!

набережная quay, embankment

наби(ва)ть stuff, pack

наби(и)рать gather; recruit; _typ._ set up; **_ номер** dial a number

наблюда|тель _m_ observer; **_ательный** observant;

~**áть** observe; (*за* Т) look after; supervise; ~**éние** observation

набóйк|а heel (of shoe); **набúть** ~**y** put a heel on, heel

набóр set, collection; recruitment; type-setting; ~**щик** type-setter

набрáсывать[1], **наброcáть** sketch, outline; draft

набрáсывать[2], **набрóсить** (*на* В) throw (on, over); **-ся** (*на* В) fall (up)on; assault

набрáть → **набирáть**

набрóсок sketch, draft; rough copy

навáл|ивать, ~**úть** (*на* В) heap upon; *person* (over)load (with В)

навéк(и) for ever

навéрно|(е) probably; certainly; ~**якá** *coll.* for sure

навéрстывать, **наверстáть** make up (for); catch up (with); ~ **упýщенное врéмя** make up for the lost time

навéрх up; upstairs; ~**ý** above; upstairs

навéс shelter; awning

навести́ → **наводи́ть**

навещáть, ~**сти́ть** visit, come or go to see

навлекáть, ~**чь** draw or bring on; ~ **на себя́** incur

наводи́ть, **навести́** (*на* В) direct or aim (at); **bridge** build; ~ **на мысль** suggest an idea; ~ **спрáвки** make enquiries

наводне́ние flood

навóз manure; dung

навóло(ч)ка pillow-case

навсегдá for ever, for good

навстре́чу: идти́ ~ (Д) go to meet; *fig.* meet half-way

нáвык skill, experience

навя́зчивый obtrusive; ~**ывать**, ~**áть** (Д) force upon; thrust on

нагибáть, **нагнýть** bend; **-ся** stoop

нагишóм *adv.* stark naked

нáглухо tightly

нáглый insolent

нагля́дный clear; obvious, graphic; ~**е пособия** *pl.* visual aids

нагóй naked; ~**отá** nakedness

нагото́ве in readiness

нагрá|да reward; award; decoration; ~**ждáть**, ~**ди́ть** reward; (**- óрденом**) decorate

нагре́(вá)ть warm, heat; **-ся** get warm or hot

нагру|жáть, ~**зи́ть** load; freight; ~**зка** loading(-up)

над (Т) over; above; at; on

надвигáться, **-нуться** draw near, approach

надé(вá)ть put on

надéжда hope

надёжн|ость reliability (*a. tech.*); ~**ный** reliable; trustworthy

наде́лать pf. (B or P) make, get ready; coll. cause, give; do

наделя́ть, **-и́ть** (T) provide or endow (with)

наде́яться (**на** B) hope (for)

надзе́мный overground; rail. elevated

надзо́р supervision; surveillance

надлежа́щий proper, due

надме́нный haughty

на́до[1] it is necessary; **мне ~** I must; I need or want; **так ему́ и ~!** serves him right!; **-бность** f necessity, need

на́до[2] → **над**

надое|да́ть, **-сть** (Д) pester, bore (with T); **мне э́то надое́ло** I am fed up with it

на́дпись f inscription; legend

надрыва́ться, **надорва́ться** overstrain o.s.

наду́(ва́)ть inflate; coll. cheat

надувно́й inflatable

надуши́ть → **души́ть**[2]

нае|да́ть, **-е́сться** eat one's fill

наём hire; rent

нажи́вка (fishing) bait

наж(им)а́ть (B) (or **на** B) press, push

наза́д back(wards); **год тому́ ~** a year ago

назва́|ние name; title; **-ть**

→ **называ́ть**

назло́ adv. (Д) to spite a person

назнач|а́ть, **-и́ть** fix, set; appoint; prescribe; **-е́ние** fixing; appointment; prescription; purpose; **ме́сто -е́ния** destination

наз(ы)ва́ть call, name; **-ся** call o.s.; impf. be called

наибо́л|ее adv. most; **-ьший** greatest, largest

наи́вный naïve

наизна́нку inside out

наизу́сть by heart

найти́ → **находи́ть**

наказа́|ние punishment; **-ывать**, **-а́ть** punish

нака́лывать, **наколо́ть** prick; (**на** B) pin (to)

накану́не the day before; (P) on the eve (of)

нака́чивать, **-а́ть** pump up or full

накладн|а́я invoice, waybill; **-но́й**: **-ны́е расхо́ды** m/pl. overhead expenses; **-ыва́ть**, **наложи́ть** put or lay on; impose; apply

накле́и(ва)ть glue or paste on

наклон|я́ть, **-и́ть** incline; bend; bow; **-ся** stoop; bend forward

наконе́ц at last; finally

накры́(ва́)ть cover; **~ (на) стол** lay the table

налага́ть, **наложи́ть** (**на** B) inflict (on); impose (on); **наложенным платежо́м** cash on delivery (C.O.D.)

нале́во (*от* P) on or to the left (of)

напи́(ва́)ть cup of tea pour out; (T) fill (with)

нали́вка fruit liqueur; *вишнёвая* ~ cherry brandy

налицо́: *быть* ~ be present or on hand

нали́чие availability; presence; **~ный** available; **~ные де́ньги** *f/pl.* ready money, cash

нало́г tax

наложи́ть → **накла́дывать** *a.* **налага́ть**

нам (to) us

намёк hint, allusion

намек(а́ть, ~ну́ть (*на* B) hint (at), allude (to)

намерева́ться intend

наме́рен|ие intention; **~ный** intentional, deliberate; **он** ~ he intends

намеча́ть, наме́тить plan; have in view

на́ми through or by us; us; **она́** ~ **дово́льна** she is pleased with us

нанима́ть, наня́ть rent, hire

наноси́ть, нанести́ (Д) inflict, cause; (на B) mark; coat; *snow or sand* drift

наоборо́т the other way round; on the contrary

наотре́з: *отказа́ться* ~ re-

fuse point-blank

напа|да́ть, ~сть (*на* B) attack; assault; *feeling*: come over; **~де́ние** attack (of)

напереко́р (Д) in defiance (of)

напёрсток thimble

напеча́тать → **печа́тать**

напи́(ва́)ться quench one's thirst; get drunk

напи́льник *tech.* file

написа́ть → **писа́ть**

напи́т|ок drink, beverage; *прохлади́тельные* **~ки** soft drinks

наполн|я́ть, ~ить *v/t.* fill; **-ся** *v/i.* fill, be filled

наполови́ну *adv.* half; by halves

напомин|а́ть, ~нить (Д) remind (of *о* П)

напо́р pressure

направ|ле́ние direction; *fig.* trend; order, assignment; **~ля́ть, ~ить** direct; send; refer; **-ся** (*в, на* B) go; (*к* Д) make for; be bound for

напра́во (*от* P) on or to the right (of)

напра́сн|о in vain; wrongfully; **~ый** vain, useless; wrongful

наприме́р for example

напрока́т for or on hire; **взять** ~ hire

напро́тив *adv.* opposite, across the street; (P) opposite; on the contrary

напряг|а́ть, ~чь strain;

~же́ние effort; *tech.* voltage; tension; strain; stress; ~же́нность *f pol.* tension; tenseness

напу́тствие parting words

наравне́ (*с* T) on a level (with); ~ (*с* T) along with

нараст|а́ть, ~и́ *v/i.* grow, increase; accumulate

наре́чие dialect; adverb

нарисова́ть → рисова́ть

нарко́|з narcosis, anaesthesia; *ме́стный ~з* local anaesthetic; ~ма́н drug addict; ~тики narcotics

нар- *in compounds* = наро́дный

наро́д people; nation; crowd; ~ный national, popular; folk...; ~ный суд People's Court; ~онаселе́ние population

наро́чно on purpose; *в э́тот день как ~* that day of all days

нару́ж|ность *f* appearance; ~ный external, outward; ~у outside; вы́йти ~у come to light

наруш|а́ть, 'ить violate, infringe; disturb; break; ~е́ние violation; breach; ~е́ние пра́вил у́личного движе́ния infringement of traffic regulations

нары́в abscess

наря́д¹ order; warrant

наря́д² dress, attire; ~ный smart, well-dressed

наряду́ (*с* T) side by side

(with)

нас us

насеко́мое insect

населе́ние population; inhabitants; ~я́ть, ~и́ть populate, settle; *impf.* inhabit

наси́лие violence, force

наскво́зь *adv.* through (-out); through and through

наско́лько *adv.* to what extent; *conj.* as far as

на́скоро hastily; in a slapdash way

насла|жда́ться, ~ди́ться (T) enjoy, relish; delight (in); ~жде́ние delight; enjoyment

насле́д|ие heritage, legacy; ~ник (, ~ница) heir (, ~ess); ~овать inherit; (Д) succeed (to); ~ственный hereditary; ~ство inheritance

насме|ха́ться (*над* T) mock *or* sneer (at); '~шка mockery

на́сморк *med.* cold; подхвати́ть ~ catch a cold

насо́с pump

на́спех hastily; carelessly

наста́(ва́)ть *time, season:* come

наста́ивать¹, настоя́ть draw, infuse; ~ся *tea:* draw

наста́ивать², настоя́ть (*на* П) insist (on); persist (in)

на́стежь *adv.* wide open

насто́йка (*not distilled*) liqueur; *med.* tincture

настойчивый (*person*) persistent; urgent

настолько so much; to such a degree; ~ **наcколько** as much as

настольный table…, desk; ~ **теннис** table tennis

настоятельный urgent, pressing; ~ть → **наcтаивать**; ~щий genuine, real; (*time*) present

настраивать, **настроить** *mus.* tune; *radio* tune in; *person* dispose, make, incline

настроение mood, humour

наступать, ~ить *time:* come; (**на** B) tread (upon); *impf. mil.* attack, be on the offensive; ~ление offensive, attack; coming, beginning

насчёт (P) concerning; *как ~ …?* what about …?; ~ *чего?* what about?

насчитывать(ся) number

насыпь *f mst. rail.* embankment

насыщать, ~тить satiate; saturate

натирать, **натереть** rub; rub sore; polish

натиск impact; onslaught

НАТО NATO

натощак on an empty stomach

натура nature; *art.* model, sitter; *писать с ~ы* paint

from life; ~альный natural; genuine

натюрморт *paint.* still-life

натягивать, ~нуть stretch, draw; pull on

наугад, **наудачу** at random, haphazard

наука science; *это тебе ~* let this be a lesson to you

научить teach; ~ся (Д) learn; '~ный scientific

наушники *m/pl.* ear-phones

нахал(ка) impudent fellow (woman); ~ьный impudent

находить, **найти** find; think; (**на** B) come over or across; ~ся be found, turn up; *impf.* be; '~ка find; *fig.* boon; '~чивый resourceful, quick-witted

национализм nationalism

национальность *f* nationality; ~ый national

нация nation

начало beginning; source; origin; ~ьник head, chief; superior; ~ьный initial; elementary; ~ьство authorities; superiors; *coll.* boss

начертить → **чертить**

начин(ин)ать (*v/i.* ~ся) begin, start

начинка *cul.* filling; ~ять, ~ить fill, stuff

начитанный well-read

наш ~а, '~е, *pl.* '~и our(s)

нашатырный: ~ *спирт* liquid ammonia

нашéствие invasion

наявý adv. awake; in reality

не not; not a, no; **нé за что!** not at all!; **не раз** more than once

не- un-, non-, dis-, in-

небéсный celestial; heavenly

неблагодáрный ungrateful; thankless

неблагожелáтельный ill-disposed, malevolent

нéбо sky; heaven; **~свóд** firmament; **~склóн** sky (just above horizon); **~скрёб** skyscraper

нёбо anat. palate

небрéжный careless; slipshod

небывáлый unprecedented; fantastic

невáжный unimportant; bad, poor; **это ~о** that does not matter

невéж|а m/f boor, lout; **~да** m/f ignoramus; **~ество** ignorance; **~ливый** impolite

невéрный wrong; unfaithful

невероя́тный improbable; incredible; **~о!** it's incredible!

невесóмость weightlessness

невéста bride; fiancée

невéстка daughter-in-law; sister-in-law

невидáнный never seen

нéвидимый before; unusual; **~имый** invisible

невúнный innocent; harmless; virgin; **~óвный** jur. not guilty

невмешáтельство non-intervention

невнимáние inattention; thoughtlessness; **~тельный** inattentive; thoughtless

невозмóжный impossible

невозмутúмый imperturbable

невóльный involuntary; **~я** captivity

невредúмый unharmed

невыносúмый unbearable, intolerable

негатúв photo. negative

нéгде (there is) nowhere

негó him; **у ~** he or it has

негóдный unfit; worthless

негодовáние indignation; **~ующий** indignant

негодя́й(ка) scoundrel

неграмотный illiterate

недалёк|ий near; (person) short-witted; **~о, недалекó** adv. not far

недáром not without reason

недействúтельный ineffective; jur. invalid

недéл|я week; **~ю (тому) назáд** a week ago; **на этóй ~е** this week; **чéрез ~ю** in a week's time

недовéр|ие distrust; **~чивый** distrustful

недоеда́ние malnutrition

недоразуме́ние misunderstanding

недосмо́тр oversight

недоста́|(ва́)ть: ему́ недостаёт терпе́ния he lacks patience; мне о́чень недостава́ло вас I missed you very much; э́того ещё недостава́ло that would be the last straw; ~ток lack, shortage; shortcoming, defect; ~точный insufficient

недоуме́ние bewilderment; быть в ~и be in a quandary

неё her; у ~ she or it has

нежда́нный unexpected

нежена́тый (man) unmarried

нежило́й uninhabited; unfit for habitation

не́жн|ость f tenderness; delicacy; ~ый tender; delicate

незабу́дка forget-me-not

незави́сим|ость f independence; ~ый independent

незадо́лго ~ до shortly before

незако́нный illegal; illegitimate

незамени́мый irreplaceable

незаме́тный imperceptible; inconspicuous

незаму́жняя (woman) unmarried

незауря́дный outstanding

нездоро́вый unhealthy; unwholesome; sickly

незнако́м|ец, ~ка stranger; ~ый unknown

неизбе́жный inevitable

неизве́стный unknown

неизлечи́мый incurable

неиспра́вный defective, faulty, out of order

нейстовство frenzy, fury

ней: о ~ about her or it

нейтралите́т neutrality

не́кий a certain

не́когда[1] there is no time; мне ~ I have no time

не́когда[2] in former times

не́который some

некроло́г obituary

некста́ти inopportunely; not to the point

не́кто someone; a certain

некуря́щий non-smoker

неле́пый preposterous

нело́вк|ий awkward; чу́вствовать себя́ ~ be ill at ease

нельзя́ it is impossible or forbidden; мне ~ I cannot

нём: о ~ about him or it

нема́ло not a little, much; not a few; many; ~ва́жный of no small importance

неме́дленно immediately

не́м|ец, ~ка; ~е́цкий German

немно́го a little, a few; some(what)

немо́й dumb; su. mute

нему́: к ~ to(wards) him or it

it

ненави́деть hate

не́нависть f hatred

ненадёжный unreliable; untrustworthy

ненападе́ние non-aggression

нена́стный rainy, foul

ненорма́льный abnormal; *coll.* mad

нену́жный unnecessary

необду́манный rash, thoughtless

необосно́ванный unfounded, groundless

необходи́мый necessary; indispensable

необыкнове́нный unusual, uncommon

неограни́ченный unlimited

неодобре́ние disapproval

неожи́данный unexpected

неопра́вданный unjustified

нео́пытный inexperienced

неосторо́ж|ность f imprudence; **~ый** imprudent

неотло́ж|ный urgent, pressing; **~ная по́мощь** urgent medical aid rendered at home

неохо́т|а reluctance; **~но** reluctantly

неплодоро́дный barren; infertile

непобеди́мый invincible

неповинове́ние disobedience, insubordination

непово́ротливый clumsy;

sluggish

непого́да bad weather

неподви́жный motionless; fixed

неподходя́щий unsuitable

непоня́тный unintelligible

непосле́довательный inconsistent

непослу́шный disobedient, naughty

непосре́дственный immediate, direct (*a. fig.*); spontaneous

непостоя́нный inconstant; (*weather*) changeable

непра́вда untruth; **~ильный** wrong; irregular (*a. gr.*); **~ый: он** he is wrong

непреме́нно *adv.* without fail

непреры́в|ный, **~ста́нный** uninterrupted, incessant, continuous

непривы́чный unusual; unaccustomed

неприго́дный unfit; useless

неприе́млемый unacceptable

неприкоснове́нн|ость f inviolability; **дипломати́ческая ~ость** diplomatic immunity; **~ый** inviolable; **~ый капита́л** reserve capital

неприли́чный indecent

непринуждённый free and easy, unconstrained

неприя́|знь f enmity; **~тель** m enemy; **~тность** f annoyance; unpleasantness; trouble; ~тный disagreeable, unpleasant

непромокаемый waterproof...

непроходимый impassable

неравенство inequality

неразборчивый not fastidious; illegible

нервничать feel nervous; ~ный nervous; irritable; nerve...

нередко not seldom, often

нерешительный irresolute; indecisive

неряшливый slovenly

несвежий not fresh; stale

несговорчивый intractable

несгораемый fireproof

несколько several; some; somewhat

нескромный immodest; indiscreet

неслыханный unheard of

несмотря: ~ **на** (B) in spite of

несовершенн|олетний minor, under age; ~ый imperfect(ive); incomplete

несогласие non-agreement; dissent; discord; **он ~ен** he disagrees

несомненный undoubted

несостоятельный unfounded

неспособный (**на** B) incapable (of)

несправедлив|ость f injustice; ~ый injust

нести, по~ (→ a. **носить**) carry; fig. bear, suffer; incur; impf. duties perform ~сь, по~ rush along

несчаст|ный unhappy; unlucky; ~ный случай accident; ~ье misfortune; к ~ью unfortunately

нет no; (P) there is no; **его ~** he is not here; **у меня ~ денег** I have no money

нетерп|ение impatience; ~еливый impatient

нетерпим|ость intolerance; ~ый intolerant

неточный inaccurate

нетрудоспособный disabled

нетто indecl. adj. comm. net

неуверенный uncertain; ~ **в себе** diffident

неудача failure; ~ный unsuccessful; lame, poor

неудержимый irrepressible

неудоб|ный uncomfortable; inconvenient; ~ство discomfort; inconvenience

неужели really?

неуклюжий clumsy

неуловимый elusive; subtle

неумелый unskilful; ~ние lack of skill

неуместный misplaced; irrelevant

неурожай bad harvest

неустойка jur. forfeit

неусто́йчивый unstable

неутеши́тельный not comforting, depressing

неутоми́мый untiring

нефт|епрово́д oil pipe-line; **-ь** f (mineral) oil; **-яно́й** oil...

неча́янно accidentally; inadvertently

не́чего (+ inf.) there is nothing or no need (to); it is no use

нечелове́ческий superhuman; inhuman

нече́стный dishonest; unfair

нечётный (number) odd

не́что something

не́ю: **с ~** with her or it

нея́сный vague

ни: **ни одна́ звезда́** not a single star; **я не по́мню ни (одного́) сло́ва** I do not remember a single word; **ни ... ни** neither nor; **ни с того́, ни с сего́** without any reason

ни́же comp. of **ни́зкий**; shorter; as prep. below

низ bottom

ни́зкий low; short; poor, inferior

ни́зменность geogr. lowland

ника́к: **~ не(т)** by no means; **~ нельзя́** it is quite impossible; **как-~** after all; **-о́й** not any, no (whatever)

никогда́ never

никто́ nobody, no one; **ни с кем** with no one

никуда́ nowhere; **~ не го́дится** is no good at all

ним: **с ~** with him or it; **к ~** to(wards) them

ни́ми with them

ниско́лько not in the least

ни́т|ка thread; **-ь** f thread; filament; med. suture

них: **о ~** about them

ничего́ nothing; so-so or quite nice(ly)

ниче́й (**ничья́, ничьё**) nobody's

ничто́ (P: **ничего́,** Д: **ничему́** etc.) nothing

ничто́|жество a nobody; **-жный** insignificant

ничу́ть adv. coll. not a bit

ничья́ (sports) draw

нищ|ета́ poverty; **'-ий** beggar

НЛО (= **неопо́знанный лета́ющий объе́кт**) UFO

но but

нов|а́тор innovator; **-изна́, -и́нка** novelty; **-ичо́к** novice, beginner

нове́лла short story; (law) new clause

ново|бра́чные newly-married couple; **-го́дний** New Year's; **~ ме́сяц** new moon; **-рождённый** newborn; **-се́лье** house-warming

но́в|ость f newness, novelty; news; **-шество** innovation; **-ый** new

ног|а́ leg; foot; **идти́ в '_у** keep step; *fig.* keep abreast

но́готь (finger-, toe-) nail

нож, '_и́к knife

но́жка *dim. of* **нога́**; (*table etc.*) leg

но́жн|ицы f/pl. scissors

ноздря́ nostril

ноль = **нуль**

но́мер number; (*hotel*) room; (*newspaper, magazine*) issue; **_о́к** cloak-room ticket *or Am* check

норве́ж|ец, _ка; _ский Norwegian

но́рма norm; rate, quota

нос nose; (*ship*) bow; **_ик** (*pot*) spout

носи́л|ки f/pl. stretcher; **_ьщик** porter

носи́тель: **_ да́нных** *tech.* data medium

носи́ть (→ *a.* **нести́**); wear; *name, traces* bear; *arms, watch* carry; **_ся** → **нести́сь;** *material* wear

носки́ m/pl. → **носо́к**

носово́й nasal; nose...; **_ платок** handkerchief

носо́к toe(-cap); sock

но́та *mus., pol.* note

нота́риус notary

ноч|ева́ть (*im*)*pf.* pass the night; **_лёг** lodging for the night; **_но́й** night(ly)...; **_ь** f night; **'_ью** by night

но́ша burden

ноя́брь m November

нрав disposition; temper; **'_иться, по-** (Д) please; **мне _ится э́тот дом** I like this house; **_ственный** moral; **_ы** m/pl. customs, manners

нужда́ need; necessity; poverty; **_ться** (в П) need, require; be hard up; **_ющийся** needy, poor; requiring

ну́жно it is necessary; **мне _но** I need, I must; **что вам _но?** what do you want?; **мне _ен каранда́ш** I need a pencil

нуль m zero; nought

ныря́ть, _ну́ть v/i. dive

ню́хать, по- v/t. smell

ня́ня (*mst. children*) nurse

О

о (П) of, about; (В) against, upon; **бок о́ бок** side by side

об *in certain positions* = **о**

о́ба m/n, **о́бе** f both

обая́ние fascination, charm; **'_тельный** fascinating, charming

обва́л collapse; avalanche; land-slide

обвести́ → обводи́ть

обвин|е́ние accusation; charge; ~и́тель accuser; prosecutor; ~я́емый accused; defendant, ~я́ть, ~и́ть (в П) accuse (of)

обводи́ть, обвести́ (вокру́г P) lead (round); – глаза́ми look around

обворо́вывать, обворова́ть coll. rob

обгоня́ть, обогна́ть outdistance; leave behind; outstrip

обделя́ть, ~и́ть do s.b. out of his share

обду́м|(ыва)ть think over

обе́ → о́ба

обе́д (early) dinner; ~ать, по- have dinner; ~енный dinner...

обезору́жи(ва)ть disarm

обезья́на monkey, ape

обели́ск obelisk

обере|га́ть, ~чь (от Р) guard (against); protect (from)

обёрт|ка wrapper; ~ывать, оберну́ть wrap up; turn

обеспе́чение guarantee(ing); safeguarding; ensuring; maintenance; ~ение социа́льное social security; ~и(ва)ть ensure; safeguard; person provide for; (Т) provide (with)

обеща́|ние promise; ~ть, по- promise

обжа́лование jur. appeal

обжига́ться, обже́чься

burn o.s.

обжо́ра m/f glutton

обзо́р survey; (press) review

оби́д|а offence; pf. ~еть, impf. обижа́ть offend; ~ся take offence; ~чивый touchy

оби́л|ие abundance; ~ьный abundant

обита́т|ель(ница) m inhabitant; ~ь inhabit, dwell

обихо́дный everyday...; household...

обко́м (= областно́й комите́т) regional committee

обла́ва round-up

облага́ть, обложи́ть ассess; – штра́фом fine; – нало́гом tax

облада́ть (Т) possess

о́блако cloud

о́бласть f region; district; fig. field

о́блачный cloudy

облегч|а́ть, ~и́ть make easier; lighten; alleviate

обли|(ва́)ть (Т) pour or spill (on, over В)

о́блик look, aspect

облич|а́ть, ~и́ть (в П) expose, unmask; impf. reveal

обложе́ние (нало́гами) taxation; ~и́ть → облага́ть; ~ка cover; dust-jacket

обло́мок fragment

облуче́ние irradiation

обма́н deception; fraud; **_чивый** deceptive; **_щик**, **_щица** deceiver; '**_ывать**, **_у́ть** deceive; _hopes_ betray

обме́н exchange; barter; **_ веще́ств** _biol._ metabolism; **_ивать(ся** T), **_я́ть(ся** T) exchange; swop

о́бморок fainting fit, swoon; **упа́сть в _** faint

обнаж|а́ть, **_и́ть** bare; uncover; _fig._ lay bare, reveal

обнару́жи(ва)ть reveal; find; discover; detect; display; **_ся** be revealed; come to light

обнима́ть, **обня́ть** embrace

обновле́ние renovation, renewal; **_ля́ть**, **_и́ть** renovate; renew

обо → _о_

обобща́ть, **_и́ть** generalize

обогна́ть → _обгоня́ть_

ободр|я́ть, **_и́ть** encourage, cheer up; **_ся** take heart

обожа́|ние adoration; **_ть** adore

обознач|а́ть, '**_ить** designate; mark; _impf._ mean; **_е́ние** designation

обозрева́тель columnist

обозре́ние (_press_) review

обо́и _m/pl._ wall-paper

оболо́чка cover, jacket; **сли́зистая _** mucous membrane

обора́чивать, **оберну́ть** wrap up; **_ся** turn round

оборва́ть → _обрыва́ть_

оборо́н|а _mil._ defence; **_и́тельный** defensive; **_я́ть**, **_и́ть** defend

оборо́т reverse (side); turn of speech; _tech._ revolution; _comm._ turnover '**_ный** капита́л working capital

обору́дова|ние equipment; outfit; **_ть** (_im_)_pf._ equip; fit out

обосно́ванн|ый well-founded, sound; **э́то вполне́ _о** there are good reasons for it

обособ|ля́ть, '**_ить** isolate; **_ся** keep apart _or_ aloof

обостре́ние aggravation; _med._ exacerbation

обою́дный mutual

обраб|а́тывать, **_о́тать** work (up), process; _land_ cultivate; **_о́тка** processing; cultivation; **_ да́нных** data processing

обра́довать → _ра́довать_

о́браз image; shape; mode, way; **гла́вным _ом** chiefly; **таки́м _ом** thus; **_е́ц** model; sample, specimen; pattern; **_ова́ние** formation; education; **_о́ванный** well-educated; **_о́вывать**, **_ова́ть** form, make up; **_цо́вый** model...

обра́тно back; inversely; **_ый** reverse; opposite;

(ticket) return...

обраща́ть, ~ти́ть turn; (в В) turn into; (в на́ что) turn into; (**в** В) pay attention to; **~ чьё-либо внима́ние на** (В) draw s.o. attention to; **~ся** (к Д) apply to, address; (**в** В) turn into; *impf.* (с Т) treat, handle; **~ще́ние** address, appeal; treatment; *fin.* circulation

обремен|я́ть, ~и́ть burden

обры́в precipice; *tech.* break; **~а́ть, оборва́ть** tear off; pluck; break; snap; cut short; **~ся** tear; fall; stop suddenly

обря́д rite, ceremony

обслу́жи|вание service; *tech.* servicing, maintenance; **~(ва)ть** serve, attend; *tech.* service

обстано́вка furniture; conditions; set-up

обстоя́тель|ный detailed; **~ство** circumstance

обстоя́ть: де́ло обстои́т так the matter stands as follows; **как обстоя́т ва́ши дела́?** how are you getting on?

обсужда́ть, ~ди́ть discuss; **~жде́ние** discussion

обтира́ть, оберте́ть wipe (dry); (Т) rub (with)

обу́(ва́)ться put on shoes

о́бувь f foot-wear

обусло́в|ливать, ~ить condition, stipulate; call forth

обуча́ть, ~и́ть teach (*something* Д); train (in Д); **~а́ться** (Д) learn; **~е́ние** teaching; instruction; training

обхо́д (*daily*) round; roundabout way; evasion *of law*; **~и́ть, обойти́** go round; *question* pass over; *law* evade; **~и́ться, обойти́сь** cost; **- без** (Р) do without; (Т) manage (with); **~ с** (Т) treat

обши́рный vast; extensive

обща́ться (с Т) associate, mix (with)

обще|жи́тие hostel; **~изве́стный** generally known; well-known; **~челове́ческий** common to all mankind

обще́ние intercourse, contact; **~е́ственность** f the broad public; **~е́ственный** public; social; **'~ество** society; *comm.* company; **'~ий** common, general; **'~ая су́мма** total sum; **в ~ем** on the whole; **~и́тельный** convivial, sociable; **'~ность** f (*abstract*) community

объедине́ние unification; union; association; **~я́ть, ~и́ть** unite

объе́зд circuit, detour

объезжа́ть, объе́хать travel (all) over; make a detour; go round; *mot.* overtake, pass

объе́кт object, **~и́вный** objective

объём volume (*a. fig.*); **~истый** voluminous, bulky

объявле́ние declaration, announcement; advertisement; **~я́ть**, **~и́ть** declare, announce; publish

объясне́ние explanation; **~е́ние в любви́** declaration of love; **~я́ть**, **~и́ть** explain; **-ся** be explained; make o.s. understood

объя́тие embrace

обы́грывать, **~а́ть** (*game*) beat

обы́денный everyday, commonplace

обыкнове́ние: име́ть ~е be in the habit (of); **~ный** usual; ordinary; customary

о́быск (*people, places*) search; **'~ивать**, **~а́ть** search (all over)

обы́чай custom; **~ный** customary; usual; ordinary

обя́занность f duty, obligation; **~анный** obliged; indebted (*a. fig.*); **~но** without fail; **~ательный** obligatory; (*person*) reliable; **~ательство** obligation; pl. comm. liabilities; **~ывать**, **~а́ть** oblige; **-ся** pledge or commit o.s.

ове́с oats

овладе́(ва́)ть (T) seize;

take possession (of); master

о́вощи m/pl. vegetables; **~но́й: ~но́й магази́н** greengrocery

овра́г ravine

овся́нка oatmeal; porridge

овца́ sheep

оглавле́ние table of contents

оглаша́ть, **огласи́ть** announce

оглуша́ть, **~и́ть** deafen; stun

огля́дывать, **~е́ть** look over, examine; **-ся** look round; **~ываться**, **огляну́ться** look back

огне|опа́сный inflammable; **~туши́тель** m fire-extinguisher; **~упо́рный** fireproof

огова́риваться, **~ори́ться** make a reservation; make a slip (*in speaking*)

огово́рка reservation; slip of the tongue

ого́нь m fire

огоро́д kitchen-garden

огорча́ть, **~и́ть** grieve; **~е́ние** grief; chagrin; disappointment

огра́да fence, wall

ограниче́ние limitation; restriction; **'~енный** limited; narrow-minded; **~и(ва́)ть** limit; restrict

огро́мный huge, enormous; vast

огуре́ц cucumber

ода́лживать, одолжи́ть lend

одарённый gifted

оде́(ва́)ть dress, clothe; **~ся** dress; **~жда** clothes; **~я́ло** blanket

одеколо́н eau-de-cologne

оде́рживать ~а́ть gain

оди́н, одна́, одно́ pl. **одни́** one; alone; a certain; **оди́н на оди́н** tête-a-tête; **оди́н раз** once; **одни́м сло́вом** in a word; **одно́ вре́мя** at one time; **одно́ и то́ же** the same thing

одина́|ковый equal; identical; **~надцатый** eleventh; **~надцать** eleven; **~о́кий** lonely; (unmarried) single; **~о́чество** loneliness; solitude

одна́|жды once, one day; **~ко** however, yet

одно|вре́менный simultaneous; **~обра́зие** monotony; **~ро́дный** homogenuous; **~сторо́нний** one-sided (a. fig.); unilateral; one-way; **~сторо́ннее движе́ние** one-way traffic; **~эта́жный** one-storeyed

одобре́|ние approval; **~я́ть, ~ить** approve

одоле́(ва́)ть overcome; cope with

одолже́ние favour

оду́маться pf. change one's mind

оды́шка short breath

ожере́лье necklace

ожесточённый bitter; embittered; fierce, desperate

ожи́(ва́)ть come to life; revive (a. fig.); **~вле́ние** animation; **~влять, ~ви́ть** revive; enliven

ожида́|ние expectation; **обма́ну~ния** disappoint; **сверх~ния** unexpectedly; **зал~ния** rail. waiting room; **~ть** (P) expect; wait (for)

ожо́г med. burn; scald

озабо́|ченный preoccupied; anxious, worried; **~чивать, ~тить** cause anxiety to

озада́чи(ва)ть puzzle, perplex

о́зеро lake

озлобле́ние animosity, embitterment

ознаком|ля́ть, ~ить acquaint, familiarize

означа́ть impf. mean, signify, stand for

озно́б shivering; chill

ока́з|ывать, ~а́ть render, show, exert; **~де́йствие (на B)** have an effect (on); **~ся** (T) prove (to be); turn out; find o.s.

ока́нчивать (v/i. **~ся**), **око́нчить** (v/i. **~ся**) end, finish

океа́н ocean

о́кись f oxide

окла́д salary

окно́ window

óкол|о (P) near, by; around; about, nearly

оконч|áние termination; end; *gr.* ending; **-áтельный** final; definitive; **'-ить → оконча́ивать**

óкорок ham, gammon

окóшко window; (*bank etc.*) counter

окра́ина outskirts; outlying districts

окра́|ска colouring; dyeing; colouration; **-шивать, -сить** colour, paint; tint

окре́стн|ость *f* environs; neighbourhood, vicinity

óкруг district; *избира́тельный* **-** constituency

окруж|а́ть, -и́ть surround; encircle; **-е́ние** surroundings; milieu; **-но́й** district...; **-ность** circumference; circle

октя́брь *m* October; **-ский** October...

окули́ст eye specialist

окун|а́ть, -у́ть dip, plunge

óкунь (*fish*) perch

оку́рок cigar(ette)-end, stub

оку́т(ыв)ать wrap up; *fig.* cloak, shroud

ола́дья fritter

оле́нь *m* deer; *се́верный* **-** reindeer

олимп|иа́да olympiad, competition; **-ийский** olympic; **-ийские и́гры** Olympic Games

олицетвор|я́ть, -и́ть personify; embody

óлов|о (*metal*) tin

ома́р lobster

омле́т omelette

он, она́, онó, *pl.* **они́** he, she, it, they

онда́тра musk-rat; musquash

ООН (= *Организа́ция Объединённых На́ций*) *pol.* UNO

опа́зд|ывать, -а́ть (на В) be late (for)

опас|а́ться (P) apprehend, fear; **-е́ние** apprehension, fear; **'-ность** *f* danger; **'-ный** dangerous

óпера opera

опера́ция operation

опере|жа́ть, -ди́ть get ahead of; forestall

опере́тта operetta, musical comedy

опери́ровать (*im*)*pf.* operate (on)

óперный opera...; **-теа́тр** opera-house

опеча́тка misprint

опира́ться, опере́ться (*на* В) lean (on, against) (*a. fig.*); rest upon

опис|а́ние description; **'-ывать, -а́ть** describe

óпись *f* inventory; list

опла́|та payment, remuneration; **-чивать, -ти́ть** pay, remunerate

опозда́|ние being late; delay; **-ть → опа́здывать**

опозна(ва)ть identify, recognize

опомниться *pf.* come to one's senses

опор|а support; **точка ~ы** fulcrum

опора́|жнивать, ~о́жнить empty

оправа setting, mounting; (*glasses*) rim

оправда́|ние justification; **~ывать, ~а́ть** justify; **~ся** justify o.s.; prove to be correct

опра́шивать, опроси́ть interrogate, examine

определе́|ние determination; definition; **~ённый** definite (*a. gr.*); certain; **~я́ть, ~и́ть** determine; define

опровер|га́ть, ~гнуть refute; **~же́ние** refutation; denial

опроки́|дывать, ~нуть *v/t.* overturn, topple

опро́с interrogation; **~ обще́ственного мне́ния** (public opinion) poll

опря́тный tidy, neat

опт|о́вый wholesale...; **'~ом** *adv.* wholesale

опублико́в|ывать, ~а́ть publish

опуска́|ть, ~ти́ть lower, let down; drop; **~ся** go down; lower o.s.; fall, sink; degenerate

опусто́ша|ть, ~ить devastate

о́пухоль *med.* tumor

о́пыт experience; experiment; **~ный** experienced; experimental

опя́ть again

ора́нжевый orange (*colour*)

оранжере́я greenhouse, hothouse

ора́тор orator, speaker

орби́т|а orbit; **вы́вести на ~у** put into orbit

орга́н *mus.* organ

о́рган *anat., pol.* organ; **~изо́вывать, ~изова́ть** (*a. impf.*) organize; **~иза́ция** organization

о́рден order, decoration

орёл eagle

оре́х nut; **лесно́й ~** hazelnut; **гре́цкий ~** walnut; **муска́тный ~** nutmeg

оригина́л; ~ьный original

орке́стр orchestra

ороша́|ть, ~си́ть irrigate; **~ше́ние** irrigation

ору́дие implement, tool; *mil.* gun; **~жие** arms, weapon(s)

орфогра́фия spelling

оса́ wasp

оса́док sediment; (*weather*) precipitation; **радиоакти́вные ~и** *pl.* radioactive fall-out

осва́ивать, осво́ить assimilate; master; develop; **~ся** acclimatize; (**с** T) make o.s. familiar with

осведомл|ённость knowledge, possession of information; **~ённый** knowledgeable; **~ять, осведомить** notify, inform; **-ся** (*o* II) inquire (about)

освежа́|ть, ~и́ть refresh, freshen; **~а́ющий** refreshing

осве|ща́ть, ~ти́ть light; illuminate; *fig.* throw light upon; **~ще́ние** light(ing); illumination

освобо|жда́ть, ~ди́ть free, liberate; release; **~жде́ние** liberation; release

осво́ить → осва́ивать

оседа́ть, осе́сть settle (down); sink, subside

осёл donkey

осе́нний autumn(al)...

о́сень *f* autumn; **~ю** in autumn

осётр, *cul.* **осетри́на** sturgeon

оси́на asp(en)

оско́лок splinter, fragment

оскорбле́ние insult; **~ля́ть, ~и́ть** insult; **-ся** take offence

ослаб|е́(ва́)ть *v/i.* weaken; slacken; **~ля́ть, '~ить** *v/t.* weaken; loosen, relax

осложн|я́ть, ~и́ть complicate

ослы́шаться *pf.* mishear

осма́тривать, осмотре́ть view, inspect, examine; look round

осме́|ивать, ~я́ть ridicule

осме́ли(ва)ться dare, venture, make bold

осмо́тр inspection, examination; **~и́тельный** circumspect

осно́в|а base, basis; foundation; *pl.* fundamentals; **~а́ние** foundation, ground, reason; **~а́тель** *m* founder; **~а́тельный** well-grounded; thorough; solid; **~но́й** fundamental; basic; **~ывать, ~а́ть** found

осо́б|енно especially, particularly; **~енность** *f* peculiarity; **~енный** peculiar, particular, special; **~ня́к** detached house; **~няко́м** *adv.* by oneself or itself; **~ый 1.** **~енный; 2.** separate

осозна́(ва́)ть realize, understand

о́спа smallpox

оспа́ривать, оспо́рить dispute, call in question; *impf.* contend for

оста́|(ва́)ться remain, stay; **~вля́ть, ~вить** leave; let; give up; **~льно́й** remaining, the rest of ...; *pl.* the others; **~навливать, ~нови́ть** stop, bring to a standstill; **~навливаться, ~нови́ться** stop (short); (*in hotel*) put up; **~но́вка** stop, halt; stoppage; **~ток** remainder, rest; remnant

остерега́ться (P) beware (of)

осторо́жн|о carefully; cautiously; **_o!** look out!; **_ость** f caution, prudence; **_ый** careful, cautious, prudent

остри|ё point, edge; **_ить** crack jokes

о́стров island

острота́[1] sharpness; acuteness; keenness

острота́[2] joke, witticism

остроу́м|ие wit; **_ный** witty

о́стрый sharp; acute; keen

осты|ва́ть get cold; cool down

осу|жда́ть, **_ди́ть** condemn; blame; **_жде́ние** condemnation

осуществ|ля́ть, **_и́ть** realize, accomplish, bring about

ось f axis; axle

осяза́|ние (sense of) touch; feel(ing); **_тельный** tangible; tactile

от (P) from; of; out of; *дрожа́ть – хо́лода* tremble with cold; *пла́кать – ра́дости* cry for joy; *сре́дство – ка́шля* cough mixture

ота́пливать, **отопи́ть** room heat

отбира́ть, **отобра́ть** take away; choose, pick

о́тблеск reflection, gleam

отбо́р|ный selected, choice...; **_очный** (*sports*) knock-out...

отбро́сы m/pl. garbage, re-

fuse

отбы|ва́ть depart; *time or sentence* serve

отва́|га bravery; **_жный** brave, valiant

отвезти́ → отвози́ть

отверг|а́ть, **'_нуть** reject

отве́рстие opening, hole, slot

отвёрт|ка screw-driver; **_ывать(ся)**, **отвер-ну́ть(ся)** (get) unscrew (-ed); turn away (*a. fig.*)

отвести́ → отводи́ть

отве́т answer; **_ить →** отве-ча́ть

отве́тственн|ость f responsibility; **_ый** responsible; **_ый рабо́тник** executive

отве|ча́ть, **'_тить** (**на** В) answer; be responsible (for **за** В); *impf* (Д) meet, answer, be up to

отви́н|чивать, **_ти́ть** unscrew

отвле|ка́ть, **'_чь** distract; divert; abstract; **_чённый** abstract

отводи́ть, **отвести́** lead, take, conduct; *blow* parry; *room* allot

отвози́ть, **отвезти́** drive or take (away)

отвор|я́ть, **_и́ть** open

отврати́тельный disgusting **_ще́ние** disgust, aversion; *пита́ть* **_ще́ние** loathe

отвык|а́ть, **'_нуть** (**от** Р) get out of the habit (of), become unused (to)

отвя́з|ывать, ~а́ть untie; ~ся get loose; (от P) get rid of

отга́д|ывать, ~а́ть riddle, etc. guess

отгова́рива|ть, ~ори́ть (от P) dissuade (from); ~о́рка (lame) excuse, pretext

отголосок echo

отда(ва́)ть give back, return; give (up); devote; ~ себе́ отчёт в (П) be aware (of); ~ся (Д) give o.s. up (to); devote o.s.

отдалённый remote, distant; ~я́ть, ~и́ть remove; postpone; alienate; ~я́ть (от P) move away (from)

отде́л department; ~ ка́дров personnel department; ~е́ние separation; compartment; department; ~е́ние мили́ции police station; ~е́ние свя́зи post office; ~(ыв)а́ть (от P) get rid of; ~ьный separate; individual; ~я́ть, ~и́ть separate

отде́лка finishing; finish

о́тдых rest, recreation; дом ~а holiday home; ~а́ть, отдохну́ть take a rest; be resting; be on holiday; ~а́ющий su. holiday-maker

отёк swelling

оте́ц father; ~чественный patriotic; home...; ~че-

ство fatherland

о́тзыв comment, review

отзы́в pol. recall; ~а́ть, отозва́ть call aside; diplomat recall; ~ся (на B) answer; (на П) tell (upon health etc.); (о П) comment (upon)

отка́з refusal; tech. failure; ~ывать, ~а́ть (в П) refuse, deny; ~ся (от P) refuse, decline; abandon

отки́д|ывать, ~нуть throw aside or back; fold back; ~ся lean back

откла́дывать, отложи́ть put aside; put off, adjourn

о́тклик response; comment

отклоне́ние deviation; digression; declination; rejection; ~я́ть, ~и́ть reject; deflect; decline; ~ся deviate; diverge; digress

открове́нный frank

откры|(ва́)ть open; discover; reveal; inaugurate; ~ся v/i. open; come to light; ~тие discovery; revelation; opening; inauguration; ~тка postcard; ~тый open

отку́да from where; whence

откупо́ри(ва)ть uncork; open

отку́с|ывать, ~и́ть bite off

отли́в ebb; ~(ва́)ть pour off

отлича́|ть, ~и́ть distinguish; ~ся distinguish

o.s.; (**от** P) differ (from); '**-ие** distinction; difference; '**-ный** excellent; (**от** P) different (from)

отло́гий sloping

отложи́ть → **откла́дывать**

о́тмель f (sand-)bank, shallow

отме́на abolition; cancellation; jur. repeal; **-я́ть,** **-и́ть** abolish; cancel; repeal

отме́тка (school) mark; note; **-ча́ть, -тить** mark (off); note

отмы(ва́)ть wash off or clean

отнести́ → **относи́ть**

отнима́ть, отня́ть take away; take (from **у** P); coll. amputate

относи́тельно adv. relatively; prep. (P) concerning; **-ельный** relative (a. gr.); **-ь, отнести́** carry away; (**в** B or **к** Д) take (to); **-ся** (**к** Д) treat; impf. (**к** Д) concern; date back to

отноше́ние relation (a. pol.); attitude; treatment; ratio; **не име́ет -я** have nothing to do (with); **в не́которых -ях** in some respects; **по -ю к** with respect (to)

отню́дь (**не**) by no means

отня́ть → **отнима́ть**

ото → **от**

отобра́ть → **отбира́ть**

отовсю́ду from everywhere

отозва́ть → **отзыва́ть**

отойти́ → **отходи́ть**

отомсти́ть → **мсти́ть**

отопле́ние heating

оторва́ть → **отрыва́ть**

отосла́ть → **отсыла́ть**

отпа́|дать, '-сть fall off or away; drop off; pass

отпеча́ток imprint; (finger-)print; **-(ыв)ать** print; imprint

отпира́ть, отпере́ть unlock

отпла́та repayment; requital; **-чивать, -ти́ть** repay; requite

отплы(ва́)ть swim or sail off (or out)

отпо́р repulse; rebuff

отправ|и́тель(ница) m sender; **-ле́ние** sending; departure; **-ля́ть, '-ить** send, forward; **-ся** set out; train: depart

о́тпуск leave, holiday; **-а́ть, отпусти́ть** let go or off; beard grow; sin remit

отпуще́ние: **козёл -я** scapegoat

отравля́ть, -и́ть poison

отра|жа́ть, -зи́ть repel; parry; **-ся** be reflected; (**на** B) affect; **-же́ние** reflection, reflex; repulse

о́трасль f fig. branch

отре́з (material) length; **-а́ть, -**́ать cut off

отрезвля́ть, -и́ть sober

отре́зок segment, section; piece; **~ вре́мени** space of time

отре|ка́ться, **'~чься** (*от* Р) renounce; disavow; **~ от престо́ла** abdicate

отрица́|ние denial; negation; **~тельный** negative; **~ть** deny; negate; disclaim

отрыва́|ть, **оторва́ть** tear off *or* away; distract, divert; **-ся** tear off; tear o.s. away; lose contact; **'~истый** abrupt; jerky; **~но́й** tear-off...; **'~ок** fragment; (*text*) passage

отря́д mil., etc. detachment

отсро́ч|и(ва)ть postpone; **~ка** postponement

отста́(ва́)ть fall behind; lag behind; *watch*: be slow

отста́ивать, **отстоя́ть** defend, assert, stand up for (*one's rights etc.*)

отста́лый backward

отстёгивать, **отстегну́ть** unfasten, unbutton

отстоя́ть v/i. (*от* Р) be distant (from); → a. **отста́ивать**

отстран|я́ть, **~и́ть** remove; dismiss; **-ся** move *or* keep away; keep aloof (from)

отступ|а́ть, **~и́ть** step back; mil. retreat; (*от* Р) deviate (from); **~ле́ние** retreat; deviation

отсу́тстви|е absence;

~овать be absent

отсыл|а́ть, **отосла́ть** send away *or* back; (*к* Д) refer (to); **'~ка** dispatch; reference

отсю́да from here; hence

отте́нок nuance, shade

отте́пель f thaw

о́ттиск impression, imprint; reprint

оттого́ (*и* ...) that's why; **~ что** because

отту́да from there; thence

отуч|а́ть, **~и́ть** (*от* Р) break *or* wean (from)

отхо́д departure; deviation; **~и́ть**, **отойти́** go *or* walk away; move away (*a. fig.*); transport: leave

отцо́в|ский paternal; **~ство** paternity

отча́|иваться, **~яться** (*в* П) despair (of)

отча́ли(ва)ть mar. cast off

отча́сти partly

отча́я|ние despair; **~нный** desperate

отчего́ why

о́тчество patronymic

отчёт account; **~ливый** distinct, clear

о́тчим stepfather

отчисл|я́ть, **'~ить** deduct; assign; dismiss

отчи́тываться, **отчита́ться** give an account (of); report

отчу|жда́ть jur. alienate; estrange; **~жде́ние** jur. alienation; estrangement

отъéзд departure; *быть в ~е* be away

отъезжáть, отъéхать depart; drive off

отыскивать, ~áть find; *impf.* search for

отягчáть, ~ить aggravate

офицéр *mil.* officer; **~иáльный** official; **~иáнт(ка)** waiter (waitress)

оформлять, ~ить mount; register, legalize; **–** *витрину* dress a shopwindow; **–** *докумéнт* draw up a paper

охóт|а readiness, wish, desire; hunt(ing); **~иться** (*за* T *or* на B) hunt, chase; **~ник** hunter; **~но** readily, gladly

охрáн|а guard(ing); protection; *личная ~а* bodyguard; **~ять, ~ить** (*от* P) guard, protect (from)

охрипнуть become hoarse

оцен|ивать, ~ить value; estimate; appraise; **~ка** estimation; appraisal; (*school. etc.*) mark

оцеплять, ~ить cordon off

очáг hearth; *fig.* breeding-ground, centre

очаров|áние charm, fascination; **~áтельный** charm-ing; **~ывать, ~áть** charm, fascinate

очевид|ец eye-witness; **~ный** obvious, evident

óчень very, very much

очередн|óй next (in turn); recurrent, usual

óчеред|ь *f* (*order of succession*) turn; queue; *в пéрвую ~* in the first place

óчерк essay, sketch

очертáние outline, contour

очищ|áть, ~стить clean; clear; purify; refine

очк|и́ *n/pl.* spectacles; *солнцезащи́тные ~и́* sunglasses; **~ó** (*cards*) pip; (*sports*) point

ошеломлять, ~ить stun, stupefy

ошиб|áться, ~иться be mistaken, make a mistake; **~ка** mistake, error (*a. tech.*)

оштрафовáть → штрафовáть

ощути|мый, ~тельный perceptible, tangible; appreciable

ощущ|áть, ~ти́ть perceive, feel; sense; **~щéние** perception, sensation

П

павли́н peacock
па́губный pernicious, fatal
па́д|ать, упа́сть fall (down); *pf.* пасть *mst. fig.* fall; die; ~ёж *gr.* case; ~е́ние fall, drop; downfall
па́дчерица stepdaughter
пай *comm.* share
паке́т parcel, packet
пакова́ть pack
пакт *pol.* pact
пала́т|а chamber; (hospital-)ward; оруже́йная ~ Armoury Museum; ~а о́бщин House of Commons; ~а представи́телей House of Representatives; Торго́вая ~а Chamber of Commerce; ~ка tent; stall
па́лец finger; toe; большо́й ~ thumb; big toe
палиса́дник front garden
пали́тра palette
пали́ть, с~ burn; о~ *v/t.* singe; sun: scorch
па́лка stick; cane; ~о двух конца́х it cuts both ways
па́лтус halibut
па́луба deck
па́льма palm(-tree)
пальто́ *n indecl.* (over-)coat
па́мят|ка memorandum; instruction; ~ник monument, memorial; ~ный memorable; ~ь *f* memory; постоя́нная ~ь *tech.* read-only memory (ROM); ~ь

с произво́льной вы́боркой random access memory (RAM)
пане́ль *f* panel; pavement, side-walk
па́ника panic
панихи́да requiem mass; гражда́нская ~ civil funeral
пансиона́т hotel with board
па́па pope; *coll.* dad(dy)
папиро́са cigarette
па́пка folder, file
пар steam
па́ра pair, couple
пара́д parade; ~ный: ~ая (дверь) front door
парализова́ть (*im*)*pf.* paralyse; ~ич paralysis
парашю́т parachute
па́рень *m* lad, fellow
пари́ *n indecl.* bet; держа́ть ~ bet
пари́к wig; ~ма́хер barber, hairdresser; ~ма́херская barber's saloon, hairdresser's
парите́т parity; на ~ных нача́лах on a par (with)
пари́ть soar
па́рить steam; stew; ~ся, по~ take a vapour bath
парк park
парке́т parquet
парла́мент parliament
парни́к hotbed
па́рный twin...; (*sports*)

double
паро|во́з steam-engine; **~во́й** steam...; **~во́е отопле́ние** central heating; **~хо́д** steamer
паро́м ferry(-boat)
парт- in compounds = **парти́йный** party...
партёр thea. pit, stalls
па́ртия pol. party; batch, lot; game; mus. part
партнёр partner
па́рус sail; nav. canvas; **~ник** sailing-boat; **~ный** sailing...
парфюме́рия perfumery
парча́ brocade
па́сека apiary
па́смурный (weather) dull, gloomy
па́спорт passport
пассажи́р|(ка) passenger; **~ский** passenger...
па́ста paste
па́стбище pasture
пасте́ль pastel (drawing)
пасти́| herd, shepherd; **~сь** graze; **~ух** shepherd, herdsman
пасть¹ → **па́дать**
пасть² f zo. jaws
па́сха Easter
па́сынок stepson
пат (chess) stalemate
пате́нт patent (for); licence (for); **~овладе́лец** patentee
патро́н mil. cartridge; lamp-socket
патру́ль m patrol

па́уза pause, interval
пау́к spider
паути́на spider's web
пах anat. groin
паха́ть plough
па́х|нуть (T) smell (of); **~учий** fragrant, sweet-smelling
пацие́нт(ка) patient
па́чка bundle; batch; packet, pack
па́чкать, ис-, за- soil; stain
па́шня field, ploughland
паште́т pâté
ПВО (= **противовозду́шная оборо́на**) anti-aircraft defence
пев|е́ц, ~и́ца singer; **~у́чий** melodious; **'~чий** adj. singing, song...; noun chorister
пейза́ж scenery; landscape
пек|а́рня bakery; **'~арь** m baker
пел|ена́ть, с- swaddle; **~ёнка** swaddling-cloth
пе́на foam; froth; suds
пе́ние singing
пе́ниться, вс- foam; froth
пенопла́ст foamed plastics
пенсио|не́р pensioner; **~о́нный** adj; **~я** pension
пень m (tree-)stump
пе́пел ashes; **~ьница** ashtray
пе́рвенство superiority; (sports) championship
перво|бы́тный primitive; **~кла́ссный** first-class;

_~нача́льный primary; initial, original

перв|ый first; **в ~ую о́чередь** in the first place

перебй(ва́)ть interrupt; break

переб(и)ра́ть finger; sort out; look through

перебо́й interruption; stoppage; hold up

перева́л (mountain-)pass

перева́р|ивать, _~ить digest; _fig._ stand

перевезти́ → перевози́ть

пере|вёртывать, _~верну́ть turn over; turn inside out

перевести́ → переводи́ть

перево́д transfer(ence); translation; **де́нежный _~** money order; **_~и́ть, перевести́** transfer; translate; remit; **_~чик, _~чица** translator, interpreter

перевози́ть, перевезти́ transport; take across; **_~ка** transport(ation)

переворо́т upheaval, revolution; **госуда́рственный _~** coup d'état

перевы́боры re-elections

перевя́з|ка bandaging, dressing; tying up; **_~ывать, _~а́ть** bandage; dress; tie up

перегна́ть → перегоня́ть

перегов|а́ривать, _~ори́ть (_о_ П) talk over; **_~о́рный: _~о́рный пункт** trunk-call office; **_~о́ры** _m/pl._ negotiations

пере|гоня́ть, _~гна́ть outdistance; overtake; surpass; _chem._ distil

перегру|жа́ть, _~зи́ть overload; _fig._ overwork; transship; **_~зка** overload; overwork; transshipping

пе́ред (T) before; in front of; **извини́ться _~ ке́м-либо** apologize to s. o.

переда|ва́(ва́)ть pass, hand (over); communicate; **_~ по ра́дио** broadcast; **_~тчик** (_radio_) transmitter; **_~ча** transfer, transmission; broadcast; gearing

передви|га́ть, '_~нуть (_v/i._ **-ся**) move, shift; **_~же́ние** movement; **сре́дства _~же́ния** means of conveyance

переде́л|ка alteration; **_~(ыв)ать** alter; do over again

пере́дн|ий fore..., front..., first; **_~ик** pinafore, apron; **_~яя** (entrance-)hall; anteroom

пере́д|о → пе́ред; _~ово́й foremost; advanced; progressive; **_~ова́я (статья́)** editorial

переду́м(ыв)ать change one's mind

переды́шка breathing-space, respite

пере|е́зд passage, crossing; removal; **_~езжа́ть, _~е́хать** (В _or_ че́рез В)

cross; *pf.* run over; *v/i.*
(re)move (*to new place*)

пережи|(ва́)ть experience,
go through; outlive; *impf.*
a. worry; **~ток** survival,
relic

пере|изб(и́)ра́ть re-elect;
~изда́(ва́)ть republish

переименов|ывать, ~а́ть
re-name

перейти́ → переходи́ть

перекла́д|ина cross-beam;
(*sports*) horizontal bar;
~ывать, переложи́ть put
(elsewhere); shift (off)

переключа́тель *m* switch;
~а́ть, ~и́ть switch (over to
на B)

перекрёсток cross-roads,
crossing

пере|лага́ть, ~ложи́ть *mus.*
arrange, transpose; **~ на
му́зыку** set to music

перелёт *av.* flight; **беспо-
са́дочный** ~ non-stop
flight; *zo.* migration

перели|(ва́)ть pour (else-
where); let overflow; *med.*
transfuse; **-ся** overflow

**переложи́ть → перекла́-
дывать** *or* **перелага́ть**

перело́м *med.* fracture; *fig.*
turning-point

переме́н|а change; (*school*)
break; **~ный** variable;
el. alternating; **~чивый**
changeable; **~я́ть(ся), ~и́ть-
(ся)** change

переме|ща́ть, ~сти́ть
move; transfer; shift

переми́рие armistice

перено́с carrying over; *typ.*
division (of words); **~и́ть,
перенести́** carry over;
transfer; postpone; endure

переоде́(ва́)ться change
one's clothes

переоце́н|ивать, ~и́ть over-
estimate; reappraise; **~ка**
overestimation; reapprai-
sal

перепеча́тка reprint (-ing)

перепи́с|ка copying; corre-
spondence; **~ывать, ~а́ть**
copy; rewrite; **-ся** *no pf.* be
in correspondence

пе́репись *f* census; **про-
вести́** ~ make a census

переплёт binding; **~чик**
book-binder

пере|плыва́ть, ~плы́ть swim
or sail across

переполн|я́ть, '~ить over-
fill; overcrowd; **-ся** (T)
overflow (with)

переправ|а passage, cross-
ing; ford; **~ля́ть, ~ить** take
across; ferry; transport
(to); mail forward

перепрода́жа resale

перепу́т(ыва)ть entangle;
coll. mix up

перераб|а́тывать, ~о́тать
process; work (into); convert; treat; **~о́тка** processing;
**~о́тка вторичного
сырья́** recycling

переры́в interruption;
break, interval

пере|са́дка *rail.* change;

med. grafting; transplantation; ~**саживаться**, **'-сесть** change one's seat; (*trains etc.*) change

пересе|ка́ть(ся), **'-чь(ся)** cross, intersect

пересел|е́нец emigrant; immigrant; settler; ~**я́ться**, **~и́ться** migrate; move

пере|се́сть → ~**са́живаться**

пересла́ть → **пересыла́ть**

переста́|(ва́)ть cease, stop; ~**вля́ть**, **~вить** move; shift; rearrange; — **часы́ вперёд (наза́д)** put one's watch forward (back)

перестро́йка rebuilding, reorganisation; perestroika

перес|(ы́)ла́ть send, forward; ~**ы́лка** sending; carriage (*of goods*); forwarding; ~**ы́лка де́нег** remittance; ~**ы́лка беспла́тно** carriage paid; post free

переу́лок by-street; lane

перехо́д transition; passage, crossing; ~**и́ть**, **перейти́** (*в or че́рез* В) go over, cross; (*к* Д) pass (to); (*в* В) turn (into); ~**ный** transition(al)...; *gr.* transitive

пе́рец pepper; *кра́сный* ~ paprika

пе́речень *m* enumeration, list

перечисл|я́ть, **'-ить** enumerate, list; (*money*) transfer

пе́речница pepper-pot

перешёек isthmus

пери́ла *n/pl.* railing; banisters

пери́на feather-bed

пери́од period; *geol.* age

перо́ feather; pen; ~**чи́нный нож(ик)** penknife

перро́н *rail.* platform

пе́рсик peach

персона́л personnel, staff

перспекти́в|а perspective; prospect; ~**ный** having prospects; promising

пе́рстень *m* (finger-)ring

перча́тка glove

пёс dog

песе́ц polar fox

пе́сня song

песо́к sand; (*са́харный*) ~ granulated sugar

пёстрый gay-coloured; motley

песча́ный sandy

пе́тля loop (*a. av.*); noose; buttonhole; (*hook*) eye; hinge; stitch; run (*in a stocking*)

петру́шка parsley

пету́х cock

петь, **с~**, **про~** sing; crow

пехо́та infantry

печа́л|ить, **о~** sadden, grieve; ~**ся** be sad, grieve; ~**ь** *f* grief, sorrow; ~**ьный** sad, grievous

печа́т|ать, **на~** print; type; ~**ь** *f* the press; print (-ing);

seal, stamp; **вы́йти из ~и** come out, be published

печёнка *cul.* liver

печёный *cul.* baked

пе́чень *f anat.* liver

пече́нье biscuit; **минда́льное ~** macaroon; **овся́ное ~** oatcake

пе́чка *coll.* stove

печь *f* stove; oven

печь, ис~. bake

пеш|ехо́д pedestrian; **'~ка** (*chess*) pawn (*a. fig.*); **~ко́м** *adv.* on foot

пеще́ра cave, cavern

пиани́но *n indecl.* (upright) piano

пив|на́я beerhouse, pub; **~но́й** beer...; **'~о** beer

пиджа́к (man's) coat *or* jacket

пи́к|а (*cards*) spade; **~овый**; **~овая да́ма** queen of spades

пила́ saw; **~и́ть** saw

пило́т *av.* pilot

пионе́р(ка) pioneer

пиро́|г pie; tart; **~жное** pastry; (*fancy*) cake; **~жо́к** pasty, patty

пис|а́ние writing; **свяще́нное ~а́ние** Holy Scripture; **~а́тель** *m* writer; **~а́ть, на~.** write; **picture paint**; **~чий** writing...

письм|енно in writing; **~енный** writing...; **~о́** letter; **заказно́е ~о́** registered letter; writing

пита́|ние nourishment, nutrition; **обще́ственное ~ние** public catering; **~ельный** nourishing; nutrient; **~ь** feed; nourish (*a. fig.*); **~ься** (T) feed (on)

пить, вы́~. drink; **~ за чьё-либо здоро́вье** drink to s. o.'s health

пи́шущая: **~ маши́нка** typewriter

пи́ща food

пищ|еваре́ние digestion; **~во́д** *anat.* gullet

пла́ва|ние swimming; navigation; **~ть** (*impf.*), *pf.* **поплы́ть** swim; float; sail; **~ить(ся)** melt, fuse; **~ник** fin; **~ный** smooth; **~учий** floating...

пла́вки swimming trunks

плака́т poster

пла́кать weep, cry

пла́мя *n* flame

план plan; scheme; **передний ~** foreground

план|ёр *av.* glider; **~и́ровать[1], с~.** glide; **~и́ровать[2], с~, за~.** plan; **~иро́вать[3], рас~.** lay out

пласти́нка *photo.* plate; *mus.* record, disc

пластма́сса plastic

пла́стырь *m med.* plaster

пла́т|а pay; fee; **зарабо́тная ~а** wages; **кварти́рная ~а** rent; **~ёж** payment; **нало́женным ~ежо́м** cash on delivery; **~ёжеспосо́бность** *comm.*

solvency; **~ёжный: ~ёж-
ный бала́нс** comm. bal-
ance of payments; **~йть,
за-, у-** pay

платóк kerchief; shawl;
носовóй ~ handkerchief

платфóрма rail., pol. platform

плáтье clothes; dress,
gown, frock

плацкáрта rail. ticket for a
sleeping place

плащ cloak; raincoat

плевáть, плю́нуть spit;
coll. (**на** B) not care a
hang (about)

плед plaid blanket

племя́нник nephew; **~ни-
ца** niece

плен captivity; **попадáть
(попáсть) в ~** be taken
prisoner

плёнка film; (tape-recorder)
tape

пле́нный (noun) prisoner;
~йть, ~йть captivate, fas-
cinate

плéсень f biol. mould

плестú, с~ braid; plait;
weave

плетёный wattled; wick-
er...

плечó shoulder

плешь f bald patch

плитá plate; kitchen-
-range; **гáзовая ~á** gas-
stove; **~ка** tile; (chocolate) bar

пловéц, ~чúха swimmer

плод(ы́ pl.) fruit (a. fig.);

~óвый fruit...; **~орóдный**
fertile; **~отвóрный** fruit-
ful

плóмб|а seal, (lead) stamp;
(tooth) stopping; **~ирó-
вáть, за-** seal; tooth stop

пломбúр (type of icecream)
plombières

плóский flat (a. fig.);
plane; **~ость** f flatness;
plane; platitude

плот raft; **~úна** dam; dyke;
'~ник carpenter; **'~ность** f
compactness; density;
'~ный compact, dense; **~ь**
f flesh

плотвá (fish) roach

плохóй bad; poor

плóщад|ка (sports) av.
ground; **дéтская ~áдка**
children's playground;
пусковáя ~áдка launch-
ing pad; **стройтельная
~áдка** building site;
(stairs) landing; **штраф-
нáя ~áдка** penalty area;
'~адь f area (a. math.);
(town-)square

плуг plough

плыть → плáвать

плю́нуть → плевáть

плюралúзм mst. pol. plural-
ity (of views, etc.)

плюс plus; coll. advantage

плющ ivy

пляж beach

пляс|áть dance; **'~ка**
dance; dancing

по prep. (Д) on, along; (all)
over; by; according to; (B)

up to; (П) after, on; ~ **утрáм** in the morning; ~ **десятú человéк** in groups of ten; ~ **дéсять** in tens

по...[1] *verbal prefix. When used to form the perfective aspect, it is usually not translated:* **посмотрéть** look, *perfective of* **смотрéть** *look; but when at the same time it indicates a short duration, it is translated:* **поспáть** *have a sleep*

по...[2] *prefix of comparatives:* **покорóче** *a bit shorter;* **побóльше** *a bit more*

по...[3] *prefix, used to form adverbial expressions:* **по-дрýжески** *in a friendly way;* **по-мóему** *in my opinion;* **по-нóвому** *in a new manner;* **по-рýсски** (in) Russian

побéг flight, escape; *bot.* shoot

побéд|а victory; ~**úтель** *m* victor; winner

побе|ждáть, ~**дúть** defeat; win, triumph

побéрежье sea coast

поблúзости near at hand

побу|ждáть, ~**дúть** induce, prompt

побывáть have visited; *coll.* look in, visit

повáр cook

поведéние conduct, be-

haviour

повезтú → **возúть**

повéренный: ~ **в делáх** charge d'affaires

повернýть(ся) → **поворáчивать(ся)**

повéрхность *f* surface; ~**ный** superficial

повéсить → **вéшать**

повéстка *jur.* summons; ~ **дня** agenda

пóвесть *f* tale, story

по-вúдимому apparently

повúдло jam

повиновáться (*im*)*pf.* (Д) obey

пóвод (*pl.* пóводы) occasion, cause; *по ~у* as regards, concerning

повáрачивать(ся), повернýть(ся) turn; swing round

поворóт turn(ing); bend, curve; turning-point; ~**ливый** nimble; agile; ~**ный** turn(ing)...; rotary

повре|ждáть, ~**дúть** damage; injure, hurt; ~**ждéние** damage; injury

повседнéвный daily, day-to-day...; ~**мéстно** in all places, everywhere

повсю́ду everywhere

повторéние repetition; ~**я́ть**, ~**úть** repeat

повы|шáть, '~**сить** highten, raise; ~**ся** rise; raising; ~**шéние по слýжбе** promotion

повя́зка band; bandage

погло|ща́ть, ~ти́ть absorb; devour

погово́рка proverb

пого́да weather

пограни́чный frontier..., border...

по́греб cellar

погре́шность inaccuracy, error (a. tech.)

погру|жа́ть, ~зи́ть[1] plunge, submerge; dip

погрузи́ть → грузи́ть

под (T) under; би́тва ~ Сталингра́дом battle of Stalingrad; (B) for: ба́нка ~ варе́нье jar for jam; ~ го́ру downhill; ~ дикто́вку from dictation; ~ Петербу́ргом near St. Petersburg; ~ му́зыку (P) to the music (of); ~ Но́вый Год on New Year's Eve

пода́(ва́)ть give; hand in; serve

подав|ля́ть, ~и́ть suppress; restrain; ~ля́ющий overwhelming

пода́рок gift, present

пода́ча tech. feed; (sports) service; ~ заявле́ния handing in of an application

подбо́р selection

подборо́док chin

подва́л basement; cellar

подверг|а́ть, ~нуть (Д) expose or subject (to); ~ся (Д) be exposed (to); undergo

подвести́ → подводи́ть

по́двиг exploit, feat

подви|га́ть(ся) ~нуть(-ся) move; ~ вперёд advance; ~жно́й mobile

подво|ди́ть, ~вести́ (к Д) bring or take up (to); (под B) place (under); (B) coll. let down

подво́дный submarine..., underwater; ~ая ло́дка submarine

подво́з transport; supply; ~и́ть, подвезти́ transport, bring up; give a lift

подготови́тельный preparatory; ~ка preparation; ~ля́ть, ~и́ть (для P) prepare or train (for); ~ся (к Д) prepare (for)

подда(ва́)ться (Д) yield or give way (to)

по́дданный pol. subject; ~ство citizenship

подде́л|ка falsification; counterfeit; ~(ыв)ать falsify; counterfeit; forge; ~ный false; forged; imitation...

поддерж|ивать, ~а́ть support, back up; ~ка support, backing; prop

поджа́ри(ва́)ть fry; grill, toast

поджига́ть, подже́чь set fire (to); set on fire

подзащи́тный jur. client

подзе́мный underground...

подкла́дка lining

подко́в|а horse-shoe; ~ывать, ~а́ть shoe

подко́жный hypodermic

подкреп|ля́ть, **~и́ть** support; refresh; reinforce

по́дле (P) near; by (the side of)

подлежа́ть (Д) be liable *or* subject (to)

подли́вка sauce, gravy

по́длинн|ик (*text*), *etc.* original; **~ый** authentic, genuine, original

по́длый mean, foul

подмётка (shoe-)sole

поднести́ → **подноси́ть**

подн|има́ть, **~я́ть** lift, raise; pick up; **~ся** rise; (**на** B) climb; **~ся по ле́стнице** go upstairs

подно́жие (*hill*) foot; **~ка** foot-board

поднос tray; **~и́ть**, **поднести́** (**к** Д) bring or take (to)

подо́б|ие likeness; something similar (to P); **~но** (Д) like; **~но тому́ как** just as; **~ный** like, similar; **ничего́ ~ного** nothing of the kind

подожда́ть *pf.* (P *or* B) wait (for)

подозр|ева́ть (**в** П) suspect (of); **~е́ние** suspicion; **~и́тельный** suspect; suspicious

подойти́ → **подходи́ть**

подоко́нник window-sill

подо́нок *fig.* scum

подохо́дный: **~ нало́г** income tax

подо́шва sole

подпи́с|ка subscription; **~чик**, **~чица** subscriber; **~ывать**, **~а́ть** sign; add (*in writing*); **~ся** sign; (**на** B) subscribe (to) (*newspaper, etc.*)

по́дпись *f* signature

подполко́вник lieutenant-colonel

подпо́р(к)а prop, support

подража́ть (Д) imitate

подразделе́ние subdivision; *mil.* (sub)unit

подразумева́ть imply, mean

подро́бн|ость *f* detail; *pl.* detailed, minute

подро́сток teenager

подру́га (*female*) friend

подружи́ться (**с** T) be *or* make friends (with)

подря́д[1] *adv.* in succession; on end

подря́д[2] зонтра́зт; **~чик** contractor

подсве́чник candlestick

подсне́жник snowdrop

подсо́лн|ечник sunflower; **~ечный**: **~ечное ма́сло** sunflower oil

подставля́ть, **~ить** (**под** B) place *or* put (under)

подста́вка glass-holder (*used in drinking tea*)

подсуди́мый accused, defendant; **быть ~ным** (Д) be under the jurisdiction (of)

подтвер|жда́ть, **~ди́ть**

confirm; corroborate; —
получе́ние (P) acknowledge receipt (of)

подтя́жки f/pl. braces

поду́шка pillow; cushion

подхо́д approach; method of approach; **⁓и́ть, подойти́** (к Д) come up to, approach; (Д) fit; suit, become; **⁓я́щий** suitable, proper

под|черкивать, ⁓черкну́ть underline; emphasize

подчине́ние subordination; submission; **⁓я́ть, ⁓и́ть** subordinate; subdue; **⁓ся** (Д) submit (to)

подъ|е́зд doorway; entrance; drive; **⁓езжа́ть, ⁓е́хать** (к Д) drive up to; coll. get round (a person)

подъём lifting; ascent; rise; enthusiasm; **⁓ ноги́** instep

поеди́нок duel mst. fig.

по́езд train; **при́городный ⁓** local train; **ско́рый ⁓** fast train; **'⁓ка** journey, trip

пое́хать → **е́здить**

пожале́ть → **жале́ть**

пожа́ловать: добро́ **⁓!** welcome

пожа́луй perhaps; if you like or I don't mind; **⁓ста** please; (consent) certainly!; (acknowledgement of thanks) don't mention it

пожа́р fire; **⁓ный; ⁓ная кома́нда** fire brigade; noun fireman

пожа́ть → **пожима́ть** a. **пожина́ть**

пожела́ние wish

пожива́|ть: как вы ⁓ете? how are you?

пожило́й elderly

пож(им)а́ть press; hand shake; **⁓ плеча́ми** shrug one's shoulders

пож(ин)а́ть mst. fig. reap

позавчера́ the day before yesterday

позади́ (P) behind (a. adv.)

позвол|я́ть, '⁓ить permit, allow; **⁓я́ть себе́** permit o.s., venture; be able to afford

позвони́ть → **звони́ть**

позвоно́чник anat. spine

по́здн|ий late; **⁓о** it is (too) late; adv. late

поздрав|ле́ние congratulation; **⁓я́ть, '⁓ить** (с Т) congratulate (on)

по́зже later (on)

пози́тив photo. positive; **⁓ный** positive

пози́ция position; stand

позна|(ва́)ть get to know; experience; **⁓ние** cognition; pl. knowledge

познако́мить → **знако́мить**

позо́р disgrace, shame; **⁓ить, о-** disgrace; **⁓ный** disgraceful

по́иски m/pl. search

пои́ть, на- (Т) give to

drink

пойма́ть → **лови́ть**

пойти́ → **идти́** a. **ходи́ть**

пока́ adv. for the present; coll. so long!; conj. while; ~ (**не**) until

пока́з showing, demonstration; **~а́ние** evidence; deposition; **~а́тель** m index; pl. showing; **~а́тельный** significant; instructive; **~но́й** ostentatious; **~ывать**, **~а́ть** show

пока́тый sloping

покая́ние repentance

поки|да́ть, **~нуть** leave; abandon, forsake

покло́н bow; compliments, regards; **~я́ться** → **кла́няться**; **~ник**, **~ница** admirer, worshipper; **~я́ться** (Д) worship

поко́й rest, peace; **~ник**, **~ница** the deceased; **~ный** quiet; (dead) late

поколе́ние biol. generation

поко́р|ный submissive; obedient; **~я́ть**, **~и́ть** subjugate, subdue; conquer; **-ся** (Д) submit (to)

покрови́тель(ница) m patron, protector; **~ство** protection, patronage

покрыва́ло bed-spread; **~(ва́)ть** cover; conceal; **~шка** mot. tire-cover

покупа́|тель(ница) m buyer; customer; **~ть** buy(ing), purchase; **де́лать ~ки** go shopping;

~а́ть, **купи́ть** buy

поку|ша́ться, **~си́ться** (**на** B) life attempt; encroach upon; **~ше́ние** attempt; encroachment

пол[1] floor

пол[2] sex

пол|а́ lap, flap, skirt; **из-под ~ы́** (buy or sell) covertly

полага́ть suppose; **-ся** be due; be the custom; **-ся**, **положи́ться** (**на** B) rely on

пол|го́да half a year; **~день** m midday, noon

пол|е field; margin; **~ево́й** field...

поле́зный useful, helpful; wholesome

полёт flight; **вид с пти́чьего ~а** a bird's-eye view

полз|а́ть, **~ти́** (impf.), pf. **поползти́** creep, crawl

поли(ва́)ть (T) pour (on B); water

поликли́ника polyclinic; outpatients' department

полит... in compounds = **полити́ческий** political; **~ика** politics; policy; **~эконо́мия** political economy

полиэтиле́н polythene

поли|це́йский police...; (noun) policeman; **~ия** police

полиэтиле́н polythene

полк regiment

по́лка shelf; rail. berth

полко́вник colonel

полне́ть, по- grow stout

полно|кро́вный full-blooded; **_лу́ние** full moon; **_мо́чие** authority; plenary powers; **_це́нный** of full value, meeting all requirements

по́лно|стью adv. entirely, fully; **_та́** fulness; stoutness

по́лночь f midnight

по́лный full; complete; stout

полови́на half

полово́дье (river) flood (-time), high water

полово́й sexual

положе́ние position; situation; **_ительный** positive; **_и́ть → класть; _и́ться → полага́ться**

полоса́ stripe; strip; zone, belt; **_тый** striped

полоска́ть, про-, вы- rinse; **– го́рло** gargle

полоте́нце towel; **ку́хонное _енце** tea towel; **махро́вое _енце** Turkish towel; **_но́** linen; paint. canvas; **_ня́ный** linen...

поло́ть, вы- weed

полпре́д (= **_полномо́чный представи́тель**) m plenipotentiary

полтора́ m/n, **_ы́** f (P) one and a half

полу... in compounds: half..., semi...; **_о́стров** peninsula; **_проводни́к**

phys. semiconductor, transistor; **_фабрика́т** half-finished products or foodstuffs; **_фина́л** semi-final

получ|а́тель recipient; **_а́ть, _и́ть** receive, obtain; **-ся** come off, turn out; **_е́ние** receipt

полуша́рие hemisphere

полча́са́ half an hour

по́льза use; benefit; **в _у** (P) in favour (of); **_ова-тель** tech. user; **_ова́ться, вос-** (T) make use (of); profit (by); impf. enjoy

по́ль|ка Polish woman; polka; **_ский** Polish

полюби́ть pf. (B) grow fond (of)

по́люс geogr., phys., fig. pole

поля n/pl. margin; (hat) brim

поля́к Pole

поля́на clearing, glade

пома́да: губна́я _ lipstick

поме́тка mark, sign

поме́ха hindrance; (radio) interference

поме́ш|анный fig. coll. mad, crazy; **_а́ть → меша́ть**

поме|ща́ть, _сти́ть place; locate; accommodate; invest; **-ся** find room, go in; impf. be housed; **_ще́ние** location; accommodation; lodging; investment

помидо́р tomato

поми́мо (P) besides; apart from; without

по́мн|ить (В *о* о П) remember; *a. impers.*: **мне ~ся** (И) I remember

помо|га́ть, ~чь (Д) help; **'~щник, '~щница** help(mate); assistant

по́мощь f help; **пе́рвая ~** first aid; **ско́рая ~** ambulance

понево́ле willy-nilly; against one's will

понеде́льник Monday

понемно́гу little by little; a little at a time

понижа́ть, ~зи́ть lower; reduce; **~же́ние** lowering, drop; reduction

понима́|ние understanding; sense; **в мое́м ~нии** as I see it; **~ть, поня́ть** understand

по-но́вому in a new way

понужда́ть, '~дить force, compel

поня́т|ие notion, idea; **~но!** *coll.* I see!; **~ный** understandable; clear, intelligible; **~ь** → **понима́ть**

поочерёдно in turn, by turns

поощр|я́ть, ~и́ть encourage; stimulate

попа|да́ть, ~сть (*в* В) hit; find o.s. *inadvertently* in; get *or* fall into; **вы не туда́ '~ли** you got the wrong number; **~ся** be taken *or* caught; come

across

попа́рно in pairs

поперёк (P) across (*a. adv.*); **~ёчный** cross..., transversal

попече́ние care, charge

попола́м in two halves; half and half

пополн|я́ть, '~ить fill up; supplement; re-stock

пополу́|дни in the afternoon; **~ночи** after midnight

попра́в|ка correction; recovery; amendment; **~ля́ть, ~ить** correct; *health* restore; **~ся** correct o.s.; improve; recover

по-пре́жнему *adv.* as before; as usual

попро́бовать → **про́бовать**

попуга́й parrot

попу́т|чик, ~чица fellow-traveller (*a. fig.*)

попы́тка attempt, endeavour

пор|а́ time; (*давно́*) **~а́** high time (*to go etc.*); **до каки́х ~** how long; **до сих ~** up to now; up to here; **с тех ~** since then

пора|жа́ть, ~зи́ть strike, stun; hit; **~же́ние** defeat; **~зи́тельный** striking

порва́ть → **порыва́ть**

порица́|ние blame, censure; **~ть** (*за* В) blame (for)

по́ровну equally, in equal

parts

поро́г threshold; *geogr. mst. pl.* rapids

поро́|да race, breed; *fig.* kind; *geol.* rock; **~дистый** thoroughbred, pedigree...; **~жда́ть**, **~ди́ть** engender, give rise to

поро́к vice; defect

поросёнок piglet

поро́ть¹, вы~ flog

поро́ть², рас~ rip, unstitch; undo

по́рох (gun)powder

поро́ч|ить, о~ defame; discredit; **~ный** vicious; depraved; faulty

порошо́к powder

порт port, harbour

по́рт|ить, ис~ spoil; damage; corrupt

портни́ха dressmaker; **~о́й** tailor

портре́т portrait

порт|сига́р cigar- *or* cigarette-case

португа́л|ец, **~ка**, **~ьский** Portuguese

портфе́ль *m* brief-case

пору́|ка bail; guarantee; **~ча́ть**, **~чи́ть** (Д) charge *or* entrust (with В); **~ча́ться**, **~чи́ться за** В) guarantee, vouch for **~че́ние** (com)mission; **по ~че́нию** on behalf

порха́ть, **~ну́ть** flutter, flit

по́рция portion

по́рча spoiling; damage

по́ршень *m* piston

поры́в (*wind*) gust; impulse; fit; **~а́ть**, **порва́ть** break (off); **~истый** gusty; impetuous

поря́д|ок order; **всё в ~ке** everything is all right; **~очный** decent; honest; respectable; *coll.* fair, sizable

посади́ть → сажа́ть; **'~ка** planting; embarkation; *av.* landing; boarding; **вы́нужденная ~ка** forced landing

по-сво́ему (in) one's own way

посвя|ща́ть, **~ти́ть** devote; dedicate; consecrate; (в В) initiate (into); **~ще́ние** dedication; consecration; initiation

посе́в sowing; crops; **~но́й** sowing...; **~на́я пло́щадь** area under crops

посел|я́ть, **~и́ть** settle; lodge; *feeling* inspire; **-ся** settle down, take up residence

посёлок urban settlement; housing estate

посе|ти́тель(ница) *m* visitor; **~ща́ть**, **~ти́ть** visit; attend; frequent; **~ще́ние** visit; attendance

поскользну́ться *pf.* slip

поско́льку *conj.* so far as; since, as

посла́|нник envoy, minister; **~ть → посыла́ть**

по́сле *prep.* (Р) after; *adv.*

after(wards), later; **~военный** post-war

после́дний last; **~овательный** consecutive; consistent; **~ствие** consequence

послеза́втра *adv.* the day after tomorrow; **~обе́денный** after-dinner...

посло́вица proverb

послу́ш|**ать** → **слу́шать**; **~ный** obedient

посме́нный by turns, in shifts; **~ая рабо́та** shift-work

посме́ртный posthumous

посмотре́ть → **смотре́ть**

посо́бие allowance, benefit; text-book

посо́л ambassador; **~ство** embassy

поспе́|(ва́)ть *coll.* ripen; *coll.* arrive in time; **~шно** in a hurry

посреди́ (P) in the middle (of) (*a. adv.*); **~ник**, **~ница** mediator; **~ничать** mediate, be a go-between; **~ством** (P) by means (of)

посре́дственный mediocre; (school mark) satisfactory

пост[1] post (*esp. mil.*); position, job

пост[2] *eccl.* fast; **вели́кий ~** Lent

поставля́ть → **ста́вить**, *a.* **поставля́ть**; **~ка** delivery; supply; **~ля́ть**, **~ить** (Д)

supply (with B); **~щи́к** supplier

постано́в|**ка** set-up, organisation; *thea.* staging, production; **~ле́ние** decree; decision; resolution; **~ля́ть**, **~и́ть** decree; **'~щик** (of play) producer; (of film) director

по-ста́рому as before; as of old

посте́ль *f* bed, **'~ный**: **~ный режи́м** confinement to bed

постепе́нный gradual

пости|**га́ть**, **'~гнуть** *or* **'~чь** comprehend; *misfortune:* befall

пост(и)ла́ть spread; *bed* make

посто́льку, поско́льку *conj.* as

посторо́нний outside..., extraneous; foreign; *noun* outsider

постоя́нный constant; permanent

постри́чь → **стричь**

постро́йка building

поступ|**а́ть**, **~и́ть** act, do; (с T) treat; (в B) join, enter; **~ в прода́жу** be on sale; come on the market; **~ле́ние** entering, joining; (*taxes, etc.*) receipt; **'~ок** action, deed; behaviour

посты́дный shameful

посу́да crockery; plates and dishes; ...ware; utensils

посыла́ть, посла́ть send (for **за** Т); – *по по́чте* post; **'-ка** parcel

посыпа́ть, '-ать strew; sprinkle

посчастли́виться have the luck (to); be lucky enough (to)

посяга́ть, -ну́ть (на В) encroach *or* infringe on; **-ательство** encroachment

пот sweat

потерпе́ть → **терпе́ть**

поте́ря loss; **'-ть** → **теря́ть**

поте́ть, вс- sweat

по́тный sweaty

пото́к stream, torrent

потоло́к ceiling

пото́м then; after(wards); later (on); **-ок** descendant; **-ство** descendants, posterity; **-ý** ... *adv.* that's why ...; **-ý что** *conj.* because

потреби́тель *m* consumer; **-и́тельский: -и́тельские това́ры** consumer goods; **-ле́ние** consumption; **-ля́ть, -и́ть** consume, use; **'-ность** *f* requirement, need; necessity; **'-овать** → **тре́бовать**

потряса́ть, -ти́ (В or Т) shake; (В) shock, stagger

поучи́тельный instructive

похвала́ praise; **'-ьный** praiseworthy

похища́ть, '-тить steal; kidnap, abduct

похме́лье hangover

похо́д walking tour, hike; **-и́ть (на** В) resemble; **-ка** gait

похо́жий like, alike; similar (to **на** В)

по́хороны *f/pl.* burial, funeral

по́хоть *f* lust

поцелу́й kiss

по́чва soil; ground

почём *coll.* (*price inquiry*) how much is *or* are

почему́ why; **'-то** for some reason

по́черк handwriting

по́чести *f/pl.* honours

почёт honour; respect, esteem; **-ный** honourable; honorary

почи́нка repair(ing); mending; **-я́ть, -и́ть** repair, mend

по́чка¹ bud

по́чка² kidney

по́чта post, mail; *coll.* post-office; **-альо́н** postman; (**гла́вный**) **-а́мт** (general) post-office

почте́ние respect; deference

почти́ almost, nearly

почти́тельный respectful; **-ь** *pf.* honour, do homage to

почто́вый post...; **-ая ма́рка** (postage) stamp; **-ое отделе́ние** post office; **-ый перево́д** postal

order; **_ый я́щик** letter-
box

по́шлина customs duty

по́шлый vulgar

поща́да mercy

пощёчина slap in the face

поэ́зия poetry

поэ́т poet

поэ́тому therefore

появле́ние appearance;
_ля́ться, _и́ться appear,
show up

по́яс belt, girdle; *geogr.*
zone; **_ни́ца** small of the
back

поясня́ть, _и́ть explain

праба́бушка great-grand-
mother

пра́вд|а truth; **_и́вый**
truthful

пра́в|ило rule; regulation;
principle; **как _ило** as a
rule; **_ила у́личного движе́ния** traffic regulations;
_ильный right, true; cor-
rect; regular; **_и́тельство**
government; **_ить** (Т)
rule, govern; **_ле́ние** administration,   manage-
ment, board

пра́во[1] *coll.* really, indeed

пра́во[2] right; *pl.* license;
only sg. law; **_во́й** law...,
legal; lawful; **_наруши́тель** lawbreaker; **_писа́ние** orthography; spelling;
_сла́вный orthodox; **_су́дие** justice; **отправля́ть
_су́дие** administer the
law

пра́вый right; right-hand;
right-wing

пра́дед great-grandfather

пра́здн|ество festival; cele-
bration; **_ик** holiday; festive occasion; **с _иком!**
best wishes of the season;
_ичный holiday; fes-
tive; **_ый** idle; **_овать,** от-
celebrate

пра́кти|ка practice; **на _ке**
in practice; **'_чный** practical; efficient

пра́чечная laundry

пребыва́|ние stay, sojourn;
_ть stay, abide

превосхо́д|ить, превзойти́
excel, surpass; **'_ный** excellent; **_ство** superiority; **_я́щий** superior

превраща́ть, _ти́ть (в В)
convert or turn (into)

превыша́ть, _сить exceed

прегра́|да barrier; obsta-
cle; **_жда́ть, _ди́ть** bar,
block, obstruct

пред → пе́ред

предава́|(ва́)ть betray; com-
mit *(to earth)*; **_ гла́сности** make public; **_ суду́**
bring to trial; **_ся** (Д) give
o.s. up (to); **_ние** legend;
tradition; **_тель(ница)** *m*
traitor (traitress); **_тельство** treachery; treason

предвари́тельный preliminary

предви́деть foresee

предвы́борный pre-elec-
tion..., election ...

предел limit; **в ~ах го́рода** within the city; **положи́ть ~** (Д) put an end (to); **~ьный** utmost, maximum...

предисло́вие preface, foreword

предлага́ть, ~ложи́ть offer; propose; **~ло́г** pretext, pretence; *gr.* preposition; **~ложе́ние** offer; proposal; *gr.* sentence

предме́стье suburb

предме́т object, article; subject, topic

предназнача́ть, '~ить (pre)destine; earmark

преднаме́ренный premeditated; deliberate

пре́док ancestor

предоставля́ть, '~ить (Д) let have; leave; give, grant

предостере|га́ть, ~чь (от Р) warn (against); **~же́ние** warning

предотвраща́ть, ~ти́ть prevent, avert

предохрани́тельный preventive; safety...; **~я́ть, ~и́ть** (от Р) preserve or protect (from)

предписа́ние order; *pl.* instructions; prescription (*a. med.*); **'~ывать, ~а́ть** order; instruct; prescribe

предпо|лага́ть, ~ложи́ть suppose; *impf.* intend; **~ложе́ние** supposition

предпосле́дний last but one

предпосы́лка prerequisite

предпо|чита́ть, ~че́сть prefer; **~чте́ние** preference

предпри|и́мчивый enterprising; **~нима́тель** businessman, entrepreneur; **~нима́тельство** entrepreneurship; **~нима́ть, ~ня́ть** undertake; **~ня́ть steps** take; **~я́тие** undertaking; enterprise; business

предрассу́док prejudice

председа́тель *m* chairman

предска́з|ывать, ~а́ть foretell, forecast

представ|и́тель *m* representative; **~и́тельство** representation; delegation; *collect.* representatives; **~ле́ние** (re)presentation; idea; *thea.* performance; **~ля́ть, '~ить** (re)present; introduce; **~ себе́** imagine; **~ся** occur, arise

предстоя́щий forthcoming; impending

предупреди́тельный precautionary; obliging; **~жда́ть, ~ди́ть** (В) prevent, forestall; **(о П)** let know (about); warn (against); **~жде́ние** notice, warning; prevention

предусмотри́тельный prudent; far-sighted; provident

предчу́вств|ие presentiment, foreboding; ~овать (B) have a presentiment (of)

предше́ственни|к, ~ца predecessor

предъяви́тель(ница) m (*document*) bearer; **~ля́ть, ~и́ть** show, produce; *claim* raise

преды́дущий previous, preceding; foregoing

прее́мни|к, ~ца successor

пре́жде before (*a. prep.* P); formerly; **~ всего́** first of all; **~временный** premature

пре́жний previous, former

презира́ть[1], ~², презре́ть defy

презри́тельный contemptuous, scornful

преиму́ществе|нно mainly, chiefly; **~о** advantage

прейскура́нт price-list

прекра́сный beautiful, fine; excellent

прекра|ща́ть, ~ти́ть discontinue, break off; **~са́** end, cease; **~ще́ние** cessation; closure; stoppage; **~ще́ние платеже́й** suspension of payments

преле́стный delightful, charming

пре́лесть f charm; wonderful thing

прельща́ть, ~сти́ть entice, attract

пре́м|ия bonus, premium;

prize; **~ирова́ть** (B) give a bonus *or* prize (to)

премье́ра *thea.* first night

пренебре|га́ть, '~чь (T) neglect, disregard; **~же́ние** neglect; scorn

пре́ния n/pl. debate

преоблада́ть predominate; prevail

преобразо́в|ывать, ~а́ть transform; reform

преодоле́ва́ть overcome

препода|ва́ние teaching; **~тель(ница)** m teacher, lecturer, instructor; **~ть** teach

препя́тствие obstacle; **~овать** (Д) hinder, hamper; **(Д в П)** prevent (from)

прер(ы)ва́ть interrupt

пресле́дова|ние pursuit; persecution; prosecution; **~ть** pursue; persecute; prosecute

пресловутый notorious

пре́сный (*water*) fresh; (*bread*) unleavened; *fig.* insipid

пре́сс|а press; **~-конфере́нция** press-conference

престу́п|ление crime; **'~ник, '~ница** criminal; **'~ный** criminal

претен|дова́ть (на B) pretend (to); lay claim (to); **'~зия** pretention; claim

преувеличе́|ние exaggeration; **'~(ва)ть** exaggerate

при (П) near; by; in the

presence (of); with; ‑ **всём том** for all that; ‑ **усло́вии** under the condition (that)

приба́в|ка, ‑ле́ние addition; supplement; *получи́ть* ‑**ку** get a rise; ‑**ля́ть, ‑ить** (P) add; *wages* raise

приба́лт *coll.* native of Estonia, Latvia or Lithuania

прибе|га́ть¹, ‑жа́ть come running; ‑**га́ть², ‑гнуть** (к Д) resort to

приближ|а́ть, ‑зить bring near(er); ‑**ся** draw near, approach; ‑**зи́тельный** approximate, rough

прибо́й surf

прибо́р device, instrument; set, service

прибы|(ва́)ть (в В) arrive (in); *water:* rise

при́бы|ль f profit; *чи́стая* ‑**ль** net profit; ‑**тие** arrival

прива́л halt, stop (*for a rest*)

приватиза́ция privatisation

привезти́ → привози́ть

привести́ → приводи́ть

приве́т greeting; regards; *переда́й(те)* ‑ (Д) give my love to; ‑**ливый** affable, polite; ‑**ствие** greeting; speech of welcome; ‑**ствовать** greet; welcome

приви|(ва́)ть vaccinate; inoculate; inculcate; ‑**вка**

vaccination; inoculation

при́вкус smack; after-taste

привле|ка́тельный attractive, winning; ‑**ка́ть, ‑чь** attract

приво́д drive, gear; ‑**и́ть, привести́** bring; (к Д) lead (to); reduce (to); (в В) drive *or* bring (to), throw (into)

привози́ть, привезти́ (*transport*) bring

привы́|кать, ‑кнуть (к Д) get used (to); ‑**чка** habit; ‑**чный** habitual, usual

привя́з|ывать, ‑а́ть tie, fasten; *fig.* attach; ‑**ся** (к Д) become attached (to); *coll.* bother

пригла|ша́ть, ‑си́ть invite; ‑**ше́ние** invitation

пригов|а́ривать, ‑ори́ть (к Д) condemn (to); ‑**о́р** sentence, verdict; condemnation

пригоди́ться prove useful (to); come in handy

приго́дный fit, suitable

при́город suburb

приготов|ле́ние preparation; ‑**ля́ть(ся), ‑ить(ся)** prepare

прида|(ва́)ть (*addition*) give; add; impart, lend; ‑ *значе́ние* attach importance (to); ‑**ча:** *в* ‑**чу** in addition

приду́м|(ыв)ать (В) think of, invent

при|е́зд arrival (*by trans-*

port); **с ~ездом!** welcome!; **~езжа́ть, ~е́хать** arrive; **~езжа́ющий** noun newcomer, arrival

прие́млемый acceptable; admissible

прие́м reception; taking; method; **в оди́н ~** at one go; **~ная** reception-room; waiting-room; **~ник** radio set; **транзи́сторный ~ник** transistor (radio); **~ный** reception...; adopted; **~ные часы́** m/pl. reception hours; (doctor) surgery (hours)

прие́хать → приезжа́ть

приж(им)а́ть (к Д) clasp or press (to); _head_ nestle

приз prize

призва́|ние vocation, calling; **~ть → призыва́ть**

приземл|я́ться, ~и́ться av. land

призёр prize-winner

призна́(ва́)ть admit; acknowledge; recognize; **~ся (в П)** confess; **~ся (сказа́ть)** pf. to tell the truth

при́знак symptom, sign

призна́|ние acknowledge(e)ment; recognition; confession; **~тельный** grateful

призы́в call, appeal; mil. call-up; **~а́ть, призва́ть** call (up), summon

прийти́ → приходи́ть

прика́з order, command; **~ывать, ~а́ть (Д)** order,

command

прика|са́ться, ~косну́ться (к Д) touch

прикладн|о́й (science, art) applied; **'~ывать, приложи́ть (к Д)** put, apply (to); add, enclose

приключе́ние adventure

прикоснове́ние touch, contact

прикреп|ля́ть, ~и́ть fasten, attach, fix

прику́ривать, ~кури́ть get a light (for one's cigarette)

прила́вок (shop) counter

прила|га́ть, ~ложи́ть apply, exert; **~ все си́лы** do one's best

приле|га́ть (к Д) dress: fit closely; adjoin; **~жа́ние** industry, assiduousness; **'~жный** industrious, assiduous

прилет|а́ть, ~е́ть arrive (by air)

прили́в flood (of tide); fig. influx, surge; **~ный** tidal

прили́чие decency; **~ный** decent

приложе́|ние enclosure; supplement, appendix; application; **~ть → прикла́дывать** a. **прилага́ть**

примен|я́ть, ~и́ть apply, use

приме́р example; **~ный** exemplary; approximate; **~я́ть, ~ить (на себя́)** try on

при́месь f admixture; fig.

touch

приме́|та sign; mark; omen; ~ча́ние (foot-)note

примеши́|вать, ~а́ть admix, add

примир|е́ние reconciliation; ~а́ть, ~и́ть reconcile; conciliate; -ся (с Т) be reconciled (to); put up (with)

при|мыка́ть, ~мкну́ть (к Д) join; impf. (к Д) adjoin

принадлеж|а́ть (Д) belong (to); ~ность f belonging; membership; pl. accessories

при|нима́ть, ~ня́ть accept; take; adopt; receive; (за В) take for; – в шко́лу admit to school; ~уча́стие (в П) take part (in); -ся (за В) set to (work etc.)

при|носи́ть, ~нести́ bring; harvest, profit yield; – по́льзу be of benefit

прину|жда́ть, ~'дить compel, force

при́нцип principle; ~а́льный of principle, fundamental

приня́тие acceptance; adoption; taking; ~ь ⇒ приниⅿа́ть

приобре|та́ть, ~сти́ acquire; gain; purchase; ~те́ние acquisition; purchase

приорите́т priority

приостан|а́вливать, ~ови́ть stop (for a while);

suspend; -ся pause; ~о́вка short stoppage

припа́док fit, paroxism

припа́сы m/pl. stores, supplies; съестны́е ~ victuals; боевы́е ~ ammunition

припе́в mus. refrain

припи́ска postscript; ~ывать, ~а́ть add (in writing); ascribe

припомин|а́ть, ~'нить remember

припра́ва seasoning, spice

приро́д|а nature; ~ный natural; inborn; ~ные бога́тства natural resources

прирост increase, accretion

присва́ивать, ~сво́ить appropriate; confer; award; – себе́ right assume

приско́рб|ие regret, grief; ~ный regrettable

присла́ть ⇒ присыла́ть

прислон|я́ть(ся), ~и́ть(ся) (к Д) lean (against)

прислу́ш(ив)аться (к Д) listen (to)

присма́тривать, ~смотре́ть (за Т) look after; supervise; -ся (at); size someone up

присоедин|я́ть, ~и́ть join; annex; connect; -ся (к Д) join; -ся к мне́нию subscribe to an opinion

приспособ|ле́ние adaptation; device, contrivance;

_лять, '_ить (к Д) adapt or adjust (to)

приста(ва)ть (к Д) stick to; worry, pester; _ prefix; _влять, _вить (к Д) put or lean (against)

пристальный (look) fixed, intent

пристань f landing-stage; wharf

пристрастие weakness (for); partiality, bias; _ный partial

пристройка annex(e), out-house

приступ fit, attack; _ать, _ить start

присуждать, _дить prize award; scientific degree confer (on)

присутствие presence; _овать (на П) be present (at)

присущий (Д) inherent (in)

прис(ы)лать send

присяга oath

притворный pretended, feigned; _ться, _иться (Т) pretend to be

притеснять, _ить oppress

притихать, _нуть quiet down

приток influx, inflow; geogr. tributary

притом (and) besides

притягивать, _нуть attract

притязание claim, pretension

приусадебный: _ участок plot of land adjoining the

farm-house

приучать, _ить (к Д) train or accustom (to)

приход coming; arrival; receipts, income; _ить, прийти come; arrive; _ в ужас be horrified; _ в ярость fly into a rage; _ся (Д) по вкусу to be to one's taste; мне _ится + inf. I must

прихотливый whimsical; fanciful

прихоть f whim; fancy

прицели(ва)ться take aim

прицеп trailer; _ить hook on; waggon couple

причали(ва)ть v/t. a. v/i. moor

причастие gr. participle; _ный participial (к Д) participating or involved (in)

причём conj. moreover, and; despite the fact that; while; adv. - здесь это? what has this to do with it?

причёска hair-cut, hairdo; _ывать, причесать hair comb, brush; _ся comb; have one's hair done

причина reason, cause; _ять, _ить cause

причислять, '_ить (к Д) reckon or number (among)

приши(ва)ть sew on

приют shelter, refuge

прия́тель(ница) *m* friend;
~ный pleasant, agreeable

про (B) *speak etc.* about

про́ба trial, test; sample;
(*gold*) standard, carat
(*Am.* karat)

пробе́|г (*sports*) run, race;
~га́ть, ~жа́ть run past *or*
through; *distance* cover

пробе́л gap, blank (*a. tech.*)

проби́(ва́)ть pierce, punch;
~ся make one's way
through

про́бка cork; stopper; *el.*
fuse; *coll.* traffic jam

про́бовать, по~ try

пробо́р (*hair*) parting

пробу|жда́ть, ~ди́ть
wake(n), arouse

пробы́ть *pf.* stay, remain

прова́л downfall; failure;
~иваться, ~и́ться fall
through; collapse; fail

проведе́ние carrying out;
conducting

прове́р|ка verification, in-
spection, check(-up);
~я́ть, ~ить verify, check,
inspect

провести́ → проводи́ть

прове́три(ва)ть air, ventilate

прово́д wire; ~и́ть[1], про-
вести́ take, lead; carry
out; (*time*) spend, pass;
~и́ть[2] → провожа́ть;
~ник guide; *el.* conductor;
rail. guard; ~ы *m/pl.* see-
ing-off

прово|жа́ть, ~ди́ть accom-

pany; see off *or* home

прово́з transport, carriage

провозгла|ша́ть, ~си́ть
proclaim; ~ тост (за B)
propose the health (of)

про́волока wire

прогл|а́тывать, ~оти́ть
swallow (*a. fig.*)

прогно́з prognosis; fore-
cast

прогова́риваться, ~ори́ть-
ся let out a secret

проголода́ться grow *or* be
hungry

прого|ня́ть, ~на́ть drive
away; send away

програ́мм|а programme;
schedule; *уче́бная ~а* syl-
labus; ~и́ровать pro-
gramme; ~и́ст program-
mer

прогре́сс progress

прогу́лка walk *or* ride *or*
drive (*for pleasure*)

прода|(ва́)ть sell; ~ва́ться
on sale, for sale; ~ве́ц,
~вщи́ца shop assistant;
~жа sale; *в ~же* on sale;
ро́зничная ~жа retail

продл|ева́ть, ~и́ть prolong,
extend

продово́льст|венный: ~ен-
ный магази́н grocery
shop; ~ие foodstuffs

продолж|а́ть, ~и́ть con-
tinue; prolong; ~ся con-
tinue, go on; ~е́ние con-
tinuation; prolongation;
~и́тельный rather long;
prolonged

проду́к|т product, produce; _pl. mst._ foodstuffs; **~ти́вный** productive, fruitful; **~ция** production, output

прое́зд thoroughfare; **пла́та за ~** fare; **~но́й биле́т** monthly ticket (_bus, underground, etc._); **~ом** _adv._ in transit, passing through

прое́зжа|ть, ~ехать drive past _or_ through; **~езжий** _noun_ (passing) traveller; passer-by

прое́кт project; draft; design; **~и́ровать** _impf._ project, design

прожива́|ть, ~ть _impf._ live, reside; _pf._ live; spend

про́звище nickname

прозева́ть _pf. opportunity_ let slip, miss

прозра́чный transparent

прои́гр|ыватель record-player; **~ывать, ~а́ть** game, case lose; _record_ play

про́игрыш loss

произведе́ние (_artist, writer_) work; **~води́тель** _m_ producer; _agr._ sire; **~води́ть, ~вести́** make, carry out; produce; **~во́дство** production, manufacture; _coll._ factory

произво́л arbitrariness; (_fate_) mercy; **~ьный** arbitrary

произ|носи́ть, ~нести́ pronounce; _speech_ deliver;

~ноше́ние pronunciation

проис|ходи́ть, произойти́ happen, take place; **~хожде́ние** descent, origin; **~ше́ствие** event, happening; accident

пройти́ → проходи́ть

про|ка́лывать, ~коло́ть pierce; perforate

прока́т hire

про|клина́ть, ~кля́сть curse, damn; **~кля́тие** curse, damnation

проко́л _mot._ puncture

прокуро́р public prosecutor

пролетари|а́т proletariat(e); **~ский** _adj._ proletarian

пролета́|ть, ~ть fly past _or_ through; _distance_ cover

проли́|в strait, sound; **~(ва́)ть** spill; shed

про́мах (_shooting_) miss; _fig._ mistake; **~ну́ться** _pf._ miss the mark (_a. fig._)

промедле́ние delay; procrastination

промежу́ток interval

промока́|ть, ~нуть get wet; **~ до косте́й** get soaked to the skin

промы́шленн|ость _f_ industry; **~ый** industrial

пронзи́тельный piercing; shrill

проника́|ть, '~нуть (_в_ В) penetrate (into)

проница́тельный perspicacious

пропа|да́ть, '~сть get lost; disappear; perish; be wasted

про́пасть precipice; abyss; *coll.* mass(es) (of)

пропи́ска registration; residence permit; ~но́й: ~на́я бу́ква capital letter; ~ывать, ~а́ть register; *med.* prescribe; ~ся get registered

пропове́довать preach; *fig.* advocate

про́поведь f sermon

про́пуск (*pl.* ~и) omission; gap; *sg. only* admission; (*pl.* ~а́) permit, pass; ~а́ть, пропусти́ть let pass; admit; omit; miss

проры́в break(-through)

Просвеще́ние Enlightenment; наро́дное ~ public education

просвещённый educated, cultured

про́седь f streak(s) of grey

просёлочный: ~ая доро́га country road

проси́ть ask (for), beg

просма́тривать, ~смотре́ть look through

просну́ться → просыпа́ться

просо́вывать, ~су́нуть push *or* pass through

проспа́ть → просыпа́ть[2]

проспе́кт avenue; prospectus

просро́ченный overdue

про|стира́ть, ~стере́ть

stretch, reach (out); ~ся (до P) stretch (to)

прости́тельный pardonable; ~ь → проща́ть

про́сто *adv.* simply; merely; ~ду́шный simple-hearted; '~й simple; plain, ordinary; mere; ~ква́ша sour milk, yoghurt

просто́й standing idle; stoppage

просто́р open space; spaciousness; amplitude

просторе́чие popular speech

просто́рный spacious, roomy; ample; wide

простота́ simplicity

простра́н|ный extensive; verbose; ~ство space

просту́|да *med.* cold; ~жа́ться, ~ди́ться catch a cold

просту́пок misdeed, misconduct

простыня́ bed-sheet

просыпа́ть[1], '~ть spill

просыпа́ть[2], проспа́ть oversleep; ~ся, просну́ться wake up, awake

про́сьба request; у меня́ к вам ~ I have a favour to ask you

проте́з prosthetic appliance; artificial limb; зубно́й ~ denture

проте|ка́ть, '~чь leak; *time:* elapse; *event:* proceed; *impf. river:* flow

протестова́ть protest

про́тив (P) against; opposite, as against

проти́в|иться, вос- (Д) resist; oppose; **~ник** opponent; collect. enemy; **~ный** opposite, contrary; repulsive, nasty; **в ~ном слу́чае** otherwise

противо... in compounds: anti..., counter..., contra...; **~га́з** gas-mask; **~де́йствие** counteraction; **~зако́нный** unlawful; illegal; **~зача́точный** contraceptive; **~поло́жный** opposite; contrary; **~раке́тный** anti-missile; **~ре́чие** contradiction; **~стоя́ть** resist, withstand; **~я́дие** antidote

протоко́л minutes

протя́г|ивать, ~ну́ть stretch or hold out; extend; **~же́ние** stretch; extent; expanse

профессиона́льный professional; occupational; **~ия** profession, occupation; **~ор** professor

профсою́з (= **профессиона́льный сою́з**) trade-union

прохла́д|а cool(ness); **~ный** cool

прохо́д passage(-way); **~и́ть, пройти́** v/i. go by, pass; fig. go off; **~ ми́мо** (P) go past; fig. disregard; v/t. go through, study

прохо́жий noun passer-by

процвета́ть prosper

проце́нт per cent; percentage; rate of interest

проце́ссор tech. processor

проче́сть → чита́ть

про́чий other, remaining; **и ~ее** et cetera; **ме́жду ~им** by the way

прочита́ть → чита́ть

про́чный durable; lasting; solid

прочь adv. away, off; coll. **он не прочь** he has no objection

проше́дший past (a. gr.)

про́шл|ое (the) past; **~ый** past, bygone; (week, year) last

проща́й(те)! farewell!; **~а́ть, прости́ть** forgive, pardon, excuse; **-ся** (с T) take leave (of); **~е́ние** forgiveness; pardon

прояв|и́тель m (photo) developer; **~ля́ть, ~и́ть** display, show; photo develop

проясн|я́ться, ~и́ться clear or brighten up

пруд pond

пружи́на tech. spring (a. fig.)

пры́г|ать, ~нуть jump, leap; **~у́н(ья)** (sports) jumper

прыжо́к jump; **~ в во́ду** dive; **~ с шесто́м** pole-vault

прыщи́к pimple

пря́|дь f (hair or threads) strand; **~жа** yarn

пря́жка buckle

пря́мо *adv.* straight; right; exactly; *coll.* really; '_й straight; direct; (up)right; _та́ uprightness; _уго́льник rectangle

пря́ник spice cake; *имби́рный* _ик gingerbread; *медо́вый* _ук honey-cake; _ость *f* spice

пря́тать(ся), с- hide (o.s.); *игра́ть в* _ии play hide-and-seek

птене́ц fledgeling

пти́ца bird; *дома́шняя* _ collect. poultry

пти́чий bird's...; poultry...; _ка (mark) tick

публи́ка public; audience; _ова́ть, о- publish

публи́чный: _ая библиоте́ка public library

пуга́ть, ис- frighten, scare; -ся be frightened; _ли́вый easily frightened, shy

пу́говица button

пу́дра face-powder; _еница compact, _ить(ся), на- powder (o.s.)

пузы́рёк phial; bubble; '_ь *m* bubble; blister; *anat.* bladder

пулемёт machine-gun; '_я bullet

пункт point; item

пуп(о́к) navel

пуска́ть, пусти́ть let, allow; let in *or* out; *в ход* set going; *– ко́рни* take root; -ся + *inf.* start running, *etc.*; -ся в подро́бности go into details

пусте́ть, о- become empty; _о́й empty; hollow; vacant; idle; _ота́ emptiness; vacuum; _ы́ня desert; _я́к trifle

пусть: _ он ду́мает let him think

пу́таница confusion, mix-up

пу́тать, с-, пере- tangle; mix up, confuse; -ся get confused; get entangled

путёвка *document showing that you have booked a place on a tour, in a holiday home, etc.*

путеводи́тель *m* guide-book

путём *prep.* by means of

путеше́ств|енник, _енница traveller; _ие journey, voyage; _овать travel *v.*

путь *m* way (*a. fig.*); road; track; journey; *мне с ва́ми по пути́* we are going the same way; *на обра́тном пути́* on the way back; *на пра́вильном пути́* on the right track; *сби́ться с пути́* lose one's way; *счастли́вого пути́!* happy journey!

пух down; fluff

пу́хнуть, вс-, о- swell

пуши́стый downy; fluffy; _ни́на collect. furs, fur-skins; _но́й fur...; fur-bearing пу́шка (artillery-)gun

пчела́ bee

пшени́ца wheat; ~ó millet

пыл ardour, heat, fervour;
~а́ть blaze, flame; *face:*
glow

пылесо́с vacuum cleaner

пы́лкий ardent, fervent

пыль f dust; ~ный dusty

пыта́ться, по~ try, endeavour

пы́тка torture, *mst. fig.*

пы́шный splendid, gorgeous; luxuriant

пье́са *thea.* play

пьян|е́ть, о~ (*от* Р) get
drunk (*fig.* intoxicated)

(with); ~и́ца *m/f* drunkard; ~ство hard drinking;
~ый drunk

пюре́ *cul.* purée; **карто́-
фельное** ~ mashed potatoes

пята́к *coll.* five-copeck coin

пяти|бо́рье pentathlon;
~деся́тый fiftieth

пя́тка (*foot or stocking*) heel

пятна́дцать fifteen; ~ница
Friday

пятно́ stain (*a. fig.*); blot

пя́тый fifth

пять five; ~деся́т fifty;
~со́т five hundred

Р

раб, ~а́ slave; ~ота́ work;
job; ~о́тать work v.; *tech.*
run, operate; (*shops, etc.*)
be open; ~о́тник, ~о́тница
worker; ~о́чий *adj.*
worker's; *noun* worker; labourer

ра́в|енство equality;
~ни́на *geogr.* plain; ~но́
equals, make(s); всё ~но́
(it is) all the same

равно|ве́сие equilibrium;
balance; ~ду́шный indifferent; ~ме́рный uniform;
even; ~пра́вие equality of
rights

ра́вный equal (in *по* Д);
~я́ть, с~ make even;
equalize; ~я́ться (Д) be

equal (to); ~ (*с* Т) compete with

рад, ~а, ~ы glad (of Д)

ра́ди (Р) for the sake of

радиа́ция radiation

ра́дио *n indecl.* radio; ~акти́вный = **акти́вное за-
грязне́ние** radioactive
contamination; ~ **акти́в-
ные оса́дки** radioactive
fall-out; ~веща́ние
broadcasting; ~лока́тор
radar; ~переда́ча transmission; broadcast; ~при-
ёмник radio set

ра́д|овать, об~ make
happy, gladden; ~ся (Д) be
glad (about); ~остный
glad, joyful; ~ость f joy,

delight

ра́дуга rainbow

раду́шный cordial

раз *noun* time; *adv.* once; counting one; *conj.* since; **вся́кий** ~ each time; **'**~*а* twice; **как** ~ just, exactly; **не** ~ more than once; ~ **и навсегда́** once and for all

разбавля́ть, '~**ить** dilute

разбе́г: **прыжо́к с** ~*у* running jump

разби(ва́)ть smash; break (up); hurt badly; ~**ся** get broken; crash

разбира́ть, **разобра́ть** take to pieces; sort out; make out, understand; investigate

разбо́р analysis; ~ **де́ла** *jur.* trial; **без** ~*а* indiscriminately; ~**чивый** fastidious; legible

разбро́санный scattered

разбуди́ть → **буди́ть**

разва́л disruption; disorganization; ~**ина** *mst. pl.* ruins; *fig. coll.* (person) wreck

ра́зве *interrogative particle*: remains untransl.: ~? really?; *conj.* unless

разведе́ние breeding; cultivation

разве́дка intelligence (service); *mil.* reconnaissance

развёртывать, ~**верну́ть** unroll; unfold

развести́ → **разводи́ть**

разви́|(ва́)ть(ся) develop; ~**тие** development; ~**то́й** (well) developed

развлече́ние entertainment, diversion

разво́д divorce; ~**и́ть**, **развести́** take to separate places; divorce; breed; dilute; ~**ся** breed, multiply; (**с** Т) divorce; ~**но́й**: ~**но́й мост** draw-bridge

развра́т depravity; debauchery

развраща́ть, ~**ти́ть** corrupt; deprave

развя́зывать, ~**а́ть** untie; unleash; ~**ный** free and easy; unduly familiar

разгова́ривать converse, talk

разгово́р conversation; talk; ~**ник** phrase-book; ~**ный** colloquial; ~**чивый** talkative

разго́н dispersal; ~**я́ть**, **разгоня́ть** disperse; drive away; *fig.* dispel

разгосуда́рствле́ние denationalisation, privatisation

разгро́м crushing; defeat; havoc

разда(ва́)ть give out, distribute; ~**ся** resound, ring out

разде(ва́)ть(ся) undress

разде́л division; (*book*) section; ~**е́ние** (division) ~**я́ть**, ~**и́ть** divide; separate; share

раздо́р discord

раздраж|а́ть, **_и́ть** irritate; **_и́тельный** irritable

разду́м(ыв)ать *impf* (*о* П) ponder (over), consider; *pf.* change one's mind

разжига́ть, **_же́чь** kindle; rouse, stir up

разлага́ться, **_ложи́ться** decay, decompose

разли́(ва́)ть spill; pour *or* ladle out

различ|а́ть, **_и́ть** distinguish; discern; **-ся** *no pf.* differ; **'_ие** difference, distinction; **'_ный** different; various

разлу́ка separation, parting

разлюби́ть *pf.* cease to love *or* like

разма́х swing; scope; *с_у* with all one's might

разме́н exchange; **_ивать**, **_я́ть** *money* change

разме́р size, dimensions; rate, amount; scale

разме|ща́ть, **_сти́ть** place, accommodate; stow

размножа́ть, **'_ить** multiply; duplicate

размышля́ть (*о* П) meditate (on)

ра́зница difference

разно|ви́дность *f* variety; **_гла́сие** disagreement; discrepancy; **_сторо́нний** various, diverse; **_сторо́нний** many-sided; all-round; versatile

ра́зность *f* difference

ра́зный various, different

разоблач|а́ть, **_и́ть** unmask, expose

разобра́ть → **разбира́ть**

ра́зовый: **_ шприц** disposable syringe

разгоня́ть → **разгоня́ть**

разойти́сь → **расходи́ться**

разорва́ть → **разрыва́ть**

разоре́ние ruin; ravage

разоруж|а́ть, **_и́ть** disarm; **_е́ние** disarmament

разор|я́ть, **_и́ть** ruin; ravage

разосла́ть → **рассыла́ть**

разочаро́в|ывать, **_а́ть** disappoint

разраб|а́тывать, **_о́тать** work out, elaborate; *mine* exploit

разре́з cut; slit; section; **_а́ть**, **_ать** cut, slit; section

разреш|а́ть, **_и́ть** allow, permit; solve; **_е́ние** permission; permit; solution

разру́ха collapse; dislocation

разруш|а́ть, **'_ить** destroy; **_е́ние** destruction

разры́в rupture; break; **_а́ть**, **разорва́ть** tear asunder; break (off); **-ся** burst, explode; break; tear

разря́д[1] *el.* discharge

разря́д[2] category; class, rating

разря́дка détente

ра́зум reason, intelligence; ~е́ется it stands to reason; of course; ~ный judicious; reasonable

разу́чивать learn (to perform), study; ~ся + inf. forget how to ...

разъедин|я́ть, ~и́ть separate; disconnect

разъ|езжа́ться, ~е́хаться depart; pf. cars: pass each other

разъясн|я́ть, ~и́ть explain

разы́|скивать, ~ска́ть imp. search for; pf. find

рай paradise

райо́н region; district

рак crayfish; med. cancer

раке́та rocket, missile

раке́тка (sports) racket

ра́ковина zo. shell; sink

ра́ма frame

ра́н|а wound; ~еный injured or wounded (man)

ра́нить (im)pf. wound, injure

ра́н|ний early; ~о adv. early; ~ьше earlier; formerly

ра́са race

раска́|иваться, ~яться (в П) repent (of), regret; ~яние repentance

раскла́дывать, разложи́ть lay out; spread

раскладу́шка coll. folding bed, camp bed

раско́л split, division

раскры́(ва́)ть open; lay

bare; disclose

раску́пори(ва)ть uncork

распа|да́ться, ~сться fall to pieces; collapse

распако́вывать, ~а́ть unpack

рас|па́хивать, ~пахну́ть open wide; throw open

распеча́тка tech. hard copy

распеча́т(ыв)ать unseal; letter open

расписа́ние schedule; ~а́ние поездо́в timetable; ~ка receipt; ~ываться, ~а́ться (one's name); coll. register one's marriage; ~ в получе́нии (P) (salary, etc.) sign for

распла́та retribution; payment; ~чиваться, ~ти́ться (с Т) pay off; get even with; ~ за (В) pay for

распо|лага́ть, ~ложи́ть arrange; person win over; impf. (Т) dispose (of); ~ложе́ние arrangement; disposition; location; favour; inclination; ~ло́женный disposed; inclined; located

распоря|жа́ться, ~ди́ться order; (Т) dispose (of); deal (with); impf. be in command; ~же́ние order; disposal

распредел|я́ть, ~и́ть distribute; assess; assign, allocate, allot

распрода|(ва)ть sell out; ~жа clearance sale

распространя|ть, ~ить spread; diffuse; propagate

распус|кать, ~тить dismiss; disband; dissolve; -ся *flower* open

распут(ыв)ать untangle; disentangle

рассвет dawn; ~ать: ~ает day is breaking

рассеянный scattered; absent-minded; diffused

рассказ story, tale, ~чик, ~чица story-teller; ~ывать, ~ать tell, recount

рас|сматривать, ~смотреть consider, examine; *pf. a.* discern

рас|спрашивать, ~спросить question; make inquiries (*о* П)

рассрочк|а: в ~у by instalments

расста(ва)ться (с Т) part (with)

расставля|ть, ~ить place, arrange; post; move apart **о** П

рас|стёгивать, ~стегнуть undo, unbutton, unhook

расстояние distance

рас|страивать, ~строить disturb, unsettle; upset

расстрел execution (by shooting); ~ивать, ~ять shoot (dead *or* down)

расстройство disorder; derangement

рассу|дительный sober-minded, reasonable;

~дить *pf.* judge (between); consider; '~док reason, common sense; ~ждать reason (*о* П) argue (about); ~ждение reasoning; argument

рассчит|ывать, ~ать calculate; (**на** В) count (on); + *inf.* expect to ...; -ся по счёту pay the bill

рассыл|ать, разослать send round; circulate

раствор *chem.* solution; *tech.* mortar; ~ять, ~ить open; dissolve

растение *bot.* plant

растерянный confused, perplexed

расти, вы~ grow

рас|тирать, ~тереть grind; rub

растительность *f* vegetation

расторг|ать, '~нуть cancel; *marriage* dissolve

растра|та (wasteful) spending; embezzlement; ~чивать, ~тить spend; waste; embezzle

растя|гивать, ~нуть stretch; strain

расход (*mst. pl.*) expense; expenditure; consumption; ~иться, разойтись disperse, break up; diverge; (**с** Т) part (from); differ (from); ~овать, израсходовать spend

расцве|т bloom; flourishing, heyday; ~тать, ~сти

bloom, blossom out;
flourish

расце́нивать, ~цени́ть estimate, assess; regard,
consider; **~це́нка** price

расчёт calculation, computation; **принима́ть в ~**
take into consideration;
за нали́чный ~ paying in
cash

расширя́ть, '-ить enlarge,
widen; expand

рвать tear, rend; *flowers*
pick; *tooth* pull out; *relations* break; **'-ся** tear;
break; burst; + *inf.* long
or be dying to ...

рве́ние fervour

рво́та vomiting

реакти́вный reactive; **~ самолёт** jet plane

реа́ктор *tech.* reactor, pile

реакцио́нный *adj.* reactionary; **'-ия** reaction (*a.
pol.*)

реа́льный real; workable

ребёнок child; **~яче́ский**
childish

ребро́ rib

рёв roar; bellow; howl

реве́нь *m* rhubarb

реве́ть roar; bellow; howl

реви́зия inspection; audit;
revision

ревмати́зм rheumatism

ревни́вый jealous; **~ова́ть**
(B) be jealous (of); **'-ость**
f jealousy

револьве́р revolver

революционе́р revolu-

tionary; **~ио́нный** *adj.*;
'-ия revolution

регистра́ция registration;
~и́ровать, за- register, record

редакти́ровать, от- edit;
'-тор editor; **'-ция** editorial staff или office; editorship; wording

реди́ска red radish

ре́дкий rare; thin(ning)

ре́дька white radish

режи́м *pol.* regime; routine; *tech.* mode; **~ пита́-
ния** diet

режиссёр *thea.* producer

ре́зать cut, slice, carve

рези́на rubber; **~ка** rubber, eraser; elastic

ре́зкий sharp, harsh

результа́т result; **в ~е** (P)
as a result (of)

резь *f med.* colic; **~ба́** carving, fretwork; *tech.*
thread(ing)

рейс trip, voyage, flight

ре́йтинг *pol., sports, etc.* rating

река́ river

рекла́ма advertisement;
publicity

рекомендова́ть (*im*)*pf.*, *pf.
a.* **по-** recommend

реко́рд (*sports*) record

рели́гия religion

рельс rail

реме́нь *m* strap; belt

ремесло́ trade, handicraft

ремо́нт repair(s)

рентге́новский; **~ сни́мок**

X-ray photograph
ре́па turnip
репертуа́р repertoire
репети́ция rehearsal
репорт|а́ж reporting; account; **~ёр** reporter
репроду́кция (*art*) reproduction
респи́ца eyelash
респу́блика republic
рессо́ра (*mot., etc.*) spring
рестора́н restaurant
рефо́рма reform
реце́пт recipe; *med.* prescription
речно́й river...
речь *f* speech (*a. gr.*)
реша́|ть, **~и́ть** decide; solve (*impf. a.* try to solve); **-ся** (**на** B *or inf.*) decide (on or to ...); **~е́ние** decision; verdict; solution
решётка grating; railing; trellis; fender
реши́т|ельный decisive; resolute; **-ь →** *реша́ть*
ржаве́|ть, **по-** rust; **'~чина** rust; **'~ый** rusty
рис rice
риск risk; **~ова́ть**, **~ну́ть** risk; *pf. a.* venture
рис|ова́ть, **на-** draw; depict; **~у́нок** drawing; figure; design
ритм rhythm
ри́фма rhyme
ро́бкий shy, timid
ро́бот robot
ров ditch

рове́сник: *они́ ~и* they are of the same age
ро́вн|о *adv.* evenly; (*time*) sharp, exactly; **~ый** flat, even; equal; equable
рог horn; antler; **~а́тый:** *кру́пный ~а́тый скот* cattle
род kin, family; **~и́льный: ~и́льный дом** maternity home; **'~ина** homeland; **~и́тели** *pl.* parents; **~** **→** *рожда́ть*; **~ни́к** spring; **~но́й** native; own; **~ны́е** relatives; **~ом** by birth; **'~ственник** relative; **~ство́** relationship, kinship; **'~ы** *m/pl.* childbirth
рожда́|емость birth-rate; **~ть**, (*impf. a.* **рожа́ть**, **роди́ть** (B) give birth (to); **-ся** be born; **~е́ние** birth; **~ество́** Christmas
рожь *f* rye
ро́за rose
розе́тка *el.* socket; jam-dish
ро́зничный retail...
ро́зовый pink, rosy; rose...
ро́зыгрыш (*lottery, etc.*) drawing; (*sports*) playing off; *approx.* practical joke
ро́зыск search; *Уголо́в-ный* **~** Criminal Investigation Department
рой swarm
ро́лик roller; **~овый: ~овые коньки́** roller skates
роль *f* part, role

ром rum

рома́н novel

рома́шка *bot., med.* camomile

роня́ть, урони́ть drop, let fall

роса́ dew

роско́шный luxurious; luxuriant; splendid

ро́скошь *f* luxury; splendour

рост growth; increase, rise; height, stature

росто́к sprout, shoot

рот mouth

ро́ща grove

роя́ль *m* (grand) piano

ртуть *f* mercury

руба́шка shirt; *ни́жняя* ~ petticoat; *ночна́я* ~ nightdress

рубе́ж border, boundary; *за* ~**о́м** abroad

рубе́ц hem; scar; *cul.* tripe

руби́ть hew; chop

рубль *m* rouble

руга́ть, вы́~ scold; **-ся** swear; *impf.* abuse each other

руда́ ore; **-ни́к** mine, pit

ружьё gun

рука́ hand; arm; ~**в** sleeve; ~**ви́ца** mitten; gauntlet

руково|ди́тель *m* leader; manager; head; instructor; ~**дство** leadership; manual; instructions; ~**де́лие** needle-work

ру́ко|пись *f* manuscript;

~**плеска́ние** (*mst. pl.*) applause; ~**пожа́тие** handshake

руле|во́й rudder...; steering...; *noun* helmsman; ~**ь** *m* rudder, helm (*a. fig.*); steering-wheel; handle-bars

румы́н(ка); ~**ский** Rumanian

румя́|нец (high) colour, flush; ~**ный** rosy, ruddy

ру́сло river-bed; channel

ру́сский Russian (*adj. a. noun*)

ру́сый light brown

руча́ться, ручи́ться (*за* B) guarantee, vouch for

руче́й brook

ру́чка handle, (*door*) knob; (*chair*) arm; *pen*; *ша́риковая* ~ ball-point pen

ручно́й hand...; arm...; manual; (*animal*) tame

ры́б|а fish; ~**а́к** fisherman; ~**а́лка** *coll.* fishing; ~**ий** fish ...; ~**ий жир** cod-liver oil

рыбо́лов fisherman, angler; ~**ство** fishing; fishery

рыда́ть sob *v.*

ры́жий red-haired

ры́нок market(-place)

рысь[1] *f* lynx

рысь[2] *f* trot

рыть, вы́~ dig; **-ся, по-ся** (*в* П) rummage, burrow

ры́хлый crumbly; (*earth, snow*) loose

ры́царь *m* knight

рыча́г lever

рюкза́к rucksack, knapsack

рю́мка (wine)glass

ряби́на mountain-ash; rowan

ря́бчик hazel-grouse

ряд row; series; **_ово́й** ordinary, common; *mil.* private; **'_ом** near; side by side; next door; **_ом с** (T) next to, beside; **сплошь и _ом** more often than not

С

с (T) with; (P) from; since; with, for (*fear, etc.*); (B) about, approximately; **мы с тобо́й (вами)** you and I; **ско́лько с меня́?** how much do I owe?; **с одно́й стороны́** on the one hand

са́бля sabre

сад garden

сади́ться, **сесть** sit down; *av.* land; *sun:* set; *rail.*, *ae.* — **на** (B) take or get into (*the train etc.*)

садо́вник gardener; **_во́дство** gardening

са́жа soot

сажа́ть, **посади́ть** seat; set; plant

сала́т lettuce; salad

са́ло salted or smoked fat of a pig

салфе́тка napkin

сам (-á, -ó, '-и) self; **я _(á)** I myself; **ты _(á)** you yourself, *etc.*; **_ó собо́й разуме́ется** it goes without saying

саме́ц *zo.* male; **'-ка** *zo.* female

самова́р samovar («self-boiler»); **_де́ятельность:** **худо́жественная _де́ятельность** amateur performance; **_кри́тика** self-criticism; **_лёт** aircraft, plane; **_лю́бие** pride, self-esteem; **_облада́ние** self-control; **_обслу́живание** self-service; **_стоя́тельно** *adv.* independently, without assistance; **_стоя́тельность** independence; **_уби́йство** suicide; **_уве́ренный** self-confident; **_управле́ние** self-government; **_чу́вствие: как ва́ше _чу́вствие?** how do you feel?

са́мый 1. тот (же) _ый same (→ **тот**); **2. с _ого нача́ла** from the very beginning; **3. _ый высо́кий** highest; **4. в _ом де́ле** indeed

са́ни *f/pl.* sledge, sleigh

санкциони́ровать (*im*)*pf.* sanction; **_ия** sanction, approval; *pol. econ.* sanction sanctions

сан|техник plumber; **~узел** bathroom and toilet

сапо|г (high) boot; **~жник** shoemaker

сарай shed

сардель́ка saveloy, polony

сарди́на sardine

са́хар sugar; **~ница** sugar-basin

сбавля́ть, **'-ить** reduce

сбе|га́ть, **~жа́ть** run down; run away

сбере|га́тельный: **~га́тельная ка́сса** savings-bank; **~га́ть**, **'-чь** save; preserve; protect; **~же́ние** saving(s); economy

сби(ва́)ть knock or bring down; knock together; cream whip; **-ся с пути́** lose one's way

сближа́ть, **'-зить** draw or bring together; **-ся** approach; draw nearer; become intimate; **~же́ние** approach; rapprochement

сбо́ку at the side; from the side; sideways

сбор collection; takings; dues; **-ник** (book) collection; compendium

сбы(ва́)ть market; get rid of; **-ся** come true

сбыт market, sale

сва́дьба wedding

сва́л|ивать, **-и́ть** knock down or over; heap up; **~вину́** (**на** B) put the blame (on); **-ся** fall

(down)

све́д|ение (*mst. pl.*) information, knowledge; **~ущий** versed, well-informed

све́жий fresh

свёкла beet, beetroot

свё́кор *m* father-in-law (*husband's father*)

свекро́вь *f* mother-in-law (*husband's mother*)

сверг|а́ть, **'-нуть** *pol.* overthrow

сверк|а́ть, **~ну́ть** flash; *impf.* sparkle

сверл|и́ть bore, drill; **~о́** borer, drill

свё́ртывать, сверну́ть *v/t.* roll up; curtail; *v/i.* turn

сверх (P) over; above, beyond; **~ того́** moreover; **'-у** from above; **~уро́чный** overtime ...

свести́ → своди́ть

свет[1] world

свет[2] light; **-а́ть**: **-а́ет** it is dawning; **-и́ло** luminary; **-и́ть(ся)** shine; **-ле́ть, по-** brighten; **'-лый** light; bright; **-ово́й** light...; **~офо́р** traffic lights

свеча́ candle; *mot.* spark-plug

све́шать → ве́шать

свида́|ние appointment, *coll.* date; **до ~я** good-bye

свиде́тель|(ница) *m* witness; **~ство** evidence; certificate; **~ство о рожде-**

нии (смéрти) birth (death) certificate; **~ствовать (о П)** be evidence (of), witness; testify to

свинéц *min.* lead

свин|инá pork; **~ья́** pig, swine

свирéп|ость *f* fierceness; **~ый** fierce

свист whistle; **~áть, ~éть,** *pf.* **'~нуть** whistle; **~óк** whistle

свúтер sweater

свобóд|а freedom; **~ный** free; vacant; (*garment*) loose; (*time*) spare

свод arch; vault

сводúть, свестú *people* take down; bring together; **~ дрýжбу с (Т)** make friends with; **~ умá** drive mad; **~ на нет** bring to naught; **~ся (к Д)** come to

свóдка summary; **~ погóды** weather forecast

своеврéменный timely; **~обрáзный** peculiar, distinctive

свой, своя́, своё, *pl.* **свои** *reflexive possessive* my, your, his, *etc.*; **он сам не свой** he is not himself

свóйственный (Д) peculiar (to)

свóйство quality, property

свыкáться, ~нуться (с Т) get used (to)

свысокá *adv.* haughtily

свы́ше (Р) over, beyond;

adv. from above

свя́з|ка sheaf; bunch; *anat.* chord; **~ный** coherent; **~ывать, ~áть** tie together; bind (*a. fig.*); connect, associate; involve; **~ся (с Т)** get in touch (with); have to do (with)

связь *f* tie; connection; communication

свято́й holy; sacred; *noun* saint

свящéнн|ик priest; **~ый** sacred; holy

сгибáть, согнýть bend

сговáриваться, ~орúться arrange (things); agree; conspire

сгор|áть, ~éть *v/i.* burn down

сгу|щáть, ~стúть *v/t.* thicken, condense

сгущёнка *coll.* condensed milk

сда(вá)ть give back, return; *mail* hand in; *exam* pass; *flat* let; give change; **~ся** surrender

сдáча (*money returned*) change; letting, leasing; surrender

сдвиг *fig.* change (for the better); **~áть, '~нуть** move (aside); get moving

сдéл|ать → дéлать; ~ка deal, bargain

сдéрж|анный restrained, reserved; **~ивать, ~áть** hold back; keep in check; restrain; **~ся** restrain o.s.)

control o.s.

сдобн|ый: ~ая бу́лочка bun

сеа́нс (*cinema*) performance

себе́, себя́ *dat. a. acc. of reflexive pronoun* (to) myself, (to) yourself, *etc.*

себесто́имость *econ.* cost; cost price

се́вер north; ~ный north(ern)

севрю́га stellate sturgeon

сего́дня today; ~ у́тром this morning; ~ ве́чером tonight; ~шний today's

седе́ть, по- turn grey; ~ина́ grey hair; ~о́й grey-haired

седло́ saddle

седьмо́й seventh

сезо́н season; ~ный seasonal

сейча́с at once; very soon; just now

секре́т secret

секрета́р|ь *m*, ~ша secretary

секре́тный secret

секс sex; ~уа́льность sexuality; ~уа́льный sexual

се́ктор sector; *госуда́рственный* ~ state (-owned) sector (of economy)

секу́нда second

селёдка herring

селезёнка *anat.* spleen

се́лезень *m* drake

село́ village

сельдере́й celery

сельдь *f* herring

се́льск|ий rural, village...; ~ое хозя́йство agriculture

сельскохозя́йственный agricultural

сельсове́т village soviet

сёмга salmon

семе́йный family...; domestic

семёрка (*cards*) seven; (*bus, tram, etc.*) number seven

семе́стр term, semester

семи|деся́тый seventieth; ~со́тый seven-hundredth

семна́дцат|ый seventeenth; ~ь seventeen

семь seven; ~деся́т seventy; ~со́т seven hundred

семья́ family

се́мя *n* seed; semen

се́но hay; ~ко́с haymaking

сентя́брь *m* September

се́ра sulphur; ear-wax

серви́з service, set; *ча́йный* ~ tea service

се́рвис service

серде́чный cordial; heart...; cardiac; ~йтый angry; ~йться (*на* B) be angry (with)

се́рдце heart; ~бие́ние palpitation

серебро́ silver; ~ьяный silver...

середи́на middle

се́рия series; part

се́рна *zo.* chamois

серп sickle

се́рфинг (*sports*) surfing; **доска́ для ~а** surfboard

се́рый grey

серьга́ ear-ring

серьёзный serious; earnest

се́ссия session

сестра́ sister; **двою́родная ~** (first) cousin; (**медици́нская**) **~** nurse

сесть → **сади́ться**

се́т|ка net; rail. rack; grid; **~ь f** net

се́я|лка sowing-machine; **~ть, по~** sow

сжа́тый compressed; brief

сжига́ть, сжечь *v/t.* burn

сза́ди *adv.* (from)behind; *prep.* (P) behind

Сиби́рь f Siberia

сига́ра cigar

сигаре́та cigarette

сигна́л signal

сид|е́ть; *sit*; *clothes*: fit; **~е́ть на ко́рточках** squat; **оста́ться ~е́ть** remain seated; **~я́чий** sitting, sedentary

си́л|а strength; power; **~ы f/pl.** mil. forces; **в ~у** (P) on the strength (of); **оста́ться в ~е** remain valid; **~ьный** strong

си́мвол symbol; tech. character

симпати́чный likeable, attractive; **~ия** liking (for)

симпто́м symptom

симфони́ческий symphonic; **~ конце́рт** symphony concert

син|ева́ the blue; **~ий** (dark) blue; **~я́к** bruise

синте́ти|ка coll. synthetic cloth; **~ческий** synthetic

синхрон|иза́ция tech. synch.; **~ный** synchronous; **~ный перево́д** simultaneous interpretation

си́плый hoarse

сире́нь f lilac

сирота́ m/f orphan

систе́ма system; **~ управле́ния** tech. control system

си́тец cotton (print)

си́то sieve

сия́|ние radiance; **се́верное ~ние** northern lights; **~ть** shine; beam

сказ|а́ть → **говори́ть**; **~ка** fairy-tale; **~а́ться** (**на** or **в** П) tell upon, affect

скала́ rock

скаме́йка, скамья́ bench

скат slope

ска́терть f table-cloth

ска́т|ывать[1], **~и́ть** *v/t.* roll down; **~ывать**[2], **~а́ть** carpet roll up; *sail* furl

ска́чки f/pl. horse-race; **~о́к** skip, bound; sharp change

сква́жина: **замо́чная ~** keyhole; **нефтяна́я ~** oil well

сквер public garden

скве́рный nasty, bad

сквоз|и́ть: **здесь ~и́т** there

is a draught here; ⁓нáк draught

сквозь (B) through

скворéц starling

скúдка reduction, discount; *(с)дéлать ⁓ку на* make allowances for; ⁓ывать, **скúнуть** throw off; *coll. price* knock off

скипидáр turpentine

склад warehouse; ⁓ *умá* turn of mind; ⁓**ка** fold; pleat; ⁓**ной** folding..., collapsible; ⁓**ывать, сложúть** put together; fold; pile; add; **-ся** form, take shape

склéй(ва)ть stick *or* paste together

склон slope; ⁓**éние** declension; ⁓**ность** f inclination, propensity; ⁓**ный** inclined, disposed, ⁓**ять, ⁓úть** incline; bend

скóбка bracket

сковородá frying-pan

скользúть, ⁓нýть slip, slide, glide; ⁓**кий** slippery

скóлько how much, how many

сконча́ться pass away, die

скорб|**éть** grieve; mourn; ⁓**ный** mournful; ⁓**ь** f grief

скорлупá *(egg or nut)* shell

скорня́к furrier

скóр|**о** quickly, fast; ⁓**ость** f speed; *mot. a.* gear; ⁓**ый** quick, fast; *(time)* near; **в ⁓ом бýдущем** in the near future; **в**

⁓**ом врéмени** soon

скот cattle

скотовóдство cattle-breeding

скрипáч(ка) violinist; ⁓**éть** squeak; creak; crunch; ⁓**ка** violin

скрóмный modest

скры(вá)ть hide, conceal; **-ся** hide (o.s.); *(от* P) escape (from)

скры́тный reticent, secretive

скýдный scanty, poor

скýка boredom

скулá cheek-bone

скýльпт|**ор** sculptor; ⁓**ура** sculpture

скýмбрия mackerel

скупóй stingy

скучáть be bored; *(по* Д *or* II) miss; ⁓**ный** boring, dull

слаб|**éть, о-** *v/i.* weaken; ⁓**úтельное** *med.* laxative; ⁓**ость** f weakness; weak point; ⁓**ый** weak; faint; poor

слáв|**а** glory; fame; ⁓**а Бóгу!** thank God!; ⁓**а** *coll.* nice

славяни́н, ⁓ка, *adj.* ⁓**ский** Slav

слáдкий sweet

сладострáстие voluptuousness

слáдость f sweetness; *pl.* sweets, sweetmeats

слайд slide

слать, по⁓ send

слева from or to the left (of **от** P)

слегка slightly, somewhat

след trace, track; footprint; **~ить** (**за** T) watch; shadow; fig. follow; **~ователь** m investigator; **'~овательно** consequently; **'~овать, по-** (Д or **за** T) follow; **'~ствие** consequence; investigation; **'~ует: мне '~ует это сделать** I ought to do it; **'~ующий** following, next

слеза tear

слез(а́)ть get down; dismount; alight

слеп|о́й blind; **~ота́** blindness

сле́сарь m locksmith

сли́ва plum(-tree)

сли(ва́)ть pour out or off or together; fuse

сли́в|ки f/pl. cream; **взби́тые ~ки** whipped cream; **~очный: ~очное ма́сло** butter

сли́тно adv. (written) in one word

сли́шком too, too much

слов|а́рь m dictionary; **'~ник** vocabulary

сло́во word; **брать ~** take the floor; **~м** in short

слог syllable; style

слоёный: ~ пиро́г puff-pastry

сложе́ние addition; (body) build; **~и́ть → скла́дывать** a. **слага́ть**; **'~ный**

complicated; compound

слой layer; coating; stratum

слом pulling down; **~а́ть → лома́ть**

слон elephant; (chess) bishop; **~о́вый: ~о́вая кость** f ivory

сложи́ть → скла́дывать

служ|ащий noun employee, white-collar worker; **~ба** service, work; **~е́бный** office...; **~и́ть, по-** (Д) serve (as T); be in use

слух hearing, ear; rumour; **~ово́й** auditory, acoustic; **~ово́й аппара́т** hearing aid

слу́ч|ай case; occasion; opportunity; incident; **несча́стный ~ай** accident; **во вся́ком ~ае** in any case; **в проти́вном ~ае** otherwise; **на вся́кий ~ай** just in case; **ни в ко́ем ~ае** in no circumstances; **~а́йный** casual, chance; incidental; **~а́ться, ~и́ться** happen

слу́шатель(ница) m listener; m/pl. audience; students

слу́шать, по~ (В) listen (to); **у~** (В) obey; **слу́шаю!** (telephone) hullo!

слы́шать, у~ hear; **~ся, по-** be heard

слы́шно one can hear

слюна́ saliva

сля́коть slush

смáз(ыв)ать oil, lubricate

смáчивать, смочи́ть moisten, wet

смéжный adjacent

смéлый bold, daring

смéн|а change; replacement; shift; relief; **_я́ть, _и́ть** change; replace; relieve

смерк|áться, '-нуться get dark

смерт|éльный deadly; mortal; **_ность** f mortality; **'-ный** death...; noun mortal; **_ь** f death

смести́ → смета́ть

смести́ть → смеща́ть

смесь f mixture

смéта comm. estimate

сметáна soured cream

сметáть, смести́ sweep away

сметь, по'- dare

смех laughter

смéш|ивать, _áть mix (up)

смеш|и́ть, рас- make laugh; **_нóй** ridiculous; funny

смещáть, смести́ть displace; remove

смея́ться laugh (at **над** T)

смир|я́ться, _и́ться resign o.s., submit

смолá resin; pitch, tar

сморкáться, вы́- blow one's nose

сморо́дина currant(s)

смотр inspection

смотр|éть, по- (на B) look (at); (B) film, etc. see; **(за** T) look after; **_я́ как (когда́** и т. д.) it depends

смýглый swarthy

смущ|áть, _ти́ть embarrass; disturb; **-ся** be embarrassed; **_щéние** embarrassment

смысл sense; meaning, point

смычóк mus. bow

смягч|áть, _и́ть soften; mitigate; assuage

смятéние confusion; disarray

снаб|жáть, _ди́ть supply

снаружи from or on the outside

снаря́д mil. shell; (sports) apparatus; **_жáть, _ди́ть** fit out, equip; **_жéние** equipment, outfit

сначáла from or at the beginning

снег snow; **~ идёт** it snows; **_оочисти́тель** snow-plough; **_опáд** snowfall; **²у́рочка** Snow-Maiden

снеж|и́нка snow-flake; **'-ный** snow...; snowy; **_ная бáба** snowman; **_óк** snow-ball

снести́ → нести́ a. **сноси́ть**

сни|жáть, '-зить lower, bring down; reduce; **~ себесто́имости** cut production costs; **-ся** descend (a. av.); come down, fall

снизу (from) below

снима́ть, снять take off or down; photograph; rent; **– с рабо́ты** sack; **– фильм** shoot a film; **-ся** have one's photo taken

сни́мок photograph

снисходи́тельный condescending; indulgent

сни́ться, при_: **мне (при)сни́лось мо́ре** I dreamed of the sea

сно́ва anew

сноп sheaf

сноси́ть, снести́ take down(stairs); carry or sweep away; demolish; bring together; pile up; bear, endure

снотво́рное noun sleeping-draught

сноше́ние intercourse; relation

снять → снима́ть

со → с

соба́ка dog

собесе́дник interlocutor

соб(и)ра́ть gather, collect; pick; convoke; tech. assemble; **-ся** gather; assemble; + inf. intend to …, make ready to …

собла́зн temptation; **-я́ть, -и́ть** tempt; seduce

соблюда́ть, -сти́ observe, keep to

соболе́знование condolence(s)

со́боль m sable

собо́р cathedral

собра́ние meeting; pol. assembly; collection

собра́ть → собира́ть

со́бственн|ик, -ица owner; **_ость** f property, possession; **_ый** own; proper, true; **_о говоря́** properly speaking

собы́тие event

сова́ owl

соверш|а́ть, -и́ть accomplish; commit; **-ённый** perfect, absolute; **_ён-ство** perfection

со́весть f conscience

сове́т advice; council; CIS Soviet; ♀ **Безопа́сности** Security Council; **Верхо́вный** ♀ Supreme Soviet; **_ник** adviser; councillor; **_овать, по-** (Д) advise; **-ся (с** T) ask advice (of); consult; **_ский** hist. Soviet

совеща́|ние conference; **_ться** deliberate, confer

совмести́мость compatibility (a. tech.)

совме́стный joint, combined

Совми́н (= **Сове́т Мини́стров**) Council of Ministers

совпа|да́ть, '-сть coincide

современ|ник, -ица contemporary; **_ый** contemporary, modern

совсе́м quite, completely; **_ не** not at all

совхо́з State farm

согла́с|ие consent; concord; **~но** *adv.* in harmony; *prep.* (Д) according to; **~ный: он ~ен с этим** he agrees to it; **~овывать, ~овать** co-ordinate; make agree

согла|шаться, ~ситься (на B *or* с T) agree, consent (to); **~шение** agreement

согнуть → сгибать

согре(ва)ть warm, heat

содействие assistance; **~овать** (*im*)*pf*., *pf. a.* **по-** (Д) assist, further

содержа|ние maintenance; contents; **~ть** maintain; contain; support

содружество companionship; **Британское ~ наций** the British Commonwealth

соедин|ять, ~ить unite; connect; **~ение** connection

сожале|ние regret; pity; **к ~нию** unfortunately; **~ть** (о П) regret; deplore

сожи́тель(ница) *m* coll. room-mate; lover, mistress; **~ство** living together

созвать → созывать

созда|(ва́)ть create; found, establish; **~ние** creation; creature; **~тель** *m* creator; founder

созна|(ва́)ть realize, be aware of; **~ся** (в П) confess; **~ние** conscious-

ness; **~ние долга** sense of duty; **~тельный** consci(enti)ous

созыв convocation

соз(ы)вать convoke; summon; invite

сойти → сходить

сок juice; **~овыжима́лка** juice extractor

со́кол falcon

сокра|ща́ть, ~ти́ть shorten; abbreviate; abridge; reduce; **~ще́ние** shortening; abbreviation; reduction

сокро́вище treasure

солда́т soldier

солёный salt(ed)...; salty

соли́ст(ка) soloist

соли́ть, по- salt; pickle

со́лн|ечный sunny; sun...; solar; **~це** sun

солове́й nightingale

соло́м|а collect. straw; **~енный** straw...; thatched; **~енная вдова́** grass widow

соло́нка salt-cellar

соль *f* salt

сомне|ва́ться, усомни́ться (в П) doubt; **~ние** doubt; **~и́тельный** doubtful; dubious

сон sleep; dream

сообра|жа́ть, ~зи́ть consider, weigh; understand; **~зи́тельный** quick-witted; **'~зно** (с T) in conformity (with)

сообща́ jointly; **~а́ть, ~и́ть**

inform, report; impart; _éние report; communication; '-ник, '-ница accomplice

сооруж|áть, _дить build, erect; _жéние building; structure; installation

соотвéтствовать (Д) correspond (to); *needs* meet

соотéчественни|к, _ца compatriot

сопéрни|к, _ца rival

сопостав|ля́ть, '-ить compare, confront

сопровождáть accompany; escort

сопротивл|éние resistance; _я́ться (Д) resist

соразмéрный proportionate

сорвáть → срывáть

соревновáние competition, contest

сóрок forty; _овóй fortieth

сорóка magpie

сорóчка (man's) shirt; *ночна́я* _ night-dress

сорт sort; kind; brand; quality

сосáть suck

сосéд|(ка) neighbour; _ний neighbouring; adjacent; _ство neighbourhood

сосúска small sausage

сослужúв|ец, _ца colleague

соснá pine(-tree)

сосредотóчи(ва)ть(ся) concentrate

состáв composition; structure; staff; _лéние composition; compiling; _ля́ть, _ить put together; compose, compile; form, make up

состоя́|ние state, condition; *в _нии* in a position, able; _тельный well-off; well-grounded; _ть (Т) be; (*в П or из Р*) consist (in *or* of); _ться *pf.* take place

сострадáние compassion

состязáние contest; match

сосýд vessel

сосуществовáние coexistence

сосчú|тывать, _áть count, calculate

сóт(ы) honey-comb

сóтня a hundred

сотрýдни|к, _ца employee; collaborator; contributor; _чать cooperate; contribute; _чество co-operation

сóтый hundredth

сóус sauce

соучáстни|к, _ца accomplice; participant

сóхнуть (get) dry

сохран|éние preservation; conservation; _я́ть, _ить preserve; conserve; keep, maintain

соц... *in compounds =* **социáльный** *or* **социалистúческий**

социалисти́ческий social-
ist

социа́льный social

соцстра́х (= *социа́льное
страхова́ние*) social in-
surance

соч́льник Christmas Eve

сочета́|ние combination;
~ть (*im*)*pf.* combine; **~ся**
harmonize, match

сочине́ние writing, work;
(*school, mus.*) composi-
tion; *и́збранные ~е́ния*
selected works; **~а́ть,
~и́ть** write; compose; *coll.*
tell stories

со́чный juicy; lush, succu-
lent

сочу́вств|ие sympathy
(with *к* Д); **~овать** (Д)
sympathize (with)

сою́з union, alliance; *gr.*
conjunction; **~ник, ~ница**
ally

спа́льн|ый: **~ый ваго́н**
sleeping-car; **~я** bedroom

спа́ржа asparagus

спаса́|тельный rescue...
life(-saving)...; **~ть, ~ти́**
save; rescue; **~е́ние** rescue; escape; salvation;
~и́бо thanks, thank you;
~и́тель *m* rescuer; *eccl.*
Saviour

спать *v.* sleep; *ложи́ться ~*
go to bed

спекта́кль *m thea.* performance

спекуля́ция speculation;
profiteering

спе́лый ripe

сперва́ at first

спе́реди at *or* from the
front; in front (of)

спеть[1] ripen; **~**[2] *→* **петь**

спец... *in compounds* =
специа́льный special

специал|и́ст specialist, ex-
pert; **~иа́льность** profession; trade; **~иа́льный**
special; **~оде́жда** overalls

спеш|и́ть, по- be (in a)
hurry; *watch:* be fast;
'~ный urgent, pressing

СПИД *med.* AIDS

спин|а́ *anat.* back; **'~ка** (*fur-
niture*) back

спирт spirit, alcohol; **~но́й**
alcoholic

спис|о́к list, roll; **~ывать,
~а́ть** copy (from *с* Р)

спи́ца knitting-needle;
spoke

спи́чеч|ный: **~ечная ко-
ро́бка** match-box; **~ка**
match

сплав *tech.* alloy

спла́чивать, **сплоти́ть**
join; unite, rally

спле́т|ник, ~ница gossip;
~ичать, на- gossip; **~я**
gossip

сплош|но́й continuous;
solid, compact; *fig.* sheer;
~ь *adv.* completely; all
over; **~ь и ря́дом** very often

споко́й|ный quiet, calm;
~ной но́чи! good night!;
~ствие calm(ness); tran-

quillity

сполна́ *adv.* in full

спо́нсор sponsor, promoter

спор argument, controversy; **'_ить, по-** (*о* П) argue, dispute (about); **_ный** disputable; controversial

спорт sport; **_и́вный** sports *adj.*; **_сме́н(ка)** sportsman (-woman)

спо́соб way, mode; method; **'_ность** *f* ability; capacity; **'_ный** able; capable

спотыка́ться, споткну́ться stumble

спра́ва on the right; (*от* P) to the right (of)

справедли́в|ость *f* justice; fairness; truth; **_ый** just; fair; true

спра́в|ка information; **наве́сти́ _ку** (*о* П) inquire (about); **_ля́ться, _иться** (*о* П) inquire (about); (*с* Т) cope (with), get the better (of); **_очник** reference book; **_очный** inquiry..., reference...

спра́шивать, спроси́ть ask (about *or* for)

спрос (*на* В) demand (for); **без '_а** without permission

спря́тать → **пря́тать**

спус|к lowering; descent; slope; **_ка́ть, _ти́ть** lower; pull (down); let loose *or*

out; **-ся** (*по ле́стнице*) go down(-stairs)

спустя́ (В) after; later

спу́тник (travelling) companion; satellite, sputnik

сравн|е́ние comparison; **'_ивать¹, _и́ть** compare; **'_ивать², _я́ть** equal(ize); **'_ивать³, сровня́ть** level; **_и́тельный** comparative

сра|жа́ться, _зи́ться fight; **_же́ние** battle

сра́зу at once

сред|а́¹ Wednesday; **_а́²** environment; surroundings, milieu; **_и́** (P) among; amidst; **в '_нем** on the average; **'_ство** means; remedy

срок term; period; time; date; **в _** in time; **продли́ть _ ви́зы** extend a visa; **платежа́** date of payment

сро́чный urgent; of fixed date

срыва́ть, сорва́ть tear off *or* away; pick, pluck; *coll.* wreck, spoil

сса́дина abrasion

ссо́р|а quarrel; **_иться, по-** quarrel

ссу́да loan

ссыл|а́ться, сосла́ться (*на* В) refer to, cite; **'_ка** reference

ста́в|ить, по- put, place, set; *thea.* stage; *problem* raise; **_ка** rate; stake стадио́н stadium

ста́дия stage

ста́до herd, flock

стаж length of service; ~ёр probationer; postgraduate (*on a special non-degree course*)

стака́н (drinking-) glass

ста́лкивать, столкну́ть push out; ~ся collide, clash

сталь f steel; ~но́й steel...; *fig.* iron...

станда́рт; ~ный standard; (...)

станови́ться, стать become; (take one's) stand; – на коле́ни kneel down; → a. стать

стано́к machine(-tool); тока́рный ~ lathe

ста́нция station

стара́ние endeavour; effort; ~ться, по- try, endeavour; – и́зо всех сил do one's utmost

старе́ть, по- grow old; ~и́к old man; ~и́нный ancient, old; '~ость old age; ~у́ха old woman; '~ший older, elder; oldest, eldest; senior; '~ый old

старт (*sports*) start; ~ёр (*sports, tech.*) starter; ~ова́ть start

стать *pf.* 1. + *inf.* begin to ...; 2. → станови́ться

статья́ (*publication*) article; item; clause

стациона́р hospital; ~ный

~ный больно́й in-patient

ста́чка *pol.* strike

ста́я flock; shoal; (*wolves*) pack

ствол trunk, stem; *mil.* barrel

сте́бель m stalk

стекло́ (*material*) glass; лобово́е ~о́ *mot.* wind-screen; око́нное ~о́ window-pane; ~я́нный glass...

стена́ wall

сте́пень f degree

степь f steppe

сте́рео... *in compounds* stereo...

стере́ть → стира́ть[1]

стере́чь *impf.* guard, watch over

стесне́ние constraint; uneasiness; ~и́тельный inconvenient; shy; ~я́ть, ~и́ть hamper; embarrass; ~ся crowd together; *impf.* feel shy

стечь → стека́ть

стиль m style

сти́мул stimulus, incentive; ~и́ровать stimulate

стипе́ндия scholarship, grant

отира́ть[1], стере́ть wipe off; erase; rub sore; ~а́ть[2], вы́стирать *linen* wash; '~ка wash(ing)

стихи́йный spontaneous; ~и́ное бе́дствие natural calamity

стихотворе́ние poem

сто hundred

сто́имость f cost; value

сто́ить (B) cost (fig. with P); deserve; ~ + inf. be worth while

стол table; ~ нахо́док lost property office

столб post, pole; pillar; ~е́ц typ. column

столи́ца capital (city)

столкнове́ние collision, clash

столо́в|ая dining-room; mess; canteen; ~ый table-

сто́лько so much, so many

столя́р joiner

стона́ть groan

стоп-сигна́л mot. brake light

сто́рож watchman, guard

сторон|а́ side; part; ~ник supporter

стоя́н|ка parking, parking area; stop; ~ка такси́ taxi rank; ~ть v/i. stand

страда́|ние suffering; ~ть v/i. suffer

стран|а́ country, land; ~и́ца page; ~ный strange, odd

стра́ст|ный passionate; ~ь f passion

страх fear; ~ова́ние insurance; ~ова́ть, за- insure

стра́шный fearful, terrible

стрел|а́ arrow; ~ка pointer; (clock) hand; ~ьба́ shooting; ~и́ть (в В or по Д) shoot (at)

стреми́|тельный swift; ~ться (к Д) strive (for); + inf. seek to ...; ~ле́ние striving, aspiration

стри́жка hair-cut(ting)

стричь, по`-` cut, clip; -ся have one's hair cut

стро́гий strict; severe

строе́ние structure; building; ~и́тель m builder; ~ить, по- build; construct

строй pol. system; ~ка construction, building; ~ный well-proportioned; slender

строка́ typ. line

струя́ spurt, jet, stream; (air) current

студе́нт(ка) student; ~ия studio

сту́день aspic

стук knock; tap; ~ать, ~нуть knock; bang

стул chair

ступа́|ть, ~и́ть step; ~е́нь f (stairs) step; stage; ~ня́ foot

стуча́ть knock; bang; ~ся в дверь knock at the door

стыд shame; ~и́ть, при- shame; ~ся, по- be ashamed; ~ли́вый shamefaced; shy; мне ~но I am ashamed

сты́(ну)ть cool down

стюарде́сса air hostess

стя́|гивать, ~ну́ть tighten;

pull off
суббо́та Saturday
сугро́б snow-drift
суд law-court; trial; **_-е́б-ный_** legal; judicial; **_-и́ть_** (_о_ П) judge (about); _jur._ try; (_sports_) referee
суда́к pike-perch
су́дно ship; **_-_ на возду́шной поду́шке** hovercraft; **_-_ на подво́дных кры́льях** hydrofoil
судопроизво́дство legal proceedings
су́дорога cramp, convulsion
судо|строе́ние ship-building; **_-хо́дный_** navigable; **_-хо́дство_** navigation
судьба́ fate, destiny
судья́ _m_ judge; (_sports_) referee, umpire
суеве́р|ие superstition; **_-ный_** superstitious
суе́т|а fuss; bustle; **_-и́ться_** fuss about; bustle; **_-ли́вый_** fussy
сужде́ние judgement, opinion
сук bough
су́ка bitch
сукно́ woollen fulled cloth
сумасше́|дший mad; _noun_ madman; **_-ствие_** madness
сумато́ха turmoil
сумбу́р muddle, confusion
су́мерки _f/pl._ dusk, twilight
су́мка (hand)bag

су́мма sum
су́мрак dusk; twilight
суп soup
супру́г husband; **_-а_** a wife
суро́вый severe; stern
суста́в _anat._ joint
су́т|ки _f/pl._ day (of 24 hours); **_-очный_** daily
суть _f_ essence; main point
суха́рь _m_ rusk
сухо́й dry
сухоща́вый lean
су́ш|а (dry) land; **_-ёный_** (_fruit, etc._) dried, dry; **_-и́ть(ся), вы́-_** dry
суще́ств|енный essential; **_-о́_** essence; creature; being; **_-ова́ние_** existence; **_-ова́ть_** exist
су́щность _f_ essence, nature; **в _-и_** as a matter of fact
сфе́ра sphere
схва́т|ка skirmish; loose fight; **_-ывать, -и́ть_** grip, catch; _fig._ grasp; **_-ся (за_ В) seize
схе́ма diagram; outline
сходи́ть¹, сойти́ (_с_ Р) go down; alight from; get off; leave; **_-_ с ума́** go mad
сходи́ть² _pf._ (_за_ Т) go and fetch
схо́д|ни _f/pl._ gangway; **_-ный_** similar; **_-ство_** similarity
сце́на scene; stage; **_-рий_** scenario
счастли́вый happy; lucky; **_-ье_** happiness; luck; **к**

'~ью fortunately
счесть → **считáть**
счёт, *pl.* **счетá** calculation; account; bill; (*sports*) score; **~чик** meter
считáть, **счесть** count, compute; (*за* B or T) consider, think
считáться (T) be considered; **~ по~** (*с* T) take into consideration
съедáть, **съесть** eat up
съедóбный eatable
съезд congress
съезжáть, **съéхать** go or come down; slide down; **-ся** come together, assemble
съёмка survey; (*film*) shooting
съестнýе припáсы *m/pl.* provisions, food supplies
сыгрáть → **игрáть**
сын son
сы́п|**ать** strew, pour; **-ся** fall; pour down; run out; **~ь** *f med.* rash
сыр cheese
сыр|**óй** damp; raw; **~ьё** raw material(s)
сы́т|**ный** nourishing; nutritious; **~ый** satiated, repleted; **я сыт(á)** I have had my fill
сюдá here
сюжéт subject, plot
сюрприз surprise

Т

та → **тот**
табáк tobacco
табл|**éтка** tablet, pill; **~и́ца** table, list
таз (wash-)basin; *anat.* pelvis
таи́нственный mysterious
тайгá *geogr.* taiga
тай|**кóм** secretly; **'~на** secret; mystery; **'~ный** secret
тайм (*sports*) half, period (*of a game*)
тáймер *tech.* clock
так so; thus; **~ же** *adv.* the same way; **~ как** *conj.* as, because; **~ скáзать** so to speak; **'~же** also; either
такóй such (a); **~ же** same, of the same kind; **что такóе?** what is that?; what is the matter?
такси *n indecl.* taxi; **~ст** (*or* **таксёр**) *coll.* taxi-driver
такти́ческий tactical; **~и́чный** tactful
талáнт talent; **~ливый** talented
там there
тамóженный customs...; **~ня** custom(s) house
тáнец dance
танце|**вáльный** dancing, dance...; **~вáть** dance; **~óвщик**, **~óвщица** *thea.*

dancer
тápочки *coll.* slippers
таракáн cockroach
тарéлка (dinner-)plate; *летáющая* ~ flying saucer
ТАСС (= *Телегрáфное Агéнтство Совéтского Сою́за*) *hist.* Telegraph Agency of the Soviet Union
татáр|**ин**, ~**ка**; ~**ский** Ta(r)tar
тащи́ть, по-~ pull, drag
тáять, рас-~ melt
твердéть *v/i.* harden
твёрдый hard; firm; solid
твой, **твоя́**, **твоё**, *pl.* **твои́** your's
твор|**éние** creation; work; ~**éц** creator; ~**и́ть**, co-~ create; *miracle* work
творóг curds
творóжник curd fritter
твóрчество creative work; *collect.* works
те → **тот**
теáтр theatre; ~**áльный**; ~**áльная кáсса** box-office
тебé *dat. of* **ты** you
тебя́ *gen. and acc. of* **ты** you
текст text (*a. tech.*)
теку́|**чий** fluid; fluctuating; ~**щий** flowing; current; ~**щие собы́тия** current affairs
телеви́|**дение** television; ~**зор** TV set
телегрáмма telegram
телéжка cart
тéлекс telex

телёнок *agr.* calf
телефáкс (tele)fax
телефóн telephone; ~**-автомáт** public telephone-booth; ~**ный**: ~**ная стáнция** telephone exchange
тéло body; ~**сложéние** build, frame
теля́тина veal
тем → **тот**; ~ *бóлее что* the more so as; ~ *лýчше* so much the better; ~ *не мéнее* nevertheless
тéма subject, topic, theme, *a. mus.*; ~**тика** *collect.* subject-matter
темнé|**ть**, по-, c-~ grow dark; ~**отá** dark(ness)
тёмный dark; obscure
темп rate, pace; tempo
тен|**и́стый** shady; ~**ь** *f* shade; shadow
тéннис tennis; *настóльный* ~ table tennis; ~**и́ст** tennis-player
тепéрь now
теплó (it is) warm; warmly; *noun* warmth; ~**вóз** diesel engine; ~**хóд** motor ship
тёплый warm (*a. fig.*)
терéть rub; grate; polish
терминá**л** *tech.* terminal
термó|**метр** thermometer; ~**я́дерный** thermonuclear
тéрмос thermos (flask)
терп|**ели́вый** patient; ~**éние** patience; ~**éть** suffer; bear; have patience; tolerate; ~**и́мый** tolerable; tolerant

теря́ть, по~ lose; **-ся** be lost *or* at a loss

тесёмка tape, ribbon

тесн|ота́ lack of space; crowded state, crush; **'-ый** cramped; small; narrow; tight; close

те́сто dough

тесть *m* father-in-law (*wife's father*)

тетра́дь *f* exercise-book

тётя aunt

те́хн|ик technician; **-ика** engineering; technology; technique; equipment; **-и́ческий** technical; **-и́ческие характери́стики** specifications; **-и́ческое обслу́живание** maintenance, service

тече́ние flow; current; trend; **в ~** (P) in the course of

течь¹ flow, run; *time:* pass; leak

течь² *f* leak

тёща mother-in-law (*wife's mother*)

тигр tiger

тип type; **-и́чный** typical

типогра́фия printing-house

тир shooting-range

тира́ж (*press*) circulation; number of copies

тире́ *n indecl. typ.* dash

тиски́ *m/pl. tech.* vice

ти́тул title

тиф typhus

ти́хий quiet; still; calm;

low, soft; slow

тишина́ quiet(ness); stillness, silence

тка|нь *f* fabric, textile; *biol.* tissue; **~ть, со'-** weave

тлеть smoulder

то → а. тот; ~ есть that is to say (т. е. = i.e.); **(а) не ~** or else; **ни ~ ни сё** neither fish nor flesh; **ни с ~го́, ни с сего́** without rhyme or reason; **~ ..., ~ ...** now ..., now ...

това́р goods; commodity; *pl.* **широ́кого потребле́ния** consumer goods; **~ищ** comrade; colleague; **~ищество** comradeship; association; **~ный** goods-...; commodity...; **~ный оборо́т** commodity circulation

тогда́ then; **~ как** while, whereas

то́же also, too

ток current (*esp. el.*)

то́карь *m* turner

толк sense; use(fulness)

толк|а́ть, ~ну́ть push; **~ ядро́** put the shot

толк|ова́ть interpret; explain; talk; **~о́вый** intelligent; intelligible; sensible; **~о́вый слова́рь** explanatory dictionary

толп|а́ crowd; **~и́ться** crowd, flock (together)

то́лстый thick; stout, fat

толчо́к push; jerk; shock; impetus

толщина́ thickness

то́лько only; ~ **что** just now

том[1] volume

том[2] → *то a.* **тот**

тома́тный: ~ **сок** tomato juice

то́нк|**ий** thin; slim; fine; subtle; ~**ость** *f* thinness, *etc.*

тону́ть[1], **по-**, **за-** *v/i.* sink; ~[2], **у-** be drowned

то́п|**ать**, ~**нуть** (T) stamp

топи́ть[1], **по-** *v/t.* sink; ~[2], **у-** *v/t.* drown

топи́ть[3] heat; melt; '~**ливо** fuel; *жи́дкое* '~**ливо** fuel oil

то́поль *m* poplar

топо́р axe

то́п|**от** trampling; clatter; ~**тать** trample down; ~**ся на ме́сте** mark time

торг|**ова́ть** (T) deal, trade (in); sell; ~**ся** (*с* T) haggle (with); ~**о́вец** dealer, trader; ~**о́вля** trade, commerce; ~**о́вый** trade..., commercial; ~**пре́дство** (= **торго́вое представи́тельство** trade delegation

торже́ств|**енный** solemn; ceremonial; ~**о́** triumph; *pl.* celebrations; ~**ова́ть** triumph

то́рмоз brake; obstacle; ~**и́ть** brake; *fig.* hamper

торопи́ть, **по-** *v/t.* hurry;

hasten; ~**ся** be in a hurry; make haste; ~**ли́вый** hasty

торт fancy cake, gâteau

торф peat

торше́р standard lamp

торча́ть stick (up, out)

тоск|**а́** yearning; melancholy; dreariness; ~**ли́вый** dreary, dull; ~**ова́ть** (*по* Д *or* о П) long (for)

тот, **та**, **то** *pl.* те that; the other...; the right...; ~ **же** (**са́мый**) the same... or the same one; → **тем** *a.* **то**

точи́ть[1], **на-** sharpen; whet

то́ч|**ка** point; dot; ~**ность** *f* exactitude; precision; accuracy; ~**ный** exact; precise, accurate

тошнота́ sickness, nausea

трава́ grass; herb

трави́ть[1], **вы-** poison

трав|**и́ть**[2] persecute; '~**ля** persecution

тра́вма *med.* injury, trauma; ~**тологи́ческий**: ~**тологи́ческий пункт** outpatient unit dealing with injuries

траге́дия tragedy

тради́ция tradition

тра́ктор tractor; ~**и́ст** (~**ка**) tractor driver

трамва́й tram(-car)

трампли́н spring-board

транзи́стор transistor (radio)

транзи́т; ~**ный** transit(...)

трансля́ция broadcasting, transmitting

тра́нспорт (*vehicles*) transport; transportation

трап *mar., av.* gangway

тра́т|а expense; waste; **_ить**, **ис-**, **по-** spend; waste

тре́бован|ие demand; claim; requirement; **_ательный** exacting, exigent; **_ать**, **по-** (*P*) demand, require; (*B*) summon

трево́г|а alarm; anxiety; **_жить¹**, **по-** disturb; **_жить²**, **вс-** alarm, worry

тре́звый sober

тре́нер (*sports*) coach

тре́ние friction (*pl. a. fig.*)

тре́пет trembling, quivering; thrill; **_ать** tremble, quiver

треск crack; crackle; **_аться**, **по-** crack

треска́ cod

тре́снуть (*impf.* **треща́ть**) crack, split

тре́т|ий third; **_ь** *f* (*one*) third; **_ье** (*блю́до*) dessert

треуго́льник triangle

тре́фы *f/pl.* (*cards*) clubs

трёх... *in compounds* three-; **трёхэта́жный** three-storeyed

трёшка *coll.* three-rouble note

треща́ть (*pf.* **тре́снуть**) crack(le); creack; **_ина**

три three

трибу́на tribune, rostrum; (*sports*) stand

три́ггер *tech.* flip-flop

тридца́т|ый thirtieth; **_дцать** thirty; **_жды** three times; **_надцатый** thirteenth; **_надцать** thirteen; **_ста** three hundred

трикота́ж *collect.* knitwear

тро́г|ать, **тро́нуть** touch (*a. fig.*); **-ся** start, be off; *coll.* have a screw loose

тро́ица Trinity; Whitsun

тро́й|ка three (*as noun*); troika; **_но́й** triple

тролле́йбус trolley(-bus)

тро́нуть → **тро́гать**

тро́п|а́, **_инка** path

трост|ни́к reed; **са́харный _ни́к** sugar-cane; **_ь** *f* cane, walking-stick

тротуа́р pavement, side-walk

труб|а́ pipe; chimney; *mar.* funnel; *mus.* trumpet; **_ка** tube; (*tobacco-*) pipe; *tel.* receiver; **_опрово́д** pipe-line

труд labour; work; **с _о́м** with difficulty; **_ность** *f* difficulty; **_ный** difficult; **_ово́й** working...; **_оёмкий** labour...; **_оёмкий** labour-consuming; **_олюби́вый** industrious; **_ящийся** worker; *pl.* working people

труп dead body, corpse

трус(и́ха) coward

тру́с|ики, ~ы *m/pl.* panties, trunks, *Am.* shorts

тря́пка rag

трясти́ *v/t.* shake; ~сь (**от** P) shake, tremble, shiver (with)

туале́т toilet, lavatory

туго́й tight; taut

туда́ there; *биле́т ~ и обра́тно* return ticket

ту́ловище *anat.* trunk

тулу́п *mil.* sheepskin coat

тума́н mist, fog; ~ный misty, foggy; *fig.* vague

туне́ц tunny(-fish)

тунне́ль *m* tunnel

тупи́к blind alley; deadlock; ~о́й blunt; dull; slow-witted

тур (*sports*) round (*a. fig.*)

турба́за tourist hostel

туре́цкий Turkish

тури́ст(ка) tourist

турне́ *indecl.* trip

турни́р tournament

ту́р|ок Turk; ~ча́нка Turkish woman

ту́склый dim; (*metal*) tarnished

тут here

ту́фля shoe; slipper

ту́хнуть, по~ light: go out

ту́ча (black) cloud

ту́чный fat, stout; (*soil*) rich

тушёный stewed; ~и́ть[1] stew

туши́ть[2], по~ extinguish, put out

тща́тельный careful

тще́тный vain, futile

ты you *poet., eccl.* thou

ты́ква pumpkin

ты́сяча thousand; ~еле́тие millennium; ~ный thousandth; ... of many thousands

тьма dark(ness); *coll.* lots

тю́бик (*tooth-paste, etc.*) tube

тюк bale

тюле́нь *m zo.* seal

тюльпа́н tulip

тюрьма́ prison

тя́г|а *fig.* bent, propensity; ~остный painful, distressing; burdensome; ~оти́ть oppress, irk

тяжёлый heavy; hard; grave; '~есть *f* weight; burden; gravity; '~кий heavy; grave; painful

тяну́ть, по~ pull, draw; haul; ~ся stretch, extend; (**к** Д) reach for; strive after; *impf.* drag on

У

у (P) by, near; with, at the house of; *take, etc.* from; ~ *меня (есть)* (И) I have

убав|ля́ть, '~ить (В *or* P) diminish, reduce

убе|га́ть, ~жа́ть run away;

escape

убеди́тельный convincing; persuasive

убежа́ть → **убега́ть**

убе|жда́ть, **_ди́ть** convince; *impf. a.* try to convince; **_жде́ние** conviction, belief; persuasion

убе́жище refuge; *полити́ческое* political asylum

уби(ва́)ть kill; murder

уби́йство murder; **_ца** *m/f* murderer, **-ess**

уб(и)ра́ть take away; harvest; *room tidy*; **_ со стола́** clear the table

убо́гий poor; squalid

убо́р|ка harvesting; tidying up; **_ная** lavatory; *thea.* dressing-room; **_щица** office cleaner; charwoman

убра́ть → **убира́ть**

убы́|ль *f* decrease; **_ток** (*financial*) loss; *нести́* **_тки** incur losses; **_точный** unprofitable; (*mst. enterprises, state farms*) working at a loss

уважа́ть respect, esteem; **_ние** respect

уведом|ля́ть, **_омить** inform, notify

увезти́ → **увози́ть**

увели́чи(ва)ть increase; enlarge; magnify

увере́|ние assurance; **_нность** confidence; **_нный** assured, sure; confident; **_ять**, **_ить** assure (of *в* П); **-ся** become convinced (of *в* П)

увести́ → **уводи́ть**

уви́деть → **ви́деть**

увле|ка́тельный fascinating; **_ка́ть**, **_чь** carry away; fascinate; **-ся** be carried away; (T) be keen (on)

уводи́ть, **увести́** take or lead away

увози́ть, **увезти́** drive or take away

уволь|не́ние dismissal; **_ня́ть**, **_ить** dismiss; **_ня́ться**, **_иться** leave one's work

уга́д|ывать, **_а́ть** guess

угас|а́ть, **_нуть** *fire:* go out; *fig.* die away

углеро́д carbon

углово́й corner...

углуб|ля́ть, **_ить** deepen; *knowledge* extend; **-ся** deepen; (*в* В) go deep into, become absorbed in

угна́ть → **угоня́ть**

угнета́ть oppress; depress

угова́ривать, **_ори́ть** (*impf. a.* try to) persuade; **-ся** arrange; agree

уго́д|ливый obsequious; **_ный** agreeable, welcome; *как вам* **_но** as you like; *кто* **_но** anybody; *что* **_но** anything

угожда́ть, **_ди́ть** (Д *or на* В) please, oblige

у́гол corner; angle

уголо́вный criminal...

у́голь *m* coal; **_ный** coal...

угоня́ть, **угна́ть** (car) steal; (plane) hijack

у́горь m eel

угоща́ть, **-сти́ть** entertain, treat (to T); **-ще́ние** refreshments, fare

угро|жа́ть (Д) threaten, menace; **'-за** threat, menace

угро́зыск (= **уголо́вный ро́зыск**) Criminal Investigation Department

угрызе́ни|е: **-я со́вести** remorse

уда(ва́)ться turn out well; be a success; **мне удало́сь сде́лать э́то** I succeeded in doing it

удал|я́ть, **-и́ть** remove; send away; **tooth** extract; **-ся** (от P) move away; withdraw (from)

уда́р blow; stroke; **-е́ние** stress; **-я́ть**, **-и́ть** strike, hit; **-ся** (о B) bump (against)

уда́ча success; piece of luck; **-ный** successful; apt; lucky

удва́ивать(ся), **удво́ить(ся)** double

уде́рж|ивать, **-а́ть** retain, hold back; **-ся** hold one's ground; (от P) refrain (from)

удиви́тельный surprising, amazing; **-ле́ние** surprise, amazement; **-ля́ть**, **-и́ть** surprise, amaze; **-ся** (Д) be surprised (at), won-

der (at)

уди́ть fish, angle

удо́бный comfortable; convenient

удобре́ние fertilizer

удо́бство comfort; convenience

удовлетворе́ние satisfaction; **-и́тельный** satisfactory; **-я́ть**, **-и́ть** (B) satisfy; (Д) needs meet

удово́льствие pleasure

удостовере́ние certificate; attestation; **-е́ние ли́чности** identity card; **-я́ть**, **'-ить** certify; witness; **-ся** (в П) make sure of

у́дочка fishing-rod

удруча́ть, **-и́ть** dishearten

удуш|ли́вый stifling, suffocating; **-ье** suffocation; asthma

уедине́ние seclusion

уезжа́ть, **уе́хать** leave, depart (for **в** or **на** B)

уж[1] grass-snake

уж[2] → **уже́**

ужа́лить → **жа́лить**

у́жас horror, terror; **-а́ться**, **-ну́ться** be horrified (by P); **-а́ющий** horrifying; **-ный** horrible, terrible, awful

уже́ already; **- не(т)** no longer

у́же comp. of **у́зкий**

у́жин supper; **-ать**, по- have supper

у́зел knot; bundle

у́зкий narrow; (*garment*) tight

узна(ва́)ть know (again), recognize; learn, find out

узо́р pattern, design

у́зы f/pl. ties, bonds

уйти́ → **уходи́ть**

ука́з decree; **~а́ние** indication; instruction, direction; **~а́тель** m index; indicator; *доро́жный ~а́тель* road sign; **~ывать**, **~а́ть** (B) indicate; (*на* B) point at; point out

укла́д: **~ жи́зни** mode of life; **~ывать**, **уложи́ть** lay; put to bed; pack; **~ся** pack up; (*в* B) go into; keep within

укло́н slope; bias; **~е́ние** evasion; **~чивый** evasive; **~я́ться**, **~и́ться** (*от* P) evade

уко́л (pin-)prick; *med.* injection

укра́дкой *adv.* stealthily

Украи́н|а Ukraine; **2ец**, **2ка**; **2ский** Ukrainian

укра́сть → **красть**

укра́ш|**ать**, **'~сить** adorn, decorate

укрепл|**е́ние** strengthening; **~ля́ть**, **~и́ть** strengthen

укро́п *bot.* dill

укры́(ва́)ть cover; shelter; conceal; **~ся** cover o.s.; seek shelter; take cover

у́ксус vinegar

уку́с bite; (*insect*) sting;

~и́ть → **куса́ть**

уку́т(ыв)ать wrap or muffle up

ула́вливать, **улови́ть** *fig.* catch; perceive

ула́|живать, **~дить** settle, arrange

у́лей beehive

улет|**а́ть**, **~е́ть** fly away or off

ули́ка (piece of) evidence

ули́тка snail

у́лица street

у́личный street...

уло́в catch; **~ка** trick, subterfuge; **~и́ть** → **ула́вливать**

улучш|**а́ть**, **'~ить** improve, better; **~ся** improve, grow better; **~е́ние** improvement

улыб|**а́ться**, **~ну́ться** smile; **'~ка** smile

ум mind; intellect, wits; *прийти́ на ~* occur to one; *склад ~а́* mentality; **~е́лый** skilful, able; **~е́ние** skill, ability

уменьш|**а́ть**, **'~ить** diminish, lessen; **~ся** decrease, diminish

уме́ренный moderate; temperate

умере́ть → **умира́ть**

умер|**я́ть**, **'~ить** moderate; restrain

уме́рший dead

уме́стный pertinent; appropriate

уме́тс, с~ know (how

умира́ть

to …), be able (to)

умира́ть, умере́ть die

умножа́ть, '-ить multiply; -éние multiplication

у́мный intelligent, clever

умолка́ть, '-нуть fall silent; noise: stop

у́мственный intellectual, mental

умыва́льник washbasin; -ть(ся), умы́ть(ся) wash (o.s.)

у́мысел (mst. evil) intent(ion); '-шленный intentional

унести́ → уноси́ть

универма́г (= универса́льный магази́н) department store

универса́м (= универса́льный магази́н самообслу́живания) approx. supermarket

университе́т university

уни́жа́ть, '-зить humiliate; -ся abase o.s.

уничтожа́ть, '-ить destroy, annihilate

уноси́ть, унести́ carry or take away

уны|ва́ть lose heart; '-лый downcast; cheerless

упа́док decline, - ду́ха despondency

упако́в|ывать, -а́ть pack (up)

упа́сть → па́дать

упла́|та payment; -чивать, -ти́ть pay

уполномо́чи(ва)ть author-

ize

упомина́ть, упомяну́ть mention

упо́р prop, rest; в - pointblank; (stare) fixedly; (с)де́лать - (на В or П) lay special stress (on); -ный obstinate; stubborn; persistent

употребле́ние use, usage; -ля́ть, -и́ть use, apply

управле́ние government; control; administration; mus. conducting; -ля́ть (Т) govern; control; operate, steer; drive; mus. conduct

упражне́ние exercise; -я́ться (в, mus. на П) practise, Brit. practise

упраздня́ть, -и́ть abolish

упрёк reproach

упрека́ть, -ну́ть (в П) reproach (with)

упроща́ть, -сти́ть (over)simplify

упру́гий elastic

упря́миться be obstinate; -ство obstinacy; -ый obstinate

упуска́ть, -сти́ть let go or slip; miss, overlook; -ще́ние omission

уравни́ва|ть, -я́ть equalize

урага́н hurricane

ура́н uranium

у́ровень m level; standard

уро́д monster, ugly person; -ливый ugly

урожа́й harvest

урожён|ец, **_ка** (P) native (of)

уро́к lesson

усадьба farmstead; country-seat

уса́живать, **усади́ть** (B) seat; (T) plant(with)

уса́живаться, **усе́сться** take a seat; (*за* (B) set to *work, etc.*)

усва́ивать, **усво́ить** learn; adopt; assimilate

усе́рд|ие zeal; **_ный** zealous

усе́сться → **уса́живаться**

усили|(ва́ть strengthen; intensify; increase; aggravate; **_е** effort; **'_тель** *tech.* amplifier

ускор|я́ть, **'_ить** speed up; accelerate

усла́|вливаться, **_виться** (*о* П) arrange; agree on

усло́в|ие condition; **_ный** conditional; (*sign*) conventional

усложне́ние complication; **_я́ть**, **_и́ть** complicate

услу́|га (*good or ill*) turn; *pl.* services; **_жливый** obliging

услы́шать → **слы́шать**

усма́тривать, **усмотре́ть** notice, discern; see (in)

усмир|я́ть, **_и́ть** pacify; *rebellion* suppress

усмотре́|ть → **усма́тривать**; **_ть** discretion; **_ть** → **усма́тривать**

усну́ть *pf.* fall asleep

усоверше́нствовать → **соверше́нствовать**

усомни́ться → **сомнева́ться**

успе́|(ва́)ть find time (to); (*на* B) be in time for

успе́|х success; *pl. a.* progress; **_шный** successful

успока́|ивать, **_оить** calm, soothe; **_оительный** soothing; (*news*) reassuring

уста́в statutes, rules, regulations; *pol.* charter

уста|(ва́)ть get tired; **_лый** tired

устан|а́вливать, **_ови́ть** instal; establish; fix; mount; **_о́вка** installation; **_о́вка** mounting; directions

устаре́лый obsolete

уста́ть → **устава́ть**

у́стный oral

усто́йчивый steady, stable

устоя́ть *pf.* keep one's balance; stand one's ground; (*про́тив* P) resist

устра́ивать, **устро́ить** arrange; establish; place, fix up; **-ся** settle (down); come right

устран|я́ть, **_и́ть** remove; eliminate; **-ся** (*от* P) keep (away) from

устрем|ля́ть, **_и́ть** direct; **-ся** rush; head for; *look:* be turned; turn, direct

у́стрица oyster

устро́ить → устра́ивать

устро́йство arrangement; device; structure, system; **счи́тывающее** ~ tech. reader

уступ|а́ть, ~и́ть (B) give up; cede; (Д) yield; give in; ~**ка** concession

у́стье geogr. mouth

усы́ m/pl. moustache; (cat) whiskers

усып|ля́ть, ~и́ть lull (to sleep); med. put to sleep

утвер|ди́тельный affirmative; ~жда́ть, ~ди́ть confirm, approve; impf. affirm; ~жде́ние confirmation; assertion

утёс rock; cliff

утеш|а́ть, ~и́ть console, comfort; ~е́ние consolation; ~и́тельный comforting

утиха́ть, ~нуть quiet down

у́тка duck

утол|я́ть, ~и́ть hunger satisfy; thirst quench

утом|и́тельный tiresome; ~ля́ть, ~и́ть tire, weary

уточн|я́ть, ~и́ть make more precise, specify

утра́|та loss; ~чивать, ~тить lose; right forfeit

у́тренний morning...; ~енник morning performance or party for children; ~о morning; ~ом in the morning

утру|жда́ть, ~ди́ть trouble

утю́г (flat-)iron; ~жить,

вы́- iron, press

уха́ fish-soup

уха́живать (за T) nurse; woman court

у́хо ear

ухо́д[1] (за T) nursing; care (of); maintenance

ухо́д[2] going away; departure; ~и́ть, уйти́ go away; (с P) leave; (от P) escape; (на B) be spent on; ~ **на пе́нсию** retire

ухудш|а́ть, ~и́ть make worse; ~ся grow worse

участ|вовать (в П) participate (in); ~ие participation; sympathy; ~ник, ~ница participant, member; ~ок plot (of land); part

у́часть f lot, fate

уча́щийся student; pupil

уче́б|ник text-book; ~ный educational; training...; ~ный год school year, academic year; ~ное заведе́ние educational institution; ~е́ние learning; apprenticeship; doctrine; ~ени́к, ~ени́ца pupil; ~ёный adj. learned; noun scholar; ~ёная сте́пень (university) degree

уче́сть → учи́тывать

учёт calculation; stock-taking; registration; consideration

учи́|лище school (providing professional education at

secondary or, sometimes, higher level); **вое́нное ~лище** military (high) school; **профессиона́льно-техни́ческое ~ лище (ПТУ)** technical school; **~тель(ница)** *m* teacher

учи́тывать, **уче́сть** consider, take into account

учи́ть[1], **вы́**~ learn; **~**[2], **на**~ teach (*something* **чему́-нибудь**); **-ся** (Д) learn, study

учре|**жда́ть**, **~ди́ть** found, establish; **~жде́ние**

founding; institution

у́ш|**и** *pl.* of **у́хо**; **~ко́** (*needle*) eye; **~но́й** ear...

уши́б injury; bruise; **~а́ться**, **~и́ться** hurt o.s.; bruise o.s.

уще́лье ravine

уще́рб damage, detriment

ую́т cosiness; comfort; **~ный** cosy; comfortable

уязви́мый vulnerable; **~ое ме́сто** weak spot

уясня́ть, **~и́ть** (*себе́*) size up, understand

Ф

фа́бр|**ика** factory, mill; **~икова́ть**, **с-** *fig.* fabricate; **~и́чный** factory...; manufactured

фаза́н pheasant

файл *tech.* file

фа́кел torch

факт fact; **~и́ческий** factual; virtual

факульте́т *univ.* faculty, department

фальши́вый false, spurious; forged

фами́лия surname

фане́ра veneer; plywood

фанта́зия fantasy; imagination

фанта́стика *coll.* something unbelievable; **нау́чная ~** science fiction

фа́ра headlight

фа́ртук apron

фарфо́р china, porcelain

фарш *cul.* minced meat; stuffing

фасо́ль *f* French bean(s)

фасо́н cut (*style in clothing*); fashion

февра́ль *m* February

федера́ция federation

фейерве́рк fireworks

фельето́н satirical article

фен hair-drier

ферзь *m* (*chess*) queen

фе́рм|**а** farm; **~ер** farmer; **~ерство** farming

фестива́ль *m* festival

фетр felt

фехтова́ть (*sports*) fence

фиа́лка *bot.* violet

фигу́р|**а** figure; shape; chess-man; **~и́ст(ка)** figure skater; **~ный: ~ное катáние** figure skating

физик physicist; **~a** physics

физкультýра (= **физи́ческая культýра**) physical training

филé(й) *n indecl.* fillet

филиáл branch

филóсоф philosopher; **~ия** philosophy

фильм (*cinema*) film; **документáльный ~** documentary film; **мультипликацио́нный ~** cartoon; **худóжественный ~** feature film

финáл finale; (*sports*) final

фи́ник *bot.* date

фи́ниш (*sports*) finish; final lap

фин|н, ~ка Finn; **~ский** Finnish

фиолéтовый violet

фи́рма *comm.* firm

флаг flag (*a. tech*)

флакóн (scent-)bottle

фланéль (*cloth*) flannel

флéйта flute

фломáстер felt-tip pen

флот fleet; **воéнно-морскóй ~** navy

фля́жка flask

фойé *indecl.* foyer

фóкус[1] focus

фóкус[2] (conjuring) trick;

~ник conjurer

фольгá foil

фон background

фонáр|ик torch, flash-light; **~ m** lantern; **у́личный ~ь** street lamp

фонд *comm.* fund; stock, reserves; **~овый: ~овая би́ржа** stock exchange

фонтáн fountain

фóрм|а form; mould; *mil.* uniform; **~áльный** formal; **~енный** uniform...; *coll.* downright

фóто *n indecl.* photograph; **~аппарáт** camera; **~граф** photographer; **~графи́ровать, с-** photograph; **~графия** photograph(y); **~плёнка** film

Францýженка French woman; **~ýз** Frenchman; **~ýзский** French

фрахт freight

фрéска fresco

фронт *mil., fig.* front

фрукт fruit; **~о́вый: ~о́вый сад** orchard

фунт pound (*a. fin.*)

фурáжка (peak-)cap

футбóл football; **~и́ст** football player; **~ка** T-shirt, sports shirt

футля́р case

X

хала́т dressing-gown; overalls; doctor's smock

хала́тность carelessness, negligence

хара́ктер character; temper; **_ный** characteristic; typical

хвали́ть, по- praise

хва́ст|аться, по- (T) boast (of); **_ли́вый** boastful

хвата́ть¹, схвати́ть snatch, seize; **-ся (за** B) snatch or catch (at)

хвата́ть², хвати́ть suffice, be enough

хво́йный coniferous

хво́рост brushwood

хвост tail

хво́я bot. needles

хи́лый sickly; punny

хи́м|ик chemist; **_и́ческий** chemical; **_ия** chemistry; **_чи́стка** dry-cleaning

хиру́рг surgeon

хитр|и́ть, с- use cunning; **'_ость** f cunning; slyness; **_оу́мный** cunning; resourceful; complicated; **'_ый** cunning, sly; intricate

хи́щник beast or bird of prey

хладнокро́вн|ый cool, composed; **_о** cooly; in cold blood

хлам trash

хлеб bread; loaf; **_а́** m/pl. corn, grain; **'_ный**

bread...; corn...

хлебосо́л(ка) hospitable person

хлев cattle-shed; fig. pigsty

хло́п|ать, _нуть (T) flap; door slam; **_ать глаза́ми** look blank; **_ать в ладо́ши** clap one's hands

хло́пок cotton

хлопота́ть, по- (о П) solicit; **(за** B) intercede for; impf. take trouble

хло́поты f/pl. trouble; efforts (on s.o.'s behalf); bustle

хлопчатобума́жный cotton...

хло́пья m/pl. flakes; (wool) flocks

хмель m bot. hop; coll. intoxication

хму́рый gloomy

хо́бби hobby

хо́бот zo. trunk

ход course; pace; motion; move; **бы́ть в _у́** be in vogue or demand; **по́лным _ом** fig. in full swing; **_ мы́сли** train of thought

ходи́ть¹, идти́ (impf.), pf. **пойти́** go; walk; → **идти́; - с** (P) card play; (T) chessman move

ходи́ть²: - в (П) wear

хо́дкий coll. selling well

хозя́ин landlord; owner; host; master

хозя́й|ка landlady; hostess;

mistress; **-ничать** keep house; boss it; **-ство** economy; household; farm

хоккей hockey; **~ с шайбой** ice hockey

холм hill(ock)

хо́лод cold(ness); **-а́ть, -е́ть, по-** grow cold; **-и́льник** refrigerator; **-ный** cold

холосто́й unmarried; tech. idle; **-я́к** bachelor

холст canvas

хор chorus, choir

хорони́ть, по- bury

хоро́ш|ий good, fine; **-о́** it is fine; all right; adv. well

хоте́ть, за- (B or P or inf.) want; **мне хо́чется** I want

хоть at least; if you like; = **-я́; -я́** though; **-я́ бы** even if

хо́хот (loud) laughter; **-а́ть** roar with laughter

хра́бр|ость f bravery, valour; **-ый** brave, valiant

храм arch. temple; church

хране́ние keeping, storage; **-и́лище** storehouse; **-и́ть** keep; treasure; pre-

serve; store (a. tech.)

храпе́ть snore; snort

хребе́т mountain-ridge; anat. spine

хрен horse-radish

хри́п|лый hoarse; **-нуть, о-** get hoarse

христиан|и́н, '-ка, adj. **'-ский** Christian

Христо́с Christ

хром|а́ть limp; **-о́й** lame

хро́ника chronicle; (cinema) newsreel

хру́пкий frail; brittle; delicate

хруста́ль m crystal; cut glass; cut-glass ware

хрусте́ть, '-нуть crunch

хрящ cartilage; gristle

худе́ть, по- grow thin

худо́ж|ественный artistic; **-ественная литерату́ра** fiction; **-ник, -ница** artist, painter

худо́|й, '-щавый lean; thin; **на -й коне́ц** if the worst comes to the worst

ху́дший worse or worst

ху́же (it is) worse (a. adv.)

хулига́н hooligan

хурма́ bot. persimmon

Ц

цара́п|ать¹, по- scratch; **-ать², на-** scribble; **-ина** scratch, abrasion

царе́вич tsar's son; **-ёвна** tsar's daughter; **-и́ца**

tsar's wife; empress of Russia; **'-ство** kingdom, realm; **'-ствовать** reign; **-ь** m tsar; fig. king

цвести́ bloom, flower; be

in blossom

цвет, *pl.* **_á** colour; *fig. sg. only:* flower, cream; **в _ý** in bloom; **_ной** colour(ed); (metal) non-ferrous; **_ная капуста** cauliflower; **_ók** flower; **_ы́** *pl.* of **_ók**

целе́бный salubrious; curative; healing

целесообра́зный expedient; **_устремлённый** purposeful

целико́м *adv.* wholly

целина́ virgin soil

це́лить(ся) (в В) aim (at)

целова́ть, по_ kiss; **_ся** *v/i.* kiss

це́лый whole; intact; unbroken

цель *f* aim; purpose; object; target

цен|а́ price; value; worth;

_и́ть value; appreciate; **_ность** *f* value; *pl.* valuables; **_ный** valuable

цензу́ра censorship

центр centre; **_а́льный** central

цепь *f* chain; *el.* circuit

це́рковь *f* church

цех *tech.* shop, department

цирк circus

цити́ровать, про_ quote

цифербла́т face; dial

ци́фра figure, cipher

цифров|о́й: **_ы́е да́нные** digital data; **_во́й код** numerical code

ЦК (= **Центра́льный Комите́т**) *hist.* Central Committee

цыга́н|(ка), *adj.* **_ский** Gipsy

цыплёнок chick(en)

Ч

чай tea; **дать на _** give a tip

ча́йка sea-gull

ча́йник tea-pot; tea-kettle

час hour; **кото́рый _?** what is the time?; **в _** at one p.m.; **_о́вня** chapel; **_ово́й** *adj.* clock...; watch; an hour's; *noun* sentry; **_овщи́к** watchmaker

ча́стник *coll.* owner of a small business; self-employed person

ча́стн|ость *f* particular (-ity); detail; **в _ости** in particular; **_ый** private; particular

ча́сто *adv.* often; **_ый** frequent

часть *f* part; *mil.* unit; **_ю** partly

часы́ *m/pl.* watch; clock

ча́хнуть wither away; pine

ча́ша cup, chalice; (scales) pan; **_ка** (tea-) cup (-ful); **коле́нная _ечка** knee-cap

ча́ща thicket

ча́ще more often; ~ всего́ mostly

чего́ → что

чей, чья, чьё, pl. **чьи** whose

чек fin. cheque, check; (in shops, etc.) bill, chit; receipt

челове́к human being, person, man; ~ческий human(e); ~чество mankind; ~чность f humanity, humaneness; ~чный humane

че́люсть f jaw; **вставна́я** ~ denture

чем¹ → что

чем² conj. than; ~ бо́льше, тем лу́чше the more, the better

чём → что

чемода́н suitcase

чемпио́н (sports) champion; ~а́т championship

чему́ → что

чепуха́ coll. rot, rubbish

че́рви (cards) hearts

червя́к worm

черда́к garret

чередова́ться alternate; take turns

че́рез (B) across, over; through (a. fig.); (time) in, after; ~ день every other day

черёмуха bird cherry

че́реп skull; ~а́ха tortoise(-shell); ~и́ца (roofing) tile

чересчу́р too (much)

чере́шня cherry (-tree)

черни́ка blue|berries, -berry; ~и́ла n/pl. ink; ~ови́к rough copy; draft; ~ово́й rough; draft...

черно|зём agr. black earth; ~мо́рский Black Sea...; ~сли́в collect. prunes

чёрный black; ~ ход back entrance; на ~ день for a rainy day

чёрствый stale, dry; fig. hard-hearted

чёрт devil

черта́ line, stroke; trait; (face) feature; ~ёж drawing, draft, design; ~и́ть, на- draw, design

чеса́ть, по- scratch; impf. comb, **-ся** scratch o.s.; impf. itch; comb (v/i.); ~но́к garlic

че́ст|ность f honesty; ~ный honest; ~ное сло́во word of honour; ~ь f honour

честолюби́вый ambitious; ~ие ambition

четве́рг Thursday; ~ёрка (bus, tram, etc.) number four; (school-mark) good; (cards) four; ~ёртый fourth; ~ерть f (a) quarter; (one) forth; (school) term

чёткий clear, accurate; legible

чётный even (number)

четы́ре four; ~ста four

hundred

четырёх... *in compounds* four-...: **~мото́рный** four-engined

четы́рнадцатый fourteenth; **~ь** fourteen

чех Czech

чехо́л case; slip-cover

чечеви́ца lentil

че́шка Czech woman; **~ский** Czech

чешуя́ *no pl.*, *zo.* scale(s)

чини́ть¹, по- repair; **~², о-** sharpen, point

чино́вник official; functionary, bureaucrat

чи́сленность *f* number, quantity; **~о́** number; **в том ~é** including; **како́е сего́дня ~о́?** what is the date today?

чи́стить, по- clean; brush; *fruit* peel; *fish* scale; **~ка** cleaning

чисто|кро́вный thoroughbred; **~пло́тный** cleanly; **~серде́чный** candid

чистота́ clean(li)ness; **~ый** clean; pure; clear; sheer

чита́тель(ница) *m* reader; **~ать, про-** *a.* **проче́сть** read

чиха́ть, ~ну́ть sneeze

член member; limb; **~ский** membership...; **~ство** membership

чо́порный prim

чрезвыча́йный extraordinary; **~выча́йные ме́ры**

emergency measures; **~вычайное положе́ние** state of emergency; **~ме́рный** excessive

чте́ние reading; **~ лекций** lecturing

чтить honour

что what; *conj.* that; *adv.* why; (Р = **чего́;** Д = **чему́;** В = **что;** Т = **чем;** П = **чём**)

чтоб *a.* **что́бы** in order to, so as; that

что́|-либо, ~-нибудь something; anything; **~-то** something (definite); *adv.* somewhat; somehow

чу́вств|енный sensual; **~и́тельный** sensible; sensitive; sentimental; considerable; **~о** feeling; **~овать, по-** feel; **~овать себя́** feel (*better etc.*)

чугу́н cast iron

чуд|а́к, ~а́чка odd person; **~е́сный** wonderful; miraculous; **~ный** wonderful; **~о** miracle; wonder; **~о́вище** monster

чу́ждый alien

чужо́й somebody else's; strange, foreign

чуло́к stocking

чу́т|кий sensitive, keen; tactful; **~ь** *adv.* slightly; hardly; **~ь не** nearly; almost; **~ьё** *zo.* scent; *fig.* flair, intuition

чу́чело stuffed animal *or* bird; scarecrow

чуять, по~ scent, smell; *fig.* feel

чьё, чьи, чья →чей

Ш

шаг step, stride; pace; **~áть** step; **~нýть** *pf.* make a step; **'~ом** *adv.* at a walking pace

шáйба (*sports*) puck; *tech.* washer

шáйка gang, band

шалúть play pranks; be naughty; **'~ость** *f* prank; **~ýн(ья)** naughty boy (girl)

шаль *f* shawl

шампáнское champagne

шампýнь *m* shampoo

шанс chance

шантáж blackmail

шáпка cap

шар ball, sphere; **воздýшный ~** balloon; **земнóй ~** terrestrial globe, the Earth

шарж (well-meant) cartoon *or* caricature

шарф scarf

шатáться *v/i.* stagger; screw, *etc.*: get loose; *coll.* loaf; **'~кий** shaky; unsteady

шах shah; check; **~ и мат** checkmate; **~мáтист(ка)** chessplayer; **'~матный** chess...; **'~маты** *f/pl.* chess; *a.* chess-men

шáхта mine, pit; **~ёр** miner

шáшки *f/pl.* draughts, checkers

швéд(ка) Swede; **~ский** Swedish

швéйный sewing...

швейцáр doorkeeper; **~ец, ~ка;** **~ский** Swiss

швыря́ть, ~нýть hurl, fling

шевелúть, ~ьнýть (T *or* B) stir; **~ся** *v/i.* stir, move

шедéвр masterpiece

шéлест rustling

шёлк silk; **~овый** silk...; silken

шелухá *no pl.* husk(s); peel(s)

шёпот whisper

шептáть, про~, шепнýть whisper

шероховáтый rough (*a. fig.*)

шерсть *f* wool; *zo.* hair; **~яной** woollen; wool...

шершáвый rough; rugged

шест pole (*a.* sports)

шестёрка (*cards*) six; (*bus, tram, etc.*) number six; six-oar boat

шестидеся́тый sixtieth

шестнáдцатый sixteenth; **~ь** sixteen

шестóй sixth

шесть six; **~деся́т** sixty; **~сóт** six hundred

ше́я neck
ши́на tyre; *med.* splint
шине́ль *f mil.* greatcoat
шип thorn; _о́вник dog-rose
шип|е́ть, про- hiss; *impf.* sizzle; fizz; _у́чий fizzy
ширина́ width, breadth; _о́кий wide, broad (*a. fig.*); _ота́ width, breadth; *geogr.* latitude
шить, с_ sew
шитьё sewing; needle-work
шифр (*code*) cipher; press-mark
ши́шка *bot.* cone; bump *on head, etc.*; *coll.* big-wig
шкаф cupboard; wardrobe; *кни́жный* _ bookcase
шко́л|а school; *сре́дняя* _а secondary school; *вы́сшая* _а collect. institutions of higher education; _ник, _ьница school|boy, _-girl; _ьный school...
шку́ра hide, skin
шлагба́ум barrier (*at rail or road crossing*)
шланг hose
шлем helmet
шлюз sluice, lock
шля́па hat
шнур cord; _о́к (shoe-)lace
шов seam; *med.* suture
шокола́д chocolate
шо́рох rustle
шо́рты shorts
шоссе́ *n indecl.* highway

шотла́нд|ец, _ка; Scotch-|man, -woman; _ский Scotch; _ия Scotland
шпага́т string, cord
шпи́лька hair-pin
шпина́т spinach
шпио́н|(ка) spy; _ить (*за* T) spy (*on*)
шприц *med.* syringe
шпро́ты sprats (*smoked and tinned in oil*)
шрам scar
шрифт print, type
штаб *mil.* staff; _кварти́ра headquarters
штанги́ст weight-lifter
штаны́ *m/pl.* trousers
штат¹ (*federation*) state
штат² (*employees*) staff; _ный regular, on staff; _ский civilian *a. noun*
штемпель *m* stamp; *почто́вый* _ postmark
ште́псель *m el.* plug
што́пать, за_ darn
што́пор corkscrew
што́ра (window-)blind
шторм *mar.* storm
штраф fine; penalty; _но́й: _но́й уда́р penalty kick
шту́ка piece; item; one of a kind; *coll.* thing
штурм *mil.* storm, assault
шу́ба fur-coat
шум noise; (up)roar; _е́ть make a noise; roar; _ный noisy; boisterous; loud
шу́рин brother-in-law (*wife's brother*)
шут|и́ть joke; (*над* T)

make fun of; (*c* T) trifle with; '**-ка** joke; **-ли́вый**

joking, playful

Щ

щади́ть, по- (*mercifully*) spare
ще́бень *m* road metal
щебета́ть twitter
щего́ля|ть, -ьну́ть (T) show off, parade
ще́дрый generous
щека́ cheek
щекота́ть *v/t.* tickle
щель *f* crack; chink; crevice
щено́к puppy
щепети́льный (over-) scrupulous

ще́пка (wooden) chip
щети́на bristle
щётка brush
щи *pl.* shchi (*cabbage soup*)
щи́кол(от)ка ankle
щип|а́ть, -ну́ть pinch; **-цы́** *m/pl.* tongs
щит shield; *распредели́тельный* - switchboard
щу́ка *zo.* pike
щу́пать, по- touch, finger
щу́риться screw up one's eyes

Э

эваку|и́ровать (*im*)*pf.* evacuate
ЭВМ (= *электро́нно-вычисли́тельная маши́на*) computer
эква́тор equator
экза́мен examination; *сдава́ть* - take an examination; *сдать* - pass an examination; **-ова́ть, про-** examine
экземпля́р specimen; copy
экипа́ж (*aircraft, ship*) crew
эколог|и́ческий ecological; **-ия** ecology
эконо́м|ика economics;

economy; **-ить, с-** economize; **-ия** economy; **-ный** economical; thrifty
экра́н screen
экску́рс|ия excursion; **-ово́д** guide
экспеди́ция expedition
экспе́рт expert; **-и́за** (*expert*) examination; commission of experts
экспона́т exhibit
э́кспорт export; **-и́ровать** (*im*)*pf.* export
э́кстренный urgent; emergency; extra, special
электр|ик electrician; **-и́че-**

ский electric(al); **~йчество** electricity; **~йчка** *coll.* suburban electric train

электро́ника electronics

электроста́нция power station

элемента́рный elementary

эма́ль *f* enamel

эмба́рго *econ.* embargo; **наложи́ть ~ (на** B) place an embargo (on)

эмигра́нт(ка) emigrant; **~ция** emigration; *collect.*, *coll.* emigrants

энерги́чный energetic; **~ия** energy

энциклопе́дия encyclopaedia

эпиде́мия epidemic

эпо́ха epoch

э́р|а era; **до на́шей ~ы** Before Christ (BC); **на́шей ~ы** A.D.

эроти́ческий erotic

эруди́ция erudition

эскала́тор escalator

эскало́п *cul.* pork cutlet

эски́з sketch

эстафе́та (*sports*) relay

эстра́да platform; variety art

эта́ж floor, storey

эта́п stage, phase; (*sports*) lap

этике́тка label

э́тот (**э́та**, **э́то**, *pl.* **э́ти**) this; **э́то мои́ кни́ги** these are my books; **что э́то?** what is that?

эфи́р ether; *fig.* air; **передава́ть в ~** broadcast

эффект|и́вный effective; **~ный** spectacular

Ю

юбиле́й jubilee

ю́бка skirt

ювели́р jeweller

юг south

югосла́в, ~ка; ~ский Yugoslav(ian)

ю́жный south...; southern

ю́мор humour

ю́н|ость *f* youth, young years; **~оша** *m* youth; **~ый** youthful; young

юриди́ческий juridical; legal; **~ая консульта́ция** (office); **~ий факульте́т** *univ.* faculty of law

юри́ст lawyer; student of law

юсти́ция (*law*) justice

Я

я I
я́бло|ко apple; **~ня** apple-tree; **~чный** apple...
я́в|ка appearance, attendance; **~ле́ние** phenomenon; **~ля́ться**, **~и́ться** appear; come, arrive; (T) be; **~ный** evident
ягнёнок lamb
я́года berry
яд poison; venom; **~ови́тый** poisonous; venomous (a. fig.)
я́дерный phys. nuclear
ядро́ kernel; nucleus; **толка́ть ~** (sports) put the shot
я́зв|а ulcer; fig. sore; **~и́тельный** caustic, biting
язы́к tongue; language
яи́чница-болту́нья scrambled eggs; **~(-глазу́нья)** fried eggs
яйцо́ egg
я́корь m anchor

я́м|а pit, hole; **~очка** dimple
янва́рь m January
янта́рь m amber
япо́н|ец, **~ка**; **~ский** Japanese; **2ия** Japan
я́ркий bright; vivid; outstanding
ярлы́к label, tag
я́рмарка comm. fair
я́рость f fury, rage
я́рус thea. circle
я́сли f/pl. day nursery, crèche
я́сный clear; serene; distinct
я́стреб hawk
я́хта yacht
яче́йка cell; **~ па́мяти** tech. location, storage cell
ячме́нь m barley; med. sty
я́щерица lizard
я́щик box, chest; **выдвижно́й ~** drawer; **почто́вый ~** letter-box, pillar-box

A

a *The indefinite article does not exist in Russian. It remains untranslated*: **a table** стол; **an apple** я́блоко; **twice a day** два ра́за в день

aback: **taken ~** поражённый

abandon *leave* покида́ть [-и́нуть]; (*give up*) отка́зываться [-за́ться] от (P); **~ o.s. to** пред(ав)а́ться (Д)

abash смуща́ть [смути́ть]

abate уменьша́ть(ся) ['-ши́ть(ся)]; *pain*: ослабева́ть ['-бну́ть] жа́ть [сни́зить]; *storm*: стиха́ть ['-хнуть]

abb|ey абба́тство; **~ot** абба́т

abbreviat|e сокраща́ть [-рати́ть]; **~ion** сокраще́ние

ABC а́збука; буква́рь

abdicat|e *v/t.* отрека́ться [-е́чься] (от P); *v/i.* отрека́ться от престо́ла; **~ion** отрече́ние (от престо́ла)

abdomen брюшна́я по́лость, *coll.* живо́т; (*insect*) брюшко́

abide (*tolerate*) терпе́ть *impf.*; **~ by** приде́рживаться (P)

ability спосо́бность *f*; уме́ние

abject жа́лкий; **~ poverty** нищета́

able спосо́бный; **be ~** [с]мочь, быть в состоя́нии

abnormal ненорма́льный

aboard на борту́, на́ борт

abode жили́ще

aboli|sh отменя́ть[-ни́ть]; **~tion** отме́на

A-bomb а́томная бо́мба

abominable отврати́тельный

aboriginal иско́нный, коренно́й

abort|ion або́рт, вы́кидыш; **~ive** неуда́чный

abound (*in*) изоби́ловать (Т)

about (*approximately*) приблизи́тельно, приме́рно; (*tell, speak*) о (П); **be ~ to** + *inf.* соб(и)ра́ться + *inf.*

above над (Т); *fig.* вы́ше (P), сверх (P); *adv.* наверху́; вы́ше; **~ all** пре́жде всего́

abreast: **keep ~ of** идти́ в но́гу (с Т)

abridge сокраща́ть [-рати́ть]; **~ment** сокраще́-

ние; сокращённое издание

abroad за границей, за границу; *from ~* из-за границы

abrupt (*unexpected*) крутой, резкий; (*manner*) резкий, грубый; (*slope*) крутой

abscess нарыв

absen|ce отсутствие; **~ce of mind** рассеянность *f*; **~t** отсутствующий; **~t-minded** рассеянный

absolut|e абсолютный; **~ely** совершенно; категорически

absolve *~ from* (*sins*) отпускать [-стить] (B); (*promise*) освобождать [-бодить] (от P)

absor|b *liquid* впитывать [-тать] (*a. fig.*); **~bed in** *fig.* погружённый в (B); **~ption** впитывание; погружённость *f*

abstain (*from*) воздерживаться [-жаться] (от P)

abstention воздержание; *the motion was carried with two ~s* предложение было принято при двух воздержавшихся

abstinen|ce воздержание; **~t** воздержанный, умеренный

abstract отвлечённый, абстрактный; (*summary*) краткий обзор; резюме

absurd абсурдный, нелепый; **~ity** абсурд, неле-

пость *f*

abundan|ce (из)обилие; **~t** (из)обильный

abus|e злоупотреблять [-бить] (T); (*scold*) бранить; злоупотребление; брань *f*; **~ive** оскорбительный; **~ive language** брань

abyss пропасть *f*

acacia акация

academ|ic академический; **~ician** академик; **~y** академия

accelerat|e ускорять ['-рить']; **~ion** ускорение; **~or** *mot.* педаль газа

accent акцент; (*stress*) ударение; **~uate** акцентировать (*im*)*pf.*

accept принимать [-нять]; **~able** приемлемый; **~ance** принятие

access доступ; **~ible** доступный; **~ory** *jur.* соучастник; **~ories** принадлежности *f/pl.*; аксессуары

accident несчастный случай, авария; (*chance*) случайность *f*; **~al** случайный

acclaim шумно приветствовать

acclimatize акклиматизировать (*im*)*pf.*; **become ~d** акклиматизироваться

accommodat|e (*adapt*) приспособлять ['-бить']; (*provide lodging*) помещáть [-ести́ть], устрáивать [-ро́ить]; (billet) размещáть [-ести́ть]; (hold) вмещáть; **~ion** приспособле́ние; (room) помеще́ние; (action) размеще́ние

accompan|iment mus. сопровожде́ние, аккомпанемéнт (a. fig.); **~y** сопровождáть; аккомпани́ровать (Д)

accomplice соо́бщни|к, -ца

accomplish совершáть [-ши́ть]; **~ed** fig. превосхо́дный; **~ment** выполне́ние, заверше́ние; (feat) достиже́ние; pl. талáнты m/pl., достои́нства n/pl.

accord соглáсие; mus. аккóрд, созву́чие; соглáсовываться (im)pf.; (grant) предоставля́ть ['-вить]; **of one's own** ~ доброво́льно; **~ance** соотвéтствие; **~ing to** соглáсно (Д)

account отчёт (a. fig.); (description) сообще́ние, описáние; fin. счёт; **on no** ~ ни в кóем слу́чае; ~ **of** из-за (Р); **~ for** объясня́ть [-ни́ть]; **take** ~ **of** учи́тывать [уче́сть] (В)

accredit аккредитовáть (im)pf.

accretion приро́ст

accrue нарастáть [-сти́]

accumulat|e накáпливать (-ся) [-пи́ть(ся)]; **~ion** накопле́ние; **~or** аккумуля́тор

accura|cy тóчность f, аккурáтность f; **~te** тóчный, аккурáтный

accursed прокля́тый

accus|ation обвине́ние; **~ative** вини́тельный падéж; **~e** обвиня́ть [-ни́ть] (**of** в П)

accustom (**to**) приучáть [-чи́ть] (к Д); **get** ~**ed** (**to**) привыкáть ['-кнуть] (к Д)

ace (cards) туз; (pilot) ас

acerbity тéрпкость f

ache болéть (3. ps. sg. боли́т); боль f

achieve достигáть [-и́чь or -и́гнуть]; **~ment** достиже́ние

acid кислотá; ки́слый

acknowledge (admit) призн(ав)áть; receipt подтверждáть ['-рди́ть]; **~ment** признáние; подтвержде́ние

acorn жёлудь m

acoustic акусти́ческий; **~s** акýстика

acquaint [по]знакóмить; ~ **o.s. with** ознакóмиться (с Т); **~ance** знакóм|ый, -ая; знакóмство; **~ed: be ~ed with** быть знакóмым с (Т)

acquire приобретáть [-ести́]; **~ment** приобрете́ние

acquistion приобрете́ние

acquit jur. опрáвдывать [-дáть]; **~tal** оправдáние

acre акр (= 0,4 га)

acrid éдкий

across че́рез (В); попере́к (Р), *a. adv.*; по той стороне́, на ту сто́рону (Р), *a. adv.*

act акт, де́йствие (*a. thea.*); (*behaviour*) посту́пок; (*operate*) де́йствовать; поступа́ть [-пи́ть]; **~ing** *thea.* игра́; **~ion** де́йствие; *mil.* бой; **~ive** де́ятельный, акти́вный, энерги́чный; **~ivity** де́ятельность *f*; **~or** актёр; **~ress** актри́са; **~ual** действи́тельный; **~ually** факти́чески; на са́мом де́ле

acute о́стрый

adapt приспособля́ть ['-бить]; *text* адапти́ровать; **~ability** приспособля́емость *f*; **~ation** приспособле́ние; (*literary*) обрабо́тка; (*organism*) адапта́ция

add до-, прибавля́ть ['-вить]; **~ition** до-, приба́вле́ние; *math.* сложе́ние; *in* **~ition** вдоба́вок; **~itional** доба́вочный, дополни́тельный

address а́дрес; (*speech*) обраще́ние; (*skill*) обраще́ние *f*; адресова́ть (*im*)*pf.*, обраща́ться [-рати́ться] (к Д)

adequate адеква́тный; (*enough*) доста́точный

adhe|re (*to*) прилипа́ть ['-пнуть] (к Д); *fig.* приде́рживаться (Р); **~rent**

приве́рженец; **~sive** ли́пкий; **~sive plaster** лейкопла́стырь *m*; **~sive tape** кле́йкая ле́нта

adjacent смежный

adjective (и́мя) прилага́тельное

adjoin примыка́ть (к Д)

adjourn переноси́ть [-нести́]; (*break*) переры́в

adjust прила́живать [-ла́дить]; подгоня́ть [-догна́ть], пригоня́ть [-гна́ть]; **~ment** подго́нка, приго́нка

administ|er управля́ть, руководи́ть (Т); (*dispense*) разд(ав)а́ть; **~ration** управле́ние, администра́ция; (*government*) прави́тельство; **~rator** администра́тор

admirable замеча́тельный; превосхо́дный

admiral адмира́л; **~ty** адмиралте́йство

admir|ation восхище́ние; **~e** [по]любова́ться (Т); **~er** покло́нни|к, -ца

admiss|ible допусти́мый; **~ion** (*to univ.*) приём; (*confession*) призна́ние; (*entrance*) вход, впуск

admit допуска́ть [-сти́ть]; призн(ав)а́ть(ся); **~tance** до́пуск, до́ступ; **~tedly** по о́бщему призна́нию

admonish увещева́ть *or* увеща́ть *impf.*

adopt *boy* усыновля́ть

[-ви́ть]; *girl* удочери́ть [-ря́ть]; *(accept)* принима́ть [-ня́ть]; **~ion** усыновле́ние; приня́тие

ador|able преле́стный; **~ation** обожа́ние; **~e** обожа́ть

adorn украша́ть [-ра́сить]

adroit ло́вкий

adult взро́слый *(a. su.)*

adultery супру́жеская изме́на

advan|ce продвига́ть(ся) [-и́нуть(ся)]; *plan* выдвига́ть [вы́двинуть]; продвиже́ние; *fin.* ава́нс; **~ced** передово́й; *(student)* успева́ющий; **~tage** преиму́щество *(of, over* надт); вы́года; **~tageous** вы́годный

advent прихо́д; **~ure** приключе́ние, авантю́ра; **~urer** иска́тель приключе́ний; *b. s.* авантюри́ст; **~urous** авантю́рный

adverb наре́чие

advers|ary проти́вни|к, -ца; **~e** неблагоприя́тный; **~ity** невзго́да

advertise реклами́ровать *(im)pf.*; **~ for** помеща́ть объявле́ние о (П); **~ment** рекла́ма; *(newspaper)* объявле́ние

advice сове́т; **~sable** целесообра́зный; **~se** [по-] сове́товать (Д); **~ser** сове́тчи|к, -ца; *(official)* сове́тник, консульта́нт

advocate *jur.* адвока́т; *fig.* сторо́нни|к, -ца; *(support)* подде́рживать; выступа́ть (за В)

aerial анте́нна

aero|drome аэродро́м; **~nautics** аэрона́втика; **~plane** самолёт

affab|ility приве́тливость *f*; **~le** приве́тливый

affair де́ло; *coll.* рома́н

affect де́йствовать на (В); *indifference, etc.* притворя́ться [-ри́ться] (Т); *(touch)* тро́гать [тро́нуть]; **~ation** жема́нство; **~ed** жема́нный; притво́рный; **~ionate** люби́щий, не́жный

affinity бли́зость

affirm утвержда́ть

affliction несча́стье, го́ре; *(illness)* боле́знь

afford *luxury* позволя́ть [-во́лить] себе́; *(give)* доставля́ть ['-вить]

affront оскорбля́ть [-би́ть]; оскорбле́ние

aforesaid вышеупомя́нутый

afraid испу́ганный; *be ~ of* боя́ться (Р)

African африка́н|ец, -ка; **~ский**

after *(time)* по́сле (Р); *(place)* за (Т); *(according to)* по (Д); **~noon: in the ~noon** пополу́дни; *this ~noon* сего́дня днём; **~wards** пото́м, по́сле

again опя́ть; ~ *and* ~ сно́ва и сно́ва; *now and* ~ вре́мя от вре́мени; ~**st** про́тив (P); на, о(б) (B); к (Д); ~**st the winter** на зи́му

age во́зраст; (*period*) век; *of (under)* ~ (не)совершенноле́тний; ~**d** пожило́й

agen|cy аге́нтство; (*mediation*) посре́дничество; ~**da** пове́стка дня; ~**t** аге́нт; посре́дник

aggravate отягча́ть [-чи́ть]

aggress|ion агре́ссия; ~**ive** агресси́вный (*a. fig.*); ~**or** агре́ссор

aghast поражённый у́жасом

agile подви́жный, (*active*) живо́й; ~ *mind* живо́й ум

agitat|e агити́ровать; (*excite*) [вз]волнова́ть; ~**ion** агита́ция; волне́ние; ~**or** агита́тор

ago: *a year* ~ год тому́ наза́д; *long* ~ давно́

agrarian агра́рный

agree быть согла́сным, соглаша́ться [-ласи́ться] (*with* с T, *to* на B); (*be in harmony*) согласо́вываться [-сова́ться]; ~**able** прия́тный; согла́сный; ~**ment** соглаше́ние (*a. pol.*)

agriculture се́льское хозя́йство

ahead вперёд, впереди́

aid помога́ть; по́мощь *f*; ~**s** (*equipment*) посо́бия, прибо́ры

AIDS *med.* СПИД

aim цель *f* (*a. fig.*); *gun* наце́ли(ва)ть (*at* на B); *fig.* стреми́ться (к Д); ~**less** бесце́льный

air во́здух; (*look*) вид; *mus.* мело́дия; ~**-base** авиаба́за; ~**craft** самолёт(ы); ~**crew** экипа́ж самолёта; ~**force** вое́нно-возду́шные си́лы; ~**hostess** стюарде́сса; ~**line** авиали́ния; ~**liner** авиала́йнер; ~**mail** авиапо́чта; ~**man** лётчик; ~**plane** самолёт; ~**port** аэропо́рт; ~**raid** возду́шный налёт; ~**tight** гермети́ческий

alarm трево́га; [вс]трево́жить; ~**clock** буди́льник

Albanian алба́н|ец, -ка; -ский

alcohol алкого́ль *m*

alert бди́тельный, (*lively*) живо́й; *on the* ~ насторо́же

Algerian алжи́р|ец, -ка; -ский

alien чу́ждый; иностра́н|ец, -ка; ~**ate** отчужда́ть

alight сходи́ть [сойти́] (*from* с P); (*riding*) спе́ши(ва)ться

alignment *pol.* расстано́вка сил; *tech.* центро́вка, подго́нка

alike одина́ковый; *adv.*

одина́ково

alive живо́й, в живы́х

all (*everybody*) все *pl.*; весь, вся, всё; ~ **night** всю ночь; *after* ~ в конце́ концо́в; *not at* ~ во́все не(т); (*politeness*) не́ за что!; ~ **right!** ла́дно!

allege (голосло́вно) утвержда́ть; *illness* ссыла́ться [сосла́ться] (на В)

alleviate облегча́ть [-чи́ть]

alley переу́лок; (*garden*) алле́я; *blind* ~ тупи́к

alli|ance сою́з; ~**ed** сою́зный; (*related*) ро́дственный

allot *fin.* распределя́ть [-ли́ть]; *time, seats* отводи́ть [-вести́]; ~**ment** распределе́ние; (*share*) до́ля; (*land*) (земе́льный) уча́сток

allow позволя́ть [-во́лить], разреша́ть [-ши́ть]; (*concede*) допуска́ть [-сти́ть]; ~**ance** (*money*) посо́бие; (*ration*) рацио́н; *comm.* ски́дка; *make* ~**ance(s)** *for* принима́ть во внима́ние (В)

alloy сплав

all-purpose универса́льный

allude ~ *to* ссыла́ться, сосла́ться на (В); (*mention*) упомина́ть [-ну́ть]

allusion ссы́лка (*to* на В)

ally сою́зн|ик, -ца

almighty всемогу́щий

almond минда́льный оре́х; *pl.* минда́ль *m, collect.*

almost почти́

alone оди́н; (*lonely*) одино́кий; *leave* ~ оста́вить в поко́е; *let* ~ (*not to mention*) не говоря́ уж (о П)

along вдоль (Р); по (Д); *adv.* вперёд; ~**side** *fig.* бок о́ бок

aloof *keep* ~ держа́ться в стороне́

aloud (*read*) вслух; гро́мко

alphabet алфави́т; ~**ic** *tech.* бу́квенный (алфави́тный)

alphanumeric *tech.* бу́квенно-цифрово́й

already уже́

also та́кже, то́же

altar алта́рь *m*

alter изменя́ть [-ни́ть]; *dress* переде́л(ыв)ать

alternate чередова́ть (-ся); ~**ing current** переме́нный ток; ~**ive** альтернати́ва; альтернати́вный

although хотя́

altitude высота́

altogether всеце́ло; (*on the whole*) вообще́

aluminium алюми́ний

always всегда́

amass накопля́ть [-пи́ть]

amateur люби́тель *m*

amaz|e изумля́ть [-ми́ть]; ~**ement** изумле́ние; ~**ing** порази́тельный

ambassador посо́л

amber янта́рь *m*

ambigu|ity двусмы́сленность *f*; ~**ous** двусмы́сленный

ambitio|n честолю́бие; **_us** честолюби́вый

ambulance маши́на ско́рой по́мощи, *coll.* ско́рая по́мощь

ambush заса́да

amen ами́нь

amend исправля́ть(ся) ['-вить(ся)]; *pol.* вноси́ть попра́вки (в В); **make _s** возмеща́ть убы́тки

American америка́н|ец, -ка; -ский

amiable любе́зный

amid(st) среди́ (Р)

ammunition боеприпа́сы *m/pl.*

amnesty амни́стия

among(st) среди́ (Р), ме́жду (Т)

amorous влю́бчивый; влюблённый

amount коли́чество; *fin.* су́мма; **_ to** равня́ться (Д) (*a. fig.*)

ample просто́рный; (*abundant*) оби́льный; **_ify** дополня́ть ['-нить]; *el.* уси́ли(ва)ть

amputate ампути́ровать (*im*)*pf.*

amuse забавля́ть; развлека́ть, **_ement** заба́ва; развлече́ние; **_ing** заба́вный

an → a

anaemia малокро́вие

analogy анало́гия

analys|e [про]анализи́ровать; **_is** ана́лиз

anatomy анато́мия

ancestor пре́док

anchor я́корь *m*; стать *or* (*v./t.*) ста́вить на я́корь

ancient дре́вний; (*castle*) стари́нный

and и; (*opposing*) а

anecdote анекдо́т

anew сно́ва; за́ново

angel а́нгел

anger гнев; *v.* серди́ть

angle у́гол

Anglo-Saxon англоса́кс(онский)

angry серди́тый; **be _** серди́ться (**with** на В)

angular *math., etc.* углово́й; *fig.* углова́тый

animal живо́тное

animat|e *gr.* одушевлённый; *fig.* оживлённый ['-вить]; **_ed** оживлённый; **_ cartoon** мультфи́льм; **_ion** оживле́ние

animosity вражде́бность *f*

ankle щи́колотка, поды́жка

annals ле́топись *f*; анна́лы *m/pl.*

annex анекси́ровать (*im*)*pf.*; (*to document*) приложе́ние; **_ation** анне́ксия

annihilate уничтожа́ть ['-жить]

anniversary годовщи́на

announce объявля́ть ['-вить]; **_ment** объявле́ние; **_r** (*radio*) ди́ктор

annoy досажда́ть [досади́ть] (Д); (*irritate*) раздража́ть; **_ance** доса́да

_ing доса́дный
annual годово́й; ежего́дный
annul аннули́ровать (im)pf.
anodyne болеутоля́ющее
anomalous анома́льный
another друго́й; ещё оди́н
answer отве́т; отвеча́ть [-е́тить]; purpose соотве́тствовать (Д); _ for (be responsible) отвеча́ть [-ве́тить]; person руча́ться [поручи́ться] за (В)
ant мураве́й
anthem гимн
ant-hill мураве́йник
anti- противо..., анти...; _-aircraft противовозду́шный; _-biotic антибио́тик; _-cyclone антицикло́н; _-freeze mot. антифри́з
anticipate (foresee) предви́деть; (expect) ожида́ть; (look forward) предвкуша́ть
antipathy антипа́тия
antiquarian антиква́р; антиква́рный; _ated устаре́лый; _e анти́чный, дре́вний; _ity анти́чность f; анти́чный мир
antler оле́ний рог
anvil накова́льня
anxiety беспоко́йство, трево́га; _ous озабо́ченный; (time, etc.) трево́жный; he is _ous + inf. ему́ о́чень хо́чется + inf.
any любо́й, како́й-нибудь; _body вся-

кий, кто уго́дно; кто́-нибудь; I don't know _body here я здесь никого́ не зна́ю; _how ка́к-нибудь; во вся́ком слу́чае; _one → _body; _one → _body; he does not know _thing он ничего́ не зна́ет; _where где уго́дно; где́-нибудь
apart в стороне́, в сто́рону; _ from кро́ме (Р); _ment кварти́ра
apathetic апати́чный; _y апа́тия
ape обезья́на
apiece за шту́ку
apologize извиня́ться [-ни́ться]; _y извине́ние
apostle апо́стол
appalling ужаса́ющий
apparatus аппара́т, прибо́р
apparent я́вный; (seeming) ка́жущийся; _ly по-ви́димому
appeal обраще́ние; призы́в; jur. апелля́ция; _ to обраща́ться; призыва́ть к (Д); апелли́ровать (im)pf. к (Д)
appear появля́ться [-ви́ться]; (seem) каза́ться; _ance появле́ние; (looks) нару́жность f
appease умиротворя́ть [-твори́ть]
appendix (book etc.) приложе́ние
appetite аппети́т
applaud аплоди́ровать;

~se аплодисме́нты *m/pl.*

apple я́блоко; *adj.* я́блочный ~**-tree** я́блоня

appli|ance устро́йство; приспособле́ние; прибо́р; ~**cable** примени́мый; ~**cation** примене́ние; заявле́ние

apply применя́ть [-ни́ть]; *med.* накла́дывать [-ложи́ть] (**to** на В); *v/i.* быть примени́мым; ~ **for** подава́ть заявле́ние о (П)

appoint назнача́ть ['-чить]; ~**ment** назначе́ние; встре́ча

appraise оце́нивать [-ни́ть]

appreciat|e [o]цени́ть; ~**ion** оце́нка

apprehen|d (*understand*) понима́ть; (*fear*) опаса́ться (Р); (*arrest, seize*) аресто́вывать [-ова́ть]; ~**sion** опасе́ние; аре́ст

apprentice подмасте́рье *m*, учени́к

approach приближа́ться [-бли́зиться] (к Д); походи́ть [подойти́] (к Д *a. fig.*); приближе́ние; *fig.* подхо́д

appropriate[1] присва́ивать [-во́ить]; *fin.* ассигнова́ть (*Im*)*pf.*; ~**ion** присвое́ние; ассигнова́ние

appropriate[2] *adj.* подходя́щий, уме́стный

approv|al одобре́ние; ~**e** одобря́ть ['-рить]

approximately приблизи́тельно

apricot абрико́с

April апре́ль *m*

apron перё́дник, фа́ртук

apt спосо́бный; (*inclined*) скло́нный; ~**itude** спосо́бность *f*; скло́нность *f*

aqualung акваланг

Arab ара́б; ~**ian** ара́бский; ~**ic** ара́бский

arable (*land*) па́хотный

arbitra|ry произво́льный; ~**tion** арбитра́ж; ~**tor** арби́тр

arc дуга́

arch а́рка; (*vault*) свод

archbishop архиепи́скоп

architect архите́ктор

archives архи́в

ard|ent горя́чий, пла́менный; ~**our** горя́чность *f*

area пло́щадь *f* (*a. math.*); райо́н, о́бласть *f*

Argentine аргенти́нский

argu|e [по]спо́рить (**about** о П); ~**ment** спор; (*reason*) до́вод

arid засу́шливый; *fig.* беспло́дный

arise встава́ть [-ста́ть]; *fig.* возника́ть [-кнуть]

aristocracy аристокра́тия

arithmetik арифме́тика

arm[1] рука́

arm[2] вооружа́ть [-жи́ть]; ~**s** ору́жие; ~**ament** вооруже́ние

armchair кре́сло

Armenian армяни́н, '-ка; '-ский

armistice переми́рие

armour броня́; *(knight)* до-
спе́хи *m/pl.*; ~**ed** брониро́-
ванный, броне́…

armpit подмы́шка

army а́рмия

aroma арома́т

around вокру́г (Р) *a. adv.*

arouse [разбуди́ть], *fig.*
возбужда́ть [-буди́ть]

arrange устра́ивать [-ро́-
ить]; *(put in order)* распо-
лага́ть [-ложи́ть]; *(come to
an agreement)* догова́ри-
ваться [-вори́ться]; ~**ment**
устро́йство; расположе́-
ние; соглаше́ние, договорё-
нность; *mus.* аранжи-
ро́вка

arrears задо́лженность

arrest аресто́вывать
[-ова́ть]

arriv|al прибы́тие; прихо́д;
~**e** прибы(ва́)ть **(at** в В);
приходи́ть [прийти́] **(at** в
В, *fig.* к Д)

arrogan|ce зано́счивость *f*;
~**t** зано́счивый

arrow стрела́; *(pointer)*
стре́лка

arson поджо́г

art иску́сство

artery арте́рия

artful хи́трый; *(skilled)* ис-
ку́сный

artic|le *(printed)* статья́;
jur. пункт, пара́граф, ста-
тья́; *(thing)* вещь; *gr.*
арти́кль; ~**ulation** артикуля́ция

artificial иску́сственный

artillery артилле́рия

artist худо́жник, -ца; *thea.*
арти́ст(ка)

as *conj.* как; когда́; *(because)* так как; ***work ~ a
teacher*** рабо́тать учи́те-
лем; ~ **cold ~ ice** холо́д-
ный как лёд; ~ **a rule**
обы́чно; ~ **if** как бу́дто; ~
soon ~ так то́лько

ascen|d *hill* поднима́ться
[-ня́ться], всходи́ть [взой-
ти́] (на В); ~**sion: ₂sion
Day** Вознесе́ние; ~**t** вос-
хожде́ние; подъём

ascertain выясня́ть [вы́яс-
нить]

ash(es) пе́пел, зола́

ashamed пристыжённый;
be ~ of стыди́ться Р

ashore на берегу́, на́ берег

ash-tray пе́пельница

Asian азиа́т(ка); азиа́тский

ask спра́шивать [спро-
си́ть]; *(beg)* [по]проси́ть;
~ **a question** зад(ав)а́ть
вопро́с

asleep: be ~ спать; **fall ~**
засыпа́ть [засну́ть]

asparagus спа́ржа

aspect вид *(a. gr.)*; аспе́кт,
у́гол зре́ния

asphalt асфа́льт

aspiration *fig.* стремле́ние

ass осёл

assassin (наёмный) уби́йца

assault нападе́ние; напа-
да́ть [-па́сть] (на В)

assemb|le соб(и)ра́ть(ся);
~**y** собра́ние; *tech.* сбо́рка

узел, блок; **~y line** сборочный конвейер

assent соглаша́ться [-гласи́ться]; (**to** на В); согла́сие

assert утвержда́ть; *rights* отста́ивать [-стоя́ть]; **~ion** утвержде́ние; отста́ивание

assess *value* определя́ть [-ли́ть]; *tax, fine* определя́ть [-ли́ть] су́мму; **~ment** оце́нка; су́мма обложе́ния

assets *fin.* акти́в(ы)

assign назнача́ть ['-чить]; *room* одводи́ть [-вести́]; **~ment** назначе́ние (*duty, etc.*) зада́ние, поруче́ние

assimilate ассимили́ровать(ся)

assist помога́ть [-мо́чь] (Д); **~ance** по́мощь *f*; **~ant** помо́щник; *shop* **~ant** продаве́ц

associate ассоции́ровать(ся); (*keep company*) обща́ться; **~ion** ассоциа́ция; това́рищество

assume (*take*) принима́ть [-ня́ть]; (*usurp*) присва́ивать себе́; (*suppose*) предполага́ть [-ложи́ть]

assur|ance уве́рение; (*self-a.*) (само)уве́ренность *f*; **~e** уверя́ть ['-рить], уверя́ть ['-рить] (*of* в П)

asthma а́стма

astonish удивля́ть [-ви́ть]; **~ment** удивле́ние

astray: **go ~** сби(ва́)ться с пути́

astronaut астрона́вт

astronom|er астроно́м; **~y** астроно́мия

asunder *adv.* врозь, по́рознь; (*to pieces*) на ча́сти

asylum убе́жище; прию́т

at у (Р); на (П); в (П); **~ five o'clock** в пять часо́в; **~ home** до́ма; **~ a table** за столо́м

atheism атеи́зм

athlet|e атле́т; **~ic** атлети́ческий; **~ics** лёгкая атле́тика

atmosphere атмосфе́ра

atom а́том; *attr.* а́томный; **~ic**: **~ic age** а́томный век; **~ic bomb** а́томная бо́мба; **~ic pile** а́томный реа́ктор

atroci|ous зве́рский; **~ty** зве́рство

attach прикрепля́ть [-пи́ть]; *importance* прид(ав)а́ть; **~ment** (*affection*) привя́занность *f*

attaché атташе́ *indecl.*; **~ case** диплома́т

attack напада́ть [-па́сть] на (В); атакова́ть (*im)pf.*; нападе́ние; ата́ка; *med.* при́ступ

attain достига́ть [-и́гнуть *or* -и́чь]; **~ment** достиже́ние

attempt попы́тка; (*on life*) покуше́ние; [по-] пыта́ться; покуша́ться [-уси́ться] (на В)

attend *lessons* посеща́ть [-ети́ть]; (*serve*) обслужи-

(ва)ть; *med.* уха́живать; **~ance** посеща́емость *f*; обслу́живание; ухо́д

attention внима́ние; **~ve** внима́тельный

attic черда́к; манса́рда

attitude отноше́ние (***towards*** к Д); (*pose*) по́за

attract притя́гивать [-яну́ть]; *fig.* привлека́ть [-е́чь]; **~ion** притяже́ние; влече́ние; **~ive** *fig.* привлека́тельный

attribute сво́йство, атрибу́т; (*ascribe*) припи́сывать [-са́ть]

auction аукцио́н; **~eer** аукцио́нщик

audaci|ous сме́лый; *b.s.* де́рзкий; **~ty** сме́лость *f*; де́рзость *f*

audi|ble слы́шный, слы́шимый; **~ence** пу́блика; **~torium** аудито́рия

audio-visual аудиовизуа́льный

augment увели́чи(ва)ть (-ся); **~ation** увеличе́ние

August а́вгуст

aunt тётя

auster|e стро́гий; *b.s.* дерзкий; **~ity** стро́гость *f*

Australian австрали́|ец, -йка; -йский

Austrian австри́|ец, -йка; -йский

authentic по́длинный; (*reliable*) достове́рный; **~ity** по́длинность *f*; достове́рность *f*

author а́втор; **~itative** авторите́тный; **~ity** авторите́т; *pol.* вла́сти *f/pl.*; **~ize** уполномо́чи(ва)ть; **~ship** а́вторство

auto|graph авто́граф; **~matic** автомати́ческий; *fig.* машина́льный; **~nomy** автоно́мия

autumn о́сень *f*; **~al** осе́нний

auxiliary вспомога́тельный

avail быть поле́зным; **~ o.s. of** [вос]по́льзоваться (Т); **~able** (име́ющийся) налицо́

avalanche лави́на

avenue алле́я, проспе́кт

average сре́днее число́; сре́дний; **on an ~** в сре́днем

aver|sion отвраще́ние; **~t** **war** предотвраща́ть [-врати́ть]

aviat|ion авиа́ция; **~or** лётчик

avoid избега́ть [-ежа́ть *or* -егну́ть] (P)

avowal призна́ние

await ждать (B *or* P), ожида́ть (P)

awake *v/t.* [раз]буди́ть; *v/i.* просыпа́ться [-сну́ться]; *adj.* бо́дрствующий; **~n 1.** = **~; 2.** *fig.* пробужда́ть [-уди́ть]

award (*prize*) приз, награ́да; **~** *v.:* **he was ~ed ...** ему́ присуди́ли (B)

aware: be ~ of созн(ав)а́ть (B); (*pf. a.:* **become ~**)

away (*moving off*) прочь; (*at a distance*) **two blocks** ~ в двух кварта́лах отсю́да; **he is** ~ его́ нет до́ма; (*move in an averted direction*) **fly** ~ улета́ть (*prefix* y-); **she looked** ~

она́ отверну́лась

aw|**e** благогове́йный страх; ~**ful** стра́шный

awkward неуклю́жий; (*position*) неудо́бный

awning наве́с

ax|**e** топо́р; ~**is**, ~**le** ось *f*

B

babble бормота́ть; *brook*: журча́ть

baby младе́нец

bachelor холостя́к

back за́дняя часть *f*; оборо́тная сторона́; *anat.* спина́; (*sports*) защи́тник; *adv.* наза́д; обра́тно; подде́рживать [-жа́ть]; ~**bone** позвоно́чник; ~**ward** (*reverse*) обра́тный; *fig.* отста́лый; *adv.* наза́д

bacon копчёная груди́нка

bad плохо́й

badge значо́к

badger барсу́к

badminton бадминто́н

bag мешо́к; (*woman's*) су́мка; ~**gage** бага́ж; ~**pipes** волы́нка

bail *jur.* зало́г; **let s.b. out on** ~ отпуска́ть [-ти́ть] кого́-либо под зало́г

bait прима́нка, нажи́вка

bak|**e** [ис]пе́чь; ~**er** пе́карь *m*; ~**er's shop** бу́лочная

balance (*instrument*) весы́ *m/pl.*; равнове́сие; *comm.* бала́нс; ~**ed** *fig.* уравнове́-

шенный; (*object*) сбаланси́рованный (*a. fin.*)

balcony балко́н

bald лы́сый

bale тюк

ball[1] (*dance*) бал

ball[2] мяч; (*sphere*) шар; ~**-bearing** шарикоподши́пник; ~**-(-point) pen** ша́риковая ру́чка

ballet бале́т

ballistic баллисти́ческий

balloon возду́шный шар

ballot: **by secret** ~ та́йным голосова́нием; ~**-paper** избира́тельный бюллете́нь *m*

balm бальза́м

bamboo бамбу́к; *attr.* бамбу́ковый

ban запреща́ть [-ети́ть]; запрёт

banana бана́н

band[1] гру́ппа; (*criminals*) ба́нда, ша́йка; *mus.* орке́стр

band[2] ле́нта; ~**age** бинт; [за]бинтова́ть

bang хло́пать [-пнуть] (Т)

banish высыла́ть (из Р); *thought* гнать; ~ment вы́сылка

banisters пери́ла *n/pl.*

bank[1] на́сыпь *f*; (*river*) бе́рег

bank[2] банк; ~er банки́р; ~rupt обанкро́тившийся; *su.* банкро́т; ~ruptcy банкро́тство

banner зна́мя *n*

banquet банке́т

baptism креще́ние; ~ze [о]крести́ть

bar (*piece*) брусо́к; ~ *of chocolate* пли́тка шокола́да; *fig.* прегра́да; *jur.* адвокату́ра; (*restaurant*) бар; буфе́т

barbarian ва́рвар; ~ous ва́рварский

barbed: ~ *wire* колю́чая про́волока

barber парикма́хер

bare го́лый; (*foot*) босо́й; *adv.* босико́м; ~ly едва́, е́ле

bargain сде́лка; вы́годная поку́пка; *into the* ~ в прида́чу

barge ба́ржа

bark[1] *bot.* кора́

bark[2] ла́ять; *su.* лай

barley ячме́нь *m*

barn амба́р, сара́й

barometer баро́метр

barracks каза́рма

barrel бо́чка, бочо́нок

barren беспло́дный

barricade баррика́да

barrier барье́р, прегра́да

barter менова́я торго́вля, ба́ртер; обме́нивать [-ня́ть]

base ба́зис, осно́ва; *mil.* ба́за; ~ball бейсбо́л; ~less необосно́ванный; ~ment подва́л

bashful засте́нчивый

basic основно́й

basket корзи́на; ~ball баскетбо́л

bass бас

bastard внебра́чный (ребёнок)

bat лету́чая мышь *f*

bath (*house*) ба́ня; *take a* ~ принима́ть ва́нну; ~e [вы́]купа́ть(ся); ~room ва́нная (ко́мната); ~tub ва́нна

battalion батальо́н

battery *mil.* батаре́я; *mot.* аккумуля́тор; (*for torches, etc.*) батаре́йка

battle би́тва

bay[1] *geogr.* бу́хта

bay[2] (*colour*) гнедо́й (*a. su.*)

bay[3] *bot.* ла́вровое де́рево; ~ *leaf* лавро́вый лист

bayonet штык

be бы(ва́)ть; *there is (are)* есть; име́ется (име́ются) (И)

beach (*sea*) бе́рег; (*bathing*) пляж

beacon мая́к

beak клюв

beam луч; *arch.* ба́лка; (*shine*) сия́ть

bean боб
bear[1] *zo.* медве́дь *m*
bear[2] носи́ть, [по]нести́; *fruit* приноси́ть [-нести́]; (*endure*) выноси́ть [вы́нести]; ~ *in mind* по́мнить, име́ть в виду́
beard борода́; ~ed борода́тый
bear|er носи́тель *m*; (*letter*) предъяви́тель *m*; ~ing (*manner*) поведе́ние; (*relation*) отноше́ние
beast зверь *m*; *fig.* скоти́на
beat [по]би́ть (*a. fig.*); *heart*: би́ться; *carpet* выбива́ть [вы́бить]
beauti|ful краси́вый; прекра́сный (*a. fig.*); ~ty красота́; (*woman*) краса́вица; ~ty parlour косметический кабинет
beaver бобр; (*fur*) бобёр
because потому́ что; ~ *of* из-за (P)
become станови́ться [стать]; *suit*: идти́ к лицу́; (*morally*) подоба́ть (Д); ~ing (иду́щий) к лицу́; подоба́ющий
bed посте́ль *f*, крова́ть *f*; (*garden*) клу́мба, гря́дка; *go to* ~ ложи́ться спать; ~-linen посте́льное бельё; ~room спа́льня; ~spread покрыва́ло
bee пчела́
beech бук
beef говя́дина; ~steak бифште́кс
beehive у́лей
beer пи́во
beet *bot.* свёкла
beetle *zo.* жук
beetroot (*red beet*) свёкла
before пе́ред (T); ~ *the war* до войны́; *prp.* пре́жде; *conj.* пре́жде чем; ~hand зара́нее; *adv.* вско́ре; *long* ~ задо́лго до (P)
beg [по]проси́ть; (*beseach*) умоля́ть, упра́шивать; ~gar ни́щий
begin нач(ин)а́ть(ся); ~ner начина́ющий; ~ning нача́ло
behalf: *on* ~ *of* от и́мени; в интере́сах (P)
behave вести́ себя́; ~iour поведе́ние
behind за (T); позади́ (P); *adv.* позади́
being существо́; *human* ~ челове́к
Belgian Бельги́|ец, -йка; ~йский
belie|f ве́ра; *pl.* ве́рования *n/pl.*; ~ve [по]ве́рить (Д); (*in* в B)
bell ко́локол; (*door*) звоно́к
bellow реве́ть; ора́ть
bellows мехи́ *m/pl.*
belly живо́т
belong: ~ *to* принадлежа́ть (Д); ~ings *f/pl.*
below под (T); ни́же (P); *adv.* внизу́
belt по́яс (*a. geogr.*); реме́нь *m* (*a. tech.*)

bench скамья́, скаме́йка

bend [co]гну́ть(ся); сгиб; (*curve*) поворо́т

beneath под (T); ни́же (P); *adv.* внизу́

bene|diction благослове́ние; **~faction** благодея́ние; **~ficial** благотво́рный; **~fit** по́льза; (*allowance*) посо́бие; *thea.* бенефи́с; **~volent** благожела́тельный

bent *su.* скло́нность *f*, спосо́бность

bereave лиша́ть [-ши́ть] (*of* P); **~ment** (тяжёлая) утра́та

beret бере́т

berry я́года

berth ко́йка; *rail.* спа́льное ме́сто, по́лка; (*anchoring*) я́корная стоя́нка

beseech умоля́ть

beside ря́дом с (T), во́зле (P); **~ the mark** не по существу́; **~s** кро́ме того́

besiege осажда́ть [осади́ть]

best (наи)лу́чший; *adv.* лу́чше всего́ *or* всех; *do one's* **~** де́лать всё возмо́жное; *all the* **~** всего́ са́мого лу́чшего; *at* **~** в лу́чшем слу́чае

bet пари́ *n indecl.*; *v.* держа́ть пари́

betray пред(ав)а́ть; (*reveal*) выдава́ть [вы́дать] (*o.s.* себя́); **~al** преда́тель-

ство

betrothal обруче́ние

better лу́чший; *adv.* лу́чше; улучша́ть ['-шить]; *so much the* **~** тем лу́чше; *get the* **~** of (пре)одоле́ть, взять верх

between ме́жду (T)

beverage напи́ток

beware остерега́ться [-ре́чься] (*of* P)

beyond за; по ту сто́рону (P); (*above*) вы́ше (P); **~ doubt** вне сомне́ния; **~ me** мне недосту́пно

Bible Би́блия

bicycle велосипе́д

bid (*command*) прика́зывать [-за́ть]; (*invite*) приглаша́ть [-гласи́ть]; *a dollar* предлага́ть [-ложи́ть]

big большо́й; (*industry*) кру́пный; (*clothes*) вели́к; **~wig** *coll.* ва́жная персо́на, ши́шка

bilateral двусторо́нний

bilberry черни́ка

bile жёлчь *f*; **~ious** жёлчный

bill[1] *zo.* клюв

bill[2] счёт; (*poster*) афи́ша; *pol.* законопрое́кт; *Am.* (*bank-note*) банкно́т; **~ of exchange** ве́ксель *m*; **~ of fare** меню́

billiards билья́рд

bind связывать [-за́ть]; *book* переплета́ть [-плести́]; **~ing** переплёт

biograph|er био́граф; **~y**

биогра́фия

biology биоло́гия

birch берёза

bird пти́ца

birth рожде́ние; ~place ме́сто рожде́ния; ~rate рожда́емость; ~day день рожде́ния

biscuit пече́нье

bishop епи́скоп; *chess* слон

bit¹ кусо́чек; *a* ~ немно́жко; *not a* ~ ниско́лько

bit² *tech.* бит, двои́чная ци́фра

bitch су́ка

bite куса́ть; *dog: (be snapish)* куса́ться, *(injure)* куса́ть [укуси́ть]; *fish:* клева́ть [клю́нуть]; уку́с; *(piece)* кусо́чек; *(fish)* клёв; *let's have a* ~ дава́й переку́сим; ~ing *(caustic)* язви́тельный

bitter го́рький; ~ness го́речь *f*

black чёрный; ~berry ежеви́ка; *en fig.* очерни́ть; ~mail шанта́ж; *v.* шанта́жи́ровать; ~ *market* чёрный ры́нок; ~smith кузне́ц

bladder мочево́й пузы́рь *m*

blade *(razor)* ле́звие

blame вини́ть; вина́; ~less безупре́чный

blank пробе́л; *(sheet of paper)* чи́стый; *(look)* бессмы́сленный

blanket одея́ло

blast поры́в ве́тра; взрывна́я волна́; взрыва́ть [взорва́ть]

bleach [от]бели́ть

bleat бле́ять

bleed кровоточи́ть; ~ing *su.* кровотече́ние

blemish [за]пятна́ть; пятно́; *without* ~ безупре́чный

blend смесь *f*; сме́шивать(ся) [-ша́ть(ся)]

bless благословля́ть [-ви́ть]; ~ing благословле́ние; *coll.* бла́го

blind слепо́й; ослепля́ть [-пи́ть]; *(window)* што́ра; ~ness слепота́

blink мига́ть [мигну́ть]

bliss блаже́нство

blister волды́рь *m*

blizzard пурга́, вьюга

block *(buildings)* кварта́л; *tech.* блок; ~ *of flats* многоэта́жный дом; ~ *(up)* загражда́ть [-ради́ть]; ~ade блока́да

blood кровь *f*

bloom *(flower)* цвето́к; *in* ~ в цвету́; *v.* цвести́

blossom цвет; *(single)* цвето́к; *v.* цвести́

blot кля́кса; пятно́; ~ting paper промока́тельная бума́га

blouse блу́за, блу́зка

blow¹ уда́р

blow² *v/i.* дуть, ве́ять; ~ *up a tyre* нака́чивать [-ча́ть]

both

ши́ну; ~ **one's nose** [вы́]-сморка́ться

blue си́ний; (light) голубо́й; ~**ish** синева́тый, голубова́тый

blunder гру́бая оши́бка; де́лать гру́бую оши́бку

blunt тупо́й; fig. прямо́й, ре́зкий; притупля́ть [-пи́ть]

blush красне́ть; кра́ска стыда́

boar бо́ров; (wild) каба́н

board доска́; (meals) стол, пансио́н; ~ **of directors** дире́кция, правле́ние; ~**ing-house** пансио́н; ~**ing school** (шко́ла-) интерна́т

boast [по]хва́стать(ся) (**about** T); (be proud) горди́ться (**of** T); ~**ful** хвастли́вый; ~**ing** su. хвастовство́

boat ло́дка; (ship) су́дно; ~**race** гребны́е го́нки f/pl.; ~**man** ло́дочник

bodice лиф

body те́ло; ~**guard** телохрани́тель m

boil water [вс]кипяти́ть; v/i. кипе́ть; вари́ться; ~**er** парово́й котёл

boisterous (child, etc.) ре́звый; (sea, wind) бушу́ющий

bolt tech. болт; (door) засо́в; запира́ть на засо́в

bomb бо́мба; бомби́ть; ~**ardment** бомбарди-

ро́вка; ~**er** бомбардиро́вщик

bond comm. облига́ция; pl. у́зы f/pl.

bone кость f

bonfire костёр

bonnet капо́р, чепчик; mot. капо́т

bonus бо́нус, пре́мия

bony костля́вый

book кни́га; ticket зака́зывать [-за́ть]; hotel-room брони́ровать [за-]; ~ кни́жный шкаф; ~**ing**: ~**ing office** биле́тная ка́сса; ~**keeper** бухга́лтер; ~**keeping** бухгалте́рия; ~**shop** кни́жный магази́н

boom гул; comm. бум

boot боти́нок; (high) сапо́г; mot. бага́жник

booth бу́дка

border грани́ца; (edge) край; кайма́; ~ **on** грани́чить с (T)

bore[1] ску́ка; ску́чный челове́к; надоеда́ть [-е́сть] (Д); ~**dom** ску́ка

bore[2] сверли́ть; ~**er** сверло́

born: **be** ~ рожда́ться impf.; роди́ться (im)pf.

borrow брать взаймы́; word, idea заи́мствовать

bosom грудь f

boss coll. нача́льник, шеф, босс

botany бота́ника

both о́ба m, n, о́бе f; ~ **he**

and ... как он, так и ...

bother беспоко́ить(ся)

bottle буты́лка; (*for scent*) флако́н

bottom dng; **at the ~** внизу́; на дне (**of** P)

bough ветвь, ве́тка

bounce (*back*) отска́кивать [-скочи́ть]

bound[1] пры́гать [-гнуть]; нести́сь скачка́ми; прыжо́к

bound[2]: **be ~ to** быть обя́занным + *inf.*; **be ~ for** *mar.* направля́ться в (В)

boundary грани́ца; (*between fields, etc.*) межа́; *fig.* преде́л

bouquet буке́т (*a. fig.*)

bow[1] лук; *mus.* смычо́к; (*girl*) бант

bow[2] покло́н; *mar.* нос; кла́няться [поклони́ться]

bowels кишки́ *f/pl.*

bowl ми́ска; (*large*) таз; **~er** (*hat*) котело́к

box[1] я́щик; коро́бка; *thea.* ло́жа

box[2]: **~ sb's ears** дава́ть [дать] кому́-либо затре́щину; (*sports*) бокси́ровать; *er* боксёр; *~ing* бокс; *attr.* боксёрский

box-office театра́льная ка́сса

boy ма́льчик; (*youth*) ю́ноша; *~-friend* друг

boycott бойко́т; бойкоти́ровать (*im*)*pf.*

boyish мальчи́шеский

bra *coll.* ли́фчик, бюстга́льтер

brace *pl.* подтя́жки *f/pl.*; *~ing* *fig.* бодря́щий

bracelet брасле́т

bracket *typ.* ско́бка

brag [по]хва́статься

braid тесьма́; (*hair*) коса́

brain мозг; **~ drain** уте́чка мозго́в

brake то́рмоз; тормози́ть

branch ветвь *f*; *comm.* филиа́л, (*science*) о́трасль *f*; (*road*) ответвле́ние

brand *comm.* ма́рка, сорт; [за]клейми́ть; **~y** конья́к; бре́нди *indecl.*

brass лату́нь *f*; **~ band** духово́й орке́стр

brassiere бюстга́льтер

brave хра́брый; *v.* хра́бро встреча́ть; **~ry** хра́брость *f*

brazen ме́дный; *fig.* на́глый

Brazilian брази́л|ец, -ья́нка; -ьский

breach (*gap*) проло́м; (*duty, etc.*) наруше́ние

bread хлеб

breadth ширина́

break [с]лома́ть(ся) (*a. med.*); *law* наруша́ть [-ушить]; *resistance* сломи́ть *pf.*; **~down** ава́рия; поло́мка; *med.* не́рвное истоще́ние

breakfast за́втрак; **have ~** [по]за́втракать

breast грудь *f*

breath дыха́ние; *out of ~* запыха́вшись; **~e** дыша́ть; **~ing** дыха́ние; **~ing-space** переды́шка

breed *zo., agr.* разводи́ть (-ся) [-вести́(сь)]; **~ing** разведе́ние; (*person*) воспита́ние

breeze ветеро́к; *mar.* бриз

brevity кра́ткость *f*

brew [с]вари́ть (пи́во) (-ся)]; **~er** пивова́р; **~ery** пивова́ренный заво́д

bribe взя́тка; **~ry** взя́точничество

brick кирпи́ч; **~layer** ка́менщик

bride неве́ста; (*just married*) новобра́чная; **~groom** жени́х; новобра́чный

bridge[1] мост

bridge[2] (*cards*) бридж

bridle узда́; обу́здывать [-да́ть]

brief кра́ткий; **~-case** портфе́ль *m*, диплома́т; **~ing** *pol.* бри́финг

brigade брига́да; **~ier** брига́дный генера́л

bright я́ркий; (*child, etc.*) смышлёный; **~ness** я́ркость *f*

brilliance блеск; **~t** блестя́щий

brim край; (*hat*) поля́ *n/pl.*; *to the ~* до краёв

bring *thing* приноси́ть [-нести́]; *person* приводи́ть [-вести́]; (*by car*

привози́ть [-везти́]; *~ up* воспи́тывать [-та́ть]

brink грань *f*

brisk бо́дрый

bristle щети́на; [о]щети́ниться

British брита́нский

brittle хру́пкий

broad широ́кий; **~cast** радиопереда́ча; передава́ть по ра́дио; **~casting**: *~casting station* радиовеща́тельная ста́нция; **~en** расширя́ть(ся) [-ши́рить(ся)]

brocade парча́

broker ма́клер, бро́кер

bronze бро́нза

brooch брошь *f*

brood вы́водок; *v.* выси́живать; *fig.* размышля́ть

brook ручей́

broom метла́

broth бульо́н

brother брат; **~-in-law** (*wife's brother*) шу́рин; (*husband's brother*) де́верь *m*; (*sister's husband*) зять *m*

brow бровь *f*

brown кори́чневый

bruise синя́к

brush щётка; (*painter's*) кисть *f*; чи́стить щёткой; *hair* причёсывать щёткой; **~wood** куста́рник

Brussels: *~ sprouts* брюссе́льская капу́ста

brutal жесто́кий, зве́рский; **~ality** жесто́кость,

bubble пузы́рь *m*, пузырёк; *v.* пузы́риться

buck саме́ц (оле́ня, за́йца, кро́лика)

bucket ведро́

buckle пря́жка; застёгивать [-стегну́ть]

bud по́чка; (*flower*) буто́н

budget бюдже́т

buffalo бу́йвол

buffet буфе́т; ~ *car rail.* ваго́н-рестора́н; ~ *supper* у́жин «а-ля-фурше́т»

bug клоп; (*insect*) насеко́мое

bugle горн

build [по]стро́ить; телосложе́ние; ~**er** строи́тель *m*; ~**ing** зда́ние

bulb *bot.* лу́ковица; *el.* ла́мпочка

bulging вы́пуклый, вы́пученный

bulk основна́я ма́сса; *buy in* ~ покупа́ть о́птом; ~**y** громо́здкий

bull бык

bullet пу́ля

bulletin бюллете́нь *m*

bully задира́ *m/f*; задира́ть [-задра́ть]

bump (*blow*) стук, глухо́й уда́р; (*swelling*) ши́шка; *v. against* сту́каться [-кнуться] о (В)

bun бу́лочка

bunch пучо́к; (*flowers*) буке́т

bundle свёрток, у́зел

bunk ко́йка, *a. mar.*; *rail.* спа́льное ме́сто, по́лка

buoy буй; плаву́честь *f*; *fig.* жизнера́достность *f*

burden бре́мя *n*; обременя́ть [-ни́ть]

bureau бюро́ *n indecl.*

burglar взло́мщик, вор

burial по́хороны *f/pl.*

burn *v/i.* горе́ть; *v/t.* [с]жечь; *med.* ожо́г

burst ло́паться ['-пнуть]; (*explode*) взрыва́ться [взорва́ться]; взрыв; ~ *into room* врыва́ться [ворва́ться] в (В); ~ *into tears* распла́каться; ~ *into laughter* рассмея́ться

bury [по]хорони́ть

bus авто́бус; ~ *station* авто́вокза́л; ~**stop** авто́бусная остано́вка

bush куст

business де́ло, би́знес; *attr.* делово́й; ~**like** делови́тый; ~**man** предпринима́тель, бизнесме́н

bust бюст

bustle суета́; суети́ться

busy занято́й; (*line*) за́нятый

but но; (*after negative phrase*) *a; prep.* кро́ме (Р); ~ *for him,* ... не будь его́, ...

butcher мясни́к; *fig.* пала́ч

butler дворе́цкий

butt[1] то́лстый коне́ц; (*target*) мише́нь *f*

butt[2] *cow*: бода́ть(ся)

butter (сли́вочное) ма́сло; **_fly** ба́бочка; **_milk** па́хта́нье

button пу́говица; *tech.* кно́пка; застёгивать [-стегну́ть]; **_hole** петли́ца

buy покупа́ть [купи́ть]; **_er** покупа́тель(ница *f*) *m*

buzz жужжа́ть; жужжа́-

ние; **_er** зу́ммер

by (*near*) у, о́коло (Р); (*not later than*) к (Д); (*past*) ми́мо (Р) *a. adv.*; (*done*) ~ **my father** мои́м отцо́м; **take – the hand** брать за́ руку; **~ day** днём; **~ Jove!** ей-бо́гу!; **~ itself** само́ по себе́; **_-product** побо́чный проду́кт

byte *tech.* байт

cab *mot.* такси́ *n indecl.*

cabbage капу́ста

cabin *mar.* каю́та; (*pilot's, lorry driver's*) каби́на; хи́жина

cabinet шка́фчик, го́рка; *pol.* кабине́т

cable кана́т; трос; *el., etc.* ка́бель *m*; телегра́мма; ~ **TV** ка́бельное телеви́дение

cabman води́тель такси́

café кафе́ *n indecl.*

cage кле́тка

cake кекс; **cream-_** пиро́жное; торт

calamity бе́дствие

calculat|e рассчи́тывать [-ита́ть] (*fig. impf. only*); вычисля́ть [вы́числить]; **_ion** расчёт (*a. fig.*); вычисле́ние (*a. fig.*); **_or** *tech.* калькуля́тор

calendar календа́рь *m*

calf[1] телёнок

calf[2] *anat.* икра́

call зов; вы́зов; [по-] зва́ть; (*name*) наз(ы)ва́ть; **_box** телефо́н-автома́т; **_er** посети́тель *m*; ~ **for** [по]тре́бовать (Р); *person* заходи́ть [зайти́] за (Т); ~ **up** вы́звать по телефо́ну; *mil.* приз(ы)ва́ть

callous мозо́листый; *fig.* безду́шный

calm ти́хий, споко́йный; тишина́, споко́йствие (*mst. fig.*); успока́ивать [-ко́ить]; **~ down** утиха́ть ['-хнуть]

camel верблю́д

camera фотоаппара́т; **_-man** фоторепортёр

camomile рома́шка

camouflage маскиро́вка; [за]маскирова́ть(ся)

camp ла́герь *m*; **_ing** ке́мпинг

can бидо́н; (*tin*) ба́нка

(*petrol*) кани́стра; *v/t.* консерви́ровать; **~ned** консерви́рованый

Canadian кана́д|ец, -ка; -ский

canal кана́л

canary канаре́йка

cancel вычёркивать [вы-черкнуть]; *subscription, etc.* аннули́ровать; *order* отменя́ть [-ни́ть]

cancer *med.* рак

candid чистосерде́чный

candidate кандида́т

candied заса́харенный

candle свеча́

candy ледене́ц; (*sweets*) конфе́ты *pl.*

cane трость *f;* *bot.* трост-ни́к

canoe кано́э *n indecl.*, байда́рка

canteen (*mil., in factories, etc.*) столо́вая; (*flask*) фля́га

canvas холст (*a. painting*)

canvass: ~ *for s.b.* агити́ровать за кого́-либо; ~ *for votes* вести́ предвыбо́рную кампа́нию

cap ша́пка; (*peaked*) ке́пка; *mil.* фура́жка

capab|ility спосо́бность *f;* **~le** спосо́бный

capacity (*space*) вмести́-мость *f;* *tech.* мо́щность *f;* производи́тельность *f;* *fig.* спосо́бность *f*

cape *geogr.* мыс

capital (*city*) столи́ца; *typ.*

пропи́сная бу́ква; *fin.* капита́л; *adj. coll.* отли́ч-ный; ~ **punishment** сме́ртная казнь

capric|e капри́з; **~ious** капри́зный

capsize опроки́дывать (-ся) [-и́нуть(ся)]

captain капита́н (*a. mil.*)

capt|ivate пленя́ть [-ни́ть]; **~ive** пле́нный; **~ivity** плен; **~ure** захва́т; захва́-тывать (-и́ть)

car (*легкова́я*) автома-ши́на, *coll.* маши́на; *rail.* ваго́н; ~-**mechanic** (а́вто)меха́ник; ~-**park** авто-стоя́нка

caravan карава́н; (*for holidays*) дом-автоприце́п

caraway тмин

carbon *chem.* углеро́д; ~-**paper** копирова́льная бума́га, *coll.* копи́рка

carburettor карбюра́тор

card ка́рта; (*post*) от-кры́тка; ~-**board** карто́н

cardinal основно́й; *eccl.* кардина́л

card-index картоте́ка

care забо́та; (*~fulness*) тща́тельность *f;* ~ *of* (*по*)забо́титься о (П); ~ *of* (*c/o*) для переда́чи (Д)

career карье́ра; (*speed*) карье́р

care|ful тща́тельный; (*heedful*) осторо́жный; **~less** небре́жный; (*imprudent*) неосторо́жный

caution

caress ласка́ть; ла́ска
cargo груз; *attr.* грузово́й
carnival карнава́л
carol (рожде́ственская) пе́сня
carp карп
carpenter пло́тник
carpet ковёр
carri|age *comm.* перево́зка, транспортиро́вка; *rail.* ваго́н; (*bearing*) оса́нка; **~er** носи́льщик
carrot морко́вь *f* (*no pl.*)
carry носи́ть, [по]нести́; (*transport*) вози́ть, [по]везти́; **~ on** продолжа́ть [-до́лжить]; **~ out** выполня́ть [вы́полнить]
cart теле́га; (*hand*) теле́жка
cartel карте́ль *m/f*
cartoon (*friendly and humorous*) шарж; карикату́ра (*esp. pol.*); (*animated*) мультфи́льм
cartridge патро́н
carv|e вы́резать [вы́резать]; *meat* нареза́ть [-ре́зать]; **~ed** вырезно́й
case[1] слу́чай; *jur.* де́ло; *gr.* паде́ж; **~ history** *med.* исто́рия боле́зни; *in any* **~** во вся́ком слу́чае
case[2] (*cover*) футля́р; (*box*) я́щик; (*trunk*) чемода́н
cash нали́чные де́ньги *f/pl.*; **~ on delivery** нало́женным платежо́м; *a* **cheque** (*receive*) получа́ть

[-чи́ть] де́ньги по че́ку; (*pay out*) опла́чивать [-лати́ть]; **~ier** касси́р(ша)
cask бочо́нок
cast броса́ть [бро́сить]; *tech.* отли́(ва́)ть; *thea.* соста́в исполни́телей; **~-iron** чугу́н; **~-iron** чугу́нный
castle за́мок (*chess*) ладья́
casual случа́йный; **~ties** *mil.* поте́ри *f/pl.*; **~ty** несча́стный слу́чай; (*person*) пострада́вший, же́ртва
cat ко́шка; (*male*) кот
catalogue катало́г
cataract водопа́д; *med.* катара́кта
catastroph|e катастро́фа; **~ic** катастрофи́ческий
catch лови́ть [пойма́ть]; **~ a cold** простужа́ться [-уди́ться]; **~ up (with)** догоня́ть [-гна́ть]; **~ing** *med.* зара́зный
category катего́рия
caterpillar гу́сеница
cathedral собо́р
Catholic като́л|ик; **-и́че**ский
cattle скот
cauliflower цветна́я капу́ста
cause причи́на; причиня́ть [-ни́ть]; **~ of peace** де́ло ми́ра
cauti|on осторо́жность *f*; (*warning*) предостереже́ние; предостерега́ть [-ре́чь];

[-стере́чь]; ~ous осторо́жный

cavalry кавале́рия, ко́нница

cave пеще́ра

caviar (чёрная) икра́

cavity *anat.* по́лость *f*; (*tooth, tree*) дупло́

cease прекраща́ть(ся) [-крати́ть(ся)]

cede уступа́ть [-пи́ть]

ceiling потоло́к

celebrate [от]пра́здновать; ~ation пра́зднование; ~ity знамени́тость *f*

celery сельдере́й

cell яче́йка; *biol.* кле́тка; *eccl.* ке́лья; *el.* элеме́нт; *prison* ~ тюре́мная ка́мера; ~ar по́греб

Celtic ке́льтский

cement цеме́нт; цементи́ровать (*im*)*pf.*

cemetery кла́дбище

censor це́нзор; ~ship цензу́ра

census пе́репись *f*

cent цент; *per* ~ проце́нт (*su.*)

central центра́льный; ~e центр

century столе́тие, век

cereals *agr.* зерновы́е, хле́бные зла́ки *m/pl.*

ceremonial церемониа́л; церемониа́льный; **stand on** ~ies церемо́ниться

certain несомне́нный; (*some*) не́который, не́кий; **I am** ~ я уве́рен(а); ~ty не-

сомне́нный факт; уве́ренность *f*

certificate свиде́тельство; спра́вка; удостовере́ние; ~y удостоверя́ть [-ри́ть]

cessation прекраще́ние

chain цепь *f*; *dim.* це́почка; ~ **of shops** сеть магази́нов

chair стул; *univ.* ка́федра; ~man председа́тель *m*

chalk мел

challenge вы́зов; вызыва́ть [вы́звать]

chamber ко́мната; *tech.* ка́мера; *pol.* пала́та; ~ **of commerce** Торго́вая пала́та; ~maid го́рничная; ~ **music** ка́мерная му́зыка

champagne шампа́нское

champion чемпио́н(ка); ~ **of peace** боре́ц за мир; ~ship пе́рвенство

chance шанс, случа́йность *f*; **by** ~ случа́йно; **take a** ~ рискова́ть [-кну́ть]

chancellor ка́нцлер

change переме́на; измене́ние; *rail.* переса́дка; пере-, изменя́ть(ся) [-ни́ть(ся)]; *money* разме́нивать [-меня́ть]; *foreign currency* [об]меня́ть; (*dress*) переоде(ва́)ться; ~ **trains** *etc.* переса́живаться [-се́сть]; **small** ~ ме́лочь *f*; ~able из-, переме́нчивый

channel ру́сло; (*man-made*)

кана́л

chapel часо́вня

chapter глава́

character хара́ктер; *lit.* геро́й, персона́ж; *thea.* де́йствующее лицо́; (*letter*) бу́ква; **~istic** характе́рный

charge (*cost*) пла́та, цена́; (*load*) заря́д; (*commission*) поруче́ние; *jur.* обвине́ние; назнача́ть [-на́чить] цену, проси́ть (*for* за В); заряжа́ть [-яди́ть]; поруча́ть [-чи́ть] (Д *with* В); обвиня́ть [-ни́ть]

charit|able милосе́рдный; **~y** милосе́рдие; благотвори́тельность

charm очарова́ние; очаро́вывать [-ова́ть]; **~ing** очарова́тельный

chart морска́я ка́рта; **~er** ship [за]фрахтова́ть; *pol.* уста́в; **~er flight** ча́ртерный рейс

chase гна́ться (за Т); *hunt.* охо́титься (за Т); пого́ня; охо́та

chassis шасси́ *n indecl.*

chast|e целому́дренный; **~ity** целому́дрие

chat дру́жески бесе́довать; дру́жеская бесе́да

chatter болта́ть

cheap дешёвый; дёшево

cheat обма́н; (*person*) обма́нщик, -ца; обма́нывать [-ну́ть]

check (*stop*) приостана́в-

ливать [-нови́ть]; (*examine*) проверя́ть [-ри́ть]; шах; **~ed** в кле́тку; **~-mate** шах и мат; **~-room** ка́мера хране́ния; *thea.* гардеро́б

cheek щека́

cheer ободря́ть [-ри́ть]; **~ful** бо́дрый; **~less** уны́лый; **~s** одобри́тельные во́згласы *m/pl.*

cheese сыр

chem|ical хими́ческий; **~icals** химика́лии *f/pl.*; **~ist** хи́мик; *Brit.* апте́карь *m*; **~istry** хи́мия

cheque чек

cherish леле́ять

cherry ви́шня

chess ша́хматы *f/pl.*; **~-player** шахмати́ст

chest ларь *m*, сунду́к; *anat.* грудна́я кле́тка; **~ of drawers** комо́д; **~nut** кашта́н; кашта́новый

chew жева́ть; **~ing gum** жева́тельная рези́нка

chicken цыплёнок; *cul.* ку́рица

chief нача́льник, *coll.* шеф; гла́вный

child ребёнок (*pl.*: де́ти); **~hood** де́тство; **~ish** ребя́ческий

chill холодо́к (*a. fig.*); *med.* просту́да; **~y** холоднова́тый, прохла́дный

chimney дымова́я труба́; **~sweep** трубочи́ст

chin подборо́док

china фарфо́р; фарфо́ровая посу́да

Chinese кита́|ец, -я́нка; -йский

chip ще́пка; *pl.* карто́фель фри

chirp, chirrup чири́кать

chisel долото́; [из]ва́ять

chivalrous гала́нтный

chocolate шокола́д

choice вы́бор; альтернати́ва; *adj.* отбо́рный

choir хор

choke *v/t.* души́ть; *v/i.* задыха́ться; дави́ться [по-]

choose выбира́ть [вы́брать]

chop руби́ть; *su. cul.* отбивна́я

chord *mus.* акко́рд; *fig.* стру́нка; *vocal* ~s голосовы́е свя́зки *f/pl.*

chorus хор; *in* ~ хо́ром

Christ Христо́с; ~ian христиани́н; '-ка; '-ский; ~ian name и́мя *n*; ~ianity христиа́нство; ~mas Рождество́; ~mas Eve соче́льник; ~mas tree ёлка

chronic хрони́ческий; ~cle хро́ника

church це́рковь *f*; ~yard кла́дбище

cigar сига́ра; ~ette папиро́са, сигаре́та

cine|ma кино́ *n. indecl.*; (*building*) кинотеа́тр; ~-camera кинока́мера

cinnamon кори́ца

cipher (*code*) шифр

circle круг; (*group*) кружо́к; *thea.* я́рус

circu|it (*detour*) объе́зд; *el.* цепь *f*; **short** ~**it** коро́ткое замыка́ние; ~lar кругово́й; кру́глый; *su.* циркуля́р; ~late циркули́ровать; ~lation обраще́ние; (*newspaper*) тира́ж

circumstance обстоя́тельство

circus цирк

citizen гражда́н|ин, '-ка; горожа́н|ин, -ка; ~ship гражда́нство

city (большо́й) го́род; *attr.* городско́й

civil гражда́нский; (*polite*) ве́жливый; ~ian ста́тский (челове́к); ~ization цивилиза́ция; ~ize цивилизова́ть

clad оде́тый

claim притяза́ние, прете́нзия; претендова́ть на (В); (*assert*) утвержда́ть

clamp зажи́м; скрепля́ть [-пи́ть]; зажима́ть

clan *fig.* клан, кли́ка

clang лязг; ля́згать

clap хлопо́к; хло́пать [-пнуть]

clash столкнове́ние; ста́лкиваться [столкну́ться]

clasp (*handshake*) рукопожа́тие; (*buckle*) застёжка; пож(им)а́ть; приж(им)а́ть; застёгивать [-стегну́ть]

class класс; *attr.* кла́ссный, *pol.* кла́ссовый; **~ify** классифици́ровать *(im)pf.*; **~room** класс (-ная ко́мната)

clatter *dishes*: греме́ть

clause *jur.* статья́, пункт

claw ко́готь *m*; *(crab, etc.)* клешня́

clay гли́на

clean чи́стый; [по]чи́стить; **~ up** приб(и)ра́ть; **~er** убо́рщица; *(dry)* **~er's** химчи́стка; **~ly** чистопло́тный; **~ness** чистота́; **~se** [по]чи́стить

clear я́сный, све́тлый; *(distinct)* чёткий

clench сж(им)а́ть

clergy духове́нство; **~man** свяще́нник

clerk клерк; конто́рский слу́жащий

clever у́мный; *(skilful)* иску́сный; **~ness** ум, одарённость *f*; иску́сность *f*

client клие́нт(ка); *comm.* покупа́тель(ница *f*) *m*

cliff утёс

climate кли́мат

climb ла́зить, [по]ле́зть; взбира́ться [взобра́ться]; **~ up a hill** взбира́ться [взобра́ться] на́ гору

cling цепля́ться (*to* за В)

clinic кли́ника

clip[1] *(paper-~)* скре́пка; скрепля́ть [-пи́ть]

clip[2] *hair* [о-, под-]стри́чь; стри́жка; **~ping** *(газет-*

ная) вы́резка

cloak плащ; *fig.* покро́в; **~-room** гардеро́б; *euph.* *(W. C.)* туале́т

clock часы́ *m/pl.*; **at two o'~** в два часа́

clod ком (земли́)

cloister монасты́рь *m*

close[1] закры́(ва́)ть; *(end)* зака́нчивать [-ко́нчить]; коне́ц

close[2] *(connection)* те́сный; *(near)* бли́зкий; **~ly** те́сно; приблизи́тельно; *(fit)* пло́тно

closet камо́рка; *(water-)* туале́т; убо́рная

cloth *(fabric)* ткань *f*, мате́рия; *(table-~)* ска́терть *f*; **~e** оде́(ва́)ть; **~es** оде́жда *(no pl.)*

cloud о́блако; **~y** о́блачный

clove *cul.* гвозди́ка

clover кле́вер

clown кло́ун

club[1] клуб

club[2] дуби́н(к)а; *(sports)* клю́шка

clue ключ *(fig.)*; *coll.* **I haven't a ~** поня́тия не име́ю

clums|iness неуклю́жесть *f*; **~y** неуклю́жий; *fig.* нета́ктичный

clutch заж(им)а́ть; хвата́ться; хвати́ться *(at* за В); *mot.* сцепле́ние; **~es** *pl.* *fig.* ко́гти *m/pl.*

coach *rail.* ваго́н; *mot.* ту-

рийстский автобус
coal у́голь *m*; ~-**mine**
у́гольная ша́хта
coarse гру́бый; *fig. only*
вульга́рный; непристо́йный; (*sand*) кру́пный;
~**ness** гру́бость *f*
coast (морско́й) бе́рег;
~-**guard** береговая охра́на
coat пальто́ *n indecl.*; ~**ing**
слой
coax угова́ривать [-ри́ть];
выма́нивать [вы́манить]
(*out of* у P)
cobbler сапо́жник (*a. fig.*).
cock пету́х; (*rifle*) куро́к;
~-**chafer** ма́йский жук;
~**roach** тарака́н; ~**tail** кокте́йль *m*
cocoa кака́о *n indecl.*;
~-**nut** коко́совый оре́х
cod треска́
code код; *jur.* ко́декс
cod-liver: ~ **oil** ры́бий жир
coexist сосуществова́ть;
~**ence** сосуществова́ние
coffee ко́фе *m indecl.*;
~-**grinder** кофемо́лка;
~-**pot** кофе́йник
coffin гроб
cog: *fig.* **a small** ~ ме́лкая
со́шка
cognition позна́ние
cohe|rent свя́зный; ~**sion**
сцепле́ние
coil свёртывать спира́лью;
v/i. изви(ва́)ться; вито́к;
el. кату́шка
coin моне́та
coincide совпада́ть

[-па́сть]; ~**nce** совпаде́ние
coke кокс; *Am. coll.* ко́ка-
-ко́ла
cold холо́дный; хо́лод;
med. просту́да; **catch a** ~
простуди́ться; ~**ness** хо́-
лод(ность *f*)
collaborat|e сотру́дничать;
~**ion** сотру́дничество
collapse (*wall*) распа́д; *fig.*
распа́д; *med.* упа́док сил;
распада́ться [-па́сться]
collar воротни́к; ~-**bone**
ключи́ца
colleague колле́га, сотру́д-
н|ик, -ица
collect соб(и)ра́ть(ся); ~
tax взыма́ть нало́ги; ~**ion**
(*tax*) сбор; (*stamps, etc.*)
колле́кция; ~**or** сбо́рщик;
коллекционе́р
colliery ша́хта
collision столкнове́ние
colloquial разгово́рный
colonel полко́вник
colour цвет; (*dye*) кра́ска;
fig. колори́т; ~**ed** цветно́й; (*man*) черноко́жий;
~**s** (*flag*) зна́мя *n*
colt жеребёнок
column *arch., mil.* коло́нна;
typ. столбе́ц, коло́нка
comb гре́бень *m*; причёсы-
вать(ся) [-чеса́ть(ся)]
combat бой; ~**ant** бое́ц
combination сочета́ние;
комбина́ция; ~**e** сочета́ть(ся); [с]комбини́ро-
вать
combustible *adj.* горю́чий

come приходи́ть [прийти́]; приезжа́ть [-éхать]; ~ *about* случа́ться [-чи́ться]; ~ *back* возвраща́ться [-врати́ться]; ~ *in* входи́ть [войти́]

comedy коме́дия

comet коме́та

comfort утеше́ние; (*convenience*) удо́бство; ~**able** удо́бный; (*well-equipped*) комфорта́бельный

comic коми́ческий; (*paper*) юмористи́ческий; (*person*) ко́мик; *the* ~**s** ко́миксы

comma запята́я; *inverted* ~**s** кавы́чки f/pl.

command прика́з, кома́нда; (*authority*) кома́ндование; ~**ant** коменда́нт; ~**er** команди́р; ~**ment** eccl. за́поведь f

commence начина́ть(ся), [-ча́ть](ся)

comment комменти́ровать (*im*)*pf.*; коммента́рии m/pl.; ~**ary** коммента́рий; (*radio*) репорта́ж

commerce торго́вля; комме́рция; ~**ial** торго́вый; комме́рческий

commission поруче́ние; (*order*) зака́з; (*group*) коми́ссия; *out of* ~ в неиспра́вности

commit *crime* соверша́ть [-ши́ть]; пред(ав)а́ть (*to* Д); ~ *o.s.* обя́зываться [-за́ться]; ~**tee** комите́т

commodity collect. това́р

common о́бщий; (*ordinary*) обыкнове́нный; ~ *sense* здра́вый смысл; *House of* ~**s** пала́та о́бщин; ~**wealth** Брита́нское содру́жество на́ций

commotion смяте́ние; (*physical*) шум и кри́ки

commun|icate v*/t*. сообща́ть [-щи́ть]; v*/i*. сообща́ться [-щи́ться]; ~**ication** сообще́ние; ~**ism** коммуни́зм; ~**ist** коммуни́ст (-ка); ~**ity** общи́на; (*abstract*) о́бщность f

compact-cassette компа́кт-кассе́та

compan|ion това́рищ, f подру́га; (*travelling*) ~**ion** попу́тчик; ~**y** компа́ния; mil. ро́та

compar|able сравни́мый; ~**ative** сравни́тельный; ~**e** сра́внивать [-ни́ть]; ~**ison** сравне́ние

compartment отделе́ние; rail. купе́ n indecl.

compass ко́мпас; ~**es** ци́ркуль m

compassion сострада́ние

compel *people* принужда́ть [-у́дить]; *action* вынужда́ть [вы́нудить]

compensat|e возмеща́ть [-ести́ть]; компенси́ровать (*im*)*pf.*; ~**ion** возмеще́ние; компенса́ция

compet|e comm. конкури́ровать; (*sports*) соревнова́ться; **~ence** компете́нтность *f*; **~ent** компете́нтный; **~ition** *comm.* конкуре́нция; соревнова́ние; (*arts*) ко́нкурс; **~itor** конкуре́нт(ка)

compile составля́ть ['-вить]

complain [по]жа́ловаться (*of* на В); **~t** жа́лоба; *med.* неду́г

complete по́лный; (*finished*) зако́нченный; завершать ['-шить]; **~ely** по́лностью; **~ion** завершение

complex сло́жный; ко́мплекс; (*face*) цвет лица́; **~ity** сло́жность *f*

compliance усту́пчивость *f*; **in ~ with** в соотве́тствии (с Т)

complicate усложня́ть [-ни́ть]; **~ed** сло́жный; **~ion** усложне́ние; *med.* осложне́ние

component составно́й; составна́я часть *f*

compose составля́ть ['-вить]; *mus.* сочиня́ть [-ни́ть]; **~er** компози́тор; **~ition** составле́ние; сочине́ние (*a. school*); **~ure** споко́йствие

compound составно́й; (*word, interest*) сло́жный

comprehend постига́ть ['-гнуть]; (*comprise*) заключа́ть в себе́; **~sion** понима́ние; **~sive** исче́рпывающий

compress сж(им)а́ть; *med.* компре́сс

comprise заключа́ть в себе́

compromise компроми́сс; идти́ на компроми́сс; *name* [с]компромети́ровать

compuls|ion принужде́ние; **~ory** обяза́тельный; (*done by force*) принуди́тельный

computer компью́тер (ЭВМ)

comrade това́рищ

conceal скры(ва́)ть, укры(ва́)ть; **~ment** скры́тие; (*place*) укры́тие

conceit самомне́ние; самодово́льство; **~ed** самодово́льный

conceiv|able мы́слимый; **~e** заду́м(ыв)ать; (*imagine*) представля́ть ['-вить] себе́

concentrate сосредото́чи(ва)ть(ся), [с]концентри́ровать; **~ion** сосредото́чение; *chem.* концентра́т

conception (*concept*) поня́тие; (*artistic*) за́мысел; *biol.* зача́тие

concern каса́ться (косну́ться) (Р); интере́с; (*anxiety*) озабо́ченность *f*; *comm.* конце́рн; **~ed** заинтересо́ванный; **~ing** относи́тельно (Р)

concert конце́рт

concession усту́пка; *comm.* конце́ссия

conciliate примиря́ть;

~ion примире́ние; ~ory примири́тельный

concise кра́ткий

conclu|de [-чи́ть] заключа́ть; ~ding заключи́тельный; ~sion заключе́ние; ~sive заключи́тельный

concord согла́сие

concrete[1] конкре́тный

concrete[2] бето́н

condemn осужда́ть [-уди́ть]; ~ation осужде́ние

condensed: ~ milk сгущённое молоко́

condition усло́вие; (state) положе́ние, состоя́ние; ~al усло́вный

condolence соболе́знование

conduct води́ть, [по]вести́; mus. дирижи́ровать; поведе́ние; ~or rail., el. проводни́к; дирижёр

cone ко́нус; bot. ши́шка

confectionery (sweets, etc.) конди́терские изде́лия pl.; (shop) конди́терская

confederate сою́зный; (accomplice) соо́бщник, -ца; ~ion конфедера́ция

confer: ~ with совеща́ться с (Т); ~ on присужда́ть [-уди́ть] (Д); ~ence совеща́ние

confess призн(ав)а́ться в (П); eccl. испове́доваться (im)pf.; ~ion призна́ние; и́споведь f

confide secret доверя́ть [-е́рить]; ~ in доверя́ться, откры́ть ду́шу (Д); ~nce дове́рие; (certainty) уве́ренность f; ~nt уве́ренный; ~ntial конфиденци́альный; (document) секре́тный

confine|d ограни́ченный; (prison) заключённый; ~d to bed прико́ванный к посте́ли; ~ment ограниче́ние; заключе́ние; (accouchement) ро́ды; ~s преде́лы m/pl.

confirm подтвержда́ть [-рди́ть]; ~ation подтвержде́ние; eccl. конфирма́ция

confiscat|e конфискова́ть (im)pf.; ~ion конфиска́ция

conflict конфли́кт; ~ing противоречи́вый

conform сообразова́ть(-ся) (im)pf.; ~ity соотве́тствие

confound спу́т(ыв)ать

confront стоя́ть лицо́м к лицу́; быть поста́вленным пе́ред (with); ~ation конфронта́ция

confus|e (muddle) спу́т(ыв)ать; (embarrass) смуща́ть [смути́ть]; ~ion пу́таница; смуще́ние

congratulat|e поздравля́ть ['-вить] (on с Т); ~ion поздравле́ние

congress (party) съезд; (USA) конгре́сс; ~man

конгрессме́н

conjecture предположе́ние; предполага́ть [-ложи́ть]

conjunction gr. сою́з; in ~ with в связи́ с (T)

conjure пока́зывать [-за́ть] фо́кусы; ~r thea. фо́кусник

connect свя́зывать [-за́ть]; (telephone, etc.) соединя́ть [-ни́ть], ~ion, connexion связь f; соедине́ние

conquer завоёвывать [-ева́ть]; ~eror завоева́тель m; ~est завоева́ние

consci|ence со́весть f; ~entious добросо́вестный; ~ous: be ~ous of созн(ав)а́ть (B); ~ously созна́тельно; ~ousness созна́ние

consensus консе́нсус

consent соглаше; соглаша́ться [-си́ться] (to на B)

consequen|ce после́дствие; (importance) ва́жность f; ~tly сле́довательно; в результа́те

conservation сохране́ние; nature ~ation охра́на приро́ды; ~ative консервати́вный; консерва́тор; ~e сохраня́ть [-ни́ть]

consider рассма́тривать [-мотре́ть]; (think to be) счита́ть за (B); (allow for) учи́тывать [уче́сть]; ~able значи́тельный; ~ate вни-

ма́тельный, учти́вый; ~ation рассмотре́ние; внима́тельность f; ~ing учи́тывая (B)

consignment: ~ of goods па́ртия това́ров; груз

consist состоя́ть (of из P); заключа́ться (in в П); ~ency после́довательность f; ~ent после́довательный

consol|ation утеше́ние; ~e утеша́ть ['-шить]

consonant согла́сный (звук)

conspicuous заме́тный

conspira|cy за́говор; ~tor загово́рщик

constant постоя́нный

constellation созве́здие

consternation у́жас

constituency collect. избира́тели; избира́тельный о́круг

constitu|ent (part) составно́й; pol. учреди́тельный; ~te составля́ть ['-вить]; ~tion pol., med. конститу́ция; ~tional конституцио́нный

constrain принужда́ть [-уди́ть]; ~t принужде́ние; (feeling) напряжённость f; ско́ванность f

construct [по]стро́ить; ~ion (building) постро́йка; (action) строи́тельство; ~ive fig. конструкти́вный

construe (interpret) истолко́вывать [-кова́ть]

consul ко́нсул; ~ate ко́нсульство

consult [по]сове́товаться (с Т); *book* посмотре́ть (в П)

consum|e *goods, food* потребля́ть [-би́ть]; *time* [по]тра́тить; ~er потреби́тель *m*; ~er goods потреби́тельские това́ры; ~ption потребле́ние

contact соприкоснове́ние; *fig.* конта́кт (*a. el.*); вступи́ть в конта́кт (с Т); ~ lenses конта́ктные ли́нзы

contagious зара́зный

contain содержа́ть (в себе́); (*capable of holding*) вмеща́ть; ~er (*packing case, etc.*) та́ра; *rail, etc.* конте́йнер; (*vessel*) сосу́д

contemplat|e созерца́ть; (*think*) размышля́ть; ~ion созерца́ние; размышле́ние

contemporary совреме́нный; совреме́нни|к, -ца

contempt презре́ние; ~ible ничто́жный; ~uous презри́тельный

contend боро́ться; (*sports*) соревнова́ться; (*affirm*) утвержда́ть

content дово́льный; удовлетворя́ть [-ри́ть]; ~ *o.s.* дово́льствоваться (**with** Т)

contention спор; (*assertion*) утвержде́ние

contentment удовлетво-

рённость

contents содержа́ние; (*vessel*) содержи́мое

contest (*sports*) состяза́ние, соревнова́ние

continent контине́нт

continu|al беспреста́нный; ~e продолжа́ть(ся) ['-жить(ся)]; ~ous непреры́вный

contraceptive противозача́точное сре́дство

contract контра́кт, догово́р; (*shrink*) сж(им)а́ться; ~ion сжа́тие; (*muscle*) сокраще́ние; ~or подря́дчик

contradict противоре́чить (Д); ~ion противоре́чие; ~ory противоречи́вый

contrary противополо́жный; (*wind*) проти́вный; **on the** ~ напро́тив, наоборо́т

contrast противополо́жность *f*, контра́ст

contribut|e спосо́бствовать (**to** Д); *money* [по-]же́ртвовать (**to** на В); *writer:* сотру́дничать; ~ion взнос; *fig.* вклад; (*press*) статья́

contriv|ance (*gadget*) приспособле́ние; (*invention*) вы́думка; ~e приду́м(ыв)ать; (*manage*) ухитря́ться [-ри́ться] (Т)

control контро́ль *m*; *tech., mil.* управле́ние; контроли́ровать; управля́ть (Т)

controversy спор, поле́-

мика

convenie|nce удобство; **~nt** удобный

convent (женский) монастырь *m*; **~ion** *pol.* конвенция; (*party, etc.*) съезд; **~ional** общепринятый

convers|ation разговор; **~e** разговаривать

conversion превращение; *eccl.* обращение; (*armaments*) конверсия; **~t** превращать [-ратить]; обращать [-ратить]

convey перевозить [-везти]; (*impart*) перед(ав)ать; (*part*) передача; **~er, ~or** *tech.* конвейер

convict осуждать [-удить]; *su.* осуждённый; **~ion** осуждение; (*belief*) убеждение

convince убеждать [-едить]

cook повар(иха); [с]варить(ся); **~ing** готовка

cool прохладный; охлаждать(ся) [охладить(ся)]; **~ down** осты(ва)ть; **~ness** прохлада

co-operat|e сотрудничать; **~ion** сотрудничество; **~ive** кооператив

co-ordinate координировать (*im*)*pf*.

cope **~ with** справляться ['-виться] с (Т)

copeck копейка

copper медь *f*; медная мо-

нета; **~s** *coll.* медяки, медь

copy копия; (*book*) экземпляр; списывать [-сать]; [с]копировать (*a. fig.*); *rough* **~** черновик; **~-book** тетрадь *f*; **~right** авторское право

coral коралл

cord верёвка; *tech.* шнур; *vocal* **~s** голосовые связки *f/pl.*

cordial сердечный

core сердцевина

cork пробка; закупори(ва)ть; **~-screw** штопор

corn хлеба *m/pl.*; зерно; (*maize*) кукуруза; **~ed beef** солонина

corner угол; *attr.* угловой

coronation коронация

corporal[1] телесный

corporal[2] *mil.* ефрейтор

corporation корпорация

corps *mil.* корпус

correct правильный; по-правлять ['-вить]; **~ion** исправление, поправка; **~ness** правильность *f*

correspond соответствовать (*to* Д); переписываться (*with* с Т); **~ence** соответствие; переписка; **~ent** *su.* корреспондент; **~ing** соответствующий

corridor коридор

corrupt (*deprave*) развращать [-атить]; *adj.* развращённый; **~ion** развращённость *f*; (*of officials*) корру́пция

cosmetic косме́тика; косме́тическое сре́дство

cosmic косми́ческий

cosmonaut космона́вт

Cossack каза́к, -чка; -ций

cost сто́имость *f*; *pl.* изде́ржки; *v.* сто́ить; **at any** ~ любо́й цено́й; **~ly** дорого́й; (*valuable*) це́нный

costume костю́м

cosy ую́тный

cot де́тская крова́ть *f*; **~tage** котте́дж; (*log-house*) изба́; (*summer*) да́ча

cotton хло́пок; *attr.* хлопчатобума́жный; ~ **wool** ва́та

couch кушётка

cough ка́шель *m*; ка́шлять

council сове́т; **~lor** член городско́го сове́та

counsel сове́т; [по]сове́товать (Д); **take** ~ **with** совеща́ться (с Т); **~lor** *pol.* сове́тник

count[1] счита́ть [сче́сть]; ~ **upon** рассчи́тывать (на В)

count[2] граф

countenance лицо́, ми́на; (*composure*) самооблада́ние

counter (*shop*) прила́вок; (*café, etc.*) сто́йка

counter|**balance** уравнове́шивать [-ве́сить]; **~feit** подде́л(ыв)ать; подде́лка

covetous жа́дный, а́лчный

cow коро́ва

подде́льный; **~-revolution** контрреволю́ция

countess графи́ня

countless бесчи́сленный

country *pol.* страна́; (*area*) ме́стность *f*; (*village*) дере́вня; (*homeland*) ро́дина; **~man** се́льский жи́тель *m*; (*compatriot*) соотéчественник

county гра́фство; (*USA*) о́круг

coupl|**e** па́ра; *tech.* сцепля́ть [-пи́ть]; **~ing** сцепле́ние

courage му́жество, **~ous** му́жественный

courier курье́р

course *mar.*, *univ.* курс; (*time*) тече́ние; (*events*) ход; *cul.* блю́до; **of** ~ коне́чно

court двор; *jur.* суд; (*sports*) площа́дка; **woman** уха́живать (за Т); **~eous** ве́жливый; **~esy** ве́жливость *f*; **~-martial** вое́нный трибуна́л; **~ship** уха́живание; **~yard** двор

cousin двою́родный брат, двою́родная сестра́

cover покры(ва́)ть; (*conceal*) прикры(ва́)ть; (*book*) переплёт, обло́жка; (*jacket*) суперобло́жка; (*bed*) покрыва́ло; (*shelter*) укры́тие; (*dinner*) прибо́р

coward трус(и́ха); **~ice** трусость f; **~ly** трусли́вый

cowboy ковбо́й

cower приседа́ть [-е́сть]

coy засте́нчивый

crab краб

crack тре́щина; (sound) треск; v/i. [по]тре́скаться; v/t. щёлкать [-кнуть] (nuts B, whip T); ~ потре́скивать; потре́скивание

cradle колыбе́ль f

craft иску́сность f; (slyness) хи́трость f; (trade) ремесло́; **~sman** ма́стер; **~y** хи́трый

crag скала́

cram набива́ть [-би́ть]; coll. (learn) зубри́ть

cramp скоба́; med. су́дорога

cranberry клю́ква

crane жура́вль m; tech. кран

crank[1] mot. заводна́я ру́чка

crank[2] чуда́к

crash гро́хот; av., mot. ава́рия; (train) круше́ние (a. fig.); comm. крах; па́дать с гро́хотом; потерпе́ть ава́рию, круше́ние; **~-helmet** защи́тный шлем; **~-landing** авари́йная поса́дка

crate упако́вочный я́щик

crater кра́тер; mil. воро́нка

crave (for) стра́стно жела́ть (P), жа́ждать (P)

crawl по́лзать, [по]ползти́; по́лзание; (sports) вольный стиль

crayfish рак

craz|e помеша́тельство; **~y** помеша́нный (on, about на П)

creak скрипе́ть; скрип

cream сли́вки f/pl.; (paste) крем; снима́ть сли́вки (с P); **ice-~** моро́женое

crease скла́дка; (wrinkle) морщи́на

creat|e созд(ав)а́ть, [со-]твори́ть; **~ion** созда́ние; eccl. сотворе́ние ми́ра; **~ive** тво́рческий; **~or** созда́тель m, творе́ц; **~ure** (person) существо́; (animal) тварь f

crèche я́сли

credentials рекоменда́ции; (ambassador's) вери́тельные гра́моты

credit дове́рие; fin. креди́т; **on** ~ в креди́т; **do** ~ **to** де́лать честь (Д); **~or** креди́тор

credulous легкове́рный

creek бу́хточка

creep по́лзать, [по]ползти́; **~er** ползу́чее расте́ние

cremat|e крема́ровать; **~ion** крема́ция; **~orium** кремато́рий

crescent полуме́сяц

crest geogr., mar. гре́бень m

crevice расще́лина

crew mar., ae. экипа́ж, кома́нда

crib де́тская крова́тка; agr. я́сли f/pl.; coll. (school) шпаргалка

cricket[1] *zo.* сверчок

cricket[2] крикет

crime преступление

criminal престу́п|ни́к, -ца; (*law*) уголо́вный

crimson тёмно-кра́сный

cripple кале́ка *m/f;* [ис-] кале́чить

crisis кри́зис

crisp (*food*) хрустя́щий; (*hair*) кудря́вый; (*air*) бодря́щий

critic кри́тик; **~al** крити́ческий; **~ism** кри́тика; **~ize** критикова́ть

croak *crow:* ка́ркать [-кнуть] (*impf. a. fig.*); *frog:* ква́кать [-кнуть]

crochet вяза́льный крючо́к; вяза́ть крючко́м

crockery (гли́няная, фая́нсовая) посу́да

crocodile крокоди́л

crooked криво́й

crop урожа́й; *pl.* посе́вы *m/pl.;* **~ up** возника́ть [-ни́кнуть]

cross крест; скре́щивать(-ся) [-ести́ть(ся)]; (*intersect*) пересека́ть (-ся) [-се́чь(ся)]; *be* **~ with** *coll.* серди́ться на (В); **~ing** (*street*) (пешехо́дный) перехо́д; *rail.* (*level*) **~ing** (железнодоро́жный) перее́зд; **~roads** перекрёсток; **~wise** крест-на́крест; **~word** (*puzzle*) кроссво́рд

crow воро́на

crowbar лом

crowd толпа́; толпи́ться; **~ed** перепо́лненный

crown коро́на; *bot., fin.* кро́на; *med.* коро́нка; *fig.* [у]венча́ть(ся)

crude (*raw*) сыро́й; (*unfinished*) необрабо́танный; (*manners*) гру́бый

cruel жесто́кий; **~ty** жесто́кость *f*

cruise *mar.* кру́из; **~r** крейсер

crumb кро́шка; **~le** [по-, на-, из-] кроши́ть(ся); рассыпа́ться [-ыпа́ться]

crumple [по]мя́ть

crunch *v/i.* хрусте́ть ['-стнуть]

crusade кресто́вый похо́д

crush [раз]дави́ть; (*small pieces*) [раз]дроби́ть

crust (*bread*) ко́рка; (*earth*) кора́

crutch косты́ль *m*

cry крича́ть [кри́кнуть]; (*weep*) [за]пла́кать; крик; плач

crystal криста́лл; *min.* хруста́ль *m;* **~lize** кристаллизова́ть(ся) (*im*)*pf.*

cub детёныш

cub|e куб; **~ic** куби́ческий

cuckoo куку́шка

cucumber огуре́ц

cuddle ла́сково прижима́ть(ся)

cudgel дуби́на, дуби́нка

cue[1] ключ (к разга́дке);

thea. ре́плика
cue[2] (billiards) кий
cuff манже́та; ~link за́понка
culprit вино́вник
cult культ; ~ivate культиви́ровать; land a. возде́л(ыв)ать; ~ivator культива́тор; (person) земледе́лец; ~ural культу́рный; ~ure культу́ра; ~ured (person) культу́рный
cumbersome (unwieldy) громо́здкий
cunning хи́трый; хи́трость f
cup ча́шка; (sports) ку́бок; ~board шкаф
cupola ку́пол
curb узда́; обу́здывать [-да́ть]
curd простоква́ша; ~le свёртываться [сверну́ться]
cure излечивать [-лечи́ть], вылечивать ['-лечить]; лече́ние
curfew коменда́нтский час
curi|osity любопы́тство; (thing) дико́вина; (rare object) рарите́т; ~ous любопы́тный; курьёзный
curl ло́кон, pl. mst ку́дри pl.; v. кудря́виться; ~y ку́дрявый
currant сморо́дина no pl.
curren|cy валю́та; ~t теку́щий; (opinion) распространённый; (air, etc.) пото́к; (sea, river) тече́ние

(a. fig.); el. ток
curriculum уче́бный план
curse проклина́ть [-ля́сть]
curt кра́ткий; ~ail сокраща́ть [-рати́ть]
curtain занаве́ска; (heavier) портье́ра; thea., за́навес
curts(e)y реверанс
curve поворо́т; math. кривая́
cushion поду́шка
custody (valuables, etc.) хране́ние; into ~ под стра́жу
custom обы́чай; (habit) привы́чка; ~s тамо́женные по́шлины f/pl.; ~s office тамо́жня; ~er покупа́тель m
cut [раз]ре́зать (v/i. impf. only); hair [о-, под-]стричь; prices, costs снижа́ть, сни́зить; (wound) поре́з; (fashion) покро́й; ~ down tree сруба́ть [-би́ть]; fig. сокраща́ть [-рати́ть]; ~ off отреза́ть
cutlery ножи́, ви́лки и ло́жки
cutlet отбивна́я котле́та
cutter резе́ц, реза́к; mar. ка́тер; (fashion) закро́йщи|к, -ца
cutting (action) ре́зка; adj. ре́жущий; fig. ре́зкий
cycle цикл; (bicycle) велосипе́д; ~ist велосипеди́ст; ~one цикло́н

date

cylinder цили́ндр
cymbals таре́лки *f/pl.*
cynical цини́чный
cypress кипари́с

czar царь *m*; ~**ina** цари́ца
Czech чех, че́шка; че́шский

D

dad(dy) *coll.* па́па *m*, па́почка
daffodil жёлтый нарци́сс
dagger кинжа́л
daily ежедне́вный; (*unvarying*) повседне́вный; (*newspaper*) ежедне́вная газе́та; *adv.* ежедне́вно
dainty *cul.* ла́комый; (*pretty*) изя́щный; ла́комство
dairy (*shop*) моло́чный магази́н
daisy маргари́тка
dam плоти́на, да́мба; запру́живать [-уди́ть]
damage повреждéние; (*abstract*) уще́рб; повреждáть [-еди́ть]; наноси́ть уще́рб (Д)
damn проклина́ть [-кля́сть]; ~**ed** прокля́тый; *adv. coll.* черто́вски
damp сыро́й; сы́рость *f*; увлажня́ть [-ни́ть]
dance танцева́ть; (*folk dances*) пляса́ть; та́нец; пля́ска; (*party*) танцева́льный ве́чер; ~**er** танцо́р; *thea.* танцо́вщик|, -ца; ~**ing** та́нцы *m/pl.*

dandelion одува́нчик
dandy франт
Dane датча́н|ин, -ка
danger опа́сность *f*; ~**ous** опа́сный
dangle *v/i.* болта́ться; *v/t.* болта́ть (Т); све́шивать [све́сить] (В)
Danish да́тский
dar|e [по]сме́ть; ~**ing** сме́лый; сме́лость *f*
dark тёмный; темнота́; *in the* ~ в потёмках; *fig.* в неве́дении; ~**en** *v/t.* затемня́ть [-ни́ть]; *v/i.* [по]темне́ть; ~**ness** темнота́
darling ми́лый, ми́ленький (*adj. a. su.*)
darn штопать
dart *glance* броса́ть ['-сить]; *v/i.* мча́ться
dash (*fling*) швыря́ть [-рну́ть]; (*splash*) обры́зг(ив)ать (Т **over** В); (*break*) разбива́ть [-би́ть]; *v/i.* мча́ться; (*motion*) бросо́к, рыво́к; *typ.* тире́ *n indecl.*; ~**ing** (*horseman etc.*) лихо́й
data да́нные *n/pl.*; ~ *processing* обрабо́тка да́нных
date[1] *bot.* фи́ник

date² да́та, число́; *coll.* свида́ние; *out of ~* устаре́вший; *up-to-~* совреме́нный

dative да́тельный паде́ж

daub нама́з(ыв)ать, изза-; (*smear*) па́чкать; (*bad painting*) мазня́

daughter дочь *f*, до́чка; *~-in-law* неве́стка

dawn заря́ (*a. fig.*), рассве́т; рассвета́ть

day день *m*; *the other ~* на днях; *~break* рассве́т; *~light* дневно́й свет; *~time: in the ~time* днём

daze *fig.* ошеломля́ть

dazzle ослепля́ть [-пи́ть] (*a. fig.*); *~ing* ослепи́тельный

dead мёртвый; *adv. coll.* соверше́нно; *he is ~* он у́мер; *~lock* тупи́к; *~ly* смерте́льный

deaf глухо́й; *~ening* оглуши́тельный; *~ness* глухота́

deal *comm.* сде́лка; (*cards*) сда́ча; торгова́ть (*in* Т); *~with* име́ть де́ло с (Т); (*act*) поступа́ть [-пи́ть] с (Т); *a great ~* мно́го; *~er* торго́вец, ди́лер; *~ings* деловы́е отноше́ния *n/pl.*

dean дека́н; *eccl.* настоя́тель собо́ра

dear дорого́й, ми́лый; (*address in informal letters*) дорого́й (*a. ~ expensive*);

(*formal address*) [глубоко́]-уважа́емый; *~th* дорогови́зна; нехва́тка

death смерть *f*; *~ rate* сме́ртность *f*

debate деба́ты *m/pl.*, пре́ния *n/pl.*; дебати́ровать (*im*)*pf.*

debit де́бет

debris разва́лины *f/pl.*

debt долг; *~or* должни́к

decade десятиле́тие, дека́да

decadence упа́док

decay разложе́ние; упа́док; *fall into ~* приходи́ть, прийти́ в упа́док, *building:* [об]ветша́ть; разлага́ться [-ложи́ться]; (*rot*) [с]гнить

deceit обма́н; *~ful* лжи́вый; (*deceptive*) обма́нчивый

deceive обма́нывать [-ну́ть]

December дека́брь *m*

decen|cy прили́чие; поря́дочность; *~t* прили́чный; (*respectable*) поря́дочный; (*rather good*) прили́чный; *its very ~t of you* о́чень любе́зно с ва́шей стороны́

deception обма́н

decide реша́ть [-ши́ть]; *~d* (*resolute*) реши́тельный

decis|ion реше́ние; (*quality*) реши́тельность *f*; *~ive* реша́ющий; (*tone*) реши́тельный

deck *mar.* па́луба; *~chair**

шезло́нг

declaration заявле́ние; деклара́ция; (war) объявле́ние; *customs* **_ation** таможенная деклара́ция; **_е** заявля́ть [-ви́ть]; объявля́ть [-ви́ть]

declension склоне́ние

decline (*refuse*) отклоня́ть [-ни́ть]; *gr.* [про]склоня́ть; (*decay*) упа́док

decorate украша́ть [укра́сить]; *mil.* награжда́ть [-ради́ть] (о́рденом); **_ion** украше́ние; о́рден; **_ive** декорати́вный

decrease уменьша́ть(ся) [-шить(ся)]; уменьше́ние

decree декре́т, ука́з; постановля́ть [-ви́ть]

dedicate посвяща́ть [-яти́ть]; **_ion** (*mst. in a book*) посвяще́ние

deduce (*decide*) [с]де́лать вы́вод; **_t** вычита́ть [вы́честь]; **_tion** вы́чет; (*inference*) вы́вод

deed дея́ние, де́ло; (*heroic*) по́двиг; *jur.* **_ of purchase** догово́р ку́пли-прода́жа

deep глубо́кий; (*colour*) густо́й; (*sound*) ни́зкий; **_en** углубля́ть(ся) [-би́ть(ся)]; **_freeze** моро́зи́ль

deer оле́нь *m*

default (*absence*) нея́вка; **_ of payment** неупла́та

defeat пораже́ние; наноси́ть пораже́ние (Д)

defect недоста́ток, де-

фе́кт; (*flaw*) изъя́н; **_ive** *tech.* неиспра́вный, дефе́ктный; **_ive goods** брако́ванные това́ры

defence защи́та (*a.* tech., sports); *mil.* оборо́на; **_less** беззащи́тный

defend защища́ть [-ити́ть]; обороня́ть [-ни́ть]; **_ant** обвиня́емый; **_er** защи́тни|к, -ца

defensive оборони́тельный; оборо́на

defer (*postpone*) откла́дывать, -ложи́ть; *payment* отсро́чи(ва)ть; **_ment** отсро́чка

defiance вы́зов; *in _ce of* напереко́р (Д); **_t** вызыва́ющий

deficiency недоста́ток; **_t** недоста́точный

define определя́ть [-ли́ть]; **_ite** определённый; **_ition** определе́ние

deform деформи́ровать (*im*)*pf.*; **_ity** уро́дство

defrost *v/t.* разма́раживать [-ро́зить]

defy бро́сить вы́зов; вести́ себя́ вызыва́юще; *description* не поддава́ться (Д)

degenerate вырожда́ться [вы́родиться]; вырожда́ющийся; вы́родок; **_ion** вырожде́ние

degradation деграда́ция; **_е** дегради́ровать (*im*)*pf.*; **_ing** унизи́тельный

degree сте́пень *f* (*a. univ.*)

(*thermometer*) гра́дус; **by ~s** постепе́нно; *in some ~* до изве́стной сте́пени

deity божество́

deject|ed уны́лый; **~ion** уны́ние

delay заде́ржка; (*respite*) отсро́чка; заде́рживать [-жа́ть]; отсро́чи(ва)ть

delegat|e делеги́ровать (*im*)*pf.*; **~ion** делега́ция; (*action*) делеги́рование

deliberate (*intentional*) (пред)наме́ренный; (*unhurried*) неторопли́вый; обду́м(ыв)ать (В); **~e on** совеща́ться о (П); **~ely** (*on purpose*) наро́чно

delica|cy делика́тность *f*; (*tenderness*) не́жность *f*; (*situation*) щекотли́вость *f*; (*food*) ла́комство; **~te** делика́тный; не́жный; щекотли́вый; **~ious** (*tasty*) о́чень вку́сный; (*smell, taste*) восхити́тельный

delight восто́рг; (*enjoyment*) наслажде́ние; приводи́ть в восто́рг; **be ~ed with** быть в восто́рге от (Р); **~ful** восхити́тельный; (*sweet*) сла́достный

delinquent правонаруши́тель *m*

delirious: be ~ быть в бреду́, бре́дить

deliver (*supply*) доставля́ть [-вить]; (*free*) освобо

жда́ть [-боди́ть]; **~ance** освобожде́ние; (*saving*) спасе́ние; **~y** доста́вка; *med.* ро́ды *m/pl.*

deluge пото́п; (*heavy rain*) ли́вень

delusion заблужде́ние

demand [по]тре́бовать (Р); тре́бование; *comm.* спрос

democra|cy демокра́тия; **~t** демокра́т; **~tic** демократи́ческий

demolish разруша́ть [-ши́ть]; *building* сноси́ть [снести́]; **~tion** разруше́ние

demon де́мон

demonstrat|e демонстри́ровать (*im*)*pf.*; *math.* дока́зывать [-за́ть]; **~ion** демонстра́ция; доказа́тельство

demoralize деморализова́ть (*im*)*pf.*

demure скро́мный

den ло́гово; (*thieves'*) прито́н

denial отрица́ние; (*refusal*) отка́з

denomination *eccl.* вероисповеда́ние

denote означа́ть; (*indicate*) ука́зывать [-за́ть] (на В)

denounce (*accuse publicly*) разоблача́ть [-чи́ть]

dens|e пло́тный; (*forest*) густо́й; *coll.* тупо́й; **~ity** пло́тность *f*; густота́

dent вы́боина; вмя́тина

dent|al зубно́й; **~ist** зубно́й

врач; ~ure (*artificial*) зубно́й проте́з

deny отрица́ть; (*refuse*) отка́зывать [-за́ть] (в П)

depart *person:* уезжа́ть [уе́хать]; ~ **train:** отходи́ть [отойти́]; ~ment отде́л, отделе́ние; *pol. a.* ве́домство; ~ment store универма́г; ~ure отъе́зд; (*train*) отправле́ние

depend зави́сеть (*on* от Р); (*rely*) полага́ться [-ложи́ться] (*on* на В); ~able надёжный; ~ent зави́симый; (*a.* ~ant) иждиве́нец

depict изобража́ть [-рази́ть]

deplor|able приско́рбный; (*result*) плаче́вный; ~e сожале́ть (о П)

deport высыла́ть ['-слать]

deposit (*advance*) зада́ток; (*bank*) вклад, депози́т; *geol.* за́лежь *f*; класть, положи́ть (в банк); ~or вкла́дчик, депози́тор

depot (*storehouse*) склад; *rail. Am.* полуста́нок

depreciat|e обесце́ни(ва)ть(ся); ~ion обесце́нивание

depress подавля́ть [-ви́ть]; ~ion пода́вленность *f*; *econ.* депре́ссия; *geogr.* впа́дина

depriv|ation лише́ние; ~e лиша́ть [-ши́ть] (*of* Р)

depth глубина́; (*colour*) густота́

deputy депута́т; замести́тель(ница *f*) *m*

deri|de осме́ивать [-е́ять]; ~sion осмея́ние

deriv|ative *su.* произво́дное сло́во; ~e происходи́ть; *benefit* извлека́ть [-е́чь]

descend спуска́ться [-сти́ться] (по Д); *fig.* происходи́ть [-изойти́]; ~dant пото́мок; ~t спуск; (*slope*) склон; *fig.* происхожде́ние

descri|be опи́сывать [-са́ть]; ~ption описа́ние

desert¹ *geogr.* пусты́ня; ~ **island** необита́емый о́стров

desert² покида́ть [-и́нуть]; *mil.* дезерти́ровать (*im*)*pf.*; ~ed пусты́нный; ~er дезерти́р; ~s за́слуги *f/pl.*

deserve заслу́живать [-жи́ть]; ~dly заслу́женно

design (*pattern*) узо́р; (*plan*) прое́кт; дизайн; *art.* компози́ция; (*intention*) у́мысел; [за]проекти́ровать ['-чить]; ~ate обознача́ть ['-чить]; ~ation обозначе́ние; ~er диза́йнер

desir|able жела́тельный; ~e [по]жела́ть (Р); жела́ние

desk пи́сьменный стол

desolate запусте́лый; (*forsaken*) забро́шенный; ~ion запусте́ние; забро́шенность *f*

despair отча́яние; отча́иваться [-ча́яться]

desperate отча́янный

despise презира́ть

despite вопреки́ (Д)

despot де́спот; **~ic** (person) деспоти́чный

dessert десе́рт

destin|ation (пред)назначе́ние; ме́сто назначе́ния; **~e** предназнача́ть ['-чить]; **~y** судьба́

destitute (живу́щий) в нищете́; лишённый (of P)

destroy разруша́ть ['-шить]; **~er** mar. эсми́нец

destruction разруше́ние; **~ve** разруши́тельный

detach отделя́ть [-ли́ть]; **~ment** fig. беспристра́стность; mil. отря́д

detail подро́бность f; (trivial) **~s** ме́лочь f

detain заде́рживать [-жа́ть]

detect обнару́жи(ва)ть; **~ive** сы́щик, операти́вный рабо́тник уголо́вного ро́зыска; adj. детекти́вный

détente pol. разря́дка

deter заде́рживать, уде́рживать [-жа́ть]

detergent стира́льный порошо́к

deteriorate ухудша́ть(ся) ['-ди́ть(ся)]

determin|ation определе́ние; (firm will) реши́тельность f; **~e** определя́ть [-ли́ть]; (decide) реша́ть

[-ши́ть]; **~ed** реши́тельный

deterrent mil. сре́дство сде́рживания

detour око́льный путь m, крюк coll.

detriment уще́рб, вред; **~al** вре́дный

devaluation fin. девальва́ция

devastat|e опустоша́ть [-ши́ть]; **~ion** опустоше́ние

develop разви(ва́)ть(ся); photo проявля́ть [-ви́ть]; **~ment** разви́тие; (event) собы́тие; проявле́ние

device tech. устро́йство, приспособле́ние; (method) приём

devil дья́вол, чёрт; **~ish** чёртовский

devise приду́мывать [-ду́мать]

devoid лишённый (of P)

devolution econ. децентрализа́ция; pol. переда́ча полномо́чий

devot|e посвяща́ть [-яти́ть]; **~ed** пре́данный; **~ion** пре́данность f

devour пож(и)ра́ть; (person) [с]ъесть с жа́дностью; be **~ed by curiosity** сгора́ть от любопы́тства

devout на́божный; (sincere) и́скренний

dew роса́

dexter|ity ло́вкость f; **~ous** ло́вкий

diagnosis диа́гноз

diagram диагра́мма, схе́ма

dial циферблат; (*telephone*) диск; набира́ть но́мер

dialect диале́кт, го́вор

dialogue диало́г

diameter диа́метр

diamond бриллиа́нт; *rough* ~ алма́з; ~s (*cards*) бу́бны *f/pl.*

diarrhoea поно́с; *have* ~ страда́ть от поно́са

diary дневни́к; (*noting engagements*) календа́рь

dicta|**te** [про]диктова́ть; *pol.* дикта́т; ~**ion** дикта́нт; (*action*) дикто́вка, *or* диктатор; ~**orship** диктату́ра

dictionary слова́рь *m*

die умира́ть [умере́ть]; ~ *down sound*: замира́ть [замере́ть]

diet пи́ща; *med.* дие́та

differ различа́ться *impf.*; ~**ence** ра́зница; *math.* ра́зность *f*; (*discord*) разногла́сие; ~**ent** разли́чный, ино́й; (*diverse*) ра́зный; ~**ently** ина́че

difficult тру́дный; ~**y** тру́дность *f*

diffident неуве́ренный в себе́

dig копа́ть, [вы́]рыть

digest перева́ривать [-ри́ть]; *fig.* усва́ивать [усво́ить]; (*literary*) дайджест; ~**ion** пищеваре́ние

dignity досто́инство

digress отклоня́ться [-ни́ться] (от Р)

dike да́мба; (*ditch*) кана́ва

dilate расширя́ть(ся) [-ри́ть(ся)]

dilemma диле́мма

diligen|**ce** прилежа́ние; ~**t** приле́жный

dilute разбавля́ть [-вить]

dim ту́склый; (*vague*) сму́тный; *mot.* ~ *the headlights* включа́ть [-чи́ть] бли́жний свет

dimension *pl.*, (= *size*) разме́р

dimin|**ish** уменьша́ть(ся) [-ши́ть(ся)]; ~**utive** (*tiny*) кро́шечный; *gr.* уменьши́тельный

dimple я́мочка

din гро́хот, шум

dine [по]обе́дать, ~**r** обе́дающий; *rail. Am.* ваго́н-рестора́н

dining-**car** ваго́н-рестора́н; ~-**room** столо́вая

dinner обе́д

dip окуна́ть(ся) [-ну́ть(-ся)]; *brush* обма́кивать [-кну́ть]

diploma дипло́м; ~**cy** диплома́тия; ~**t** диплома́т; ~**tic** дипломати́ческий; (*tactful*) дипломати́чный

direct прямо́й; (*first-hand*) непосре́дственный; направля́ть [-вить]; (*control*) руководи́ть (Т), управля́ть (Т); ~**ion** направле́ние; управле́ние; ~**or** дире́ктор; (*film*) режиссёр; ~ory а́дресно-спра́вочная кни́га; телефо́нный спра́вочник

dirt грязь *f*; ~y гря́зный

disabled (*unable to work*) нетрудоспосо́бный

disadvantage невы́годное положе́ние; (*shortcoming*) недоста́ток; ~ous невы́годный

disagree не соглаша́ться [-ласи́ться]; *I ~ with you* я с ва́ми несогла́сен; ~able неприя́тный; ~ment разногла́сие; *express ~ment* выража́ть ['-азить] несогла́сие

disappear исчеза́ть [-е́знуть]; ~ance исчезнове́ние

disappoint разочаро́вывать [-ова́ть]; ~ment разочарова́ние

disapprov|al неодобре́ние; ~e не одобря́ть ['-рить]

disarm разоружа́ть(ся) [-жи́ть(ся)]; ~ament разоруже́ние

disast|er бе́дствие, катастро́фа; ~rous бе́дственный, ги́бельный; *~rous policy* ги́бельная поли́тика

disband *mil.* расформиро́вывать [-ирова́ть]

disbelief неве́рие

disc диск; *compact ~* компа́кт-диск; ~otheque дискоте́ка

discard (*reject*) отбра́сывать [-ро́сить]

discern различа́ть [-личи́ть]

discharge разгружа́ть [-узи́ть]; *el.* разряжа́ть [-яди́ть]; (*dismiss*) увольня́ть [уво́лить]; разря́д; увольне́ние; (*from hospital*) выпи́сывать ['-писать]

disciple учени́к (*a. eccl.*); ~ine дисципли́на

disclose раскрыва́ть [-кры́ть]; обнару́живать [-ру́жить]

discomfort неудо́бство, дискомфо́рт

disconnect разъединя́ть [-ни́ть]

discontent недово́льство; ~ed недово́льный

discord разногла́сие

discount (*deduction*) ски́дка; (*bank*) учёт; *~rate* учётная ста́вка

discourage обескура́живать(ва)ть

discover открыва́(ва́)ть; ~y откры́тие

discredit дискредити́ровать (*im*)*pf.*; (*throw doubt on*) ста́вить под сомне́ние; дискреди́та́ция

discreet (*tactful*) такти́чный; (*circumspect*) осмотри́тельный

discretion благоразу́мие *f*; осмотри́тельность *f*; (*choice*) усмотре́ние; *use* *your own* ~ поступа́й(те) по своему́ усмотре́нию

discrimination (*law*) дискримина́ция; (*ability to choose*) разбо́рчивость; вкус

discus диск

discuss обсужда́ть [-уди́ть]; ~**ion** обсужде́ние

disdain презира́ть; презре́ние

disease боле́знь *f*; ~**d** больно́й

disembark (*passengers*) выса́живать(ся) ['-сади́ть(ся)]

disfigure [о]безобра́зить

disgrace позо́р; (*disfavour*) неми́лость *f*; [о]позо́рить; ~**ful** позо́рный

disguise [за]маскирова́ть; (*hide*) скры(ва́)ть; маскиро́вка

disgust отвраще́ние; внуша́ть отвраще́ние (Д); ~**ing** отврати́тельный

dish суши́лка для посу́ды

dishearten обескура́живать(ва)ть

dishonest нече́стный

dishonour [о]бесче́стить; бесче́стье

disillusioned разочаро́ванный

disinterested бескоры́стный

disk диск → *disc*

dislike не люби́ть; нелюбо́вь *f* (**for** к Д); *take a* ~

to s.o. невзлюби́ть кого́- -ли́бо

dismal мра́чный, уны́лый

dismantle разбира́ть [-зобра́ть]

dismiss увольня́ть [уво́лить]; (*send away*) отпуска́ть [-сти́ть]; *fig.* отбра́сывать [-бро́сить]; ~**al** увольне́ние

dismount *tech.* демонти́ровать (*im*)*pf.*

disobe|dience непослуша́ние; ~**dient** непослу́шный; ~**y** не [по]слу́шаться (Р) *pf.*; *order* не подчиня́ться [-ни́ться] (Д)

disorder беспоря́док; (*stomach*) расстро́йство; (*public*) беспоря́дки *m/pl.*; ~**ly** беспоря́дочный

dispatch (*send*) отправля́ть ['-вить]; отпра́вка, отсы́лка; (*message*) сообще́ние

dispel разве́ивать [-ве́ить], рассе́ивать [-се́ять], *a. fig.*

dispense: ~ **with** обходи́ться [обойти́сь] (без Р)

disperse разгоня́ть [разогна́ть], рассе́ивать [-се́ять]

displace (*change the place*) переставля́ть, перекла́дывать; (*a bone*) смеща́ть [смести́ть]

display (*exhibit*) выставля́ть [вы́ставить]; *fig.* проявля́ть [-ви́ть]; выста́вка; проявле́ние; *tech.* дисплёй

displeas|e вызыва́ть недово́льство (P); **~ure** недово́льство

disposa|l: at your ~al в ва́шем распоряже́нии; **~e** располага́ть [-ложи́ть] (*fig. impf. only*); **~e of** распоряжа́ться [-яди́ться] (T); *waste* выбра́сывать ['-бросить]; **~ition** (*character*) хара́ктер

dispute (*argue*) [по]спо́рить; (*discuss*) обсужда́ть [-суди́ть]; *right* оспа́ривать [оспо́рить]; спор; диску́ссия

disqualify дисквалифици́ровать (*im*)*pf.*

disquiet (о)беспоко́ить; беспоко́йство

disregard пренебрега́ть [-бре́чь] (T); пренебреже́ние

dissatisfaction недово́льство, неудовлетворённость

dissipat|e (*disperse*) рассе́ивать [-е́ять]; *money* растра́чивать [-тра́тить]

dissolve растворя́ть(ся) [-ри́ть(ся)]; *parl.* распуска́ть [-пусти́ть]; *agreement* расторга́ть [-гнуть]

distan|ce расстоя́ние, (*sports*) диста́нция; **in the ~ce** вдали́, вдалеке́; **~t** далёкий, да́льний

distil *chem.* перегоня́ть [-гна́ть]; **~led water** ди-

стилли́рованная вода́; **~lery** спиртово́й заво́д

distinct (*clear*) отчётливый; (*different*) разли́чный; **~ion** разли́чие; **~ive** характе́рный, отличи́тельный

distinguish различа́ть [-чи́ть]; **~ o.s.** отлича́ться [-чи́ться]; **~ed** (*scientist, etc.*) ви́дный; (*guest*) почётный

distort искажа́ть [-кази́ть]; **~ion** искаже́ние

distress (*grief*) огорче́ние; *mar.* бе́дствие; **~ing** огорчи́тельный

distribut|e распределя́ть [-ли́ть]; (*deal out*) раздава́ть; **~ion** распределе́ние; разда́ча

district о́круг, райо́н

distrust не доверя́ть (Д); недове́рие

disturb [о]беспоко́ить (В), [по]меша́ть (Д); *peace, rest* наруша́ть [-'шить]; **~ance** наруше́ние (поря́дка); (*noise*) шум; *pl.* волне́ния *f/pl.*

ditch ров, кана́ва

div|e ныря́ть [-рну́ть]; *U-boat:* погружа́ться [-узи́ться]; **~er** (*professional*) водола́з; **~ing** (*sports*) прыжки́ в во́ду

diverge расходи́ться [разойти́сь]

diver|sion (*amusements*) развлече́ние; (*of atten-*

divide [раздели́ть; разделя́ть(ся)] [ли́ть(ся)] (*into* на В); ~nd *comm.* дивиде́нд

divin|e боже́ственный; ~ity божество́; (*theology*) богосло́вие

division деле́ние; разделе́ние; *mil.* диви́зия

divorce разво́д; разводи́ться [-вести́сь] (с Т); (*court*) расторга́ть брак (Р)

dizzy (*height*) головокружи́тельный; **I feel ~** у меня́ кру́жится голова́

do [с]де́лать; (*act*) поступа́ть [-пи́ть]; *that will ~* хва́тит; *how ~ you ~?* ра́д[а] с ва́ми познако́миться!; *we ~ not know* мы не зна́ем; *~ come!* приходи́те же!; *I could ~ with a cup of tea* я не отказа́л[ась, -ся бы от ча́шки ча́я; *~ without* обходи́ться [-ойти́сь] без (Р)

dock *mar.* док

doct|or врач, до́ктор; (*degree*) до́ктор; ~rine до́ктрина, уче́ние

document докуме́нт; ~ary документа́льный (фильм)

dodge уклоня́ться [-ни́ться] от (Р); уве́ртка

dog соба́ка; ~ged упо́рный

dogma до́гма

doleful ско́рбный

doll ку́кла

dollar до́ллар

dolphin *zo.* дельфи́н

domain *fig.* о́бласть *f*

dome ку́пол

domestic семе́йный; дома́шний; (*inland*) вну́тренний

domicile местожи́тельство

domin|ant гла́вный, основно́й; ~ate госпо́дствовать над (Т); ~ation госпо́дство; ~ion влады́чество; (*British*) доминио́н

don *Brit. univ.* преподава́тель

donation дар, поже́ртвование

donkey осёл

donor (*blood, etc.*) до́нор

doom обрека́ть [-е́чь] (*to* на В); (*fate*) рок; (*death, ruin*) ве́рная ги́бель *f*

door дверь *f*; *pl. typ.* ~step поро́г; ~way дверно́й проём; *in the ~way* в дверя́х

dormitory о́бщая спа́льня

dose до́за

dot то́чка; *pl.* многото́чие; ~ted line пункти́р

dote: ~ *on* души́ не ча́ять, обожа́ть

double двойно́й; удва́ивать(ся) [удво́ить(ся)]; *adv.* вдво́е, вдвойне́; ~-breasted двубо́ртный

doubt сомне́ние; сомнева́ться (в П); ~ful сомни́-

тельный; (*uncertain*) по́лный сомне́ний; **~less** несомне́нно

dough те́сто; **~nut** по́нчик

dove го́лубь *m*

down¹ пух (*no pl.*)

down² внизу́, вниз; **with ...!** доло́й (В)!; *up and ~* вверх и вниз; (*walk*) взад и вперёд; **~cast** удручённый; **~fall** (*rain*) ли́вень *m*; паде́ние *n*; **~hill** *adv.* вниз, под го́ру; **~right** (*person*) прямо́й; *it's ~right nonsense* э́то абсолю́тная чепуха́; **~stairs** вниз (по ле́стнице), внизу́; **~ward(s)** *adv.* вниз

dowry прида́ное

doze дрема́ть; *to have a ~* вздремну́ть

dozen дю́жина

draft (*sketch*) набро́сок; (*rough copy*) черновик; *comm.* тра́тта; (*bill*) законопрое́кт; набра́сывать [-роса́ть]; (*document*) составля́ть [-а́вить]; написа́ть черновик (Р); → *a.* draught

drag таска́ть(ся), [по-]ташить(ся); *on time:* тяну́ться; **~net** бре́день *m*

dragon драко́н; **~fly** стрекоза́

drain дрени́ровать (*im*)*pf.*; *fig.* истоща́ть [-щи́ть]; **~age** дрена́ж

drake се́лезень *m*

drama дра́ма; **~tic** драмати́ческий; **~tist** драмату́рг

drape драпирова́ть (*im*) *pf.*; **~ry** драпиро́вка; (*cloth goods*) тка́ни

drastic (*measures*) круто́й, суро́вый

draught (*current*) сквозня́к, (*chimney*) тя́га; (*drinking*) глото́к; **~s** ша́шки; → *a.* draft

draw [по]тяну́ть; (*drawings*) [на]рисова́ть, *tech.* [на]черти́ть; (*attract*) привлека́ть [-е́чь]; (*in game*) ничья́; **~back** ми́нус; **~er** (*box*) выдвижно́й я́щик; **~ing** рису́нок, *tech.* чертёж

dread страх; страши́ться (Р); **~ful** стра́шный

dream сон; (*day~*) мечта́; [при]сни́ться; мечта́ть; **~er** мечта́тель(ница *f*) *m*; **~y** мечта́тельный

dredge землечерпа́лка; *mar.* дра́га

drench промока́ть ['-кнуть]; *I was ~ed to the skin* я промо́к(ла) до ни́тки; прома́чивать [-мочи́ть]

dress пла́тье, оде(ва́)ть(-ся); *wound* перевя́зывать [-за́ть]; **~er** ку́хонный шкаф; **~ing** припра́ва; *cul.* припра́ва; **~ing gown** хала́т; **~maker** портни́ха; **~ rehearsal** генера́льная репети́ция

drift v/i. mar. дрейфова́ть; snow: мести́; v/t. snow, sand наноси́ть [-нести́]; дрейф; (snow-) сугро́б

drill[1] tech. сверло́; [про]сверли́ть

drill[2] (exercises) pl. упражне́ния; (sports) трениро́вка; mil. строева́я подгото́вка

drink [вы́]пить; напи́ток; *let us have a ~* вы́пьем рю́мку; **~er** (heavy) пья́ница m/f

drip ка́пать

drive cattle гнать; car води́ть, вести́ (В); (go) е́здить, [по]е́хать; (take) вози́ть, [по-, от]везти́; *~ mad* своди́ть с ума́; **~r** води́тель

drizzle мороси́ть

drone insect: жужжа́ть; motor: гуде́ть, жужжа́ние; гуде́ние; zo. тру́тень m

droop поника́ть ['-кнуть]

drop ка́пля; v/i. ка́пать; (fall) па́дать [упа́сть]; v/t. роня́ть [урони́ть]; **~in(to)** заходи́ть [зайти́]; **~per** med. пипе́тка

drought за́суха

drown v/t. [у]топи́ть; v/i. (= *be ~ed*) [у]тону́ть

drowsy со́нный

drudgery ну́дная рабо́та

drug лека́рство; нарко́тик; **~ addict** наркома́н; **~gist** апте́карь; **~store** Am. ап-

drum бараба́н; бараба́нить; **~mer** бараба́нщик

drunk пья́ный; *get ~* опьяне́ть; напи́ться; **~ard** пья́ница m/f; **~enness** опьяне́ние; (habit) пья́нство

dry сухо́й; v/t. [вы́]сушить; v/i. [вы́]со́хнуть; **~ness** су́хость

dual двойно́й

dubious сомни́тельный

duchess герцоги́ня

duck у́тка; окуна́ть(ся) [-ну́ть(ся); **~ling** утёнок

due (proper) до́лжный, надлежа́щий; *the train is ~* по́езд прибыва́ет; *~ to* (owing to) всле́дствие, из-за (Р); su. до́лжное; (harbour) pl. сбо́ры m/pl., (club) взно́сы m/pl.

duel дуэ́ль f

duke ге́рцог; **~dom** ге́рцогство

dull (knife; person) тупо́й; (weather) па́смурный; (boring) ску́чный

duly до́лжным о́бразом; (in time) своевре́менно

dumb немо́й; **~ness** немота́

dummy (tailor's) манеке́н; (baby's) пусты́шка; mil., tech. маке́т; (figure-head) подставно́е лицо́

dump load сва́ливать [-ли́ть]; (place) сва́лка; mil. склад; **~ing** comm. де́мпинг

dunce тупо́й учени́к, ту-
пи́ца *m/f*

dune дю́на

dung наво́з

dungeon темни́ца

dupe простофи́ля *m/f*;
наду́(ва́)ть

duplicate дублика́т, ко́пия;
[с]де́лать ко́пию

dur|able про́чный; ~ation
дли́тельность *f*; for the
~ation of на вре́мя (P);
~ing во вре́мя (P)

dusk су́мерки *f/pl.*

dust пыль *f*; ~bin му́сор-
ный я́щик; ~er тря́пка
для вытира́ния пы́ли; ~y
пы́льный

Dutch голла́ндский; ~man,
~woman голла́ндец *m*,
голла́ндка *f*

duty долг, обя́занность *f*;
comm. по́шлина; on ~ на
дежу́рстве; ~free не об-
лага́емый тамо́женной по́-
шлиной

dwarf ка́рлик

dwell жить, обита́ть; ~er
жи́тель(ница *f*) *m*; ~ing
жили́ще

dye кра́ска; [по]кра́сить

dynam|ic динами́ческий;
fig. динами́чный; ~ics ди-
на́мика; ~ite динами́т

dynasty дина́стия

dysentery дизентери́я

E

each ка́ждый; ~ other друг
дру́га

eager усе́рдный; be ~ to
стреми́ться + *inf.*; ~ness
усе́рдие

eagle орёл

ear у́хо; *bot.* ко́лос

earl граф

early ра́нний; *adv.* ра́но

earn зараба́тывать [-бо́-
тать]; (*deserve*) заслу́жи-
вать [-жи́ть]

earnest серьёзный; (*sin-
cere*) и́скренний; in ~
серьёзно

earnings за́работок

earphones нау́шники *m/pl.*

ear-ring серьга́

earth земля́; ~en земля-
но́й; ~enware гли́няная
посу́да; ~ly земно́й;
~quake землетрясе́ние

ease: be (ill) at ~ чу́вство-
вать себя́ (ско́ванно) не-
принуждённо (нело́вко);
(*slacken*) ослабля́ть
['-бить]; with ~ с лёгко-
стью

easel мольбе́рт

easily легко́, без труда́;
~ness лёгкость *f*

east восто́к; *attr.* восто́ч-
ный; ~ of к восто́ку от
(P); Far 2 Да́льний Вос-
то́к; 2er па́сха; ~ern вос-
то́чный

easy лёгкий; (*manners*) непринуждённый; ~ *chair* кре́сло; ~*-going* беспе́чный

eat [съ]есть; ~ *up* съеда́ть [съесть]; ~*able* съедо́бный

ebb отли́в

ebony чёрное де́рево

eccentric эксцентри́чный (челове́к); *tech.* эксцентри́ческий; ~*icity* эксцентри́чность *f*

ecclesiastical церко́вный; (*clerical*) духо́вный

echo э́хо; *fig.* отголо́сок; *v/t.* вто́рить (Д) *v/i.* отража́ться [-рази́ться]

eclair экле́р

eclipse *astron.* затме́ние; *v/t.*, *v/i.* затмева́ть [затми́ть]

economic экономи́ческий; ~*ical* эконо́мный, хозя́йственный; ~*ics* эконо́мика; ~*y* эконо́мия; эконо́мика; *national* ~*y* наро́дное хозя́йство

ecstasy экста́з; восто́рг

edge (*table*) край; (*wood*) опу́шка; (*knife*) ле́звие; ~*ing* кайма́

edible съедо́бный

edifice зда́ние; ~*ying* назида́тельный

edit [от]редакти́ровать; *book* изд(ав)а́ть; ~*ion* изда́ние; ~*or* реда́ктор; изда́тель *m*; ~*orial* передова́я статья́; ~*orial office**

реда́кция

educate дава́ть [дать] образова́ние; воспи́тывать [-та́ть]; ~*ed* образо́ванный; ~*ion* образова́ние; воспита́ние; ~*ional film* уче́бный фильм

eel у́горь *m*

efface *fig.* изгла́живать [-гла́дить]; ~ *o.s.* стушёвываться [-шева́ться]

effect де́йствие; (*consequence*) сле́дствие; *bad* ~ плохо́е влия́ние; *take* ~ вступи́ть в си́лу; ~*ive* эффекти́вный; (*law*) име́ющий си́лу; *jur.* действи́тельный; (*spectacular*) эффе́ктный

effeminate женоподо́бный

efficacious де́йственный, эффекти́вный; ~*y* де́йственность *f*

efficiency де́йственность, эффекти́вность; (*person*) уме́лость *f*; работоспосо́бность *f*; ~*t* эффекти́вный; уме́лый; работоспосо́бный; делово́й

effort уси́лие; попы́тка

e.g. наприме́р

egg яйцо́; *hard-boiled* ~ яйцо́ вкруту́ю; *soft-boiled* ~ яйцо́ всмя́тку; *fried* ~*s* яи́чница-глазу́нья; *scrambled* ~*s* яи́чница-болту́нья; ~*-shell* скорлупа́

egoism эгои́зм; ~*t* эгои́ст(ка); ~*tic* эгоисти́чный

Egyptian египтя́н|ин, -ка; еги́петский

eight во́семь; **~een** восемна́дцать; **~eenth** восемна́дцатый; **~h** восьмо́й; **~y** во́семьдесят

either тот и́ли друго́й; (both) и тот и друго́й; **I can't do it** – я то́же не могу́ э́того сде́лать; ~ ... **or** и́ли ... и́ли

elaborate разраба́тывать [разрабо́тать]; тща́тельно разрабо́танный

elapse истека́ть [-е́чь]; проходи́ть [пройти́]

elastic эласти́чный, упру́гий; (tape) рези́нка; **~ity** эласти́чность f, упру́гость f

elbow ло́коть m

elder[1] bot. бузина́

elder[2] ста́рший; **~ly** пожило́й; **~est** ста́рший

elect изб|ира́ть, [-бра́ть] [вы́брать]; **~ion** вы́боры m/pl.; **~or** избира́тель m; **~oral** избира́тельный

electri|c(al) электри́ческий; **~cian** электроте́хник; **~ic** электрик; **~city** электри́чество f; **~fy** электрифици́ровать (im)pf.

electronic электро́нный; **~s** электро́ника

elegan|ce элега́нтность f, изя́щество f; **~t** элега́нтный, изя́щный

element элеме́нт; (any of the 4) стихи́я; **~al** стихи́й-

ный; **~ary** элемента́рный; (school) нача́льный

elephant слон

elevat|ed возвы́шенный (a. fig.); **~ion** возвыше́ние, возвы́шенность f; **~or** (grain store) элева́тор; Am. лифт; tech. подъёмник

eleven оди́ннадцать; **~th** оди́ннадцатый

eliminate устраня́ть [-ни́ть]; (exclude) исключа́ть [-чи́ть]

elk лось m

elm(-tree) вяз

eloquen|ce красноре́чие; **~t** красноречи́вый

else: **what** ~ что ещё; **somebody** ~ кто́-то друго́й; **or** ~ и́ли же; (if not) а то; **~where** в друго́м ме́сте; в друго́е ме́сто

elusive (answer) укло́нчивый

embankment rail. на́сыпь f; (river) на́бережная

embargo эмба́рго n indecl.; **place an** ~ **on** наложи́ть эмба́рго на (В)

embark сади́ться [сесть] на кора́бль; ~ (up)on fig. бра́ться [взя́ться] за (В); **~ation** поса́дка; (of cargo) погру́зка

embarrass затрудня́ть [-ни́ть]; (confuse) смуща́ть [-ути́ть]; **~ing** затрудни́тельный; **~ment** затрудне́ние; смуще́ние

embassy посо́льство

embezzle (незако́нно) растра́чивать [-ра́тить]; **~ment** растра́та

emblem эмбле́ма

embody воплоща́ть [-лоти́ть]; (include) включа́ть [-чи́ть]

embrace обнима́ть [-ня́ть]; (comprise) охва́тывать [-ти́ть]; объя́тия n/pl.

embroider выши(ва́)ть; **~y** вы́шивка

embryo заро́дыш; attr. зача́точный

emerald изумру́д

emerge всплы(ва́)ть (a. fig.); **~ncy** кра́йняя необходи́мость; чрезвыча́йная ситуа́ция; attr. (exit) запасно́й, (landing) вы́нужденный

emigra|nt эмигра́нт(ка); **~te** эмигри́ровать (im) pf.; **~tion** эмигра́ция

eminen|ce geogr. возвы́шение; fig. знамени́тость f; **2ce** высокопреосвяще́нство; **~t** выдаю́щийся

emit испуска́ть [-усти́ть]

emotion чу́вство, эмо́ция; волне́ние; **~al** эмоциона́льный; (exiting) волну́ющий

empha|sis fig. подчёркивание; **~size** fig. подчёркивать [-черкну́ть]; **~tic** подчёркнутый; (gesture) вырази́тельный

empire импе́рия

employ (give work) нанима́ть [-ня́ть]; (use) применя́ть [-ни́ть]; **~ee** рабо́чий; (office worker) слу́жащий, -ая; **~er** работода́тель m; **~ment** рабо́та; заня́тие; (use) примене́ние; **full ~ment** по́лная за́нятость f

empower уполномо́чи(ва)ть

empt|iness пустота́; **~y** пусто́й (a. fig); опоража́нивать [-ро́жнить]

enable дава́ть возмо́жность [Д]

enact постановля́ть [-ви́ть]; thea. игра́ть [сыгра́ть]

enamel эма́ль f; art. эма́ль, финифть; эмалирова́ть

enchant очаро́вывать [-ова́ть]; **~ment** очарова́ние

encircle окружа́ть [-жи́ть]

enclos|e document прилага́ть [приложи́ть]; (fence in) огора́живать [-роди́ть]; **~ure** приложе́ние; agr. заго́н

encore int. бис

encounter (неожи́данно) встреча́ть [-е́тить]; встре́ча; mil. сты́чка

encourage person ободря́ть [-ри́ть]; person, action поощря́ть [-ри́ть]; **~ment** ободре́ние; поощре́ние

encroach: ~ upon (territory) вторга́ться ['-гнуться] (в

B); (*rights*) посяга́ть [-гну́ть] (на B); (*time*) отнима́ть [-ня́ть]; ~ment вторже́ние

encumber обременя́ть [-ни́ть]; (*block up*) загроможда́ть [-мозди́ть]

end коне́ц; конча́ть(ся) ['-чить(ся)]; **in the ~** в конце́ концо́в; **to that ~** с э́той це́лью

endanger подверга́ть опа́сности

endeavour [по]стара́ться; стара́ние

ending оконча́ние (*a.gr.*); ~less бесконе́чный

endorse подтвержда́ть [-рди́ть]; *cheque, etc.* подпи́сывать [-са́ть]

endurance вы́держка, выно́сливость *f*; ~e выде́рживать [вы́держать]; ~ing про́чный; до́лгий

enemy враг; вра́жеский

energetic энерги́чный

enforce заставля́ть ['-вить]; ~ **a law** применя́ть [-ни́ть] зако́н

engage (*bind. o.s.*) обя́зываться [-за́ться]; (*hire*) нанима́ть [-ня́ть]; **be ~d** быть помо́лвленным; ~ment обяза́тельство; помо́лвка; (*date*) свида́ние, встре́ча; *mil.* бой

engine дви́гатель *m*, мото́р; ~er инжене́р; *mar.* меха́ник

English англи́йский; **the ~**

англича́не; **man, ~woman** англича́н|ин, -ка

engrav|e [вы́]гравирова́ть; ~ing гравю́ра

enhance повыша́ть [-ы́сить]

enjoy получа́ть [-чи́ть] удово́льствие; (*delight in*) наслажда́ться [-лади́ться] (T); **I ~ed the book** кни́га мне понра́вилась

enlarge увели́чи(ва)ть (*a. photo*); (*extend*) расширя́ть [-ши́рить] (*a. fig.*); ~ment увеличе́ние

enlighten просвеща́ть [-ети́ть]

enlist *v/t.* (*obtain*) заручи́ться подде́ржкой; *v/i. mil.* призыва́ть [-зва́ть] (*into* в B); поступа́ть [-пи́ть] (на B)

enliven оживля́ть [-ви́ть]

enmity вражда́; (*feeling of hatred*) вражде́бность

enormous грома́дный

enough дово́льно, доста́точно

enquire → **inquire**

enrage [вз]беси́ть

enrapture приводи́ть в восто́рг

enrich обога́|ща́ть [-гати́ть]

enrol(l) → **enlist**

ensue [по]сле́довать; получа́ться в результа́те

ensure *success* обеспе́чи(ва)ть; ~ **against** предохраня́ть [-ни́ть] от (P)

entail влечь за собо́й

entangle запу́тывать(ся) ['-тать(ся)]; *fig.* впу́т(ы-в)ать

enter *room* входи́ть (войти́) (в В); *school* поступа́ть [-пи́ть] (в В); *name* вноси́ть [внести́]

enterprise предприя́тие; (*quality*) предприи́мчивость *f;* **-ing** предприи́мчивый

entertain (*amuse*) развлека́ть [-éчь]; *guests* принима́ть [-ня́ть]; (*provide a meal*) угоща́ть [угости́ть]; **-ment** развлече́ние

enthusias|m энтузиа́зм, восто́рг; **-tic** по́лный энтузиа́зма, восто́рженный

entice при-, пере-ма́нивать [-ни́ть]; завлека́ть [-ле́чь]

entire це́лый, весь; **-ly** цели́ком, всеце́ло

entitled: *be ~ to* име́ть пра́во на (В)

entrails вну́тренности *f/pl.*

entrance вход; (*for cars*) въезд; *~ hall* пере́дняя; (*in a public building*) вестибю́ль

entreat умоля́ть [-ли́ть]; **-y** мольба́

entrepreneur предпринима́тель; **-ship** предпринима́тельство

entrust доверя́ть ['-рить] (Д *with* В)

entry вход; (*for cars*) въезд; *no ~* вход (въезд) запре-

щён; (*in book*) за́пись *f;* **~ permit** разреше́ние на въезд

enumerate перечисля́ть ['-лить]

envelop (*in mist, etc.*) оку́тывать ['-тать]; *baby, etc.* завёртывать [-верну́ть]; **-e** конве́рт

enviable зави́дный

envious зави́стливый

environ|ment окруже́ние; окружа́ющая среда́; (*social*) среда́; **-ment protection** охра́на окружа́ющей среды́; **-mental:** **-mental pollution** загрязне́ние окружа́ющей среды́; **-s** окре́стность *f*

envisage представля́ть себе́; (*anticipate*) предви́деть

envoy посла́нник; (*diplomat*) полномо́чный представи́тель

envy за́висть *f;* [по]зави́довать (Д)

epidemic эпиде́мия

episode эпизо́д

epoch эпо́ха; **-making** эпоха́льный

equal ра́вный; равня́ться (Д); ровня́ *m/f;* **-ity** ра́венство; **-ize** ура́внивать [-ня́ть]; **-ly** по́ровну; (*likewise*) в ра́вной сте́пени

equanimity споко́йствие; невозмути́мость

equat|ion уравне́ние; **-or** эква́тор

equilibrium равнове́сие

equip обеспе́чивать [-чить]; (*fit out*) обору́довать (*im*)*pf.*; **~ment** обору́дование

equivalent эквивале́нт; эквивале́нтный

era э́ра

eradicate искореня́ть [-ни́ть]

erase стира́ть [стере́ть]; *tech.* стира́ние

erect *arch.* (*build*) [по]стро́ить; (*monument*) воздвига́ть [-и́гнуть]

erotic эроти́ческий

err ошиба́ться [-би́ться]

errand поруче́ние; **run ~s** быть на побегу́шках

error оши́бка, погре́шность (*a. tech.*)

eruption изверже́ние; *med.* сыпь *f*

escalator эскала́тор

escape убега́ть [убежа́ть]; (*avoid*) избега́ть ['-гнуть *or* избежа́ть]; бе́гство; побе́г

escort эско́рт; эскорти́ровать

especially осо́бенно

essay о́черк; (*a try*) попы́тка

essence су́щность *f*; суть *f*; **the ~ce of the matter** суть де́ла; **~tial** (*necessary*) необходи́мый; (*important*) суще́ственный; (*indispensable*) непреме́нный

establish (*set up*) учрежда́ть [-еди́ть]; *fact* устана́вливать [-нови́ть]; **~ o.s.** устра́иваться [-ро́иться]; **~ment** учрежде́ние; установле́ние

estate (*landed*) поме́стье; (*real*) (недви́жимое) иму́щество

esteem уважа́ть; уваже́ние

ester *chem.* эфи́р

estimate оце́нка; *fin.* сме́та; оце́нивать [-ни́ть] (*at в* B)

Estonian эсто́н|ец, -ка; эсто́нский

etc. и т. д. (= и так да́лее)

etching офо́рт

etern|al ве́чный; **~ity** ве́чность *f*

ethic эти́ческий; **~s** э́тика, мора́ль

ethnic этни́ческий

etiquette этике́т

European европе́ец; -йский

evacua|te эвакуи́ровать (-ся) (*im*)*pf.*; **~ion** эвакуа́ция

evade уклоня́ться [-ни́ться] *от* (P); *law* обходи́ть [обойти́]

evaporate испаря́ть(ся) [-ри́ть(ся)]; *fig.* развева́ться [-е́яться]; **~ion** испаре́ние

evasi|on уклоне́ние (*of от* P); **~ve** укло́нчивый

eve кану́н; **on the ~ of** накану́не (P); **Christmas** ⁓ сочёльник

even¹ ро́вный *a.*; (*development*) равноме́рный; (*number*) чётный

even² *adv.* да́же

evening ве́чер; *attr.* вече́рний; **in the** ⁓ ве́чером; *in the* ⁓ вече́ром

event собы́тие; (*outcome*) исхо́д; *in the* ⁓ *of* в слу́чае (P)

ever когда́-либо; (*as good*) **as** ⁓ как всегда́; **for** ⁓ навсегда́; **⁓green** вечнозелёный

every ка́ждый; ⁓ **other day** че́рез день; ⁓**body**, ⁓**one** все (*pl.*); ⁓**day** *adj.* повседне́вный; ⁓**where** везде́, всю́ду

eviden|ce (*indication*) при́знак; (*facts*) фа́кты, да́нные *pl.*; (*basis*) основа́ние; *jur.* свиде́тельства, показа́ния, *mst. pl.*; **give** ⁓**ce** дава́ть показа́ния; (*piece*) ули́ка; ⁓**t** очеви́дный

evil злой, дурно́й; *su.* зло

evolution эволю́ция

evolve развива́ть(ся)

ewe овца́

exact то́чный; взы́скивать [-ка́ть]; ⁓**ing** взыска́тельный; ⁓**itude** то́чность *f*; ⁓**ly** то́чно; как раз, ро́вно

exaggerat|e преувели́чи(ва)ть; ⁓**ion** преувеличе́ние

exalt (*praise*) превозноси́ть [-нести́]; ⁓**ation** (*rapture*) восто́рженность *f*

examin|ation осмо́тр (*a. med.*); (*school*) экза́мен; ⁓**e** осма́тривать [осмотре́ть]; (*check*) проверя́ть [-ве́рить]; [про]экзамено́вать

example приме́р; **for** ⁓ наприме́р

exceed (*be greater than*) превосходи́ть [-взойти́]; **speed, etc.** превыша́ть [-ы́сить]; ⁓**ingly** чрезвыча́йно, о́чень

excel *v/t.* превосходи́ть [-взойти́]; *v/i.* отлича́ться [-чи́ться]; ⁓**lence** превосхо́дство; ⁓**lency** превосходи́тельство; ⁓**lent** превосхо́дный, отли́чный

except исключа́ть [-чи́ть]; *prep.* исключа́я (B), кро́ме (P); ⁓ исключе́ние; ⁓**ional** исключи́тельный

excess изли́шек; эксце́сс; *in* ⁓ *of* сверх (P); ⁓ **fare** допла́та; ⁓ **profits duty** нало́г на сверхприбыль; ⁓**ive** чрезме́рный

exchange обме́н; *fin.* би́ржа; **bill of** ⁓ долгово́е обяза́тельство *m*; **foreign** ⁓ **rate** валю́тный курс

excite возбужда́ть [-уди́ть]; ⁓**ment** возбужде́ние

excla|im восклица́ть [-и́кнуть]; ⁓**mation** восклица́-

ние

exclu|de исключа́ть [-чи́ть];
~sion исключе́ние;
~sive исключи́тельный;
(*circle*) за́мкнутый, не
общедосту́пный

excursion экску́рсия

excuse извине́ние; (*justification*) оправда́ние; извиня́ть [-ни́ть]; ~ *me!* извини́(те)!

execut|e исполня́ть ['-нить];
criminal казни́ть (*im*)*pf.*;
~ion исполне́ние; казнь *f*;
~ive исполни́тельный;
su. администра́тор,
руководи́тель; **~or** исполни́тель завеща́ния

exemplify служи́ть приме́ром (P)

exempt освобожда́ть [-боди́ть] (от P)

exercise упражне́ние;
(*constitutional*) прогу́лка
(лече́бная *or* для о́тдыха); *mil.* уче́ние; *v.*
упражня́ть(ся); *mil.* проводи́ть уче́ния

exert *pressure, etc.* ока́зывать [-за́ть]; ~ *o.s.* прилага́ть уси́лия; **~ion** уси́лие

exhale (*breathe out*) выдыха́ть [вы́дохнуть]

exhaust *fig.* истоща́ть [-щи́ть]; *subject* исче́рпывать [-па́ть]; *tech.* вы́хлоп;
~ion истоще́ние; **~ive** исче́рпывающий

exhibit выставля́ть [вы́ставить]; экспона́т; **~ion** вы-

ста́вка

exile ссыла́ть [сосла́ть],
вы́слать; ссы́лка; (*person*)
вы́сланн|ый, -ая

exist существова́ть; **~ence**
существова́ние

exit вы́ход

exotic *adj.* экзоти́ческий

expand расширя́ть(ся)
['-ри́ть(ся)]; **~se** простра́нство; **~sion** расшире́ние; *fig.* рост; разви́тие

expect ожида́ть (P), ждать
(B *or* P); (*suppose*) ду́мать, полага́ть (*impf.*);
~ation ожида́ние

expedi|ent целесообра́зный; **~tion** экспеди́ция

expel изгоня́ть [-гна́ть];
(*from school*) исключа́ть
[-чи́ть]; (*from univ.*) отчисля́ть [-лить]

expend [из]тра́тить; **~iture**
тра́та; (*expenses*) расхо́ды
m/pl.

expens|e расхо́д; *travelling*
~es командиро́вочные
(*per day*) су́точные *pl.*;
~ive дорого́й

experience о́пыт; (*event*)
слу́чай; приключе́ние;
испы́тывать [-та́ть]; пережи(ва́)ть; **~d** о́пытный

experiment эксперимѐнт;
~al эксперимента́льный

expert экспе́рт, специали́ст; (*in arts*) знато́к;
attr. высококвалифици́рованный

expire *term*: истека́ть

[-éчь]

explai|n объ-, по-ясня́ть [-ни́ть]; **_nation** объ-, по-ясне́ние

explicit я́сный; (definite) определённый

explode взрыва́ть(ся) [взорва́ть(ся)]; (with laughter) разража́ться [-рази́ться] (T)

exploit[1] (feat) по́двиг

exploit[2] эксплуати́ровать; **_ation** эксплуата́ция

explor|ation иссле́дование; **_e** иссле́довать (im)pf.; **_er** иссле́дователь m

explos|ion взрыв; **_ve** взры́вчатый; взры́вчатое вещество́

export э́кспорт, вы́воз; экспорти́ровать (im)pf.; вывози́ть [вы́везти] (Т); экспортёр

expose goods выставля́ть [вы́ставить]; photo экспони́ровать [-чи́ть]; **_ition** вы́ставка; (school) изложе́ние; **_ure** разоблаче́ние; (photo) вы́держка

express выража́ть [вы́разить]; rail. экспре́сс; **_ion** выраже́ние; **_ive** вырази́тельный; **_ly** категори́чески; (on purpose) наро́чно

expulsion (from school) исключе́ние; (from univ.) от-

числе́ние; (from a country) вы́сылка

exquisite преле́стный, изы́сканный

exten|d расширя́ть [-ши́рить]; (stretch) простира́ться, тяну́ться; term, leave продлева́ть [-ли́ть]; **_sion** расшире́ние; продле́ние; arch. пристро́йка; **_t** протяже́ние, простра́нство; (degree) сте́пень f

exterior вне́шний, вне́шнийвид; (person) вне́шность f

exterminat|e истребля́ть [-би́ть]; **_ion** истребле́ние

extinct zo. вы́мерший

extinguish [по]туши́ть, [по]гаси́ть; **_er**: fire **_er** огнетуши́тель m

extra (additional) дополни́тельный, доба́вочный; (spare) ли́шний

extract извлека́ть [-е́чь]; tooth удаля́ть [-ли́ть]; chem. экстраги́ровать; извлече́ние; (book, etc.) отры́вок

extraordinary (unusual) необыча́йный; (remarkable) выдаю́щийся; (wonderful) удиви́тельный; (session) внеочередно́й

extrem|e кра́йний; кра́йность f; **_ity** кра́йность f; anat. коне́чность f

exult ликова́ть; **_ation** лико-ва́ние

eye глаз; (*needle*) ушко́; **~brow** бровь f; **~lash** ресни́ца; **~lid** ве́ко; **~shadow** те́ни для век; **~sight** зре́ние; **~witness** очеви́дец, -ица; *jur.* свиде́тель-очеви́дец

F

fable ба́сня
fabric (*textile*) ткань f
fabulous басносло́вный
face лицо́; лицева́я сторона́; (*clock*) цифербла́т; стоя́ть лицо́м к (Д); *truth* смотре́ть в лицо́ (Д)
facilit|ate облегча́ть [-чи́ть]; **~y** (*ease*) лёгкость f; *tech.* сре́дство; удо́бство; *pl.* (благоприя́тные) усло́вия *n/pl.*
fact факт; **in ~** на (са́мом) де́ле; **~ion** *pol.* фра́кция; **~or** фа́ктор; **~ory** фа́брика, заво́д
faculty спосо́бность f; *univ.* факульте́т
fade *flower:* увяда́ть [увя́нуть]; *colour:* выцвета́ть [вы́цвести]; (*in washing*) линя́ть
fail потерпе́ть неуда́чу; (*examination*) прова́ливаться [-ли́ться]; **he ~ed to find** ему́ не удало́сь найти́; **~ure** неуда́ча; прова́л; неуда́чник, -ца
faint сла́бый; (*idea*) сму́тный; *su.* о́бморок; упа́сть в о́бморок
fair[1] *comm.* я́рмарка; **fun ~**

аттракцио́ны *m/pl.*
fair[2] прекра́сный; (*hair*) белоку́рый; (*just*) справедли́вый; **~ly** справедли́во; (*rather*) дово́льно; **~ness** справедли́вость f
fairy фе́я; **~land** волше́бное ца́рство; **~ tale** ска́зка
faith ве́ра; (*trust*) дове́рие; **in good ~** че́стно; **~ful** ве́рный; **~less** неве́рный
falcon со́кол
fall па́дать, [у]па́сть; паде́ние; (*season*) о́сень f; *pl.* водопа́д; **~ asleep** засыпа́ть [засну́ть]; **~ back on** прибега́ть ['-гнуть] (к Д); **~ behind** отст(ав)а́ть [-ста́ть]; **~ ill** заболева́ть [-ле́ть]; **~ in love** влюбля́ться [-би́ться] (**with** в В)
false (*wrong*) оши́бочный, ло́жный; (*note, money*) фальши́вый; **~hood** ложь f
falter (*speaking*) запина́ться [-пну́ться]
fame сла́ва; **~d** изве́стность f
familiar (*known*) знако́мый; (*intimate*) бли́зкий; (*forward*) фамилья́рный; **be ~ with** хорошо́ знать (В);

_ity осведомлённость, знание; (act of licence) фамильярность f; **_ize o.s.** [о-, по-] знакомиться

family adj; attr. семейный

famine го́лод

famous знамени́тый

fan[1] ве́ер; (electric) вентиля́тор

fan[2] (sports) боле́льщи|к; thea. театра́л|ка; (zealot) фана́т|ик, -ичка; фанати́чный; **_aticism** фанати́зм

fancy воображе́ние, фанта́зия; (liking) пристра́стие (for к Д); вообража́ть [-рази́ть]

fang (wolf) клык

fantas|tic фантасти́ческий; **_y** фанта́зия

far далёкий; adv. далеко́; (go) **as _ as** до (Р); (in)as_much наско́лько; **so _** до сих пор; **_-away** отдалённый; да́льний; adv. далеко́

fare rail. пла́та за прое́зд; (food) еда́; **_well** проща́ние; проща́й(те)!

farm фе́рма, ху́тор; collective **_** колхо́з; state **_** совхо́з; **_er** фе́рмер; **_ing** се́льское хозя́йство; **_stead** уса́дьба

farsighted дальнозо́ркий; fig. дальнови́дный

farther adv. да́льше; adj. бо́лее отдалённый; **_est** adv. да́льше всего́ or

всех; adj. са́мый отдалённый

fascinat|e очаро́вывать [-ова́ть]; **_ing** очарова́тельный; **_ion** очарова́ние

fashion мо́да; (way) о́браз, мане́ра; **_able** мо́дный, фешене́бельный

fast[1] eccl. пост; v. пости́ться

fast[2] (quick) бы́стрый, ско́рый; adv. бы́стро; (colour) про́чный; (of sleep) кре́пко; **be _ watch:** спеши́ть; **_en** закрепля́ть [-пи́ть]; clothes, etc. застёгивать [-гну́ть]; **_ener** застёжка

fastidious разбо́рчивый, (about food, etc.) приве́редливый

fat жи́рный; (person) то́лстый; su. жир

fat|al (day) роково́й; (wound) смерте́льный; (accident) со смерте́льным исхо́дом; **_e** рок; (destiny) судьба́

father оте́ц; **_-in-law** (man's) тесть m; (woman's) свёкор; **_land** оте́чество; **_ly** оте́ческий

fathom fig. постига́ть [-ти́чь]

fatigue уста́лость, утомле́ние; утомля́ть [-ми́ть]

fault недоста́ток, изъя́н; (guilt) вина́; tech. неиспра́вность; **find _ with**

прид(и)ра́ться к (Д); **~less** безупре́чный; безоши́бочный; **~y** (idea, method) поро́чный; (thing) дефе́ктный

favour расположе́ние, ми́лость f; **do a ~** сде́лать одолже́ние or оказа́ть любе́зность; **~able** благоприя́тный; **~ite** люби́мый; люби́м|ец, -ица; (sports) фавори́т

fear бо́язнь f, страх; **~ful** стра́шный; **be ~ful** (of or that) боя́ться (+ inf. or что); **~less** бесстра́шный

feast (banquet) банке́т; пир; (religious festival) пра́здник

feat по́двиг

feather перо́; **~y** пе́ристый; (snow) пуши́стый

feature характе́рная черта́; осо́бенность; pl. черты́ лица́; **~ film** худо́жественный фильм

February февра́ль m

federa|l федера́льный; **~tion** федера́ция

fee пла́та, (doctor) гонора́р; (member) взнос

feeble сла́бый

feed v/t. [по-, на]корми́ть; tech. пита́ть; v/i. корми́ться, пита́ться (on T); корм; tech. пита́ние, пода́ча (электроэне́ргии)

feel v/t. [по]чу́вствовать; **~ for** fig. сочу́вствовать; (touch) [по]щу́пать; v/i.

чу́вствовать себя́; **I ~ like eating** мне хо́чется есть; **~ing** чу́вство; (sensation) ощуще́ние

feign притворя́ться [-и́ться]; **~ an excuse** приду́мывать отгово́рку

fellow (young) па́рень m; (comrade) това́рищ; **old ~** coll. дружи́ще m; **~countryman** соотéчественник; **~ship** (companionship) това́рищество; бра́тство; **~student** одноку́рсник; **~-traveller** попу́тчи|к, -ца (a. pol.); **~-worker** сотру́дник колле́га

felt фетр; attr. фе́тровый

female же́нщина; zo. са́мка; же́нский

feminine же́нский (a. gr.); (womanlike) же́нственный

fence забо́р, и́згородь f; v. (sports) фехтова́ть; **~ in** огора́живать [-роди́ть]

ferment ферме́нт; v/i. броди́ть; v/t. вызыва́ть броже́ние (P); **~ation** броже́ние (a. fig.)

fern па́поротник

feroci|ous свире́пый; **~ty** свире́пость

ferry паро́м; (place) перепра́ва; перепра́вля(ть)ся ['-вить(ся)] (на паро́ме)

fertil|e плодоро́дный; **~ity** плодоро́дие; **~ize** soil удобря́ть ['-рить]; biol. оплодотворя́ть [-ри́ть]; **~izer**

удобре́ние

fervent пы́лкий; горя́чий; **_our** пы́лкость f; (_earnestness_) рве́ние, усе́рдие

festival пра́здник; _thea._ etc. фестива́ль m; ⁓e пра́здничный

fetch (go and) ⁓ сходи́ть (за Т) pf.; thing приноси́ть [-нести́], person приводи́ть [-вести́]; (by transport) привози́ть [-везти́]

feud (family) ссо́ры f/pl.; междоусо́бица

fever (high temperature) жар; (illness) лихора́дка (a. fig.); **⁓ish** лихора́дочный

few немно́гие; ма́ло (P); a ⁓ не́сколько (P); quite a ⁓ дово́льно мно́го (P); ⁓er ме́ньше (P)

fiancé жени́х; ⁓e неве́ста

fibr|e волокно́; **⁓ous** волокни́стый

fiction вы́мысел; худо́жественная литерату́ра; **science** ⁓ нау́чная фанта́стика

fiddle coll. скри́пка; fig. маха́нации f/pl.

fidelity ве́рность f; tech. то́чность воспроизведе́ния

fidget ёрзать; (person) непосе́да m/f; **⁓y** непосе́дливый

field по́ле; attr. полево́й (a. mil.); in this ⁓ в э́той о́бласти; oil-⁓ нефтяно́е ме-

сторожде́ние

fierce лю́тый, свире́пый; (wind) си́льный; **⁓ness** лю́тость f, свире́пость f

fiery о́гненный; fig. горя́чий

fif|teen пятна́дцать; **⁓teenth** пятна́дцатый; **⁓th** пя́тый; **⁓tieth** пятидеся́тый; **⁓ty** пятьдеся́т

fig инжи́р

fight борьба́; mil. бой; (boys) дра́ка; боро́ться (for за В); дра́ться; mil. сража́ться; **⁓er** боец; av. истреби́тель m

figure фигу́ра; (arithmetic) ци́фра, число́; (person) ли́чность f; (in book) рису́нок; Am. счита́ть, полага́ть (impfs.); I can't ⁓ it out я не могу́ э́того поня́ть; **⁓ skating** фигу́рное ката́ние

file[1] tech. напи́льник; подпи́ливать [-ли́ть]

file[2] па́пка, скоросшива́тель m; делово́й архи́в; tech. файл; подши́в(а́)ть; сдава́ть в архи́в; **newspaper** ⁓ газе́тная подши́вка; **personal** ⁓ досье́ indecl.

fill наполня́ть(ся) ['-нить(-ся)]; (in a form) заполня́ть ['-нить]; **⁓ up** mot. заправля́ться ['-виться]

fillet (fish, meat) филе́ indecl.

film фильм; photo. плёнка; **⁓ director** кинорежиссёр

_ing (кино)сьёмка

filter фильтр; [про]фильтрова́ть(ся)

filth грязь *f; fig.* скверносло́вие; **_y** гря́зный; (*joke*) неприли́чный

fin плавни́к

final заключи́тельный; (*victory*) оконча́тельный; (*sports*) фина́л; *pl. univ.* выпускны́е экза́мены; **_ly** в заключе́ние; оконча́тельно

financ|e фина́нсовое де́ло; *pl.* фина́нсы *m/pl.*; фина́нсировать (*im*)*pf.*; **_ial** фина́нсовый; **_ier** финанси́ст

find находи́ть [найти́]; нахо́дка; ~ **out** разузн(ав)а́ть; **_ing** нахо́дка; (*conclusion*) *mst. pl.* вы́воды; (*jury*) реше́ние

fine[1] *jur.* штраф; [о]штрафова́ть

fine[2] прекра́сный; (*thread*) то́нкий; (*sand*) ме́лкий; (*arts*) изя́щный

finger па́лец

finish конча́ть(ся) ['-чить(-ся)]; (*polish*) отде́л(ыв)ать; (*sports*) фи́ниш

Finn фи́н|н, -ка; **_nish** фи́нский

fir ель *f*, пи́хта

fire ого́нь *m (a. mil.)*; (*damaging*) пожа́р; стреля́ть [вы́стрелить]; **be on** ~ горе́ть; **_arms** огнестре́льное ору́жие; **_brigade**

пожа́рная кома́нда; ~ **escape** пожа́рная ле́стница; ~ **extinguisher** огнетуши́тель; **_man** пожа́рный; **_place** ками́н; **_proof** огнеупо́рный; **_works** фейерве́рк

firm[1] твёрдый; (*durable*) про́чный; **_ness** твёрдость *f*; про́чность *f*

firm[2] *comm.* фи́рма

first пе́рвый; **at** ~ снерва́; ~ **aid** пе́рвая по́мощь *f*; **_-class** первокла́ссный; **_-rate** первокла́ссный

fish ры́ба; лови́ть ры́бу; (*angle*) уди́ть; **_erman** рыба́к; **_ery** ры́бный про́мысел; **_ing** ры́бная ло́вля; **_ing rod** уди́лище

fist кула́к

fit[1] *med.* припа́док (*a. fig.*)

fit[2] го́дный, подходя́щий; годи́ться (Д), быть впо́ру (Д); (*fit on*) примеря́ть ['-рить]; ~ **out** обору́довать (*im*)*pf.*; **_ness** го́дность *f*; **_ting** (*clothes*) приме́рка; **_ting(s)** армату́ра

five пять; ~ **hundred** пятьсо́т

fix (*fasten*) прикрепля́ть [-пи́ть]; (*repair*) почини́ть; (*determine*) устана́вливать [-нови́ть]; **_ed** устано́вленный; (*look*) при́стальный; **_ed storage** *tech.* постоя́нная па́мять

flag флаг (*a. tech.*)
flake|s *pl.* хло́пья *m/pl.*;
snow-~ снежи́нка
flame пла́мя *n*; *v.* пыла́ть
flank *anat.* бок; *mil.* фланг
flannel флане́ль *f*
flap (*of wing*) взмах; (*pocket*) кла́пан; (*lapel*) отворо́т; (*wings*) хло́пать [-пнуть]
flare я́ркий неро́вный свет; *mil.* освети́тельная раке́та; **~ up** вспы́хивать [-хнуть], *fig.* вспыли́ть
flash вспы́шка; **~-light** (*small torch*) фона́рик; (*photo*) вспы́шка
flask фля́га
flat[1] (*home*) кварти́ра
flat[2] пло́ский; (*even*) ро́вный; (*plate*) ме́лкий; **~ tire** спу́щенная ши́на; **~-iron** утю́г; **~ten** сплю́щи(ва)ть
flatter [по]льсти́ть (Д); **~er** льстец; **~y** лесть *f*
flavour вкус; арома́т; приправля́ть ['-вить]; **~ing** припра́ва
flaw (*crack*) тре́щина; *fig.* изъя́н; **~less** *fig.* безупре́чный
flax лён
flea блоха́
flee бежа́ть, спаса́ться бе́гством
fleet *mar.* флот
fleeting мимолётный
flesh плоть *f*; *biol.* мя́со; *bot.* мя́коть *f*; **~y** мяси́-

стый
flexible ги́бкий
flicker мерца́ть, мига́ть; мерца́ние
flight[1] бе́гство; **~ of stairs** ле́стничный марш
flight[2] полёт; *av.* рейс; **non-stop ~** беспоса́дочный перелёт; (*flock*) ста́я
flimsy непро́чный, хру́пкий
flinch (*from pain*) вздра́гивать [вздро́гнуть]
fling швыря́ть [-рну́ть]; (*rush*) броса́ться ['-ситься]
flint креме́нь *m*
flippant легкомы́сленный
flippers (*sports*) ла́сты
flirt флиртова́ть; *su.* коке́тка; **~ation** флирт
float пла́вать, [по]плы́ть; (*fishing*) поплаво́к; **~ing** плавучий
flock (*herd*) ста́до; (*flight*) ста́я; *v.* держа́ться ста́дом; *fig.* толпи́ться
flog [вы́]поро́ть
flood наводня́ть [-ни́ть]; наводне́ние; (*tide*) прили́в; *fig.* пото́к
floor пол; (*storey*) эта́ж; **ground ~** пе́рвый эта́ж
florist's цвето́чный магази́н
flounder[1] *zo.* ка́мбала
flounder[2] бара́хтаться
flour мука́
flourish (*prosper*) процвета́ть; (*brandish*) разма́хи-

вать (Т)

flow *v.* течь; течéние; *tech., fig.* потóк; (*tide*) прилúв

flower цветóк; *fig.* цвет; *v.* цвестú; **~y** цветúстый (*a. fig.*)

flu *coll.* грипп

fluctuate колебáться; **~ion** колебáние

fluent (*speech*) бéглый; **speak ~ French** свобóдно говорúть по-францýзски

fluff пух; **~y** пушúстый

fluid жúдкий; жúдкость *f*

flute флéйта

flutter *flag:* развевáться; *bird:* порхáть [-хнýть]; (*tremble*) трепетáть

fly[1] *zo.* мýха

fly[2] летáть, [по]летéть; *kite* запускáть [-стúть]; **~ into a rage** приходúть [-йтú] в ярость; **~ing** летáющий; (*weather*) лётный

flyover *mot.* путепровóд; эстакáда

foam пéна; **~y** пéнистый

focus *phys.* фóкус; *fig.* сосредотóчи(ва)ть

fodder корм

foe враг

fog тумáн; **~gy** тумáнный (*a. fig.*)

fold склáдывать [сложúть]; склáдка; **~er** скоросшивáтель *m*; **~ing** (*chair*) складнóй

foliage листвá

folk люд; *attr.* нарóдный; **~lore** фольклóр

follow [по]слéдовать (за Т); *fig.* (Д); *speaker, target* следúть (за Т); **~er** послéдователь *m*; **~ing** слéдующий

folly безрассýдство

fond: be ~ of любúть (В)

food пúща, едá; **~stuffs** продýкты (питáния) *m/pl*

fool глупéц, дурáк; [о]дурáчить; **~ish** глýпый, неразýмный

foot ногá; ступнá; **on ~** пешкóм; *attr.* ножнóй; *math.* фут; **~ball** футбóл; **~ball player** футболúст; **~hold** тóчка опóры; **~lights** рáмпа; **~note** снóска; **~path** тропúнка; **~print** след; **~step** шаг; **~wear** óбувь *f*

for для (Р); за (В); *conj.* úбо или так как; **~ life** на всю жизнь

forbear воздéрживаться [-жáться] (**from** от Р)

forbid запрещáть [-етúть]

force сúла; (*to do*) заставлять [-вить]; вынуждáть [вынудить] (В); **come into ~** вступáть [-пúть] в сúлу; **put into ~** вводúть [ввестú] в дéйствие *pf.*; (*armed*) **~s** вооружённые сúлы *f/pl*; **~d** (*labour*) принудúтельный; (*landing*) вынужденный; (*smile*) натянутый

fore|boding (*feeling*) предчýвствие; **~cast** прогнóз;

предсказа́ние; предска́зывать [-за́ть]; **~father** пре́док; **~ground** пере́дний план; **~head** лоб

foreign иностра́нный; **² Office** U.K. министе́рство иностра́нных дел; **~ trade** вне́шняя торго́вля; **~er** иностра́н|ец, -ка

fore|man ма́стер; брига-ди́р; **~most** пере́дний, передово́й; (most notable) выдаю́щийся; (chief) са́мый гла́вный; **~see** предви́деть; **~sight** предви́дение; (prudence) предусмотри́тельность f

forest лес; attr. лесно́й

forestall (anticipate) предупрежда́ть [-преди́ть]; (do s.th. first) опережа́ть [-реди́ть]

forester лесни́чий

forever навсегда́

forfeit утра́чивать [-ра́тить]; утра́та; (in game†) фант

forge кова́ть; (document) подде́л(ыв)ать; (smithy) ку́зница; **~ry** подде́лка

forget забы(ва́)ть; **~ful** забы́вчивый; **~-me-not** незабу́дка

forgive проща́ть [прости́ть]; **~ness** проще́ние

fork ви́лка; agr. ви́лы f/pl.; road развилка

form фо́рма; (document) бланк; (school) класс; обра́зовывать (-ся) [-ова́ть-

(ся)]; **~al** форма́льный; **~ality** форма́льность f; **~ation** образова́ние, формирова́ние; mil. строй

former бы́вший; (times) пре́жний; **~ly** пре́жде, в про́шлом

formidable гро́зный; (requiring great effort) о́чень тру́дный

formula фо́рмула; **~te** формули́ровать (im)pf.

forsake покида́ть [-и́нуть]

forth|coming предстоя́щий; **~with** то́тчас

fortieth сороково́й

forti|fication укрепле́ние; **~fy** укрепля́ть [-пи́ть]; **~fy o.s.** подкрепля́ться [-пи́ться]; **~tude** сто́йкость f

fortnight две неде́ли

fortress кре́пость f

fortun|ate счастли́вый, уда́чный; **~ately** к сча́стью; **~e** судьба́; (money) состоя́ние

forty со́рок

forward adj. пере́дний; передово́й; (presumptuous) развя́зный; adv. вперёд; letter перес(ы)ла́ть; plan выдвига́ть [вы́двинуть]

foster воспи́тывать [-ита́ть]; fig. леле́ять; **~ child** приёмный ребёнок

foul (weather) нена́стный; (crime) по́длый; (play) нече́стный; su. фол

found осно́вывать [-ова́ть];

~ation основа́ние; *arch.* фунда́мент; *fig.* осно́ва; **~er** основа́тель *m*

foundry лите́йный цех

fountain фонта́н; **~-pen** авто́ручка

four четы́ре; **~-engined** четырёхмото́рный; **~teen** четы́рнадцать; **~teenth** четы́рнадцатый; **~th** четвёртый

fowl дома́шняя пти́ца

fox лиса́, лиси́ца

fraction *math.* дробь *f*; (*small part*) части́ца; **~ure** *med.* перело́м; [с]лома́ть

fragile хру́пкий, непро́чный; **~ment** оско́лок (*literary*) фрагме́нт

fragrance арома́т, благоуха́ние; **~t** арома́тный, души́стый

frail хру́пкий; (*person*) тщеду́шный; **~ty** хру́пкость *f*; тщеду́шность

frame ра́ма, ра́мка; (*~work*) карка́с, о́стов; (*build*) телосложе́ние; **~ of mind** настрое́ние; вставля́ть ['-вить] в ра́м(к)у; обрамля́ть ['-мить]

frank открове́нный; **~ness** открове́нность *f*

frantic (*efforts, etc.*) отча́янный, безу́мный; **~ with pain** обезу́мевший от бо́ли

fraternal бра́тский; **~ity** бра́тство

fraud обма́н; моше́нничество (*a. jur.*); **~ulent** об-

~manный

freckles *pl.* весну́шки *f/pl.*

free свобо́дный; (*city*) во́льный; освобожда́ть [-боди́ть]; **~ of charge** беспла́тно; **~dom** свобо́да

freeze *v/i.* мёрзнуть, замерза́ть [-мёрзнуть]; *v/t.* замора́живать [-ро́зить]; **~r** моро́зильная ка́мера

freight (*pay*) фрахт; (*load*) груз, фрахт; **~er** грузово́е су́дно

French францу́зский; **~man**, **~woman** францу́з, -женка

frenzy нейстовство; **in a ~ of despair** в безу́мном отча́янии

frequency частота́ (*a. tech.*); **~t** ча́стый

fresh све́жий; (*weather*) прохла́дный; **~man** первоку́рсник; **~ness** све́жесть *f*; прохла́да; **~water** пре́сная вода́

friction тре́ние; *fig.* тре́ния *n/pl.*

Friday пя́тница

friend друг, подру́га; **~liness** дружелю́бие; **~ly** дружелю́бный, дру́жественный; **~ship** дру́жба

fright испу́г; (*fear*) страх, *coll.* страши́лище; **~en** [ис]пуга́ть; страши́ть; **~ful** стра́шный

fringe бахрома́; (*hair*) чёлка; (*of a forest*)

опу́шка; ~ **benefits** до-
полни́тельные льго́ты
frisk резви́ться; ~**у** ре́звый
fritter ола́дья
frivolous легкомы́слен-
ный; несерьёзный
fro: to and ~ взад и впере́д
frock пла́тье; *eccl.* ря́са
frog лягу́шка; ~**man** аква-
лангист
from из (Р); от (Р); с (Р);
(**be**) ~ **London** из Ло́н-
дона; **far** ~ **the town** да-
леко́ от го́рода; ~ **morning
till evening** с утра́ до ве́-
чера
front перёд, передня́я сторо-
на́; *mil., pol.* фронт; **in** ~
of пе́ред (Т)
frontier грани́ца
frost моро́з; (*hoar*~) и́ней;
~**ed** покры́тый и́нейем;
(*glass*) ма́товый; ~**у** мо-
ро́зный; *fig.* холо́дный
froth пе́на; *v.* пе́ниться
frown [на]хму́риться; хму́-
рый взгляд
frugal (*meal*) ску́дный
fruit плод (*a. fig.*); *collect.*
фру́кты *m/pl.*; ~**ful** плодо-
ви́тый; *fig.* плодотво́р-
ный; ~**less** беспло́дный
frustrate расстра́ивать
[-ро́ить]
fry [за-, под]жа́рить; ~**ing-
pan** сковорода́
fuel то́пливо; (*liquid*) жи́д-
кое то́пливо; *mot.* горю́-
чее
fugitive бегле́ц; (*from dan-*

ger) бе́женец
fulfil исполня́ть ['-нить];
~**ment** исполне́ние
full по́лный; (*hour*) це́лый;
~ **stop** то́чка; ~ вполне́;
(*completely*) по́лностью
fumble [по]ша́рить; (*rummage*) ры́ться
fume (*smoke*) дым; *pl.* ис-
паре́ния *n/pl.*; *fig.* кипе́ть
от зло́сти
fun заба́ва; весе́лье; **have**
~ хорошо́ провести́
вре́мя; **just for** ~ шу́тки
ра́ди; **make** ~ **of s.b.** вы-
сме́ивать кого́-либо; **what**
~! как ве́село!, как
смешно́!
function фу́нкция; *v.* функ-
циони́ровать; ~**ary** функ-
ционе́р
fund фонд; ~**amental**
основно́й; фундамента́ль-
ный
funeral по́хороны *f/pl.*
funnel воро́нка; (*smoke-
stack*) (дымова́я) труба́
funny заба́вный; (*ridicu-
lous*) смешно́й; (*odd*) чуд-
но́й
fur мех; *attr.* мехово́й
furious я́ростный, бе́ше-
ный; (*person*) серди́тый,
взбешённый
furnace *tech.* печь *f*;
blast-~ до́мна
furnish снабжа́ть [-ди́ть];
room меблирова́ть (*im*)*pf.*;
~**ture** ме́бель *f*
furrow борозда́; (*on ca-*

морщи́на; [из]борозди́ть
further дальне́йший; *adv.*
да́лее; *v.* продвига́ть
[-и́нуть]; **~more** кро́ме
того́
furtively укра́дкой
fury я́рость *f*, бе́шенство
fuse (*melt*) [рас]пла́вить
(-ся); (*unite*) сли(ва́)ть
(-ся); *el.* (пла́вкий) пре-

дохрани́тель *m*; *coll.*
про́бка
fuss суета́; (*row*) сканда́л;
суети́ться; **~y** суетли́вый;
(*about food*) привере́дли-
вый
futile тще́тный; **~ity** тще́т-
ность *f*
future бу́дущий; *su.* бу́ду-
щее

G

gable фронто́н
gadget *coll.* приспособле́-
ние
gag (*joke*) шу́тка, остро́та
(*a. thea.*)
gaiety весёлость *f*; (*general*) весе́лье
gain (*win*) выи́грывать [вы́-
играть]; (*acquire*) при-
обрета́ть [-ести́]; вы́-
игрыш; (*profit*) при́быль *f*
gait похо́дка
gale бу́ря, (*sea*) шторм
gall жёлчь *f*
gallant хра́брый; (*polite*)
гала́нтный; **~ry** хра́брость
f; гала́нтность *f*
gallery галере́я; *thea.* бал-
ко́н, *coll.* галёрка
gallon галло́н (= *4.5 litres*)
gallop ска́чка, гало́п; ска-
ка́ть гало́пом
gamble аза́ртная игра́; *fig.*
риско́ванное де́ло; **~r**
игро́к, картёжник
game[1] игра́

game[2] *zo.* дичь *f*; **~ reserve**
запове́дник
gang (*criminals*) ша́йка;
(*workers*) брига́да; **~ster**
га́нгстер; **~way** схо́дни *f/
pl.*
gap брешь *f*, проры́в;
(*blank*) пробе́л (*a. fig.*)
gape (*stare*) *coll.* смотре́ть
рази́нув рот
garage гара́ж
garbage му́сор
garden сад; (*kitchen~*) ого-
ро́д; **~er** садо́вник; **~ing**
садово́дство
gargle полоска́ть го́рло
garland гирля́нда
garlic чесно́к
garment оде́жда
garnish гарни́р; гарни́ро-
вать (*im*)*pf.*
garret черда́к; манса́рда
garrison гарнизо́н
gas газ; *attr.* га́зовый; *Am.*
бензи́н; **~ main** газопро-
во́д; **~olene** *Am.* бензи́н

get

~-stove га́зовая плита́

gasp v. задыха́ться, дыша́ть (с трудо́м); говори́ть задыха́ясь

gate воро́та n/pl.; (in a fence) кали́тка; **~way** подворо́тня

gather (collect.) соб(и)ра́ть; (assemble) соб(и)ра́ть(ся); (conclude) заключа́ть [-чи́ть]; **~ing** собра́ние

gaunt то́щий

gauntlet рукави́ца

gauze ма́рля

gay весёлый; (colours) пёстрый; (bright) я́ркий

gaze при́стальный взгляд; при́стально смотре́ть (at на В)

gear mot. ско́рость f, переда́ча; **change ~** переключа́ть [-чи́ть] ско́рость

gelatine желати́н

gem драгоце́нный ка́мень m; fig. драгоце́нность f

gender gr. род

gene biol. ген; **~tics** гене́тика

general (все)о́бщий; (usual) обы́чный; **~ practitioner** (врач-)терапе́вт; **~ store** универса́льный магази́н; coll. универса́м; mil. генера́л; **in ~** вообще́; **~ize** обобща́ть [-щи́ть]; **~ly** обы́чно; вообще́

generate el., etc. генери́ровать; производи́ть [-вести́]; hatred порожда́ть [породи́ть]; **~ion** поколе́ние

genero|sity ще́дрость f; (nobleness) великоду́шие; **~us** ще́дрый; великоду́шный

genial (welcome) раду́шный; (temper) доброду́шный

genius ге́ний; (spirit) дух; (talent) гениа́льность f

gentle мя́гкий; (quiet) ти́хий; (character) кро́ткий; **~man** джентльме́н; **~ness** мя́гкость f; кро́тость f

genuine настоя́щий, по́длинный; (sincere) и́скренний

geograph|er гео́граф; **~ic** географи́ческий; **~y** геогра́фия

geolog|ical геологи́ческий; **~ist** гео́лог; **~y** геоло́гия

geometry геоме́трия

Georgian грузи́н(ка); грузи́нский

germ микро́б; (embryo) заро́дыш

German не́м|ец, -ка; -е́цкий; pol. герма́нский

germinate v/i. прораста́ть [-сти́]

gesture жест

get (obtain) дост(ав)а́ть; (receive) получа́ть [-чи́ть]; (become) станови́ться [стать]; (to a place) доезжа́ть [-е́хать] (до P); (buy) покупа́ть [купи́ть]; (fetch) приноси́ть [-нести́]; (~ unexpectedly into) попа-

дать [-па́сть] (в В); ~ up
встава́ть; ~ tired уст(ава́)ть

geyser (natural spring) гéй-
зер; (apparatus) га́зовая
колóнка

ghastly ужа́сающий

ghost привидéние, при́зрак; дух (a. eccl.)

giant велика́н; fig. гига́нт

giddiness головокружéние; ~y (height) головокружи́тельный; ~ легкомы́сленный, вéтреный

gift подáрок; (talent) дар,
дарова́ние; ~ed одарённый, спосо́бный

gigantic гига́нтский

giggle хихи́кать; хихи́канье

gild [по]золоти́ть

gill жáбра

gin (spirit) джин

ginger имби́рь m; ~bread
имби́рный пря́ник

gipsy цыгáн(ка); цыга́нский

giraffe жирáф

girdle пояс; (sash) кушáк

girl дéвушка, (little) дéвочка; ~hood дéвичество; ~-hood дéвичество

give [по]дáть; ~ away от-
д(ав)áть; ~ in уступáть
[-пи́ть]; ~ up smoking бросáть [бро́сить]; (surrender)
сд(ав)áться

glacier ледни́к

glad (news) ра́достный; I
am ~ я рад(а); ~ly охóтно

~ness ра́дость f

glamorous очаровáтель-
ный; ~our очаровáние

glance (быстрый взгляд;
взгля́дывать [-яну́ть] (at
на В)

gland железá

glass стекло́; (drinking-~)
стакáн, (wine) рю́мка;
(mirror) зéркало; attr. сте-
кля́нный; ~es очки́ pl.;
~ware издéлия из стеклá;
~works стекóльный завóд

glaze глазу́рь f; глазирó-
вáть (im)pf.; window за-
стекля́ть [-ли́ть]; ~ier сте-
кóльщик

gleam луч, прóблеск (a.
fig.); слáбый свет; мер-
цáть

glide скользи́ть; av. пла-
ни́ровать; скольжéние;
плани́рование; ~er пла-
нёр

glimmer мерцáние, слáбый
свет; мерцáть, слáбо све-
ти́ться

glimpse (short look) бы́-
стрый взгляд; catch a ~
уви́деть мéльком (of В)

glisten, glitter блестéть,
сверкáть

globe (sphere) шар; (earth)
земнóй шар; (with map)
глóбус

gloom мрак; fig. уны́ние;
~y мрáчный (a. fig.)

glorify прославля́ть
[-'вить]; ~ious слáвный;
(splendid) великолéпный;

~y сла́ва; великоле́пие
gloss гля́нец; *(hair, etc.)* блеск; лоск *(a. fig.)*; ~ гля́нцевый; блестя́щий

glove перча́тка; ~ **compartment** *mot.* перча́точный я́щик; *coll.* бардачо́к

glow *(shine red)* рде́ть; *(sunset, distant fire, etc.)* свет; за́рево; *(flush)* румя́нец

glue клей; [с]кле́ить

gnat кома́р

gnaw глода́ть

go ходи́ть, идти́ [пойти́]; *(by transport)* е́здить, [по]е́хать; ~ **in** проходи́ть [пройти́]; ~ **in** входи́ть [войти́]; вмеща́ться [вмести́ться] (в В); ~ **in for sport** занима́ться спо́ртом; ~ **on** продолжа́ть (with В); ~ **up** *(mountain)* поднима́ться [-ня́ться]; *(prices)* повыша́ться [-вы́ситься]; ~ **without** обходи́ться [обойти́сь] без (Р)

goal цель f; *(sports)* воро́та n/pl.; *(scoring)* гол; ~**keeper** врата́рь m

goat коза́

go-between посре́дник

god бог; *a.* Бог; ~**child** кре́стник, -ца; ~**dess** боги́ня; ~**mother** кре́стная мать; **thank ~!** сла́ва Бо́гу!; ~ **forbid!** не дай Бог!

golf гольф; **игра́ть в гольф**

good хоро́ший, до́брый; *su.* добро́; бла́го; *pl.* това́р(ы); ~ **afternoon!** до́брый день!, здра́вствуй(те)!; ~ **morning!** до́брое у́тро!; ~ **night!** споко́йной но́чи!; ~**bye!** до свида́ния!, *(farewell)* проща́й(те)!, *coll.* счастли́во!; ~**-for-nothing** никчёмный *(челове́к)*; ~**-natured** доброду́шный; ~**will** до́брая во́ля

goose гусь m; ~**berr**|**y**, -**ies** крыжо́вник

gorge *geogr.* уще́лье

gorgeous великоле́пный

gospel Ева́нгелие

gossip спле́тня; [на]спле́тничать; *(person)* спле́тник, -ца

govern управля́ть *(a. gr.)*, пра́вить (Т); ~**ment** прави́тельство; *(management)* правле́ние; ~**or** губерна́тор

gown пла́тье

grab хвата́ть [схвати́ть]

grac|**e** гра́ция, изя́щество; ~**eful** грацио́зный, изя́щ-ный

grad|**e** *(degree)* сте́пень f; *Am.* *(school)* класс; *(mark)* оце́нка; *(quality)* сорт; [рас-] сортирова́ть; ~**ual** постепе́нный; ~**uate** конча́ть университе́т

grain зерно́

gram грамм

gramma|**r** грамма́тика; ~**tical** граммати́ческий

gramophone про́игрыватель; **~ record** грампласти́нка, диск

granary зернохрани́лище

grand вели́чественный, грандио́зный; *coll.* отли́чный; **~daughter** вну́чка; **~father** дед, де́душка; **~mother** ба́бушка; **~son** внук

granite грани́т

grant предоставля́ть ['-вить]; (*admit*) допуска́ть [-сти́ть]; *fin.* субси́дия; (*student*) стипе́ндия

granulated: **~ sugar** са́харный песо́к

grape|s *pl.* виногра́д; **~-fruit** грейпфру́т

graphic графи́ческий; *fig.* нагля́дный; **~ arts** гра́фика

grasp схва́тывать [-ти́ть]; хвата́ть; (*understand*) понима́ть [-ня́ть]; хва́тка; понима́ние

grass трава́; (*plot*) лужа́йка; (*field*) па́стбище; **keep off the ~!** по газо́ну не ходи́ть!; **~hopper** кузне́чик; **~ widow** соло́менная вдова́; **~y** травяни́стый

grateful благода́рный

gratif|ication удовлетворе́ние; **~y** удовлетворя́ть [-ри́ть]

grating решётка

gratitude благода́рность *f*

grave[1] моги́ла; **~yard** кладбище

grave[2] серьёзный; (*situation*) тяжёлый

gravit|ation тяготе́ние; **~y** серьёзность *f*; *phys.* притяже́ние; **force of ~y** си́ла тя́жести

gravy (*мясна́я*) подли́вка

gray → grey

graze *agr.* пасти́(сь)

greas|e жир; (*lubricant*) (консисте́нтная) сма́зка; сма́з(ыв)ать; **~y** жи́рный

great вели́кий; (*difference*) большо́й; **that is ~** э́то замеча́тельно; **~grandfather** пра́дед; **~ly** о́чень; **~ness** вели́чие; (*size*) величина́

greed жа́дность *f*; **~y** жа́дный

Greek гре|к, -ча́нка; гре́ческий

green зелёный; (*unripe*) незре́лый, зелёный (*a. fig.*); **~grocery** овощно́й магази́н; **~house** тепли́ца; (*conservatory*) оранжере́я; **~ish** зеленова́тый

greet приве́тствовать; (по)здоро́ваться (с Т); **~ing** приве́тствие, приве́т

grey се́рый; (*hair*) седо́й; **~hound** борза́я

grief го́ре

griev|ance оби́да; печа́ль *f*; **~e** *v/i.* горева́ть; *v/t.* [о]печа́лить; **~ous** огорчи́тельный; (*crime*) тя́жкий; (*pain*) си́льный

grill ра́шпер; гриль; жа́-
рить(ся) на ра́шпере

grim суро́вый, жесто́кий

grimace грима́са; грима́с-
ничать

grin усмеха́ться [-ну́ться];
усме́шка

grind *axe* [на]точи́ть; *coffee*
[с]моло́ть; **~stone** точи́ло

grip схва́тывать [-ти́ть];
хва́тка; *(handle)* ру́чка;
(of machine, etc.) руко-
я́тка; *(travelling bag)* до-
ро́жная су́мка

grit кру́пный песо́к; *fig.
coll.* твёрдость хара́ктера

groan стона́ть; стон

grocer|ies [s] ба-
кале́йный магази́н

groom ко́нюх; *(bride~)* же-
ни́х; *horse* уха́живать за
(T); **well-~ed** ухо́женный

groove желобо́к; *(rut)* ко-
ле́я *(a. fig.)*

grope иска́ть о́щупью *(for
B)*; **~ one's way** проби-
ра́ться о́щупью

gross *(coarse)* гру́бый;
(glaring) вопию́щий, я́в-
ный; *comm.* валово́й;
(weight) бру́тто *indecl.*; in
~ о́птом

ground земля́; *(soil)* по́чва;
(reason) основа́ние; обо-
сно́вывать [-ова́ть]; **~less**
необосно́ванный

group гру́ппа; *attr.* группо-
во́й; [с]группирова́ть;
(gather) *v/i.* соб(и)ра́ться

grouse ря́бчик; *(black)* те́-

терев

grove ро́ща

grow *v/i.* расти́; *(become)*
[с]де́латься; *v/t.* выра́щи-
вать [вы́растить]

growl ворча́ть *(at* на B);
fig. ворча́ть себе́ под нос

grown-up *adj. a. su.* взро́с-
лый

growth рост

grudge зата́ённая оби́да;
have a ~ against име́ть
зуб про́тив (P); **he ~s a bit
of bread** ему́ жаль куска́
хле́ба

gruff грубова́тый; *(voice)*
хри́плый

grumble ворча́ть; **~r** ворч-
у́н(ья)

grunt *(person)* бурча́ть;
(pig) хрю́кать [-кнуть]

guarantee гара́нтия;
comm. гаранти́йное обя-
за́тельство; *(person)* га-
ра́нт; гаранти́ровать
(im)pf. *(against* от P); *I ~
that ...* я руча́юсь за то,
что ...

guard охраня́ть [-ни́ть];
(protection) охра́на, стра́-
жа; *(on duty)* карау́л, *(single)* часово́й; **be on one's
~** быть начеку́; **catch s.b.
off his ~** заста́ть кого́-
ли́бо враспло́х; *pl.* гва́р-
дия; **~ian** опеку́н

guess *(угада́ть)* [угада́ть];
дога́дываться [-да́ться],
Am. coll. *(suppose)* пола-
га́ть; дога́дка

guest го́сть(я) m (f)
guid|ance руково́дство; ~e руководи́ть (T); проводни́к, (for tourists) гид, экскурсово́д; (book) путеводи́тель m
guile хи́трость f, кова́рство
guilt вина́; ~less невино́вный; ~y вино́вный
guitar гита́ра
gulf geogr. зали́в
gulp (большо́й) глото́к; v. глота́ть; at one ~ за́лпом
gum: (chewing-) ~ жева́тельная рези́нка, coll. жва́чка
gun (rifle) ружьё; (cannon)

ору́дие; (pistol) пистоле́т, револьве́р; ~ner артиллери́ст; ~powder по́рох
gurgle бу́лькать; бу́лька́нье
gush си́льный пото́к, струя́; хлы́нуть pf.
gust поры́в (a. fig.)
gut кишка́; pl. he has plenty of ~s он му́жественный, волево́й челове́к
gutter сто́чная кана́ва
gymnas|ium спорти́вный зал; (school) гимна́зия; ~tic гимнасти́ческий; ~tics гимна́стика

H

haberdashery галантере́я
habit привы́чка; (custom) обы́чай; ~ation жильё; ~ual привы́чный; обы́чный; ~ually по привы́чке, привы́чно
hack руби́ть; ~ down сруба́ть [-би́ть]
haemorrhage кровоизлия́ние
haggard измождённый
hail¹ град; it ~s идёт град
hail² оклика́ть ['-кнуть]; ~ a taxi подозва́ть такси́
hair во́лос(ы); ~cut стри́жка; ~do причёска; ~dresser парикма́хер; ~dresser's парикма́херская; ~-drier фен

half полови́на; adj. полови́нный; adv. наполови́ну; in compounds: пол-, полу-; ~way adv. на полпути́
halibut па́лтус
hall пере́дняя; (concert, etc.) зал; ~ of residence общежи́тие
halt остано́вка, (hikers) прива́л; ~ остана́вливать(ся) [-нови́ть(ся)]
ham ветчина́; (whole) о́корок
hamlet дереву́шка
hammer молото́к, (big) мо́лот; рабо́тать молотко́м; ~ in вби(ва́)ть
hammock гама́к

hamper затрудня́ть [-ни́ть] (B), [по]меша́ть (Д)

hand рука́ f; вруча́ть [-чи́ть]; *change* ~s переходи́ть [перейти́] из рук в ру́ки; *lend a* ~ помога́ть [помо́чь]; ~ *back* возвраща́ть [возврати́ть]; ~ *down* передава́ть (из поколе́ния в поколе́ние); ~ *in* подава́ть [-да́ть]; ~ *over* перед(ав)а́ть; *at* ~, *on* ~ (*within reach*) налицо́; (*available*) налицо́; *on the other* ~ с друго́й стороны́; ~*bag* су́мочка f; ~*ful* горсть f; ~*shake* рукопожа́тие

handicap помо́ха f; (*physical*) физи́ческий недоста́ток, уве́чье; (*sports*) гандика́п

handkerchief носово́й плато́к

handle руко́ятка f; (*touch*) тро́гать руко́й; (*treat*) обраща́ться [-рати́ться] (с Т)

hand-rail по́ручень m

handsome краси́вый; (*sum*) поря́дочный

handwriting по́черк m

hang v/i. висе́ть; v/t. ве́шать [пове́сить]; ~*ings* драпиро́вка f; ~*over* похме́лье

haphazard случа́йность f; случа́йный; *at* ~ науда́чу

happen случа́ться [-чи́ться]; ~*ing* слу́чай, собы́тие

happ|iness сча́стье; ~*y* счастли́вый; (*lucky*) уда́чный

harass [вс]тревóжить

harbour га́вань f

hard твёрдый, жёсткий; (*difficult*) тру́дный; (*time*) тяжёлый; ~*-boiled*: ~*-boiled egg* яйцо́ вкруту́ю; ~ *copy* tech. маши́нный докуме́нт; распеча́тка f; ~*en* v/i. [за-] тверде́ть; v/t. закаля́ть [-ли́ть]; ~*ly* едва́; (*unlikely*) едва́ ли; ~*ness* твёрдость f; ~*ship* лише́ния n/pl.; ~*ware* tech. аппара́тное обеспе́чение

hardy (*strong*) си́льный, выно́сливый; (*bold*) сме́лый

hare за́яц

harm вред; [по]вреди́ть (Д); ~*ful* вре́дный; ~*less* безоби́дный

harmon|ious гармони́чный; ~*y* гармо́ния; *fig. a.* согла́сие

harness у́пряжь f; запряга́ть [-я́чь]

harp а́рфа

harrow борона́; [вз]борони́ть

harsh (*voice*) ре́зкий; (*climate*) суро́вый; (*taste*) те́рпкий

harvest (*yield*) урожа́й; (*action*) убо́рка f; собира́ть урожа́й; ~*er* комба́йн

hast|e спе́шка f; ~*en* [по]спеши́ть; ~*y* торопли́-

вый; (*rash*) поспе́шный

hat шля́па

hatch *mar.* люк

hatchet топо́рик

hat|e ненави́деть; **~eful** ненави́стный; **~red** нена́висть *f*

haughty надме́нный

haul тяну́ть; (= **~age**) перево́зка; (*catch*) уло́в

haunch бедро́

have *possibility, idea, etc.* име́ть; **they ~ a house** у них (есть) дом; **they ~ no house** у них нет до́ма; **I ~ a headache** у меня́ боли́т голова́; **they ~ come** они́ пришли́

haven *fig.* убе́жище

hawk я́стреб

hay се́но; **~-making** сеноко́с

hazard риск; (*danger*) опа́сность; *life* рискова́ть [-кну́ть] (Т); **~ous** риско́ванный; опа́сный

haze ды́мка

hazel-nut лесно́й оре́х

hazy подёрнутый ды́мкой; *fig.* тума́нный

he он

head голова́; (*leader*) глава́; **~ache** головна́я боль *f*; **~light** фа́ра; (*газе́тный*) заголо́вок; **~long** опроме́тчиво; очертя́ го́лову; **~quarters** штаб-кварти́ра

heal *v/t.* выле́чивать [-чи́ть]; *v/i.* зажи́(ва́)ть

~th здоро́вье; **~thy** здоро́вый

heap ку́ча; *pl. fig. coll.* ку́ча, ма́сса; **~ up** нава́ливать [-ли́ть]

hear [у]слы́шать; *witness* слу́шать; (*learn*) узн(ав)а́ть; (*sense*) слух; *jur.* слу́шание

heart се́рдце; **by ~** наизу́сть; **~en** ободря́ть [-ри́ть]

hearth оча́г

heart-rending ду́шердздира́ющий

hearty серде́чный, раду́шный; (*meal*) оби́льный

heat жара́; *fig.* пыл; *v. t.* пои́ть; *metal* нагре́(ва́)ть

heath ве́ресковая пу́стошь

heathen язы́чник; *adj.* язы́ческий

heating отопле́ние

heave поднима́ть [-ня́ть]; *waves:* подыма́ться

heaven небеса́ *n/pl.*; (*sky*) не́бо; **for ~'s sake** ра́ди Бо́га; **~ly** небе́сный

heav|iness тя́жесть *f*; **~y** тяжёлый; (*rain, blow*) си́льный

hedge жива́я и́згородь *f*, **~hog** ёж

heed внима́ние; **take ~ of** быть осторо́жным, обраща́ть внима́ние на (В); **~less** невнима́тельный, беспе́чный

heel каблу́к; *anat.* пя́тка

heifer тёлка

height высота́; *geogr.* возвы́шенность *f*; **~en** повыша́ть [-бы́сить]

heir, **~ess** насле́дни|к, -ца

helicopter вертолёт

hell ад

helm штурва́л

helmet шлем

help помога́ть [-мо́чь] (Д); по́мощь *f*; **~!** помоги́те! (*at table*) бери́(те), пожа́луйста!; **~er** помо́щник, -ца; **~ful** поле́зный; **~less** беспо́мощный

hem (*sewing*) рубе́ц; подруба́ть [-би́ть]

hemisphere полуша́рие

hemp пенька́; *bot.* конопля́

hen ку́рица

hence отсю́да; (*from now*) с э́тих пор; (*therefore*) сле́довательно; **~forth** впредь

her *pers. pron.* её (= B); (= Д); *poss. pron.* её, *reflex.* свой; **~ son was ...** её сын был ...; **she likes ~ son** она́ лю́бит своего́ сы́на; **by ~** е́ю; **with ~** с не́й

herald (пред)ве́стник; предвеща́ть [-ве́стить]

herb *med.* целе́бная трава́; *cul.* пря́ная зе́лень

herd ста́до; (*horses*) табу́н; **~sman** пасту́х; табу́нщик

here здесь, тут; (*hither*) сюда́; **~ I am!** вот и я́!; (*after*) в бу́дущем; (*document*) в дальне́йшем; **~by**

jur., comm. настоя́щим; (*thus*) таки́м о́бразом; **~inafter** здесь и да́лее

hereditary насле́дственный; **~y** насле́дственность *f*

herewith **~by** (= *in annex*) при э́том (прилага́ется)

heritage насле́дство; *fig.* насле́дие

hero геро́й; **~ic** герои́ческий; **~ine** геро́йня; **~ism** герои́зм

heron ца́пля

herring сельдь *f*, *cul. mst.* селёдка

hers её; свой; → **her**

herself себя́, -ся; (*emphatic*) сама́

hesitate колеба́ться; (*to do, etc.*) затрудня́ться [-ни́ться]; **~ion** колеба́ние

hew руби́ть

hide[1] [с]пря́тать(ся) (*keep secret*) скрыва́ть [-ры́ть]

hide[2] шку́ра; *comm.* коже́венное сырьё

high высо́кий; (*official*) вы́сший; (*command*) верхо́вный; (*sea*) откры́тый; *adv.* высоко́; **~lands** го́рная ме́стность; **~ly** в вы́сшей сте́пени; **~ness** высо́чество; **~way** шоссе́ *indecl.*; автостра́да; **~way Code** пра́вила доро́жного движе́ния

highjack (*plane*) угоня́ть [-на́ть]; (*rob*) соверша́ть

[-ши́ть] ограбле́ние

hike турпохо́д; ~r пе́ший тури́ст

hill холм; *down*~ под го́ру; ~y холми́стый

him его́ (= В); ему́ (= Д); *by* ~ им; *with* ~ с ним; ~**self** сам, -ся; (*emphatic*) сам

hind[1] за́дний

hind[2] *zo.* лань *f*

hind|er [по]меша́ть (Д); ~**rance** поме́ха

Hindu инду́с(ка), инди́ец, -иа́нка; инду́сский, инди́йский

hinge (*door*, *window*) пе́тля; *tech.* шарни́р

hint намёк; намека́ть [-кну́ть] (*at* на В)

hip *anat.* бедро́

hire *worker* нанима́ть [-ня́ть]; *thing* брать на прока́т; наём; прока́т

his его́; *refl.* свой; *this is* ~ *house* э́то его́ дом; *he sees* ~ *house* он ви́дит свой дом

hiss *v.* шипе́ть; (*catcall*) осви́стывать [-ста́ть]

histor|ian исто́рик; ~**ic(al)** истори́ческий; ~у исто́рия

hit ударя́ть [-́рить]; *aim* попада́ть [попа́сть] (в В); уда́р; попада́ние; *the new play is a* ~ но́вая пье́са по́льзуется больши́м успе́хом

hither сюда́; ~**to** до сих пор

hive у́лей

hoard запаса́ть [-сти́]; (*secretly*) запа́с

hoarfrost и́ней

hoarse хрипу́лый

hobby хо́бби *indecl.*

hockey хокке́й; *attr.* хокке́йный; *ice* ~ хокке́й с ша́йбой

hog бо́ров

hoist поднима́ть [-ня́ть]; подъёмник

hold держа́ть; *positions* уде́рживать [-жа́ть]; *meeting* проводи́ть [-вести́]; (*contain*) вмеща́ть [-сти́ть]; ~**er** (*owner*) владе́лец; *fin.* держа́тель *m*; ~**ing** владе́ние

hole дыра́; (*in ground*) я́ма, (*small*) я́мка

holiday *public, eccl.* пра́здник; (*day off*) выходно́й день *m*; (*leave*) о́тпуск; (*school*) *pl.* кани́кулы *f/pl.*

hollow по́лый, пустоте́лый; (*cheek*) впа́лый; (*tree*) дупли́стый; *su.* дупло́

holly па́дуб

holy свято́й

home *su.; maternity* ~ роди́льный дом; *orphans'* ~ де́тский дом, *coll.* детдо́м; (~*land*) ро́дина; *adv.* до-мо́й; *at* ~ до́ма; *make o.s. at* ~ чу́вствовать себя́ как до́ма; ~**less** бездо́мный; 2 *Office U.K.* министе́рство вну́тренних дел; ~**sick:**

be **~sick** тосковать по дому *or* родине; **~ trade** внутренняя торговля; **~work** домашняя работа

honest честный; **~y** честность *f*

honey мёд; **~comb** соты *m/pl.*; **~moon** медовый месяц

honorary почётный

honour честь *f*; *pl. mil.* почести *f/pl.*; *v.* почитать; **~able** (*person*) благородный; (*task*) почётный

hood (*coat*) капюшон; *mot.* капот

hoof копыто

hook крючок; (*large*) крюк; (*fish*) поймать (на крючок) (*a. fig.*); **~ed** крючковатый

hoop обруч

hooping-cough коклюш

hoot гудеть; **~er** гудок

hop¹ [по]скакать (на одной ноге); скачок

hop² *bot.* хмель *m*

hope надежда; надеяться (**for** на В); **~ful** надеющийся; (*talented*) многообещающий; **~less** безнадёжный

horizon горизонт; **~tal** горизонтальный

horn рог; *mus.* рожок; *mot.* звуковой сигнал

horr|ible, **~id** ужасный; **~ify** ужасать [-снуть]; **~or** ужас

hors: **~ d'œuvres** *pl.* закус-

ки *f/pl.*

horse лошадь *f*, конь *m*; **~back: on ~back** верхом; **~man** всадник; **~-power** лошадиная сила; **~-race** скачки *f/pl.*; **~-radish** хрен; **~shoe** подкова

hose шланг

hosiery чулочные изделия

hospita|ble гостеприимный; **~l** больница, *mil.* госпиталь *m*; **~lity** гостеприимство; **~lize** госпитализировать

host хозяин; **~age** заложни|к, -ца; **~el** общежитие; **~ess** хозяйка

hostil|e враждебный; **~ity** враждебность *f*; *pl.* военные действия *n/pl.*

hot горячий; (*weather*, *day*) жаркий

hotel гостиница, отель *m*; *take a room in a* **~** снять комнату в гостинице

hothouse теплица

hound гончая (*собака*)

hour час; **~ly** ежечасный; *adv.* ежечасно

house дом; *v.* обеспечивать жильём; **~ of Commons** *U.K.* палата общин; **~hold** (*people*) семья, домочадцы *m/pl.*; **~holder** (*owner*) домовладелец; (*tenant*) квартиросъёмщик; **~-warming** новоселье; **~wife** домашняя хозяйка

how как; **~ many**, **~ much**

ско́лько; **~ever** одна́ко;
~ever that may be как бы
то ни́ было

howl выть; (*cry*) реве́ть;
вой; рёв

hue отте́нок

hug обнима́ть [-ня́ть]; объя́тие

huge грома́дный

hull *mar.* ко́рпус су́дна

hum жужжа́ть; **~ a tune**
напева́ть пе́сенку

human челове́ческий; **~e**
челове́чный, гума́нный;
~ity (*mankind*) челове́чество; гума́нность *f*; **the
~ities** гуманита́рные нау́ки; **~ize** гуманизи́ровать

humble смире́нный; (*condition*) скро́мный; *pride*
смиря́ть [-ри́ть]

humidity вла́жность *f*

humiliat|e унижа́ть [уни́зить]; **~ing** унизи́тельный; **~ion** униже́ние

humo|rous юмористи́ческий; **~ur** ю́мор; (*mood*)
настрое́ние; **sense of ~r**
чу́вство ю́мора

hump горб; [с]го́рбить;
~back горбу́н(ья);
~backed горба́тый

hundred сто; **~s** со́тни *f/pl.*;
~th со́тый; **~weight** це́нтнер

Hungarian венг|р, -е́рка;
-е́рский

hung|er го́лод; *v.* голода́ть;
~er strike голодо́вка; **~ry**
голо́дный

hunt охо́титься (за Т) (*a. ~
for fig.*); **~er** охо́тник; **~ing**
охо́та

hurdle барье́р; **~-race** бег с
препя́тствиями

hurl швыря́ть [-ну́ть]

hurricane урага́н

hurr|iedly поспе́шно, торопли́во; **~y** *v/i.* [по]спеши́ть, [по]торопи́ться; *v/t.*
[по]торопи́ть

hurt *v/t.* ушиба́ть [-би́ть];
(*offend*) обижа́ть [оби́деть]; *v/i.* боле́ть

husband муж, супру́г

husk шелуха́, лузга́

hustle (*push*) толка́ть(ся);
(*hurry*) торопи́ть; су́толока; суета́

hut хи́жина

hyacinth гиаци́нт

hybrid гибри́д

hydrogen водоро́д; *attr.* водоро́дный

hygiene гигие́на

hymn (церко́вный) гимн

hyphen дефи́с, чёрточка

hypocri|sy лицеме́рие; **~te**
лицеме́р(ка); ханжа́

hypothe|sis гипо́теза; **~tical** гипотети́ческий

hyster|ia исте́рия; **~cal** исте́рический; **~cs** исте́рика

I

I я; **you and ~** мы с тобой [с вáми]; **~ feel cold** мне хóлодно; **~ have a headache** у меня болит головá

ice лёд; **~berg** áйсберг
~-breaker ледокóл;
~-cream морóженое

icicle сосýлька; **~ing** (сáхарная) глазýрь; **~у** ледянóй, холóдный (a. fig.)

idea идéя, мысль f; (notion) понятие; **~l** идеáл; идеáльный

identical такóй же, идентичный; **~fy** распознавáть [-знáть]; (establish identity) опознавáть [-знáть], **~ty** идентичность; (person) лчность

ideological идеологический; **~у** идеолóгия

idiom идиоматическое выражéние; (dialect) гóвор

idiot идиóт(ка); med. слабоýмный; **~ic** идиóтский

idle прáздный (a. fig.); (lazy) ленивый; tech. холостóй; **~ness** прáздность f

idol кумир

if éсли; (whether) ли; **I don't know ~ he is rich** я не знáю богáт ли он; **as ~** как будто

ignition mot. зажигáние; **~ key** ключ зажигáния

ignoble неблагорóдный

ignorance невéжество;

(lack of information) невéдение; **~ant** невéжественный, несвéдущий (of в П); **~e** игнорировать (im)pf.

ill (sick) больнóй; **fall ~** заболéть; (evil) дурнóй, злой; adv. плóхо; su. зло; **~-advised** неблагоразýмный; **~-bred** плóхо воспитанный; **~-founded** необоснóванный

illegal, illicit незакóнный
illiterate неграмотный
illness болéзнь f
illuminate [-éтить], освещáть; **~ion** освещéние; mst. pl. иллюминáция

illusion иллюзия
illustrate [(про)иллюстрировать]; **~ation** иллюстрáция; **~ious** знаменитый

image (ideal) óбраз; (concrete) изображéние; (likeness) подóбие, кóпия

imaginable вообразимый; **~ary** воображáемый; **~ation** воображéние; **~e** воображáть [-разить], представлять [-'вить] себé

imitate (try to be like) подражáть (Д); (copy) имитировать; **~ion** подражáние; имитáция

immature незрéлый
immediate (quick) немéдленный; (direct) непосрéдственный

immense безме́рный, грома́дный, необъя́тный; ~ly чрезвыча́йно

immigra|nt иммигра́нт (-ка); ~tion иммигра́ция

imminent надвига́ющийся

immobile неподви́жный

immoderate непоме́рный

immoral безнра́вственный

immortal бессме́ртный; ~ity бессме́ртие

immovable неподви́жный; (property) недви́жимый

immunity med., pol. иммуните́т

impact (a strong hit) уда́р; (collision) столкнове́ние; fig. влия́ние

impart сообща́ть [-щи́ть]; ~ial беспристра́стный; ~iality беспристра́стие

impatien|ce нетерпе́ние; ~t нетерпели́вый

impediment препя́тствие

impel (force) вынужда́ть ['-удить]; (urge) побужда́ть [-уди́ть]

impending предстоя́щий; (danger) надвига́ющийся

imperative повели́тельный (a. gr.); (need) насто́ятельный

imperfect несоверше́нный; ~ion несоверше́нство; ~ive gr. несоверше́нный вид

imperial импе́рский; ~ism империали́зм

impersonal беспристра́стный

impertinent де́рзкий, на́глый

imperturbable невозмути́мый

impetus и́мпульс; fig. a. толчо́к

implement ору́дие; выполня́ть [вы́полнить]

implic|ate person впу́т(ыв)ать; (imply) подразумева́ть; ~it подразумева́емый; (obedience) безусло́вный

implore умоля́ть

imply → **implicate**

impolite неве́жливый

import ввози́ть [ввезти́], импорти́ровать impf.; ввоз, и́мпорт; ~ licence лицензия на и́мпорт

importan|ce ва́жность f; ~t ва́жный

importation ввоз, и́мпорт

impos|e tax облага́ть [-ложи́ть] (T, on B); fine налага́ть [наложи́ть]; decision навя́зывать [-за́ть] (B, upon Д); ~ing внуши́тельный

impossib|ility невозмо́жность f; ~le невозмо́жный

impress people производи́ть впечатле́ние (на В); (imprint) отпеча́т(ыв)ать; fig. запечатлева́ть [-ле́ть]; ~ion впечатле́ние; от-тиск; ~ive внуши́тельный, впечатля́ющий

imprint → **impress**

281   **inconceivable**

imprison заключа́ть [-чи́ть]
(в тюрьму́); **~ment** заключе́ние

improbable маловероя́тный, невероя́тный

improper неуме́стный; (*indecent*) неприли́чный

improve улучша́ть(ся) ['-чшить(ся)]; **~ment** улучше́ние

impruden|ce неблагоразу́мие; **~t** неблагоразу́мный

impuden|ce на́глость; **~t** на́глый

impuls|e и́мпульс; **~ive** импульси́вный

impunity: with ~ безнака́занно

impur|e нечи́стый; гря́зный; **~ity** *pl.* загрязне́ние; при́меси *f/pl.*

in в (П; = *into* В); *adv.* внутри́, внутрь; **~ the street** на у́лице; **~ summer** ле́том; **~ my opinion** по моему́ мне́нию; **come ~** входи́ть [войти́] (*prefix* в(о), *like in many other verbs*)

inability неспосо́бность *f*

inaccessible недосту́пный

inaccurate нето́чный

inadequate недоста́точный; **~ excuse** неубеди́тельная отгово́рка

inadmissible недопусти́мый

inanimate неодушевлённый

inaudible неслы́шный

inaugurat|e *exhibition* торже́ственно открыва́ть; **~ion** торже́ственное откры́тие; инаугура́ция

inborn врождённый, приро́дный

incalculable неисчисли́мый

incapable неспосо́бный

incentive сти́мул

inch дюйм (= *25.4 mm*)

incident происше́ствие; *mil., pol.* инциде́нт; **~al** случа́йный; *pl.* непредви́денные расхо́ды *m/pl.*

incite подстрека́ть [-кну́ть]

inclin|ation накло́н; *fig.* скло́нность *f*; **~e** склоня́ть(ся) [-ни́ть(ся)]; **be ~ed to** быть скло́нным к (Д)

inclose → **enclose**

includ|e включа́ть [-чи́ть]; **~ding** включа́я (В); **~sion** включе́ние (В); **~sive** включи́тельно

income дохо́д; **~tax** подохо́дный нало́г

incomparable несравни́мый

incompatible несовмести́мый

incompetent некомпете́нтный: (*incapable*) неспосо́бный

incomplete непо́лный; (*unfinished*) незако́нченный

incomprehensible непоня́тный; непостижи́мый

inconceivable невообрази́-

inconsisten|cy непоследовательность *f*; ~t непосле́довательный; *(with)* противоре́чащий (Д)

inconvenien|ce неудо́бство; ~t неудо́бный

incorporate включа́ть [-чи́ть]

incorrect непра́вильный

incorrigible неисправи́мый

increase увели́чи(ва)ть(ся); увеличе́ние

incred|ible невероя́тный; ~ulous недове́рчивый

incur *danger* подверга́ться [-е́ргнуться] (Д); *suspicion* навлека́ть [-е́чь] на себя́; *losses* [по]нести́

incurable неизлечи́мый

indebted в долгу́ (*to* у Р); *fig.* обя́занный

indecent неприли́чный

indecision нерешительность

indeed в са́мом де́ле; ~! неуже́ли!

indefinite неопределённый

indemnity возмеще́ние, компенса́ция

independen|ce незави́симость *f*; ~t незави́симый

index указа́тель *m*; *math., comm.* показа́тель *m*

Indian инди́|ец, -а́нка; -и́йский; ~ **summer** ба́бье ле́то; **Red** ~ инди́ец, -и́анка; -е́йский

indicate ука́з|ывать [-за́ть] (на В); ~ion указа́ние; *(sign)* при́знак; *tech.* пока-

за́ние

indictment обвине́ние

indifferen|ce безразли́чие; ~t безразли́чный; *(poor)* посре́дственный

indigestion несваре́ние желу́дка

indigna|nt негоду́ющий; ~tion негодова́ние

indirect ко́свенный

indispensable необходи́мый

indisputable бесспо́рный

indistinct неотчётливый

individual индивидуа́льный; *su.* ли́чность *f*; ~ity индивидуа́льность *f*

indolent лени́вый

indoor *(plant, games)* ко́мнатный; ~s в до́ме, до́ма

induce побужда́ть [-уди́ть]; вынужда́ть [вы́нудить]; ~ment побужде́ние, сти́мул

indulge *child* балова́ть; ~ *in* балова́ться (Т); ~nce *(too much)* баловство́; *(lenience)* снисходи́тельность *f*; ~nt снисходи́тельный

industr|ial промы́шленный; ~ious трудолюби́вый; ~y промы́шленность *f*; трудолю́бие; **tourist** ~y тури́зм

ineffective неэффекти́вный

inefficient *(person)* неуме́лый; *(machine)* ни́зкой производи́тельности

inequality неравенство

inert инертный (a. fig.)

inestimable неоценимый

inevitable неизбежный

inexhaustible неисчерпаемый

inexorable неумолимый

inexpensive недорогой

infallible непогрешимый; (method, etc.) надёжный

infam|ous позорный; ~y позор

infan|cy младенчество; ~t младенец

infantry пехота; attr. пехотный

infatuated до безумия влюблённый

infect заражать [-разить] (a. fig.); ~ion инфекция; ~ious инфекционный, заразный; fig. заразительный

infer заключать [-чить]; ~ence умозаключение, вывод

inferior неполноценный; (in rank) подчинённый; ~ to хуже, чем...; ~ity неполноценность f; (goods) низкого качества

infernal адский

infest: be ~ed with кишеть (Т)

infinit|e бесконечный; ~y бесконечность f

inflame воспламенять(ся) [-нить(ся)]; med. воспалять(ся) [-лить(ся)]; ~mation воспаление

inflat|e надувать [-дуть]; (tyre) накачивать [-чать]; ~ed prices взвинченные [-нтить] цены; ~ion econ. инфляция

inflection gr. флексия; (in speech) модуляция

inflexible несгибаемый

inflict wound, blow наносить [-нести] (upon Д); pain причинять [-нить] (upon Д)

influen|ce влияние; влиять на (В); ~tial влиятельный

influenza грипп

influx приток

inform сообщать [-щить] (Д; of о П), информировать; (denounce) доносить [-нести] (against на В); ~al неофициальный; ~ation сообщение, информация

infringement нарушение

infuriate [вз]бесить

ingen|ious изобретательный; ~uity изобретательность f

ingratitude неблагодарность f

ingredient ингредиент

inhabit обитать; ~ant житель(ница) m

inhale вдыхать [вдохнуть]

inherent присущий (in Д)

inherit [у]наследовать; ~ance наследство

inhuman бесчеловечный

initial (перво)начальный; (person's) pl. инициалы

m/pl.; ~te положи́ть нача́ло (Д); посвяща́ть [-яти́ть] (*into* в В); ~tive инициати́ва, почи́н

inject впры́скивать [-снуть]; *med.* [с]де́лать инъе́кцию; ~ion впры́скивание; *med.* инъе́кция, *coll.* уко́л

injunction *jur.* постановле́ние суда́

injure (*wound*) ра́нить (im)*pf.;* (*damage*) повреждать [-еди́ть]; (*harm*) [по]вреди́ть (Д); (*wrong*) обижа́ть [оби́деть]; ~ious (*harmful*) вре́дный; (*insulting*) оби́дный; ~y ране́ние; (*sports, etc.*) тра́вма, поврежде́ние; оби́да

injustice несправедли́вость *f*

ink черни́ла *n/pl.*

inland вну́тренний

inn гости́ница

inner вну́тренний

innocen|ce неви́нность *f*; *jur.* невино́вность *f*; ~t невинный; невино́вный (*of* в П)

innovation но́вшество

innumerable бесчи́сленный

inoculate [с]де́лать приви́вку; ~ion приви́вка

inoffensive безоби́дный

inopportune несвоевре́менный

in-patient стациона́рный больно́й

inquire справля́ться [-ви́ться], спра́шивать [спроси́ть] (*about* о П); ~ry вопро́с, запро́с; *jur.* рассле́дование; ~ry office спра́вочное бюро́; ~sitive пытли́вый; (*prying*) любопы́тный

insane *med.* психи́чески больно́й; *coll.* сумасше́дший; *fig.* безу́мный; ~ity психи́ческое заболева́ние; *coll., fig.* сумасше́ствие; *fig.* безу́мие

inscribe надпи́сывать [-са́ть]; ~ption на́дпись *f*

insect насеко́мое; ~ **bite** уку́с насеко́мого

insensible нечувстви́тельный; (*unconscious*) без созна́ния; (*unsympathetic*) бесчу́вственный

inseparable неотдели́мый; (*friends*) неразлу́чный

insert вставля́ть [-вить]; *advertisement* помеща́ть [-ести́ть]; ~ion вста́вка

inside вну́тренняя сторона́; *adj.* вну́тренний; *adv.* внутрь, внутри́

insight *fig.* проница́тельность *f*; прозорли́вость *f*

insignificant незначи́тельный

insinuate намека́ть [-кну́ть]; ~ion намёк, инсинуа́ция

insist наста́ивать [-стоя́ть] (*on* на П); ~ence настоя́ние; (*quality*) настойчи-

вость *f*; ~**ent** насто́йчи-
вый

insolen|ce на́глость *f*; ~**t**
на́глый

insoluble нераствори́мый;
(*problem*) неразреши́мый

insomnia бессо́нница

inspect осма́тривать [ос-
мотре́ть]; *tech.* проверя́ть
[-ве́рить]; (*officially*) ин-
спекти́ровать; ~**ion** ос-
мо́тр; инспе́кция; ~**or** ин-
спе́ктор

inspir|ation вдохнове́ние;
~**e** вдохновля́ть [-ви́ть];
hope, etc. вселя́ть [-ли́ть];
fear, etc. внуша́ть [-ши́ть]

install устана́вливать [-но-
ви́ть]; *el.* проводи́ть [-ве-
сти́]; ~**ation** *tech.* (*action*)
монта́ж; (*action, appara-
tus*) устано́вка; прово́дка

instalment *fin.* очередно́й
взно́с; **by** ~**s** в рассро́чку

instance приме́р; **for** ~ на-
приме́р

instant мгнове́ние; *adj.* не-
ме́дленный; (*need*) неот-
ло́жный; *comm.* теку́щего
ме́сяца; ~**aneous** мгно-
ве́нный

instead вме́сто (**of** Р); *adv.*
вме́сто того́

instinct инсти́нкт; ~**ive** ин-
стинкти́вный

institut|e институ́т; учреж-
да́ть [-еди́ть]; *custom,
rule* устана́вливать [-но-
ви́ть]; ~**ion** учрежде́ние;
установле́ние

instruct обуча́ть [-чи́ть];
~**ion** обуче́ние; *pl.* ин-
стру́кции; ~**ive** поучи́-
тельный; ~**or** учи́тель *m*,
инстру́ктор

instrument инструме́нт (*a.
mus.*); (*apparatus*) при-
бо́р; (*tool*) ору́дие

insufficient недоста́точный

insula|r островно́й; ~**te** изо-
ли́ровать (*im*)*pf.*

insulation *tech.* изоля́ция;
~ **tape** изоляцио́нная
ле́нта

insult оскорбля́ть [-би́ть];
оскорбле́ние

insurance страхова́ние;
(*money paid*) страхова́я
су́мма; ~**e** [за]страхова́ть

insurgent *su.* повста́нец;
~**rection** восста́ние

intact (*untouched*) нетро́ну-
тый; (*undamaged*) непо-
вреждённый

integral це́льный; (*part*)
неотъе́млемый

intell|ect ум, интелле́кт;
~**ectual** у́мственный; *su.*
интеллиге́нт, *pl.* интелли-
ге́нция; ~**igence** ум; (*information*) све́дения; *mil.
etc.* разве́дка; ~**igent**
у́мный

intend намерева́ться; (*des-
tine*) предназнача́ть
['-чить]

intens|e напряжённый;
(*pain, desire*) си́льный;
~**ify** усили(ва)ть; ~**ity**
интенси́вность *f*; си́ла; ~**ive**

интенси́вный

intent (*purpose*) наме́рение; (*design, mst. b. s.*) у́мысел; **~ion** наме́рение; **~ional** (пред-)наме́ренный; **~ionally** наро́чно; **~ly** внима́тельно

interact взаимоде́йствовать

inter|cept перехва́тывать [-ти́ть]; **~changeable** взаимозаменя́емый; **~course** (*social*) обще́ние; (*sexual*) сноше́ния *n/pl.*

interest интере́с; *fin.* проце́нты *m/pl.*; **~ed** заинтересо́ванный; **be ~ed** интересова́ться (**in** T); **~ing** интере́сный

interfere вме́шиваться [-ша́ться] (**in** в В); [по]меша́ть (**with** Д); **~nce** вмеша́тельство; (*radio*) поме́хи *f/pl.*

interior вну́тренний, *a. pl.*; вну́тренность *f*, вну́тренняя сторона́; (*of building*) интерье́р

inter|lude *mus.* интерлю́дия; **~mediate** *adj.* промежу́точный; (*in degree*) сре́дний; **~mission** переры́в; **~mittent** преры́вистый

intermediary посре́дник

internal вну́тренний

inter|national междунаро́дный; **the 2national** интернациона́л; **~pret** толкова́ть; (у́стно) переводи́ть;

~pretation интерпрета́ция; **~preter** (*translator*) у́стный перево́дчик; **~rogation** *jur.* допро́с; (*mark*) вопроси́тельный (знак); **~rupt** прер(ы)ва́ть; **~ruption** переры́в; **~section** пересече́ние; промежу́ток; интерва́л, *a. mus.*; **~vention** вмеша́тельство; интерве́нция; **~view** интервью́ *n indecl.*, бесе́да; брать интервью́

intestine кишка́; *pl.* кише́чник

intima|cy бли́зость *f*, инти́мность *f*; **~te** бли́зкий, инти́мный

intimidate запу́гивать [-га́ть]

into → **in**

intolera|ble нестерпи́мый, невыноси́мый; **~nt** нетерпи́мый

intoxicat|e опьяня́ть [-ни́ть] (*a. fig.*); **~ion** опьяне́ние; *med.* интоксика́ция

intrepid неустраши́мый

intricate сло́жный, запу́танный

intrigue интри́га; интригова́ть (**against** про́тив В); (*interest*) (за)интригова́ть

introduce вводи́ть [ввести́]; (*present*) представля́ть ['-вить]; **~tion** введе́ние; **letter of ~tion** рекоменда́тельное письмо́

intrude *v/i* вторга́ться

['-гнуться] (*into*, *upon* в B)

intuition интуи́ция

invade *mil.* вторга́ться ['-гнуться] (в B); ∼r захва́тчик

invalid[1] инвали́д; инвали́дный

invalid[2] *jur.* недействи́тельный

invaluable бесце́нный, неоцени́мый

invariable неизме́нный; ∼ly неизме́нно

invasion вторже́ние

invent изобрета́ть [-ести́]; ∼ion изобрете́ние; ∼or изобрета́тель *m*; ∼ory инвента́рная ве́домость

invest *fin.* вкла́дывать [вложи́ть]; ∼igate иссле́довать (*im*)*pf.*; ∼igation иссле́дование; (*inquiry*) рассле́дование; (*law*) сле́дствие; ∼ment *fin.* капиталовложе́ние, инвести́ция; ∼or вкла́дчик капита́ла, инве́стор

invisible неви́димый

invitation приглаше́ние; ∼e приглаша́ть [-ласи́ть]

invoice накладна́я, факту́ра

involuntary нево́льный

involve (*include*) включа́ть в себя́; (*bring into*) вовлека́ть [-е́чь] (в B); (*entangle*) впу́т(ыв)ать

inward вну́тренний; *adv.* внутрь; ∼ly внутрь, внутри́; (*in the mind*) вну́-

тренне

iodine йод

iris *bot.* и́рис

Irish ирла́ндский; ∼man, ∼woman ирла́ндец, -ка

irksome ну́дный; ску́чный

iron желе́зо; *attr.* желе́зный; (*flat-∼*) утю́г; [от]утю́жить

ironic ирони́ческий; (*person*) ирони́чный; ∼y иро́ния

irregular нерегуля́рный, непра́вильный; ∼ity нерегуля́рность *f*, непра́вильность *f*

irrelevant не относя́щийся к де́лу

irreparable непоправи́мый

irreplaceable незамени́мый

irreproachable безупре́чный

irresistible неотрази́мый

irresponsible безотве́тственный

irrigate ороша́ть [ороси́ть]; ∼ion ороше́ние

irritable раздражи́тельный; ∼te раздража́ть [-жи́ть]; ∼tion раздраже́ние

island, ∼e о́стров

isolate изоли́ровать (*im*)*pf.*; ∼ion изоля́ция

issue *typ.* вы́пуск, изда́ние; (*result*) исхо́д; *v/t.* выпуска́ть [вы́пустить]; изда́(ва́)ть; *v/i.* (*come out*) выходи́ть [вы́йти], (*flow out*)

вытека́ть [вы́течь]
it оно́, его́ (= B); (*referring to m and f nouns*: он, она́ и т. д.); ~ **is late** по́здно; ~ **snows** идёт снег
Italian италья́нец, -ка; -ский
itch зуд; чеса́ться *impf.*

item пункт, статья́
itinerary маршру́т
its его́ (её → **it**); *reflex.* свой, своя́ *and so on*
itself себя́, -ся; *emphatic* само́ (сам, сама́)
ivory слоно́вая кость *f*
ivy плющ

J

jab *coll.* толчо́к; внеза́пный уда́р; *v.* толка́ть [-кну́ть]; ты́кать [ткнуть]
jack *tech.* домкра́т; поднима́ть домкра́том
jackal шака́л
jacket (*lady's*) жаке́т, (*man's*) пиджа́к; (*casual*) ку́ртка; *book* суперобло́жка
jack-knife складно́й нож
jagged зубча́тый
jail тюрьма́
jam¹ (*pinch*) защемля́ть [-ми́ть], (*block*) загроможда́ть [-мозди́ть]; (*traffic~*) зато́р
jam² *cul.* варе́нье; джем
January янва́рь *m*
Japanese япо́нец, -ка; -ский
jar кувши́н; (*jam, etc.*) ба́нка
jaundice *med.* желту́ха
javelin копьё
jaw *anat.* че́люсть *f*; *pl. zo.* пасть *f*
jazz джаз; ~ **band** джаз-ор-

ке́стр
jealous ревни́вый; ~**y** ре́вность *f*
jeans джи́нсы
jeer глуми́ться (*at* над Т)
jelly желе́ *n indecl.*; ~**-fish** меду́за
jerk *su.* (*pulling*) рыво́к, (*pushing*) толчо́к
jersey (*garment*) сви́тер
jest шути́ть; шу́тка; ~**er** шутни́к
jet (*stream*) струя́; *av. attr.* реакти́вный
Jew евре́й; ~**ess** евре́йка
jewel драгоце́нный ка́мень *m*; ~**ler** ювели́р; ~**lery** f/*pl.*; (*on sale*) ювели́рные изде́лия
Jewish евре́йский
jingle *coins, keys* звене́ть (Т); звон
job рабо́та, заня́тие, де́ло; **it's a good ~ that** хорошо́, что; **it's a ~ to** + *inf.* тру́дно
jockey жоке́й
join *v/t.* (при)соединя́ть [-ни́ть]; *person:* (при-) со-

единя́ться [-ни́ться] (к Д); *party* вступа́ть [-пи́ть] (в В); **~er** столя́р; **~t** *anat.* суста́в; **~t** *venture* совме́стное предприя́тие

joke шу́тка, анекдо́т; [по]шути́ть

jolly весёлый, ра́достный

jolt толчо́к; *v.* трясти́; **~ing** *su.* тря́ска

jot *v*: **~ down** бы́стро запи́сывать [-са́ть], набра́сывать [-роса́ть]

journal журна́л; (*record*) дневни́к; **~ist** журнали́ст(ка)

journey путеше́ствие, пое́здка

jovial весёлый

joy ра́дость *f*; **~ful, ~ous** ра́достный

jubilee юбиле́й

judge судья́ *m*; (*in contests, etc.*) член жюри́; *fig.* цени́тель(ница) *m*; суди́ть (о П); (*decide*) реша́ть [-ши́ть]; **~ment** сужде́ние; реше́ние

judicial суде́бный; (*impartial*) беспристра́стный

judicious (благо)разу́мный

judo дзюдо́ *indecl.*

jug кувши́н

juggle жонгли́ровать (*a. fig.*); **~r** жонглёр

juic|e сок; **~y** со́чный

July ию́ль *m*

jump пры́гать [-гнуть]; (*to one's feet*) вска́кивать [вскочи́ть]; прыжо́к; **~er** прыгу́н(ья); (*garment*) дже́мпер

junction соедине́ние; (*crossroads*) перекрёсток; *rail.* узлова́я ста́нция

June ию́нь *m*

jungle джу́нгли *pl.*

junior мла́дший (*a. mil.*)

jurisdiction юрисди́кция

jur|or прися́жный (заседа́тель); **~y** прися́жные (заседа́тели); (*in contests*) жюри́ *indecl.*; *trial by* **~y** суд прися́жных

just справедли́вый; (*exact*) то́чный; **~ enough** как раз доста́точно; **he has ~ come** он то́лько что пришёл; **~ice** справедли́вость *f*; *jur.* правосу́дие

justi|fication оправда́ние; **~y** оправда́ть [-да́ть]

jut: ~ out выступа́ть, торча́ть

juvenile ю́ношеский; *jur.* малоле́тний

K

keel киль *m*

keen о́стрый; (*eager*) стра́стный; **be ~ on** стра́стно увлека́ться (Т)

keep держа́ть; *money, secret* храни́ть; *family* содержа́ть; ~ *laughing* не переста́вая смея́ться; ~ *silent* молча́ть; ~ *s.o. waiting* заставля́ть кого́-либо ждать; ~ *to* приде́рживаться [-жа́ться] (P); ~ *up* подде́рживать [-жа́ть]

kernel (*nut, etc.*) ядро́; зерно́

kerosene кероси́н

kettle (*tea-~*) ча́йник; ~*-drum* лита́вра

key ключ; (*piano, typewriter*) кла́виш(а); *attr. fig.* ключево́й; *tech.* коммута́тор; ~*board* клавиату́ра; ~*hole* замо́чная сква́жина

kick *horse*: брыка́ть(ся) [-кну́ть(ся)]; *person*: ударя́ть уда́р (ного́й), *coll.* пино́к, (*horse*) уда́р копы́том

kid козлёнок; (*leather*) ла́йка; *coll.* ребёнок; ~*nap* похища́ть [-хи́тить]

kidney *anat., cul.* по́чка; ~ *bean* фасо́ль

kill уби(ва́)ть; *animals* забива́ть [-би́ть]; ~*er* уби́йца *m/f*

kilo(*gram*) кило́(гра́мм) *n indecl.*; ~*meter* киломе́тр

kin: *next of* ~ ближа́йшие ро́дственники *m/pl.*

kind[1] до́брый, любе́зный; *would you be so* ~ бу́дьте добры́ (+ *inf. or imp.*)

kind[2] сорт; (*race*) поро́да; *nothing of the* ~ ничего́ подо́бного

kindergarten де́тский сад

kindle *v/t.* разжига́ть [-же́чь] (*a. fig.*); *v/i.* загора́ться [-ре́ться]

kindness доброта́

king коро́ль *m*; ~'s короле́вский; ~*dom* короле́вство

kiss поцелу́й; [по]целова́ть(ся)

kit набо́р, компле́кт; *first-aid* ~ апте́чка

kitchen ку́хня; *attr.* ку́хонный

kite возду́шный змей; *zo.* ко́ршун

kitten котёнок

knack сноро́вка

knapsack рюкза́к

knead меси́ть

knee коле́но; ~*I* стоя́ть на коле́нях; (= ~*I down*) стать на коле́ни

knife нож; (*stab*) уда́рить ножо́м

knight ры́царь *m*; (*chess*) конь *m*

knit [c]вяза́ть (спи́цами); ~ *one's brows* нахму́рить бро́ви; ~*ted* вя́заный; ~*ting* вяза́ние; ~*ting machine* вяза́льная маши́на; ~*ting needles* спи́цы; ~*wear* трикота́жные изде́лия

knob (*door*) кру́глая ру́чка; (*radio, etc.*) ру́чка

knock стуча́ть(ся) (*at* в В); сту́кнуть(ся), уда́риться (*against* о(б) В); ~ *down* сбива́ть с ног; **~ out** (*sports*) нокаути́ровать (*im*)*pf.*

knot у́зел (*a. mar.*)

know знать; (*recognize*) узн(ав)а́ть

know-how уме́ние; *tech.* ноу-ха́у

knowledge зна́ние; *collect.* зна́ния *n/pl.*; **have a good ~ of** хорошо́ знать (В); **to the best of my ~** на́сколько мне изве́стно

knuckle (*finger*) коста́шка (суста́в па́льца)

kopeck копе́йка

L

label ярлы́к (*a. fig.*); (*tied on*) би́рка; (*stuck on*) накле́йка; (*on goods*) этике́тка

laboratory лаборато́рия

labour труд; *collect.* рабо́чие; *attr.* трудово́й, *pol.* лейбори́стский; *v.* труди́ться; **~er** рабо́чий; ** Exchange** би́ржа труда́; ** Party** лейбори́стская па́ртия

lace кру́жево; (*string*) шнуро́к; [за]шнурова́ть

lack недоста́ток; (*absence*) неиме́ние; (*shortage*) нехва́тка; недост(ав)а́ть; **he ~s patience** ему́ недостаёт терпе́ния (= Р)

lacquer лак

lad па́рень *m*

ladder (приставна́я) ле́стница; **~-proof** с неспуска́ющимися пе́тлями

laden гружёный

ladle поло́вник

lady да́ма, госпожа́; (*rank*) ле́ди *f indecl.*

lag отст(ав)а́ть; отстава́ние; **~gard** медли́тельный челове́к

lake о́зеро

lamb ягнёнок; (*meat*) бара́нина; **~-skin** (*fur*) мерлу́шка

lame хромо́й; **~ness** хромота́

lament причита́ть (*over* над Т); **~able** приско́рбный; **~ation** причита́ние

lamp ла́мпа, свети́льник; (*street*) фона́рь *m*; **~-shade** абажу́р

land *agr.* земля́; (*dry~*) су́ша; (*country*) страна́; **by ~** сре́дствами назе́много тра́нспорта; *av.* приземля́ть [-ли́ться]; *mar.* выса́живать(ся) [вы́садить(ся)]; **~ing** приземле́ние; вы́садка; **~lady** хозя́йка; **~lord** хозя́ин; **~mark** ве́ха; (*guide*) ориенти́р; **~owner** землевладе́лец; **~scape** ландша́фт; (*picture*, *scenery*) пейза́ж

lane переу́лок

language язы́к (*a. tech.*)

languish томи́ться

lap (*mother's*) коле́ни *n/pl.*; (*nature's*) ло́но; (*sports*) круг

lard лярд

large большо́й; кру́пный (*a.* **~-scale**)

lark жа́воронок

larva личи́нка

larynx горта́нь *f*

lash (*eye*) ресни́ца

lass де́вушка

last[1] после́дний; **~ night** вчера́ ве́чером; **~ week** на про́шлой неде́ле; **~ but one** предпосле́дний; **at ~** наконе́ц(-то!)

last[2] дли́ться

latch щеко́лда, защёлка

late по́здний; (*dead*) поко́йный; **be ~** опа́здывать [опозда́ть] (*for* на В); *of ~*, **~ly** неда́вно; **~st** после́дний

lateral боково́й

lathe (*тока́рный*) стано́к

lather мы́льная пе́на; намы́ли(ва)ть

Latin лати́нский (*язы́к*)

latitude *geogr.* широта́

latter после́дний; (*part*) второ́й

lattice решётка

Latvian латы́ш(ка); латы́шский; *geogr., pol.* латви́йский

laugh смех; смея́ться;

make *s.b.* **~** (рас)смеши́ть; **~ter** смех

launch *mar.* спуска́ть [-сти́ть] на во́ду; *rocket* запуска́ть [-сти́ть]; спуск на во́ду; за́пуск; **~ing pad** пускова́я площа́дка

laundry пра́чечная

laurel лавр

lava ла́ва

lavatory туале́т

lavender лава́нда

lavish (*liberal*) ще́дрый; (*abundant*) оби́льный; расточа́ть [-чи́ть] (В *on* Д)

law зако́н; (*science*) пра́во; **~ful** зако́нный; **~less** беззако́нный

lawn газо́н

law|suit суде́бный проце́сс; **~yer** юри́ст; адвока́т

lay класть [положи́ть]; *egg* [с]нести́; **~ the table** накрыва́ть [-ры́ть] на стол; **~ aside**, **~ by** откла́дывать [положи́ть]; **~ off** *workers* (вре́менно) увольня́ть; **~er** слой

lay-by *mot.* стоя́нка (на обо́чине)

laz|iness лень *f*; **~y** лени́вый

lead[1] води́ть, [по]вести́ (*manage, direct*) руководи́ть [(Т)

lead[2] свине́ц; **~en** свинцо́вый

leader руководи́тель *m*; глава́; *pol.* ли́дер *m*;

∼ship руково́дство

leading веду́щий

leaf[1] лист; *(gas)* утёчка *(a. fig.)*; *v.* течь; **∼ out** вытека́ть ['∼течь]; *(ooze)* проса́чиваться [∼сочи́ться] *(a. fig.)*

lean[1] прислоня́ть(ся) [∼ни́ть(ся)] **(against** к Д); **∼ out** высо́вываться [вы́сунуться]

lean[2] то́щий; *(meat)* нежи́рный

leap пры́гать [∼гнуть]; прыжо́к; **∼-year** високо́сный год

learn изуча́ть [∼чи́ть] (В), научи́ться (Д) *pf.*; *(get to know)* узна(ва́)ть; **∼ed** учёный

lease аре́нда; арендова́ть *(im)pf.*

leash *(dog)* поводо́к

least наиме́ньший; *adv.* ме́ньше всего́; **at ∼** по кра́йней ме́ре

leather ко́жа; *attr.* ко́жаный

leave *v/i.* уходи́ть [уйти́], *(by transport)* уезжа́ть [уе́хать] **(for** в В); *v/t.* оставля́ть ['∼вить]; *(room)* выходи́ть [вы́йти] (из Р); *family* покида́ть [∼и́нуть]; **∼ it to me** предоста́вь(те) э́то мне; *su. (consent)* разреше́ние; *(holiday)* о́тпуск

lecture ле́кция; чита́ть ле́кции; **∼r** ле́ктор; *(univ. staff)* преподава́тель

ledge усту́п; *(shelf)* по́лка, по́лочка; **window ∼** подоко́нник

leech пия́вка

left ле́вый; **on** *or* **to the ∼** нале́во **(of** от Р)

leg нога́; *(dimin., a. furniture)* но́жка

legacy насле́дство; *fig.* насле́дие

legal правово́й, юриди́ческий; *(lawful)* зако́нный

legend леге́нда; **∼ary** легенда́рный

legislat|ion законода́тельство; **∼ve** законода́тельный

legitimate зако́нный; узако́ни(ва)ть

leisure досу́г

lemon лимо́н; **∼ade** лимона́д

lend ода́лживать [одолжи́ть]; *money* дава́ть взаймы́

length длина́; *(time)* дли́тельность; **at ∼** подро́бно; *(at last)* наконе́ц; **∼en** удлиня́ть(ся) [∼ни́ть(ся)]

lens ли́нза; *(photo)* объекти́в; **contact ∼es** конта́ктные ли́нзы

leprosy прока́за

less ме́ньше; *(= ∼er)* ме́ньший; **∼ important** ме́нее ва́жный; **more or ∼** бо́лее или ме́нее; **~en** уменьша́ть(ся) ['-ши́ть(ся)]

lesson уро́к

let пуска́ть [-сти́ть]; (allow) разреша́ть [-ши́ть]; room сдава́ть внаём; **~ him think that!** пусть он ду́мает э́то!; **~ us go!** пойдём or пойдёмте!; **~ down** (lower) спуска́ть [-сти́ть]; coll., fig. подводи́ть [-вести́]; **~ in** впуска́ть [-сти́ть]; **~ know** дать знать (Д); **~ out** выпуска́ть [вы́пустить]

lethal лета́льный

letter бу́ква; (writing) письмо́; **~-box** почто́вый я́щик

lettuce сала́т

level у́ровень m; ро́вный; выра́внивать [вы́ровнять]

lever рыча́г

levy (taxes) взима́ние; v. взима́ть

liab|ility отве́тственность f; pl. обяза́тельства n/pl.; pl. (debts) задо́лженность f; **~le** отве́тственный; (subject to) подлежа́щий, подве́рженный (Д)

liar лгу́н(ья), лжец

libel оскорбле́ние че́сти и досто́инства n/pl.

liber|al (generous) ще́дрый; pol. либера́льный; либера́л; **~ate** освобожда́ть [-боди́ть]; **~ty** свобо́да

(conduct ignoring civility) во́льность f, бесцеремо́нность

librar|ian библиоте́карь m; **~y** библиоте́ка

licence comm. лице́нзия; **driving ~** води́тельские права́ n/pl.

lick лиза́ть [лизну́ть]

lid кры́шка; (eye) ве́ко

lie¹ лежа́ть; **~ down** ложи́ться [лечь]

lie² ложь f; [со]лга́ть, coll. [со]вра́ть

lieutenant лейтена́нт

life жизнь f; **~-boat** спаса́тельная шлю́пка; **~less** безжи́зненный; **~long** пожи́зненный; **~time** (вся) жизнь, век

lift поднима́ть [-ня́ть]; tech. лифт; **give a ~** подвози́ть [-везти́] (В)

light¹ лёгкий

light² свет; (~ing) освеще́ние; све́тлый; светло́-; (kindle) зажига́ть(ся) [-же́чь(ся)]; **please, give me a ~** позво́льте прикури́ть; **~en¹** освеща́ть [-ети́ть]; (cigarette) **~er** зажига́лка

lighten² облегча́ть [-чи́ть]; fig. смягча́ть [-чи́ть]

light|house мая́к; **~ning** мо́лния

like¹ v. люби́ть (В or + inf.); [по]нра́виться; **I ~ her face** её лицо́ мне нра́вится; **he ~d the film**

фильм ему́ понра́вился

like[2] *adj.* подо́бный (Д), по-
хо́жий (на В); *conj.* как;
and the ~ и тому́ подо́б-
ное (и т. п.); **~ this
(that)** так; **~ly** *adv.* вероя́тно; *adj.* вероя́тный;
~ness подо́бие, схо́дство

lilac сире́нь *f*

lily ли́лия; **~ of the valley**
ла́ндыш

limb коне́чность *f*

lime и́звесть *f*; **~stone** из-
вестня́к

lime-tree ли́па

limit преде́л, грани́ца;
ограни́чи(ва)ть; **~ time**
преде́льный срок; **~ation**
ограниче́ние

limp[1] хрома́ть

limp[2] вя́лый, дря́блый

line ли́ния; *typ.* строка́;
hold the ~ не кладите
тру́бку; *paper* [на]лино-
ва́ть; *coat* подбива́ть
[-би́ть] (**with** Т)

linen (*cloth*) льняно́е по-
лотно́; (*sheets, etc.*) бельё

liner *mar., av.* ла́йнер

linger заде́рживаться, *coll.*
ме́шкать

lingerie же́нское бельё

lining подкла́дка

link звено́; *pl. fig.* у́зы *f/pl.*;
свя́зывать [-за́ть]

lion лев

lip губа́; **~stick** губна́я по-
ма́да

liqueur ликёр; **~id** жи́д-
кий; жи́дкость *f*; **~or**

спиртно́й напи́ток

list спи́сок, пе́речень *m*

listen [по]слу́шать (**to** В);
~er слу́шатель(ница *f*) *m*

literal буква́льный; **~ry** ли-
терату́рный; **~ture** литера-
ту́ра

litre литр

litter му́сор; **~-bin** у́рна;
(за)му́сорить, (на)сори́ть

little ма́ленький; (*quantity*)
ма́ло (Р), а ма́ло не-
мно́го, *coll.* немно́жко; **~
by** постепе́нно

live[1] жить

live[2] живо́й; **~liness** жи́-
вость *f*; **~ly** живо́й, ожив-
лённый

livelihood сре́дства суще-
ствова́ния

liver *anat.* пе́чень *f*; *cul.* печёнка

living живо́й; *su.* о́браз
жи́зни; **earn one's ~** зара-
ба́тывать себе́ на жизнь

lizard я́щерица

load груз; [по]грузи́ть; *rifle*
заряжа́ть [-яди́ть]

loaf[1] (*brown*) буха́нка;
(*white*) бато́н

loaf[2] *v/i.* слоня́ться

loan (*state*) заём; (*bank*)
ссу́да; да(ва́)ть ссу́ду;
(*personal*) ода́лживать,
одолжи́ть

loathe не выноси́ть *impf.*
(Р)

lobby (*hotels, etc.*) вести-
бю́ль *m*

lobster ома́р

loca|| ме́стный; (*train*) при́городный; **~lize** ме́стность *f*; **~lize** локализова́ть; **~te** определя́ть расположе́ние (P); **~tion** местонахожде́ние (P); *tech.* яче́йка па́мяти

lock[1] (*curl*) ло́кон

lock[2] замо́к; запира́ть [-пере́ть]; шлюз; **~er:** *left luggage* **~er** автомати́ческая ка́мера хране́ния; **~smith** сле́сарь *m*

locomotive локомоти́в

locust саранча́

lodge *v/t.* помеща́ть [-ести́ть]; *complaint* под[ав]а́ть; *v/i.* посели́ться [-ли́ться]; **~r** квартира́нт(ка); **~ing** ко́мната (сня́тая у ча́стного лица́)

loft (*attic*) черда́к; *agr.* сенова́л; **~y** (*mountain*) высо́кий; *fig.* возвы́шенный

log бревно́

logic ло́гика; **~al** логи́чный

loin *cul.* филе́йная часть *f*; *pl. anat.* поясни́ца

loiter слоня́ться

lonel|**iness** одино́чество; **~y** одино́кий

long[1] дли́нный; (*years*) до́лгий; *two feet* **~** два фу́та в длину́; *adv.* **~** до́лго; **~ ago** давно́; *before* **~** вско́ре; *no* **~er** бо́льше не; **~sighted** дальнозо́ркий; **~-term** долгосро́чный

long[2] тоскова́ть (*for* по Д *or* П); (*to do*) стра́стно жела́ть + *inf.*; **~ing** стра́стное жела́ние

longitude *geogr.* долгота́

look [по]смотре́ть (*at* на В); (*seem*) вы́глядеть; (*appearance*) вид, нару́жность *f*; **~ after** следи́ть *or* присма́тривать за (Т); **~ for** иска́ть (В *or* Р); **~ forward to** с ра́достью ожида́ть (Р); **~ over** просма́тривать [-смотре́ть]; **be on the ~-out** (*look for*) иска́ть

loop пе́тля; **~hole** *fig.* лазе́йка

loose (*hair, morals*) распу́щенный; (*screw, tooth*) шата́ющийся; (*clothing*) свобо́дный; (*earth*) ры́хлый

lord лорд; 2 *eccl.* Госпо́дь *m*; **~ly** высокоме́рный

lorry грузови́к

lose [по]теря́ть; *game, case* прои́грывать [-ра́ть]; **~ one's way** заблуди́ться *pf.*

loss поте́ря; про́игрыш (→ *lose*); *at a* **~** в затрудне́нии

lost: **~ property office** стол *or* бюро́ нахо́док

lot жре́бий; (*destiny*) уча́сть *f*; *agr.* уча́сток; (*goods*) па́ртия; *a* **~ of** мно́го (Р); **~tery** лотере́я

loud гро́мкий; (*colour*) крича́щий; *adv.* гро́мко;

~-speaker динáмик

louse вошь f

love любóвь f; любúть; *fall in* ~ влюбля́ться [-бúться] (*with* в В); ~liness пре́лесть f; ~ly прелéстный, прекрáсный; ~r любóвник m; pl. влюблённые; (*art, etc.*) люби́тель m

low ни́зкий (a. fig.); (*voice*) ти́хий; adv. ни́зко; ти́хо; ~er v. спускáть [-стúть]; price, tone снижáть [сни́зить]; ~land ни́зменность f; ~paid низкооплáчиваемый

loyal лоя́льный; вéрный; ~ty лоя́льность f, вéрность f

lubricant смáзочное вещество́; ~e смáз(ыв)ать

luck удáча, сча́стье; bad ~ неудáча; ~y удáчный, счáстливый; (*person*) удáчливый

ludicrous смешнóй

luggage багáж

lukewarm чуть тёплый

lull убаю́к(ив)ать (a. fig.); ~aby колыбéльная пéсня

lumber хлам; (*timber*) Am. строевóй лес; лесоматериáл

luminous светя́щийся

lump комóк; ~ *sugar* кусковóй сáхар

lunatic сумасшéдший (a. su.)

lunch обéд в пóлдень

lung лёгкое

lure fig. соблáзн; замáнивать [-нúть]

luscious (*fruit*) сóчный и слáдкий

lust пóхоть f

lustre гля́нец

luxuriant пы́шный; ~ious роскóшный; ~y рóскошь f

lynx рысь f

lyrical лири́ческий; ~s ли́рика

M

macaroni макарóны m/pl.

macaroon миндáльное печéнье

machine станóк, маши́на; ~-gun автомáт; (*large*) пулемёт; ~ry collect. маши́ны f/pl.; механи́змы m/pl. (a. fig.)

mad сумасшéдший; (*furious*) бéшеный, взбешён-ный

madam госпожá

madden [взбеси́ть; ~man сумасшéдший; ~ness сумасшéствие

magazine журнáл

maggot личи́нка

magic волшебствó; ~al волшéбный; ~ian волшéбник

magistrate *approx.* судья
magnet магни́т; **_ic** магни́тный
magnificen|ce великоле́пие; **_t** великоле́пный
magnif|y увели́чи(ва)ть; **_fying glass** лу́па; **_tude** величина́; (*importance*) ва́жность
magpie соро́ка
mahogany кра́сное де́рево
maid (*hotel*) го́рничная; (*servant*) служа́нка; *old* ~ ста́рая де́ва; **_en** *adj.* (*first*) пе́рвый; (*name*) де́ви́чий
mail по́чта; *attr.* почто́вый; посыла́ть по́чтой
maim изуве́чить
main гла́вный; (*pipe*) магистра́ль *f*; **_land** матери́к; **_ly** гла́вным о́бразом
maintain содержа́ть в испра́вности; *opinion, contact* подде́рживать [-жа́ть]; **_enance** содержа́ние; *tech.* техни́ческое обслу́живание
maize кукуру́за, маи́с
majest|ic вели́чественный; **_y** вели́чество
major (*main*) гла́вный; (*larger*) бо́льший; *mil.* майо́р; **_-general** генера́л-майо́р; **_ity** большинство́
make [с]де́лать; *noise, impression* производи́ть [-вести́]; (*manufacture*) производи́ть [-вести́]; выпус

ка́ть ['-пусти́ть]; *su.* ма́рка; *of British* ~ произво́дства Великобрита́нии; ~ *out cheque, etc.* выпи́свать ['-писать]; *document* составля́ть [-ста́вить]; ~ *up* (*total*) составля́ть ['-вить]; (*become friends again*) помири́ться; *women*: (вос)по́льзоваться косме́тикой; **_r** производи́тель *m*; **_-up** косме́тика
malaria маляри́я
male мужско́й; *su.* мужчи́на *m*; *zo.* саме́ц
malic|e зло́сть *f*; **_ious** злой
malignant зло́бный; *med.* злока́чественный
malnutrition недоста́точное пита́ние
malt со́лод
mammal *zo.* млекопита́ющее
mammoth ма́монт; *attr.* грома́дный
man мужчи́на *m*; (*general sense*) челове́к
manage управля́ть (Т); руководи́ть (Т); *problem, person* справля́ться ['-виться] (с Т); **_ment** (*action*) управле́ние; (*hotel, etc.*) администра́ция; (*factory, etc.*) дире́кция; **_r** управля́ющий; ме́неджер
mandat|e манда́т; **_ory** обяза́тельный, принуди́тельный

mane гри́ва
manhood зре́лый во́зраст
mania ма́ния
manicure маникю́р
manifest я́вный, очеви́дный; проявля́ть [-ви́ть]; **~ation** проявле́ние
man|kind челове́чество; **~ly** му́жественный
manner о́браз, спо́соб; *pl.* мане́ры *f/pl.*
manoeuvre манёвр; маневри́ровать
manor поме́стье
manpower рабо́чая си́ла
mansion особня́к
manual руково́дство, уче́бник; *tech.* инстру́кция; *adj.* ручно́й; (*work*) физи́ческий
manufacture произво́дство; *v/t.* производи́ть *mst. impf.*; **~r** производи́тель *m*, изготови́тель *m*
manure наво́з; удобря́ть ['-рить] наво́зом
manuscript ру́копись *f/pl.*
many мно́гие; *often a.* мно́го (P); **how ~** ско́лько (P); **a great ~** большо́е число́, ма́сса
map ка́рта, (*town*) план
maple клён
mar [ис]по́ртить
marble мра́мор; *attr.* мра́морный
march марш; марширова́ть
March март
mare кобы́ла

margarine маргари́н
margin (*edge*) край; *typ.* поля́ *n/pl.*; **~ of profit** чи́стая при́быль
mar|ine морско́й; (торго́вый) флот; солда́т морско́й пехо́ты; **~ner** моря́к; **~time** морско́й; (*town*) примо́рский
mark ме́тка, (*sign*) знак; (*trace*) след; (*school*) отме́тка, балл; **~ trade ~** торго́вая ма́рка; отмеча́ть [-е́тить]; **~ed** заме́тный; **~er** *tech.* ма́ркер
market(-place) ры́нок
marketing марке́тинг
marmalade (апельси́новое) варе́нье
marr|iage брак, (*ceremony*) сва́дьба, (*official*) бракосочета́ние; **~ied** жена́тый, заму́жняя; **~ied couple** супру́жеская па́ра; **~y** *man:* жени́ться (на П), *woman:* выходи́ть за́муж (за П); *priest:* [по]венча́ть; *couple: coll.* пожени́ться (*im*)*pf.*
marsh боло́то
marshal *mil.* ма́ршал
marten куни́ца
martial: **~ law** вое́нное положе́ние
martyr му́чени|к, -ца
marvel чу́до, **~lous** чуде́сный
masculine мужско́й (*a. gr.*)
mash *cul.* пюре́ *n indecl.*; размина́ть [-мя́ть]

mask ма́ска; [за]маскирова́ть; *fig.* скрыва́ть

mason ка́менщик; (*freemason*) масо́н; **~ry** ка́менная кла́дка

mass[1] ма́сса; *attr.* ма́ссовый; **~ media** сре́дства ма́ссовой информа́ции

mass[2] *eccl.* ме́сса

massacre ма́ссовое уби́йство

massage масса́ж; масси́ровать (*im*)*pf.*

massive масси́вный; *fig.* огро́мный

mast ма́чта

master (*owner*) хозя́ин; (*expert*) ма́стер; (*teacher*) учи́тель *m;* **~ly** ма́стерски́й, *adv.* **~ piece** шеде́вр; **~ship, ~y** мастерство́

mat цино́вка, мат

match[1] чета́, па́ра (*for* Д); (*sports*) матч, соревнова́ние

match[2] спи́чка; *attr.* спи́чечный

mate (*fellow*) това́рищ; *mar.* помо́щник капита́на

material материа́л; (*textile*) мате́рия; **raw ~** сырьё; материа́льный; (*essential*) суще́ственный

maternity матери́нство; **~ hospital** роди́льный дом (*coll.* роддо́м)

mathematics матема́тика

matrimony супру́жество

matter (*substance*) веще-ство́; (*affair*) де́ло; *v.* име́ть значе́ние; **as a ~ of fact** вообще́-то; **it doesn't ~** не име́ет значе́ния; **what is the ~?** в чём де́ло?

mattress матра́с

mature (*fruit, age*) зре́лый; *v/i.* созре(ва́)ть; **~ity** зре́лость *f*

maximum ма́ксимум; *v/i.* максима́льный

may: **~ I ask …** могу́ я и́ли мо́жно мне спроси́ть …; **he ~ have said so** он, мо́жет быть, э́то сказа́л

May май; **~ Day** Пе́рвое ма́я

maybe мо́жет быть

mayonnaise майоне́з

mayor мэр

me меня́ (= В); мне (= Д); → **I**

meadow луг

meal еда́ (за́втрак, обе́д, у́жин)

mean[1] (*average*) сре́дний; *su.* середи́на

mean[2] (*signify*) зна́чить; (*intend*) име́ть в виду́; (*imply*) подразумева́ть; **~ing** значе́ние, смысл; **~less** бессмы́сленный

mean[3] (*stingy*) скупо́й; (*low*) ни́зкий, по́длый

means сре́дство *or* сре́дства *n/pl.* (*a. fig.*); **by ~ of** посре́дством (Р)

meant: **~ for** предназна́ченный для (Р)

mean|time, **_while** тем временем, между тем

measles корь f

measure мера (a. fig.); v/t. измерять ['-рить]; (tailor) снимать мерку с (P); **_ment** (action) измерение; **_ments** (size) размеры m/pl.

meat мясо, attr. мясной

mechanic механик; **_al** механический; **_al engineering** машиностроение; **_s** механика

medal медаль f

meddle вмешиваться ['-шаться] (в B)

mediat|e посредничать; **_ion** посредничество; **_or** посредник

medical медицинский; (doctor) врачебный; **_ student** студент-медик

medicine медицина; (drug) лекарство

medieval средневековый

mediocre посредственный

meditat|e размышлять; **_ion** размышление

medium (means) средство; phys. среда; adj. средний

meek кроткий; **_ness** кротость f

meet (fig. **_ with**) встречать ['-етить] (B); (mutually) встречаться ['-етиться]; wishes встречать ['-рить]; **_ing** встреча; (gathering) собрание; pol. митинг; (session) заседа-

ние

melancholy грусть f; adj. грустный

melody мелодия

melon дыня

melt v/i. snow: [рас]таять (a. fig.); metal: [рас]плавиться; v/t. [рас]плавить, [рас]плавлять, топить; fat растапливать [-топить]

member член; **_ship** членство

memor|able памятный; **_ial** su. памятник; **_ize** запоминать ['-мнить], память f, a. tech.

menace угроза; угрожать (Д)

mend [по]чинить; (improve) улучшаться ['-шиться]

ment|al умственный; (disease) психический; **_al hospital** психиатрическая больница; **_ion** упоминать ['-мянуть]; упоминание

menu меню n indecl.

merchan|dise товар(ы); **_t** торговец; attr. торговый

merci|ful милосердный; **_less** беспощадный

mercury ртуть f

mercy милосердие; (clemency) пощада

mere простой; **the _ smell** один уже запах; **_ly** просто; (only) только, всего лишь

merge v/i. сли(ва́)ться; **_r**

слияние

merit (*worth*) достоинство; (*desert*) заслуга; заслуживать [-жить]

merr|iment весе́лье; **~y** весёлый; **~y-go-round** карусе́ль *f*

mess *mil.* столо́вая; *coll.* (*muddle*) пу́таница; (*disorder*) беспоря́док

mess|age посла́ние; (*information*) сообще́ние (*a. tech.*); **~enger** (*boy*) посыльный

metal мета́лл; *attr.* металли́ческий; **~lic** (*sound, colour*) металли́ческий

meteor метео́р

meter счётчик

method ме́тод, спо́соб; **~ical** методи́чный

metre метр

metric: **~ system** метри́ческая систе́ма мер

metro метро́

metropoli|s столи́ца; **~tan** столи́чный

mew мяўкать; мяўканье

Mexican мексика́н|ец, -ка; -ский

micro|phone микрофо́н; **~processor** микропроце́ссор; **~scope** микроско́п; **~wave** микроволна́ *f*; **~wave oven** микроволно́вая печь *f*

midday по́лдень *m*

middle сре́дний; середи́на; **~-aged** сре́дних лет; **⌕ Ages** средневеко́вье

midge мо́шка

mid|night по́лночь *f*; **~wife** акуше́рка

might¹ → **may**

might² могу́щество, мощь *f*; **~y** могу́чий, мо́щный

migrate переселя́ться [-ли́ться]; *zo.* мигри́ровать; **~ion** переселе́ние; мигра́ция

mild (*weather, temper*) мя́гкий; (*slight*) лёгкий

mile ми́ля

milit|ant вои́нствующий; **~ary** вое́нный; (*unit, service*) во́инский; *su.* вое́нные *pl.*; **~ia** мили́ция

milk молоко́; *attr.* моло́чный; **condensed ~** сгущённое молоко́; **~bar** моло́чное кафе́; **~y: ⌕y Way** Мле́чный путь *m*

mill ме́льница; (*factory*) заво́д

millet про́со; *cul.* пшено́

million миллио́н; **~aire** миллионе́р

mimic подража́ть

mince *meat, etc.* пропуска́ть [-сти́ть] че́рез мясору́бку; (= **~d meat**) фарш; **~r** (*mincing machine*) мясору́бка

mind *su.* (*opinion*) мне́ние; **be in two ~s** быть в нереши́тельности, колеба́ться; **change one's ~** переду́м(ыв)ать; **keep in ~** по́мнить; **⌕ out!** Осторо́жно!; **never ~!** Все-

or пустяки́!; **to my ~** по
моему́ мне́нию; **I don't ~**
я не возража́ю; **~ful** за-
бо́тливый

mine¹ мой, моя́, моё, *pl.*
мои́

mine² ша́хта; *coal* добы-
ва́(ть); **~r** шахтёр; **~ral**
минера́л; минера́льный;
~ral resources поле́зные
ископа́емые

mini|ature миниатю́ра; ми-
ниатю́рный; **~bus** микро-
авто́бус; **~mum** ми́нимум;
минима́льный

minist|er мини́стр; *eccl.*
свяще́нник; **~ry** мини-
сте́рство

mink но́рка; *attr.* но́рковый

minor ме́ньший; незначи́-
тельный; второстепе́н-
ный; (*under age*) несовер-
шенноле́тний; **~ity** ме́нь-
шинство́

minus ми́нус

minute¹ мину́та; **any ~** с
мину́ты на мину́ту; **just a
~** (одну́) мину́точку; **record the ~s** вести́ прото-
ко́л

minute² (*detailed*) подро́б-
ный; (*tiny*) мельча́йший,
кро́шечный

mirac|le чу́до; **~ulous** чу-
де́сный

mirror зе́ркало

mirth весе́лье

misapprehend неве́рно ис-
толко́вывать [-ова́ть]

miscalculate ошиба́ться

[-би́ться] в подсчёте; про-
счита́ться *mst. pf.*

miscarriage *med.* вы́кидыш

mischie|f озорство́, прока́-
зы *f/pl.;* **~vous** (*naughty*)
озорно́й

miser скря́га *m/f*

miserable несча́стный;
(*abject*) жа́лкий; (*squalid*)
убо́гий; (*nasty*) скве́рный;
~y страда́ние; (*poverty*)
нищета́

mis|fortune неуда́ча, беда́;
~giving опасе́ние; **~inform**
дезинформи́ровать (*im-
*)*pf.*; **~lead** вводи́ть в за-
блужде́ние; **~placed** *fig.*
неуме́стный; **~print** опе-
ча́тка

miss¹ мисс; де́вушка

miss² *opportunity* упуска́ть
[-сти́ть]; *mother, friends*
тоскова́ть (по Д *or* П); *lecture* пропуска́ть [-сти́ть];
→ **~ing**; *su.* про́мах; **~a
chance** упуска́ть [-сти́ть]
возмо́жность; **~the train**
опозда́ть на по́езд

missile *mil.* раке́та; **guided
~** управля́емая раке́та

missing недостаю́щий, от-
су́тствующий; *mil.* про-
па́вший бе́з вести

mission ми́ссия; (*task*) за-
да́ча; **~trade** торго́вое
представи́тельство
(= торгпре́дство)

mist тума́н; (*haze*) ды́мка

mistake оши́бка; **~for**
(оши́бочно) принима́ть за

(B); **by** ~ по оши́бке; ~**n: be** ~**n** ошиба́ться [-би́ться]

Mister ми́стер, господи́н

mistress (*house*) хозя́йка; (*school*) учи́тельница; (*lover*) любо́вница; (= *Mrs.*) ми́ссис, госпожа́

mistrust недове́рие; не доверя́ть (Д)

misty тума́нный

misunderstand непра́вильно понима́ть; ~**ing** недоразуме́ние

misuse злоупотребля́ть [-би́ть] (Т); злоупотребле́ние

mitten рукави́ца, (*mst. knitted*) ва́режка

mix сме́шивать(ся) [-ша́ть(ся)]; ~ **up** перепу́т(ыв)ать; ~**ture** смесь *f*

moan стон; *v.* стона́ть

mob сбо́рище, толпа́

mobil|e подви́жно́й; ~**ity** подви́жность *f*; ~**ization** мобилиза́ция

mock насмеха́ться (**at** над Т); ~**ery** насме́шка

mode спо́соб; (*fashion*) мо́да; *tech.* режи́м, мо́да

model моде́ль *f*; *fig.* образе́ц; *attr.* образцо́вый; (*painter*) нату́рщи|к, -ца; модели́ровать (*im*)*pf.*

moderat|e уме́ренный; умеря́ть ['-рить']; ~**ion** уме́ренность *f*

modern совреме́нный; *in ~ times* в на́ше вре́мя

modest скро́мный; ~**y** скро́мность *f*

modif|ication модифика́ция; ~**y** модифици́ровать *im*(*pf.*), изменя́ть [-ни́ть]

modulate *tech.* модули́ровать (*a. voice*); ~**ation** модуля́ция; ~**e** мо́дуль

moist вла́жный; ~**ure** вла́га

Moldavian молдава́н|ин, -ка; молда́вский

mole[1] *zo.* крот

mole[2] (*breakwater*) мол

mole[3] (*on skin*) роди́нка

moment моме́нт, мгнове́ние; ~**ary** момента́льный, мгнове́нный; ~**ous** значи́тельный, ва́жный

monarch мона́рх; ~**y** мона́рхия

monastery монасты́рь *m*

Monday понеде́льник

money де́ньги *f/pl.*; ~ *order* де́нежный перево́д

Mongolian монго́л|(ка); -ьский

monitor *tech.* монито́р; контроли́ровать

monk мона́х

monkey обезья́на

monopol|y монопо́лия; ~**to-nous** моното́нный, однообра́зный; ~**tony** моното́нность *f*

monst|er чудо́вище; ~**rous** чудо́вищный

month ме́сяц; ~**ly** (еже-)ме́сячный; (*magazine*) ежеме́сячник

monument монумент, памятник; ~al монументальный

mood настроение; *gr.* наклонение

moon месяц, луна; ~light лунный свет

moor *mar.* причали(ва)ть (*a. v/i.*); ~ing (*place*) причал

mop швабра; *floor* мести *or* мыть шваброй; *sweat* стирать [стереть]

moral нравственный, моральный; морель *f*; ~e моральное состояние; ~s нравственность *f*

morbid болезненный

more больше (P); (*greater*) больший; ~ complicated сложнее, (*attr.*) более сложный; ~ or less более или менее; *once* ~ ещё раз; *the* ~ *so* тем более, что; ~over кроме того

morgue морг

morning утро; *attr.* утренний

morsel кусочек

mortal смертный (*a. su.*); (*wound, enemy*) смертельный; ~ity смертность *f*

mortar (*kitchen*) ступ(к)а; *arch.* известковый раствор

mortgage (*money lent*) ссуда; заклáдывать [заложить]

mortify обижать [обидеть]

Moscow *attr.* московский

mosque мечеть *f*

mosquito комар; (*tropical*) москит

moss мох; ~y мшистый

most больше всего; больше всех; *the* ~ complicated сложнейший *or* самый сложный; *a* ~ complicated очень *or* весьма сложный; *three* ~ at ~ самое большее три; ~ly по большей части

moth мотылёк; (*clothes-*) моль *f*

mother мать *f*; ~ of pearl перламутр; ~-in-law (*husband's mother*) свекровь *f*; ~ly материнский; ~ tongue родной язык

motif *art.* мотив

motion движение; ~less неподвижный

motivate мотивировать

motive мотив, повод; ~ power движущая сила

motley пёстрый

motor мотор, двигатель *m*; *attr.* моторный; ~-car автомобиль *m*; ~-coach (междугородный) автобус; ~-cycle мотоцикл; ~ist автомобилист; ~-ship теплоход; ~-scooter моторóллер; ~way автострáда

motto девиз

mould *biol.* плесень *f*; ~y заплесневелый

mound (*small hill*) холмик

mount (*horse*) верховая лошадь *f*; *geogr.* = _**ain**; (*as-cend*) взбира́ться, взо-бра́ться (на В); *horse* са-ди́ться [сесть] (на В); *tech.* [с]монти́ровать; *costs*: повыша́ться [-ы́ситься]

mountain гора́; _**eer** альпини́ст(ка); (*dweller*) го́рец; _**ous** го́рный, гори́стый

mourn скорбе́ть (*over* о П); (*wear black*) носи́ть тра́ур; _**ful** ско́рбный, печа́льный; _**ing** тра́ур

mouse мышь *f*; _**trap** мышело́вка

moustache усы́ *m/pl.*

mouth рот; *geogr.* у́стье

mov|e дви́гать(ся) [дви́-нуть(ся)]; (*affect*) тро́гать [тро́нуть]; (*change abode*) переезжа́ть [перее́хать]; движе́ние; (*games*) ход; _**ement** движе́ние; _**ing** дви́жущийся; тро́гательный

mow [с]коси́ть (траву́, и т.д.); _**er** (*for hay*) сеноко-си́лка; (*lawn*) газоноко-си́лка

much мно́го (Р), *a. adv.*; **very** _ *adv.* о́чень; **how** _ ско́лько (Р); **I'm much obliged to you** я вам о́чень обя́зан(а); **I thought as** _ так я и ду́мал(а)

mud грязь *f*; _**dle** (*mix up*) перепу́т(ыв)ать; беспоря́док; пу́таница; _**dy** гря́зный; (*mud-coloured*) му́тный

muffle заку́т(ыв)ать; _**d** *sound* приглу́шенный (звук)

mug кру́жка

mulberry ту́товая я́года; (*tree*) ту́товое де́рево

mule мул

multi|ple многокра́тный; кра́тное число́; _**plication** умноже́ние; _**ply** умножа́ть(ся) ['-жить(ся)]; _**tude** мно́жество, ма́сса

mumble [про]бормота́ть

mummy му́мия

municipal муниципа́льный, городско́й

mural стенна́я ро́спись; фре́ска

murder уби́йство; уби-(ва́)ть; _**er**, _**ess** уби́йца *m/f*; _**ous** уби́йственный

murmur *stream*: журча́ть; (*whisper*) [про]шепта́ть; журча́ние; шёпот

muscle мы́шца, му́скул; _**ular** мы́шечный; (*strong*) мускули́стый

muse размышля́ть

museum музе́й

mushroom гриб; *U.K. mst.* шампиньо́н

music му́зыка; (*score*) но́ты *f/pl.*; _ **hall** мю́зик-холл; _**al** музыка́льный; *su.* мю́зикл; _**ian** музыка́нт

must: **I** _ я до́лж|ен, -на́; **I have forgotten** я, должно́ быть, забы́л(а)

mustard горчи́ца

musty за́тхлый
mute (*dumb*) немо́й; (*silent*) молчали́вый
mutilate [из]уве́чить, [ис]калéчить
mutter [про]бормота́ть; бормота́ние
mutton бара́нина; *attr.* бара́ний
mutual взаи́мный; ~ **aid** взаимопо́мощь *f*
muzzle *zo.* мо́рда; (*straps to prevent biting*) намо́рдник; *mil.* ду́ло
my мой, моя́, моё, *pl.* мои́; *reflex.* свой, *etc.*
myself себя́, -ся; *emphatic* сам(á)
myst|erious таи́нственный; ~**ery** та́йна; (*secrecy*) таи́нственность *f*; ~**ify** мистифици́ровать (*im*)*pf.*
myth миф *m*; ~**ology** мифоло́гия

N

nag *v/t.* пили́ть *impf.*
nail гвоздь *m*; *anat.* но́готь *m*; заби(ва́)ть; зака́лчивать [-лоти́ть]
naked наго́й, го́лый; ~**ness** нагота́
name и́мя *n*; (*surname*) фами́лия; (*things*) назва́ние; (*call*) наз(ы)ва́ть; (*list*) перечисля́ть ['-лить]; **by** ~ по и́мени; **in the** ~ **of** от и́мя (P); **what is your** ~? как вас (тебя́) зову́т?; **full** ~ фами́лия + и́мя + о́тчество; ~**less** безымя́нный; ~**ly** а и́менно
nap коро́ткий сон; **take a** ~ вздремну́ть *pf.*
napkin салфе́тка
narcissus нарци́сс
narcotic нарко́тик; нарко́тический
narrat|ive повествова́ние; ~**or** расска́зчик

narrow у́зкий (*a. fig.*); ~**-minded** ограни́ченный; ~**ness** у́зость *f*
nasty скве́рный
nation на́ция; ~**al** национа́льный; (*debt, anthem*) госуда́рственный; ~**alist(ic)** националисти́ческий; ~**ality** национа́льность *f*; (*citizenship*) гражда́нство, подда́нство
native *adj.* родно́й; (*indigenous*) ме́стный, коренно́й; *su.* ме́стный жи́тель
natur|al есте́ственный, натура́льный; (*resources*) приро́дный; ~**al science** есте́ственные нау́ки *pl.*; ~**e** приро́да; (*essence*) нату́ра; (*quality*) хара́ктер; (*kind*) род
naught|iness озорство́; ~**y** озорно́й; **be** ~**y** озорнича́ть, капри́зничать

nausea тошнота́

nautical морско́й

naval вое́нно-морско́й

naviga|ble судохо́дный; **_tion** морепла́вание; (act) навига́ция; **_tor** морепла́ватель m; штурма́н

navy (вое́нно-морско́й) флот

near бли́зкий; adv. бли́зко, вблизи́; prep. бли́зко от (P), о́коло (P); **~ by** adv. побли́зости; **_ly** почти́; **_-sighted** близору́кий

neat (work) аккура́тный; (appearance) опря́тный; **_ness** аккура́тность; опря́тность f

necessary необходи́мый; **_ity** необходи́мость f

neck ше́я; (bottle) го́рлышко; **_lace** ожере́лье; **_tie** га́лстук

need нужда́, (necessity) на́добность f, pl. потре́бности f/pl.; нужда́ться в (П); **you ~ not (have) come** вам нет (не́ было) на́добности приходи́ть

needle игла́ (a. bot.)

need|less нену́жный; **_y** нужда́ющийся

negative отрица́тельный

neglect duties пренебрега́ть [-ре́чь]; house запуска́ть [-сти́ть]; (state) запу́щенность f; (action) пренебреже́ние; **_igence** небре́жность f; **_igent** не-

бре́жный; хала́тный

negotiat|e вести́ перегово́ры; **_ions** перегово́ры m/pl.

negro негр; негритя́нский

neigh ржать; ржа́ние

neighbour сосе́д(ка); attr. сосе́дний; **_hood** сосе́дство; **_ing** сосе́дний

neither adj. ни тот ни друго́й; adv. та́кже не; **~ ... nor ...** ни ... ни ...; **~ of us** никто́ из нас

nephew племя́нник

nerv|e нерв; **_ous** не́рвный; (situation) нерво́зный; **_ousness** не́рвность; нервно́сть f

nest гнездо́; v. гнезди́ться

net¹ сеть f; (hair, tennis) се́тка; (fishing) се́ти f/pl. (a. fig.)

net² чи́стый; не́тто indecl.; **~ weight** вес не́тто

nettle крапи́ва

network сеть f

neuter gr. сре́днего ро́да, su. сре́дний род

neutral нейтра́льный; **_ity** нейтра́льность; pol. нейтралите́т; **_ize** нейтрализова́ть (im)pf.

never никогда́; **~ mind** нева́жно, ничего́; **_theless** тем не ме́нее

new но́вый; **2 Testament** Но́вый заве́т; **_born** новорождённый; **_ly** неда́вно; вновь

news но́вость f; (informa-

tion) изве́стия *n/pl.*; ~ **media** *pl.* сре́дства ма́ссовой информа́ции; ~**paper** газе́та; ~**reel** кинохурна́л; ~ **stand** газе́тный кио́ск

next сле́дующий; (*nearest*) ближа́йший; *adv.* зате́м; *prep.* о́коло (Р); ~ **to**, ~ **door** ря́дом; ~ **year** в бу́дущем году́; ~ **of kin** ближа́йшие ро́дственники *m/pl.*

nice (*fine*) хоро́ший, *coll.* сла́вный; (*sweet*) ми́лый; (*subtle*) то́нкий; ~**ty** то́нкость *f mst. pl.*

niche ни́ша

nickel ни́кель *m*

nickname про́звище

niece племя́нница

night ночь *f*; *good* ~! споко́йной но́чи!; *last* ~ вчера́ ве́чером; ~**dress** ночна́я руба́шка; ~**ingale** солове́й; ~**ly** по ноча́м; ~**mare** кошма́р

nimble подви́жный, прово́рный

nine де́вять; ~**teen** девятна́дцать; ~**teenth** девятна́дцатый; ~**tieth** девяно́стый; ~**ty** девяно́сто

ninth девя́тый

nip щипа́ть [ущипну́ть]; ~ *in the bud* пресе́чь в ко́рне

nitrate *chem.* нитра́т

nitrogen азо́т

no нет; (*not a*) никако́й; *in* ~ *book* ни в одно́й кни́ге;

there is ~ *doubt* нет сомне́ния (= Р); ~ *one* никто́

nobi|lity дворя́нство; (*nobleness*) благоро́дство; ~**le** благоро́дный; ~**leman** дворяни́н

nobody никто́

nocturnal ночно́й

nod кива́ть [кивну́ть]; киво́к

noise шум; *make a* ~ шуме́ть; ~**less** бесшу́мный; ~**y** шу́мный

nomina|l номина́льный; ~**te** *pol.* выдвига́ть ['-нуть] кандидату́ру (Р); (*appoint*) назнача́ть ['-чить]; ~**tion** выдвиже́ние; назначе́ние

noncommittal (*answer*) укло́нчивый

nondescript невзра́чный

none (*nobody*) никто́; (*not any*) никако́й; *adv.* ниско́лько

nonpayment неплатёж, неупла́та

nonsense бессмы́слица, но́нсенс, вздор, *coll.* чепуха́

non-stop безостано́вочный; *av.* беспоса́дочный

nook уко́мное месте́чко; (*in room*) ую́тный уголо́к

noon по́лдень *m*

noose пе́тля

nor и не, та́кже не; *neither* … ~ … ни … ни …

norm но́рма; ~**al** норма́льный; ~**alize** нормализовáть

north сéвер; attr. сéверный; ~ of к сéверу от (P); ~-east сéверо-востóк; attr. сéверо-востóчный; ~ern сéверный; ~ward(s) к сéверу, на сéвер; ~west сéверо-зáпад; attr. сéверо-зáпадный

Norwegian норвéж|ец, -ка; -ский

nose нос; (flair) нюх

nostril ноздря́

not не; he is ~ at home егó нет дóма

nota|ble выдаю́щийся; (occasions) знаменáтельный; ~ry нотáриус

note запи́ска, замéтка (in book, etc.) примечáние; pol., mus. нóта; запи́сывать [-сáть]; (notice) замечáть [-éтить]; ~book записнáя кни́жка; ~d извéстный; ~worthy примечáтельный

nothing ничтó, mst. often: ничегó (= P); for ~ зря, напрáсно; with ~ он с этим заявлéние (об ухóде); at short ~ в корóткий срок, незамедли́тельно; take no ~ of не обращáть внимáния; ~able замéтный

notify извещáть [-ести́ть]

notion поня́тие

notorious пресловýтый

notwithstanding несмотря́ (на B); adv. всё же

nought нуль m; bring (come) to ~ своди́ть (своди́ться) к нулю́

noun и́мя существи́тельное

nourish питáть (a. fig.); ~ment пи́ща, питáние

novel нóвый, необы́чный; ромáн; ~ist романи́ст; ~ty новизнá, (new thing) нови́нка, (new method) нóвшество

November ноя́брь m; attr. ноя́брьский

novice новичóк

now тепéрь; just ~ тóлько что; up to ~ до сих пор; ~adays в нáше врéмя, ны́нче coll.

nowhere нигдé, никудá

nozzle tech. соплó

nucle|ar я́дерный; ~ar power plant áтомная электростáнция (АЭС); ~ar reactor áтомный реáктор; ~us ядрó

nude нагóй; paint. обнажённая фигýра

nuisance неприя́тность f; (person) надоéдливый человéк

null adj. недействи́тельный; ~ify аннули́ровать

numb оцепенéлый, онемéвший; (with cold) окоченéлый

number число; (*No.*) номер; (*reach the ~*) насчитывать; (*give number*) нумеровать; (*reckon*) причислять ['-лить] (*among* к Д); **~less** бесчисленный; **~plate** *mot.* номерной знак

numeral *gr.* числительное; **~ous** многочисленный

nun монахиня

nurse *med.* медсестра, сиделка; (*child's*) няня; pa-tient ухаживать за (Т); child [по]кормить; **~ry** (*day ~ry*) детский сад

nut *bot.* орех; *attr.* ореховый; *tech.* гайка; **~cracker** щипцы для орехов; **~meg** мускатный орех

nutrition питание

nutshell ореховая скорлупа

nylon нейлон; *pl.* нейлоновые чулки *m/pl.*

O

oak дуб; *attr.* дубовый

oar весло

oasis оазис

oath клятва, присяга

oatmeal овсянка

oats овёс

obedien|ce послушание, повиновение; **~t** послушный

obey [по]слушаться (Р), повиноваться (Д) (*im*)*pf.*

object предмет, объект; (*aim*) цель *f*; *gr.* дополнение; возражать [-азить] (*to* против Р); **~ion** возражение; **~ive** цель *f*; *photo.* объектив; *adj.* объективный

oblig|ation обязательство; **~atory** обязательный; (*gift*) обязывать [-зать]; *I am much ~ed to you* я вам очень благодарен; **~ing**

услужливый, любезный

oblique косой

oblivion забвение

oblong продолговатый

obscene непристойный; **~ity** непристойность *f*

obscur|e (*not clear*) неясный; (*not well known*) малоизвестный; затемнять [-нить]; **~ity** неизвестность *f*

observ|ance соблюдение; **~ation** (*gift*) наблюдательность *f*; (*remark*) замечание; **~atory** обсерватория; **~e** наблюдать; *law, rite* соблюдать [-юсти]; замечать [-етить]; **~er** наблюдатель *m*

obsolete устарелый, (*word*) устаревший

obstacle препятствие

obstina|cy упрямство; **~te**

упря́мый

obstruct (*impede*) препя́тствовать [вос-]; (*block*) загора́живать [-роди́ть]

obtain получа́ть [-чи́ть]; доста́(ва́)ть; **_able** досту́пный

obvious очеви́дный, я́вный

occasion (удо́бный) слу́чай; (*cause*) по́вод; вызыва́ть ['-звать]; *festive* ~ пра́здник; *on the* ~ *of* по слу́чаю (P); **_al** случа́йный, ре́дкий

occupation заня́тие; *mil.* оккупа́ция; **_y** занима́ть [-ня́ть]; оккупи́ровать (*im*)*pf.*

occur происходи́ть [-изойти́]; *it _red to him* у него́ возникла мысль (*that* что); **_rence** слу́чай, происше́ствие

ocean океа́н

o'clock: (*at*) *two* ~ (в) два часа́

October октя́брь *m*

odd стра́нный; *math.* нечётный; *forty* ~ *roubles* со́рок рубле́й с ли́шним; **_ity** стра́нность *f*; **_s** *in favour* (*of*) ша́нсы в по́льзу (P); *be at* ~*s* не ла́дить; (*disagree*) расходи́ться во мне́ниях

odious отврати́тельный

odour за́пах

of: *a piece* ~ *bread* кусо́к хле́ба; *the roof* ~ *the house* кры́ша до́ма; *but*:

the city ~ *Berlin* го́род Берли́н; (= *made* ~) из (P); *one* ~ *them* оди́н из них; *speak, hear* ~ (= *about*) о (П); *guilty, sure, confident* ~ в (П)

off: *day* ~ выходно́й день; *a long way* ~ далеко́ отсю́да; *I must be* ~ мне пора́ идти́; *wash* ~ от- *or* смы́(ва́)ть

offen|ce оби́да; *jur.* правонаруше́ние; **_d** оскорбля́ть [-би́ть]; (*feelings*) оскорбля́ть [-би́ть]; за́ оби́дчик; правонаруши́тель *m*

offer предлага́ть [-ложи́ть]; предложе́ние

offhand *adv.* сейча́с, то́тчас

office *comm.* конто́ра; (*room*) кабине́т, о́фис; (*ministry*) министе́рство; (*position*) до́лжность *f*, пост; **_e hours** часы́ рабо́ты; приёмные часы́ *m/pl.*; **_er** *mil.* офице́р; **_ial** официа́льный; *su.* должностно́е лицо́, *b. s.* чино́вник

offspring о́тпрыск

often ча́сто

oil ма́сло; (*petroleum*) нефть *f*; *diesel* ~ соля́рка; *fuel* ~ жи́дкое то́пливо; *vegetable* ~ расти́тельное ма́сло; сма́з(ыв)ать; **_cloth** клеёнка; **_paint** ма́сляная кра́ска; **_y** масляни́стый

ointment мазь

O.K. ла́дно, оке́й

old ста́рый; **_ grow** = [по]-
старе́ть; **_ age** ста́рость
f; **_ man, woman** стари́к,
-у́ха; **_ people's home**
дом для престаре́лых; 2
Testament Ве́тхий заве́т

olive масли́на, оли́вка;
attr. оли́вковый

olympic олимпи́йский; 2
Games Олимпи́йские
и́гры *f/pl.*

omi|ssion про́пуск; (*by neg-
lect*) упуще́ние; **_t** пропус-
ка́ть [-сти́ть], упуска́ть
[-сти́ть]

on на (П *or* В); **_ Sunday** в
воскресе́нье; **_ the fifth of
May** пя́того ма́я; **and so _**
и так да́лее (и т.д.); **go _!**
продолжа́й(те)!

once (оди́н) раз; **at _** не-
ме́дленно; **_ more** ещё
раз

one оди́н, одна́, одно́; **_ another** друг дру́га; **no _** ни-
кто́

oneself себя́, -ся; **be _**
быть сами́м собо́й

one-way-street у́лица с
односторо́нним движе́-
нием

onion лук; (*single*) лу́ко-
вица

only то́лько; *adj.* еди́н-
ственный

onset (*beginning*) нача́ло

onward(s) *adv.* вперёд,
впереди́

ooze сочи́ться, проса́чи-
ваться [-сочи́ться]

opaque непрозра́чный

open откры́тый; (*frank*) от-
крове́нный; откры(ва́)ть-
(ся); **_ing** отве́рстие; (*action*) откры́тие

opera о́пера; **_-house**
о́перный теа́тр

operat|e *v/i.* де́йствовать;
comm., med. опери́ровать
(*med. on* В); *v/t.* управ-
ля́ть (Т); *tech.* рабо́тать;
_ing time *tech.* рабо́чее
вре́мя; **_ion** де́йствие;
опера́ция; рабо́та; **_ion
manual** инстру́кция по
эксплуата́ции

opinion мне́ние; **in my _** по
моему́ мне́нию

opium о́пий, о́пиум

opponent проти́вник, оппо-
не́нт

opportunity удо́бный слу́-
чай, возмо́жность *f*

oppos|e [вос]проти́виться
(Д); **_ite** противополо́ж-
ный; противополо́жность
f; *prep.* напро́тив (Р). (*a.
adv.*); **_ition** сопротивле́-
ние; *pol.* оппози́ция

oppress угнета́ть; угнете́-
ние; гнёт; **_ive**
(*heat*) гнету́щий (*a. fig.*)

optical опти́ческий; **_ian**
о́птик; **_s** о́птика

option вы́бор

or и́ли; **_ else** а (не) то

oral у́стный

orange апельси́н; (*colour*)

орáнжевый
orator орáтор
orbit орбúта; *put into* ~ выводúть ['-вести] на орбúту
orchard фрýктовый сад
orchestra оркéстр
orchid орхидéя
ordeal тяжёлое испытáние
order порядок; (*command*) прикáз; *comm.* закáз; (*brotherhood; decoration*) óрден; прикáзывать [-зáть]; закáзывать [-зáть]; *money* ~ дéнежный перевóд; *in* ~ *to* чтóбы; акку рáтный; *med.* санитáр, -ка
ordinary обычный; (*average*) срéдний, заурядный
ore рудá
organ óрган; *mus.* оргáн; ~ic органúческий; ~ization организáция; ~ize организовáть (*im*)*pf.*
orient Востóк; ~ *or* ~ate (*o.s.*) ориентúровать(ся) (*im*)*pf.*
origin происхождéние; ~al первонáчальный; (*text*) пóдлинный, *su.* оригинáл *or* пóдлинник; ~ate возникáть ['-кнуть]
ornament украшéние; украшáть [украсить]; ~al декоратúвный
orphan сиротá *m/f*
orthodox ортодоксáльный; *eccl.* правослáвный, (*a. su.*)
ostentatious показнóй

ostrich стрáус
other другóй, инóй; *every* ~ *day* чéрез день; *the* ~ *day* на днях; ~*wise* инáче; (*or else*) в протúвном слýчае
otter выдра
ought: *you* ~ *to* вам (тебé) слéдует (*or:* слéдовало бы) + *inf.*
ounce ýнция (= 28.3 *gr.*)
our(s) наш, '-а, '-е, *pl.* '-и; ~*selves* себя, -ся; *emphatic* сáми
out (*prep., mst.* ~ *of*) из (P); *adv.* нарýжу; ~ *of turn* вне óчереди (= P); ~ *with him!* вон егó!; *often the verb takes a prefix, such as:* вы-, из-, из-у; *fly* ~ вылетáть [выlететь] (*of* из P); ~*burst* взрыв; *fig.* вспышка; ~*come* исхóд; ~*cry fig.* протéст; шум; ~*door(s)* на открытом вóздухе; ~*fit* (*equipment*) снаряжéние; ~*line* очертáние; *fig.* обрисовáть *mst. pf.*; ~*live* переживá(ть); ~*look* вид, перспектúва; (*point of view*) взгляд *mst. pf.*; ~*patient* амбулатóрный больнóй; ~*put* выпуск; продýкция; *min.* добыча; *el.* выходнáя мóщность *f*; ~*rage* возмутúтельное явлéние; возмущáть [-утúть]; ~*rageous* возмутúтельный
out|side вне (P); *adv.* нарýжу; внéшняя сторонá;

~skirts окра́ина; ~standing выдаю́щийся; (debt) неуплаченный; ~ward adj. нару́жный, вне́шний
oven духо́вка

over над (T); (across) че́рез (B); (more than) свы́ше, бо́лее (P); it is all ~ всё ко́нчено; all ~ the country по всей стране́; ~alls комбинезо́н sg.; ~board за борт, за бо́ртом; ~coat пальто́ n indecl.; ~come преодоле(ва́)ть; ~crowded переполненный; ~do утри́ровать (im)pf.; meat пережа́ри(ва)ть; ~draw превыша́ть [-ы́сить] креди́т (в ба́нке); ~estimate переоце́нивать [-ни́ть]; ~flow v/i. разли(ва́)ться; разли́в; fig. избы́ток; ~grown (wall, path) заро́сший (T)

overhead над; вверху́, наверху́; ~ expenses накладны́е расхо́ды m/pl.

over|hear подслу́ш(ив)ать; (unintentionally) неча́янно услы́шать pf.; ~load tech. su. перегру́зка; ~look обозре́(ва́)ть; (miss) не заме́тить, проглядеть pf.; ~night adv. (change) за ночь; stay ~night ночева́ть; ~power одолева́ть

[-ле́ть]; ~rate переоце́нивать [-ни́ть]; ~seas adj. иностра́нный; adv. за границей, за рубежо́м; ~sight недосмо́тр; ~take обгоня́ть, обогна́ть; storm: застига́ть [-и́чь or -и́гнуть]; ~throw pol. сверга́ть ['-гнуть]; ~time adj. сверхуро́чный

overture mus. увертю́ра

over|turn опроки́дывать(ся) [-и́нуть(ся)]; ~whelm подавля́ть [-ви́ть]; (feelings) ошеломля́ть [-ми́ть]; ~work переутомля́ться рабо́той; переутомле́ние

owe: I ~ you two pounds я вам до́лж|ен, -на́ два фу́нта; we ~ this to him э́тим мы обя́заны ему́

owing: ~ to всле́дствие (P), благодаря́ (Д)

owl сова́

own со́бственный; (possess) име́ть (T); (admit) призн(ав)а́ть; ~er владе́л|ец, -ица; хозя́ин; ~ership владе́ние; (right) пра́во со́бственности

ox вол

oxygen кислоро́д

oyster у́стрица

ozone озо́н

P

pace (*step*) шаг; (*speed*) темп; *v.* шага́ть

pacif|ic ми́рный; **~y** умиротворя́ть [-ри́ть]

pack (*bale*) тюк; (*rucksack*) рюкза́к; (*mule's*) вьюк; (*cards*) коло́да; *v/t.* упако́вывать [-ова́ть]; *trunk* укла́дывать [уложи́ть]; **~age** свёрток, паке́т; **~et** (*cigarettes, letters*) па́чка; небольшо́й паке́т; **small ~et** (*mail*) бандеро́ль

pact пакт

pad мя́гкая наби́вка, прокла́дка; наби(ва́)ть

paddling: **~ pool** coll. лягуша́тник

padlock вися́чий замо́к

pagan язы́ческий

page страни́ца

pail ведро́

pain боль *f*; причиня́ть боль (Д); **take ~s** [по]стара́ться; **~staking** стара́тельный

paint кра́ска; *wall, lips* [по]кра́сить; *picture* [на]писа́ть; **~er** маля́р; (*artist*) худо́жник, живопи́сец; **~ing** карти́на; (*art*) жи́вопись *f*

pair па́ра; соединя́ть по́ двое; *biol.* спа́ри(ва)ть(ся); **~ off** разделя́ться [-ли́ться] на па́ры

pal coll. друг

palace дворе́ц

palate нёбо; *fig.* вкус

pal|e, **~lid** бле́дный; **~lor** бле́дность *f*

palm[1] *bot.* па́льма

palm[2] *anat.* ладо́нь *f*

paltry ничто́жный

pamper [из]балова́ть

pamphlet брошю́ра; *mst. pol.* памфле́т

pan (*frying ~*) сковорода́; (*sauce~*) кастрю́ля; **~cake** бли́нчик; (*of batter made with yeast*) блин

pane око́нное стекло́

panel пане́ль *f*; *mot.* прибо́рная доска́; *tech.* **control ~** пульт управле́ния

pang о́страя боль *f*; **~s of remorse** угрызе́ния со́вести

panic па́ника; *v/i.* панико́вать *impf.*

pansy аню́тины гла́зки *pl.*

pant *v/i.* тяжело́ дыша́ть *impf.*

pant|s трусы́; *Am.* брю́ки; **~y**: **~y hose** *Am.* колго́тки

paper бума́га; *attr.* бума́жный; (*news~*) газе́та; **~back** кни́га в мя́гком перепле́те

par: **at ~** *fin.* по номина́льной сто́имости; **on a ~** на парите́тных нача́лах

parachute парашю́т; **~ist** парашюти́ст(ка)

parade пара́д; (*show off*) щеголя́ть [-льну́ть] (Т)

para|dise рай; **~dox** парадо́кс; **~graph** _typ._ абза́ц; **~llel** паралле́ль _f_ (_a. geogr._); паралле́льный; **~lyse** парализова́ть (_im_)_pf._; **~lysis** парали́ч; **~mount** первостепе́нный; **~pet** парапе́т; **~site** парази́т

parcel паке́т; (_postal_) посы́лка

parch: ~ing heat паля́щий зной; **~ed lips** запёкшиеся гу́бы _f/pl._

pardon проще́ние; _jur._ поми́лование; проща́ть [прости́ть]; поми́ловать _pf._; **I beg your ~** прости́(те); **~?** как вы сказа́ли?

pare (_trim_) подстрига́ть [-ри́чь] (но́гти, и т. д.); (_peel_) [по]чи́стить

parent|al роди́тельский; **~s** роди́тели _pl._

parish церко́вный прихо́д; _attr._ прихо́дский

park парк; _car_ ста́вить на стоя́нку; **~ing lot** _Am._ автостоя́нка; **no ~ing!** стоя́нка запрещена́

parliament парла́мент; **~ary** парла́ментский

parlour гости́ная

parquet парке́т

parrot попуга́й

parsley петру́шка

parson свяще́нник

part часть _f_; _thea._ роль _f_; _v/t._ разделя́ть [-ли́ть]

friends разлуча́ть [-чи́ть]; **fighters** разнима́ть [-ня́ть]; _v/i._ расст(ав)а́ться (**with** с Т); **take ~** принима́ть уча́стие; **~ial** части́чный; (_biased_) пристра́стный; **~iality** пристра́стие (**for** к Д)

particip|ant уча́стни|к, -ца; **~ate** уча́ствовать; **~ation** уча́стие; **~le** _gr._ прича́стие

particle части́ца; **~ular** (_special_) осо́бенный, осо́бый; (_exacting_) притяза́тельный; _su. pl._ подро́бности _f/pl._

parting расстава́ние; _attr._ проща́льный; (_hair_) пробо́р; **~ition** разде́л; (_wall_) перегоро́дка; **~ly** части́чно, отча́сти; **~ner** _sports, thea., comm._ партнёр; **~ owner** совладе́лец

partridge куропа́тка

party _pol._ па́ртия, _attr._ парти́йный; (_group_) гру́ппа; (_team_) отря́д; **evening ~** вечери́нка; **dinner ~** обе́д

pass (_go by_) проходи́ть [пройти́] (**a house** ми́мо до́ма = Р); (_in a car_) проезжа́ть [-е́хать] (ми́мо); (_overtake_) обогна́ть; (_cross, change over_) переходи́ть [перейти́]; _holiday_ проводи́ть [провести́] _pf._; _examination_ сдать _pf._; (_sports_) пасова́ть; (_cards_) [с]пасова́ть; _geogr._ перевал; (= ~port) паспорт; (permit) пропуск; (sports) пас; ~age (way) проход, проезд; mar. рейс; av. перелёт; (book) отрывок, ~enger пассажир; attr. пассажирский

passion страсть f; ~ionate страстный; ~ive пассивный; gr. страдательный (залог)

passport паспорт

past prep. мимо (P) a. adv.; adj. прошлый; su. прошлое; gr. прошедшее время n; ten ~ two десять минут третьего

paste (glue) клей; паста; приклеи(ва)ть

pastime времяпрепровождение

pastor пастор

pastry (dough) тесто; (cake) пирожное

pasture пастбище

pat похлопывать; хлопать

patch заплата; [за]латать

pâté cul. паштет

patent патент; (за)патентованный; (obvious) явный; ~-leather лакированный

paternal отцовский; (fatherly) отеческий

path тропинка, дорожка

patience терпение; ~t терпеливый; med. пациент(ка)

patriot патриот(ка); ~ic патриотический

patrol патруль m; патрулировать

patron покровитель m; ~age покровительство; ~ize покровительствовать (Д); b.s. относиться свысока

patter rain: барабанить; (feet) звук шагов

pattern (model, sample) образец; (design) узор; (tailoring) выкройка

patty (little pie) пирожок

pause (speech, mus.) пауза; (work) перерыв; приостанавливаться [-новиться]

pavement (sidewalk) тротуар

paw лапа

pawn (chess) пешка (a. fig.); закладывать [заложить]; ~-shop ломбард

pay v/i. [за-, у]платить (for за В); v/t. worker [за]платить; (for losses) возмещать [-местить]; debt, tax уплачивать [уплатить] (В); заработная плата; ~ a bill платить по счёту; ~ment платёж; уплата; ~ment on delivery наложенным платежом; defer ~ment откладывать, отложить срок платежа

pea(s) горох; attr. гороховый; (single ~) горошина

peace мир; ~able, ~ful мирный

peach персик

peacock павлин

perch

peak *geogr.* пик; (*cap*) козырёк; *fig.* разгар

peal (*bells*) звон; (*thunder*) раскат грома; звонить; греметь

peanut арахис

pear груша

pearl жемчужина; *pl. collect.* жемчуг; *attr.* жемчужный; **~ barley** перловая крупа, *coll.* перловка

peasant крестьянин; *attr.* крестьянский; **~ woman** крестьянка

peat торф; *attr.* торфяной

pebble(s) галька

peck клевать [клюнуть]

peculiar особенный; (*strange*) странный; **~ to** свойственный (Д); **~ity** особенность *f*; странность *f*

pedal педаль *f*

pedestal пьедестал

pedestrian пешеход; *adj.* пешеходный

pedigree родословная; **~ dog** породистая собака

peel кожура, (*thin*) кожица; [o-, по]чистить; **~ings** очистки *m/pl.*; шелуха *sg.*

peep смотреть украдкой; **~ in** заглядывать [-януть]

peer вглядываться [-деться] (*at, into* в В)

peg колышек; (*clothes*) прищепка

pen ручка; **ball-point ~** шариковая ручка; **felt-tip ~**
фломастер

penal (*law*) уголовный; **~ offence** наказуемое правонарушение; **~ty** наказание; **~ty kick** штрафной удар

pencil карандаш

pendulum маятник

penetrate проникать ['-кнуть] (в *or* сквозь В); (*soak, pierce*) пронизывать [-зать] (В); **~ion** проникновение; (*insight*) проницательность *f*

peninsula полуостров

penitent кающийся; **~iary** *Am.* тюрьма

penny пенни *n indecl.*, пенс

pension пенсия; **~er** пенсионер(ка)

pensive задумчивый

people люди *pl.*; (*nation*) народ; населять [-лить]

pepper перец; [на]перчить; **~pot** перечница

peppermint (*sweet*) мятный леденец

perambulator детская коляска

perceive (*see*) различать [-чить]; (*understand*) понимать [-нять]

percent, per cent процент; **~ five** пять процентов

percentage процент

perceptible (*discernable*) различимый; (*noticeable*) ощутимый; **~on** восприятие

perch[1] *zo.* окунь *m*

perch² садиться *or* сидеть высоко

percolator кофеварка

perfect (*absolute*) совершенный; (*excellent*) превосходный; [у]совершенствовать; **~ion** совершенство

perform duty, promise, role исполнять ['-нить]; *actor*: выступать [выступить]; **~ance** исполнение; (*acting*) игра; (*show*) спектакль, (*cinema*) сеанс; (*sports*) достижение; *tech*. работа; **~er** исполнитель(ница *f*) *m*

perfume аромат; (*liquid*) духи *m/pl.*; надушить; *put* **~ on** [на]душиться

perhaps может быть, пожалуй

peril опасность *f*; **~ous** опасный

period период *m*; (*full stop*) точка; **~ical** периодический; *su.* периодическое издание

perish погибать ['-бнуть], **~able** *able goods* скоропортящиеся продукты *m/pl.*

perjury лжесвидетельство

permanen|**ce** постоянство; **~t** постоянный

permi|**ssion** позволение, разрешение; **~t** позволять ['-лить] (Д), разрешать [-шить] (Д); *su.* разрешение, (*pass*) пропуск

perpetua|**l** вечный, непрерывный; **~te** увековечи(ва)ть

perplex озадачи(ва)ть; **~ity** озадаченность *f*; (*situation*) затруднение

persecut|**e** преследовать; **~ion** преследование

persever|**ance** настойчивость *f*; **~e** проявлять настойчивость

Persian персидский

persist упорствовать (**in** в П); (*continue*) продолжать(ся) *mst. impf.*; **~ence** упорство; **~ent** упорный; (*unceasing*) непрерывный

person лицо (*a. gr., jur.*): человек, особа; **~age** *thea., lit.*, персонаж; персона, особа; **~al** личный; **~ality** личность *f*; **~ify** олицетворять [-рить]; **~nel** персонал, штат; **~nel department** отдел кадров

perspective перспектива

persua|**de** уговаривать [-ворить]; (*convince*) убеждать [-едить]; **~sion** уговор *mst. pl.*; (*belief*) убеждение; (*power*) убедительность *f*; **~sive** убедительный

perver|**se** извращённый; (*wilful*) своенравный; (*wrong*) превратный; **~sion** извращение; **~t** извращать [-ратить]

pessimist пессимист(ка)

~ic пессимисти́ческий

pest *agr.* вреди́тель *m*; ~er докуча́ть [-чи́ть]

pet люби́м|ец, -ица; (*animal*) люби́мое живо́тное; балова́ть, ласка́ть; ~ **name** ласка́тельное и́мя *n*

petition *jur.* ход́атайство; пети́ция; ход́атайствовать (о П); обраща́ться [-ати́ться] с пети́цией

petrol *Brit.* бензи́н; ~ **station** автозапра́вочная ста́нция; ~**eum** (*raw oil*) нефть *f*

petty ме́лкий, малова́жный; (*mean*) ме́лочный

phase фа́за (*a. el.*)

pheasant фаза́н

phenomen|al феномена́льный; ~**on** фено́мен, явле́ние

philosoph|er фило́соф; ~**y** филосо́фия

phone *v/t., v/i.* [по]звони́ть (по телефо́ну) (Д)

phonebooth телефо́нная бу́дка

photocopy фотоко́пия

photograph фо́то(гра́фия) *n indecl.*; ~**er** фото́граф; ~**ic** фотографи́ческий; ~**y** фотогра́фия

phrase фра́за, оборо́т ре́чи; *v.* [с]формули́ровать (*im*)*pf.*

physic|al физи́ческий; ~**ian** терапе́вт, врач; ~**ist** фи́зик; ~**s** фи́зика

physique телосложе́ние

pian|ist пиани́ст(ка); ~**o** ро́яль *m*; (*upright*) пиани́но *n indecl.*

pick (*gather*) соб(и)ра́ть; (*pluck*) рвать, срыва́ть [сорва́ть]; *su.* (*choice*) вы́бор; ~ **out** подбира́ть [подобра́ть], отбира́ть [отобра́ть]; ~ **up** поднима́ть [-ня́ть]; ~**ed** (*choice*) отбо́рный; ~**up** *mot.* гру́зови́к

pickle рассо́л; (*with vinegar*) марина́д; *pl.* соле́нья; марино́ванные о́вощи; [за]маринова́ть

pickpocket карма́нный вор

picnic пикни́к

picture карти́на; фотогра́фия; (кино)фи́льм; (*image*) изображе́ние; изобража́ть [-рази́ть]; (*describe*) опи́сывать [-са́ть]; **the** ~**s** кино́ *n indecl.*; ~**sque** живопи́сный

pie пиро́г

piece (*bit, fragment*) кусо́к; (*small*) кусо́чек, (*paper*) клочо́к; (*single article*) вещь *f*; шту́ка; (*in a set*) предме́т; **by the** ~ пошту́чно; **break to** ~**s** разби́ть на куски́; **take to** ~**s** разбира́ть [-обра́ть] на ча́сти; ~**work** сде́льная рабо́та

pier *mar.* пирс, при́стань *f*

pierc|e протыка́ть [-ткну́ть]; прока́лывать [-коло́ть]; пронза́ть

[-зи́ть]; *cold:* прони́зывать [-за́ть]; **~ing** (*voice*) пронзи́тельный

pig свинья́

pigeon го́лубь *m*

pike *zo.* щу́ка

pile (*heap*) ку́ча, гру́да, (*of books*) сто́пка; (*beam*) сва́я; *v/t.* (с)вали́ть в ку́чу; **~ up** нагроможда́ть(ся) [-мозди́ть(ся)]; *money* накопля́ть [-пи́ть]

pilgrim пало́мник; **~age** пало́мничество

pill табле́тка

pillar столб; *fig.* столп

pillow поду́шка; **~-case** на́волочка

pilot пило́т, лётчик; *mar.* ло́цман; пилоти́ровать; *ship* проводи́ть [-вести́]

pimple пры́щик, прыщо́к

pin була́вка; (*hair*) шпи́лька; *tech.* штифт; **drawing ~** кно́пка; прика́лывать була́вкой

pincers пинце́т; (*larger*) клещи́ *pl.*

pinch щипа́ть [щипну́ть]; *shoe:* жать; щипо́к; (*salt*) щепо́тка

pine (*away*) ча́хнуть

pine *bot.* сосна́; **~apple** анана́с; **~-cone** сосно́вая ши́шка

pink ро́зовый (цвет); *bot.* гвозди́ка

pint пи́нта (= 0,57 ли́тра)

pioneer пионе́р

pip (*grape, orange*) зёр-

нышко; (*apple, pear*) се́мечко

pipe труба́; (*smoker's*) тру́бка; **~-line** трубопро́вод; (*gas*) газопрово́д; (*oil*) нефтепрово́д

piracy пира́тство; **~te** пира́т

pistol пистоле́т, револьве́р

pit я́ма; *min.* ша́хта; *thea.* за́дние ряды́ парте́ра

pitch *mus., arch.* высота́; (*degree*) сте́пень *f*; (*thread*) *tech.* шаг резьбы́; (*throw*) броса́ть ['-сить]; **tent** разби(ва́)ть

pitcher кувши́н

pitfall западня́ (*mst. fig.*)

pitiful жа́лкий; (*compassionate*) жа́лостливый; **~less** безжа́лостный; **~y** жа́лость *f*; **it is a ~y** о́чень жаль; **what a ~y!** как жаль!

pivot *tech.* ось враще́ния

placard плака́т

place ме́сто; (*put*) [по]ста́вить, класть [положи́ть]; (*lodge, locate*) помеща́ть [-ести́ть]

placid споко́йный

plague *v/t.* [из-, за]му́чить

plaice ка́мбала

plaid плед; (*material*) шотла́ндка

plain (*simple*) просто́й; (*clear*) я́сный, поня́тный; (*uncomely*) невзра́чный; *geogr.* равни́на

plaintiff исте́ц, -и́ца; **~ve**

жа́лобный

plait коса́; (*short*) коси́чка; заплета́ть [-ести́]

plan план; прое́кт (*a. arch.*); [за]плани́ровать (В *or inf.*)

plane¹ пло́ский, ро́вный; пло́скость *f*; (*tool*) руба́нок; *v.* строга́ть

plane² *av.* самолёт

planet плане́та

plank у́зкая то́лстая доска́

plant *bot.* расте́ние; (*seedling*) са́женец; (*mill*) заво́д; сажа́ть [посади́ть]; ~ation планта́ция

plaster *med.*; *arch.* штукату́рка; [о]штукату́рить; ~ **cast** *med.* ги́псовая повя́зка

plastic (*made of plastic*) пластма́ссовый; *su.* пластма́сса

plate (*dish*) таре́лка; (*silver* ~e) столо́вое серебро́; ~eau плато́, плоского́рье; ~form rail. платфо́рма (*a. pol.*); (*on tram*) площа́дка; **the train departs from** ~**form 2** по́езд отправля́ется с платфо́рмы 2

platinum пла́тина

plausible правдоподо́бный

play игра́; *thea.* пье́са *f*, *v/i.* игра́ть [сыгра́ть] (*game* в В: в ка́рты, в футбо́л); *instrument* на П: на скри́пке); ~er игро́к (*not mus.*); ~ful игри́вый; (*joking*) шутли́вый;

plead *case* защища́ть *impf.*; ~ **ignorance** опра́вдываться незна́нием; ~ **guilty (not guilty)** признава́ть себя́ вино́вным (не вино́вным)

pleas|**ant** прия́тный; ~e [по]нра́виться (Д); ~e! пожа́луйста!; ~ure удово́льствие

pleat скла́дка

pledge (*as security*) зало́г (*a. fig.*); (*promise*) обеща́ние; обеща́ть

plenti|**ful** изоби́льный; ~y (из)оби́лие; ~y of о́чень мно́го (Р)

pliable податливый (*a. fig.*)

plight бе́дственное положе́ние

plod (*walking*) плести́сь с трудо́м; (*toil*) труди́ться (*at* над Т)

plot¹ интри́га, *pol.* за́говор; (*literary*) сюже́т

plot² (*land*) участо́к

plough плуг; [вс]паха́ть; ~land па́шня

pluck *flowers* рвать; *fowl* ощи́пывать [-па́ть]; (*courage*) хра́брость *f*; ~ **up courage** набра́ться хра́брости

plug про́бка, *coll.* затьі́чка; *el.* ште́псель *m*; затыка́ть

[заткну́ть]; **sparking ~**
mot. свеча́ (зажига́ния)

plum сли́ва; attr. сли́вовый

plumber санте́хник, coll.
водопрово́дчик

plump пу́хлый, по́лный;
v/i. (grow stout) [рас]полне́ть; (drop down) бу́хаться [бу́хнуться]

plunder грабёж; (booty) добы́ча; v. гра́бить

plunge окуна́ть(ся)
[-ну́ть(ся)]

plural мно́жественное
число́; **~ity** мно́жественность f

plus плюс

plywood фане́ра; attr. фане́рный

pneumonia пневмони́я,
воспале́ние лёгких

poach занима́ться браконье́рством; **~er** браконье́р

**PO Box (= Post Office
Box)** почто́вый я́щик
(п/я)

pocket карма́н; attr. карма́нный; класть в карма́н; (steal) прикарма́нивать(ва)ть

pod стручо́к

poem стихотворе́ние, поэ́ма; **~t** поэ́т; **~try** поэ́зия,
стихи́ m/pl.

point math., typ. то́чка;
(place, item) пункт; (needle) остриё; (sports) очко́;
~ at, out ука́зывать [-за́ть]
на (В); **a sore ~** больно́й
вопро́с; **come to the ~** до-

йти́ до су́ти де́ла; **~ of
view** то́чка зре́ния; **that's
beside the ~** э́то к де́лу
не отно́сится; **~ed**
о́стрый, остроконе́чный;
~er tech. указа́тель m;
стре́лка

poise (body) оса́нка;
(mind) уравнове́шенность
f

poison яд; отравля́ть
[-ви́ть]; **~ous** ядови́тый (a.
fig.)

poke ты́кать [ткнуть]; fire
меша́ть кочерго́й; совать [су́нуть]; **~r** кочерга́

polar поля́рный; **~ bear** бе́лый медве́дь m

polarity поля́рность

Pole поля́к, по́лька

pole шест, столб; geogr.
по́люс

police поли́ция; **~man** полице́йский; **~-station** полице́йский уча́сток

policy поли́тика; (insurance) по́лис

Polish по́льский

polish wood [от]полирова́ть; shoes [по]чи́стить;
полиро́вка; **shoe ~** крем
для о́буви

polite ве́жливый; **~ness**
ве́жливость f

politic|al полити́ческий;
~ian полити́ческий де́ятель m; **~s** поли́тика

poll (voting) голосова́ние;
~ opinion ~ опро́с обще́ст-

венного мне́ния; **~ing:**
~ing day день вы́боров;
~ing station избира́тель-
ный уча́сток

pollut|e *water* загрязня́ть
[-ни́ть]; **~ion** загрязне́ние;
~ion of environment за-
грязне́ние окружа́ющей
среды́

polythene полиэтиле́н;
~ bag полиэтиле́новый ме-
шо́к

pond пруд

ponder *v/t.* взве́шивать
[взве́сить]; **~ous** тяжело-
ве́сный

pool¹ пруд; (*puddle*) лу́жа;
swimming ~ пла́ватель-
ный бассе́йн

pool² *v/t.* объединя́ть
(-ни́ть); *comm.* объедине́-
ние; *fin.* о́бщий фонд

poor бе́дный (*a. fig.*);
(*scanty*) ску́дный; (*quality*) ни́зкий, плохо́й

Pope па́па *m* (ри́мский)

poplar то́поль *m*

poppy мак; *attr.* ма́ковый

popul|ar популя́рный; **~ar-**
ity популя́рность *f*;
~ation населе́ние; **~ous**
гу́сто населённый

porcelain фарфо́р; *attr.*
фарфо́ровый

porcupine дикобра́з

pore *biol.* по́ра

pore over *books* корпе́ть
над (T); *problem* размыш-
ля́ть над (T)

pork свини́на; **~ chop** сви-

на́я отбивна́я

porous по́ристый

porridge овся́ная ка́ша

port¹ *mar.* порт, га́вань *f*;
(*side*) ле́вый борт

port² (*drink*) портве́йн

portable портати́вный, пе-
рено́сный

portal порта́л

porter носи́льщик; (*hotel*)
швейца́р

portion (*part*) часть *f*;
(*share*) до́ля; (*helping*)
по́рция; дели́ть на ча́сти;
~ out разделя́ть [-ли́ть]

portrait портре́т

Portuguese португа́л|ец,
-ка; -ьский

pos|e по́за; пози́ровать;
~ition положе́ние; пози́-
ция; (*job*) до́лжность *f*;
~itive положи́тельный

possess владе́ть (T), обла-
да́ть (T); **~ion** владе́ние,
облада́ние; *pl.* (= *property*) иму́щество; **~or**
владе́лец, облада́тель *m*

possibility возмо́жность *f*;
~le возмо́жный

post¹ (*pillar*) столб

post² по́чта; *v/t.* отправ-
ля́ть ['-вить]; **~age stamp**
почто́вая ма́рка; **~al** по-
что́вый; **~al order** почто́-
вый перево́д; **~card** от-
кры́тка; **~code** почто́вый
и́ндекс

poster плака́т, афи́ша

posterity пото́мство

post|man почтальо́н;

~mark почто́вый штéмпель *m*; **~office** отделéние свя́зи, *coll.* по́чта; **general ~office** почта́мт

postpone откла́дывать, отложи́ть; *(payment, etc.)* отсро́чи(ва)ть; **~ment** перенóс; отсрóчка

pot горшóк; *(jar)* бáнка

potato(es) карто́фель *m*; *attr.* карто́фельный

potent *med.* эффекти́вный; *(drink)* крéпкий; **~ial** потенциáльный; *su.* потенциáл

potter: **~ about** вози́ться

pottery *(objects)* керáмика

pouch *(under eyes)* мешóк

poultry *collect.* домáшняя пти́ца

pounce: **~ upon** набрáсываться [-рóситься] на (В)

pound[1] фунт (= *0.454 kg*) *(a. fin.)*

pound[2] *(beat)* колоти́ть (-ся); *(crush)* [рас]толóчь

pour ли́ть(ся); **~ out** разли́(ва)ть, *a cup of tea* нали́(ва)ть

pout надувáть гýбы

poverty бéдность *f*

powder порошóк; *(face)* пýдра; [на]пýдрить; **~ed:** **~ed milk** сухóе молокó

power *(might)* мощь *f*; *tech.* мóщность *f*; *(force)* си́ла; *(nation)* держáва; *(control)* власть *f*; **nuclear ~** áтомная энéргия; **~ful** мóщный, могýществен-

ный; **~station** электростáнция

practi|cable осуществи́мый; реáльный; **~cal** практи́ческий; *(person)* практи́чный; **~ce** прáктика; *(habit)* привы́чка; *(exercise)* упражнéние; *v.* *(Brit.* **~se)** занимáться; *(sports)* тренировáться; *(learn)* упражня́ться в (П), *mus.* на (П)

praise похвалá; [по]хвали́ть

prance *child:* пры́гать

prank шáлость *f*

prayer моли́тва

preach проповéдовать; **~er** проповéдник

precarious *(insecure)* ненадёжный; *(dangerous)* опáсный

precaution предосторóжность *f*; *(measure)* мéра предосторóжности

precede предшéствовать (Д); **~nt** предшéствующий; *su.* прецедéнт

precious драгоцéнный

precip|ice обры́в; **~tate** *(hasten)* [по]торопи́ть; ускоря́ть [-рить]; *chem.* осáдок

precise тóчный; *tech.* прецизиóнный; **~ion** тóчность *f*

predatory хи́щный

predecessor предшéственник

predicament затрудни́-

pretence

тельное положёние

predict предскáзывать [-зáть]; ~**ion** предсказáние

predomina|nt преоблáдающий; ~**te** преоблáдать

preface предислóвие

prefer предпочитáть [-чéсть]; ~**able** предпочти́тельный; ~**ence** предпочтéние

pregnan|cy бéременность f; ~**t** берéменная

prehistoric доистори́ческий

prejudice предрассýдок, предубеждéние; (harm) [по]вреди́ть (Д); ~d **against** настрáивать [-рóить] против (Р)

preliminary предвари́тельный

prelude прелю́дия

premature преждеврéменный

première премьéра

premise (logical) предпосы́лка; pl. помещéние

premium comm. прéмия (a. = reward)

preoccupation озабóченность f

prepar|ation приготовлéние; (training) подготóвка; (mixture) препарáт; ~**atory** подготови́тельный; ~**e** [при]готóвить; подготовля́ть(ся) [-тóвить(ся)]

preposition gr. предлóг

preposterous нелéпый

prerogative прерогати́ва

prescri|be предпи́сывать [-сáть]; ~**ption** med. рецéпт

presen|ce прису́тствие; ~t[1] прису́тствующий; (time) настоя́щий; su. настоя́щее врéмя

present[2] (gift) подáрок; [по]дари́ть (Д; **with** В); (introduce) представля́ть [-ви́ть]; ~**ation** представлéние; (exposition) изложéние

preserv|ation сохранéние; охрáна; ~**e** сохраня́ть [-ни́ть]; fruit консерви́ровать (im)pf.; zo. запóведник; pl. cul. варéнье

preside председáтельствовать; ~**nt** председáтель m; президéнт; ~**ntial** президéнтский

press (weigh on) дави́ть; (squeeze) сж(им)áть; (push) наж(им)áть на (В); (journalism) прéсса, печáть f; typ. типогрáфия; (tool) пресс; ~**ure** давлéние; нажи́м

prestige прести́ж

presum|able предположи́тельный; ~**e** предполагáть [-ложи́ть]; (venture) осмéли(ва)ться; ~**ption** предположéние; (arrogance) занóсчивость f; ~**ptuous** занóсчивый

preten|ce (sham) притвóрство; (pretext) предлóг;

~**d** притворя́ться [-ори́ться] (*to be ill* больны́м); ~**sion** претéнзия; ~**tious** претенцио́зный

pretext предло́г

pretty хоро́шенький; *adv. coll.* дово́льно, весьма́

prevail преоблада́ть; (*be victorious*) взять верх (*over* над Т)

prevent предупрежда́ть [-упреди́ть]; (*hinder*) [по]меша́ть (Д; *from coming* прийти́); ~**ion** предупрежде́ние; ~**ive** предупреди́тельный; *med.* профилакти́ческий

previous прéжний; ~ **to** прéжде (Р); пéред (Т)

prey добы́ча; *bird of ~* хи́щная пти́ца

price цена́; *goods* оце́нивать [-ни́ть]; ~**less** бесце́нный

prick коло́ть [кольну́ть, уколо́ть]; уко́л (иглóй); (*hole*) проко́л; ~ **le** коло́чка, шип; ~**ly** колю́чий

pride го́рдость *f*

priest свяще́нник

primary (*main*) основно́й; (*first*) первоочередно́й; (*original*) первонача́льный

prim|e: ~**e minister** премье́р-мини́стр; *in one's* ~**e** в расцвéте сил; ~ **cost** себесто́имость *f*; ~**itive** примити́вный; (*primeval*) первобы́тный

primrose при́мула

princ|e князь *m*; (*royal*) принц; ~**ess** княги́ня; княжна́; принце́сса; ~**ipal** гла́вный; *su.* (*school*) дире́ктор; *univ.* ре́ктор; ~**iple** при́нцип

print *typ.* печа́ть *f*, шрифт; (*mark*) отпеча́ток; *art.* эста́мп; (на)печа́тать; *er tech.* при́нтер; ~**ing** печа́тание; *attr.* печа́тный

priority приорите́т

prism при́зма

prison тюрьма́; ~**er** заключённый; *mil.* военноплéнный; **be taken** ~**er** попа́сть в плен

priva|cy (*seclusion*) уедине́ние; (*tell*) **in** ~**cy** по секре́ту; ~**te** ча́стный; (*personal*) ли́чный; *mil.* рядово́й; ~**tely** ча́стным о́бразом; ~**tion** лише́ние; ~**ti-zation** приватиза́ция, (*large enterprises*) разгосударствление

privilege привиле́гия

prize приз; ~**-winner** (*sports*) призёр; *mst. mus.* лауреа́т; *Nobel* ~ *Winner* лауреа́т Нобелевской прéмии

proba|bility вероя́тность *f*; ~**le** вероя́тный

prob|ation испыта́тельный срок; *a med.* зонд; зонди́ровать (*a. fig.*)

problem пробле́ма; *math.* зада́ча

promotion

procedure процеду́ра

proceed (*go on*) продолжа́ть ['-жить] (*with* B); (*issue*) исходи́ть *impf.* (*from* из P); **~ing** де́йствие; *pl. jur.* судопроизво́дство; (*records*) труды́ *m/pl.*; **~s** вы́ручка

process проце́сс; (*treat*) обраба́тывать [-бо́тать]; **~ion** ше́ствие, проце́ссия

proclaim провозглаша́ть [-гласи́ть]; **~mation** провозглаше́ние

procure добы(ва́)ть, дост(ав)а́ть

prodigal: **~al son** блу́дный сын; (*huge*) грома́дный; **~y** чу́до; *child* **~y** вунде́ркинд

produc|e производи́ть [-вести́]; *ticket* предъявля́ть [-ви́ть]; *play* [по]ста́вить; *su.* проду́кты *m/pl.*; **~er** производи́тель *m*; *thea.* постано́вщик; (*cinema*) продю́сер; **~t** проду́кт, изде́лие; **~tion** (*output*) проду́кция; (*action*) произво́дство; *attr.* произво́дственный; **~tive** производи́тельный; *fig.* продукти́вный; (*writer*) плодови́тый

profession профе́ссия; **~ional** профессиона́л; профессиона́льный; **~or** профе́ссор

proficient иску́сный, уме́лый

profile про́филь *m*

profit *comm.* при́быль *f*; *gross* **~** валова́я при́быль; *net* **~** чи́стая при́быль; *fig.* по́льза; (*be*)[вос]по́льзоваться (*by* T); **~able** вы́годный, при́быльный; поле́зный; **~eer** спекуля́нт

profound глубо́кий (*a. fig.*)

programme програ́мма; *tech.* программи́ровать; **~r** программи́ст

progress прогре́сс, продвиже́ние; продвига́ться [-и́нуться]; *make* **~** [c]де́лать успе́хи *m/pl.* (*study*); **~ive** прогресси́вный

prohibit запреща́ть [-ети́ть]; **~ion** запреще́ние

project прое́кт; [с]проекти́ровать (*a. opt.*); (*stick out*) выступа́ть; **~ion** прое́кция; вы́ступ

prolific плодови́тый (*a. fig.*)

prologue проло́г

prolong продлева́ть [-ли́ть]; **~ation** продле́ние; *jur.* пролонга́ция; **~ed** *adj.* дли́тельный

prominent выдаю́щийся (*a. fig.*)

promis|e обеща́ние; [по]обеща́ть; **~ing** многообеща́ющий

promot|e *trade* соде́йствовать разви́тию (P); *people* повыша́ть по слу́жбе; **~ion** соде́йствие разви́тию; повыше́ние по слу́жбе

prompt бы́стрый, неме́дленный; побужда́ть [-уди́ть]; (school) подска́зывать [-за́ть]

prone (inclined) скло́нный; **lie** ~ лежа́ть ничко́м

pronoun местоиме́ние

pronounce произноси́ть [-нести́]; ~d adj. я́рко вы́раженный, заме́тный

pronunciation произноше́ние

proof доказа́тельство; ~s typ. гра́нки; **put to the** ~ проверя́ть [-ри́ть]

prop подпо́рка; ~ **up** подпира́ть [-пере́ть]

propaganda пропага́нда; ~te biol. размножа́ть(ся) [-жи́ть(ся)]; (spread) распространя́ть [-ни́ть]

propel дви́гать or толка́ть вперёд; ~ler av. пропе́ллер; mar. гребно́й винт

proper (right) пра́вильный; (suitable) до́лжный, надлежа́щий; (decent) прили́чный; ~ **name** и́мя со́бственное; ~ly как сле́дует; надлежа́щим о́бразом; ~ly speaking со́бственно говоря́; ~ty со́бственность f, иму́щество

prophe|cy проро́чество; ~sy проро́чить; ~t проро́к; ~tic проро́ческий

proportion пропо́рция; **in** ~ **to** в соотве́тствии с (Т); ~al пропорциона́льный

propos|al предложе́ние; ~e

предлага́ть [-ложи́ть]; (intend) предполага́ть; (to woman) сде́лать предложе́ние (Д)

proprietary: ~ **rights** права́ со́бственности

proprietor владе́лец, хозя́ин

propulsion движе́ние вперёд; tech. дви́жущая си́ла

prose про́за

prosecu|te пресле́довать суде́бным поря́дком; ~ion суде́бное пресле́дование; (side in court) обвине́ние; ~or обвини́тель m; (public) прокуро́р

prospect (view) вид; fig. перспекти́ва; ~us проспе́кт

prosper процвета́ть; ~ity процвета́ние; ~ous процвета́ющий

prostitute проститу́тка

protect (shield) охраня́ть [-ни́ть]; (defend) защища́ть [-ити́ть]; ~ion (patronage) покрови́тельство; охра́на; защи́та; ~ive покрови́тельственный; защи́тный; предохрани́тельный (a. tech.); ~or покрови́тель m; защи́тник

protest проте́ст; v. протестова́ть; **~ant** протеста́нт(ка); протеста́нтский

protrude выступа́ть, торча́ть

proud го́рдый

prove дока́зывать [-за́ть]; (~ *to be*) оказываться [-за́ться] (T)

proverb посло́вица

provide: ~ *for family* обеспе́чивать [-чить]; *winter* запаса́ть(ся) [-сти́(сь)] на (B); ~ *with* снабжа́ть [-бди́ть] (T); (*law*) ~ *s for* (зако́н) предусма́тривает (B); ~ *d that* при усло́вии, что

province прови́нция; о́бласть *f* (*a. fig.*)

provision (*act*) обеспече́ние; *pl.* проду́кты *m./pl.*; *jur.* усло́вие; *v.* снабжа́ть продово́льствием; ~**al** вре́менный

provo|cation провока́ция; ~**ke** [с]провоци́ровать (*im*)*pf.*

proximity бли́зость

pruden|ce предусмотри́тельность *f*; ~**t** предусмотри́тельный

prunes *collect.* черносли́в

psalm псало́м

psychological психологи́ческий; ~**y** психоло́гия

public обще́ственный; (*library*) публи́чный; ~ *conveniences* обще́ственные туале́ты; *su.* пу́блика; (*broad*) обще́ственность *f*; ~ *house* паб, пивно́й бар; ~**ation** (*edition*) изда́ние; (*issuing*) опублико́вание; ~**ity** *comm.* рекла́ма

publish опублико́вывать [-ова́ть]; *books* изд(ав)а́ть; ~**er** изда́тель *m*; ~**ing:** ~**ing house** изда́тельство

pudding пу́динг

puddle (*pool*) лу́жа

puff *v.* пыхте́ть; (*wind*) поры́в ве́тра

pull [по]тяну́ть; (*row*) грести́; ~ *o.s. together* взять себя́ в ру́ки; ~ *through* (*recover*) вы́здороветь; (*overcome*) преодоле́ть; ~ *up* (*car*) остана́вливать(ся) [-нови́ть(ся)]

pulley *tech.* шкив; блок

pullover пуло́вер

pulp *bot.* мя́коть *f*; (*wood*) древе́сная ма́сса

pulse *med.* пульс; *tech.* и́мпульс, *feel s.o.'s* ~ [по]щу́пать пульс

pulverize превраща́ть(ся) в порошо́к; (*spray*) распыля́ть [-ли́ть]

pump насо́с; *v.* кача́ть насо́сом; ~ *up* нака́чивать [-ча́ть]

pumpkin ты́ква

punch уда́рить кулако́м; *ticket* [про]компости́ровать; уда́р кулако́м; компо́стер

punctual пунктуа́льный; ~**ality** пунктуа́льность *f*; ~**ation** пунктуа́ция; ~**re** проко́л (ши́ны); прока́лывать [-коло́ть]

pungent о́стрый, е́дкий

punish нака́зывать [-за́ть];

_ment наказа́ние
pup(py) щено́к
pupil[1] учени́|к, -ца
pupil[2] anat. зрачо́к
puppet ку́кла; марионе́тка (a. fig.); **_-show** ку́кольный теа́тр
purchase поку́пка; покупа́ть [купи́ть]; **_r** покупа́тель(ница f) m
pure чи́стый; **_gative** med. слаби́тельный; **_ify** очища́ть [очи́стить]; **_itan** пуритански́й; **_ity** чистота́
purple багря́ный, пурпу́рный
purpose цель f, наме́рение; **for what** _ с како́й це́лью; **on** _, **_ly** наро́чно; **_ful** целеустремлённый; **_less** бесце́льный
purr v. мурлы́кать; мурлы́канье
purse кошелёк; Am. су́мочка; lips подж(им)а́ть
pursue пресле́довать (B), гна́ться (за T); policy проводи́ть [-вести́]; **_it** пресле́дование; (occupation)

заня́тие
push толка́ть [-кну́ть]; **_ aside** отта́лкивать [-толкну́ть]; fig. отмета́ть [-ести́]; **_ one's way** прота́лкиваться [-толкну́ться] (**through** че́рез B)
put [по]ста́вить, класть [положи́ть]; (express) выража́ть [вы́разить]; **_ by** money откла́дывать [отложи́ть]; **_ down** класть, [по]ста́вить, (write) запи́сывать [-са́ть]; **_ on** clothes наде(ва́)ть; weight [по]полне́ть; (defer) отсро́чи(ва)ть; **_ through** (telephone) соединя́ть [-ни́ть] (с T); **_ up** (in hotel) остана́вливаться [-нови́ться]; **_ up with** [при]мири́ться с (T)
puzzle зага́дка; **crossword _e** кроссво́рд; v/t. озада́чи(ва)ть; (look) недоуме́нный; **be _ed** недоумева́ть
pyjamas пижа́ма
pyramid пирами́да

Q

quack[1] кря́кать; кря́канье
quack[2] med. шарлата́н
quail zo. пе́репел
quaint причу́дливый
quake трясти́сь
quali|fication квалифика́ция; (restriction) ого-

во́рка; **_fied** квалифици́рованный; **_fy** получи́ть квалифика́цию; огова́ривать [-вори́ть]; **_ty** ка́чество
quantity коли́чество
quarantine каранти́н

quarrel ссо́ра; *v.* ссо́-
риться; **~some** сварли́-
вый

quarry *tech.* каменоло́мня

quart|er *math.* че́тверть *f*;
(*3 months*) кварта́л; **~erly**
кварта́льный; **~et** кварте́т

quaver (*voice*) дрожа́ть;
дрожь *f*

quay при́стань

queen короле́ва; (*chess*)
ферзь *m*; (*cards*) да́ма

queer стра́нный

quench *fire* [по]туши́ть;
thirst утоля́ть [-ли́ть]

question вопро́с; задава́ть
вопро́сы; *jur.* допра́ши-
вать [-роси́ть]; (*doubt*)
подверга́ть сомне́нию;
beyond ~ вне сомне́ния;
~able сомни́тельный;
~-mark вопроси́тельный
знак; **~naire** анке́та; (*for
polls*) вопро́сник

queue о́чередь *f*; стоя́ть в
о́череди

quick бы́стрый; (*lively*)
живо́й; (*~-minded*) сооб-
рази́тельный; *adv.* бы́ст-
ро; **~en** *race* ускоря́ть
['-рить]; **~silver** ртуть *f*

quiet споко́йный, ти́хий;
успока́ивать(ся) [-ко́ить-
(ся)]; **~ness** споко́йствие,
тишина́

quilt стёганое одея́ло; **~ed**
стёганый

quince *bot.* айва́; *attr.* айво́-
вый

quinine хини́н

quite совсе́м; (*rather*) до-
во́льно; **~ so!** соверше́н-
но ве́рно!

quiver тре́пет; *v.* трепета́ть

quiz: *TV ~ programme* теле-
викторина

quota кво́та; **~ation** ци-
та́та; *fin.* котиро́вка;
~ation marks кавы́чки *f*/
pl.; **~e** [про]цити́ровать;
comm. коти́ровать (*im*)*pf.*

R

rabbit кро́лик

rabble сброд

race[1] (*car, boat*) го́нки *f/pl.*;
(*horse*) ска́чки *f/pl.*; (*ath-
letic*) [за]бе́г; состяза́ться
в ско́рости; (*speed along*)
мча́ться; **~-course** ипподро́м; **~-track** (*for runners*)
бегова́я доро́жка; (*for cy-
cles, etc.*) трек

race[2] ра́са; **human ~e** род
челове́ческий; **~ial** ра́со-
вый

rack (*clothes*) ве́шалка;
rail. се́тка; (*hay*) кор-
му́шка; *v.* пыта́ть, му́чить

racket[1] (*noise*) шум; (*blackmail*) рэ́кет

rack|et[2], **~quet** (*sports*) ра-
ке́тка

radar *tech.* рада́р

radia|nce сия́ние; **~nt** сия́ющий; **~te** *v/t.* излуча́ть *impf.* (*a. fig.*); **~tion** радиа́ция; излуче́ние; **~tor** батаре́я, радиа́тор (*a. mot.*)

radical коренно́й, радика́льный; *su. math., pol.* радика́л

radio ра́дио *n indecl.*; передава́ть по ра́дио; *mar., av.* радии́ровать (*im*)*pf.*; **~-activity** радиоакти́вность; **~graph** рентгеногра́мма; **~operator** ради́ст

radish ре́дька, (red) реди́ска

raft плот

rag (*wiping*) тря́пка; (*scrap*) лоску́т; *pl.* (*old clothes*) ве́тошь *f*

rage я́рость; *person, wind, sea:* бушева́ть

ragged (*clothes*) рва́ный; (*uneven*) неро́вный

raid *av.* налёт; (*police*) обла́ва; де́лать налёт (на B); (на В)

rail рельс; пери́ла *n/pl.*; (*fence*) огра́да; **~road**, **~way** желе́зная доро́га

rain дождь *m*; **it's ~ing** идёт дождь; **~bow** ра́дуга; **~-coat** дождеви́к, плащ; **~y** дождли́вый

raise (*lift*) поднима́ть [-ня́ть]; (*increase*) повыша́ть [-ы́сить]; (*rear, grow*) выра́щивать [вы́растить]; *child* воспи́ты-

raisin(s) изю́м

rake гра́бли *pl.*

rally сбор, съезд; соб(и)ра́ть(ся); **~ round** спла́чивать(ся) [сплоти́ть(ся)] вокру́г (P)

ram *zo.* бара́н

ramble броди́ть, прогу́ливаться

ramp *mot., etc.* па́ндус; **~art** вал

ranch фе́рма (скотово́да), ра́нчо

random вы́бранный наугад *or* произво́льно; **at ~** наугад

range (*row*) ряд; (*scope*) диапазо́н; ста́вить в ряд; (*extend*) простира́ться; **mountain ~** го́рный хребе́т; **shooting ~** тир, стре́льбище

rank ранг; *mil.* (*line*) шере́нга, (*grade*) зва́ние, чин; **~ high** занима́ть ви́дное ме́сто

rape [изнаси́ловать; изнаси́лование

rapid бы́стрый, ско́рый; *pl. geogr.* поро́ги *m/pl.*

rapt восхищённый; **~ure** восхище́ние

rare ре́дкий; (*air*) разрежённый; **~ity** ре́дкость *f*; (*thing*) рарите́т

rascal подле́ц; (*child*) плути́шка

rash опроме́тчивый; **~ness** опроме́тчивость *f*

rasp (*tool*) ра́шпиль *m*; **~berry, ~ies** мали́на; *attr.* мали́новый

rat кры́са

rate (*speed*) ско́рость; **birth** ~ рожда́емость *f*; **~ of exchange** валю́тный курс; **~ of profit** но́рма при́были

rather скоре́е, предпочти́тельно; (*somewhat*) дово́льно; **~!** коне́чно, да!

ratif|ication ратифика́ция; **~y** ратифици́ровать (*im*)*pf.*

rating (*popularity*) рейтинг

ratio *math.* отноше́ние; **~n** паёк; **~n card** продово́льственная ка́рточка; **~nal** рациона́льный; (*person*) рассу́дочный

rattle *v/i.* дребезжа́ть; *v/t.* греме́ть (Т); (*toy*) погрему́шка

ravage опустоша́ть [-ши́ть]; опустоше́ние

rave бре́дить (**about** П); (*angrily*) неи́стовствовать

raven во́рон

ravine уще́лье

raw сыро́й; (*unwrought*) необрабо́танный; **~ material** сырьё

ray луч

rayon иску́сственный шёлк, виско́за

razor бри́тва; **electric** ~ электробри́тва; **~-blade** ле́звие

reach (*stretch out*) протя́гивать(ся) [-яну́ть(ся)]; **peak** достига́ть ['-гнуть *or* -и́чь]; (*travelling*) доезжа́ть [-е́хать] до (Р), (*on foot*) доходи́ть [дойти́] до (Р); **~ an agreement** приходи́ть [-ийти́] к соглаше́нию; **within** ~ в преде́лах досяга́емости

react реаги́ровать; **~ion** реа́кция; **~ionary** реакцио́нный; реакционе́р; **~or** реа́ктор

read [про]чита́ть [прочте́сть]; **~er** чита́тель (-ница *f*) *m*; **~ing** чте́ние; **~ing-room** чита́льный зал

read|iness гото́вность *f*; **~ily** охо́тно; **~y** гото́вый; **~ money** нали́чные де́ньги; **~-made** **~y-made clothes** гото́вая оде́жда

real действи́тельный, реа́льный; (*genuine*) настоя́щий; **~ coffee** натура́льный ко́фе; **~istic** реа́льный; *art.* реалисти́ческий; **~ity** действи́тельность *f*; **~ization** осуществле́ние; **~ize** осуществля́ть [-ви́ть]; (*become aware*) осозн(ав)а́ть

realm *fig.* о́бласть *f*

reap [с]жать; *fig.* пож(ин)а́ть

rear за́дняя сторона́, *attr.* за́дний; *mil.* тыл

reason причи́на; (*argument*) до́вод; (*common sense*) ра́зум; **for this** ~ по э́той причи́не; ~**able** разу́мный; (*moderate*) уме́ренный; ~**ing** рассужде́ние

reassure успока́ивать [-ко́ить]

rebel бунтова́ть [взбунтова́ться]; повста́нец; ~**lion** бунт, восста́ние

rebuff отпо́р; дава́ть отпо́р (Д)

rebuke вы́говор, упрёк; де́лать вы́говор (Д)

recall (*remember*) вспомина́ть ['-мнить]; *envoy* отзыва́ть [отозва́ть]; *order* отменя́ть [-ни́ть]; отзы́в; отме́на

recei|pt (*receiving*) получе́ние; *fin.* квита́нция, распи́ска; *pl.* де́нежные поступле́ния *n/pl.*; ~**ve** получа́ть [-чи́ть]; *visitor* принима́ть [-ня́ть]; *idea* воспринима́ть [-ня́ть]; ~**ver** получа́тель *m*; (*телефо́нная*) тру́бка; (*radio*) (ра́дио-)приёмник

recent неда́вний; ~**ly** неда́вно

reception (*social*) приём; (*hotel, hospital*) регистрату́ра (*a.* ~ **desk**)

recess переры́в; (*parliament*) кани́кулы; *arch.* ни́ша; *pl. fig.* глубины́ *f/pl.*; ~**ion** *econ.* спад

recipe *cul.* реце́пт

recital подро́бный расска́з; *mus.* со́льный кон-

це́рт

reckless безрассу́дный; ~ **driving** лиха́чество (води́теля)

reckon счита́ть *impf.*; ~ **upon** рассчи́тывать на (В); ~ **with** [по]счита́ться с (Т)

reclaim заб(и)ра́ть обра́тно; *neglected land* реку́льтиви́ровать [В]

recline полулежа́ть

recogni|tion (*realization*) осозна́ние; (*acknowledgment*) призна́ние; ~**ze** (*identify*) узн(ав)а́ть; созна(ва́)ть; призн(ав)а́ть

recoil отпря́нуть *pf.*

recollect вспомина́ть ['-мнить]; ~**ion** воспомина́ние

recommend [по]рекомендова́ть; ~**ation** рекоменда́ция

recompense вознагражда́ть [-ради́ть]; вознагражде́ние

reconcile примиря́ть [-ри́ть]

reconnaissance разве́дка

reconsider пересма́тривать [-мотре́ть]

reconstruct реконструи́ровать (*im*)*pf.*; ~**ion** реконстру́кция

record запи́сывать [-са́ть], за́пись *f*; (*disk*) пласти́нка; (*sports*) реко́рд; *attr.* реко́рдный; ~**ing** за́пись

recourse: *have ~ to* прибегáть к пóмощи (P)

recover *v/t.* получáть обрáтно, *debt* взыскивать [-кáть]; *v/i. med., fin.* выздорáвливать ['-здороветь]; **~y** выздоровлéние; **~y of damages** *jur.* возмещéние убытков

recreation развлечéние

recruit *mil. approx.* призывник; *soldiers, workers* наб(и)рáть

rectangle прямоугóльник

rectify исправля́ть ['-вить]

recycling перерабóтка вторичного сырья́

red крáсный; ⌀ **Cross** крáсный крест; **~ tape** волокита; **~dish** краснóватый

redeem *goods* выкупáть [выкупить]; **~ption** *eccl.* искуплéние

reduce сокращáть [-ратить]; *price* снижáть [снизить]; (*to tears*) доводить [-вести] до (P); **~tion** сокращéние; снижéние; (*amount*) скидка

reed тростник

reef риф

reel катушка; намáтывать [-мотáть]; (*stagger*) шатáться

refer *v/t.* (*direct*) направля́ть ['-вить]; *v/i.* in *statement*) ссылáться [сослáться] (**to** на B); (*for information*) посмотрéть (**to**

в П); **~ee** (*sports*) судья́ *m*; **~ence** ссылка; спрáвка; (*mention*) упоминáние; (*testimonial*) характеристика; **~ence book** спрáвочник

refine (*sugar*) рафинировать (*im*)*pf.*; (*oil*) очищáть [-истить]; **~ment** *fig.* утончённость *f*; **~ry** (*oil*) нефтеперерабáтывающий завóд

reflect отражáть [отразить]; (*meditate*) размышля́ть (**on** о П); **~ion** отражéние; размышлéние

reform реформировать (*im*)*pf.*; (*morally*) исправля́ть(ся) ['-вить(ся)]; рефóрма; **~er** реформáтор

refrain[1] воздéрживаться [-жáться] (**from** от P)

refrain[2] *mus.* припéв, рефрéн

refresh освежáть [-жить]; **~ o.s.** (*by food, drink*) подкрепля́ться [-питься]; **~ing** освежительный; **~ment** едá

refrigerator холодильник; (*on boat, etc.*) рефрижерáтор

refuel заправля́ться ['-виться]

refuge убéжище; **~e** бéженец, -ка

refusal откáз; **~e** *help, visa* откáзывать [-зáть] в (П); (*to do*) откáзываться [-зáться] + *inf.*

refut|ation опроверже́ние;
~**e** опроверга́ть ['-гнуть]

regard (esteem) уваже́ние;
(consideration) внима́ние;
pl. приве́т; ~**s** что каса́ется
(В); **as ~s** что каса́ется
(Р); **with due ~ for** с
до́лжным учётом (Р)

regardless несмотря́ (**of** на
В), незави́симо (**of** от Р)

reg|ent ре́гент; ~**ime** ре-
жи́м; ~**iment** полк

region о́бласть f, регио́н;
~**al** областно́й

regist|er реги́стр (a. mus.),
рее́стр; [за]регистри́ро-
вать; ~**ered letter** зака́з-
но́е письмо́; ~**ration** реги-
стра́ция

regret сожале́ть; сожале́-
ние; ~**able** приско́рбный

regula|r регуля́рный (a.
mil.); (features) пра́виль-
ный; (customer) постоя́н-
ный; ~**rity** регуля́рность
f; ~**te** регули́ровать
(im)pf.; ~**tion** регули́рова-
ние; pl. пра́вила n/pl., mil.
уста́в

rehabilitation jur. реабили-
та́ция (a. med.)

rehears|al thea. репети́ция;
~**e** [про]репети́ровать

reign ца́рствование; ца́р-
ствовать, fig. a. цари́ть

rein по́вод, узда́ (a. fig.);
~**deer** се́верный оле́нь m

reinforce подкрепля́ть
[-пи́ть]; ~**ment** подкрепле́-

reject (goods) брак; отвер-
га́ть ['-гнуть]; ~**ion** отка́з;
(goods) брако́вка

rejoice [об]ра́довать(ся)

relapse med., jur. рециди́в

relat|e (tell) расска́зывать
[-за́ть]; (connect) соотно-
си́ть(ся), свя́зать ['-зы-
вать]; (concern) отно-
си́ться; ~**ed** (connected)
свя́занный; состоя́щий в
родстве́; ~**ion** отноше́ние,
связь f; (a. connected)
~**ionship** родство́; ~**ive**
(notion) относи́тель-
ный (a. gr.); (comparative)
сравни́тельный; su.
ро́дственни|к, -ца

relax tension: осла́бе(ва́)ть;
person: отдыха́ть [-дох-
ну́ть]; ~**ation** осла́бле́ние;
о́тдых

release (free) освобожда́ть
[-боди́ть]; film выпуска́ть
[вы́пустить]; освобожде́-
ние; вы́пуск

relent смягча́ться [-чи́ться]

relevant относя́щийся к
чему́-либо, уме́стный

reliab|ility надёжность f;
~**le** надёжный

relic eccl. рели́квия

relief[1] arch. релье́ф

relie|f[2] облегче́ние; (aid)
по́мощь f; (next shift)
сме́на; (help) посо́бие;
~**ve** облегча́ть [-чи́ть];
сменя́ть [-ни́ть]

religio|n рели́гия; ~**us** ре-
лиги́озный

relinquish (hope, etc.) оставля́ть ['-вить]; (*rights, etc.*) уступа́ть [-пи́ть]

reluctan|ce нежела́ние; **~tly** неохо́тно

rely: **~ upon** полага́ться [-ложи́ться] на (В)

remain ост(ав)а́ться; **~der** оста́ток; (*people*) остальны́е *pl*; **~s** оста́нки *m/pl*

remark замеча́ние; замеча́ть [-ме́тить]; **~able** замеча́тельный

remedy сре́дство; *situation* исправля́ть ['-вить]

remember по́мнить, вспомина́ть ['-мнить]; **~rance** па́мять *f*; (*gift*) пода́рок на па́мять

remind напомина́ть ['-мнить]; *of* В, о П); **~er** напомина́ние

remit пересы(ла́ть, *money* переводи́ть [-вести́]; **~tance** пересы́лка, де́нежный перево́д

remnant оста́ток

remorse угрызе́ния со́вести

remote отдалённый; **~ control** дистанцио́нное управле́ние

remov|al удале́ние, устране́ние; (*change of place*) перее́зд; **~e** удаля́ть [-ли́ть], устраня́ть [-ни́ть]; переезжа́ть [перее́хать]

Renaissance эпо́ха Возрожде́ния, Ренесса́нс

rend разрыва́ть(ся) [разорва́ть(ся)]

render difficult [с]де́лать (тру́дным); *help*, *service* ока́зывать [-за́ть]; *comm.* **~ an account** представля́ть ['-вить] счёт

renew возобновля́ть [-ви́ть]; *contract* продлева́ть [-ли́ть]; **~al** возобновле́ние

renown сла́ва, изве́стность

rent[1] (*tear*) дыра́, проре́ха

rent[2] (*flat*) кварти́рная пла́та; (*office, etc.*) аре́ндная пла́та

repa|ir ремо́нт, почи́нка; [от]ремонти́ровать, [по]чини́ть; **~ration** возмеще́ние; *pol.* репара́ция

repay *money* возвраща́ть [-рати́ть]

repeal отменя́ть [-ни́ть]; отме́на

repeat повторя́ть [-ри́ть]; **~ed** *adj.* многокра́тный

repel отта́лкивать [оттолкну́ть]; *attack* отража́ть [-рази́ть]

repent раска́иваться [-ка́яться]; **~ance** раска́яние

repetition повторе́ние

replace заменя́ть [-ни́ть], замеща́ть [-ести́ть]; (*put back*) ста́вить обра́тно; **~ment** заме́на, замеще́ние

report отчёт, докла́д; (*account*) сообще́ние; сообща́ть [-щи́ть]; докла́дывать [доложи́ть]; **~er** (*press*) репортёр

represent (*show, describe*) представля́ть ['-вить]; (*depict*) изобража́ть [-ази́ть]; (*stand for*) представля́ть собо́й; **∼ation** представи́тельство; (*art*) изображе́ние; **∼ative** представи́тель *m* (*a. comm.*); *adj.* (*typical*) характе́рный

repress подавля́ть [-ви́ть]; **∼ion** подавле́ние

reprimand вы́говор; де́лать вы́говор [-ить]

reprint перепеча́тка

reproach укоря́ть [-ри́ть] (*for* в П); укор; **∼ful** укори́зненный

reproduc|e воспроизводи́ть [-вести́]; **∼tion** воспроизведе́ние; *art.* репроду́кция

reproof упрёк

reptile пресмыка́ющееся

republic респу́блика; **∼an** республика́нец; республика́нский

repuls|e *mil., fig.* отпо́р; дава́ть отпо́р [-разить]; *attack* отража́ть [-рази́ть]; **∼ive** отта́лкивающий

reputation репута́ция

request про́сьба; [по]проси́ть (о П); **at his ∼** по его́ про́сьбе; **on ∼** по тре́бованию; **∼ programme** конце́рт по зая́вкам

require [по]тре́бовать (P); **∼ment** тре́бование; (*need*) потре́бность *f*

requisit|e *adj.* тре́буемый; **∼ion** реквизи́ция

rescue спасе́ние; спаса́ть [-сти́]

research иссле́дование; *attr.* иссле́довательский

resembl|ance схо́дство; **∼e** походи́ть *or* быть похо́жим (на В)

resent обижа́ться [оби́деться] (на В); **∼ment** чу́вство оби́ды, возмуще́ние

reservation (*mental*) огово́рка; (*Indian*) резерва́ция; **∼e** запа́с, *mil. a.* резе́рв; (*nature*) запове́дник; (*reticence*) за́мкнутость *f*; *table in restaurant, ticket* зака́зывать [-за́ть]; *room, ticket* (за)брони́ровать

reside прожива́ть; **∼nce** (*place of*) местожи́тельство; (*house*) дом; (*official*) резиде́нция; **∼nt** прожива́ющий; *su.* жи́тель(ница *f*) *m*

resign (*retire*) уходи́ть в отста́вку; **∼ o.s.** смиря́ться [-ри́ться] (*to* с Т); **∼ation** отста́вка; смире́ние

resin *chem., bot.* смола́

resist сопротивля́ться (Д); **∼ance** сопротивле́ние

resolu|te реши́тельный; **∼tion** (*formal decision*) реше́ние, резолю́ция; (*firmness*) реши́мость *f*; **∼ve** реша́ть [-ши́ть]

resort (*health*) куро́рт; **∼ to** прибега́ть [-гну́ть] к (Д); **in the last ∼** в кра́йнем случае

resound звучать; (echo) вторить (Д); ~ **with** оглашаться [огласиться] (Т)

resource (wealth, goods) mst. pl. ресурсы m/pl.; запасы m/pl.; (means of comfort) утешение; (skill) находчивость f; ~ful находчивый

respect уважение; **in every** ~ во всех отношениях; ~**able** (person) порядочный (a. fairly good); ~**ful** почтительный; ~**ive** соответственный

respiration дыхание

respite передышка; jur. отсрочка

respond отвечать [-етить], fig. отзываться [отозваться], (pro)реагировать (**to** на В); ~**se** ответ; ответная реакция; ~**sibility** ответственность f; ответственность f; ~**sible** ответственный; ~**sive** отзывчивый

rest[1] остальное, остаток; (people) остальные pl.

rest[2] (from work) отдых; (peace) покой; mus. пауза; отдыхать [-дохнуть]; (lean) прислоняться [-ниться] (**against** к Д); ~ **upon** опираться [опереться] на (В)

restaurant ресторан

restless неспокойный, неугомонный

restoration (health, rights)

восстановление; art, pol. реставрация; ~**e** восстанавливать [-новить]; реставрировать (im)pf.

restrain сдерживать [-жать]; ~**t** сдержанность f

restrict ограничи(ва)ть; ~**ion** ограничение

result результат; ~ **from** являться [явиться] следствием (Р); ~ **in** приводить [-вести] к (Д)

resume возобновлять [-вить]

resurrection воскресение

retail розничная продажа; ~ **price** розничная цена; v. продавать в розницу

retain удерживать [-жать] (в памяти **in mind**); interest сохранять [-нить]

retaliate отплачивать тем же; ~**ion** возмездие

retard замедлять [-лить]; ~**ed**: (mentally) ~**ed child** умственно отсталый ребёнок

reticence неразговорчивость f; ~**t** неразговорчивый

retinue сопровождающие лица, свита

retire (from office) уходить в отставку; (because of age) уходить [уйти] на пенсию; (seclude o.s.) уединяться [-ниться]; Q mil. отставной; находящийся на пенсии; ~**men**

отста́вка; ухо́д на пе́нсию; **_ment age** пенсио́нный во́зраст

retort отвеча́ть [-ве́тить]; (ре́зко) возража́ть [-рази́ть]; отве́т; ре́зкое возраже́ние

retreat отступа́ть [-пи́ть]; отступле́ние; (*walk away*) удаля́ться [-ли́ться]

return возвраща́ть(ся) [-врати́ть(ся)], *pf. a.* верну́ть(ся); возвраще́ние; (*money*) возвра́т; *pl.* дохо́д(ы); _ **ticket** обра́тный биле́т; **tax _** нало́говая декла́рация

reunion воссоедине́ние; *meeting* встре́ча

reveal обнару́жи(ва)ть

revelation *fig.* открове́ние; (*something secret*) разоблаче́ние

revenge месть *f*; [ото]мсти́ть (*for* за В); **_ o.s. on** [ото]мсти́ть (Д)

revenue дохо́д(ы)

revere благогове́ть пе́ред (Т); **_nce** благогове́ние; **_nt** почти́тельный; благогове́йный

reverse (*motion*) обра́тный; *su.* (*side*) обра́тная *or* оборо́тная сторона́ (*a. fig.*); (*opposite*) противополо́жное; **_t** возвраща́ться [-врати́ться]

review (*study again*) пере-

смотре́ть [-смотре́ть]; *book* [про]рецензи́ровать; *text* перераба́тывать [-бо́тать]; обзо́р; (*journal*) обозре́ние; реце́нзия

revis|ed (*edition*) испра́вленный; **_ion** пересмо́тр; (*text*) перерабо́тка; испра́вленное изда́ние

reviv|al оживле́ние; (*art*) возрожде́ние; **_e** *v/t. person* приводи́ть в чу́вство; *trade* оживля́ть [-ви́ть]; *v/i.* приходи́ть в чу́вство, *fig.* ожи(ва́)ть

revol|t восста(ва́)ть; восста́ние; **_ting** отврати́тельный; **_ution** револю́ция; *tech.* враще́ние; (*one turn*) оборо́т; **_utionary** революцио́нный; *su.* револю́ция, революционе́р; **_ve** враща́ть(ся); **_ver** револьве́р

reward награ́да; награжда́ть [-ради́ть]

rheumatism ревмати́зм

rhinoceros носоро́г

rhubarb реве́нь *m*

rhyme ри́фма; рифмова́ть(ся)

rhythm ритм

rib ребро́

ribbon ле́нта

rich бога́тый; (*harvest*) оби́льный; (*cake*) сдо́бный; **_es** бога́тство

rid: get _ of отде́л(ыва)ться от (Р)

riddle зага́дка

ride е́здить, [по]е́хать (*on horseback* верхо́м); (верхова́я) езда́; ~r вса́дник

ridge geogr. гряда́, хребе́т; (*roof*) конёк

ridicul|e высме́ивать [вы́-смеять]; ~ous смешно́й, неле́пый

rifle винто́вка

rift тре́щина; разры́в (*a. fig.*); geol. разло́м

rig (*oil*) бурова́я (вы́шка)

right (*correct*) пра́вильный; (~-*hand*) пра́вый; *adv.* пра́вильно, (*straight*) пря́мо; *su.* пра́во; **all** ~! ла́дно!; *put* ~ (*correct*) исправля́ть ['-вить]; (*order*) навести́ поря́док; *to the* ~ напра́во, спра́ва; ~ *away* неме́дленно, сейча́с (*of* то P); *you are* ~ вы пра́вы, ты прав(а́); ~ful зако́нный

rigorous (*control, etc.*) стро́гий; (*severe*) суро́вый

rim о́бод, ободо́к; (*glasses*) опра́ва

rind (*fruit*) кожура́; ко́рка (*cheese*)

ring¹ кольцо́; (*boxing*) ринг; *wedding* ~ обруча́льное кольцо́

ring² (*bells*) звон; (*telephone, door*) звоно́к; [по]звони́ть; *words*: звуча́ть

rinse [вы́]полоска́ть

riot волне́ния *pl.*

rip (*tear*) [по]рва́ть; проре́ха; ~ *off* сдира́ть [содра́ть]

ripe зре́лый (*a. fig.*), спе́лый; ~*n v/i.* зреть, поспе́(ва́)ть; *mst. fig.* созре́(ва́)ть

ripple (*on water*) рябь *f*; (*sound*) журча́ние; *v/t.* покры́(ва́)ться ря́бью; *v/i.* журча́ть

rise поднима́ться [-ня́ться]; (*stand up*) встá(ва́)ть; *price*: повыша́ться [-ы́ситься]; *sun*: восходи́ть [взойти́]; подъём; повыше́ние; восхо́д

risk риск, рискова́ть [-кну́ть] (T); ~y риско́ванный

rite обря́д

rival сопе́рни|к, -ца; (*competitor*) конкуре́нт; *v.* сопе́рничать; ~ry сопе́рничество

river река́; *attr.* речно́й

rivet заклёпка

road доро́га; *dirt* ~ грунтова́я доро́га; ~-block доро́жное загражде́ние; ~map ка́рта автомоби́льных доро́г; ~side *attr.* придоро́жный; ~way прое́зжая часть

roam броди́ть

roar *storm, lion*: реве́ть; *cannon*: грохота́ть; рёв, гро́хот; ~ *with laughter* пока́тываться от хо́хота

roast [из]жа́рить(ся); *su.* жарко́е; *attr.* жа́реный

rob [у]кра́сть; *shop* [о]гра́бить; ~ber граби́тель *m*;

~bery грабёж

robe (*bath*~) хала́т

robot ро́бот

robust кре́пкий, здоро́вый

rock¹ скала́; *min.* го́рная поро́да

rock² скали́стый

rocket раке́та; *attr.* раке́тный

rocking-chair (кре́сло-)кача́лка

rod прут; (*fishing*) уди́лище

roe¹ (*deer*) косу́ля

roe² (*fish*) икра́; (*soft*) моло́ки *pl.*

rogue моше́нник; *little* ~ плути́шка *m*

roll (*paper, cloth*) руло́н; *cul.* бу́лочка; ката́ть(ся), [по]кати́ть(ся); ~ *up* свёртывать(ся); ~**er** (*cylinder*) ва́лик; (*wheel*) ро́лик; ~**ing-mill** прока́тный стан; ~**ing-pin** ска́лка

Rom|**an**: ~*an numeral* ри́мская ци́фра; ²**ance** (*poem, love affair*) рома́н; (*mood*) рома́нтика; ²**antic** романти́чный

romp *v.* резви́ться, шали́ть

roof кры́ша; ~**rack** *mot.* бага́жник

rook *zo.* грач; (*chess*) ладья́

room ко́мната; (*space* ме́сто; (*elbow-*~) просто́р; *waiting* ~ (*rail.*) зал ожида́ния; (*doctor's, etc.*) при-

ёмная; ~**y** просто́рный

root ко́рень *m* (*a. fig.*); (**deep-**)~**ed** укорени́вшийся

rope верёвка, (*thick*) кана́т; свя́зывать [-за́ть] верёвкой

rose ро́за

roster: *duty* ~ расписа́ние дежу́рств

rosy ро́зовый; (*cheeks*) румя́ный

rot [c]гни́ть; гние́ние

rotate враща́ть(ся), ~**ion** враще́ние

rotten гнило́й; (*eggs, meat*) тухлый; *coll.* дрянно́й

rouble рубль *m*

rouge румя́на *n/pl.*

rough (*surface*) шерша́вый; (*manners*) гру́бый; (*sea*) бу́рный; (*weather*) нена́стный; (*sketch*) чернови́й; (*estimate*) приблизи́тельный

round кру́глый; округля́ть [-ли́ть]; *prep.* вокру́г (*P*); *adv.* круго́м; *su.* (*duties*) круг; (*doctor's*) обхо́д; (*sports*) тур, (*boxing*) ра́унд; (*talks*) эта́п, тур; ~**about** *Am.* кольцева́я тра́нспортная развя́зка; *Brit.* карусе́ль

rouse [раз]буди́ть; *fig.* возбужда́ть [-буди́ть]

route маршру́т; ~**ine** режи́м, поря́док; *attr.* обы́чный

rove броди́ть

row[1] (*quarrel*) ссóра
row[2] (*line*) ряд
row[3] (*sports*) *v/i.* грести́;
_ing гребля́; _ing boat
гребна́я ло́дка
rowan *bot.* ряби́на
royal короле́вский; _ty
член короле́вской семьи́;
(*author*) *pl.* гонора́р
rub тере́ть; (*massage*) рас-
тира́ть [-тере́ть]; _ in вти-
ра́ть [втере́ть]; _ off or
out стира́ть(ся); _ber ре-
зи́на; (*eraser*) рези́нка;
_bish хлам; *coll.* чепуха́
ruby руби́н; *attr.* руби́но-
вый
rudder руль *m*
rude гру́бый; _ness гру́-
бость *f*
rudiment рудиме́нт; *pl. fig.*
осно́вы *f/pl.*; _ary *fig.*
рудимента́рный; *fig.* элемен-
та́рный
ruffian хулига́н
rug ковёр, (*small*) ко́врик
ruin (*fall*) ги́бель *f*; (*wreck,
debris*) руи́ны *f/pl.*; *comm.*
разоре́ние; [по]губи́ть;
разоря́ть [-ри́ть]; _ous гу-
би́тельный; разори́тельный
rul|e пра́вило; *pol.* власть;
as a _e как пра́вило; _e
out исключа́ть [-чи́ть]; *v.*
госпо́дствовать; _er пра-
ви́тель *m*; (*tool*) лине́йка;
_ing *adj.* госпо́дству-
ющий; *su.* постановле́ние
Rumanian румы́н(ка);

-ский
rumble громыха́ть; громы-
ха́ние
rummage *drawer* [по]ры́ть-
ся (в П)
rumour слух, молва́; *it is
_ed* хо́дят слу́хи
run *v/i.* бе́гать, [по]бежа́ть;
fluid: течь; *machine:* ра-
бо́тать; *train:* ходи́ть; *text:*
гласи́ть; *v/t. of-
fice* управля́ть (Т); *firm*
возглавля́ть (В); *distance*
пробега́ть [-ежа́ть]; *su.*
бег, пробе́г; _ across
(*meet*) случа́йно встре́-
тить; _ away убега́ть
[-ежа́ть]; _ over pedes-
trian задави́ть, сбить *pf.*;
_ out supply: истоща́ться
[-щи́ться]; _away бегле́ц;
_ner (*sports*) бегу́н(ья);
_ning (*account, water*) те-
ку́щий; (*in a row*) подря́д;
su. бег; (*here and there*)
беготня́; _ning: _ning water водопрово́д; _way
взлётно-поса́дочная поло-
са́
rural се́льский
rush *v.* мча́ть(ся); (*hurry*)
торопи́ть(ся); *v.* (*haste*)
спе́шка; (*customers*) на-
плы́в; _ hour(s) час(ы́)
пик; _ order сро́чный за-
ка́з
Russian *su., adj.* ру́сский;
(*language*) ру́сский язы́к;
speak _ говори́ть по-
ру́сски

rust ржа́вчина; заржаве́ть
rustic дереве́нский
rustle ше́лест; шелесте́ть

rut колея́ (*a. fig.*)
ruthless безжа́лостный
rye рожь *f; attr.* ржано́й

S

sabbatical *univ.* академи́ческий о́тпуск преподава́теля
sable со́боль *m;* (*fur*) собо́лий мех
sabotage сабота́ж; саботи́ровать (*im*)*pf.*
sack мешо́к
sacr|ament та́инство; **~ed** свято́й; (*writings*) свяще́нный; **~ifice** же́ртва; [по]же́ртвовать (Т)
sad печа́льный, гру́стный; *be or feel* ~ грусти́ть; **~den** огорчи́ть(ся)
saddle седло́; [о]седла́ть
sadness печа́ль *f,* грусть *f*
safe безопа́сный; (*unharmed*) невреди́мый; (*dependable*) надёжный; *n.* сейф; **~guard** *fig.* гара́нтия; **~ty** безопа́сность *f;* невреди́мость *f;* **~ty belt** *mot., an.* пристяжно́й реме́нь; **~ty pin** англи́йская була́вка; **~ty razor** безопа́сная бри́тва; **~ty valve** предохрани́тельный кла́пан
sag (*droop*) обвиса́ть ['-снуть]; (*sink*) провиса́ть ['-снуть]
sagacious прозорли́вый

sail па́рус; пла́вать, [по]плы́ть (под паруса́ми); **~ing** морепла́вание; па́русный спорт; **~ing-boat** па́русная ло́дка; **~or** моря́к, матро́с
saint свято́й (*a. su.*)
sake: *for the* ~ *of* ра́ди (Р)
salad сала́т
salary зарабо́тная пла́та, окла́д
sale прода́жа; *for* ~ продаётся; *on* ~ в прода́же; *clearance* ~ распрода́жа; **~s(wo)man** продаве́ц, -щи́ца
saliva слюна́
salmon ло́сось *m; cul.* лососи́на
salon: *beauty* ~ космети́ческий кабине́т
salt соль *f; attr.* соляно́й; **~-cellar** соло́нка; **~y** солёный
salut|ation приве́тствие; **~e** [по]приве́тствовать; *artillery:* салю́т
salvage *mar.* спасе́ние, (*cargo*) спасённый груз; *v.* спаса́ть [-сти́]; **~tion** (*a. eccl.*) спасе́ние
same тот же (са́мый); (*same kind*) тако́й же; *the*

~ **thing** то же са́мое, одно́ и то же; **all the** ~ безразли́чно; (*nevertheless*) всё--таки

sample образе́ц (*water, etc.*) про́ба; [по]про́бовать

sanatorium санато́рий

sanct|ify освяща́ть [-яти́ть]; **~ion** согла́сие, разреше́ние, (*official*) са́нкция; разреши́ть [-ши́ть], санкциони́ровать (*im*)*pf*; **~uary** (*place of safety*) убе́жище; (*animals, birds*) запове́дник

sand песо́к

sandwich бутербро́д

sanit|ary санита́рный; **~y** ра́зум; (*judgement*) здра́вомы́слие

Santa: ~ **Claus** Дед-моро́з

sap *bot.* сок; **~ling** молодо́е де́рево

sarcastic саркасти́ческий

sardine сарди́на

sash (*garment*) куша́к

satellite спу́тник; **~ communications** спу́тник свя́зи

satin атла́с

satire сати́ра

satis|faction удовлетворе́ние; **~factory** удовлетвори́тельный; **~fied** *adj.* дово́льный; (*convinced*) убеждённый; **~fy** удовлетворя́ть [-ри́ть]

saturate (*soak*) пропи́тывать [-та́ть]; *market* насыща́ть [-ы́тить]

Saturday суббо́та

sauce со́ус, подли́вка; **~pan** кастрю́ля; **~r** блю́дце; **flying** ~ лета́ющая таре́лка

sausage колбаса́, (*frankfurter*) сосиска

savage ди́кий; (*ferocious*) свире́пый

save спаса́ть [-сти́]; *money, strength* сберега́ть [-ре́чь]; **~ings** сбереже́ния *n/pl.*; **~ings-bank** сберка́сса = сберега́тельная ка́сса; **~iour** спаси́тель *m*

savour пика́нтность *f*, (*taste*) вкус; *v/i. mst. fig.* отдава́ть *or* па́хнуть (*of* Т); **~y** пика́нтный, вку́сный

saw пила́; **~dust** опи́лки *f/pl.*; **~mill** лесопи́лка

say говори́ть [сказа́ть]; **he ~s** он говори́т; **he said** он сказа́л; **I dare ~** (вполне́ возмо́жно; **I should ~ so!** ещё бы!; **that is to ~** то́ есть; (*frequent*) погово́рка; **it goes without ~ing** само́ собо́й разуме́ется

scaffolding строи́тельные леса́ *m/pl.*

scald обва́ривать [-ри́ть]; (*injury*) ожо́г

scale[1] (*thermometer, wages*) шкала́; (*map*) масшта́б (*a. fig.*); *pl.* (= *balance*) весы́ *m/pl.*; **on a large** ~ в больши́х масшта́бах (*a.* в больши́х масшта́бах)

scale[2] *zo.* чешуя́; (*in boiler*)

на́кипь f; ~ **off** v/i. шелуши́ться

scandal сканда́л, позо́р; (gossip) спле́тня; ~**ous** сканда́льный, позо́рный

Scandinavian скандина́в(ка); -ский

scant, ~**y** ску́дный

scar рубе́ц, шрам; v/i. рубцева́ться

scarc|e (goods) дефици́тный; (rare) ре́дкий; ~**ely** едва́ ли, вряд ли; ~**ity** нехва́тка; ре́дкость f

scare [ис]пуга́ть; ~**crow** пуга́ло (a. fig.)

scarf шарф; (head) плато́к, косы́нка; (necktie) га́лстук

scarlet adj. а́лый; ~ **fever** скарлати́на

scatter рассе́ивать(ся) [-е́ять(ся)]; (by throwing) разбра́сывать [-броса́ть]

scen|ario сцена́рий; ~**e** (part of play) сце́на; (story) ме́сто де́йствия; **behind the ~es** за кули́сами; ~**ery** пейза́ж; thea. декора́ция f/pl.

scent (smell) за́пах; (sense of smell) нюх; (liquid) духи́ m/pl.; (track) след

sceptical скепти́ческий

schedule (time-table) расписа́ние; (plan) план, гра́фик

scheme прое́кт, план, (plot) интри́га; проекти́ровать [-]

scholar учёный; ~**ship** эруди́ция; (money) стипе́ндия

school шко́ла; attr. шко́льный; ~**book** уче́бник; ~**boy** шко́льник; ~**girl** шко́льница; ~**master** учи́тель; ~**mistress** учи́тельница

scien|ce нау́ка; (natural) естествозна́ние; ~**ce fiction** нау́чная фанта́стика; ~**tific** нау́чный; ~**tist** учёный

scissors но́жницы f/pl.

scold [вы]брани́ть

scoop ковш, черпа́к; (shovel) сово́к; зачёрпывать [-пну́ть]

scooter mot. моторо́ллер

scope (field of action) сфе́ра де́ятельности; **beyond my ~** вне мое́й компете́нции; **give full ~ to** дава́ть просто́р (Д)

scorch v/i. пали́ть; v/t. [с]пали́ть; earth, grass выжига́ть [вы́жечь]

score (count) счёт (a. sports); mus. партиту́ра; **on that ~** по э́тому по́воду; ~ **point** получа́ть [-чи́ть] (очко́); ~ **goal** заби(ва́)ть

scorn презира́ть; ~**ful** презри́тельный

Scot шотла́ндец; ~**ch** шотла́ндский; шотла́ндское ви́ски; ~**ch(wo)man** шотла́нд|ец, -ка; ~**ch tape**

скотч
scoundrel подлец
scourge бич
scout *mil.* разведчик; *(boy)* (бой)скаут
scowl [на]хмуриться; хмурый взгляд
scramble *(fight)* драка, свалка; *v.* драться; *(clamber)* карабкаться; **~d:** **~d eggs** яичница-болтунья
scrap клочок; *(metal, etc.)* утиль *m,* вторичное сырьё; *v.* пускать на слом; **~-iron** железный лом
scratch *v/t.* [о]царапать; *(scribble)* [на]царапать; *itching spot* [по]чесать; *su.* царапина
scream пронзительный крик, вопль *m; v.* пронзительно кричать, вопить
screen ширма; *(film, etc.)* экран
screw винт; *attr.* винтовой; **~ up** завинчивать(ся) [-нтить(ся)]; **~ up one's eyes** щурить глаза; **~-driver** отвёртка
scribble *(hastily)* писать наскоро; *(carelessly)* [на]царапать; каракули *f/pl.*
script *(film)* сценарий; *(play)* текст; 2**ure:** **Holy** 2**ure** Священное писание
scrub *v.* мыть (щёткой)
scrupulous точный, скрупулёзный; *(conscientious)* добросовестный; *(over~)*

щепетильный
sculptor скульптор; **~ure** скульптура; [из]ваять
scythe коса
sea море; *attr.* морской; **on the high ~s** в открытом море; **~-gull** чайка
seal[1] *zo.* тюлень *m, (fur ~)* котик
seal[2] печать *f (a. fig.);* запечатывать [-тать]; **~ing-wax** сургуч
seam шов
seaman моряк
search *house, person* обыскивать [-кать]; обыск; поиски *m/pl.;* **~ for** искать (B); **~light** прожектор
seashore побережье; **~side** взморье; *attr.* приморский
season *(spring, etc.)* время года; *(period)* сезон; *cul.* приправлять ['-вить]; **~ing** приправа; **~-ticket** *(concert, etc.)* сезонный билет; абонемент
seat стул, сиденье; *thea.* место; *(residence)* местопребывание; *hall:* вмещать [вместить]; **take a ~** садиться [сесть]
seaweed морские водоросли *f/pl.*
seclu|de ~de o.s. уединяться [-ниться]; **~sion** уединение
second второй; *su.* секунда; **~ary** вторичный; *(lesser)* второстепенный;

ary _school_ сре́дняя
шко́ла; _-hand_ поде́ржан-
ный; (information) из вто-
ры́х рук; _-ly_ во-вторы́х
secre|cy секре́тность f; _-t_
та́йна, секре́т; та́йный,
секре́тный; _-tary_ секре-
та́р|ша, -ь m; _-tive_ скры́т-
ный
sect се́кта; _-ion_ (part)
часть f; law разде́л, пункт;
(division) отде́л; tech. се-
че́ние; _-ional_ (made of
parts) разбо́рный, сек-
цио́нный; _-or_ се́ктор
secur|e безопа́сный; (so-
cially) обеспе́ченный;
-ity безопа́сность f; (social) обеспе́ченность f;
mil., comm. обеспе́чение;
pl. це́нные бума́ги f/pl.;
-ity _Council_ Сове́т Безо-
па́сности; _social_ _-ity_
социа́льное обеспе́чение
sedative med. успока́ивающее
сре́дство
seduce|e соблазня́ть
[-ни́ть]; _-tion_ собла́зн
see (у)ви́деть; _- to it that_
_..._ [про]следи́ть за тем,
что́бы...; _I ._! понима́ю;
let me .! дай(те) мне
поду́мать; _go to ._ наве-
ща́ть [-ести́ть]; _. s.o._
home провожа́ть домо́й; _._
off провожа́ть [-води́ть];
_- to_ позабо́титься [о Т];
заня́ться [Т]
seed bot. се́мя n; _-ling_ се́-
янец; расса́да collect.

seek (look for) иска́ть (Р);
wealth стреми́ться (к Д);
(to do) [по]стара́ться
seem [по]каза́ться; _-ing_
ка́жущийся; _-ingly_ по-ви́-
димому
seethe v/i. кипе́ть (a. fig.)
seize хвата́ть [схвати́ть]
self: _my own ._ я сам(а́);
my better . со́весть;
-confidence самоуве́рен-
ность f; _-confident_ само-
уве́ренный; _-conscious_
засте́нчивый; _-control_
самооблада́ние; _-em-_
ployed занима́ющийся
индивидуа́льной трудо-
во́й де́ятельностью; _-evi-_
dent очеви́дный; _-ish_ эго-
исти́чный; _-portrait_ ав-
топортре́т; _-service_ са-
мообслу́живание
sell прод(ав)а́ть(ся); _-er_
продаве́ц, торго́вец
semblance подо́бие
semi|circle полукру́г; _-_
colon то́чка с запято́й
senat|e сена́т; _-or_ сена́тор
send пос(ы)ла́ть; _- for_
(doctor, taxi) вызыва́ть
['-звать]; _-er_ отправи́тель
senior ста́рший; _John_
Parker _-_ Джон Па́ркер
ста́рший
sensation сенса́ция; biol.
ощуще́ние; _-al_ сенса-
цио́нный
sens|e (feeling) чу́вство;
(meaning) смысл; ощу-
ща́ть [-ути́ть]; _good ._e_

здра́вый смысл; *in a _e* в како́й-то сте́пени; *man of _e* разу́мный челове́к; _eless бессмы́сленный; _ible *(reasonable)* разу́мный; *(noticeable)* заме́тный; _itive чувстви́тельный, *(person)* чу́ткий; _ual чу́вственный; _uality чу́вственность *f*

sent|ence *gr.* предложе́ние; *jur.* пригово́р; _imental сентимента́льный

sentry часово́й; _ duty карау́льная слу́жба

separa|te отделя́ть(ся) [-ли́ть(ся)]; *(friends)* разлуча́ть(ся) [-чи́ть(ся)]; _tion отделе́ние; разлу́ка

September сентя́брь *m*

septic септи́ческий; _ wound инфици́рованная *or* гно́йная ра́на

seque|l *(consequence)* после́дствие; *(book)* продолже́ние; _nce после́довательность *f*; *(series)* ряд, цикл

sergeant сержа́нт

serial: _ film многосери́йный телефи́льм, сериа́л

series се́рия, ряд

serious серьёзный; _ness серьёзность *f*

sermon про́поведь *f*

serpent змея́

serv|ant слуга́ *m*, служа́нка; *civil _ant* госуда́рственный слу́жащий;

_e [по]служи́ть (Д; *as* Т); *diner, clients* обслу́живать [-йть] (В); *dish* по-да(ва́)ть; _ice слу́жба; обслу́живание, се́рвис; *tech.* техобслу́живание; *(set)* серви́з; *at your _ice* к ва́шим услу́гам; _ice station *mot. Am.* ста́нция техобслу́живания; _iceable практи́чный; про́чный; _iceman военно-слу́жащий

session заседа́ние; *(period)* се́ссия

set [по]ста́вить; *med.* вправля́ть ['-вить]; *jewel* оправля́ть ['-вить]; *sun:* сади́ться [сесть]; *(instruments)* компле́кт; *(dishes)* серви́з; _ *about work* приступа́ть [-пи́ть] к (Д); _ *forth* излага́ть [-ложи́ть]; _ *up* устана́вливать [-нови́ть]

settle *(go and live)* поселя́ться [-ли́ться]; *(in life)* устра́ивать(ся) [-ро́ить(ся)]; *question, quarrel, claim* разреша́ть [-ши́ть]; _ *one's accounts* рассчи́тываться *or* (-ита́ться]; _ment поселе́ние; реше́ние; *fin.* расчёт; _ *r* посе-ле́нец

seven семь; _ *a* (*cards, number of bus, etc.*) семёрка; _teen семна́дцать; _teenth семна́дцатый; _th седьмо́й; _tieth семи-

деся́тый; **~ty** се́мьдесят
several не́сколько (P)
sever|e (strict) стро́гий; (harsh) суро́вый; **~ity** стро́гость f; суро́вость f
sew [c]шить; **~ on** приши́(ва́)ть
sex пол; секс; attr. полово́й; **~ual** полово́й сексуа́льный
shabby потрёпанный, поно́шенный
shad|e тень f; (nuance) отте́нок; (lamp-~) абажу́р; затени́ть [-ни́ть]; drawing [за]штрихова́ть; **~ow** тень f; (twilight) су́мерки f/pl.; затени́ть [-ни́ть]; (follow) следи́ть (за T); **~owy** тени́стый; (dim) сму́тный; **~y** тени́стый; (business) нечи́стый
shaft tech. вал
shaggy лохма́тый
shak|e трясти́(сь); (shock, weaken) потряса́ть [-сти́]; **~e down** [-хну́ть]; **~e off** стря́хивать [-хну́ть]; **~e up** встря́хивать [-хну́ть]; **~y** ша́ткий
shall I ~ say я скажу́; **what ~ I say?** что мне сказа́ть?; **he ~ work** он до́лжен рабо́тать
shallow ме́лкий; fig. пове́рхностный; (shoal) mst. pl. мелково́дье
sham притво́рный; притво́рство; притворя́ться [-ри́ться]

shame стыд; (disgrace) позо́р; [при]стыди́ть; **what a ~ that ...** как жаль, что ...; **~ful** посты́дный; **~less** бессты́дный
shampoo шампу́нь m
shape о́браз, фо́рма; v/t. придава́ть фо́рму (Д); v/i. (develop) развива́ться; **~less** бесфо́рменный; **~ly** хорошо́ сложённый
share до́ля; fin. а́кция; [раз]дели́ть B) or [по]дели́ться (T); **~holder** акционе́р
shark аку́ла
sharp о́стрый; (turn) круто́й; (wind, change, tone) ре́зкий; adv.: **at 3 o'clock ~** то́чно (or ро́вно) в три часа́; **~en** v/t. заостря́ть [-ри́ть], [на]точи́ть
shatter разбива́ть вдре́безги; plans, nerves расстра́ивать [-ро́ить]
shave бритьё; [по]бри́ть(ся); wood строга́ть [-хну́ть]; **~ing** бритьё; attr. бри́твенный; **~ing cream** крем для бритья́; pl. стру́жки f/pl.
shawl шаль f
she она́
shear [о]стри́чь; **~s** (больши́е) но́жницы f/pl.
shed¹ (building) сара́й
shed² tears, blood проли́(ва́)ть; leaves ро́нить mst. impf.
sheep овца́

shorts

sheer абсолютный, сплошной; (*steep*) отвесный; **by ~ chance** по чистой случайности

sheet лист; (*bedding*) простыня; **~ iron** листовое железо

shelf полка

shell (*oyster*) раковина; (*nut, egg*) скорлупа; (*artillery*) снаряд; **~fish** моллюск

shelter (*refuge*) убежище, приют; приютить (В) *pf.*

shepherd пастух

sherry херес

shield щит; (*protect*) защищать [-итить]

shift (*change*) менять(ся); (*move*) перемещать(ся) [-естить(ся)]; перемещение; (*working*) смена; **~work** сменная работа

shilling шиллинг

shin *anat.* голень *f*

shine *v/i. sun:* светить, сиять; (*glitter*) блестеть; *su.* свет, сияние; блеск

shingle (*pebbles*) галька

shiny блестящий

ship судно, корабль *m;* *attr.* судо-, судовой; (*send*) отправлять ['-вить]; **~ment** отгрузка; отправка; (*load*) груз; **~ping** (морские) перевозки *pl.;* (*navigation*) судоходство; **~ping company** судоходная компания; **~wreck** кораблекрушение; **~yard**

verf *f*

shirk: **~ work** прогуливать [-лять]; (*avoid*) уклоняться [-ниться] (от Р)

shirt рубашка

shiver дрожать; дрожь *f*

shock потрясать [-сти]; (*scandalize*) шокировать; потрясение; *med.* шок, нервное потрясение; **~absorber** *mot.* амортизатор, *coll.* ужасный

shoe туфля, (*high*) ботинок; (*horse's*) подкова; **~shop** обувной магазин

shoot стрелять [выстрелить]; (*execute*) расстреливать [-лять]; **~ down plane** сби(ва)ть; **~ing:** **~ing season** охотничий сезон

shop магазин; *tech.* цех; **~assistant** продавец, **-щица;** **~window** витрина; **~ping: go ~ping** делать покупки

shore морской берег

short короткий, (*person*) невысокий; (*brief*) краткий; **for ~** для краткости; **in ~** вкратце; (*summing up*) короче говоря; **~age** недостаток; (*goods*) дефицит; **~en** укорачивать(ся) [-ротить(ся)]; **~hand** стенография; **~ness** краткость *f;* **~-sighted** близорукий; **~-term** краткосрочный

shorts шорты

shot вы́стрел; (*person*) стрело́к

should: *I ~ say* я сказа́л бы; *you ~ go there* вам ну́жно (бы) пойти́ туда́; *you ~ not have gone* вам не ну́жно бы́ло (*or:* не сле́довало) идти́

shoulder плечо́

shout крик; крича́ть; *~ at* [на]крича́ть на (В)

shove сова́ть [су́нуть]; (*push*) толка́ть [-кну́ть]; *~l* сово́к, (*big*) лопа́та

show пока́зывать [-за́ть]; *interest* проявля́ть [-ви́ть]; (*appear*) появля́ться [-ви́ться]; зре́лище, спекта́кль *m*; *comm.* вы́ставка; *~case* витри́на

shower ли́вень *m*; *fig.* град; *(~-bath)* душ

shred клочо́к, лоску́ток

shrill пронзи́тельный

shrimp *zo.* креве́тка

shrine *fig.* святы́ня

shrink *material:* сади́ться [сесть]; *fig.* сокраща́ться [-ати́ться]

shrivel *v/i.* съёжи(ва)ться

shrub (декорати́вный) куст; *~bery* куста́рник (в саду́)

shrug: *~ one's shoulders* пожима́ть плеча́ми

shudder содрога́ться [-гну́ться]; содрога́ние

shuffle *feet* ша́ркать [-кнуть] (Т); *cards* (пере)тасова́ть; ша́рканье

shun избега́ть (Р)

shut закры(ва́)ть(ся), затворя́ть(ся) [-ри́ть(ся)]; *~ter* (*window*) ста́вень *m*; *photo* затво́р

shy засте́нчивый, ро́бкий; *~ness* ро́бость *f*; засте́нчивость *f*

sick больно́й; *I feel ~* меня́ тошни́т; *it makes me ~* меня́ тошни́т от э́того; *~ pay* вы́плата по больни́чному листу́

sickle серп

sickly боле́зненный

sickness боле́знь *f*; (*nausea*) тошнота́

side сторона́, бок; *attr.* боково́й, побо́чный; *~ by ~* бок о́ бок; *from all ~s* со всех сторо́н; *~ with* быть на стороне́ (Р); *~-car* *mot.* коля́ска; *~walk* тротуа́р

siege оса́да

sieve си́то, решето́

sift просе́ивать [-е́ять]

sigh вздыха́ть [вздохну́ть]; вздох

sight (*power*) зре́ние; (*spectacle*) зре́лище, вид; *pl.* достопримеча́тельности *f/pl.*; *catch ~ of* уви́деть *pf.*, *lose ~* потеря́ть и́з виду (*of* В)

sign знак; (*life etc.*) при́знак; (*shop*) вы́веска; *v.* подпи́сывать(ся) [-са́ть(ся)]; *~al* сигна́л; *~ature* по́дпись *f*; *~ification* значе́ние, значи́тельность *f*;

~ify знáчить; **~post** дорóжный указáтель

silen|ce молчáние; (*night*) тишинá; **~t** молчалúвый; тúхий; *be or keep ~t* молчáть

silk шёлк; *attr.* шёлковый; **~y** шелковúстый

sill (*window*) подокóнник; (*door*) порóг

sill|iness глýпость *f;* **~y** глýпый

silver серебрó; *attr.* серéбряный; **[по]**серебрúть**(**ся**)**; **~y** серебрúстый

similar схóдный, схóжий, подóбный; **~ity** схóдство, подóбие

simpl|e простóй; (*food, dress*) скрóмный; (*mind*) простодýшие; **~icity** простотá; **~ify** упрощáть **[**-остúть**]**

simultaneous одновремéнный

sin грех

since *prep.* с (P); *adv.* с тех пор; *conj.* с тех пор, как; (*because*) так как

sincer|e úскренний; **~ity** úскренность *f;* **~ yours ~ely** (*semiformal*) úскренне Ваш, -а, (*formal*) с глубóким уважéнием

sinew сухожúлие; **~y** жúлистый

sing **[**с**]**петь

singe опалúть

sing|er певéц, -úца; **~ing** *su.* пéние

singl|e (*case, fact*) единúчный; (*will*) едúный; (*person*) холостóй, незамýжняя; (*separate*) отдéльный; *not a ~le* ни одúн; **~ular** *gr.* едúнственное числó

sinister зловéщий

sink *v/i. ship:* **[**за**]**тонýть; (*drop*) опускáться **[**-стúться**]**; *sun:* заходúть **[**зайтú**]**; *v/t. ship* (зa-, по)топúть; *kitchen ~* рáковина

sinner грéшни|к, -ца

sir (*title*) сэр; *Dear 2* Сэр; *Dear 2s* уважáемые господá

sirloin филéйная часть

sister сестрá; **~-in-law** (*woman's*) невéстка; (*man's*) своячéница

sit сидéть; **~ down** садúться **[**сесть**]**

site мéсто, местоположéние; *arch.* строúтельная площáдка

situat|ed располóженный; **~ion** (*location*) **(**рас**)**положéние; *fig.* положéние; (*job*) мéсто

six шесть; *a ~* (*cards, number of bus, tram*) шестёрка; **~teen** шестнáдцать; **~teenth** шестнáдцатый; **~th** шестóй; **~tieth** шестидесятый; **~ty** шестьдесят

size величинá; (*shoe, glove*) размéр

skate конёк; ката́ться на конька́х; ~r конькобе́жец

skeleton скеле́т, *tech.* о́стов

sketch (*art*) набро́сок, этю́д, эски́з; де́лать набро́сок (-ся) (Р)

ski лы́жа; ходи́ть на лы́жах

skid *mot.* заноси́ть [-нести́]

ski|er лы́жни|к, -ца; ~ing лы́жный спорт

skil|ful уме́лый; ~l уме́ние, мастерство́; ~led (*worker*) квалифици́рованный

skim *cul.* снима́ть (пе́нку, сли́вки и т. п.) (с Р); ~med milk снято́е молоко́

skin ко́жа; (*hide*) шку́ра; ~diver аквала́нгист

skip *v/i. impf.* скака́ть; пры́гать [-гнуть]; (*omit*) пропуска́ть [-сти́ть]; ~ping rope скака́лка

skipper капита́н

skirmish сты́чка

skirt ю́бка

skull че́реп

sky не́бо; ~-scraper небоскрёб

slab плита́

slack *adj.* (*rope*) сла́бо натя́нутый; (*work, business*) вя́лый; (*behaviour*) расхля́банный

slam *door* хло́пать [-пнуть] (Т)

slander клевета́; ~ous клеве́тнический

slang жарго́н; сленг

slant накло́н; укло́н (*a. fig.*); ~ing накло́нный, косо́й

slap шлепо́к; (*in the face*) пощёчина; шлёпать [-пнуть], хло́пать [-пнуть]

slate *geol.* сла́нец; (*roof*) ши́фер

slaughter забива́ть, [за]ре́зать; *su.* убо́й; *fig.* резня́; ~-house бо́йня

Slav славя́н|ин, '-ка; '-ский

slave раб(ы́ня); ~ry ра́бство

slay убива́ть

sledge са́ни *f/pl.*; (*child's*) са́нки *pl.*; *v/i.* ката́ться на саня́х, '-ках

sleek гла́дкий и блестя́щий

sleep сон; *v.* спать; ~ing-car спа́льный ваго́н; ~less бессо́нный; ~y со́нный, сонли́вый

sleeve рука́в

sleigh са́ни *f/pl.*; ~-bell бубе́нчик

slender (*shapely*) стро́йный; (*thin*) то́нкий

slice ло́мтик, (*bread*) ло́моть *m*; *v.* [на]ре́зать ло́мтиками

slide скользи́ть; скольже́ние; *photo.* слайд

slight лёгкий, незначи́тельный; (*figure*) то́нкий; ~ing *adj.* пренебрежи́тельный; ~ly слегка́

slim стро́йный, то́нкий

slime (*secretion*) слизь *f*

357   **snap**

sling *med.* пе́ревязь *f;*
(*throw*) *v.* швыря́ть
[-рну́ть];
slip (*slide*) скользи́ть [по-
скользну́ться]; (*put
secretly*) всо́вывать [всу́-
нуть]; скольже́ние;
(*tongue*) обмо́лвка; (*pen*)
опи́ска; ~ **on jacket** наки́-
нуть на себя́; ~ **s.o.'s
memory** вы́лететь из голо-
вы; ~**pers** ко́мнатные
ту́фли; ~**pery** ско́льзкий
slogan ло́зунг
slop|e укло́н; *geogr.* отко́с,
косого́р; ~**ing** *adj.* отло́-
гий
slot щель *f*, разре́з; ~ **machine** (*selling*) торго́вый
автома́т; (*amusement*)
игра́льный автома́т
slow ме́дленный; (*dull*) ту-
по́й; *adv.* ме́дленно, ти́хо;
my watch is ~ мои́ часы́
отстаю́т; ~ **down** замед-
ля́ть(ся) ['-ли́ть(ся)];
~**ness** ме́дленность *f*
sluice шлюз
slum трущо́ба *mst. pl.*
slush сля́коть *f*
sly хи́трый
small ма́ленький, неболь-
шо́й; (~-*scale*) ме́лкий;
(~-*minded*) ме́лочный
smart *wound:* боле́ть; боль
f; adj. (*dress*) элега́нтный,
наря́дный; (*clever*) у́м-
ный, толко́вый
smash разби́(ва́)ть(ся);
enemy [раз]громи́ть; *car:*

smell за́пах; (*sense*) обоня́-
ние; *v/i.* па́хнуть (*of* Т);
[по]нюхать (В); *v/t.* [по]-
чу́ять
smile улы́бка; улыба́ться
[-бну́ться]
smith кузне́ц
smoke дым; *v/t.* [по]ку-
ри́ть; *fish* копти́ть; *v/i.*
дыми́ться; ~**ed** *cul.* копчёный; ~**er** куря́щий; ~**e-
-stack** дымова́я труба́;
~**ing: no** ~**ing!** кури́ть вос-
преща́ется!; ~**ing room**
ко́мната для куре́ния; ~**y**
(*room*) ды́мный, наку́рен-
ный
smooth гла́дкий; (*voice*)
ро́вный; (*take-off, etc.*)
пла́вный; (*voyage*) благо-
полу́чный; ~ **out** разгла́-
живать [-ла́дить]
smother *v/t.* [за]души́ть;
anger подавля́ть [-ви́ть];
v/i. задыха́ться
smoulder (*fire*) *v.* тлеть (*a.
fig.*)
smuggle занима́ться кон-
траба́ндой; *v/t.* провози́ть
контраба́ндой; ~**r** контра-
банди́ст
snack заку́ска; ~-**bar** заку́-
сочная
snail ули́тка
snake змея́
snap (*break*) *v/t.* [с]лома́ть;
v/i. ло́паться [-пнуть]; ~
at огрыза́ться [-зну́ться];
(*sound*) треск; *photo., coll.*

сни́мок

snarl рыча́ть (*at* на В); рыча́ние

snatch *v/t.* хвата́ть [схвати́ть], (*away*) вырыва́ть ['-рвать]; *v/i.* хвата́ться [схвати́ться] (*at* за В); **work by _es** рабо́тать урывка́ми

sneak *v.* кра́сться

sneakers кроссо́вки *f/pl.*

sneer (*unpleasant smile*) ухмы́лка; (*remark*) насме́шливое замеча́ние; *v.* **~ at s.o.** насмеха́ться (над Т)

sneeze чиха́ть [-хну́ть]; чиха́нье

snore храп; *v.* храпе́ть

snort фы́ркать [-кнуть]

snout (*dog, etc.*) мо́рда

snow снег; **it _s** идёт снег; **_ball** снежо́к; **_fall** снегопа́д; **_flake** снежи́нка; **_storm** мете́ль *f*; **_white** белосне́жный; **_y** сне́жный

snug ую́тный

so так; (*therefore*) поэ́тому; **_ am I** и я то́же; **_ far** пока́; **_ much, _ many** сто́лько (Р), **_** и́ли о́коло э́того

soak *washing* [за]ма́чивать [-мочи́ть]; (*get wet*) промока́ть ['-кнуть]

soap мы́ло; намы́ли(ва)ть

sob рыда́ние; рыда́ть

sober тре́звый (*a. fig.*)

so-called так называ́емый

soccer футбо́л

soci|able общи́тельный; **_al** обще́ственный; *pol.* социа́льный; **_alism** социали́зм; **_alist(ic)** социали́ст(и́ческий); **_ety** о́бщество (*a. comm.*)

sociology социоло́гия

sock носо́к

socket (*bulb*) патро́н; (*wall*) розе́тка; *tech.* штепсельное гнездо́

soda со́да; (*drink*) газиро́ванная вода́

sofa дива́н

soft мя́гкий; (*voice*) ти́хий; **_ drink** безалкого́льный напи́ток; **_en** смягча́ть(ся) [-чи́ть(ся)]

software *tech.* програ́ммное обеспе́чение

soil¹ *agr.* по́чва, земля́

soil² [ис]па́чкать(ся)

solder *v.* пая́ть

soldier солда́т

sole¹ подо́шва, (*shoe a.*) подмётка; *v.* ста́вить подмётки (на В)

sole² еди́нственный

solemn торже́ственный; **_ity** торже́ственность *f*

solicitor *jur. approx.* юрисконсульт

solid *phys.* твёрдый; *fig.* (*weighty*) ве́ский; (*mass*) пло́тный, сплошно́й; **_arity** солида́рность *f*

solit|ary одино́кий; **_ude** одино́чество

soloist соли́ст(ка)

sol|uble (*puzzle*) разреши́-
мый; (*liquid*) раствори́-
мый; **~ution** раство́р;
раство́р; **~ve** (раз)реша́ть
[-ши́ть]; **~vent** раствори́-
тель *m*; *adj. comm.* платёже-
спосо́бный

some не́который; (*not much*) немно́го (P); (*any*) како́й-нибудь; **~ of them** не́которые из них; **~body** кто́-то; (*no matter who*) кто́-нибудь; **~how** ка́к-то; ка́к-нибудь; **~one** = **~body**; **~thing** что́-то; что́-нибудь; **~time** когда́-нибудь; **~times** иногда́; **~what** слегка́, немно́го; **~where** где́-то, куда́-то; где́-нибудь, куда́-нибудь

son сын

song пе́сня

son-in-law зять *m*

soon ско́ро, вско́ре; (*too ~*) ра́но; *~ for you* мне жаль; ~ as то́лько ...; *as ~ as possible* как мо́жно скоре́е

soot са́жа

soothe успока́ивать [-ко́-ить]

sophisticated изы́скан-
ный; (*person*) све́тский; (*tech.*) сло́жный

sore больно́й, воспалён-
ный; ра́на, боля́чка; **~ point** *fig.* больно́е ме́сто; *I have a ~ throat* у меня́ боли́т го́рло

sorrow го́ре; горева́ть (*over* о П); **~ful** го́рест-

ный; **~y: be ~y that** [по]жале́ть, что ...; *I am ~y for you* мне жаль её; **~y!** прости́(те); **~y?** прости́(те), не расслы́-
шал(а), *coll.* что?

sort сорт; *all ~s of* вся́кие

soul душа́

sound[1] звук; (*noise*) шум; *v.* [про]звуча́ть; **~proof** звуконепроница́емый

sound[2] (*healthy*) здоро́вый; (*firm*) про́чный; (*sleep*) кре́пкий; (*sensible*) здра́-
вый

soup суп

sour ки́слый; **~ cream** смета́на; **~ milk** просто-
ква́ша; *turn ~* прокиса́ть [-сну́ть]

source исто́чник

south юг; *attr.* ю́жный; **~ of** к ю́гу от (P); **~east** юго-восто́к; *attr.* юго-вос-
то́чный; **~west** юго-за́-
пад; *attr.* юго-за́падный

souvenir сувени́р

sovereign коро́ль *m*, короле́ва; *adj.* сувере́нный; **~ty** суверените́т

Soviet *hist.* сове́тский

sow[1] (*pig*) свинья́

sow[2] [по]се́ять; *field* засе-
ва́ть [-е́ять]

spa|ce простра́нство; (*in-terval*) промежу́ток; **~e craft** косми́ческий кора́бль; **~ious** просто́рный

spade лопа́та; *queen of ~s* пи́ковая да́ма

span *fig.* промежу́ток; (*bridge*) пролёт

Span|iard испа́н|ец, -ка; **_ish** испа́нский

spank *v/t.* шлёпать [-пну́ть]

spanner га́ечный ключ

spare *life, person* [по]щади́ть; *minutes* уделя́ть [-ли́ть]; (*do without*) обойти́сь без (P); **_ part** запасна́я часть *f*; **_ time** свобо́дное вре́мя *n*

spark и́скра; **_le** и́скри́ться, сверка́ть

sparrow воробе́й

spatter бры́згать [-зну́ть]

speak говори́ть, сказа́ть; (*talk*) [по]говори́ть (**to** с Т); **_er** докла́дчи|к, -ца; *parl.* председа́тель *m*; *U.K.* спи́кер

special специа́льный, осо́бенный; (*edition*) экстренный; **_ delivery** сро́чная доста́вка; **_ powers** *pol.* чрезвыча́йное положе́ние; **_ist** специали́ст; **_ity** специа́льность *f*; осо́бенность *f*

speci|fic специфи́ческий; *phys.* уде́льный; **_fy** специфици́ровать (*im*)*pf.*; **_men** образе́ц, экземпля́р

speck пя́тнышко; (**_le**) крапи́н(к)а

specta|cle зре́лище; (**_cles**) очки́ *n/pl.*; **_tor** зри́тель (-ница *f*) *m*

spectrum спектр

speculat|ion размышле́ние; (*supposition*) предположе́ние; *comm.* спекуля́ция; **_ve** умозри́тельный; спекуляти́вный

speech речь *f*

speed ско́рость *f*; **_ limit** преде́льная ско́рость *f*; **_ up** ускоря́ть ['-рить]

spell[1] (*charm*) очарова́ние; (*time*) коро́ткий пери́од; **under the _ of** под очарова́нием (P), очаро́ванный (Т)

spell[2]: **how do you _ ...** как пи́шется (И); **_ing** орфогра́фия

spend *money* [ис]тра́тить; *time* проводи́ть [-вести́]

sphere *math.* шар; *fig.* сфе́ра

spice пря́ность *f*; **_y** пря́ный

spider пау́к; **_'s web** паути́на

spike (*shoes*) шип; *bot.* ко́лос

spill проли́(ва́)ть(ся)

spin (*turn*) кружи́ть(ся); *wool* [с]пря́сть; круже́ние

spinach шпина́т

spine *anat.* позвоно́чник; *bot.* колю́чка; *zo.* игла́

spinster незаму́жняя же́нщина

spiral спира́ль *f*; *attr.* спира́льный; **_ staircase** винтова́я ле́стница

spire *arch.* шпиль *m*

spirit дух; (*soul*) душа́; (liquor) спирт, *pl.* спиртны́е напи́тки *m/pl.*; *pl.* (*humour*) настрое́ние; **~ual** духо́вный

spit плева́ть [плю́нуть]

spite зло́ба; (*do*) **to ~ him** назло́ ему́; **in ~ of** вопреки́ (Д)

spittle слюна́

splash (*water*) плеска́ть(ся); (*mud*) бры́згать(ся); плеск; *pl.* бры́зги *f/pl.*

spleen *anat.* селезёнка; *fig.* хандра́

splend|id великоле́пный; **~our** великоле́пие

splinter ще́пка; (*metal, glass*) оско́лок; (*foot*) зано́за; расщепля́ть(ся) [-пи́ть(ся)]

split раска́лывать(ся) [-коло́ть(ся)]; раско́л; **~ hairs** копа́ться в мелоча́х

spoil [ис]по́ртить(ся)

spoke спи́ца

spokesman представи́тель *m*

sponge гу́бка; (*clean*) мыть гу́бкой; **~ cake** бискви́т; **~ on** жить за счёт (Р)

sponsor спо́нсор (*in Russia = one who supports financially*)

spoon ло́жка

sport спорт; *adj.* спорти́вный; **~sman** спортсме́н; **~swoman** спортсме́нка

spot пятно́; (*place*) ме́сто; **on the ~** на ме́сте, тут же; **~ted** *adj.* пятни́стый

spray распыля́ть [-ли́ть]; **~er** распыли́тель *m*

spread (*news*) распространя́ть(ся) [-ни́ть(ся)]; (*cloth*) расстила́ть [разостла́ть]; (*butter*) нама́з(ыв)ать; распростране́ние

sprig *bot.* ве́точка

spring (*season*) весна́; (*wire*) пружи́на; (*source of water*) родни́к; **~ to one's feet** вскочи́ть на но́ги; **~board** трампли́н; **~time** весе́ннее вре́мя *n*

sprinkle (*with liquids*) обры́згивать [-згать]; (*with sugar, etc.*) посыпа́ть [-ыпать]

sprinter спри́нтер

spur шпо́ра; **~ on** *fig.* подстёгивать [-егну́ть]

spurt струя́; *v.* бить струёй

spy шпио́н(ка); -ить (**on** за Т)

squad гру́ппа, отря́д; **~ron** *mar.* эска́дра; *av.* эскадри́лья

square *math.* квадра́т; (*town*) пло́щадь *f*; *adj.* квадра́тный; (*deal*) че́стный

squash разда́вливать [-ви́ть]; (*drink*) фрукто́вый сок

squat сиде́ть на ко́рточках

squeak *mouse*: пища́ть; *wheel*: скрипе́ть; писк;

скрип

squeeze (*compress*) сж(и-)
ма́ть; (*cram*) вти́скивать
[-снуть]; ~ *out* выжима́ть
[вы́жать]

squint *v.* коси́ть; (*at a
bright light*) щу́риться

squirrel бе́лка

stab коло́ть; (*kill*) зака́лы-
вать [-коло́ть]; уда́р (но-
жо́м); (*wound*) коло́тая
ра́на

stab|ility усто́йчивость *f*,
стаби́льность *f*; ~le[1]
усто́йчивый, стаби́льный

stable[2] коню́шня

stack *agr.* стог; (*books,
etc.*) сто́пка

stadium стадио́н

staff (*employees*) штат, пер-
сона́л

stage *thea.* сце́на; (*development*) ста́дия, эта́п; *thea.*
[по]ста́вить

stagger *v/i.* шата́ться; *v/t.
fig.* поража́ть [-рази́ть],
потряса́ть [-сти́]

stain пятно́; [за]пятна́ть;
~**less:** ~**less steel** нержа-
ве́ющая сталь *f*

stair ступе́нька; ~**case**
ле́стница

stake[1] ста́вка; *money* [по]-
ста́вить (**on** на В); *be at* ~
fig. быть поста́влен-
ным на ка́рту

stake[2] кол

stale (*bread*) чёрствый;
(*beer*) вы́дохшийся; (*joke*)
изби́тый

stalk *bot.* сте́бель *m*

stall сто́йло; *comm.* ларёк;
~**s** *thea.* парте́р

stallion жеребе́ц

stammer заика́ться; заика́-
ние

stamp (*trampling*) то́пот;
(*mail*) ште́мпель *m*; (*ru-
ber*) печа́ть; (*postage*)
почто́вая ма́рка; *v.* то́-
пать нога́ми; ште́мпе-
лева́ть; [по]ста́вить печа́ть

stand *v/i.* стоя́ть; *v/t.* (*put*)
[по]ста́вить; (*endure*) тер-
пе́ть; (*position*) ме́сто; *fig.*
пози́ция; (*sports*) три-
бу́на; (*news*) кио́ск; *take
a firm* ~ заня́ть твёрдую
пози́цию; ~ *for* (*mean*)
означа́ть; (*defend*) стоя́ть
за (В); ~ *up* встава́ть; ~
up for заступа́ться
[-пи́ться] за (В)

standard *tech. comm.* стан-
да́рт, но́рма; (*level*) у́ро-
вень; (*flag*) зна́мя *n*; ~ *of
life* жи́зненный у́ровень
m; ~**ize**
стандартизи́ровать (*im*) *pf.*

standpoint то́чка зре́ния

staple *adj.* основно́й

star звезда́ (*a. fig.*)

starboard пра́вый борт

starch крахма́л; [на]крах-
ма́лить

stare при́стально смотре́ть
(*at* на В); при́стальный
взгляд

starling скворе́ц

start (*begin*) нач(ин)а́ть(ся); (*set off*) отправля́ть(ся) ['-виться]; (*in surprise*) вздра́гивать [вздро́гнуть]; (*sports, etc.*) стартова́ть (*im*)*pf.*; нача́ло; старт; **~le** (ис-, на)пуга́ть

starv|ation го́лод; голода́ние; **die of ~ation** умере́ть от го́лода; **~e** *v/i.* голода́ть; *v/t.* мори́ть го́лодом

stat|e госуда́рство; (*of a union*) штат; (*condition*) состоя́ние; (*declare*) заявля́ть [-ви́ть]; *case* излага́ть [-ложи́ть]; **2e Department** Госуда́рственный департа́мент; **~ement** заявле́ние; **~esman** госуда́рственный де́ятель *m*; **~ion** radio, el., rail. ста́нция; (*building for passengers*) вокза́л; **~ionary** неподви́жный; стациона́рный; (*condition*) зая́вле́ние; **~ionary** неподви́жный; стациона́рный; **~ionery** канцеля́рские това́ры; **~istics** стати́стика; **~ue** ста́туя; **~us** ста́тус, положе́ние; **~ute** зако́н; *pl.* уста́в

staunch ве́рный, сто́йкий, непоколеби́мый

stay (*remain*) ост(ав)а́ться; (*live*) жить, гости́ть (**with** у Р); *su.* пребыва́ние

stead|fast сто́йкий; **~y** усто́йчивый; (*even*) равноме́рный; (*even-tempered*)

уравнове́шенный

steal [у]кра́сть; **~thily** укра́дкой

steam пар; *v/i.* испуска́ть пар; *v/t. cul.* па́рить, [с]вари́ть на пару́; **~ing hot** о́чень горя́чий; **~ship** парохо́д

steed верхова́я ло́шадь, конь

steel сталь *f*; *attr.* стально́й; **~ beam** стальна́я ба́лка

steep *adj.* круто́й

steeple колоко́льня; **~chase** ска́чки с препя́тствиями

steer *v.* пра́вить, управля́ть (Т); **~ing-wheel** *mar.* штурва́л; *mot.* руль *m*

stem (*plant*) сте́бель *m*; *gr.* осно́ва

stenographer стенографи́стка

step шаг (*a. tech.*); (*stair, rung*) ступе́нька; *v.* шага́ть [-гну́ть]; **~ on** наступа́ть [-пи́ть] на (В); **take ~s** принима́ть ме́ры; **~father** о́тчим; **~mother** ма́чеха

steppe степь *f*

stereo стереофони́ческий; **~ set** стереофони́ческий прои́грыватель

steril|e *tech., med.* стери́льный; *fig.* беспло́дный; **~ize** стерилизова́ть (*im*)*pf.*

stern *adj.* стро́гий

stew *cul.* туши́ть; *su.* тушёное мя́со

steward *mar.* стюа́рд; *av.* бортпроводни́к; **~ess** бортпроводни́ца, стюарде́сса

stick[1] па́лка; (*walking-*) трость *f*

stick[2] *v/i.* прилипа́ть ['-пнуть] (**to** к Д); *fig.* приде́рживаться (**to** Р); *v/t.* *stamp* накле́ива)ть (on на В); **~ing plaster** лейкопла́стырь *m*; **~y** кле́йкий, ли́пкий

stiff неги́бкий, жёсткий; (*limbs*) одеревене́лый; (*jelly*) засты́вший; (*manners*) чо́порный; (*drink*) кре́пкий; (*exam*) тру́дный

stifle *v/t.* [за]души́ть; *fig.* подавля́ть [-ви́ть]; *v/i.* задыха́ться

still (*motionless*) неподви́жный; (*quiet*) ти́хий; *adv.* ещё; *conj.* одна́ко, всё же

stimul|ate стимули́ровать (*im*)*pf.*; **~ating** стимули́рующий; **~us** сти́мул

sting (*organ*) жа́ло; (*wound*) уку́с; *v/t.* [у]жа́лить; *nettle:* [об]же́чь; *v/i.* уязвля́ть [-ви́ть]

stingy скупо́й

stink злово́ние; *v.* воня́ть (**of** Т)

stipulate предусма́тривать [-мотре́ть]

stir шевели́ть(ся) [-льну́ть-

(ся)]; (*excite*) возбужда́ть [-уди́ть]; *sugar* разме́шивать [-ша́ть]; *su.* шевеле́ние; возбужде́ние

stitch стежо́к; (*knitting*) пе́тля; *med.* шов; *v.* [с]ши́ть; (*wound*) накла́дывать [-ложи́ть] шов

stock (*supply*) запа́с; *cul.* бульо́н; *pl. fin.* а́кции *f/pl.*; **~ live** поголо́вье скота́; **~breeder** животново́д; **≈ Exchange** фо́ндовая би́ржа; **~holder** акционе́р

stocking чуло́к

stoker кочега́р

stomach желу́док; (*belly*) живо́т

stone ка́мень *m*; (*fruit*) ко́сточка; *precious* **~** драгоце́нный ка́мень; *attr.* ка́менный; *v.* забра́сывать камня́ми; **~d** (*fruit*) без ко́сточки

stool табуре́т, -ка

stoop *v/i.* наклоня́ться [-ни́ться]; (*habit*) [с]суту́литься; *fig.* унижа́ться [уни́зиться] (**to** до Р); суту́лость *f*

stop остано́вка (*a. rail.*); остана́вливать(ся) [-нови́ть(ся)]; *work, payment* прекраща́ть [-рати́ть]; (*doing*) переста(ва́)ть + *inf.*; *hole* затыка́ть [-ткну́ть]; **full ~** то́чка; **~page** остано́вка; прекраще́ние; **~per** заты́чка;

(*bottle*) пробка; **~ping** (*tooth*) пломба; **~watch** секундомер

stor|age хранение; (*place*) склад; **~e** (*supply*) запас; *Am.* магазин; *v.* хранить *impf.*; **~ehouse** склад; хранилище; **~ey** этаж

stork аист

storm буря (*a. fig.*); *mar.* шторм; (*rage*) бушевать; **~y** бурный (*a. fig.*)

story рассказ, повесть *f*; *coll.* выдумка, сказка

stout (*strong*) крепкий; (*corpulent*) тучный

stove (*cooking*) плита; (*heating*) печь *f*, печка

stow goods укладывать [уложить]

straight прямой; *adv.* прямо; **~ away** *coll.* сразу; сейчас; **put** ~ приводить в порядок; **~en** выпрямлять(ся) [выпрямить(ся)]

strain rope натягивать [-януть]; *tendon* растягивать [-януть]; *soup* процеживать [-едить]; **~ every nerve** напрягать все силы

straits *pl. geogr.* пролив *f*; *fig.* бедственное положение

strand (*rope, hair*) прядь *f*

strange (*odd*) странный; (*unknown*) чужой, незнакомый; **~r** незнаком|ец, -ка

strap (*leather*) ремень *m*, ремешок; *mil.* погон

strateg|ic стратегический; **~y** стратегия

straw солома, (*single*) соломинка; *attr.* соломенный; **~berry, -ies** клубника; (*wild*) земляника

stray *adj.* бездомный, бродячий; *v.* забрести *pf.*

streak (*stripe*) полоса; (*layer*) прослойка; *fig.* черта характера

stream поток (*a. fig.*); (*brook*) ручей; (*current*) течение; *v.* течь, струиться; **~-lined** обтекаемый

street улица; *attr.* уличный; **~-map** план города

strength сила; **~en** усили(ва)ть(ся)

strenuous напряжённый

stress напряжение (*a. tech.*); (*psychological*) стресс; *gr.* ударение; *v.* делать ударение на (П) (*underline*) подчёркивать [-черкнуть]

stretch (*draw out*) вытягивать(ся), рас- [вытянуть (-ся), рас-]; (*extend*) простирать(ся) [-переть(ся)]; (*tighten*) натягивать(ся) [-януть(ся)]; *su.* рас-, вытягивание; (*extent*) протяжение; (*fancy*) натяжка; **~er** носилки *f/pl.*

strew посыпать, [-ыпать], усыпать [-ыпать]

strict строгий; (*precise*)

то́чный; **~ness** стро́гость f

stride большо́й шаг; v. шага́ть

strik|e (*hit*) ударя́ть ['-рить]; *fig.* поража́ть [-рази́ть]; *workers:* бастова́ть [про]би́ть; *clock:* [про]би́ть; **~ a match** зажига́ть [-же́чь] спи́чку; забасто́вка; **~er** забасто́вщик; **~ing** поража́ющий

string бечёвка, шпага́т; (*shoe*) шнуро́к; *mus.* струна́; (*pearls*) ни́тка; *tech.* строка́; *pearls* нани́зывать [-за́ть]; **~y** (*meat*) жи́листый

strip у́зкая полоса́; v. (*undress*) раздева́ть(ся); *skin, bark* сдира́ть [содра́ть]

stripe полоса́, поло́ска; *mil.* наши́вка (на рукаве́); **~d** полоса́тый

strive **~ against** боро́ться с (Т); **~ for** стреми́ться [к Д], добива́ться (P); **~ to +** *inf.* [по]стара́ться + *inf.*

stroke уда́р (*a. med.*); (*pencil*) штрих; (*oar*) взмах; v. [по]гла́дить

stroll прогу́лка; прогу́ливаться **~** -ля́ться]

strong си́льный; (*cloth, tea, build*) кре́пкий; **~hold** кре́пость f; *fig.* опло́т; **~-willed** волево́й

structure структу́ра, строе́ние

struggle борьба́; v. боро́ться

stub (*tree*) пень m; (*pencil*) огры́зок; (*cigarette*) оку́рок

stubble *agr.* стерня́; *coll.* щети́на

stubborn упо́рный; (*person*) упря́мый

student студе́нт(ка); **~io** сту́дия; **~ious** приле́жный; стара́тельный; **~y** изуча́ть [-чи́ть] (В), занима́ться (Т); изуче́ние; (*piece of writing*) иссле́дование; (*science*) нау́ка; (*art*) этю́д

stuff материа́л, вещество́; (*textile*) мате́рия, ткань; **~ and nonsense!** *coll.* ерунда́!; v. наби(ва́)ть; *cul.* [на]фарширова́ть; **~ing** наби́вка; фарш

stumble спотыка́ться [-ткну́ться] (**over** о В); **~ upon** натыка́ться [-ткну́ться] на (В)

stump (*tree*) пень m; (*tail*) обру́бок; (*leg*) культя́; v. (*walking*) ковыля́ть

stun оглуша́ть [-ши́ть]; *fig.* ошеломля́ть [-ми́ть]; *coll.* **~ning** сногсшиба́тельный

stup|endous изуми́тельный; **~id** глу́пый; **~idity** глу́пость f

sturdy кре́пкий; (*firm*) сто́йкий

sturgeon осётр; *cul.* осетри́на

stutter заика́ться

styl|e стиль *m*; (*fashion*) фасо́н; **set the ~e** задава́ть тон; **~ish** мо́дный, *coll.* сти́льный

subconscious подсозна́тельный

subdivide подразделя́ть

subdue *nation* покоря́ть [-ри́ть]

subject (*topic*) предме́т, те́ма; *jur.* по́дданный; *gr.* субъе́кт; *gr.* подлежа́щее; *v.* подверга́ть ['-гнуть] (**to** Д); *adj.* подве́рженный; **~ive** субъекти́вный

submarine подво́дный; подво́дная ло́дка

submerge погружа́ть(ся) [-узи́ть(ся)]

submi|ssion подчине́ние; (*obedience*) поко́рность *f*; **~t** *v/i.* подчиня́ться [-ни́ться]; *v/t.* представля́ть ['-вить] (**for** на В)

subordinate подчиня́ть [-ни́ть]; *su., adj.* подчинённый

subscri|be подпи́сываться [-са́ться] (**to** на В); (*good cause*) же́ртвовать [по]же́ртвовать (**to** на В); **~ber** подпи́счик; -ца; (*telephone*) абоне́нт; **~ption** подпи́ска; (*to concerts, etc.*) абонеме́нт; *attr.* подписно́й

subsequent после́дующий; **~ly** впосле́дствии

subside *water*: убы(ва́)ть;

(*abate*) утиха́ть ['-хнуть]; (*sink*) оседа́ть [осе́сть]; **~ize** субсиди́ровать; **~y** субси́дия

subsist существова́ть; (*feed*) пита́ться (**on** Т); **~ence** существова́ние; **means of ~ence** сре́дства существова́ния; **~ence wage** прожи́точный ми́нимум

substan|ce *chem.* вещество́; *fig.* су́щность *f*, содержа́ние; **~tial** суще́ственный; **~tive** и́мя существи́тельное *n*

substitute (*person*) замести́тель *m, a.* заме́на; (*material*) замени́тель *m*; замеща́ть [-ести́ть], заменя́ть [-ни́ть]

subtle (*delicate*) то́нкий; (*hardly noticeable*) неулови́мый; (*refined*) утончённый; **~ty** утончённость *f*; неулови́мость *f*

subtract вычита́ть [вы́честь]; **~ion** вычита́ние

suburb при́город; **~an** при́городный

subway (*path under a road*) подзе́мный перехо́д; *rail.* метро́ *n indecl.*

succeed име́ть успе́х; уд(ав)а́ться; (*take the place of*) быть прее́мником, сменя́ть; **I ~ed in finding it** мне удало́сь найти́ э́то

success успе́х; **~ful** успеш-

ный; ~**ion** после́дователь-
ность *f*; *in* ~**ion** подря́д;
~**or** прее́мник, насле́дник
such (*or* ~ **a**) тако́й; тако́в,
-á, -ó, *pl.* -ы́: ~ **are the
facts** таковы́ фа́кты
suck соса́ть; ~**le** *v/t.* кор-
ми́ть гру́дью
sudden внеза́пный; ~**ly**
вдруг, внеза́пно
sue *jur.* предъявля́ть иск;
возбужда́ть де́ло
suede за́мша; *attr.* за́мше-
вый
suffer *v/i. med.* страда́ть
(**from** T *or* от P); *fig.*
[по]страда́ть; *v/t.* [по]-
терпе́ть; ~**ing** страда́ние
sufficient доста́точный
suffix су́ффикс
sugar са́хар; (*granulated*)
(са́харный) песо́к; *attr.*
са́харный; ~**basin** са́хар-
ница
suggest предлага́ть [-ло-
жи́ть]; ~**ion** предложе́ние
suicide самоуби́йство
suit (*man's*) костю́м; *jur.*
гражда́нское суде́бное
де́ло; (*cards*) масть *f*; под-
ходи́ть [подойти́] (Д);
dress a.: быть к лицу́;
~**ability** приго́дность *f*;
~**able** подходя́щий;
~**case** чемода́н; ~**ed** го́д-
ный; *be* ~**ed for,** *to* го-
ди́ться для (P), на (B)
sulk ду́ться; ~**y** наду́тый,
угрю́мый
sullen хму́рый

sulphur се́ра; ~**ic**: ~**ic acid**
се́рная кислота́
sultry зно́йный
sum (*amount*) су́мма; (*total*) ито́г; ~ **up** подводи́ть
[-вести́] ито́г (Д); ~**marize**
сумми́ровать (*im*)*pf.*; ре-
зюми́ровать (*im*)*pf.*;
~**mary** резюме́ *n indecl.*
summer ле́то; *attr.* ле́тний;
~ **resort** куро́рт
summit верши́на; ~ **meeting** встре́ча в верха́х
summon [по]зва́ть; *council*
созы(ва́)ть; *witness* вызы-
ва́ть [вы́звать]; ~**s** вы́зов
sumptuous роско́шный
sun со́лнце; *attr.* со́лнеч-
ный; ~**bathe** загора́ть;
~**burn** зага́р; ~**day** воскре-
се́нье; *attr.* воскре́сный;
~**flower** подсо́лнечник;
~**glasses** тёмные очки́
sunken (*ship*) затону́вший;
(*eyes*) впа́лый
sun|ny со́лнечный; ~**rise**
восхо́д со́лнца; ~**set** за-
ка́т; ~**shine** со́лнечный
свет; *in the* ~**shine** на
со́лнце; ~**stroke** со́лнеч-
ный уда́р
superb прекра́сный
superficial пове́рхностный
superfluous изли́шний
superintend (*manage*) руко-
води́ть (Т); ~**ent** руко-
води́тель
superior (*forces*) превосхо-
дя́щий; (*quality*) вы́сший;
su. нача́льник; ~**ity** пре-

восхо́дство

super|market универса́м; **_sonic** (plane) сверхзвуко́вой

supersede заменя́ть [-ни́ть]

superstitio|n суеве́рие; **_us** суеве́рный

supervis|e work руководи́ть (Т); **_ion** надзо́р; **_or** инспе́ктор; univ. нау́чный руководи́тель

supper у́жин

supplant вытесня́ть [вы́теснить], заменя́ть

supple ги́бкий

supplement дополня́ть [-нить]; дополне́ние; (to paper) приложе́ние; **_ary** дополни́тельный

supply снабжа́ть [-бди́ть]; (deliver) поставля́ть [-ви́ть]; снабже́ние; поста́вка; (stock) запа́с, pl. a. припа́сы m/pl.; **_ and demand** спрос и предложе́ние

support (back) подде́рживать [-жа́ть]; (prop) подпира́ть [-пере́ть]; family соде́ржать; подде́ржка; подпо́рка; tech., fig. опо́ра; **_er** сторо́нник, -ца

suppos|e полага́ть, предполага́ть [-ложи́ть]; **_ed** предполага́емый; **_ition** предположе́ние

suppress подавля́ть [-ви́ть]; **_ion** подавле́ние

supreme pol., mil. верхо́вный

sure (reliable) ве́рный; (convinced) уве́ренный (of в П); adv. коне́чно; **make _** (check) прове́рить; (arrange so) позабо́титься; **_ enough** и действи́тельно

surface пове́рхность f

surge|on хиру́рг; **_ry** хирурги́я

surmise предположе́ние; выска́зывать [-казать] предположе́ние

surmount (rise above) возвыша́ться над (Т); (overcome) преодоле́(ва́)ть

surname фами́лия

surpass превосходи́ть [-взойти́]

surplus изли́шек, избы́ток; избы́точный, [из]ли́шний

surpris|e удивля́ть [-ви́ть]; enemy заста́ть враспло́х; удивле́ние; (fact or gift) сюрпри́з; **_ing** удиви́тельный; (unexpected) неожи́данный

surrender сд(ав)а́ться; mil. сда́ча, капитуля́ция

surround окружа́ть [-жи́ть]; **_ings** (place) окре́стности; окруже́ние; среда́

survey (examine) осма́тривать [осмотре́ть]; **_or** (land) землеме́р

surviv|al выжива́ние; (remnant) пережи́ток; **_e** v/i. сохрани́ться [-ня́ться], уцелеть *pf.*, *person a.*: выживать [выжить]; *v/t.* пережи(ва́)ть

susceptible восприймчивый

suspect подозревать (*of* в П); подозрительный; *su.* подозреваемый

suspend подвешивать [-сить]; *work* приостанавливать [-новить]; **~ders** *Am.* подтяжки

suspicion подозрение; **~us** подозрительный

sustain (*support*) поддерживать [-жать]; (*suffer*) перенести, понести

swallow[1] *zo.* ласточка

swallow[2] глотать, проглатывать [-лотить] (*a. fig.*)

swamp болото, топь *f*

swan лебедь *m*

swarm (*bees*) рой; (*birds*) стая; *fig.* толпа; роиться; (*teem*) кишеть (**with** Т); *crowd*: [с]толпиться

swarthy смуглый

sway *grass, flame*: колыхать(ся) [-хну́ть(ся)]; (*swing*) качать(ся); *person* [по]колебать; **be easily ~ed** легко поддаваться [Д]

swear *v/i.* [по]клясться; (*curse*) [вы]ругаться

sweat пот; *v/i.* [вс]потеть; **~er** свитер

Swede швед(ка); **~ish** шведский

sweep подметать [-мести]; **~ away**, **~ off** сметать [смести]; **~ past** промчаться мимо *pf.*; (*curve*) изгиб

sweet сладкий; (*smell*) душистый; (*child*) милый; *su.* конфета; *pl. coll.* сласти *f/pl.*; **~heart** возлюбленн[ый, -ая; (*address*) дорог[ой, -ая

swell *med.* распухать [-хнуть]; *bud, wood*: набухать [-хнуть]; *sound*: нарастать [-сти]; **~ing** *su.* отёк; (*slight*) припухлость

swerve *car*: резко сворачивать (свернуть) в сторону

swift быстрый; **~ness** быстрота

swim плавать, [по]плыть; **go for a ~** пойти купаться; **~mer** пловец; **~ming** *su.* плавание; **~ming costume** купальный костюм; **~ming trunks** плавки

swindle [с]мошенничать; **~r** мошенник

swine *fig. coll.* свинья

swing качать(ся) [-чнуть(ся)]; *arm* размахивать (Т); размах; (*child's*) качели *f/pl.*; **in full ~** в полном разгаре

Swiss швейцар[ец, -ка; -ский

switch *el.* выключатель *m*; (*radio, etc.*) переключатель; **~ on** включать

[-чи́ть]; ~ **off** выключа́ть [вы́ключить]
sword меч
syllable слог
symbol си́мвол
symmetry симметри́я
sympath|etic сочу́вственный; ~**ize** сочу́вствовать (**with** Д); ~**y** сочу́вствие
symphony симфо́ния
symptom симпто́м

synagogue *eccl.* синаго́га
synonym сино́ним
syntax си́нтаксис
synthe|sis си́нтез; ~**tic** синтети́ческий
syringe шприц; **disposable** ~ однора́зовый шприц
syrup сиро́п
system систе́ма; ~**atic** системати́ческий

T

table стол; (*list*) табли́ца; *attr.* столо́вый; ~ **of contents** оглавле́ние; ~-**cloth** ска́терть *f*; ~ **d'hôte** *approx.* ко́мплексный обе́д
tablet (*pill*) табле́тка; (*slab*) плита́; (*memorial*) мемориа́льная доска́
tack гвоздь; (*thumb*~) *Am.* кно́пка; *v.* прикрепля́ть [-пи́ть] (гвоздя́ми); прика́лывать [-коло́ть] (кно́пками); (*sew*) смётывать, при- [-мета́ть]
tackle: **fishing** ~ рыболо́вные принадле́жности *f/pl.*
tact такт; ~**ful** такти́чный; ~**ics** та́ктика; ~**less** беста́ктный
tag бирка, этике́тка; **price** ~ це́нник; прикрепля́ть [-пи́ть] (би́рку, и т. д.)
tail хвост; ~-**coat** фрак; ~-**light** *mot.* за́дний свет

tailor портно́й
take брать [взять]; **bath, medicine, measures** принима́ть [-ня́ть]; **time** отнима́ть [-ня́ть]; ~ **account of** учи́тывать [уче́сть] (В); ~ **along** брать, взять с собо́й; ~ **care of** [по]забо́титься о (П); ~ **in** *fig.* понима́ть [-ня́ть]; ~ **place** происходи́ть, случа́ться [-чи́ться]; ~ **a seat** сади́ться [сесть]; ~ **off** *garment, hat* снима́ть [снять]; *av.* взлета́ть [-ете́ть]
tale расска́з; (*fairy*-, **a. lie**) ска́зка
talent тала́нт; ~**ed** тала́нтливый
talk [по]говори́ть (**to** с Т); (*informally*) бесе́довать, разгова́ривать (с Т); *su.* бесе́да, разгово́р; *pl. pol.* перегово́ры *m/pl.*; ~**ative** разгово́рчивый

tall (*person*) высо́кий, ро́слый

tame приручённый, ручно́й; прируча́ть [-чи́ть]; *fig.* укроща́ть [-оти́ть]

tan hide [вы́]ду́бить; (*sun*) загора́ть; зага́р

tangerine мандари́н

tangible осяза́емый

tangle пу́таница; *v/t.* запу́т(ыв)ать

tank бак; цисте́рна; *mil.* танк; **petrol** ~ бензоба́к

tap (*water*) кран; (*knock*) ти́хий стук; *v.* тихо постуча́ть (**at** в В)

tape ле́нта; (*recording*) плёнка; ~**-measure** руле́тка; (*cloth*) сантиме́тр; ~**-recorder** магнитофо́н

tapestry гобеле́н

tar (*roads*) гудро́н; (*to preserve wood*) смола́

tardy (*slow*) медли́тельный; (*belated*) запозда́лый

target (*for practice*) мише́нь *f* (*a. fig.*); *objective* цель *f*

tariff тари́ф; (*list of fixed prices*) прейскура́нт

tart ки́слый, тёрпкий; *su.* пиро́г с фру́ктами

Ta(r)tar тата́р|ин, -ка; ~ский

task зада́ние, зада́ча; **take to** ~ руга́ть за [В]

tassel ки́сточка

taste вкус; *v/t.* [по]про́бовать; ~**less** безвку́сный;

~**у** вку́сный

taunt дразни́ть (**with** за В); язви́тельное замеча́ние

tax нало́г; облага́ть нало́гом; *strenght* испы́тывать [-пыта́ть]; ~**ation** нало́говое обложе́ние; ~**-free** необлага́емый нало́гом; ~**payer** налогопла́тельщик

taxi такси́ *n indecl.*; **take a** ~ взять такси́; ~**-driver** води́тель такси́; ~**rank** стоя́нка такси́

tea чай; *attr.* ча́йный

teach [на]учи́ть (*a student* студе́нта *English* англи́йскому языку́); преподава́ть; ~**er** учи́тель (-ница *f*) *m*; *univ.* преподава́тель(ница *f*) *m*; ~**ing** преподава́ние; (*doctrine*) уче́ние

team (*workers*) брига́да; (*sports*) кома́нда; ~**work** совме́стная рабо́та

tea-pot ча́йник

tear слеза́

tear[2] [по]рва́ть(ся); *su.* проре́ха; ~ **away** отрыва́ться; ~ **down** сорва́ть [срыва́ть]; *building* сноси́ть [снести́]; ~ **up** разрыва́ть [разорва́ть]

tease (*person*) зади́ра *m/f*; *v.* дразни́ть

teaspoon ча́йная ло́жка

technic|al техни́ческий; ~**cian** те́хник; ~**que** те́хника

373   **terrific**

technology техноло́гия;
(*scence*) те́хника
tedious ску́чный
teem: ~ **with** кише́ть (T)
tele|fax (теле)фа́кс; ~**gram**
телегра́мма; ~**graph** телег-
ра́ф; телеграфи́ровать
(*im*)*pf.*; ~**phone** телефо́н;
[по]звони́ть по телефо́ну;
~**phone booth** телефо́н-
-автома́т; ~**printer** теле-
та́йп; ~**scope** телеско́п;
~**vision** телеви́дение; ~**vision set** телеви́зор
telex те́лекс; *v.* пос[ы]ла́ть
те́лекс
tell говори́ть [сказа́ть] (Д);
story расска́зывать
[-за́ть]; (*order*) веле́ть (Д);
~**er** (*bank*) касси́р
temper (*disposition*) нрав,
хара́ктер; (*mood*) настро-
е́ние; (*irritation*) раздра-
же́ние; **keep one's** ~
сде́рживаться [-жа́ться];
loose one's ~ вы́йти из
себя́; *v.* **steel**, *will* зака-
ля́ть [-ли́ть]; ~**ament** тем-
пера́мент; ~**ance** уме́рен-
ность *f*; ~**ate** уме́ренный;
~**ature** температу́ра
tempest бу́ря
temple[1] храм
temple[2] *anat.* висо́к
temporal временно́й;
(*wordly*) све́тский; ~**ry**
вре́менный
tempt искуша́ть [-уси́ть];
(*attract*) соблазня́ть
[-ни́ть]; ~**ation** искуше́-

ние; собла́зн
ten де́сять; (*cards, number
of bus, tram*) деся́тка
tenant аренда́тор; (*flat*)
квартиросъёмщик
tend *patients* уха́живать
(за T); (*to do*) име́ть тен-
де́нцию + *inf.*; ~**ency** тен-
де́нция, скло́нность *f*
tender не́жный; ~ **spot**
больно́е ме́сто; ~**ness**
не́жность *f*
tendon сухожи́лие
tenement: ~ **house** мно-
гокварти́рный дом
tennis те́ннис
tenor о́бщий смысл; *mus.*
те́нор
tense напряжённый; ~**ion**
напряже́ние (*a. el.*); *pol.*
напряжённость *f*
tent пала́тка
tenth деся́тый
term (*date, period*) срок;
(*expression*) те́рмин; *univ.*
семе́стр; *pl.* (*conditions*)
усло́вия *n/pl.*; (*relations*)
отноше́ния *n/pl.*; **be on
good (bad)** ~ быть в хо-
ро́ших (плохи́х) отноше́-
ниях (**with** с T)
termin|al коне́чный; *su. el.*
кле́мма; ~**ate** оканчи-
ва́ть(ся) [око́нчить(ся)];
~**ation** оконча́ние; ~**us**
(*bus*) коне́чная оста-
но́вка; *rail.* коне́чная
ста́нция
terrace терра́са
terri|ble ужа́сный; ~**fic** coll.

потряса́ющий; **~fy** ужаса́ть [-сну́ть]

territory террито́рия

terror (*violence*) терро́р; (*fear*) у́жас; **~ism** террори́зм

test испыта́ние; *attr.* испыта́тельный; испы́тывать [-та́ть]; (*check*) проверя́ть [-е́рить]

testament завеща́ние; **New (Old)** 2 Но́вый (Ве́тхий) Заве́т

test|ify *v/i.* дава́ть показа́ния; *v/t.* свиде́тельствовать; **~monial** характери́стика, о́тзыв; **~mony** показа́ние; (*proof*) доказа́тельство

test-tube проби́рка

text текст (*a. tech.*); **~book** уче́бник

textile тексти́льный; (*cloth*) ткань; тексти́льное изде́лие

than чем

thank [по]благодари́ть; **~ful** благода́рный; **~s** благода́рность *f*; **~s!** спаси́бо!; **~s to** благодаря́ (Д)

that *dem. pron.* (э́)тот, (э́)та, (э́)то; *rel. pron.* кото́рый, *conj.* что, **~ is** (*i. e.*) то́ есть (т. е.)

the *The definite article does not exist in Russian. It remains untranslated.* **~ ... ~** чем ... тем

theatre теа́тр

pl. свои́; **I see ~ house** я ви́жу их дом; **they see ~ house** они́ ви́дят свой дом

them их (= В), *after prep.* них; им (= Д)

theme те́ма

themselves себя́, -ся; *emphatic* са́ми

then (*at that time*) тогда́; (*next*) зате́м, пото́м; (*in that case*) в тако́м слу́чае, зна́чит; **by ~** к тому́ вре́мени; **since ~** с того́ вре́мени

theological богосло́вский; **~y** богосло́вие

theor|etical теорети́ческий; **~y** тео́рия

there там, (*thither*) туда́; **~ is (are)** есть *or* име́ется (име́ются) (*in translation these Russian verbs are often replaced by other verbs or omitted*) **~ was a strong wind** дул си́льный ве́тер; **~ is a man in the room** в ко́мнате како́й-то мужчи́на; **~fore** поэ́тому; **~upon** зате́м

thermometer термо́метр

thermonuclear термоя́дерный

they они́

thick то́лстый; (*forest, hair, soup*) густо́й; **~en** утолща́ть(ся) [-лсти́ть(ся)]; сгуща́ть(ся) [сгусти́ть(ся)] **~et** ча́ща; **~ness** толщина́; густота́

thie|f вор; **~ve** воровáть

thigh бедрó

thimble напёрсток

thin тóнкий; (*hair*) рéдкий; (*soup*) жи́дкий; *v.* ~ (*out*) [по]рéдеть

thing вещь *f*; *the best* ~ (*to do*) cáмое лýчшее; *poor* ~*!* бедня́жка!; *how are* ~*s?* как делá?

think [по]дýмать (*of, about* о П); ~ *over* обдý-м(ыв)ать; ~ *up* придý-м(ыв)ать; ~**able** мысли́-мый; ~**er** мысли́тель *m*

third трéтий

thirst жáжда; *v.* жáждать (*for* P); ~**y**: *be* ~**y** хотéть пить

thirteen трина́дцать

thirt|eenth трина́дцатый; ~**ieth** тридца́тый; ~**y** три́дцать

this э́тот, э́та, э́то

thistle чертополóх

thorn шип, колю́чка; ~**y** колю́чий; (*path*) терни́-стый

thorough основáтельный; ~**fare** у́лица, магистрáль; *no* ~ *fare* проéзда нет

those те, э́ти

though хотя́; (*however*) однáко (же); *as* ~ как бýдто

thought мысль *f*; *v.* задýмчивый; (*heedful*) внимáтельный (*of* к Д); ~**less** невнимáтельный; (*action*) необдýманный

thousand ты́сяча; ~**th** ты́-сячный

thread нить (*a. fig.*), ни́тка; *needle* вдевáть ни́тку (в В); *pearls* нани́зывать [-зáть]; ~**bare** изнóшен-ный

threat угрóза; ~**en** грози́ть *or* угрожáть (Д; *with* Т)

three три; *a* ~ (*in cards, number of bus, tram*) трóйка

thresh [с]молоти́ть

threshold порóг

thrift бережли́вость *f*; ~**y** бережли́вый

thrill трéпет; *v/i.* трепетáть (*with* от P); *v/t.* достав-ля́ть рáдость, наслажде́-ние; вызывáть трéпет у (P); ~**er** приключéнче-ский *or* детекти́вный фильм (ромáн), три́ллер

thrive процветáть

throat гóрло

throb би́ться, пульси́ро-вать

throne престóл, трон

throng толпá; *v.* толпи́ться; *v/t.* заполня́ть [-пóлнить]

throttle *engine* глуши́ть; *su. tech.* дрóссель *m*

through чéрез, сквозь (В); (*because of*) из-за (P); ~ *train* прямóй пóезд

throw бросáть ['-сить], *jave-lin, discus* метáть [мет-нýть]; ~ *away* or *out* вы-брáсывать ['-росить] бросо́к

thrush дрозд

thrust сова́ть (*су́нуть*); *knife* вонза́ть [-зи́ть]; ~ **aside** отта́лкивать [-толкну́ть]

thumb большо́й па́лец (*руки́*)

thump (*blow*) уда́р, уда́рить, (*sound*) стуча́ть [-у́кнуть]; *heart*: колоти́ться

thunder гром; *v.* греме́ть; ~**clap** уда́р гро́ма; ~**storm** гроза́; ~**struck** ошеломлённый

Thursday четве́рг

thus таки́м о́бразом; ~ **far** до сих пор

thwart *plan* расстра́ивать [-ро́ить], [по]меша́ть

tick *clock*: ти́кать; ти́канье; (*mark*) га́лочка

ticket биле́т; (*price*-~) це́нник; ~**-machine** биле́тный автома́т; ~**-office** биле́тная ка́сса

tickl|e [по]щекота́ть; ~**ish** *fig.* щекотли́вый

tide: *high* ~ прили́в; *low* ~ отли́в

tidy опря́тный; (*room*) при́бранный; (*sum*) соли́дный; ~ *up* уб(и)ра́ть

tie (*fasten*) привя́зывать [-за́ть] (*to* к Д); (*link*) свя́зывать [-за́ть]; связь *f*; (*neck*-~) га́лстук; *pl. fig.* [у́зы *f/pl.*]

tiger тигр

tight (*knot, spring*) туго́й; (*rope*) натя́нутый; (*shoe*) те́сный; *su. pl.* колго́тки; *thea., sports* трико́ *n* в *indecl.*; ~**en** *v/t.* belt, knot затя́гивать [-яну́ть]

tile (*roof*) черепи́ца; (*stove, floor*) кафель *m*; ~**d** черепи́чный; ка́фельный

till[1] *prep.* до (Р); *conj.* до тех пор пока́

till[2] *land* возде́л(ыв)ать

timber лесоматериа́л

time вре́мя *n*; (*first, second*) раз; *it is* ~ *to go* пора́ идти́; *in* ~ во́время; *what's the* ~? кото́рый час?; ~**ly** своевре́менный; ~**table** *rail.* расписа́ние поездо́в

timid ро́бкий; ~**ity** ро́бость *f*

tin о́лово; (*container*) консе́рвная ба́нка; *v/t.* консерви́ровать; ~**foil** фольга́; ~**opener** консе́рвный нож *f*; (*box*) жестя́нка

tinge лёгкая окра́ска; *fig.* отте́нок

tinsel мишура́

tint отте́нок; *v.* придава́ть отте́нок (Д)

tiny кро́хотный, кро́шечный

tip (*finger*) ко́нчик; (*umbrella*) наконе́чник; (*waiter*) чаевы́е *pl.*; *v.* дава́ть на чай (Д); ~ *over* опроки́дывать(ся) *v/i.*

нуть(ся); **on ~toe** на цы́-
почках

tire[1] *mot.* ши́на

tire[2] *v/t.* утомля́ть [-ми́ть];
v/i. уст(ав)а́ть; **~d** уста́-
лый; **~less** неуста́нный;
(*person*) неутоми́мый;
~some утоми́тельный

tissue ткань *f* (*a. biol.*)

title (*book*) назва́ние, за-
гла́вие; (*rank*) ти́тул, зва́-
ние; **~-holder** чемпио́н

to *prep.* (*to person*) к (Д); (*a*
(Д); (*to place*) в (В), на
(В); **ten ~ one** (*o'clock*)
без десяти́ час; **~ the
right** напра́во

toad жа́ба

toast *cul.* грено́к; (*drink*)
тост; с[де́лать гренки́];
~er то́стер

tobacco таба́к; *attr.* таба́ч-
ный

toboggan са́нки *f/pl.*; *v.*
ката́ться на са́нках

today сего́дня; **~'s** сего́д-
няшний

toe па́лец (ноги́); (*shoe*)
носо́к

together вме́сте

toil тяжёлый труд; *v.* труди́ться

toilet туале́т; (*W.C.*) туа-
ле́т, убо́рная; **~-paper**
туале́тная бума́га

token (*gift*) пода́рок
на па́мять

tolera|ble сно́сный; **~nce**
терпи́мость *f*; **~nt** терпи́-
мый; **~te** (*endure*) тер-

пе́ть; *allow* допуска́ть
[-сти́ть]

tomato помидо́р; *attr.* то-
ма́тный

tomb моги́ла

tomorrow за́втра

ton то́нна

tone тон

tongs щипцы́ *m/pl.*

tongue язы́к (*a. fig.*)

tonic *med.* тонизи́рующее
сре́дство; (*water*) то́ник

tonight сего́дня ве́чером

tonsil минда́лина

too (+ *adj.*) сли́шком;
(*also*) та́кже, то́же

tool инструме́нт; *fig.* ору́-
дие

tooth зуб; **~ache** зубна́я
боль *f*; **~-brush** зубна́я
щётка; **~-paste** зубна́я
па́ста

top верх; (*summit*) вер-
ши́на; (*toy*) волчо́к; (*cover*) кры́шка; *attr.* ве́рх-
ний; (*highest*) вы́сший;
from ~ to bottom све́рху
до́низу

topic предме́т, те́ма; **~al**
злободне́вный

topple: **~ over** опроки́ды-
вать(ся) [-и́нуть(ся)]

torch фа́кел; *el.* карма́н-
ный фона́рь *m*

torment му́ка; *v.* [из-, за]-
му́чить

torpedo торпе́да

torrent пото́к

tortoise черепа́ха; **~-shell**
черепа́ховый

torture пытка; *v.* пытáть; *fig.* [за]мýчить

toss брóса́ть ['-сить]; *coin* подбрáсывать [-брóсить]; *head* вскидывать [вскинуть]; *(in bed)* метáться

total итóг; *adj.* óбщий; *(in all)* итогó *(adv.);* *v. figures:* составля́ть ['-вить]; **_itarian** тоталитáрный

touch прикаса́ться [-косну́ться] к (Д); *(affect)* трóгать [трóнуть]; *(hurt)* заде(вá)ть; **_ down** *ae.* приземля́ться [-ли́ться]; **_ on** затрáгивать [-рóнуть]; **_** прикосновéние; *fig.* контáкт; *(art)* штрих; **_ing** трóгательный; **_y** оби́дчивый

tough *(material)* прóчный; *(meat)* жёсткий; *hardy* выно́сливый; *(hard)* трýдный

tour турнé *n indecl.,* поéздка; *thea.* гастрóли; **_ coach** автóбусная экскýрсия; *v. country* соверша́ть турнé (поéздку) по Д); **_ist** тури́ст(ка); **_na-ment** турни́р

tow *(act)* букси́ровка; *v.* букси́ровать

towards *a.;* *(for)* для (Р)

towel полотéнце

tower бáшня

town гóрод; **_ council** горoдскóй совéт; **_-dweller** горожáн|ин, **_**ка

toy игру́шка; *attr.* игрý-

шечный

trace след *(a. fig.);* *animal* высле́живать [вы́следить]; *fig.* прослéживать [-еди́ть]

track *(trace)* след; *rail.* колея́; *(sports)* бегова́я доро́жка, *(cycle or motor racing)* трек, *(ski)* лы́жня; **_suit** трениро́вочный костю́м

trade ремесло́, профéссия; *comm.* торго́вля; *v.* торгова́ть; **_-mark** заводскáя мáрка; **_ mission** торгпрéдство (= торго́вое представи́тельство); **_r** торго́вец; **_ union** профсою́з

tradition тради́ция; *(story)* предáние; **_al** традицио́нный

traffic *mot., rail.* движéние; трáнспорт; *mar., ae.* сообщéние; *comm.* торгóвля; **_ jam** прóбка; **_ lights** светофóр; **_ police** ГАИ (= госудáрственная автомоби́льная инспéкция); **_ sign** дорóжный знак

tragedy трагéдия; **_ic** траги́ческий

trail *v.* волочи́ть(ся) *(on* по Д); *after* за Т); *(trace)* след; *(path)* тропá; **_er** *mot.* прицéп, трéйлер

train *rail.* пóезд; *suburban* **_** при́городный пóезд; *coll.* электри́чка; шлейф; *(instruct)* обуча́ть [-чи́ть]

trait черта́ (хара́ктера)

traitor преда́тель *m*

tram трамва́й; *attr.* трамва́йный

tramp тяжёлый то́пот; (*hobo*) бродя́га *m*; *v/i.* то́пать нога́ми; бродя́жничать; **~le** *v/t.* раста́птывать [растопта́ть]; **~le on** наступи́ть [-пи́ть] на (В); *feelings* задева́ть [-де́ть]

tranquillizer *med.* транквилиза́тор

transaction сде́лка *f*; *pl.* (*science*) труды́ *m/pl.*

transfer перево́д; переводи́ть [-вести́]

transform преобразо́вывать [-зова́ть]; **~ation** преобразова́ние; **~er** *el.* трансформа́тор

transfusion (*blood*) перелива́ние кро́ви

transgress *law* преступа́ть [-пи́ть]

transient преходя́щий; *v.* транзи́т; *attr.* транзи́тный; **~t visa** транзи́тная ви́за; **~tion** перехо́д; *attr.* перехо́дный; **~tive** *gr.* перехо́дный

translate переводи́ть [-вести́]; **~ion** перево́д; **~or** перево́дчик *m*, -ца

transmission переда́ча; **~t** переда(ва́)ть; **~tter** переда́тчик

transparent прозра́чный

transplant переса́живать [-сади́ть]

transport тра́нспорт, перево́зка; *v.* перевози́ть [-везти́]; **be ~ed with joy** быть вне себя́ от ра́дости

trap лову́шка (*a.* *fig.*); (*spring-~*) капка́н; (*pitfall*) западня́

trash хлам; *fig. coll.* дрянь *f*

travel путеше́ствовать; *v.* путеше́ствие; **~ agency** туристи́ческое аге́нтство; **~er** путеше́ственик, -ца; *comm.* коммивояжёр; **~ling:** **~ling speed** ско́рость движе́ния

trawler тра́улер

tray подно́с

treacherous преда́тельский; **~y** преда́тельство

tread ступа́ть [-пи́ть]; (*gait*) по́ступь *f*; (*stair, rung*) ступе́нька; **~ on** наступа́ть [-пи́ть] на (В)

treason (госуда́рственная) изме́на

treasure сокро́вище; *v.* (*value*) высоко́ цени́ть; (*store*) храни́ть [-нить]; **~y** *fin.* казна́; **the ~y** *U.K.* мини́стерство фина́нсов; *fig.* сокро́вищница

treat (*handle*) обраща́ться [-рати́ться] (с Т); *med.* лечи́ть; (*discuss*) рассма́тривать(ся) (*of* В, И); **~ise** нау́чный труд; (*for a degree*) диссерта́ция; **~ment** обращение; обработка; лечение; трактовка; ~y договор

treble тройной; *v.* утрашивать(ся) [утроить(ся)]

tree дерево

trem|ble дрожать; ~endous огромный; (*wonderful*) *coll.* потрясающий; ~or дрожь f

trench (*ditch*) канава

trend направление, тенденция, тренд

trial (*test*) испытание; *jur.* судебный процесс; *attr.* испытательный, пробный

triangle треугольник

tribe племя n

tribun|al трибунал; ~e (*stand*) трибуна

tribut|ary *geogr.* приток; ~e дань f *mst. fig.*

trick трюк; (*deceiving*) уловка; *v.* обманывать [-нуть]

trickle *v/t.* (*drop*) капать; (*ooze*) сочиться; (*run down*) стекать

trif|le пустяк, мелочь f; ~ing пустяковый

trigger спусковой крючок

trim *hair, hedge* подрезать [ёзать]; *dress* отдел(ыва)ть; *adj.* опрятный

Trinity Троица

trip поездка, экскурсия; *mar., av.* рейс; *v/i.* (*stumble*) спотыкаться [-ткнуться]

triple тройной

triumph торжество; *v.* [вос]торжествовать; ~ant торжествующий

trivial мелкий, незначительный

trolley (*bus*) троллейбус; тележка

troop (*people*) толпа; *pl. mil.* войска n/pl.

trophy трофей

tropic тропик; ~al тропический

trot *v.* бежать рысью

trouble беспокойство, хлопоты f/pl.; беспокоить(ся); утруждать(ся); *get into* → попасть в беду; *take the* → брать [взять] на себя труд + *inf.*; *what's the* ~? в чём дело?; ~some хлопотный; (*child*) беспокойный

trousers брюки f/pl.

trout форель f

truant прогульщик

truce *pol.* перемирие

truck *mot.* грузовик

true верный; (*genuine*) истинный, подлинный; (*right*) правильный; *yours* ~ly искренне Ваш(а) (*signature*)

trump козырь m

trumpet *mus.* труба; *v.* трубить; ~er трубач

truncheon (*police*) дубинка

trunk *anat.* туловище; *bot.* ствол; *zo.* хобот; (*case*) чемода́н

trunks трусы́

trust *person* доверя́ть (Д); *thing* вверя́ть ['-рить] (В; **to** Д); (*rely*) наде́яться; *su.* дове́рие; *comm.* трест; **~ee** опеку́н; **~ful** дове́рчивый; **~worthy** надёжный

truth пра́вда, *pl.;* **~ful** правди́вый

try [по]про́бовать (В *or* + *inf.*); (*test*) испы́тывать [-пыта́ть]; (*attempt*) [по]пыта́ться; (*law*) суди́ть; *~ on clothes* приме́рять [-ме́рить]

tsar царь *m;* **~itza** цари́ца

T-shirt футбо́лка

tub (*bath*) ва́нна; (*vat*) ка́дка

tube *tech.* труба́; (*toothpaste*) тю́бик; *Brit.* метро́ *indecl.;* **~ inner ~** *mot.* ка́мера

tuberculosis туберкулёз

tuck (*hide*) [с]пря́тать; **~ up** *sleeve* засу́чивать [-чи́ть]

Tuesday вто́рник

tug дёргать [дёрнуть] (**by** за В); (*boat*) букси́р

tulip тюльпа́н

tumult шум, сумато́ха

tuna *zo.* туне́ц

tune мело́дия; *v.* настра́ивать [-ро́ить]; *out of ~* расстро́енный

tunnel тунне́ль *m*

turban тюрба́н; (*Muslim*) чалма́

turbine турби́на

turbulent бу́рный (*a. fig.*)

turf (*soil with grass*) дёрн; (*peat*) торф

Turk тю́рок, -ча́нка; **~ey** Ту́рция; **2ey** инде́йка, инде́йк; **~ish** туре́цкий

turn (*revolve*) верте́ть(ся), враща́ть(ся); (*reverse*) повора́чивать(ся) [поверну́ть(ся)]; (*become*) станови́ться [стать]; *su.* поворо́т; оборо́т; **~ on** включа́ть [-чи́ть]; **~ off** выключа́ть [вы́ключить]; **~ out** (*expel*) выгоня́ть [вы́гнать]; *products* выпуска́ть [вы́пустить]; *it ~ed out that ...* оказа́лось, что ...; **~er** то́карь *m;* **~ing-point** поворо́тный пункт

turnip ре́па

turpentine скипида́р

turtle черепа́ха

tusk би́вень *m*

tutor (*private*) репети́тор; *univ. approx.* нау́чный руководи́тель

twel|**fth** двена́дцатый; **~ve** двена́дцать

twent|**ieth** двадца́тый; **~y** два́дцать

twice два́жды

twig ве́точка

twilight су́мерки *f/pl.*

twin близне́ц; **~ towns** города́-побрати́мы

twine бечёвка

twinkle мерца́ние; *v.* мерца́ть

twirl верте́ть

twist rope скру́чивать [-ути́ть]; ring крути́ть; (distort) искажа́ть [-кази́ть]; way, river: извива́ться; su. (bend) изги́б

twitch дёргать(ся) [дёрнуть(ся)]; дёрганье

twitter щебет; v. щебета́ть

two два, две; su. (in cards, number of bus, tram): дво́йка; ~ of us дво́е из нас; ~ hundred две́сти;

~-way mot. двусторо́нний

type тип; typ. шрифт; v. [на]печа́тать (на маши́нке); ~writer пи́шущая маши́нка

typhus тиф

typical типи́чный

typist машини́стка

tyran|ny тирани́я; ~t тира́н

tyre mot. ши́на; flat ~ спу́щенная ши́на

tzar → **tsar**

U

udder вы́мя n

ugly некраси́вый, уро́дливый, безобра́зный

Ukrainian украи́н|ец, -ка; -ский

ulcer я́зва

ultimate|te (aim) коне́чный; (result) оконча́тельный; ~um ультима́тум

ultra-high: ~ frequency коротковолно́вый; ~-violet ультрафиоле́товый

umbrella зо́нтик; **telescopic ~** складно́й зо́нтик

umpire (sports) судья́ m

unable неспосо́бный; не в состоя́нии; be ~ to не [c]мочь

unaccustomed непривы́кший; (unusual) необы́чный

unanimous единоду́шный,

единогла́сный

unarmed невооружённый

unavoidable неизбе́жный

unaware: be ~ of не сознава́ть; не знать (P); ~s неча́янно; (by surprise) враспло́х

unbearable невыноси́мый

unbelievable невероя́тный

unbind развя́зывать [-вяза́ть]

unbroken (whole) неразби́тый, це́лый; (continuous) непреры́вный

unbutton расстёгивать [-тёгну́ть]

uncanny жу́ткий

uncertain (not confident) неуве́ренный; (not definitely known) неопределённый; ~ty неуве́ренность f; неопределённость f

unchanged неизме́нный;

his condition remains ~ его состояние не изменилось

uncle дя́дя *m*

uncomfortable неудо́бный

uncommon необы́чный; необыча́йный

unconscious бессозна́тельный; *(fainted)* без созна́ния

uncouth гру́бый

uncover *v/t. head, flank* обнажа́ть [-жи́ть]; *pot* снима́ть кры́шку (с Р); *fig.* откры́(ва́)ть

undeniable бесспо́рный

under *prep.* под (Т *or* В); *(below)* ни́же (Р); *(less than)* ме́ньше (Р); ~ *the condition* при усло́вии; ~ *the agreement* по соглаше́нию

underbrush подле́сок

underdeveloped нера́звитый; *econ.* развива́ющийся

underdone *cul.* недожа́ренный

underestimate недооце́нивать [-ни́ть]; недооце́нка

undergo *changes, hardships* претерпе́(ва́)ть; *operation* подверга́ться ['-гнуться] (Д)

underground подзе́мный; *pol.* подпо́льный; *su.* метро́ *n indecl.*

underline подчёркивать [-черкну́ть]

underlying *fig.* лежа́щий в осно́ве

undermine подры́(ва́)ть; *fig.* подрыва́ть [подорва́ть]

underneath *adv.* внизу́, вниз; *prep.* под (Т *or* В)

understand [-ня́ть]; ~**ing** понима́ние; *(agreement)* соглаше́ние

undertak|e предпринима́ть [-ня́ть]; *(pledge o.s.)* обя́зываться [-за́ться]; ~**ing** предприя́тие; обяза́тельство

undertone полуто́н; *fig.* отте́нок; *in an* ~ вполго́лоса

underwear ни́жнее бельё

underworld ад; *(social)* дно о́бщества

undesirable нежела́тельный

undoubted несомне́нный

undress разде́(ва́)ть(ся)

uneas|iness *(anxiety)* беспоко́йство; *(situation)* нело́вкость *f*, неудо́бство; *(feeling)* стеснённость *f*; ~**y** обеспоко́енный; неудо́бный; стеснённый

unemploy|ed безрабо́тный; ~**ment** безрабо́тица

unequal нера́вный

uneven *(surface)* неро́вный; *(number)* нечётный

unexpected неожи́данный

unfair несправедли́вый; *(means)* нече́стный

unfamiliar незнако́мый

unfavourable неблагоприя́тный

unfinished незакóнченный; (*rough*) неотдéланный, необрабóтанный

unfit негóдный

unfold развёртывать(ся) [-вернýть(ся)]

unforgettable незабывáемый

unfortunate несчáстный; (*enterprise*) неудáчный; **~ly** к несчáстью

unfriendly недружелю́бный, непривéтливый

unhappy несчáстный, несчастли́вый

unheard-of неслы́ханный

uniform единообрáзный; *phys., tech.* равномéрный; *su.* мунди́р, фóрменная одéжда

unimportant невáжный

union объединéние (*a. action*), сою́з

unique еди́нственный в своём рóде, неповтори́мый, уникáльный

unit *math., phys.* едини́ца; *mil.* часть *f*, подразделéние; *tech.* блок, агрегáт; **~e** со-, объ-единя́ть(ся) [-ни́ть(ся)]; **~ed**: **~ed Nations** Организáция Объединённых Нáций (= ООН); **~y** еди́нство; (*harmony*) соглáсие

universal универсáльный (*a. tech.*); (*general*) всеóбщий; (*world-wide*) всеми́рный; **~e** вселéнная, мир; **~ity** университéт

unjust несправедли́вый

unkind недóбрый, недружелю́бный

unknown неизвéстный

unlike: *he is ~ his father* он не похóж на отцá; *~ his father, he ...* в отли́чие от отцá, он ...; **~ly** маловероя́тный

unlimited неограни́ченный

unload *vehicle* разгружáть [-узи́ть]; *goods, people* выгружáть [вы́грузить]

unlock отпирáть [-перéть]

unmoved: *she remained ~* это её не трóнуло

unnatural неестéственный; (*instinct*) противоестéственный

unnecessary ненýжный

unpack распакóвывать [-овáть]

unpleasant неприя́тный

unqualified неквалифици́рованный; (*unreserved*) безоговóрочный

unreasonable неразýмный; (*excessive*) чрезмéрный

unrest беспокóйство; *pol.* волнéния, беспоря́дки *pl.*

unruly непокóрный, непослýшный

unselfish бескоры́стный

unsettled (*problem*) не(раз)решённый; (*weather*) неустóйчивый; (*account*) неоплáченный

unskilf**ul** неумéлый; **~ed** неквалифици́рованный

unspeakable вели́кий, неопису́емый

unsteady неусто́йчивый

untidy неопря́тный; (*room*) неубранный

until → **till**

untimely *adj.* (*ill-timed*) несвоевре́менный; (*too early*) преждевре́менный

untouched нетро́нутый

untrue неве́рный

unused неиспо́льзованный; ~**ual** необыкнове́нный

unwise неразу́мный

unworthy недосто́йный

up *adv.* наве́рх, наве́рх; *prep.* вверх по (Д); (*right*) ~ **to** (вплоть до (Р)

upbringing воспита́ние

uphill *adv.* в го́ру

uphold подде́рживать [-жа́ть]; *decision* подтвержда́ть [-рди́ть]

upholster оби(ва́)ть; ~**y** оби́вка

upon → **on**

upper ве́рхний; (*higher*) вы́сший; ~**most** са́мый ве́рхний; наивы́сший

upright прямо́й, вертика́льный; (*honest*) че́стный; *adv.* сто́я́

uprising *pol.* восста́ние

uproar шум, гам; (*violent*) сканда́л

upset (*overturn*) опроки́дывать(ся) [-и́нуть(ся)]; *person, plan* расстра́ивать [-ро́ить]

upside: ~ **down** вверх дном

upstairs наве́рх (по ле́стнице); наве́рху (в ве́рхнем этаже́)

up-to-date совреме́нный; **be** ~ быть в ку́рсе

upward *adv.* вверх; *adj.* напра́вленный вверх

urban городско́й

urgen|cy сро́чность *f*, неотло́жность *f*; ~**t** (*matter*) сро́чный, неотло́жный; (*request*) настоя́тельный

urine мочá

us нас (= В); нам (= Д)

usage испо́льзование, употребле́ние; (*custom*) обы́чай

use употребля́ть [-би́ть] (В); (*avail o.s.*) [вос]по́льзоваться (Т); (*apply*) применя́ть [-ни́ть] (В); употребле́ние; по́льзование; **make** ~ **of** испо́льзовать (*im*)*pf.*; **we** ~ **d to play** мы, быва́ло, игра́ли; **I am** ~ **d to it** я привы́к(ла) к э́тому; **get** ~ **d to** привыка́ть ['-кнуть] к (Д); ~**ful** поле́зный; ~**less** бесполе́зный; ~**r** по́льзователь

usual обыкнове́нный, обы́чный; ~**ly** обы́чно

utensils *pl.* у́тварь *f*

utili|ty (*usefulness*) поле́зность *f*; **public** ~**ties** комму́на́льные услу́ги *f/pl.*; ~**ze** испо́льзовать (*im*)*pf.*

utmost преде́льный (*a. fig.*); (*importance*) вы-

сочáйший; **do one's** ~ дéлать всё возмóжное
utter¹ крáйний, совершéнный, пóлный
utter² *opinion* выскáзывать

[выскáзать]; *sound* изд(ав)áть; ~**ance** выскáзывание
U-turn *mot.* разворóт

V

vaca|ncy (*office*) вакáнсия; ~**nt** вакáнтный; (*empty*) пустóй (*a. fig.*); свобóдный; (*look*) отсýтствующий; ~**tion** (*school*) канѝкулы *f/pl.*; (*holiday*) óтпуск
vaccination вакцинáция, привѝвка
vacuum вáкуум; *fig.* пустотá; ~ **cleaner** пылесóс; ~ **flask** тéрмос
vague (*indefinite*) неопределённый; (*dim*) смýтный; (*sense*) неясный
vain тщеслáвный; (*futile*) тщéтный, напрáсный; *in* ~ тщéтно, напрáсно
valet слугá
valiant дóблестный
valid (*passport*) действѝтельный; (*reason, claim*) обоснóванный; ~**ity** действѝтельность *f*
valley долѝна
valu|able цéнный; *su. pl.* цéнности *f/pl.*; ~**ation** оцéнка; ~**e** цéнность *f*; значéние (*a. tech.*); *v.* [о]ценѝть; *market* ~**e** рыночная стóимость *f*

valve клáпан, вéнтиль; *el.* электрóнная лáмпа
van *mot.* (автó)фургóн
vandalism вандалѝзм
vane лóпасть *f*; (*weather* ~) флюгер
vanguard авангáрд
vanilla ванѝль *f*
vani|sh исчезáть ['-знуть]; ~**ty** тщеслáвие; ~**ty case** косметѝчка
vapour пар
vari|able перемéнчивый, перемéнный; ~**ant** *su.* вариáнт; ~**ation** изменéние, колебáние; *mus.* вариáция; ~**ety** разнообрáзие; *biol.* разновѝдность *f*; (*sort*) сорт; ~**ous** (*different*) разлѝчный; (*with pl.* = *several*) рáзные *pl.*
varnish лак; [от]лакировáть
vary (*differ*) расходѝться, (*change*) изменять(ся) [-нѝть(ся)]; (*diversify*) разнообрáзить
vase вáза
vast (*wide*) обшѝрный; (*huge*) огрóмный; ~**ness** обшѝрность *f*; огрóм-

ность f

vat чан, бак

vault свод; (*cellar*) подвал; (*burial*) склеп; ~**ing horse** конь; ~**ing pole** шест

veal телятина

vegeta|ble овощ; *adj.* растительный; ~**ble garden** огород; ~**rian** вегетарианец, -ка; ~**tion** растительность f

vehemen|ce страстность f, сила; (*passion*) сильный

vehicle *mot.* автомашина; *mst.* наземное транспортное средство; *fig.* средство

veil вуаль f; *fig.* завеса; **bridal** ~ свадебная фата; *fig.* [за]вуалировать

vein жила (*a. min.*), вена; *fig.* жилка (*a. bot.*)

velocity скорость f

velvet бархат; *attr.* бархатный

veneer (*wood*) фанеровка

venereal венерический

venison оленина

venom *zo.* яд; *fig.* злоба; ~**ous** ядовитый (*a. fig.*)

vent отверстие, отдушина; **give** ~ *fig.* изли(ва)ть (**to** В); ~**ilate room** проветри(ва)ть; ~**ilation** вентиляция; ~**ilator** вентилятор

venture предприятие; **joint** ~ совместное предприятие; *v. life* рисковать [-кнуть] (Т); (*dare*) отва-

жи(ва)ться

Venus Венера

veranda(h) веранда

verb *gr.* глагол; (*oral*) устный; (*verbatim*) дословный

verdict (*law*) приговор

verge (*edge*) край; *fig.* грань f; ~ **on** граничить (с Т)

veri|fication проверка; (*confirmation*) f подтверждение; ~**fy** проверять ['-рить]; подтверждать [-рдить]

vermicelli вермишель f

vermouth вермут

versatile разносторонний

vers|e (*Bible*) стих; (*poetry*) стихи *m/pl.*; (*stanza*) строфа; ~**ion** версия; вариант; (*translation*) перевод

vertical вертикальный

very *adv.* очень; ~ *much interested* очень заинтересованный; ~ *the* ~ *same* тот же самый; *the* ~ *thing* как раз то, что нужно; *the* ~ *thought* одна уже мысль

vessel сосуд (*a. anat.*); *mar.* судно

vest майка; *Am.* жилет

vestige след

veteran ветеран (войны); ~**inary** ветеринарный; *su.* ветеринар (*a. vet*)

veto вето *n indecl.*; наложить вето (на В)

vex [раз]доса́довать (В);
~**ation** доса́да; доса́дное
обстоя́тельство

via че́рез (В)

vibrate вибри́ровать; ~**ion**
вибра́ция

vice[1] tech. тиски́ m/pl.

vice[2] поро́к

vice-president вице-прези-
де́нт

vicinity сосе́дство; (area)
окре́стности f/pl.; **in the** ~
побли́зости (**of** от Р)

vicious злой, зло́бный; ~
circle поро́чный круг

victim же́ртва

victor победи́тель m; ~**ious**
победоно́сный; ~**y** побе́да

video ви́део, ~**tape recorder** видеомагнитофо́н

Vienna Ве́на

view (aspect, prospect) вид;
(opinion) взгляд, мне́ние;
v. осма́тривать [осмо-
тре́ть]; fig. рассма́тривать
[-мотре́ть]; **in** ~ **of** ввиду́
(Р); **with a** ~ **to** с це́лью
(+ inf.); ~**point** то́чка зре́-
ния

vigilan|ce бди́тельность f;
~**t** бди́тельный

vigo|rous энерги́чный; ~**ur**
си́ла, эне́ргия

vile ме́рзкий, по́длый

villa ви́лла

village дере́вня, село́; ~**r**
се́льский жи́тель m

vine виногра́дная лоза́; ~
gar у́ксус; ~**yard** виног-
ра́дник

vintage вино́ (**of 1963** уро-
жа́я 1963-го го́да); ~ **wine**
ма́рочное вино́

violate law, peace нару-
ша́ть [-ши́ть]; woman
[из]наси́ловать; ~**ation** на-
руше́ние; изнаси́лование;
~**ence** (brute force) наси́-
лие; (intensity) неи́стовая
си́ла; **outbreak of** ~ бес-
поря́дки pl.; ~**ent** наси́-
льственный; неи́сто-
вый

violet фиа́лка; adj. фиоле́-
товый

violin скри́пка; ~**ist** скри-
па́ч

viper гадю́ка

virgin де́вственница; **the** ⁀
де́ва Мари́я; ~**al** де́в-
ственный

virtual факти́ческий; ~**e**
доброде́тель f; (advan-
tage) досто́инство; **by** ~
of в си́лу (Р)

visa ви́за

visib|ility ви́димость f;
~**ible** ви́димый; ~**ion** biol.
зре́ние; (dream) мечта́;
~**it** визи́т, посеще́ние; v.
посеща́ть [-ети́ть]; ~**itor**
посети́тель m; (private)
гость m; ~**ual** зри́тельный

vital жи́зненный; (person)
живо́й, энерги́чный; ~**ity**
жи́зненность f; энерги́ч-
ность f

viva|cious живо́й, ожив-
лённый; ~**acity** жи́вость
f; ~**id** (colour, description)

389

wake

я́ркий

voca|bulary (*in a book*) слова́рь; (*of a dictionary*) слóвник; (*stock of words*) запáс слов; **~l** *mus.* вокáльный; **~l cords** голосовы́е свя́зки; **~tion** профéссия; (*inner call*) призвáние

vogue мóда; популя́рность *f*

voice гóлос; *gr.* залóг

void пустóй; *jur.* недействи́тельный; *su.* пустотá; (*gap*) пробéл; **~ of** лишённый (Р)

volcano вулкáн

volley *fig.* град; *v.* сы́паться грáдом

volleyball волейбóл

volt вольт; **~age** напряжéние

volume (*size*) объём; (*capacity*) ёмкость *f*; (*book*) том

volunt|ary добровóльный; **~eer** добровóлец; (*to do*) вызывáться [вы́зваться] + *inf.*

vomit *v/t.*, *v/i.* [вы́]рвать; **~ing** рвóта

voracious *fig.* ненасы́тный

vote (*voting*) голосовáние; (*single*) гóлос; *v/i.* голосовáть (*for* за В); *v/t.* [про]голосовáть; **~r** избирáтель *f*

vouch ручáться [поручи́ться] (*for* за В); **~er**: **luncheon ~er** талóн на обéд

vow [по]кля́сться

vowel глáсный (звук)

voyage путешéствие; *v.* путешéствовать

vulgar вульгáрный

vulnerable язви́мый

vulture стервя́тник

W

wade *river* переходи́ть вброд; (*a. ~ through*) *weeds, mud* проб(и)рáться по (Д)

wafer вáфля

waffle вáфля

wage: **~ war** вести́ войну́

wage(s) зарáботная плáта

wag(g)on (*cart*) повóзка; *rail.* товáрный вагóн; (*flat*) платфóрма

wail *person:* вопи́ть, плáкать; *wind:* выть; *su.*

вопль *m*; вой

waist тáлия; **~coat** жилéт

wait ждать (*for* В *or* Р); (*expect*) ожидáть (*for* Р); **~ a moment** подожди́(те) мину́тку!; **~ on** обслу́живать (В); **~er** официáнт; **~ing-room** зал ожидáния; **~ress** официáнтка

wake *v/i.* (*awake*) просыпáться [-сну́ться]; *v/t.* [раз]буди́ть; *fig.* пробужда́ть [-уди́ть]

walk ходи́ть, идти́ [пойти́] (пешко́м *on foot*); (*stroll*) прогу́лка; (*gait*) похо́дка; **go for a ~** пойти́ прогуля́ться; **ten minutes ~** де́сять мину́т ходьбы́

wall стена́

wallet бума́жник

wallpaper обо́и *m/pl.*

walnut гре́цкий оре́х

walrus морж

waltz вальс

wander [по]броди́ть; *thoughts*: блужда́ть

wane *moon*: убы(ва́)ть; *fig.* ослабева́ть

want (*wish*) хоте́ть (В *or* P *of inf.*); (*need*) нужда́ться (в П); (*lack*) не хвата́ть (Р); *su.* нужда́; недоста́ток; *pl.* потре́бности *f/pl.*; **for ~ of** за неиме́нием (Р)

war война́; **~ Office (Department)** вое́нное министе́рство

ward (*hospital*) пала́та; (*prison*) ка́мера; (*under ~ship*) опека́емый; **~ off** отвраща́ть [-рати́ть]; (*hostel*) коменда́нт; *Am.* нача́льник тюрьмы́; *eccl.* церко́вный ста́роста *m*; **~er** тюре́мный надзира́тель

wardrobe (*furniture*) платяно́й шкаф; (*clothes*) гардеро́б

ware изде́лия *n/pl.*; *pl.* това́р(ы *pl.*); **~house** склад

това́ров

warm тёплый; (*reception*) серде́чный; (*support*) горя́чий; **I am ~** мне тепло́; *v/t.* греть; *fig.* согрева́ть [-гре́ть]; *v/i.* нагрева́ться [-е́ться]; **~th** теплота́; серде́чность *f*

warn предостерега́ть [-ре́чь] (*against* от Р); (*let know*) предупрежда́ть [-упреди́ть]; **~ing** предостереже́ние; предупрежде́ние

warp *wood*: [по]коро́биться

warrior во́ин; **~ship** вое́нный кора́бль *m*

wary осторо́жный

wash *v/t.* [вы́]мыть, умы́(ва́)ть; *linen* [вы́]стира́ть; *sea*: омы(ва́)ть; *v/i.* умы(ва́)ться; стира́ться; *su.* мытьё; сти́рка; **~basin** умыва́льник; **~ing:** **~ing machine** стира́льная маши́на

washer *tech.* ша́йба

wasp оса́

waste [по]тра́тить зря; пуста́я тра́та; (*refuse*) отбро́сы *m/pl.*; (*manufacture*) отхо́ды *m/pl.*; **~ful** расточи́тельный

watch следи́ть за (Т), наблюда́ть; (*guard*) сторожи́ть (В); *su.* охра́на; *mar.* ва́хта; (*instrument*) часы́ *m/pl.*; **~ for** *chance* выжида́ть [вы́ждать]; **~ful** бдительный; ~-maker часовщи́к; ~-man (night) сто́рож; вахтёр

water вода́; attr. водяно́й, (sports) во́дный; v/t. street, flowers поли(ва́)ть; ~-colour акваре́ль; ~-fall водопа́д; ~-melon арбу́з; ~-tight водонепроница́емый; ~-way водяно́й путь m; ~-y водяни́стый

watt ватт

wave волна́ (a. el.); (hair) зави́вка; v/t. маха́ть [махну́ть] (Т); v/i. колыха́ться [-хну́ться]; ~-r (hesitate) колеба́ться

wax воск; (ear) се́ра; attr. восково́й

way путь m, доро́га; ~ of life о́браз жи́зни; by the ~ (incidentally) кста́ти; in a friendly ~ ми́рным путём; give ~ (yield) уступа́ть [-пи́ть]; have one's ~ поступа́ть [-пи́ть] по своему́; on the ~ по доро́ге; the other ~ round наоборо́т; ~-side обо́чина; attr. придоро́жный

we мы

weak сла́бый; ~-ly adj. хи́лый; adv. сла́бо; ~-ness сла́бость f

wealth бога́тство; (plenty) изоби́лие; ~-y бога́тый

weapon ору́жие

wear носи́ть(ся); (clothes) оде́жда; ~ (and tear) mst. tech. изно́с; ~ off fig.

проходи́ть, пройти́; ~ out изна́шивать(ся) [-носи́ть(ся)]; (exhaust) fig. утомля́ть [-ми́ть], изнуря́ть [-ри́ть]

wear‖iness уста́лость f; ~-y уста́лый; (tiring) утоми́тельный; v/t. утомля́ть [-ми́ть]

weasel zo. ла́ска

weather пого́да; ~-cock флю́гер; ~-forecast прогно́з пого́ды

weave [со]тка́ть; ~-r тка́чиха

web (spider) паути́на (a. fig.)

wedding сва́дьба; church венча́ние; attr. сва́дебный; ~ ceremony бра́чная церемо́ния

wedge клин

Wednesday среда́

weed сорня́к; v. [вы́]полоть

week неде́ля; this ~ adv. на э́той неде́ле; this day ~ че́рез неде́лю; ~-day бу́дний день; ~-end уике́нд; ~-ly еженеде́льный; adv. еженеде́льно; su. еженеде́льник

weep пла́кать

weigh v/i. ве́сить; v/t. взве́шивать [-е́сить] (a. fig.); ~-t вес; (piece) ги́ря; (sports) шта́нга; ~-ty ве́ский

welcome v. приве́тствовать; (speech) приве́тст-

вие; (*reception*) раду́шный
приём; *adj.* жела́нный,
прия́тный; ~! добро́ по-
жа́ловать!

weld *tech.* сва́ривать
[-ри́ть]; ~**er** сва́рщик

welfare (*person*) благопо-
лу́чие; (*nation*) благосо-
стоя́ние; *public* ~ соци-
а́льное обеспече́ние

well[1] коло́дец

well[2] *adv.* хорошо́; *int.* ну!;
I am ~ я чу́вствую себя́
хорошо́; ~**-being** благосо-
стоя́ние; ~**-bred** хорошо́
воспи́танный; ~**-off** зажи́-
точный; ~**-read** начи́тан-
ный

Welsh валли́йский; ~**man**
валли́ец

west за́пад; *attr.* за́падный;
~ *of* к за́паду от (P);
~**ward** *adj.* (*journey*) в за́-
падном направле́нии;
adv. на за́пад

wet мо́крый, сыро́й; *v/t.*
(*soak*) сма́чивать [-мо-
чи́ть]; (*moisten*) увлаж-
ня́ть [-жни́ть]; *get* ~ промо-
ка́ть [-кнуть]

whale кит

wharf (грузова́я) при́стань
f

what что; (~ *kind of*) ка-
ко́й; ~ *is the time?* кото́-
рый час?; ~ *is the mat-
ter?* в чём де́ло?; ~**ever**
happens что бы ни случи́-
лось; ~ *for?* заче́м?

wheat пшени́ца

wheel колесо́; *v/t.* ката́ть,
[по]кати́ть

when когда́; (*whither*) куда́
бы ни

where где, (*whither*) куда́;
~**as** тогда́ как; ~**upon** по́-
сле чего́; ~**ver** где бы ни,
куда́ бы ни

whet [на]точи́ть, ~**stone**
точи́льный ка́мень

whether ли; ~ *he will come*
придёт ли он

which кото́рый

while: *for a* ~ не́которое
вре́мя, на вре́мя; *once in
a* ~ вре́мя от вре́мени;
wait a ~ подожди́(те) не-
мно́жко; *conj.* пока́;
(*though*) хотя́

whim при́хоть *f*

whimper *v.* хны́кать; *mst.
dog:* скули́ть

whip кнут; (*riding*) хлыст;
cream взби(ва́)ть; ~**ped:**
~**ped cream** взби́тые
сли́вки

whirl *v.* кружи́ть(ся), ~**pool**
водоворо́т; ~**wind** смерч

whisk (*a.* ~ *away*) юркну́ть *pf.*; *egg* взби(ва́)ть;
mouse: юркну́ть *pf.*; ~**ers**
усы́ *m/pl., a. zo.*

whisper шёпот; *v.* [про]-
шепта́ть

whistle свист; (*instrument*)
свисто́к; *v.* свисте́ть
[сви́стнуть]

white бе́лый; *su.* бе́лый
цвет; (*egg, eye*) бело́к; ~
coffee ко́фе с молоко́м;

~n v/t. [по]бели́ть; v/i. [по]беле́ть; ~wash [по]бели́ть; fig. обеля́ть [-ли́ть]

Whitsun Тро́ица

who кто; rel. pron. кото́рый; ~ever кто бы ни

whole весь, вся, всё (mst. the ~); це́лый (mst. **a** ~); ~sale опто́вый; опто́вая торго́вля; adv. о́птом; ~some благотво́рный; (food, etc.) здоро́вый, поле́зный

wholly целико́м, всеце́ло

whom кого́; **to** ~ кому́; rel. pron. кото́рого; кото́рому

whore проститу́тка

whose чей, чья, чьё, pl. чьи

wick фити́ль m

wicked (evil) злой; (very bad) плохо́й, дурно́й; (immoral) безнра́вственный

wide широ́кий; ~ **open** широко́ откры́тый; ~ **n** расширя́ть(ся) [-ри́ть(ся)]; (~roký) распространённый

widow вдова́; ~er вдове́ц

width ширина́

wife жена́

wig пари́к

wild ди́кий; (frenzied) бе́шеный, нейстовый; ~ness ди́кая ме́стность f, глушь

wilful своево́льный; ~l su. во́ля; jur. завеща́ние; ~ling гото́вый, согла́сный; ~lingly охо́тно, с го-

то́вностью; ~lingness гото́вность f

willow ве́рба, и́ва

win game выи́грывать [вы́играть]; medal, freedom завоёвывать [-ева́ть]; victory одержа́ть pf.; su. вы́игрыш

wince вздра́гивать [-ро́гнуть]

wind[1] v/i. river, path: извива́ться; plant: ви́ться; v/t. yarn нама́тывать [-мота́ть]; clock заводи́ть [-вести́]

wind[2] ве́тер; ~-instrument духово́й инструме́нт; ~mill ветряна́я ме́льница; ~ow окно́; ~screen mot. ветрово́е стекло́; ~screen wiper стеклоочисти́тель m, coll. дво́рник; ~y ве́треный

wine вино́

wing крыло́ (a. fig.); pl. thea. кули́сы f/pl.; ~ed крыла́тый

wink морга́ть [-гну́ть]; ~ **at** подми́гивать [-гну́ть] (Д)

winner победи́тель(ница f) m; (prize-~) призёр

winter зима́; attr. зи́мний; **in** ~er зимо́й; ~ry зи́мний

wipe face, dishes вытира́ть [вы́тереть]; ~ **off**, ~ **out** стира́ть [стере́ть]

wire про́волока; телегра́мма; el. про́вод; телеграфи́ровать (im)pf.; ~y fig. жи́листый

wis|dom му́дрость *f*; **~e** му́дрый

wish жела́ние; *v.* [по]жела́ть (P *or inf.*); *I ~ he'd been there* жаль, что его́ там не́ было; *best ~es* наилу́чшие пожела́ния *n/pl.*

wistful (*pensive*) заду́мчивый; (*look*) гру́стный

wit ум; (*wittiness* остроу́мие; (*person*) остря́к

witch ве́дьма

with с (T); (*by means of* T, *e. g.*: *write ~ a pen* писа́ть перо́м); *~ cold* дрожа́ть от хо́лода

withdraw *v/t.* hand уб(и)ра́ть; (*from use*) изыма́ть [изъя́ть]; (*cancel*) отменя́ть [-ни́ть]; *v/i.* mil. отходи́ть [отойти́]; **~al** отхо́д

wither *v/i.* увяда́ть [-я́нуть]

withhold (*information*) скры(ва́)ть; (*from s.o.'s pay*) уде́рживать [-жа́ть]; (*deny*) отка́зывать [-за́ть] (в P)

with|in внутри́ (P) *a adv.*; **~in a year** не по́зже ме́ньше чем че́рез год; **~out** *prep.* без (P); *adv.* снару́жи; **~stand** противостоя́ть (Д)

witness свиде́тель(ница *f*) *m*; (*evidence*) свиде́тельство; *v.* засвиде́тельствовать *pf.*; *accident* быть свиде́телем (P)

witty остроу́мный

wolf волк

woman же́нщина; **~ly** же́нственный, же́нский

womb утро́ба; *anat.* ма́тка

wonder чу́до; (*amazement*) изумле́ние, удивле́ние; *v.* удивля́ться [-ви́ться] (at Д); *I ~ what…* интере́сно (знать), что …; *it's no* ничего́ удиви́тельного; **~ful** чуде́сный

wood лес; (*material*) де́рево; (*fire~*) дрова́ *n/pl.*; **~cutter** лесору́б; (*artist*) гравёр по де́реву; **~ed** леси́стый; **~en** деревя́нный; **~pecker** дя́тел

wool шерсть *f*; **~len** шерстяно́й

word сло́во (*a.* tech.)

work рабо́та; (*labour*) труд; (*art*) произведе́ние; *pl.* (= *mill*) заво́д; *v/t. v/i.* рабо́тать; *mechanism*: де́йствовать; *v/t.* (*soil*) обра́батывать [-бо́тать]; *~ out plan* разраба́тывать [-бо́тать]; *out of work* безрабо́тный; *complete ~s of* по́лное собра́ние сочине́ний (P); **~er** рабо́чий; (*wider sense*) рабо́тни|к, -ца; **~ing** *adj.* рабо́чий; *in ~ing order* в испра́вности; **~shop** мастерска́я

world мир, свет; *attr.* мирово́й; **~ly** све́тский; **~ly wisdom** жите́йская му́дрость; **~wide** всеми́рный

worm червь *m*, червя́к

med. глист

worry *v/i.* беспокóиться (**about** о П); *v/t.* прист-а(в)áть к (Д; **with** с Т); *su.* беспокóйство; забóта

worse хýдший, *pred.*, *a. adv.* хýже

worship *eccl.* богослужéние; *v.* почитáть; ⁓(p)er почитáтель(ница *f*) *m*

worst наихýдший, *pred.*, *a adv.* хýже всегó (*или:* всех)

worth *su.* стóимость *f*; (*moral*) достóинство; **be ⁓** стóить; **it is ⁓ reading** стóит прочéсть это; ⁓less ничегó не стóящий; ⁓y достóйный (**of** Р); **it is ⁓y of note** это достóйно внимáния

wound рáна; *v.* рáнить (*im*)*pf.* (*a. fig.*)

wrangle перекáние; *v.* пререкáться

wrap *v/t. person* закýт(ыв)ать; *book* обёрт(ыв)ать [обернýть]; *parcel* завёртывать [завернýть]; ⁓per обёртка

wrath гнев

wreath венóк; (*smoke*) клуб

wreck (корабле)крушéние; (*remains*) обломки *m/pl.*; (*human*) развáлина; *v.* разрушáть [⁓шить]; *car* разбить; ⁓age (*remains*)

обломки *m/pl.*; **be ⁓ed** *ship, train, plan:* потерпéть крушéние

wrench *tech.* гáечный ключ; *v. foot* вывихнуть; → *a.* **wrest**

wrest вырывáть [вырвать] (**from** у Р); ⁓le (*sports*) борóться (*a. fig.*); ⁓ler борéц; ⁓ling борьбá

wretched жáлкий

wriggle *worm:* извивáться; ⁓ **out** *fig.* увиливать [-льнýть] (**of** от Р)

wring выжимáть [выжать]; (*extort*) вымогáть (**from** у Р); *hands* ломáть

wrinkle морщина; *v.* [с]мóрщить(ся)

wrist запястье; ⁓-watch ручные часы *m/pl.*

writ|e [на]писáть (*v/i. impf.*); ⁓e **out** *cheque* выписывать ['-исать]; ⁓er писáтель(ница *f*) *m*; *su.* (*writer*) литерáтурный труд; письмó; (*text*) пóчерк; ⁓ing **paper** писчая бумáга; **in ⁓ing** письменно

wrong (*answer*) непрáвильный; (*train, person*) не тот (та, то); *su.* зло; несправедливость; обида; **the ⁓ side** (*textile*) изнáнка; **you are ⁓** ты непрáв(á), вы непрáвы

wry кривóй

X, Y

xerox ксёрокс; *v.* ксерокопи́ровать

X-ray *attr.* рентге́новский; (с)де́лать рентге́новский сни́мок; рентге́новский сни́мок, рентгеногра́мма

yacht я́хта

yard двор; *(measure)* ярд; **~stick** *fig.* мери́ло

yarn пря́жа

yawn зево́та, *(single)* зево́к; *v.* зева́ть [-вну́ть]

year год; **this ~** в э́том году́; **many ~s ago** мно́го лет тому́ наза́д; **he is five ~s old** ему́ пять лет; **academic, school ~** уче́бный год; **~ly** ежего́дный; *adv.* ежего́дно; **~ly income** годово́й дохо́д

yearn *v.* тоскова́ть *(for* по Д или П)

yeast дро́жжи *pl.*

yell гро́мкий крик; *v.* гро́мко крича́ть

yellow жёлтый

yelp тя́вканье; *v.* тя́вкать

yes да

yesterday вчера́; **the day before ~** позавчера́; **~'s**

вчера́шний *(adj.)*

yet ещё; *(already)* уже́; *(however)* одна́ко (же); **not ~** ещё не(т); **as ~** до сих пор

yield *agr.* урожа́й; *tech.* вы́ход, добы́ча; *fin.* дохо́д; *v. harvest* дава́ть, дать; *profit* приноси́ть [-нести́]; *(give in)* уступа́ть [-пи́ть]

yoga йо́га

yog(h)ourt йо́гурт; *approx. a.* кефи́р, простоква́ша

yolk желто́к

you ты, *pl.* (*a. polite sg.*) вы; тебя́, вас (= В); тебе́, вам (= Д)

young молодо́й; **~ people** молодёжь *f;* **the ~** *zo.* детёныши *m/pl.*

your(s) ваш, **~а**, **~е**, *pl.* **~и**; твой, твоя́, твоё; *pl.* твой; **~self**, **~selves** себя́, -ся; *emphatic* сам(а́), са́ми *m/pl.*

youth *(age)* ю́ность *f; (boy)* ю́ноша *m; (people)* молодёжь *f*

Yugoslav югосла́в|(ка), -ский

Z

zeal усе́рдие; **~ous** усе́рдный

zebra зе́бра; **~ crossing** (пешехо́дный) перехо́д

zenith зени́т *(a. fig.)*

zero нуль *m,* ноль; *attr.* нулево́й

zigzag *su.* зигза́г; *adj.* зиг-

загообра́зный
zinc цинк; *attr.* ци́нковый
zip-fastener (застёжка)-мо́лния

zone зо́на; *attr.* зона́льный
zoo зоопа́рк; **_logy** зооло́гия

Числительные – Numerals

Количественные Cardinals

0	ноль ог нуль *m* naught, zero, cipher	40	со́рок *forty*
1	оди́н *m*, одна́ *f*, одно́ *n* one	50	пятьдеся́т *fifty*
		60	шестьдеся́т *sixty*
2	два *m/n*, две *f* two	70	се́мьдесят *seventy*
3	три *three*	80	во́семьдесят *eighty*
4	четы́ре *four*	90	девяно́сто *ninety*
5	пять *five*	100	сто (а и́ли one) hundred)
6	шесть *six*		
7	семь *seven*	200	две́сти *two hundred*
8	во́семь *eight*	300	три́ста *three hundred*
9	де́вять *nine*		
10	де́сять *ten*	400	четы́реста *four hundred*
11	оди́ннадцать *eleven*		
12	двена́дцать *twelve*	500	пятьсо́т *five hundred*
13	трина́дцать *thirteen*		
14	четы́рнадцать *fourteen*	600	шестьсо́т *six hundred*
15	пятна́дцать *fifteen*	700	семьсо́т *seven hundred*
16	шестна́дцать *sixteen*		
17	семна́дцать *seventeen*	800	восемьсо́т *eight hundred*
18	восемна́дцать *eighteen*	900	девятьсо́т *nine hundred*
19	девятна́дцать *nineteen*		
20	два́дцать *twenty*	1.000	(одна́) ты́сяча *f* (a и́ли one) thousand
21	два́дцать оди́н *m* (одна́ *f*, одно́ *n*) twenty-one	60.140	шестьдеся́т ты́сяч сто со́рок *sixty thousand one hundred and forty*
22	два́дцать два *m/n* (две *f*) twenty-two	1.000.000	(оди́н) миллио́н *m* (a и́ли one) million
23	два́дцать три twenty-three	1.000.000.000	(оди́н) милли́ард ог биллио́н *m* milliard, Am. billion
30	три́дцать *thirty*		

1st	пе́рвый *first*	50th	пятидеся́тый *fiftieth*
2nd	второ́й *second*	60th	шестидеся́тый *sixtieth*
3rd	тре́тий *third*	70th	семидеся́тый *seventieth*
4th	четвёртый *fourth*	80th	восьмидеся́тый *eightieth*
5th	пя́тый *fifth*	90th	девяно́стый *ninetieth*
6th	шесто́й *sixth*	100th	со́тый *(one) hundredth*
7th	седмо́й *seventh*	200th	двухсо́тый *two hundredth*
8th	восьмо́й *eighth*	300th	трёхсо́тый *three hundredth*
9th	девя́тый *ninth*	400th	четырёхсо́тый *four hundredth*
10th	деся́тый *tenth*	500th	пятисо́тый *five hundredth*
11th	оди́ннадцатый *eleventh*	600th	шестисо́тый *six hundredth*
12th	двена́дцатый *twelfth*	700th	семисо́тый *seven hundredth*
13th	трина́дцатый *thirteenth*	800th	восьмисо́тый *eight hundredth*
14th	четы́рнадцатый *fourteenth*	900th	девятисо́тый *nine hundredth*
15th	пятна́дцатый *fifteenth*	1.000th	ты́сячный *(one) thousandth*
16th	шестна́дцатый *sixteenth*	60.140th	шестьдеся́т ты́сяч сто сороко́вой *sixty thousand one hundred and fortieth*
17th	семна́дцатый *seventeenth*		
18th	восемна́дцатый *eighteenth*		
19th	девятна́дцатый *nineteenth*		
20th	двадца́тый *twentieth*	1.000.000th	миллио́нный *millionth*
21st	два́дцать пе́рвый *twenty-first*		
22nd	два́дцать второ́й *twenty-second*		
30th	тридца́тый *thirtieth*		
40th	сороково́й *fortieth*		